SUSE Linux Enterprise Server Administration (Course 3037)

Novell & Jason W. Eckert

COURSE TECHNOLOGY
CENGAGE Learning

Australia • Brazil • Japan • Korea • Mexico • Singapore • Spain • United Kingdom • United States

**SUSE Linux Enterprise Server
Administration (Course 3037)**

Novell & Jason W. Eckert

Vice President, Technology and Trades:
Dave Garza

Managing Editor: William Pitkin III

Product Manager: Amy Lyon

Technical Editor: Ed Sawicki

Manufacturing Coordinator: Susan Carroll

Text Design: GEX Publishing Services

Editorial Director: Sandy Clark

Acquisitions Editor: Nick Lombardi

Product Manager: John Bosco

Marketing Director: Deborah Yarnell

Senior Editorial Assistant: Dawn Daugherty

Compositor: GEX Publishing Services

Executive Editor: Stephen Helba

Product Manager: Manya Chylinski

Production Editor: Brooke Booth

Senior Channel Marketing Manager:
Dennis Williams

Cover Design: Laura Rickenbach

For product information and technology assistance, contact us at
Cengage Learning Customer & Sales Support, 1-800-354-9706

For permission to use material from this text or product,
submit all requests online at **cengage.com/permissions**
Further permission questions can be emailed to
permissionrequest@cengage.com

ISBN-13: 978-1-4188-3731-0
ISBN-10: 1-4188-3731-8

Course Technology
25 Thomson Place
Boston, Massachusetts, 02210
USA

Cengage Learning is a leading provider of customized learning solutions
with office locations around the globe, including Singapore, the United
Kingdom, Australia, Mexico, Brazil, and Japan. Locate your local office at:
international.cengage.com/region

Cengage Learning products are represented in Canada by Nelson
Education, Ltd.

For your lifelong learning solutions, visit **course.cengage.com**

Visit our corporate website at **cengage.com**

The Novell and SUSE names and trademarks are the exclusive property
of, and are licensed from, Novell, Inc. Linux is a registered trademark of
Linus Torvalds.

Printed in Canada
2 3 4 5 6 7 8 9 09 08

BRIEF
Contents

TABLE OF
Contents

Preface

Open Source Software such as Linux has radically changed how the computer industry approaches software development. One of the largest changes since 2000 was Novell's switch to SUSE Linux as their main enterprise platform. Today, there are millions of Linux users, administrators, and developers, and this community continually grows as companies adopt Linux and Open Source technologies. To provide benchmarks for hiring, many vendors such as CompTIA, Novell, Red Hat, and the Linux Professional Institute (LPI) have released Linux certification exams geared towards different skill sets required for common Linux job functions. The Novell Certified Linux Professional (CLP) certification is practicum-based, and focuses on the in-depth administration of SUSE Linux systems. Using carefully constructed examples, questions, and practical exercises, the *SUSE Linux Enterprise Server Administration (Course 3037)* text introduces you to the concepts required to successfully use and administer a Linux system. Alongside *Advanced SUSE Linux Enterprise Server Administration (Course 3038),* this text provides you with the information that is tested on the CLP certification exam.

The Intended Audience

This book is appropriate for anyone who wishes to learn how to administer SUSE Linux systems as well as those who are working towards obtaining the Novell CLP, LPI Level 1, or LPI Level 2 certifications. The concepts introduced in this book do not assume prior SUSE Linux experience, but a general knowledge of Linux and System Administration concepts is assumed. Many of the concepts and procedures introduced in this book are transferable to most other Linux distributions.

Section Descriptions

Section 1, "Introduction to Managing the SUSE Linux Enterprise Server," introduces the major features of the SUSE Linux Enterprise Server (SLES). This section also discusses how to perform basic system administration using YaST, as well as the utilities that are commonly used to monitor SLES systems.

Section 2, "Manage User Access and Security," discusses the various tools and concepts surrounding security and access control in SLES. Focus is placed on file and directory permissions, user account management, and Pluggable Authentication Modules (PAM).

Section 3, "Manage the Linux File System," examines the various file system types that are supported in SLES as well as their configuration. More specifically, this section discusses disk partitioning, LVM partitioning, file system creation, file system management, user and group restrictions using disk quotas, and the creation of file system backups.

Section 4, "Manage Software for SUSE Linux Enterprise Server," walks through the procedures used to install and manage RPM software packages. In addition, this section discusses the management of shared libraries and the configuration of the YaST Online Update (YOU) services.

Section 5, "Manage System Initialization," covers the structure of the Linux boot process and management of system runlevels. This section also introduces the management of the Linux kernel, kernel modules, the GRUB boot loader, system hardware settings, and power management.

Section 6, "Manage Linux Processes and Services," discusses the various utilities and procedures used to manage daemon and user processes in SLES. Furthermore, this section discusses the configuration of daemons at system startup, process scheduling, and the management of system and daemon log files.

Section 7, "Connect the SUSE Linux Enterprise Server to the Network," focuses on the commands and procedures used to configure and test TCP/IP network interfaces in SLES. In addition, this section discusses the configuration of routing tables and name resolution for the SLES computer.

Section 8, "Enable Infrastructure Services," discusses the configuration and administration of commonly used network services. These include CUPS printing services, NFS file sharing services, Samba file and printer sharing services, NIS services, and LDAP services.

Section 9, "Enable Internet Services," covers the configuration and administration of NTP time services, Apache web services, and FTP file services. In addition, this section examines the configuration of the Internet Super Daemon (xinetd).

Section 10, "Manage Remote Access," discusses how to configure remote administration to SLES systems using YaST as well as OpenSSH. The configuration of network-based installations is also discussed.

Section 11, "LiveFire Exercise," allows you to configure many of the technologies discussed in previous sections as part of a real-world exercise. This exercise is good practice for the Novell CLP certification candidates.

Appendix A details the installation steps for SUSE Linux Enterprise Server 9.

Appendix B covers basic networking terminology and concepts with a focus on the TCP/IP protocol.

Appendix C maps the concepts introduced in this course to the Novell CLP and LPI certification examinations.

Appendix D introduces the management of SLES using Novell ZENworks.

Features

To ensure a successful learning experience, this book includes the following pedagogical features:

- **Section Objectives:** Each section in this book begins with a detailed list of the concepts to be mastered within that section. This list provides you with a quick reference to the contents of that section, as well as a useful study aid.

- **Screenshots, Illustrations, and Tables:** Wherever applicable, screenshots and illustrations are used to aid you in the visualization of common installation, administration, and management steps; theories; and concepts. In addition, many tables provide command options that may be used in combination with the specific command being discussed.

- **Exercises:** Exercises are distributed throughout the body of each section. They contain specific step-by-step instructions that enable you to apply the knowledge gained in the section.

- **End-of-Chapter Material:** The end of each section includes the following features to reinforce the material covered in the section:

  - **Chapter Summary:** Gives a brief but complete summary of the section

  - **Key Terms List:** Lists all new terms and their definitions

  - **Review Questions:** Test your knowledge of the most important concepts covered in the section

  - **Discovery Exercises:** Include theoretical, research, or scenario-based projects that allow you to expand on your current knowledge of the concepts that you learned in the section

Text and Graphic Conventions

Wherever appropriate, additional information and exercises have been added to this book to help you better understand what is being discussed in the section. Icons throughout the text alert you to additional materials. The icons used in this textbook are as follows:

Notes present additional helpful material related to the subject being discussed.

The Caution icon identifies important information about potential mistakes or hazards.

Each Discovery Exercise in this book is preceded by the Discovery Exercise icon.

On the DVD: On the DVDs included with this text you will find a copy of SLES 9, VMWare emulation software for lab setup, the Student Manual PDF, files used for section exercises, and a Self Study Workbook.

Instructor's Materials

The following supplemental materials are available when this book is used in a classroom setting. All of the supplements available with this book are provided to the instructor on a single CD-ROM.

- **Electronic Instructor's Manual:** The Instructor's Manual that accompanies this textbook includes additional instructional material to assist in class preparation, including suggestions for classroom activities, discussion topics, and additional projects.

- **Solutions:** Answers to all end-of-chapter materials are provided, including the Review Questions, and, where applicable, Discovery Exercises.

- **ExamView®:** This textbook is accompanied by ExamView, a powerful testing software package that allows instructors to create and administer printed, computer (LAN-based), and Internet exams. ExamView includes hundreds of questions that correspond to the topics covered in this text, enabling students to generate detailed study guides that include page references for further review. The computer-based and Internet testing components allow students to take exams at their computers, and also save the instructor time by grading each exam automatically.

- **PowerPoint presentations:** This textbook comes with Microsoft PowerPoint slides for each section. These are included as a teaching aid for classroom presentation, to make available to students on the network for section review, or to be printed for classroom distribution. Instructors, please feel at liberty to add your own slides for additional topics you introduce to the class.

- **Figure Files:** All of the figures in this textbook are reproduced on the Instructor's Resource CD in bit-mapped format. Similar to the PowerPoint presentations, these are included as a teaching aid for classroom presentation, to make available to students for review, or to be printed for classroom distribution.

LAB REQUIREMENTS

The following hardware is required for the Discovery Exercises at the end of each section and should be listed on the Hardware Compatibility List available at *www.novell. com/linux/suse/*:

- Pentium CPU (Pentium II 400 or higher recommended)
- 256 MB RAM (512 MB RAM recommended)
- 4 GB hard disk
- A DVD drive (or a combination CD/DVD drive)
- Network Interface Card
- Internet connection

Similarly, the following lists the software required for the Discovery Exercises at the end of each section:

- SUSE Linux Enterprise Server 9

ACKNOWLEDGMENTS

First, I wish to thank the staff at Course Technology and Novell for an overall enjoyable writing experience. More specifically, I wish to thank my Project Managers, Manya Chylinski and Amy Lyon, for their coordination and insight, as well as my Project Editor, Brooke Booth, for the long hours spent pulling everything together to transform the text into its current state. As well, I wish to thank Frank Gerencser, of triOS College for freeing me up to write this textbook and Apple Computer Inc. for the amazing computer I wrote it on.

Readers are encouraged to e-mail comments, questions, and suggestions regarding *SUSE Linux Enterprise Server Administration (Course 3037)* to Jason W. Eckert: jason. eckert@trios.com

INTRODUCTION

This text is based on Novell Authored Courseware *SUSE Linux Enterprise Server Administration (Course 3037)*, which Novell sells and distributes to commercial and acedemic institutions, as well as selfstudy customers.

Utilizing the strength of Novell's original content, software, and hands-on exercises, Course Technology has reformed and enhanced the texts for an academic audience. Additional end-of-chapter exercises, student labs, and instructor tools — including test banks, slide decks, and online deliverables — have been added to produce quality courseware based on Novell's SUSE Linux.

The Novell course developers have reviewed the manuals from Course Technology to ensure that, although in a new format, the content is consistent with Novell's own manuals, meeting the objectives to prepare students to take the Certification Exams.

To learn more about Novell Academic Programs, visit *www.novell.com/natp*.

In the *SUSE Linux Enterprise Server Administration* (3037) course, you learn basic SUSE Linux Enterprise Server 9 (SLES 9) administration skills.

These skills, along with those taught in the *SUSE Linux Fundamentals* (3036) and *Advanced SUSE Linux Enterprise Server Administration* (3038) courses, prepare you to take the Novell® Certified Linux® Professional (Novell CLP) certification practicum test.

The contents of your student kit include 2 DVDs. The first DVD is your Course DVD and contains the following:

- *SUSE Linux Enterprise Server Administration (3037)* Student Manual
- *SUSE Linux Enterprise Server Administration (3037)* Self-Study Workbook
- *SUSE Linux Enterprise Server Administration (3037)* Self-Study Files
- SLES 9 VMWare Server

The second DVD contains a full evaluation version of SUSE Linux Enterprise Server 9. To accommodate this academic deliverable, the original software has been modified from CD to DVD and is distributed on an "AS IS" basis. Please note that this software is for classroom use only and is not to be used in a production environment.

To download a fully functional, supported, and upgradeable version of the SUSE Linux Enterprise Server and other Novell Open Source products, visit *www.novell.com/downloads*.

The *SLES 9 VMware Server DVD* contains a VMware Workstation SLES 9 server that you can use with the *SUSE Linux Enterprise Server Administration Self-Study Workbook* (in PDF format on your Course CD) outside the classroom to practice the skills you need to take the Novell CLP practicum.

Instructions for setting up a self-study environment are included in the *SUSE Linux Enterprise Server Administration Self-Study Workbook*.

If you do not own a copy of VMware Workstation, you can obtain a 30-day evaluation version at *www.vmware.com*. If you want to dedicate a machine to install SLES 9, instructions are also provided in the Self-Study Workbook.

COURSE OBJECTIVES

This course teaches you how to perform the following Linux system administration tasks for SLES 9:

- Update and check the health of a SLES 9 server
- Perform administrative tasks with YaST
- Manage users and groups
- Provide basic system security
- Manage the Linux file system
- Manage software installation
- Manage system initialization, processes, and services
- Connect the server to the network
- Provide basic network services (such as printing and Web access)
- Remotely access a SLES 9 server

These are administrative skills common to an entry-level administrator or help desk technician in an enterprise environment.

The last half of the final day of class is reserved for building a SLES 9 solution on your own to prepare for taking the Novell CLP Practicum.

AUDIENCE

While the primary audience for this course is the current Novell CNE[SM], Linux professionals, and administrators with experience in other operating systems can also use this course to help prepare for the Novell CLP Practicum.

LINUX CERTIFICATION

With Novell® and Linux, you are going places! Industry-recognized certification exams are available to leverage your Linux experience and training. Novell's commitment to the open source community is evident by our support of CompTIA's Linux+ vendor-neutral exam.

CompTIA Linux+

The CompTIA Linux+ certification is an international industry credential that validates the knowledge of individuals with at least six months of practical Linux experience. Professionals who want to certify their technical knowledge in basic installation, operation, and troubleshooting for Linux operating systems should consider this certification. The skills and knowledge measured by this examination were developed with global input to assure accuracy, validity, and reliability. Earning the CompTIA Linux+ designation means that the candidate can explain fundamental open source resources/licenses, demonstrate knowledge of user administration, understand file permissions/software configurations, and manage local storage devices and network protocols.

Novell Certified Linux Professional (Novell CLP)

The Novell Certified Linux Professional certification is for people interested in being Linux administrators. Skills demonstrated by someone holding a Novell CLP certification include: installing Linux servers into a network environment, managing users and groups, managing the SUSE® Linux file system, managing printing, managing software, and managing network processes and services — just to name a few. As with all Novell certifications, course work is never required, but you must pass a Novell Practicum exam (050-689) in order to achieve the certification. Visit *www.novell.com/training/certinfo/* for more information.

Novell Certified Linux Engineer 9 (Novell CLE 9)

This certification is for those wanting engineer-level skills to operate SUSE Linux Enterprise Servers in a network. The Novell Certified Linux Engineer 9 certification will help you master those aspects of SUSE Linux Enterprise Servers that are not already covered in the CLP curriculum. With this certification, you will be in high demand as more and more employers seek talented Linux engineers. This certification will require you to have completed your Novell CLP certification before you take the Novell Practicum for your Novell CLE 9 certification. (So if you're already a Novell CLP, you're more than halfway done with the Novell CLE 9 certification.) You can find more information online at *www.novell.com/training/certinfo/*.

Novell Practicum Exams

Both Novell CLP and CLE 9 certifications employ Practicum exams. These performance-based exams are designed to test not only students' knowledge but also their skills. The 2.5-hour exam requires students to perform real-world tasks on one or more SUSE Linux servers. At the end of the exam, each server environment is evaluated and each student is scored with a pass or fail grade. These exams are available through testing partners world-wide. See *http://practicum.novell.com* for more information.

Novell and SUSE are registered trademarks of Novell, Inc. in the United States and other countries.

Figure I-1 illustrates the training/testing path for Novell CLP.

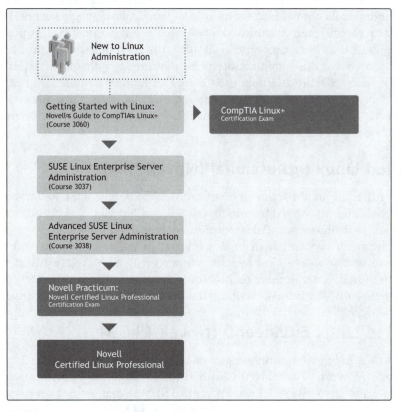

Figure I-1

SLES 9 SUPPORT AND MAINTENANCE

The copy of SUSE Linux Enterprise Server 9 (SLES 9) you receive in your student kit is a fully functioning copy of the SLES 9 product.

However, to receive official support and maintenance updates, you need to do one of the following:

- Register for a free registration/serial code that provides you with 30 days of support and maintenance.
- Purchase a copy of SLES 9 from Novell (or an authorized dealer).

You can obtain your free 30-day support and maintenance code at *www.novell.com/products/linuxenterpriseserver/eval.html*.

You will need to have or create a Novell login account to access the 30-day evaluation.

SLES 9 ONLINE RESOURCES

Novell provides a variety of online resources to help you configure and implement SLES 9.

These include the following:

- www.novell.com/products/linuxenterpriseserver/

  This is the Novell home page for SLES 9.

- www.novell.com/documentation/sles9/index.html

  This is the Novell Documentation Web site for SLES 9.

- http://support.novell.com/linux/

  This is the home page for all Novell Linux support, and includes links to support options such as the Knowledgebase, downloads, and FAQs.

- www.novell.com/coolsolutions

  This Novell Web site provides the latest implementation guidelines and suggestions from Novell on a variety of products, including SUSE Linux.

AGENDA

Table I-1 shows the agenda for this 5-day course.

Table I-1

	Section	Duration
Day 1	**Introduction**	00:30
	Section 1: Introduction to Managing the SUSE Linux Enterprise Server	02:00
	Section 2: Manage User Access and Security	03:00
Day 2	**Section 3:** Manage the Linux File System	03:00
	Section 4: Manage Software for SUSE Linux Enterprise Server	02:00
	Section 5: Manage System Initialization	02:00
Day 3	**Section 6:** Manage Linux Processes and Services	03:00
	Section 7: Connect the SUSE Linux Enterprise Server to the Network	03:00
Day 4	**Section 8:** Enable Infrastructure Services	03:00
	Section 9: Enable Internet Services	03:00
Day 5	**Section 10:** Manage Remote Access	02:00
	Section 11: LiveFire Exercise	04:00

SCENARIO

As system administrator for your Digital Airlines office, you have been tasked by the company to migrate several network services to SLES 9 servers over the next year.

As part of the rollout plan, you would like to install SLES 9 on a prototype/staging server that you can use to do the following:

- Become familiar with basic administrative tasks on the local host (such as providing user access and security)
- Connect to the network to test a variety of services you will be migrating (such as file and print)
- Provide limited access for training others in your office (such as the database group) who will be using or configuring these services
- Test updating and remote administration of SLES 9

Once you complete this initial testing of services and administrative tasks, you will then be in a position to begin rolling out SLES 9 according to guidelines from Digital Airlines corporate headquarters.

Exercise Conventions

When working through an exercise, you will see conventions that indicate information you need to enter that is specific to your server.

The following describes the most common conventions:

- *italicized/bolded text*. This is a reference to your unique situation, such as the host name of your server.

  For example, if the host name of your server is DA50, and you see the following:

  hostname.digitalairlines.com

  you would enter

  DA50.digitalairlines.com

- **10.0.0.xx**. This is the IP address that is assigned to your SLES 9 server.

  For example, if your IP address is 10.0.0.50, and you see the following:

  10.0.0.xx

  you would enter:

  10.0.0.50

- **Select.** The word *select* is used in exercise steps to indicate a variety of actions, including clicking a button on the interface and selecting a menu item.

- **Enter and Type.** The words *enter* and *type* have distinct meanings.

  The word *enter* means to type text in a field or at a command line and press the Enter key when necessary. The word *type* means to type text without pressing the Enter key.

  If you are directed to type a value, make sure you do not press the Enter key or you might activate a process that you are not ready to start.

1

Introduction to Managing the SUSE Linux Enterprise Server

In this section, you learn about the features of SUSE Linux Enterprise Server 9 (SLES 9), how to use YaST, and how to monitor your current installation.

♦ Describe SLES 9

♦ Access and Use YaST

♦ Monitor Your SLES 9 System

Objective 1   Describe SLES 9

Backed by an extensive Novell support infrastructure and partner network, SLES 9 is a secure, reliable platform for open source computing in the enterprise.

The new 2.6 kernel, scalability and availability, management tools, and developer tools make SLES 9 the most flexible, most convenient, most scalable version yet.

SLES 9 also provides open application programming interfaces (APIs) and other development tools that simplify Linux™ integration and customization.

And, since SLES 9 is backed by Novell, you can deploy it with confidence, knowing that you've got the help of hundreds of software engineers, support staff, and consultants who are dedicated to Linux, open source, and customer success.

In this objective, you learn the following about SLES 9:

- What's New in SLES 9
- Hardware Support and System Requirements
- Service and Support
- Linux Standards and SLES 9

NOTE

For a complete list of SLES 9 technical features, download the file *sles9_featurelist_technical.pdf* at www.suse.de/en/business/products/server/sles/index.html.

What's New in SLES 9

Although the list of exclusive and open source features in SLES 9 is extensive, knowing what's new in SLES 9 helps you understand the possibilities for integrating or migrating to a SUSE Linux Enterprise Server environment.

The following are feature categories that cover the new functionality of SLES 9:

- New Kernel
- New Scalability and Available Features
- New Systems Management Tools
- New Developer Tools
- New Software

CAUTION
Many of these new features are advanced topics and are not discussed in this basic Linux Administration course.

However, by becoming familiar with these technical features, you are in a better position to meet requirements and plans for introducing SLES 9 into your enterprise network environment.

New Kernel

SLES 9 includes the Linux kernel version 2.6, a dramatic improvement over earlier systems in terms of scale, speed, and power.

USB 2.0 and Bluetooth are supported. In addition, Hotplug support exists for SCSI, USB, Firewire, PCI, and CPU (the latter only on PowerPC). The support of Ipv6 has improved, and the ALSA sound system is now part of the kernel.

Table 1–1 provides an overview of improvements directly related to the new kernel.

Table 1-1

Feature	Description
Kernel 2.6 scalability enhancements	These enhancements include the following: • **More processors:** More than 128 CPUs have been tested on available hardware but, theoretically, there is no limit on the number that will work. • **More users:** Systems can now have more than 4 billion unique users. • **More processes:** Run up to 65,535 user-level processes, plus additional kernel-level processes that represent threads. • **More open files:** SLES 9 automatically tunes resource usage dynamically to support the maximum number of simultaneous open files.
Kernel 2.6 device enhancements	These enhancements include the following: • **More device types:** 4,095 major device types and more than a million subdevices per type make larger storage arrays, print farms, and tape units more feasible. • **More devices:** The server can now manage more devices. For example, it can control up to 32,000 SCSI disks. • **Faster devices:** Support for high-speed USB 2.0 and Firewire* (IEEE 1394 and 1394b). • **Higher throughput:** High-speed Serial ATA (SATA) device support enables transfer rates up to 150 MB/sec.

Table 1-1   (continued)

Feature	Description
Non-Uniform Memory Access (NUMA)	NUMA lets SUSE Linux Enterprise Server scale more efficiently for systems with dozens or hundreds of CPUs because CPUs can access a dedicated memory bus for local memory. It also supports multiple interconnected memory nodes, each supporting a smaller number of CPUs. The result is greater scalability for applications that use local memory.
NUMA development tools	For x86-64 (Opteron) and IA-64 (Itanium*), the NUMA tools allow developers to fine-tune applications for NUMA usage. Both Oracle and DB2 are developing NUMA API support, and Oracle already uses it in testing—one reason that SUSE Linux Enterprise Server has surpassed other distributions in database benchmarks.
Hyperthreading	Hyperthreading enables multithreaded server software applications to execute threads in parallel within each individual server processor, dramatically improving transaction rates and response times.

Table 1-1 (continued)

Feature	Description
Flexible I/O scheduler	The new I/O scheduler lets you tune the server to match its usage with four I/O behavior policies: • **Complete Fair Queuing:** CFQ is suitable for a wide variety of applications, especially desktop and multimedia workloads. It is the default I/O scheduler. CFQ treats all competing processes equally by assigning each process a unique request queue and giving each queue equal bandwidth. • **Deadline:** The deadline I/O scheduler implements a per-request service deadline to ensure that no requests are neglected. Deadline policy is best for disk-intensive database applications. • **Anticipatory:** The anticipatory I/O scheduler uses the deadline mechanism plus a heuristic to anticipate the actions of applications. This provides greater disk throughput but slightly increases latency. The anticipatory heuristic is suitable for file servers but does not work as well for database workloads. • **No-Op:** This "no-operation" mode does no sorting and is used only for disks that perform their own scheduling or are randomly accessible. The first three behaviors group and merge requests to maximize request sizes, cutting down on the amount of seeking performed.
Class-based Kernel Resource Management(CKRM)	CKRM lets you provide differentiated service at a user or job level and prevent denial-of-service attacks. It also increases the accuracy of resource-consumption metering.

New Scalability and Available Features

Delivering rapid scalability and high availability, SLES 9 is well suited to meet the demands of the datacenter.

SLES 9 provides the rapid scalability and high performance systems that today's businesses require, and includes those listed in Table 1–2.

Table 1-2

Feature	Description
Heartbeat high-availability system	The Heartbeat system provides core cluster membership and messaging infrastructure.

It implements the Open Clustering Framework APIs (a subset of the Service-Availability Forum APIs) to provide low-level services for node fencing, fault isolation, and basic two-node failover.

The node failure detection time can be tuned to under one second, allowing for subsecond failovers in some environments.

In the case of a node failure, the Heartbeat system checks I/O to ensure data integrity, then moves resources to the alternate node.

Return to action of failed nodes can be set to automatic or manual, depending on your preference. |
| Enterprise Volume Management System (EVMS) | EVMS lets you handle storage through one mechanism. RAID, LVM, various file system formats, disk checking and maintenance, bad block relocation and more are handled by a single tool. |
| Distributed Replicated Block Device (DRBD) | This networked disk-management tool constructs single partitions from multiple disks that mirror each other. It is similar to a RAID1 system but runs over a network. The partition size can be changed at runtime. |

New Systems Management Tools

SLES 9 simplifies system administration. Table 1–3 lists the new systems management tools available.

Table 1-3

Feature	Description
Novell ZENworks® Linux Management support	Novell ZENworks Linux Management lets you deploy software enterprise-wide. It includes Red Carpet Daemon in the box, and specifically distributes YaST patches and updates from Novell and SUSE Linux.

Table 1-3   (continued)

Feature	Description
Novell ZENworks Linux Management server support	Novell ZENworks Linux Management includes the bundled SUSE Linux Enterprise Server and Novell ZENworks Linux Management.
	It enables onsite hosting of the server and offers granular administration, with tight control over software and patch deployment.
	It also provides integration into IT Service Management (such as ITIL) change-control processes and offers scriptable or Web-based administration.
New YaST Modules	YaST has several new modules in SLES 9, including the following:
	• A mail server configuration tool that lets you create secure servers with IMAP and POP service, quotas, access control lists, name spaces, routing, local mail delivery, server-side filtering of viruses and junk mail, and other enterprise-level mail system features.
	• A VPN configuration assistant for both client and server. The VPN is compatible with Linux and Windows clients and can be configured without additional software.
	• Full Samba 3 configuration.
Improved YaST Tools	The following YaST configuration tools have been enhanced and updated in this release, and range from user-interface improvements to new features and capabilities:
	• Improved network-configuration tools, including DNS, DHCP, LDAP, NIS, Postfix, and TFTP
	• NFS and Samba network file system settings
	• Automated default certificate authority (CA) for servers, including LDAP, Apache*, and Postfix
	• Virtual Private Network (VPN)
	• Installation server
	• Boot server
	• CD creation
	• User-Mode Linux installation and virtualization setup
	• Apache
	• Wake on LAN
	• High-availability tools expanded to work with Heartbeat
	• Update server
	• User-management-tool support for plugins for external back-ends, including IMAP and Samba

New Developer Tools

Developers trust SUSE Linux Enterprise Server to supply a dependable platform and offer rich software-development capabilities through built-in network services and protocols, including CUPS, DNS, DHCP, IMAP, NTP, SLP, Postfix, PXE, Proxy, Samba, SNMP and SMTP.

SLES 9 also includes application and database services and supports popular solutions from hundreds of vendors.

Table 1-4 lists new developer tools included in SLES 9.

Table 1-4

Feature	Description
C# and .NET	The SUSE Linux SDK has always provided state-of-the-art Linux software-development tools for a stable, multiplatform codebase. The newest addition to the toolbox, the Mono™ project, lets developers build and run .NET applications on Linux and other operating systems. Application frameworks supported include ASP.NET, ADO.NET and gtk#.

New Software

Like its predecessors, SLES 9 supports the best of new software as well as updated favorites. Table 1-5 lists some of the new software provided with SLES 9.

Table 1-5

Feature	Description
Samba 3	The latest version of the Samba package supports Unicode* and Active Directory* and offers improved authentication and printing tools. Other improvements include migration tools, support for establishing trust relationships with Windows NT* 4.0 domain controllers, improved ACL settings, and better performance.

Table 1-5 (continued)

Feature	Description
User-Mode Linux	User-Mode Linux (UML), originally developed as a kernel debugging tool, is a tool that allows a Linux instance to run as a regular process under Linux. In other words, UML makes it possible to run several instances of Linux at once. UML is the virtualization tool of choice for the Linux kernel and VPN development and can be used to provide extra systems in labs, testing environments, or hosting providers. It also makes an excellent secondary firewall. After installing the UML package like any other application binary, you can create additional Linux instances that are installed into directories and managed using the same tools and applications as the non-virtual instance of Linux. While virtual performance is not as optimal as its non-virtual counterpart, and although UML systems require significant amounts of memory, UML instances can generally be used for the same tasks as nonvirtual Linux instances.

Hardware Support and System Requirements

The following are hardware support and system requirement specifications for SLES 9:

- Supported Processor Platforms
- Supported Hardware Extensions
- SLES 9 Hardware Requirements

NOTE

To avoid unnecessary waste of resources, see http://cdb.suse.de/ to find out if a particular piece of hardware is supported by SLES 9 before you buy it or try to get it to work.

Supported Processor Platforms

The supported processor platforms are shown in Table 1-6.

Table 1-6

Feature	Description
*x*86	The *x*86 platform, the most common personal computer hardware platform, is the basis for chips from Intel, AMD, VIA, and Transmeta. Supported processors include Intel Pentium and Xeon processors, AMD Athlon and K7 series, and the AMD Opteron and Athlon64 chips in 32-bit mode.
*x*86-64 (AMD-64)	The *x*86-64 architecture was created by AMD and is a 64-bit extension of the x86 platform that also runs 32-bit legacy code. Supported processors include the AMD Athlon64 and Opteron, and the forthcoming Intel Xeon EM64T. Note that not all 32-bit applications are certified to run perfectly in this environment; check with your ISV or perform extensive testing before deployment.
Itanium Processor Family	SUSE Linux Enterprise Server supports the Itanium processor family, a 64-bit platform from Intel and HP that includes an emulator for x86 32-bit hardware. Because 32-bit support relies on an emulator, 32-bit performance can suffer. However, 64-bit performance benefits from a clean break with the *x*86 platform.
IBM POWER (iSeries and pSeries systems)	SLES 9 is available for 64-bit IBM POWER series hardware. The IBM POWER 64-bit architecture is used in systems from Apple and IBM. It supports execution of code built for the 32-bit edition of the POWER platform. POWER systems include IBM iSeries and pSeries servers.
IBM zSeries (S/390*x*)	The IBM zSeries is a 64-bit platform mostly used in the S/390*x* mainframe series. zSeries hardware can also run code built for the earlier 31-bit S/390 systems. SUSE Linux Enterprise Server running on zSeries hardware can be used for zVM and LPAR virtualization of both 31-bit and 64-bit systems.

Table 1-6   (continued)

Feature	Description
IBM S/390 (31-bit)	The IBM S/390 architecture is an anomaly in that it uses 31 bits, rather than the more common 32. In these systems, the 32nd processor bit is used by the chip itself instead of being made available to the software. SLES 9 is available in a 31-bit compile for S/390 mainframes. SLES 9 on S/390 hardware can be used for zVM and LPAR virtualization of 31-bit systems only.

Supported Hardware Extensions

Table 1-7 lists the supported hardware extensions for SLES 9.

Table 1-7

Feature	Description
InfiniBand (Exclusive)	InfiniBand technology is used for intersystem and interprocess communications (IPC) within a single system. IPC is used in parallel clustering systems, where it provides greater performance, lower latency, faster data sharing, improved usability, and built-in security and reliability.
USB 2.0	USB 2.0 is a powered connection with bandwidth of up to 480 megabits per second.
Firewire (IEEE 1394)	Firewire (IEEE 1394) is a powered connection with bandwidth of up to 400 megabits per second.
ACPI	The ACPI system handles low-level hardware control and configuration, including power management, processor speed, and temperature management.

SLES 9 Hardware Requirements

Table 1-8 lists the hardware requirements for SLES 9.

Table 1-8

Feature	Description
For installation	The following are memory requirements for installation: • **Local Installation:** 256 MB RAM • **SSH-based network install, graphical:** 256 MB RAM • **VNC-based network install using FTP:** 512 MB RAM

Table 1-8 (continued)

Feature	Description
For operation	The following are minimum requirements for running the SLES 9 operating system: • 256 MB RAM • 500 MB hard-disk space for software
Recommended	The following are general recommendations for running services on SLES 9: • A Pentium® III or AMD 750 Mhz or faster computer • 512 MB to 3 GB RAM, at least 256 MB per CPU • 4 GB hard-disk space • Network interface (Ethernet, wireless, or modem)
Suggestions for specific uses	The following are recommendations for specific services: • **Print servers:** If rendering is done on a server, a faster processor or additional processors. • **Web servers:** Additional RAM can improve caching. Additional processors will improve web application performance. • **Database server:** Additional RAM can improve caching. Using multiple disks permits parallel I/O. • **File servers:** Additional disks or a RAID system can improve I/O throughput.

Service and Support

Many of you have relied on Novell to provide the best enterprise level services in the industry. Now you can depend on Novell to provide that same level of service for Linux technologies provided by Novell.

- Support Programs
- Bug Fixes and Security Patches
- Maintenance Contract

Support Programs

The following are current support programs provided by Novell:

- **Premium Service.** Premium Service provides the high level of customized service needed for mission-critical systems and covers all your Novell products and technologies.

  You choose the level of support that makes the most sense for your business—from occasional telephone support to dedicated support engineers who bring full time support, knowledge, and expertise to your organization for business-critical or highly customized solutions.

- **SUSE Linux Server Support.** SUSE Linux Server Support lets you access Novell's expertise for the ongoing support of a single SUSE Linux server.

- **Novell Linux Small Business Support.** The Novell Linux Small Business Support program supports a range of Novell Linux products, offering direct access to Novell Linux support experts, fast response times, and additional support resources for preventing and resolving technical issues.

- **Remote and Managed Services.** Reduce system down time, control your costs, and free up your IT resources with Novell's Remote and Managed Services.

  Novell's experts can proactively monitor and manage all your Novell technologies, freeing up your IT staff for more strategic and profitable projects.

- **Novell Technical Subscriptions.** These subscriptions make it easier to manage today's complex networks. By subscribing, you'll receive the latest information and resources, including new Novell software, advanced technical resources, exclusive online tools, and much more.

- **Online support options.** These include the Knowledgebase (TIDs), support forums, downloadable files, patches and drivers, product tips and tricks, documentation, and much more.

Additional free and fee-based services are available for issues not covered during the warranty period as well as for ongoing support of Novell's Linux consumer products.

NOTE

You can access all of Novell's Linux support options at http://support.novell.com/linux/.

For a list of frequently asked questions (FAQs) about SLES 9 support, see http://support.novell.com/linux/linux_faq.html.

Bug Fixes and Security Patches

From a business perspective, it is important that an operating system and its associated software are maintained over a long period of time. This means that security patches or bug fixes need to be available for several years.

Bug fixes and security patches for SLES 9 are provided for five years to those customers with a valid maintenance contract or registration code for updates.

This is not the case with SUSE Linux products such as SUSE Linux Professional or Personal (the Linux distributions for the consumer market).

Maintenance Contract

Another aspect of product support is certification of the operating system by other software vendors. For example, Oracle and SAP do not support their software if it is run on an operating system not certified by them.

Such certifications are not done for the SUSE consumer products, but only for the SUSE Linux Enterprise Server.

Because maintenance and certifications require considerable know-how and manpower, this service is not provided for free.

This is the reason why there is a fee for a maintenance contract, despite the fact that the Linux kernel and most of the software that accompanies SLES 9 (such as Postfix and Apache) are contributed voluntarily by thousands of developers around the globe.

The maintenance contract assures an up-to-date product throughout its product life cycle.

Linux Standards and SLES 9

SLES 9 adheres to the following Linux standards:

- Linux Standard Base (LSB)
- File System Hierarchy Standard (FHS)
- TeX Directory Structure (TDS)

Linux Standard Base (LSB)

SUSE actively supports the efforts of the Linux Standard Base (LSB) project. The currently valid LSB specification is version 1.3.*x* and only covers the *x*86 architecture.

Apart from the File System Hierarchy Standard (FHS), which is now part of the LSB, the specification defines items such as the package format and details of the system initialization.

NOTE   For up-to-date information about the LSB project, see www.linuxbase.org.

File System Hierarchy Standard (FHS)

In accordance with the LSB specification, SUSE Linux Enterprise Server is also compliant with the File System Hierarchy Standard or FHS (package *fhs*).

For this reason, in some cases it has been necessary in SUSE Linux Enterprise Server to move files or directories to their correct places in the file system, as specified by the FHS.

For example, one aim of the FHS is to define a structure in which */usr/* can be mounted as read-only.

NOTE   For up-to-date information about FHS, see www.pathname.com/fhs/.

TeX Directory Structure (TDS)

TeX is a comprehensive typesetting system that runs on various platforms. It can be expanded with macro packages, like LaTeX, and consists of numerous files that must be organized according to the TeX Directory Structure (TDS).

teTeX is a compilation of current TeX software. On a SUSE Linux system, teTeX is installed in a way that ensures compliance with the requirements of both the TDS and the FHS.

NOTE

For additional information on TDS, see ftp://ftp.dante.de/tex-archive/tds/.

Exercise 1-1   Explore Your KDE Desktop

When you first install SLES 9 and log in to a desktop environment, you probably want to take a few minutes to explore your desktop and check available resources.

In this course, SLES 9 has been installed for you, and you use the KDE desktop.

In this exercise, you log in as geeko (the normal user), and then explore and prepare your KDE desktop for performing the rest of the exercises in the course

NOTE

In this (and other exercises), you switch between using Kate and vi as text editors. If you would prefer using vi, feel free to do so.

Do the following:

1. Log in to your SLES 9 server as **geeko** with a password of **N0v3ll** (a zero; not an uppercase O).

   Several messages appear during the initial login, including the following:

   - New Hardware found message

   - Welcome to SLES 9 message

   - "Warning" message about the powersave daemon not running or that you are not a member of the powersave system group

   - Kandolf's Useful Tips – KTip

2. From the New Hardware found message, deselect **Keep me informed about new hardware**.

3. Skip configuring the hardware device (such as a sound card) by selecting **No**.

4. Close the Welcome to SLES 9 message.

   You can display this message at any time by selecting the **SUSE** icon on the KDE desktop.

5. From the Kandolf's Useful Tips dialog box, view some of the tips by selecting **Previous** or **Next**.

6. When you finish, select **Show tips on startup** to deselect the option; then select **Close**.

   The Warning message about powersave appears for a few seconds each time you log in to the KDE desktop (by now it should have disappeared).

7. Disable the powersave Warning message by doing the following:

   a. Open a terminal window by selecting the **Terminal Program** icon on the panel at the bottom of the screen.

      A Tip of the Day - Konsole dialog box appears.

   b. Select **Show tips on startup** to deselect the option; then select **Close**.

   c. From the terminal window, su (switch user) to root by entering **su -**; then enter a password of **novell**.

   d. Edit the file /opt/kde3/share/autostart/kpowersave.desktop by entering the following;

      vim /opt/kde3/share/autostart/kpowersave.desktop

      The file kpwersave.desktop appears in the vi editor.

   e. Scroll down to the bottom of the file (use the down arrow) until you find the following line:
      ```
      X-KDE-autostart-condition=kpowersaverc:General:
      AutoStart:true
      ```
      You need to change the "true" value to "false."

   f. Press the Insert key; then make the change.

   g. When you finish, press **Esc**; then save the change and exit the vi editor by typing **:wq** and pressing **Enter**.

      You are returned to the command line.

8. View the vi tutorial by entering **vimtutor**.

   A text file with several short lessons is opened in the vi editor. If you are new to vi or need to refresh your basic skills, try some of the lessons after finishing this exercise.

9. Close the vi editor without saving any changes by pressing **Esc**; then type **:q!** and press **Enter**.

10. (Optional) If you are connected to the Internet, you can test the connectivity from the command line by entering the following:

    ping –c 3 www.novell.com

    If there is no Internet access, you receive an "unknown host" message.

11. From the terminal window, check the IP address configured for eth0 by entering **ifconfig**.

    Because your network card is currently configured for automatic IP address setup through DHCP, you do not have an IP address assigned unless you are connected to a network that provides a DHCP server.

    In this case, the only IP address available is 127.0.0.1 (the localhost loopback address).

12. Check the SLES 9 help resources available by doing the following:

    a. From the panel at the bottom of the desktop, select the **SUSE HelpCenter** icon (the lifesaver).

       The SUSE HelpCenter provides a central location for viewing and searching many of the manuals installed with SLES 9.

    b. On the left, make sure the **Content** tab is selected, then select **SLES 9 Adminguide**.

       Notice the variety of topics available, including documentation for YaST administration tool (which you will be using in this course).

    c. Close the HelpCenter window.

    d. From the desktop, select the **SUSE** icon.

       The Welcome to SUSE Linux Enterprise Server 9 dialog box appears.

    e. (Conditional) If you have Internet access, try selecting the **SUSE Hardware Database** link.

       The SUSE Hardware Database is especially critical for finding out if the hardware you have or the hardware you plan on purchasing is supported by SLES 9.

       There are also links on the left for finding out more about support issues.

    f. (Conditional) If you have Internet access, try selecting the **Novell and Linux** link.

       This is Novell's home page for Linux products.

    g. From the menu on the left, select **get involved > download**.

       This is Novell's download page for accessing the latest downloads for all products.

h. From the top of the page, select **SUPPORT > Knowledgebase**.

From here you can access Novell's support database for information about SLES 9.

i. When you finish exploring, close all open windows.

13. Check your current hardware configuration against the hardware requirements for SLES 9:

   - A Pentium® III or AMD 750 Mhz or faster computer
   - 512 MB to 3 GB RAM, at least 256 MB per CPU
   - 4 GB hard-disk space
   - Network interface (Ethernet, wireless, or modem)

   Do the following:

   a. From the panel at the bottom of the screen, select the **KDE Start Menu** icon (the green circle with the red N); then select **System > Monitor > Info Center**.

   The KDE Info Center appears.

   Use this tool to check your hardware configuration against the Recommended category in the SLES 9 Hardware Requirements table.

   b. On the left, select categories such as **Processor**, **Memory**, **Storage Devices**, and **Network Interfaces**.

   c. When you finish, close the KDE Info Center window.

14. Log out as geeko by selecting **KDE Menu > Logout > Logout**.

   You are returned to the GUI login screen.

15. Log in again as **geeko** (password of **N0v3ll**) to test the changes you made to the desktop.

   Notice that the messages no longer appear. If you left the terminal window open when logging out, a new terminal window opens for you when you log back in again.

NOTE

The same Welcome message and other dialog boxes appear the first time you log in as any local user from the GUI login screen, and you will need to perform the same tasks to suppress the messages from appearing again.

Objective 2   Access and Use YaST

YaST stands for Yet another Setup Tool. You can use YaST to complete many configuration tasks as a SUSE Linux Enterprise Server administrator.

To effectively use YaST for configuring SLES 9, you need to know the following:

- YaST Basics
- The Role of SuSEconfig

YaST Basics

Although you use YaST to install SLES 9, it has a much greater role as a system management and configuration tool.

You can use YaST to configure various services, to install software, to configure hardware, to manage users, and to complete many other administrative tasks.

To perform basic administrative tasks with YaST, you need to know:

- How to Start YaST with a GUI Interface
- How to Start YaST with a Text Interface (ncurses)

How to Start YaST with a GUI Interface

You can start YaST by doing one of the following:

- Select the **YaST** icon from the desktop, and then enter the root *password* (if you are not already logged in as root).
- From a terminal window, switch to root by entering **sux –** and the root *password*; then enter **yast2**.
- Press **Alt+F2**, type **yast2**, select **Options**, select **Run as a different user**, and enter the root *password*; then select **Run** (KDE only).

After using one of these three methods to start YaST, the dialog box shown in Figure 1-1 appears.

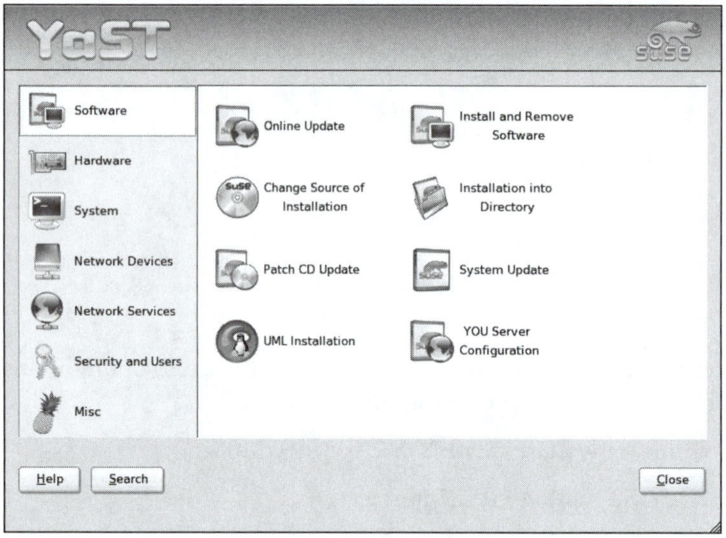

Figure 1-1

This is the main dialog box of YaST, sometimes called the *YaST Control Center*.

From here you can select a category on the left (such as Software or System) and a module on the right (such as Online Update) to configure and manage your system from a GUI interface.

When you finish making changes with a YaST module, YaST uses backend services such as SuSEconfig (see *The Role of SuSEconfig*) to implement the changes in the system.

Beside starting a module from the YaST Control Center, you can also start the module from a command line.

Make sure you are logged in to a terminal window as root with the command **sux –**; then list the names of the available modules by entering **yast2 –l**. Start a module by entering **yast2** *module_name*.

How to Start YaST with a Text Interface (ncurses)

As root, you can run YaST without a graphical user interface by entering **yast**. This starts the *ncurses* interface. If there is no X Windows running, the command yast2 also launches the ncurses interface.

Figure 1-2 shows the YaST Control Center ncurses interface.

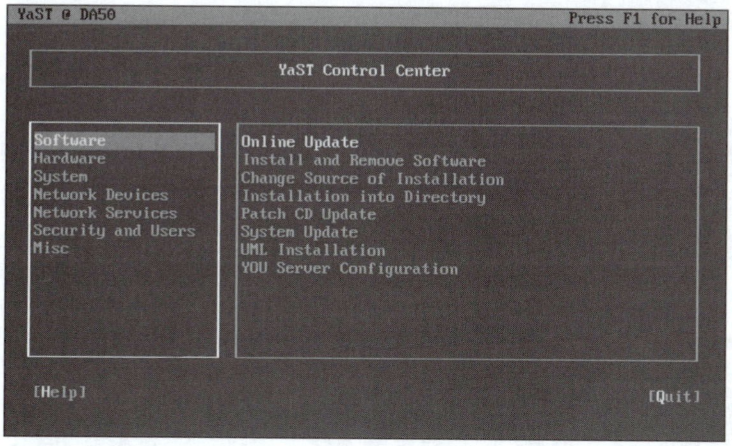

Figure 1-2

You can use the Tab key, Up and Down Arrow keys, or Alt+*letter* to navigate. Except for the navigation, there is no functional difference between the YaST GUI and ncurses interface.

The Role of SuSEconfig

You can consider YaST as a front end to various other programs, such as a front end to RPM (RPM Package Manager) software management, a front end to user management, or a front end to various configuration files of different services (like a mail or web server).

Sometimes YaST writes the configuration changes you make directly into the final configuration file.

In many other cases, there is an additional intermediate step, where the information you enter is first written to a file in the directory /etc/sysconfig/ and then written to its final destination.

This is where the program SuSEconfig becomes important.

SuSEconfig is a tool used in SUSE Linux Enterprise Server to configure the system according to the variables that are set in the various files in /etc/sysconfig/ and its subdirectories.

These files contain variables such as SYSLOGD_PARAMS="" in /etc/sysconfig/syslog and SMTPD_LISTEN_REMOTE="no" in */etc/sysconfig/mail*.

Some of these variables are used directly (such as in some start scripts). For example, if SYSLOGD_PARAMS is set to "-r," the daemon that logs system messages is directed to listen on port 514 for system messages from other hosts.

Other variables are used to modify other files. For example, if SMTPD_LISTEN_ REMOTE is set to "yes," the variable INET_INTERFACES in /etc/postfix/main.cf is set to "all" by the script /sbin/SuSEconfig and the scripts in /sbin/conf.d/.

SuSEconfig acts as a back end for YaST and activates the configuration changes you make when using a YaST module.

If you modify files in /etc/sysconfig/ using an editor, all you might need to do is restart a service for the change to take place. However, you might also need to run SuSEconfig.

For this reason, we recommend running SuSEconfig after manually editing files in /etc/ sysconfig/.

Additional details about SuSEconfig are provided throughout this and other SUSE Linux administration courses. You can also display the manual pages for SuSEconfig by entering **man suseconfig**.

NOTE

Exercise 1-2   Customize Your SLES 9 Installation with YaST

In this exercise, you customize your SLES 9 installation using the YaST text user interface and the YaST graphical user interface.

1. Set the language and time zone with the YaST text user interface:

   During classroom setup, your SLES 9 server was configured to use US English.

   To check and change this setting with YaST (ncurses), do the following:

   a. From the KDE desktop, open a terminal window by selecting the **Terminal Program** icon from the bottom panel.

   b. Switch to the root user by entering **su –**; then enter a password of **novell**.

   c. Start YaST by entering **yast2**.

      The text version of the YaST Control Center appears with a list of categories on the left and a list of modules on the right.

   d. (Optional) You might want to expand the terminal window for a larger view of the YaST Control Center.

   e. From the YaST Control Center, select the **System** category and the **Choose Language** module.

      A Language selection dialog box appears.

   f. Select *your language*; then select **Accept** by pressing **Alt+A**.

      You are returned to the YaST Control Center.

   g. Close the YaST Control Center by selecting **Quit**.

2. Change the date and time settings by using the YaST graphical user interface:

   During classroom setup, your SLES 9 server was configured to use Mountain Standard Time (US).

   To check and change this setting with YaST (GUI), do the following:

   a. From the terminal window, logout as root by entering **exit**.

   b. Log in as root by entering **sux –**; then enter a password of **novell**.

   c. List the available modules for YaST by entering **yast2 –l**.

   d. Scroll through the list to find the module you would use to set the time zone.

   e. Start the module by entering **yast2 timezone**.

      The Clock and Time Zone Configuration dialog box appears.

   f. Select *your region* and *your time zone*; then from the Hardware clock drop-down list, select **UTC**.

   g. When you finish, select **Accept**.

      Notice that YaST uses SuSEconfig to configure all the necessary files and services for the clock and time zone settings.

      When the configuration is complete, YaST closes. Because you directly accessed the YaST module, the YaST Control Center is not displayed.

3. Check and set the monitor and resolution for your SLES 9 server:

   During installation, YaST selects a graphics card driver and resolution automatically.

   However, you might want to change these as YaST dialog boxes (and the terminal window) display best at an 1152 × 768 or a 1024 × 768 resolution.

   a. Right-click the desktop and select **Configure Desktop**.

      The Configure – Desktop dialog box appears.

   b. On the left, select **Size & Orientation**.

   c. On the right, from the Screen size drop-down list, select **1152 × 768** or **1024 × 768**.

   d. Do one of the following:

      ■ After selecting the screen size, select **OK > Accept Configuration**; then continue on to Step 4.

      or

      ■ If either of these settings is not available, continue on to Step e.

e. Start YaST from the desktop by selecting the **YaST** icon.

A Run as root dialog box appears.

f. Enter a password of **novell**; then select **OK**.

The YaST Control Center appears.

g. Select **Hardware > Graphics Card and Monitor**.

A Desktop Settings dialog box appears with Graphical desktop environment selected and your graphics card and monitor settings listed.

h. Select **Change**.

An SaX2 dialog box appears.

i. On the left, expand **Desktop**; then use the **Monitor**, **Graphics card**, and **Color and Resolution** options (with the **Change configuration** button) to make any adjustments to your graphics configuration.

j. When you finish, select **Finalize**; then select **Test**.

k. Do one of the following:

- If the test screen appears properly, select **Save**; then select **OK**.

or

- If the test screen does not display properly (or at all), return to the SaX2 dialog box by pressing **Ctrl+Alt+Backspace** and change the Desktop settings.

l. When you finish, select **Accept**.

4. Close the YaST Control Center.

5. (Conditional) If you changed the graphics settings, do the following:

a. Log out as geeko by selecting **KDE Menu > Logout > Logout**.

You are returned to the GUI login screen.

b. Log in again as **geeko** (password of **N0v3ll**) to see the changes you made to the graphics settings.

OBJECTIVE 3   MONITOR YOUR SLES 9 SYSTEM

After installation, you probably have questions similar to the following:

- Did the system boot normally?
- What is the kernel version?
- What services are running?
- What is the load on the system?

In this objective, you are introduced to the following information that helps you discover information about your hardware and Linux system:

- Boot Log Information (/var/log/boot.msg)
- Hardware Information (/proc/)
- Hardware Information (Command-Line Utilities)
- System and Process Information (Command-Line Utilities)
- GUI Desktop Utilities

NOTE

These tools are covered in more detail in later sections of this course, and in other Novell SUSE Linux administration courses.

Boot Log Information (/var/log/boot.msg)

When SLES 9 starts, some lines scroll by too quickly for you to read easily. If there is an error message, it might be nearly impossible to read it.

However, because these messages are kept in a buffer and saved to /var/log/boot.msg, you can view them after booting by entering **dmesg | less**, as in the following:

```
Linux version 2.6.5-7.97-default (geeko@buildhost) (gcc  version 3.3.3
(SuSE Linux)) #1 Mon Jul 2 14:21:59 UTC 2007
BIOS-provided physical RAM map:
 BIOS-e820: 0000000000000000 - 00000000000a0000 (usable)
 BIOS-e820: 00000000000f0000 - 0000000000100000 (reserved)
 BIOS-e820: 0000000000100000 - 000000001fdf7000 (usable)
 BIOS-e820: 000000001fdf7000 - 000000001fe16000 (ACPI data)
 BIOS-e820: 000000001fe16000 - 0000000020000000 (reserved)
 BIOS-e820: 00000000fec00000 - 00000000fec10000 (reserved)
 BIOS-e820: 00000000fee00000 - 00000000fee10000 (reserved)
 BIOS-e820: 00000000ffb00000 - 0000000100000000 (reserved)
503MB vmalloc/ioremap area available.
0MB HIGHMEM available.
509MB LOWMEM available.
On node 0 totalpages: 130551
  DMA zone: 4096 pages, LIFO batch:1
  Normal zone: 126455 pages, LIFO batch:16
  HighMem zone: 0 pages, LIFO batch:1
DMI 2.3 present.
ACPI: RSDP (v000 DELL                                       ) @  0x000fd6d0
ACPI: RSDT (v001 DELL     GX150    0x00000005 ASL  0x00000061) @  0x000fd6e4
```

```
ACPI: FADT (v001 DELL    GX150   0x00000005 ASL  0x00000061) @  0x000fd718
ACPI: SSDT (v001   DELL    st_ex 0x00001000 MSFT 0x0100000b) @  0xfffe7465
lines 1-22
```

By using the command less, you can scroll up and down through the messages. The output of dmesg shows messages generated during the initialization of the hardware by the kernel or kernel modules.

For each line displayed at the console during startup, there is one or several lines in the file /var/log/boot.msg.

Although the file /var/log/boot.msg can be somewhat difficult to read, it contains additional information beyond what you can display with dmesg.

This information includes data such as the messages the various scripts generated at boot time and exit status codes, as in the following:

```
/dev/fd0 on /media/floppy type subfs (rw,nosuid,nodev,sync, fs=floppyfss,procuid)
/dev/hda3 on /apps type ext2 (rw,acl,user_xattr)
/dev/hda5 on /export/data1 type vfat (rw)
/dev/hda6 on /export/data2 type ext3 (rw,usrquota,grpquota)
/dev/hda7 on /export/data3 type reiserfs (rw)
/dev/mapper/project1-pilot on /project1/pilot type reiserfs  (rw,acl,user_xattr)
/dev/mapper/project1-prod on /project1/prod type reiserfs (rw, acl,user_xattr)
done<notice>exit status of (boot.localfs) is (0)
<notice>run boot scripts (boot.crypto)
<notice>exit status of (boot.crypto) is (0)
<notice>run boot scripts (boot.scpm boot.restore_permissions  boot.loadmodules)
Loading required kernel modules
doneRestore device permissionsdone
<notice>exit status of (boot.scpm boot.restore_permissions boot.loadmodules) is (0 0 0)
<notice>run boot scripts (boot.swap boot.idedma)
Activating remaining swap-devices in /etc/fstab...
done<notice>exit status of (boot.swap boot.idedma) is (0 0)
<notice>run boot scripts (boot.cycle boot.clock)
```

These additional messages can be useful when troubleshooting.

Besides using the commands dmesg and less from the command line to view the contents of /var/log/boot.msg, you can also use YaST to view the file contents by doing the following:

1. From the KDE desktop, start the YaST View System Log module by doing one of the following:

   ■ Select the **YaST** icon, enter the root *password*, and select **OK**; then select **Misc > View Start-up Log**.

   or

   ■ Open a terminal window and enter **sux –** and the root *password*; then enter **yast2 view_anymsg;** then, from the drop-down list, select **/var/log/boot.msg**.

   The log file appears as shown in Figure 1-3.

```
/var/log/boot.msg                                    ⬦

System log (/var/log/boot.msg)
Starting service kdmdone                                              ⬆
Starting mail service (Postfix)done
<notice>exit status of (xdm postfix) is (0 0)
<notice>start services (xinetd cron)
<notice>startproc: execve (/usr/sbin/xinetd) [ /usr/sbin/xinetd ], [ CONSOLE=/dev/console TERM=linux
SHELL=/bin/sh progress=45 INIT_VERSION=sysvinit-2.85 REDIRECT=/dev/tty1 COLUMNS=80
PATH=/usr/local/sbin:/sbin:/bin:/usr/sbin:/usr/bin RUNLEVEL=5 PWD=/ PREVLEVEL=N LINES=25 HOME=/ SHLVL=2
splash=silent sscripts=47 _=/sbin/startproc DAEMON=/usr/sbin/xinetd ]
<notice>startproc: execve (/usr/sbin/cron) [ /usr/sbin/cron ], [ CONSOLE=/dev/console TERM=linux SHELL=/bin/sh
progress=45 INIT_VERSION=sysvinit-2.85 REDIRECT=/dev/tty1 COLUMNS=80
PATH=/usr/local/sbin:/sbin:/bin:/usr/sbin:/usr/bin RUNLEVEL=5 PWD=/ PREVLEVEL=N LINES=25 HOME=/ SHLVL=2
splash=silent sscripts=47 _=/sbin/startproc DAEMON=/usr/sbin/cron ]
Starting CRON daemondone
Starting INET services. (xinetd)failed
<notice>exit status of (xinetd cron) is (7 0)
<notice>start services (splash_late)
<notice>exit status of (splash_late) is (0)
Master Resource Control: runlevel 5 has been reached
Failed services in runlevel 5: xinetd
Skipped services in runlevel 5: smbfs nfs splash
<notice>killproc: kill(780,3)                                         ⬇

                              OK
```

Figure 1-3

2. When you finish reading through the log file, exit by selecting **OK**.

Hardware Information (/proc/)

The directory /proc/ lets you view hardware information stored in the kernel memory space.

For example, if you enter cat /proc/cpuinfo, output is generated from data stored in kernel memory that gives you information such as the CPU model name and cache size.

You can view the available information by using commands such as cat, more, or less with a filename (such as **cat /proc/cpuinfo**).

The following list shows some of the filenames that are commonly used to generate information:

- **/proc/devices.** View the devices used on your Linux system.

- **/proc/cpuinfo.** View processor information.

- **/proc/ioports.** View the I/O ports on your server. The I/O ports are the addresses of various hardware devices.

- **/proc/interrupts.** View the IRQ (hardware interrupt signal) assignments for your Linux system.

- **/proc/dma.** View the DMA (Direct Memory Access) channels used on your Linux system.

- **/proc/bus/pci/devices.** View the PCI (Peripheral Component Interconnect) information on your Linux system.

- **/proc/scsi/scsi.** View a summary of the SCSI (Small Computer System Interface) information on your Linux system.

- **/proc/bus/usb/devices.** View information about the USB (Universal Serial Bus) devices on your Linux system.

- **/proc/bus/usb/drivers.** View information about the USB drivers on your Linux system.

For a list of all the available filenames, enter **ls -al /proc**.

Hardware Information (Command-Line Utilities)

The following are utilities you can use from the command line to view information about the hardware on your Linux system:

- **hwinfo.** Entering this command generates and displays a list of specific information about the devices installed on your Linux system.

  To view one page of information at a time, enter **hwinfo | less**. For a summary listing, entering **hwinfo --short**.

  To write the information to a log file, enter **hwinfo --log** *filename*.

- **hdparm.** Entering this command with various options lets you view information about your hard drive and manage certain hard drive parameters.

  For example, the option –i displays hard drive identification information available at boot time. The option –l requests information directly from the hard drive.

  For a summary list of available options, enter **hdparm** or **hdparm –h**.

1

- **fdisk.** While this command is primarily used for managing the partition table on a Linux system, you can also use options such as –l (list partition tables), and –s (size of partition) to view hard drive information.

- **iostat.** Entering this command displays CPU and input/output (I/O) statistics for devices and partitions.

  This command generates reports that can be used to change system configuration to better balance the input/output load between physical disks.

  The first report generated provides statistics concerning the time since the system was booted. Each subsequent report covers the time since the previous report.

  You can generate two types of reports with the command—the CPU usage report and the device usage report.

  The option –c generates only the CPU usage report; the option –d generates only the device usage report.

- **lspci.** Entering this command displays information about all PCI buses in your Linux system and all devices connected to them.

  The options –v and –vv generate verbose reports. The option –b gives you a bus-centric view of all the IRQ numbers and addresses as seen by the cards (instead of the kernel) on the PCI bus.

- **siga.** This is a SUSE Linux tool for gathering hardware information.

System and Process Information (Command-Line Utilities)

The following are commonly-used command line tools for viewing system information, and viewing and managing system processes:

- top
- uptime
- ps
- netstat
- uname

top

The top utility gives you a summary of various system statistics (such as memory and CPU usage, uptime, and number of users) in the top part of the screen, as shown in Figure 1-4.

```
top - 14:00:36 up 15 days,  2:31,  1 user,  load average: 1.16, 1.15,
Tasks:  95 total,   1 running,  89 sleeping,   5 stopped,   0 zombie
Cpu(s): 97.0% us,  2.6% sy,  0.0% ni,  0.0% id,  0.0% wa,  0.3% hi,  0
Mem:    514712k total,   434520k used,    80192k free,   118432k buffe
Swap:  1028120k total,       8k used,  1028112k free,    82884k cache

  PID USER      PR  NI  VIRT  RES  SHR S %CPU %MEM    TIME+  COMMAND
 7182 root      15   0 26276  13m  17m S  3.0  2.7 602:19.49 y2base
16379 root      15   0 85772  17m  68m S  1.3  3.5  1:45.69 X
13676 geeko     16   0  1876  876 1520 S  1.0  0.2  0:34.41 ksysgua
13675 geeko     16   0 26760  15m  23m S  0.7  3.1  1:11.70 ksysgua
16513 geeko     15   0 26212  13m  23m S  0.3  2.8  0:10.33 kdeinit
14127 geeko     15   0 33220  21m  26m S  0.3  4.3  0:15.30 kdeinit
17114 root      16   0  1752  920 1536 R  0.3  0.2  0:00.45 top
    1 root      16   0   588  244  444 S  0.0  0.0  0:05.15 init
    2 root      34  19     0    0    0 S  0.0  0.0  0:00.06 ksoftir
    3 root       5 -10     0    0    0 S  0.0  0.0  0:00.13 events/
    4 root       5 -10     0    0    0 S  0.0  0.0  0:00.00 kacpid
    5 root       5 -10     0    0    0 S  0.0  0.0  0:00.00 kblockd
    6 root       7 -10     0    0    0 S  0.0  0.0  0:00.07 khelper
    7 root      15   0     0    0    0 S  0.0  0.0  0:23.73 pdflush
    8 root      15   0     0    0    0 S  0.0  0.0  0:04.74 pdflush
   10 root      10 -10     0    0    0 S  0.0  0.0  0:00.00 aio/0
    9 root      16   0     0    0    0 S  0.0  0.0  0:12.64 kswapd0
  163 root      23   0     0    0    0 S  0.0  0.0  0:00.00 kseriod
```

Figure 1-4

In the lower part of the display, processes running on the server are sorted by CPU usage. The screen is updated every 2 seconds.

You can sort the processes by fields such as % Memory (type **m**) or by user (type **u** and then enter the *user ID*).

You can change the sorting and send signals to a process (such as suspending or killing a process). When you finish, type **q** to end top.

NOTE

For additional information on top, type **h** while in top or enter **man top** from a command line.

uptime

Although the command top gives you system information in the header, there might be times when you only want specific information without starting a utility.

For example, you can use the command uptime to display the current time, the length of time the system has been running, the number of users on the system, and the average number of jobs in the run queue over the last 1, 5, and 15 minutes.

The following is an example of entering the command uptime:

```
geeko@DA50:~> uptime
  1:44am  up 11 days 18:56,   2 users,   load average: 0.05, 0.09, 0.08
geeko@DA50:~>
```

For additional information on the uptime command, enter **man uptime**.

ps

The utility ps displays the processes running on the system sorted by process ID. You can change the output using one of several options.

For example, to see a display with detailed information, enter **ps aux** (as in the following):

```
geeko@DA50:~> ps aux
USER       PID %CPU %MEM   VSZ  RSS TTY      STAT START   TIME COMMAND
root         1  0.0  0.0   588  244 ?        S    Aug20   0:05 init [5]
root         2  0.0  0.0     0    0 ?        SN   Aug20   0:00 [ksoftirqd/0]
root         3  0.0  0.0     0    0 ?        S<   Aug20   0:00 [events/0]
root         4  0.0  0.0     0    0 ?        S<   Aug20   0:00 [kacpid]
root         5  0.0  0.0     0    0 ?        S<   Aug20   0:00 [kblockd/0]
root         6  0.0  0.0     0    0 ?        S<   Aug20   0:00 [khelper]
root         7  0.0  0.0     0    0 ?        S    Aug20   0:00 [pdflush]
root         8  0.0  0.0     0    0 ?        S    Aug20   0:12 [pdflush]
root        10  0.0  0.0     0    0 ?        S<   Aug20   0:00 [aio/0]
root         9  0.0  0.0     0    0 ?        S    Aug20   0:05 [kswapd0]
root       169  0.0  0.0     0    0 ?        S    Aug20   0:00 [kseriod]
root       530  0.0  0.0     0    0 ?        S<   Aug20   0:00 [reiserfs/0]
root       707  0.0  0.0     0    0 ?        S<   Aug20   0:00 [kcopyd]
root       769  0.0  0.0     0    0 ?        S    Aug20   0:00 [kjournald]
root      1426  0.0  0.0     0    0 ?        S    Aug20   0:00 [khubd]
root      1843  0.0  0.1  1584  720 ?        Ss   Aug20   0:27 /sbin/resmgrd
bin       1846  0.0  0.1  1432  624 ?        Ss   Aug20   0:37 /sbin/portmap
```

If there is more information than can fit on one screen, you can use the command less (such as **ps aux | less**).

netstat

While the command ps provides information on a process level, you can use netstat to find out which network ports are offering services and what connections are established, as in the following:

```
geeko@DA50:~> netstat -patune
(Not all processes could be identified, non-owned process info
 will not be shown, you would have to be root to see it all.)
Active Internet connections (servers and established)
Proto Recv-Q Send-Q Local Address      Foreign Address      StateUser  Inode      PID/Program name
tcp      0      0 0.0.0.0:2049         0.0.0.0:*LISTEN       0         1288996    -
tcp      0      0 0.0.0.0:32776        0.0.0.0:*LISTEN       0         1248510    -
tcp      0      0 0.0.0.0:139          0.0.0.0:*LISTEN       0         1324989    -
tcp      0      0 10.0.0.50:427        0.0.0.0:*LISTEN       0         5032       -
tcp      0      0 127.0.0.1:427        0.0.0.0:*LISTEN       0         5031       -
tcp      0      0 0.0.0.0:111          0.0.0.0:*LISTEN       0         2844       -
tcp      0      0 0.0.0.0:752          0.0.0.0:*LISTEN       0         1274848    -
tcp      0      0 0.0.0.0:785          0.0.0.0:*LISTEN       0         1275487    -
tcp      0      0 0.0.0.0:21           0.0.0.0:*LISTEN       0         1352119    -
...
```

Table 1-9 shows some useful options for customizing the output of netstat.

Table 1-9

Option	Description
-p	Show processes (as root)
-a	Show listening and non listening sockets (all)
-t	Show tcp information
-u	Show udp information
-n	Do not resolve hostnames
-e	Display additional information (extend)
-r	Display routing information

uname

You can use the command uname to find out about the current kernel version, as in the following:

```
geeko@DA50:~> uname -a
Linux DA50 2.6.5-7.97-default #1 Mon Jul 2 14:21:59 UTC 2007 i686 i686
i386 GNU/Linux
geeko@DA50:~>
```

GUI Desktop Utilities

The following are utilities you can use from the desktop to view information about your hardware and Linux system:

- KDE System Guard
- Xosview
- SuSEPlugger

KDE System Guard

KDE System Guard is the KDE desktop task manager and performance monitor. With KDE System Guard, you can monitor system load performance (CPU load, load average, physical memory, and swap memory) or processes.

To access KDE System Guard, from the system menu select **System > Monitor > KDE System Guard** (see Figure 1-5).

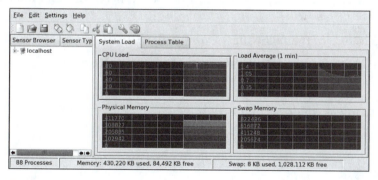

Figure 1-5

Selecting **Process Table** displays the tab shown in Figure 1-6.

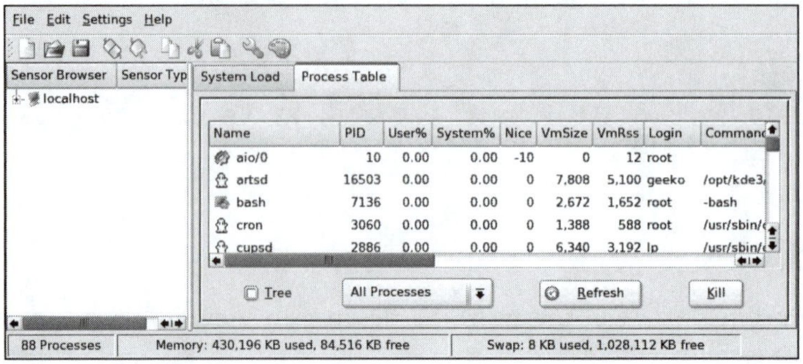

Figure 1-6

From the process table, you can monitor and stop (kill) processes.

> For additional information on KDE System Guard, from the program menu select **Help > KDE System Guard Handbook**.
>
> **NOTE**

Xosview

You can use the utility Xosview to display the status of several system-based parameters such as CPU usage, load average, memory usage, swap space usage, network usage, interrupts, and serial port status.

To start Xosview, do one of the following:

- From the KDE menu, select **System > Monitor > Xosview**.

  or

- From a terminal window, enter **xosview**.

A window similar to that shown in Figure 1-7 appears.

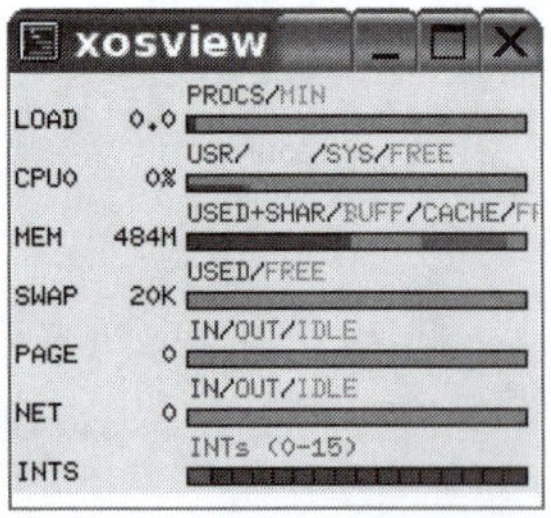

Figure 1-7

Each parameter status is displayed as a horizontal bar separated into color-coded regions. Each region represents a percentage of the resource that is being put to a particular use.

When you finish viewing the information, you can quit by closing the window or by typing **q**.

SuSEPlugger

You can use the utility SuSEPlugger to view details about specific hardware on your Linux system, and to launch the appropriate YaST module for configuring the hardware.

To start SuSEPlugger, do one of the following:

- From your desktop panel (bottom of the screen), select the **SuSEPlugger** icon.

    or

- From a terminal window, enter **suseplugger**.

The SuSEPlugger utility opens, as shown in Figure 1-8.

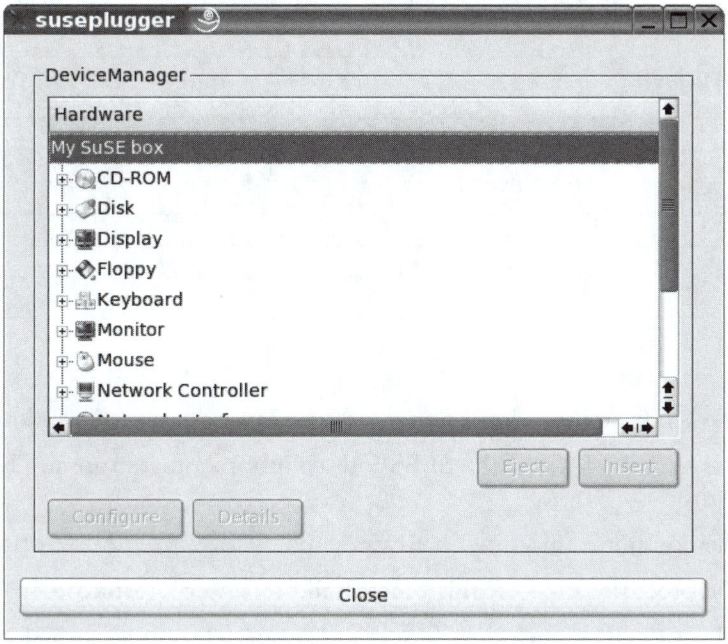

Figure 1-8

From the SuSEPlugger window, you can expand a hardware category and select a specific hardware device.

After selecting the hardware device, you can view details about the device by selecting **Details**, or launch a YaST module to configure the device by selecting **Configure**.

When you finish using SuSEPlugger, close the window by selecting **Close**.

Exercise 1-3   Gather Information About Your SLES 9 Server

After installing SLES 9, you decide to use several of the administration tools available to gather information about your SLES 9 server.

Enter information in Table 1-10 by following Steps 1-10 below.

Table 1-10

System Parameter	Value
OS	
Hardware Architecture	
Processor Type	
Hostname	
Kernel Release	
Kernel Version (include date and time)	
System Up Time	
Load Averages	
SLES 9 Version	
System Date and Time	
Model Name of Processor	
Free Memory	

Do the following:

1. From the KDE desktop (logged in as geeko), open a terminal window.

2. View the kernel release of the SLES 9 distribution you are running by entering **uname -r**.

3. View the computer (machine) hardware architecture by entering **uname -m**.

4. View the processor type for this Linux build by entering **uname -p**.

5. View all information including hostname, kernel release, and kernel version by entering **uname -a**.

6. View how long the system has been running and the load averages by entering **uptime**.

7. View the version of the SLES 9 distribution by entering **cat /etc/ SuSE-release**.

8. View the system date and time by entering **date**.

1

9. View information about the current running processor by entering **cat /proc/cpuinfo**.

10. View the current memory statistics by entering **cat /proc/meminfo**.

11. Start Xosview to monitor system resource usage:

    a. Press **Alt+F2**.

       The Run Command - KDesktop dialog box appears.

    b. Enter **xosview**; then select **Run**.

12. Use SuSEPlugger to view unknown devices:

    a. From the System Tray, select the **SuSEPlugger** icon (SUSE Hardware Tool).

       SuSEPlugger is similar to the Device Manager in Windows.

    b. View the unconfigured devices on your SLES 9 server by expanding the **Unknown** category.

13. Launch the YaST Network Card module from SuSEPlugger:

    a. Expand **Network Controller**; then select *your network device*.

    b. Select **Configure**.

       The Run as root dialog box appears.

    c. Enter a password of **novell**; then select **OK**.

       The Network cards configuration dialog box appears.

    d. Close the dialog box without changing any settings by selecting **Abort**; then select **Yes**.

14. Close all open windows on your desktop.

CHAPTER SUMMARY

- SLES 9 uses the new 2.6 version of the Linux kernel, which has more hardware support and better scalability. In addition, SLES 9 hosts many new development tools, YaST management utilities, and software packages.

- By providing support for many different hardware platforms and hardware extensions, such as USB 2.0 and Firewire, SLES is an attractive choice for a server-based network operating system.

- You must have 256 MB RAM and 500 MB available hard disk space to install SLES. Depending on the server role, you will almost always need to exceed these minimum requirements.

- SLES versions are certified by many major software vendors, and support the LSB, FHS, and TDS standards.

- Each SLES version has a five-year period of software support and several support options.

- Most system configuration is performed using YaST in graphical mode (yast2) or text mode (yast). YaST typically saves information to the /etc/sysconfig directory and uses SuSEconfig to configure the information on the system.

- The /var/log/boot.msg file contains hardware and software information from system initialization and may be viewed using the **dmesg** command.

- You may view the files in the /proc directory to obtain hardware information for your SLES system. Alternatively, you may use the **hwinfo**, **hdparm**, **fdisk**, **iostat**, **lspci**, and **siga** commands or the KDE System Guard, Xosview, and SuSEPlugger graphical utilities to view information about various hardware devices or display hardware statistics.

- The **top**, **uptime**, **ps**, **netstat**, and **uname** commands display system and process-related information about your system.

Key Terms

/proc — A directory stored in RAM that contains information about system hardware and processes exported by the Linux kernel.

/var/log/boot.msg — A text file that stores information regarding system initialization.

Application Programming Interfaces (APIs) — Sets of routines in an operating system that are available to software programs.

fdisk command — Used to view and change hard disk partitions.

Filesystem Hierarchy Standard (FHS) — A Linux standard that defines the names, locations, and contents of key directories on the system.

hdparm command — Used to view and change hard disk settings.

hwinfo command — Used to display a hardware device report.

iostat command — Displays Input/Output statistics for various system devices.

KDE System Guard — A graphical utility that can be used to display and manage processes on the system as well as view system load statistics.

kernel — The core component of the operating system. Different kernels provide different hardware features. The version of the Linux kernel in SLES is 2.6.

Linux Standard Base (LSB) — A standard that defines the system and package structure for Linux systems.

lspci command — Displays information about devices using the PCI bus on your system.

ncurses — A text-based menuing interface in Linux.

netstat command — Displays network statistics for network interfaces on the system.

ps command — Displays process information.

scalability — The ease with which a system is able to support larger sets of hardware, data, and users.

1

siga command — Displays information about system hardware devices and installed software applications.

SuSEconfig — A software utility that configures the system using entries in the /etc/sysconfig directory.

SuSEPlugger — A graphical utility that displays hardware device information by category.

TeX Directory Structure (TDS) — A Linux standard for the implementation of the TeX typesetting system.

top command — Used to view and manage the processes on your system that are using the most CPU time.

uname command — Displays brief system information such as host name and kernel version.

uptime command — Displays system uptime and process activity.

Xosview — A small graphical utility that displays CPU, memory, swap, and network statistics.

YaST — The main configuration tool in SLES. It may be run in graphical or text (ncurses) mode.

REVIEW QUESTIONS

1. Which of the following are features of the 2.6 Linux kernel? (Choose all that apply.)
   a. UML virtualization
   b. Support for NUMA and Hyperthreading
   c. Ability to scale to 4 billion users, 65,535 processes, and over 128 CPUs
   d. High throughput for data devices and system busses

2. What are the recommended minimum CPU, RAM, and hard disk requirements in SLES 9?
   a. Pentium I, 256 MB RAM, 500 MB hard disk
   b. Pentium II, 256 MB RAM, 500 MB hard disk
   c. Pentium III, 512 MB RAM, 4 GB hard disk
   d. Pentium IV, 512 MB RAM, 10 GB hard disk

3. What is the default support lifespan for SLES?
   a. 1 year
   b. 2 years
   c. 5 years
   d. 10 years

4. Which of the following server roles will likely require more RAM than outlined in the recommended minimum installation requirements? (Choose two answers.)

   a. Print server

   b. Web server

   c. Database sever

   d. File server

5. Which Linux standard defines the location of key directories and files?

   a. LSB

   b. FHS

   c. TDS

   d. LSD

6. What command would you type at a command prompt within a desktop environment to start the text-based yast interface? _____

7. What utility should you run after changing content in the /etc/sysconfig directory?

   a. YaST

   b. suseconfig

   c. uname

   d. KDE System Guard

8. What command can you use to quickly view the contents of the system initialization log file? _____

9. Which of the following may be used to view CPU, memory, and swap usage information? (Choose all that apply.)

   a. uptime

   b. top

   c. Xosview

   d. iostat

10. What file in the /proc directory contains information on IRQ usage? _____

DISCOVERY EXERCISES

Updating SLES

All operating systems today require constant and consistent updating to reduce security breaches and application problems. Use the Internet to search for and install the latest bug fixes and security patches for SLES 9.

1

Scaling SLES

One of the key reasons why enterprise organizations use SLES for their operating system is its ability to scale to large systems. Use the Internet to research three organizations that use SLES in a large-scale system and summarize the features of their technologies and how they were implemented.

Creating a System Baseline

Following a SLES installation, it is important to create a baseline of system performance to aid in troubleshooting future performance problems related to system hardware and software. Use the utilities introduced in this chapter to create a baseline of typical CPU load, memory usage, swap usage, and process load. Then use local or Internet resources to find three other Linux utilities that may be used to obtain performance data, and summarize their usage and features.

2

MANAGE USER ACCESS AND SECURITY

In this section you learn how to perform basic user and group management tasks that provide users with a secure and accessible SUSE Linux Enterprise Server environment.

- ◆ Describe Basic Linux User Security Features
- ◆ Manage Linux Users and Groups
- ◆ Manage and Secure the Linux User Environment
- ◆ Secure Files and Directories with Permissions
- ◆ Configure User Authentication with PAM
- ◆ Implement and Monitor Enterprise Security Policies

OBJECTIVE 1 DESCRIBE BASIC LINUX USER SECURITY FEATURES

One of the main characteristics of a Linux operating system is its ability to handle several users at the same time (multiuser) and to allow these users to perform several tasks on the same computer simultaneously (multitask).

To maintain an environment where data and applications are secure, you need to understand the following:

- File System Security Components
- Users and Groups
- Ownership and Access Permissions

File System Security Components

As with other operating systems, you control access to files in a Linux file system by implementing the following types of components:

- **Users.** Users are individual accounts on the Linux system.

- **Groups.** Groups are collections of users. Users are assigned to a group when they are created. Only root or the owner can change the group to which the file or directory is assigned. Every user must belong to at least one group.

- **Ownership.** The user who creates a file or directory is automatically assigned as its owner. Ownership can only be changed manually by root.

- **Permissions.** Permissions determine user access to a file or directory.

Users and Groups

Because Linux is a multiuser system, several users can work on the system at the same time. For this reason the system uniquely identifies all users through user accounts that require a user name and password to log in to the system.

In addition, Linux provides groups that let you associate users together that require the same type of access privileges to data and applications.

To manage users and groups, you need to know the following:

- User and Group ID Numbers
- Regular vs. System Users
- Public vs. Private Group Schemes
- User Accounts and Home Directories
- User and Group Configuration Files
- How to Check /etc/passwd and /etc/shadow

User and Group ID Numbers

Because an operating system can handle numbers much better than strings, users and groups are administered internally as numbers on a Linux system.

The number that a user receives is called a *user ID* (UID). Every Linux system has a privileged user, the user root. This user always has a UID of 0. UID numbering for normal users starts (by default) at 1000 for SUSE Linux.

As with users, groups are also internally allocated a number, called the *group ID* (GID).

Normal users are usually included in the group users. Other groups also exist (and can be created) for special roles or tasks.

For example, all users who intend to create Web pages can be placed in the group webedit. Of course, file permissions for the directory in which the Web pages are located must be set so that members of the group webedit are able to write and read files.

You can use the command id to display information about a user's UID and the groups to which she is assigned. For example, entering **id geeko** provides information about the user geeko:

```
geeko@earth:~> id geeko
uid=1000(geeko) gid=100(users)
groups=100(users),14(uucp),16(dialout),17(audio), 33(video)
```

This information includes the following:

- **User ID:** uid=1000(geeko)

- **Current default (effective) group:** gid=100(users)

- **All groups of which geeko is a member:** groups=100(users),14(uucp), 16(dialout),...

If you want information on the groups in which you are a member, enter **groups**. You can specify a particular user by entering **groups** *user*.

You can display additional information about local users by entering **finger** *user*, as illustrated in the following:

```
geeko@earth:~> finger geeko
Login: geeko                              Name: geeko
Directory: /home/geeko                    Shell: /bin/bash
On since Tue Oct 23 13:21 (CEST) on pts/0 from 192.168.5.16
New mail received Mon Oct 22 11:54 2007 (CEST)
          Unread since Mon Oct 22 11:54 2007 (CEST)
No Plan.
geeko@earth:~ >
```

Regular vs. System Users

In a Linux operating system, there are two basic kinds of user accounts:

- **Regular (normal) users.** These are user accounts you create that allow employees and others to log in to the Linux environment. This type of login gives people a secure environment for accessing data and applications.

  These user accounts are managed by the system administrator.

- **System users.** These are user accounts created during installation that are used by services, utilities, and other applications to run effectively on the server.

Regular users are stored in the files /etc/passwd and /etc/shadow; system users are created by scripts that are part of rpm packages.

Public vs. Private Group Schemes

When you create a user in a Linux (or UNIX) environment, that user is assigned a default group using one of two basic methods (schemes):

- **Private scheme.** In this scheme, the user is assigned his own group that he can manage.

  For example, if you create the user **cgrayson**, a group **cgrayson** is also created.

- **Public scheme.** In this scheme, the user is assigned to a general, public group such as **users**.

  Because the group includes all new users, the group is normally managed by the system administrator.

SUSE Linux Enterprise Server uses the public scheme for assigning new users to a group.

User Accounts and Home Directories

Each user has a user account identified by a login name and a personal password for logging in to the system.

By having user accounts, you are able to protect a user's personal data from being modified, viewed, or tampered with by other users. Each user can set up her own working environment and always find it unchanged when she logs back in.

As part of these security measures, each user in the system has her own directory in the directory /home/, as shown in Figure 2-1.

bin	2.9 KB	Folder
boot	544 B	Folder
dev	175.3 KB	Folder
etc	8.5 KB	Folder
home	96 B	Folder
geeko	984 B	Folder
bin	48 B	Folder
Desktop	344 B	Folder
Documents	80 B	Folder
public_html	80 B	Folder
snapshot1.png	24.1 KB	PNG Image
tux	568 B	Folder
bin	48 B	Folder
Documents	80 B	Folder
public_html	80 B	Folder
lib	3.5 KB	Folder
media	96 B	Folder
mnt	48 B	Folder
opt	176 B	Folder
proc	0 B	Folder
root	848 B	Locked Folder
sbin	10.3 KB	Folder
srv	96 B	Folder

Figure 2-1

The exception to this rule is the account root. It has its own home directory in /root/.

Home directories allow personal data and desktop settings to be secured for user access only.

You should avoid using the root account when performing day-to-day tasks that do not involve system management.

User and Group Configuration Files

The Linux system stores all user and group configuration data in the following files:

- /etc/passwd
- /etc/shadow
- /etc/group

NOTE Whenever possible, you should not modify these files with an editor. Instead, use the Security and Users modules provided in YaST or the command-line tools described in *Manage User Accounts from the Command Line*.

Modifying these files with an editor can lead to errors (especially in /etc/ shadow), such as a user—including the user root—no longer being able to log in.

/etc/passwd

The file /etc/passwd stores information for each user such as the user name, the UID, the home directory, and the standard shell.

In the past, /etc/passwd also contained the encrypted password. However, because the file needs to be readable by all (especially to find out the UID of a particular user), the encrypted password is now stored in /etc/shadow, which is only readable by root.

Figure 2-2 shows a sample /etc/passwd file.

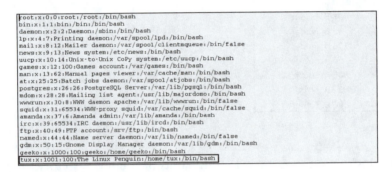

```
root:x:0:0:root:/root:/bin/bash
bin:x:1:1:bin:/bin:/bin/bash
daemon:x:2:2:Daemon:/sbin:/bin/bash
lp:x:4:7:Printing daemon:/var/spool/lpd:/bin/bash
mail:x:8:12:Mailer daemon:/var/spool/clientmqueue:/bin/false
news:x:9:13:News system:/etc/news:/bin/bash
uucp:x:10:14:Unix-to-Unix CoPy system:/etc/uucp:/bin/bash
games:x:12:100:Games account:/var/games:/bin/bash
man:x:13:62:Manual pages viewer:/var/cache/man:/bin/bash
at:x:25:25:Batch jobs daemon:/var/spool/atjobs:/bin/bash
postgres:x:26:26:PostgreSQL Server:/var/lib/pgsql:/bin/bash
mdom:x:28:28:Mailing list agent:/usr/lib/majordomo:/bin/bash
wwwrun:x:30:8:WWW daemon apache:/var/lib/wwwrun:/bin/false
squid:x:31:65534:WWW-proxy squid:/var/cache/squid:/bin/false
amanda:x:37:6:Amanda admin:/var/lib/amanda:/bin/bash
irc:x:39:65534:IRC daemon:/usr/lib/ircd:/bin/bash
ftp:x:40:49:FTP account:/srv/ftp:/bin/bash
named:x:44:44:Name server daemon:/var/lib/named:/bin/false
gdm:x:50:15:Gnome Display Manager daemon:/var/lib/gdm:/bin/bash
geeko:x:1000:100:geeko:/home/geeko:/bin/bash
tux:x:1001:100:The Linux Penguin:/home/tux:/bin/bash
```

Figure 2-2

Each line in the file /etc/password represents one user, and contains the information shown in Figure 2-3.

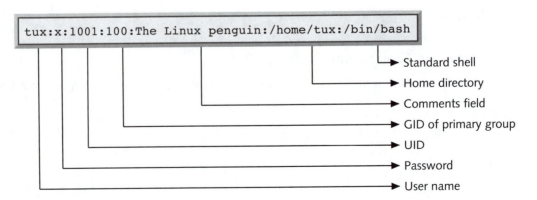

```
tux:x:1001:100:The Linux penguin:/home/tux:/bin/bash
```

- ➤ Standard shell
- ➤ Home directory
- ➤ Comments field
- ➤ GID of primary group
- ➤ UID
- ➤ Password
- ➤ User name

Figure 2-3

Note the following about the fields in each line:

- **User name.** This is the name a user enters to log in to the system (login name).

  Although Linux can handle longer user names, in this file they should be restricted to a maximum of 8 characters for backward compatibility with older programs.

- **Password.** The x in this field means that the password is stored in the file /etc/shadow.

- **UID.** In compliance with the Linux standards, there are two number ranges which are reserved:

  - **0–99** for the system itself
  - **100–499** for special system users (such as services and programs)

  Normal users start from UID 1000.

- **Comments field.** Normally, the full name of the user is stored here. Information such as a room number or telephone number can also be stored here.

- **Home directory.** The personal directory of a user is normally in the directory /home/ and is the same name as the user (login) name.

- **Standard shell.** This is the shell that is started for a user after he or she has successfully logged in. In Linux this is normally bash (Bourne Again Shell).

  The shell must be listed in the file **/etc/shells**. Each user can change his standard shell with the command chsh (see **man chsh**).

For additional information on this file, enter **man 5 passwd**.

/etc/shadow

The /etc/shadow file stores encrypted user passwords and password expiration information. Most Linux systems use *shadow passwords*. Shadow passwords are stored in /etc/shadow instead of /etc/passwd.

The file can only be changed by the user root and read by the user root and members of the group shadow. Figure 2-4 shows a sample /etc/shadow file.

```
mailman:!:12608:0:99999:7:::
man:*:8902:0:10000::::
mdom:!:12 08:0:99999:7:::
mysql:!:12608:0:99999:7:::
named:!:12608:0:99999:7:::
news:*:8902:0:10000::::
nobody:*:8902:0:10000::::
ntp:!:12608:0:99999:7:::
pop:!:12608:0:99999:7:::
postfix:!:12608:0:99999:7:::
postgres:!:12608:0:99999:7:::
quagga:!:12608:0:99999:7:::
radiusd:!:12608:0:99999:7:::
root:XOQeyibhsgHj2:12608:0:10000::::
snort:!:12608:0:99999:7:::
squid:!:12608:0:99999:7:::
sshd:!:12608:0:99999:7:::
stunnel:!:12608:0:99999:7:::
uucp:*:8902:0:10000::::
vscan:!:12608:0:99999:7:::
wwwrun:*:8902:0:10000::::
tux:svSIYQsFoEwKg:12608:0:99999:7:-1::
geeko:mostSt1zdI45I:12623:1:99999:14:-1:12134:
```

Figure 2-4

Each line in the file /etc/shadow belongs to one user and contains the fields shown in Figure 2-5.

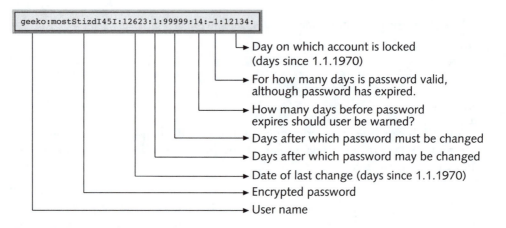

Figure 2-5

The above illustration shows the entry for the user **geeko** with an encrypted password. The plain text password was **suse**.

The encrypted password is coded with the crypt function and is always 13 characters in length. The encrypted word consists of letters, digits, and the special characters "." and "/."

If an invalid character (such as "*" or "!") occurs in the password field, then that user has an invalid password.

Many users, such as wwwrun (Apache Web server) or bin have an asterisk ("*") in the password field. This means that these users do not log in to the system, but instead play a role for specific programs.

If the password field is empty, then the user can log in to the system without entering a password. A password should always be set in a multiuser system.

/etc/group

The file /etc/group stores group information. Figure 2-6 shows a sample /etc/group file.

```
root:x:0:
bin:x:1:daemon
daemon:x:2:
sys:x:3:
tty:x:5:
disk:x:6:
lp:x:7:
www:x:8:
kmem:x:9:
uucp:x:14:geeko,tux
shadow:x:15:
dialout:x:16:geeko,tux
audio:x:17:geeko,tux
floppy:x:19:
cdrom:x:20:
console:x:21:
utmp:x:22:
at:!:25:
postgres:!:26:
mdom:!:28:
public:x:32:
video:x:33:geeko,tux
nobody:x:65533:
nogroup:x:65534:nobody
users:x:100:
novell:!:1000:
```

Figure 2-6

Each line in the file represents a single group record, and contains the group name, the GID (group ID), and the members of the group. For example

```
video:x:33:geeko,tux
```

This is the entry for the group video in /etc/group and has a GID of **33**. The users geeko and tux are members of this group. The second field (**x**) is the password field.

The /etc/groups file shows secondary group memberships, but does not identify the primary group for a user.

In older versions of SUSE Linux (such as SUSE Linux Enterprise Server 8), group passwords are stored in the file /etc/gshadow.

CAUTION

How to Check /etc/passwd and /etc/shadow

Because user configuration is handled with two files (/etc/passwd and /etc/shadow), these files match each other. This includes an entry for each user in both files.

However, discrepancies can occur—especially if you are configuring these files in an editor. In these cases, there are programs you can use to check /etc/passwd and /etc/shadow.

For example, to view the contents of both files at once, you can enter the following:

```
earth:~ # tail -3 /etc/passwd /etc/shadow
==> /etc/passwd <==
cyrus:x:96:12:User for cyrus-imapd:/usr/lib/cyrus:/bin/bash
tux:x:1000:100:tux:/home/tux:/bin/bash
geeko:x:1001:100:geeko:/home/geeko:/bin/bash
==> /etc/shadow <==
postfix:!:12543:0:99999:7:::
cyrus:!:12543:0:99999:7:::
tux:0C9zaAMz3p72g:12551:0:99999:7:::
earth:~ #
```

In the above example, the user geeko is entered in /etc/passwd but not in /etc/shadow.

In order to correct this type of error, you can enter the command pwconv:

```
earth:~ # pwconv
earth:~ # tail -3 /etc/passwd /etc/shadow
==> /etc/passwd <==
cyrus:x:96:12:User for cyrus-imapd:/usr/lib/cyrus:/bin/bash
tux:x:1000:100:tux:/home/tux:/bin/bash
geeko:x:1001:100:geeko:/home/geeko:/bin/bash
==> /etc/shadow <==
cyrus:!:12543:0:99999:7:::
tux:0C9zaAMz3p72g:12551:0:99999:7:::
geeko:x:12566:0:99999:7:::0
earth:~ #
```

You can also use the command pwck:

```
earth:~ # pwck
Checking '/etc/passwd'
User 'geeko': directory '/home/geeko' does not exist.
Checking '/etc/shadow'.
earth:~ #
```

Exercise 2-1   Check User and Group Information on Your Server

Check the user and group information on your SLES 9 server by doing the following from a command line:

1. Make sure you are logged in as **geeko** to the KDE desktop.

2. From a terminal window, su to root (**su -**) with a password of **novell**.

3. Display all information in the file /etc/group by entering **cat /etc/group**.

4. Display only the group name and group number fields in the file by entering **cat /etc/group | cut -d: -f1,3 | less**.

   You see entries similar to root:0 and bin:1.

5. Scroll through the file by pressing the **spacebar**; then exit by typing **q**.

6. Display the contents of the file /etc/passwd by entering **less /etc/passwd**.

7. Scroll through the file by pressing the **spacebar**; then exit by typing **q**.

8. Display the identity information of the logged-in user by entering **id**.

   Because you are su'd to root, you see UID, GID, and group information for root.

9. Exit the su state and return to the geeko user by entering **exit**.

10. Enter **id** again.

    Notice that the groups displayed for geeko are different from those displayed for root.

11. Close the terminal window by entering **exit**.

Ownership and Access Permissions

Each file and directory in the file system is assigned access permissions. The permissions assigned determine the level of access a given user has. Permissions are assigned at 3 levels:

- **Owner.** The permissions assigned to a file or directory's owner determine the owner's level of access.

- **Group.** Permissions assigned to the group determine the level of access group members have to the file or directory.

- **Others.** Permissions assigned to this entity apply to authenticated users who are not members of the group that has been associated with the file or directory.

For details on assigning permissions, see *How to Set Permissions from the Command Line*.

OBJECTIVE 2   MANAGE LINUX USERS AND GROUPS

To manage Linux user accounts and groups from your SUSE Linux Enterprise Server, you need to know how to do the following:

- Create and Edit User Accounts with YaST
- Create and Edit Groups with YaST
- Edit User Account Properties
- Configure Account Password Settings
- Manage User Accounts from the Command Line
- Manage Groups from the Command Line
- Create Text Login Messages

Create and Edit User Accounts with YaST

You can use the Edit and Create Users module in YaST to create, edit, and delete Linux user accounts by doing the following:

1. From the KDE desktop, start the YaST Edit and create users module by doing one of the following:

    - Select the **YaST** icon, enter the root *password*, and select **OK**; then select **Security and Users > Edit and create users**.

        or

    - Open a terminal window and enter **sux –** and the root *password*; then enter **yast2 users**.

The User and Group Administration dialog box appears, as shown in Figure 2-7.

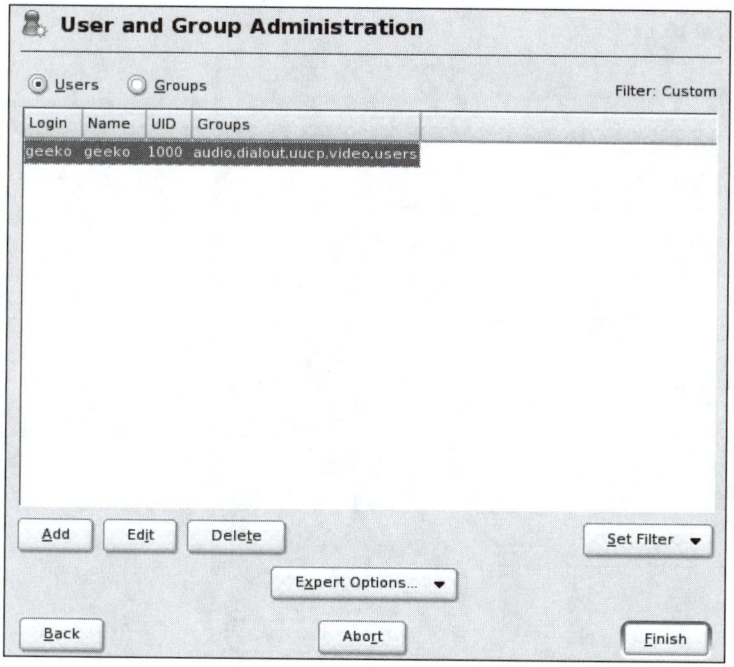

Figure 2-7

A list of users (accounts on your server) appears with information such as login name, full name, UID, and associated groups included for each user.

2. Select **Set Filter**; then select one of the following to change the users listed:

- **Local Users.** User accounts you have created on your local server for logging into the server.

- **System Users.** User accounts created by the system for use with services and applications.

- **Custom.** A customized view of users based on the settings configured with **Customize Filter**.

- **Customize Filter.** This option lets you combine listed user sets (such as **Local Users** and **System Users**) to display a customized view (with **Custom**) of the users list.

Additional sets of users (such as LDAP users) are added to the Set Filter drop-down list as you configure and start services on your server.

3. You can create a new user account or edit an existing account by selecting **Add** or **Edit**.

The Add a New Local User dialog box appears, as shown in Figure 2-8.

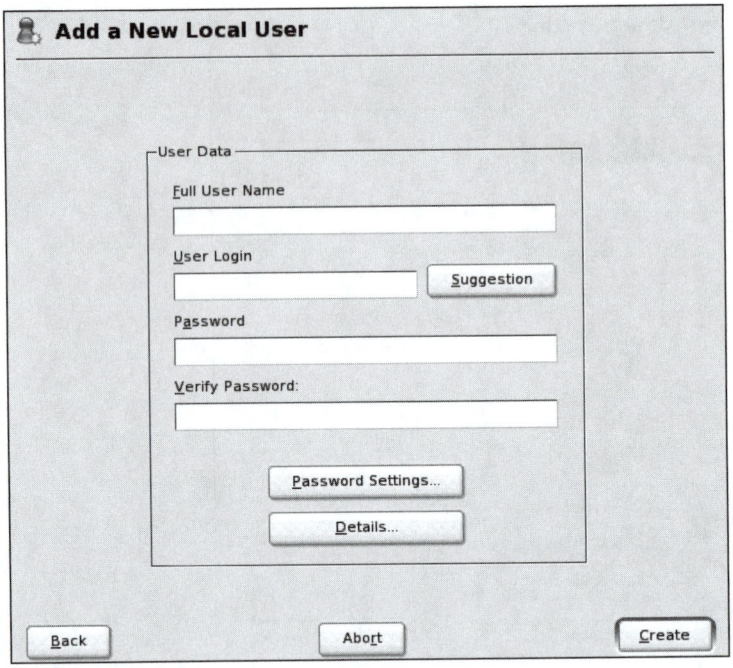

Figure 2-8

4. Enter or edit information in the following fields:

- **Full User Name.** Enter a descriptive user name (such as **Sandy Geeko**).

- **User Login.** Enter a user name that can be used to log in to the system (such as **geeko**).

- **Password** and **Verify Password.** Enter and reenter a password for the user account.

    When entering a password, distinguish between uppercase and lowercase letters.

    Valid password characters include letters, digits, blanks, and #*,.;:._-+!$%&/|?{[()]}=.

    The password should not contain any special characters (such as accented characters), as you might find it difficult to type these characters on a different keyboard layout when logging in from another country.

    With the current password encryption (DES), the password length should be between 5 and 8 characters.

NOTE

For information on creating longer passwords, see the Password Settings configuration settings under *Configure Security Settings*.

5. Save the settings for the new or edited user by selecting **Create** or **Next**.

   The new user appears in the list.

6. Configure your server with the new settings by selecting **Finish**.

Create and Edit Groups with YaST

You can use the Edit and create groups module in YaST to create, edit, and delete Linux groups by doing the following:

1. From the KDE desktop, start the YaST Edit and create groups module by doing one of the following:

   - Select the **YaST** icon, enter the root *password*, and select **OK**; then select **Security and Users > Edit and create groups**.

     or

   - Open a terminal window and enter **sux –** and the root *password*; then enter **yast2 groups**.

The User and Group Administration dialog box appears, as shown in Figure 2-9.

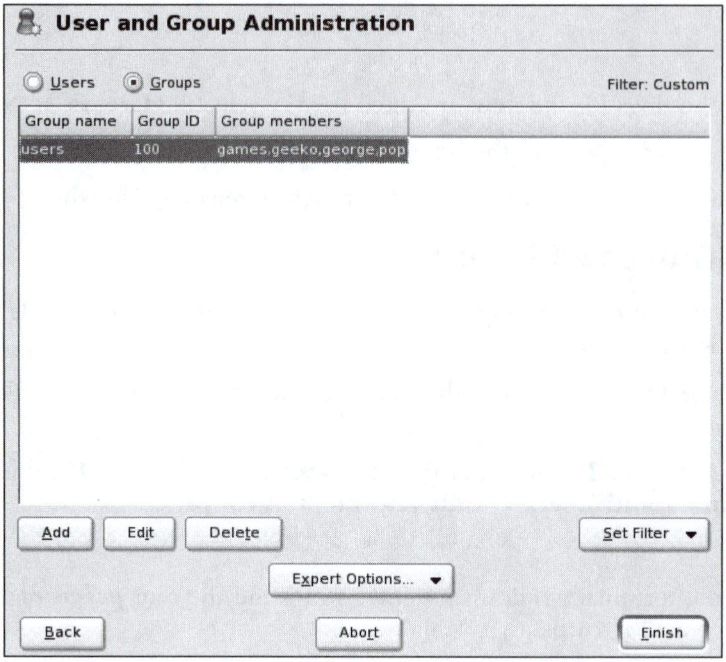

Figure 2-9

A list of groups appears with information such as group name, Group ID (GID), and group members.

2. Select **Set Filter**; then select one of the following to change the groups listed:

- **Local Groups.** Groups created on your local server to provide permissions for members assigned to the group.

- **System Groups.** Groups created by the system for use with services and applications.

- **Custom.** A customized view of groups based on the settings configured with **Customize Filter**.

- **Customize Filter.** This option lets you combine listed group sets (such as **Local Groups** and **System Groups**) to display a customized view (with **Custom**) of the groups list.

Additional sets of groups (such as LDAP) are added to the Set Filter drop-down list as you configure and start services on your server.

3. You can create a new group or edit an existing group by selecting **Add** or **Edit**.

When you select Add, the Add a New Local Group dialog box appears, as shown in Figure 2-10.

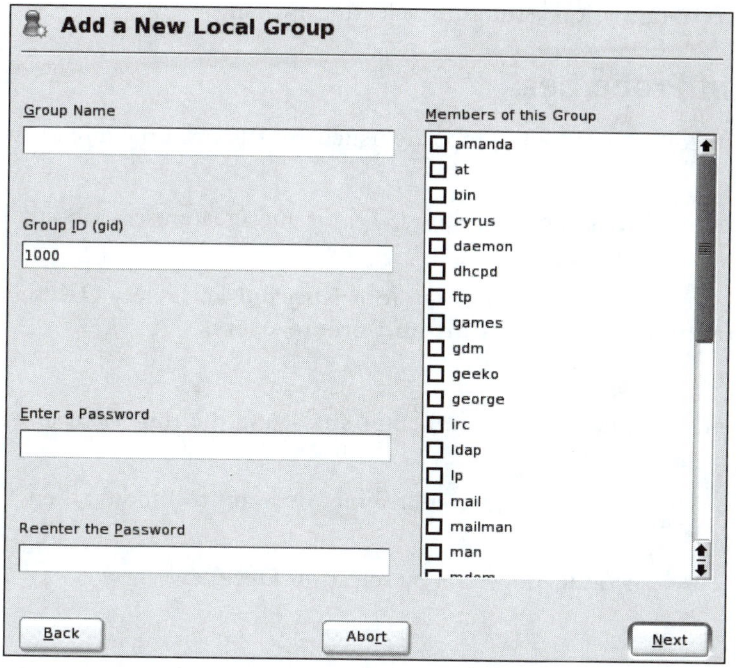

Figure 2-10

4. Enter or edit information in the following fields:

- **Group Name.** The name of the group. Avoid long names. Normal name lengths are between 2 and 8 characters.

- **Group ID (gid).** The GID number assigned to the group. The number must be a value between 0 and 60000. YaST warns you if you try to use a GID that is already in use.

- **Enter a Password** (optional). Require the members of the group to identify themselves while switching to this group (see **man newgrp**). To do this, assign a password.

  For security reasons, the password is represented by asterisks (*).

- **Reenter Password.** Enter the password a second time to avoid typing errors.

- **Members of This Group.** Select which users should be members of this group.

  A second list appears (when you select Edit) that shows users for which this group is the default group. This list cannot be edited from YaST.

5. When you finish entering or editing the group information, select **Next**.

   You are returned to the Group Administration dialog box.

6. Save the configuration settings by selecting **Finish**.

Edit User Account Properties

You can use YaST to edit user account properties (such as UID or home directory) by doing the following:

1. From the KDE desktop, start the YaST Edit and create users module by doing one of the following:

   ■ Select the **YaST** icon, enter the root *password*, and select **OK**; then select **Security and Users > Edit and create users**.

   or

   ■ Open a terminal window and enter **sux –** and the root *password*; then enter **yast2 users**.

2. From the user list, select the *user account* you want to modify; then select **Edit**.

3. Edit the user account properties by selecting **Details**.

The Add/Edit User Properties – Details dialog box appears, as shown in Figure 2-11.

2

Add/Edit User Properties - Details

Detailed Profile for User "geeko"

User ID (uid)	Additional Group Membership
1000	

☐ users
☐ at
☑ audio
☐ bin
☐ cdrom
☐ console
☐ daemon
☑ dialout
☐ disk
☐ floppy
☐ ftp
☐ games
☐ kmem
☐ ldap
☐ lp
☐ mail

Home Directory

/home/geeko   Browse...

Additional User Information:

Login shell

/bin/bash ▼

Default group

users ▼

| Back | Abort | Next |

Figure 2-11

4. Enter or edit information in the following fields:

- **User ID (uid).** For normal users, you should use a UID greater than 499 because the smaller UIDs are used by the system for special purposes and pseudo logins.

  If you change the UID of an existing user, the rights of the files this user owns must be changed. This is done automatically for the files in the user's home directory, but not for files located elsewhere.

NOTE

If this does not happen automatically, you can change the rights of the user files in the home directory (as root) by entering **chown -R *username* /home/*username*.**

- **Home Directory.** The home directory of the user. Normally this is **/home/*username*.**

  You can select an existing directory by selecting **Browse**.

- **Additional User Information.** This field can contain up to three parts separated by commas. It is often used to enter *office, work phone, home phone.*

  This information is displayed when you use the **finger** command on this user.

- **Login shell.** From the drop-down list, select the default login shell (command interpreter) for this user from the shells installed on your system.

- **Default Group.** This is the group to which the user belongs. Select a group from the list of all groups configured on your system.

- **Additional group membership.** Select all additional memberships you want to assign to the user.

5. When you finish configuring the user account properties, continue by selecting **Next**.

6. Save the configuration settings by selecting **Next > Finish**.

Configure Account Password Settings

You can use YaST to configure password settings (such as expiration date) for individual user accounts by doing the following:

1. From the KDE desktop, start the YaST Edit and create users module by doing one of the following:

   - Select the **YaST** icon, enter the root *password*, and select **OK**; then select **Security and Users > Edit and create users**.

     or

   - Open a terminal window and enter **sux –** and the root *password*; then enter **yast2 users**.

2. From the user list, select a *user account*; then select **Edit**.

3. Select Password Settings.

The dialog box shown in Figure 2-12 appears.

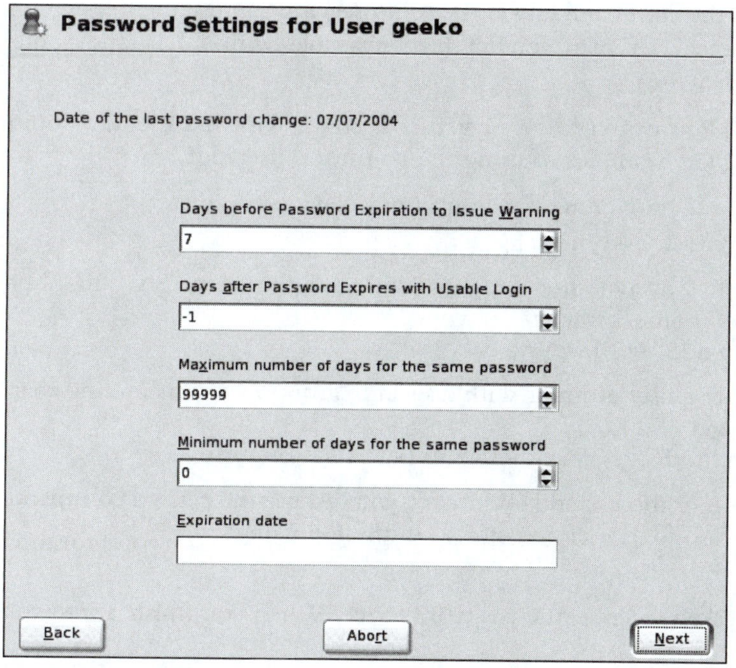

Password Settings for User geeko

Date of the last password change: 07/07/2004

Days before Password Expiration to Issue **W**arning

```
7
```

Days **a**fter Password Expires with Usable Login

```
-1
```

Ma**x**imum number of days for the same password

```
99999
```

Minimum number of days for the same password

```
0
```

Expiration date

```
```

[**B**ack]   [Abo**r**t]   [**N**ext]

Figure 2-12

4. Enter or edit information in the following fields:

- **Days before Password Expiration to Issue Warning.** Enter the number of days before password expiration that a warning is issued to users.

  Enter **–1** to disable the warning.

- **Days after Password Expires with Usable Login.** Enter the number of days after the password expires that users can continue to log in.

  Enter **–1** for unlimited access.

- **Maximum number of days for the same password.** Enter the number of days a user can use the same password before it expires.

- **Minimum number of days for the same password.** Enter the minimum age of a password before a user can change it.

- **Expiration date.** Enter the date when the account expires. The date must be in the format YYYY-MM-DD.

  Leave the field empty if the account never expires.

5. Save the password configuration settings by selecting **Next > Next > Finish**.

Manage User Accounts from the Command Line

When logged into the command line as the root user, you can use the following commands to perform the same user management tasks available with YaST (and some tasks not available with YaST):

- **useradd.** You can create a new user account with the useradd command. The following are examples of using the command useradd:

  - Create a bwayne user account (with default parameters):
    ```
    useradd bwayne
    ```
  - Create a bwayne user account (with default parameters) and a home directory (/home/bwayne/):
    ```
    useradd -m bwayne
    ```
  - Create a user account with a specific group membership, and that expires at the end of 2007:
    ```
    useradd -g temp -e 2007-12-31 bwayne
    ```

  In addition to the useradd command, you can use the passwd command to change the password for a user account, as in the following:
  ```
  passwd bwayne
  ```

  You are asked to enter the password twice. When you finish, a Password changed message appears.

- **userdel.** This command lets you delete an existing user account. It provides a single option, **-r**, which deletes the user's home directory and the user's account.

  Before using **userdel -r**, it is important that you determine the user's UID (**id user**). The UID enables you to locate files outside the user's home directory that are assigned to the user (such as **/var/mail/$USER**).

  To delete these files, enter the command:
  ```
  find / -uid user_UID -exec rm {} \;
  ```

- **usermod.** This command lets you modify settings (such as UID, standard shell, home directory, and primary group) for an existing user account.

  The usermod options are basically the same as those for the useradd command.

  The following are examples:

  - Change the home directory:
    ```
    usermod -d /newhome/geeko -m geeko
    ```
  - Change the UID:
    ```
    usermod -u 1001 geeko
    ```

2

- **passwd.** This command lets you change a user's password.

  When logged in, any user can change his password by entering **passwd** without options; root can change the password of any user by entering **passwd** *username*.

  Besides changing a user's password, you can also use the command to do the following:

  - **Lock a user account.** With the option –l (lock), you can deactivate a user account, and then reactivate the account with the option *–u* (unlock),

    For example, to deactivate the user account geeko, enter **passwd –l geeko**.

  - **Display the password status of a user account.** The option –S lets you display the status of a user account. For example, entering **passwd –S geeko** might display the following:

    geeko L 09/04/2007 0 99999 7 0

    The status follows directly after the username. **L** means that the user is locked out. Other options are NP (no password) or P (valid password).

    This is followed by the date of the last password change, the minimum length of validity, the maximum length of validity, and the warning periods and inactivity periods when a password expires.

  - **Change password times.** You can use options such as –n and –w to change expiration times for user passwords.

    For example, entering **passwd –x 30 –w 5 geeko** changes the maximum number of days to **30** for which the password is valid and warns the user **5** days in advance of the password expiration.

You can learn more about these commands by referring to the online manual pages (such as **man useradd**).

NOTE

Manage Groups from the Command Line

You can use the following commands to perform the same group management tasks available with YaST (and some tasks not available with YaST):

You need to be logged in as root (or switch to root by entering **su -**) to use these commands.

CAUTION

- **groupadd.** You can create a new group by entering **groupadd** *group_name*. In this case, the next free GID is used.

  Using the option -g (such as **groupadd -g 200 sports**) lets you specify a GID.

  Using the option -p (such as **groupadd -p novell sports**) lets you specify a password. You can use the command mkpasswd to create the encrypted password.

  You can verify that the group has been added to the system by entering **tail /etc/group**.

- **groupdel.** You can delete a group by entering **groupdel** *group_name*. There are no options for this command.

  You can only delete a group if no user has this group assigned as a primary group.

- **groupmod.** You can modify the settings (such as GID, group name, and users) for an existing group.

  The following are examples:

  - Change the GID:
    ```
    groupmod -g 201 sports
    ```
  - Change the group name from sports to water:
    ```
    groupmod -n water sports
    ```
  - Add the user tux to the group:
    ```
    groupmod -A tux sports
    ```

NOTE

You can learn more about these commands by referring to the online manual pages (such as **man groupadd**) or online help page (such as **groupadd --help**).

Create Text Login Messages

You can create text login messages that are useful for displaying information when a user logs in from a terminal window, a virtual terminal, or remotely (such as an ssh login).

You can modify the following files to provide these messages:

- **/etc/issue.** Edit this file to configure an initial message for users logging into the system.

  The following is an example of an edited /etc/issue file:
  ```
  Welcome to SUSE Linux Enterprise Server 9 (i586) Kernel \r (\l).

  ================================================================
                      The SUSE Linux Web Server
  ================================================================
  ```

- **/etc/motd.** Edit this file to configure an initial message of the day.

  The following is an example of an edited /etc/issue file:

  ```
  This server is currently being maintained by the Web Master
  at webmstr@enterprise.com. If you would like to know how
  to upload files to this server, contact Human Resources
  for training.

  Recent additions to this server include web portals for
  Finance and Customer Relations.
  ```

  Make sure you add one or two empty lines at the end of the message, or it will run into the command line prompt.

Exercise 2-2   Create and Manage Users and Groups from the Command Line

You need to set up your SLES 9 server with user accounts and groups to help train the database administrators in your Digital Airlines office.

Do the following:

- Part I: Customize User Account Default Settings
- Part II: Create Login Messages
- Part III: Create Users with YaST
- Part IV: Create a User Account at the Command Line
- Part V: Manage Groups with YaST
- Part VI: Manage Groups from the Command Line
- Part VII: Manage User Accounts from the Command Line
- Part VIII: Restore the Default Group Assignment for New Users

Part I: Customize User Account Default Settings

In this part of the exercise, you customize the user environment for a new project for database administrators in your Digital Airlines office.

1. From the KDE desktop, open a terminal window and su to root (**su -**) with a password of **novell**.

2. Create a new group named dba by entering the following:

   groupadd dba

3. Edit the file /etc/default/useradd to change the default location for home directories and the list of groups:

   a. From the KDE Menu, select **System > File Manager > File Manager – Super User Mode**.

   b. Enter the password **novell**; then select **OK**.

   c. In the Location field, enter **/etc/default**.

   d. Right-click **useradd**; then select **Open With > Kate**.

   The file useradd opens in the Kate editor.

   e. Change the HOME= parameter to the following setting:

   HOME=**/export/home**

   f. Add dba to the GROUPS= parameter:

   GROUPS=dialout,uucp,video,audio,**dba**

   g. Save the changes by selecting **File > Save**; then close the file by selecting **File > Close** (keep the Kate window open).

   h. From the terminal window, verify the change by entering **cat /etc/default/useradd**.

   The database administrator accounts need to have dba and .dba directories created when a new account is created. You can do this by creating the directories in /etc/skel.

4. To create these directories in the directory /etc/skel, enter the following commands:

   cd /etc/skel

   mkdir dba

   mkdir .dba

5. Verify that the directories exist by entering **ls –al**.

6. Create an /export/data2/db directory for storing project files by entering **mkdir -p /export/data2/db**.

7. Verify that the directory exists by entering **ls –al /export/data2**.

Part II: Create Login Messages

Because your server will be used as a database server, you decide to set the initial message for the database administrators at system login to include a message.

1. Edit the file /etc/issue by doing the following:

   a. From the Kate window, select **File > Open**.

2

b. Browse to and open the file **/etc/issue**.

c. Scroll to the end of the file; then add the following text:

==

The DBA System

==

d. Add some space at the end of the file by pressing **Enter** twice.

e. Save the file by selecting **File > Close**; then select **Save**.

2. Set an initial message of the day (upon a successful login) by editing the file /etc/motd:

a. From the Kate window, select **File > Open**.

b. Browse to and open the file **/etc/motd**.

The file is empty.

c. Enter the following message:

Team,

Welcome to the SLES 9 staging server.

Your project files are in: /export/data2/db

For questions call me at: 555–1212

Thanks,

Project Manager

d. Add some space at the end of the file by pressing **Enter** twice.

e. Delete any tabs or spaces at the beginning of the last line.

f. Save the file by selecting **File > Close**; then select **Save**.

3. Close the Kate window by selecting **File > Quit**.

Part III: Create Users with YaST

Now that you've created a new group and changed the default home directory for new users, you are ready to create the database administrator user accounts.

Start by using YaST to create two user accounts.

Do the following:

1. From the KDE desktop, select the **YaST** icon; then log in as root by entering a password of **novell** and selecting **OK**.

The YaST Control Center appears.

2. Select **Security and Users > Edit and create users**.

   The User and Group Administration dialog box appears.

3. Create a new user account by selecting **Add**.

   The Add a New Local User dialog box appears.

4. Enter the following information:

   - Full User Name: **Database Admin 1**
   - User Login: **dba1**
   - Password: **suse1**
   - Verify Password: **suse1**

5. Select **Password Settings**.

   A Password Settings for User dba1 dialog box appears.

6. In the Expiration date field, enter a *date* (YYYY-MM-DD) for 5 days from today.

   For example, if today's date is 2007-07-01, you would enter **2007-07-06**.

7. When you finish, continue by selecting **Next**.

   You are returned to the Add a New Local User dialog box.

8. Select **Details**.

   An Add/Edit User Properties – Details dialog box appears.

9. Make sure that the default Home Directory is **/export/home/dba1**.

   Because you changed the HOME= parameter in the file /etc/default to /export/home, YaST uses the setting to create a default directory for dba1 in /export/home.

10. In the Additional Group Members list, make sure the group **dba** (at the top of the list) is selected.

11. When you finish, continue by selecting **Next**.

12. Select **Create**.

    You are returned to the User and Group Administration dialog box.

13. Create a second database administrator account with the parameters shown in Table 2-1.

Table 2-1

Field	Value
Full User Name	Database Admin 2
User Login	dba2
Password	suse2

Table 2-1   (continued)

Field	Value
Groups	default groups plus the **dba** group
Expiration Date	5 days from today (such as 2007-07-06)
Home Directory	**/export/home/dba2**

14. When you finish creating both dba1 and dba2, complete the process by selecting **Finish**.

15. Verify that user account dba1 works:

   a. Switch to virtual console 2 by pressing **Ctrl+Alt+F2**.

   b. Log in by entering **dba1** and a password of **suse1**.

   Notice that the team welcome message (in the file /etc/motd) appears.

   c. Log out by entering **exit**.

   Notice that the message from the file **/etc/issue** appears.

   d. Log in again by entering **dba2** and a password of **suse2**; then log out by entering **exit**.

   e. Return to the KDE desktop by pressing **Ctrl+Alt+F7**.

   The user dba1 is the project lead for the database administrator group, and should have ownership rights to the directory /export/data2/db.

16. From the terminal window, make the user dba1 the owner of the directory /export/data2/db and make dba the group owner by entering the following:

   chown dba1:dba /export/data2/db

17. Verify the changes by entering **ls –l /export/data2**.

Part IV: Create a User Account at the Command Line

Do the following:

1. Using the useradd command, create a user with the information shown in Table 2-2.

Table 2-2

Field	Value
Full User Name	**Database Admin 3**
User Login	**dba3**
Password	**suse3**
Groups	default groups plus the **dba** group
Expiration Date	5 days from today (such as 2007-07-06)
Home Directory	**/export/home/dba3**

Enter the following (all on one line):

useradd –c "Database Admin 3" –d /export/home/dba3 –m

–e *date* **–G users,uucp,dialout,audio,video,dba dba3 ; passwd dba3**

The parameter *date* should be the same expiration date you used for the other accounts (5 days from today).

NOTE

This expiration date is for the user account; it is not the expiration date of the password. After the expiration date, the account becomes locked and cannot be accessed.

When the password expires, you are prompted to enter a new password.

After entering the command, you are prompted for a new password.

2. Enter a password of **suse3** twice.

   You are prompted that the password is too simple, but you are allowed to enter the password a second time.

   A Password changed message appears.

3. Switch to virtual console 2 (**Ctrl+Alt+F2**) and login as **dba3**; then exit the login (**exit**) and return to the desktop (**Ctrl+Alt+F7**).

Part V: Manage Groups with YaST

Do the following:

1. From the YaST Control Center, select **Security and Users > Edit and create groups**.

   The User and Group Administration dialog box appears.

2. Create a new group by selecting **Add**.

   An Add a New Local Group dialog box appears.

3. In the Group Name field, enter **dbabackup**; then select **Next**.

   You are returned to the User and Group Administration dialog box.

4. Add all existing dba users to the group dbabackup:

   a. Select the group **dbabackup**; then select **Edit**.

      An Edit an Existing Local Group dialog box appears.

   b. In the Members of this Group list, select **dba1**, **dba2**, and **dba3**.

   c. Continue by selecting **Next**.

   d. Complete the group configuration by selecting **Finish**.

e. Switch to virtual console 2 (**Ctrl+Alt+F2**) and log in as **dba1** with a pass-word of **suse1**.

f. Verify that the new group was added by typing **groups**.

Notice that dbabackup is listed for the user dba1.

g. Log out by entering **exit**; then switch back to the desktop by pressing **Ctrl+Alt+F7**.

5. Make the group dbabackup the default group when creating a new user:

a. From the YaST Control Center, select **Security and Users > Edit and create groups**.

b. From the Expert Options drop-down list, select **Defaults for New Users**.

c. From the Default Group drop-down list, select **dbabackup**.

You might need to scroll up to find the group in the list.

d. Continue by selecting **Next**.

e. Save the configuration change by selecting **Finish**.

6. Create a new user from **YaST** to test the configuration changes:

a. From the YaST Control Center, select **Security and Users > Edit and create users**.

b. Create a new user account by selecting **Add**.

c. Create a fourth database administrator account with the parameters shown in Table 2-3.

Table 2-3

Field	Value
Full User Name	Database Admin 4
User Login	dba4
Password	suse4
Groups	Default group (dbabackup) plus the **dba, audio, dialout, uucp,** and **video** groups
Expiration Date	5 days from today (such as 2007-07-06)
Home Directory	/export/home/dba4

Notice that the preselected default group for dba4 is dbabackup.

d. When you finish, save the new configuration by selecting **Finish**.

Part VI: Manage Groups from the Command Line

From the terminal window, do the following:

1. Create a group named party by entering **groupadd party**.

2. Add dba1, dba2, and dba3 to the group party by entering the following commands:

   usermod –G uucp,dialout,audio,video,dba,party,dbabackup dba1

   usermod –G uucp,dialout,audio,video,dba,party,dbabackup dba2

   usermod –G uucp,dialout,audio,video,dba,party,dbabackup dba3

   Make sure each command is on a single line with no spaces after the commas.

3. Verify that these users were added to the party group by entering the following commands:

   groups dba1

   groups dba2

   groups dba3

Part VII: Manage User Accounts from the Command Line

From the terminal window, do the following:

1. Check the entry in the file shadow for dba3 by entering the following:

   grep dba3 /etc/shadow

2. Lock the dba3 account using the command passwd:

   passwd –l dba3

3. Check the entry in shadow again by entering the following:

   grep dba3 /etc/shadow

   Notice the "!" after "dba3:". This indicates that the account is locked.

4. Verify that the account is locked by switching to a virtual console and attempting to log in as dba3.

   A Login incorrect message is displayed.

5. Return to the KDE desktop (**Ctrl+Alt+F7**) and unlock the dba3 account by entering the following:

   passwd –u dba3

6. Check the entry in shadow by entering the following:

   grep dba3 /etc/shadow

   Notice that the "!" has been removed from the account information.

7. Verify that the account is unlocked by switching to a virtual console and attempting to log in as dba3.

   You can now log in. Notice the number of failed attempts since the last login.

2

8. Log out as dba3 by entering **exit**.

9. Return to the KDE desktop (**Ctrl+Alt+F7**).

10. Change the information about the dba2 account in GECOS format by entering **passwd –f dba2**.

11. When you are prompted for a full name, continue by pressing **Enter**.

12. Enter the following information (as prompted):

    ▪ Room Number: **Classroom**

    ▪ Work Phone: **555–1212**

    ▪ Home Phone: **444–1212**

    ▪ Other: **Level 2 DBA**

13. Verify the information you added for dba2 by entering **finger dba2**.

14. Delete the group party by entering **groupdel party**.

15. Delete the account dba3 and the account home directory by entering **userdel –r dba3**.

    An informational message appears indicating that no crontab job exists for dba3.

16. View password policy information about the account dba2 by entering **chage –l dba2**.

Part VIII: Restore the Default Group Assignment for New Users

To restore the group users as the default group when creating a new user, do the following:

1. From the YaST Control Center, select **Security and Users > Edit and create groups**.

2. From the Expert Options drop-down list, select **Defaults for New Users**.

3. From the Default Group drop-down list, select **users**.

4. Continue by selecting **Next**.

5. Save the configuration changes by selecting **Finish**.

6. Close all open windows.

OBJECTIVE 3   MANAGE AND SECURE THE LINUX USER ENVIRONMENT

Besides managing individual user accounts, you also need to know how to do the following to manage and secure the Linux user environment:

- Perform Administrative Tasks as root
- Delegate Administrative Tasks with sudo
- Set Defaults for New User Accounts
- Configure Security Settings

Perform Administrative Tasks as root

As a system administrator, you are advised to log in as a normal user and only switch to root to perform tasks that require root permissions.

To switch between a normal user and root while performing administrative tasks, you can do the following:

- Switch to Another User with su
- Switch to Another Group with newgrp
- Start Programs as Another User from KDE

Switch to Another User with su

You can use the command **su** (switch user) to assume the UID of root or of other users.

The following is the su syntax:

su [*options*] ...[–] [*user*[*argument*]]

For example, to change to the user geeko, enter **su geeko**; to change to the user root, enter **su root** or **su** (without a user name).

Root can change to any user ID without knowing the password of the user.

CAUTION

If you want to start a login shell when changing to the user root, you can enter **su –**.

To change to the user root and execute a single command, you can use the option **–c**:

su – –c "grep geeko /etc/shadow"

For additional information on the command su, enter **su --help**.

Switch to Another Group with newgrp

A user can be a member of many different groups, but only one GID is his *effective* (current) group at any one time. Normally this is the *primary group*, which is specified in the file /etc/passwd.

If a user creates directories or files, then they belong to the user and to the effective group.

You can change the effective group GID with the command newgrp or sg (such as **sg video**).

Only group members may perform this group change, unless a group password is defined. In this case, any user that knows the group password can make the change.

You can undo the change (return to the original effective GID) by entering **exit** or by pressing **Ctrl+D**.

Start Programs as Another User from KDE

In KDE you can start any program with a different UID (as long as you know the password) by doing the following:

1. From the KDE desktop, open a command line dialog box by pressing **Alt+F2**; then select **Options**.

The dialog box shown in Figure 2-13 appears.

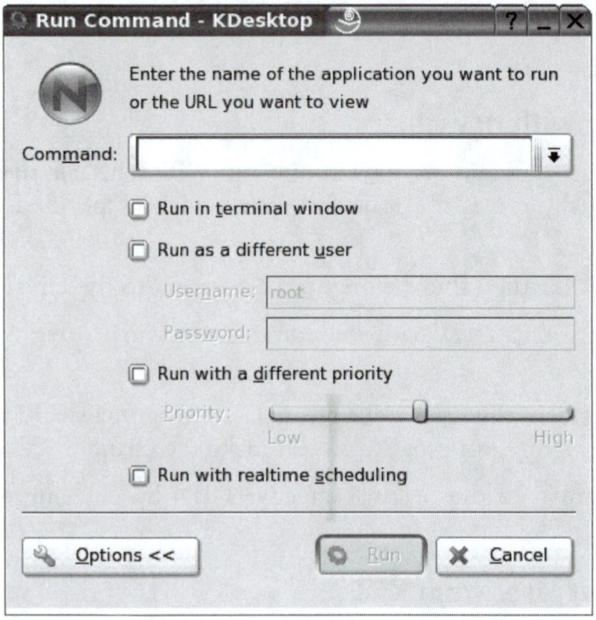

Run Command - KDesktop

Enter the name of the application you want to run or the URL you want to view

Command:

☐ Run in terminal window

☐ Run as a different user

Username: root

Password:

☐ Run with a different priority

Priority: ───────────●───────────
Low   High

☐ Run with realtime scheduling

Options <<   Run   ✗ Cancel

Figure 2-13

From this dialog box, you can enter a command that you want to run (or enter a URL to view).

There are also several options, including the option to run the command as a different user.

2. Select **Run as a different user**; then enter the *username* (such as **root**) and the *password*.

3. Enter the command you want to run as root; then select **Run**.

NOTE

You can also enter **kdesu *program_name*** to start a program as root. You are prompted for the root password before the program starts.

Delegate Administrative Tasks with sudo

Sometimes it is necessary to allow a normal user access to a command which is usually reserved for root. For example, you might want a coworker to take over tasks such as shutting down the computer and creating users while you are on vacation.

To enable a command to be run by a normal user, you can use the command sudo (as illustrated in the following):

```
geeko@earth:~ > sudo /sbin/shutdown -h now
We trust you have received the usual lecture from the local System
Administrator. It usually boils down to these two things:
#1) Respect the privacy of others.
#2) Think before you type.
Password:
```

You are prompted for a password, which is the user password.

As administrator, you can specify which commands a user can or cannot enter by configuring the file /etc/sudoers. You can modify the configuration by using the command visudo.

> In SLES 8, sudo expected the password of the user executing sudo. To change to this default setting, put comment signs (#) in front of the lines "Defaults targetpw" and "%users ALL=(ALL) ALL" in the file /etc/sudoers using the command visudo.

The following is the general syntax of an entry in the configuration file:

user/group host = command1, command2 ...

For example

```
geeko ALL = /sbin/shutdown
```

In this example, the user geeko is able to carry out the command **/sbin/shutdown** with the permissions of root on all computers (**ALL**).

Figure 2-14 shows a more complex example that illustrates the flexibility of sudo.

```
  User_Alias  ADMINS    = tux, geeko
2 User_Alias  WEBMASTER  = john
  User_Alias  SUBSTITUTE = olli, klaas
4
  # Cmnd alias specification
6
  Cmnd_Alias  PRINTING = /usr/sbin/lpc, /usr/bin/lprm
8 Cmnd_Alias  SHUTDOWN = /sbin/shutdown
  Cmnd_Alias  APACHE   = /etc/init.d/apache
10
12 # User privilege specification
  root     ALL=(ALL) ALL
14
  ADMINS      ALL = NOPASSWD: !/usr/bin/passwd, /usr/bin/passwd [A-z]*,
16 !/usr/bin/passwd root
  WEBMASTER  ALL = APACHE
18 SUBSTITUTE ALL = SHUTDOWN, PRINTING
```

Figure 2-14

Lines 1 to 9 define aliases. You can do this for the following:

- Users with User_Alias (lines 1–3)
- Commands with Cmnd_Alias (lines 7–9)
- Hosts with Host_Alias

Lines 14–17 in this example show how these aliases can be used in the actual rules:

- **ADMINS.** This is the User_Alias for the users tux and geeko (see line 1).

  The following are additional parameters:

  - **!/usr/bin/passwd, /usr/bin/passwd [A-z]*.** This indicates that both users are allowed to run the command passwd with one single argument and change the passwords for user accounts.
  - **!/usr/bin/passwd root.** This indicates that both users are not allowed to change the password for root. However, they can change the passwords of other users.

With this configuration, tux and geeko could still lock out root by entering **sudo /usr/bin/passwd root -l**.

- **WEBMASTER.** This is the User_Alias for the user account john (see line 2). This user can start and stop the Web server (APACHE).
- **SUBSTITUTE.** This is the User_Alias for the user accounts olli and klaas (see line 3). These users can execute commands summarized in sections SHUT-DOWN and PRINTING (see lines 7 and 8).

For additional documentation and configuration examples, enter **man 5 sudoers**.

Set Defaults for New User Accounts

You can use YaST to select default settings to be applied to new user accounts by doing the following:

1. From the KDE desktop, start the YaST Edit and create users module by doing one of the following:

   - Select the **YaST** icon, enter the root *password*, and select **OK**; then select **Security and Users > Edit and create users**.

     or

   - Open a terminal window and enter **sux –** and the root *password*; then enter **yast2 users**.

2. Select **Expert Options > Defaults for New Users**.

   The New User Defaults dialog box appears, as shown in Figure 2-15.

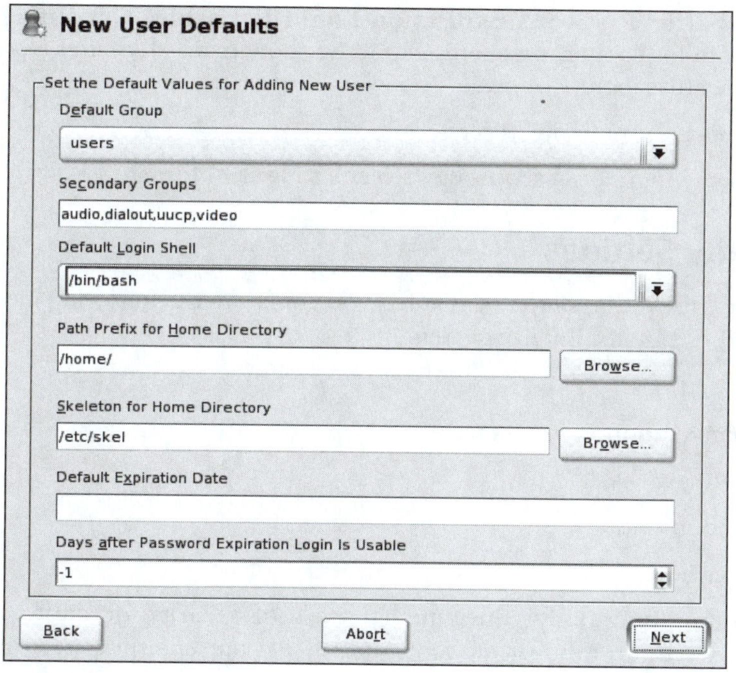

New User Defaults

Set the Default Values for Adding New User

Default Group

users

Secondary Groups

audio,dialout,uucp,video

Default Login Shell

/bin/bash

Path Prefix for Home Directory

/home/   Browse...

Skeleton for Home Directory

/etc/skel   Browse...

Default Expiration Date

Days after Password Expiration Login Is Usable

-1

Back   Abort   Next

Figure 2-15

3. Enter or edit information in the following fields:

   - **Default Group.** From the drop-down list, select the primary (default) group.

- **Secondary Groups.** Enter a list of secondary groups (separated by commas) to assign to the user.

- **Default Login shell.** From the drop-down list, select the default login shell (command interpreter) from the shells installed on your system, or enter your own path to the shell.

- **Default Home.** Enter or browse to the initial path prefix for a new user's home directory. The user's name will be appended to the end of this value to create the default name of the user's home directory.

- **Skeleton Directory.** Enter or browse to the skeleton directory. The contents of this directory will be copied to the user's home directory when you add a new user.

- **Default Expiration Date.** Enter the date on which the user account is disabled. The date must be in the format YYYY-MM-DD.

  Leave the field empty if this account never expires.

- **Days after Password Expiration Login Is Usable.** This setting enables users to log in after passwords expire. Set how many days after a password expires that login is allowed.

  Enter **–1** for unlimited access.

4. Save the configuration settings by selecting **Next > Finish**.

Configure Security Settings

Yast provides a Security Settings module that lets you configure the following local security settings for your SUSE Linux Enterprise Server:

- Password settings
- Boot configuration
- Login settings
- User creation settings
- File permissions

You can select from (or modify) three preset levels of security, or create your own customized security settings to meet the requirements of your enterprise security policies and procedures.

To use the Security Settings module, do the following:

1. From the KDE desktop, start the YaST Security Settings module by doing one of the following:

   - Select the **YaST** icon, enter the root *password*, and select **OK**; then select **Security and Users > Security Settings**.

   or

   - Open a terminal window and enter **sux –** and the root *password*; then enter **yast2 security**.

   The Local Security Configuration dialog box appears, as shown in Figure 2-16.

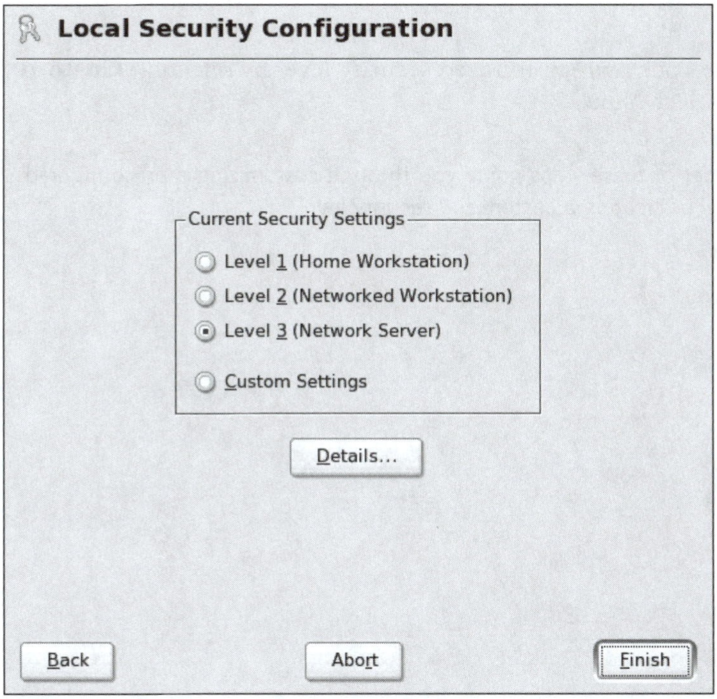

⌘ Local Security Configuration

┌─ Current Security Settings ──────────────────┐
│   │
│   ○ Level 1 (Home Workstation)   │
│   ○ Level 2 (Networked Workstation)   │
│   ⊙ Level 3 (Network Server)   │
│   │
│   ○ Custom Settings   │
│   │
└──┘

                  [Details...]

[Back]   [Abort]   [Finish]

Figure 2-16

From this dialog box, you can select one of the following preset configurations:

- **Level 1 (Home Workstation).** Select for a home computer not connected to any type of network.

- **Level 2 (Networked Workstation).** Select for a computer connected to any type of network or the Internet.

■ **Level 3 (Network Server).** Select for a computer that provides any type of service (network or otherwise).

You can also select **Details** or **Custom Settings** to modify an existing security level or create your own configuration.

2. Do one of the following:

■ Select a preconfigured **security level** setting; then configure your server by selecting **Finish**.

   or

■ Select a preconfigured **security level** setting; then customize the level by selecting **Details**.

   or

■ Create your own customized security level by selecting **Custom Settings**; then select **Next**.

NOTE

The remainder of these steps guide you through customizing a preconfigured security level or creating a customized security level.

The Password Settings dialog box appears, as shown in Figure 2-17.

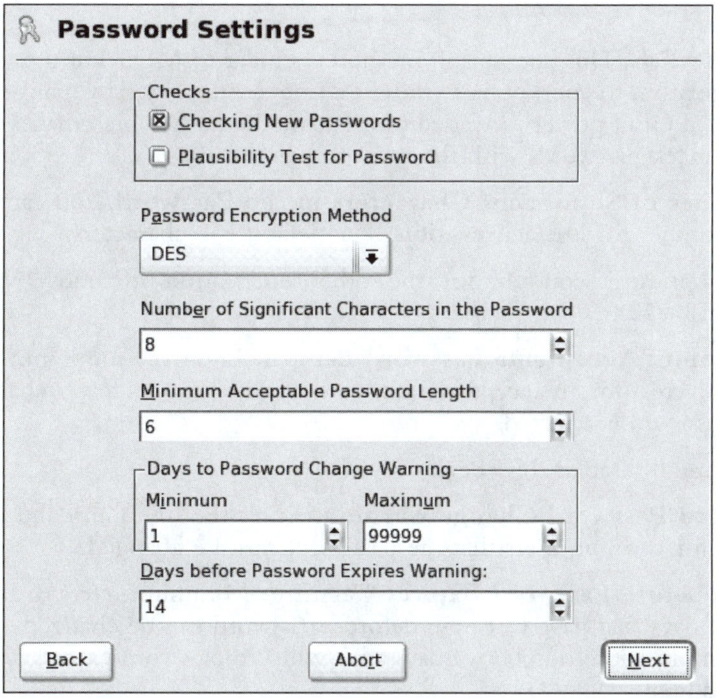

Figure 2-17

From this dialog box, you can select or enter the following password settings (mainly stored in /etc/login.defs):

- **Checking New Passwords.** It is important to choose a password that cannot be found in a dictionary and is not a name or other simple, common word. By selecting this option, you enforce password checking in regard to these rules.

- **Plausibility Test for Password.** Passwords should be constructed using a mixture of characters. This makes it very difficult to guess the password. Select this option to enable additional checks.

- **Password Encryption Method.** From the drop-down list, select one of the following encryption methods:

  - **DES.** This is the Linux default method. It works in all network environments, but it restricts you to passwords no longer than eight characters. If you need compatibility with other systems, select this method.

- **MD5.** This encryption method allows longer passwords and is supported by all current Linux distributions, but not by other systems or older software.

- **Blowfish.** This encryption method is similar to MD5, but uses a different algorithm to encrypt passwords. It is not yet supported by many systems. A lot of CPU power is needed to calculate the hash, which makes it difficult to crack passwords with the help of a dictionary.

- **Number of Significant Characters in the Password.** You can only set this number for DES encryption. The default is **8** characters.

  This option is ignored for the other encryption methods (MD5=**127**; Blowfish=**72**).

- **Minimum Acceptable Password Length.** Enter the minimum number of characters for an acceptable password. If a user enters fewer characters, the password is rejected.

  Entering **0** disables this check.

- **Days to Password Change Warning.** Enter the minimum and maximum times for warning users that the password must be changed.

- **Days before Password Expires Warning.** Minimum refers to the number of days that have to elapse before a password can be changed again. Maximum is the number of days after which a password expires and must be changed.

NOTE

Although root receives a warning when setting a password, she can still enter a bad password despite the above settings.

3. When you finish configuring password settings, continue by selecting **Next**.

The Boot Settings dialog box appears, as shown in Figure 2-18.

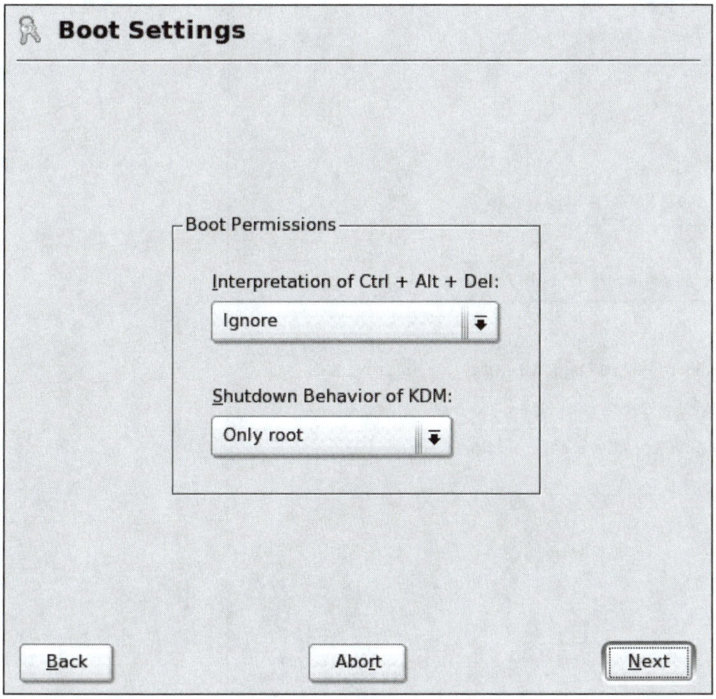

Boot Settings

┌─ Boot Permissions ──────────────────────────┐
│   │
│   Interpretation of Ctrl + Alt + Del: │
│   ┌──────────────────────────────┐ ┌───┐   │
│   │ Ignore   │ │ ▼ │   │
│   └──────────────────────────────┘ └───┘   │
│   │
│   Shutdown Behavior of KDM: │
│   ┌──────────────────────┐ ┌───┐   │
│   │ Only root   │ │ ▼ │   │
│   └──────────────────────┘ └───┘   │
│   │
└──┘

[Back]   [Abort]   [Next]

Figure 2-18

From this dialog box, you can select the following boot settings (which update the file /etc/inittab):

- **Interpretation of Ctrl + Alt + Del.** When someone at the console presses the **Ctrl+Alt+Del** keystroke combination, the system usually reboots.

  Sometimes you want to have the system ignore this keystroke combination, especially when the system serves as both workstation and server.

  You can select from **Ignore**, **Reboot**, or **Halt**. If you select Halt, the system shuts down.

- **Shutdown Behavior of KDM.** You use this option to set who is allowed to shut down the computer from KDM.

  You can select from **Only root**, **All users**, **Nobody**, **Local users**, and **Automatic**.

  If you select Nobody, you can only shut down the system from a text console.

4. When you finish configuring boot settings, continue by selecting **Next**.

The Login Settings dialog box appears, as shown in Figure 2-19.

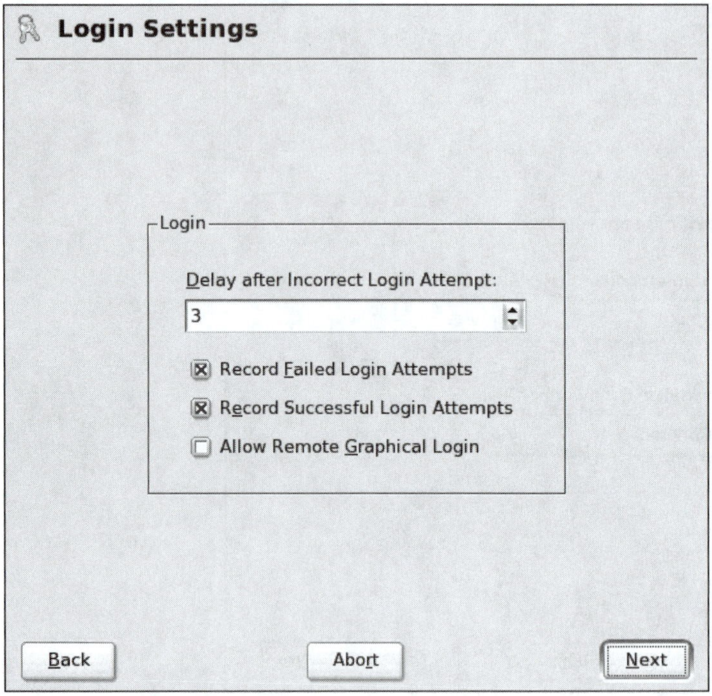

Figure 2-19

From this dialog box, you can enter and select the following login settings (mainly stored in /etc/login.defs):

■ **Delay after Incorrect Login Attempt.** Following a failed login attempt, there is typically a waiting period of a few seconds before another login is possible. This makes it more difficult for password crackers to log in.

This option lets you adjust the time delay before another login attempt.

Make the time small enough so users do not need to wait too long to retry if a password is mistyped. A reasonable value is **3** seconds.

■ **Record Failed Login Attempts.** It is useful for you to know if somebody tried to log in and failed, especially when that person is trying to guess other users' passwords.

Select this option to specify whether failed login attempts should be recorded in /var/log/faillog. To view failed login attempts, enter the command **faillog**.

■ **Record Successful Login Attempts.** Logging successful login attempts can be useful, especially in warning you of unauthorized access to the system (such as a user logging in from a different location than normal).

Select this option to record successful login attempts in the file /var/log/ wtmp. You can use the command **last** to view who logged in at what time.

■ **Allow Remote Graphical Login.** You can select this option to allow other users access to your graphical login screen via the network.

Because this type of access represents a potential security risk, it is inactive by default.

5. When you finish configuring login settings, continue by selecting **Next**.

The Adding User dialog box appears, as shown in Figure 2-20.

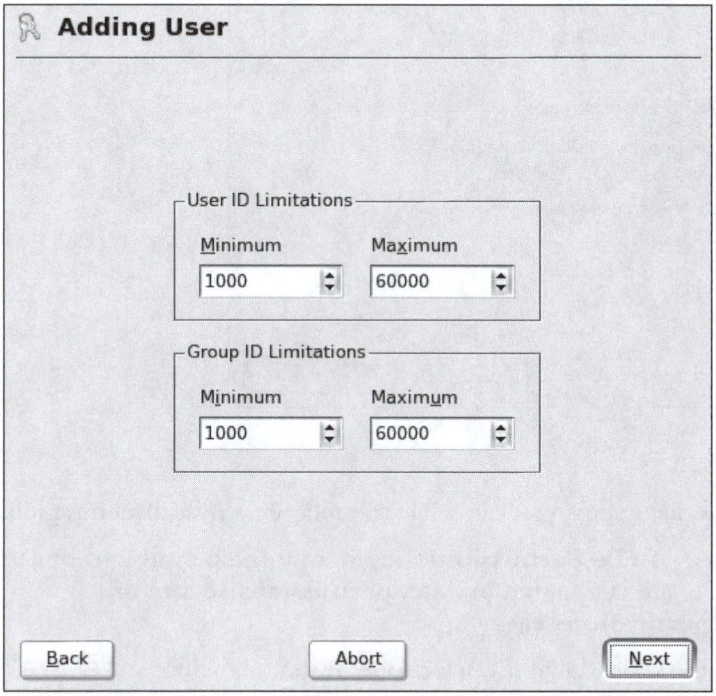

ℛ Adding User

┌─User ID Limitations─────────────────┐
│   │
│ Minimum   Maximum   │
│ 1000   ⬍   60000   ⬍   │
│   │
└─────────────────────────────────────┘

┌─Group ID Limitations────────────────┐
│   │
│ Minimum   Maximum   │
│ 1000   ⬍   60000   ⬍   │
│   │
└─────────────────────────────────────┘

[Back]   [Abort]   [Next]

Figure 2-20

From this dialog box, you can enter the following ID settings:

■ **User ID Limitations.** Enter a minimum and maximum value to config-ure a range of possible user ID numbers. A minimum of 500 is suitable for users.

■ **Group ID Limitations.** Enter a minimum and maximum value to con-figure a range of possible group ID numbers.

6. When you finish configuring user and group ID limitations, continue by selecting **Next**.

The Miscellaneous Settings dialog box appears, as shown in Figure 2-21.

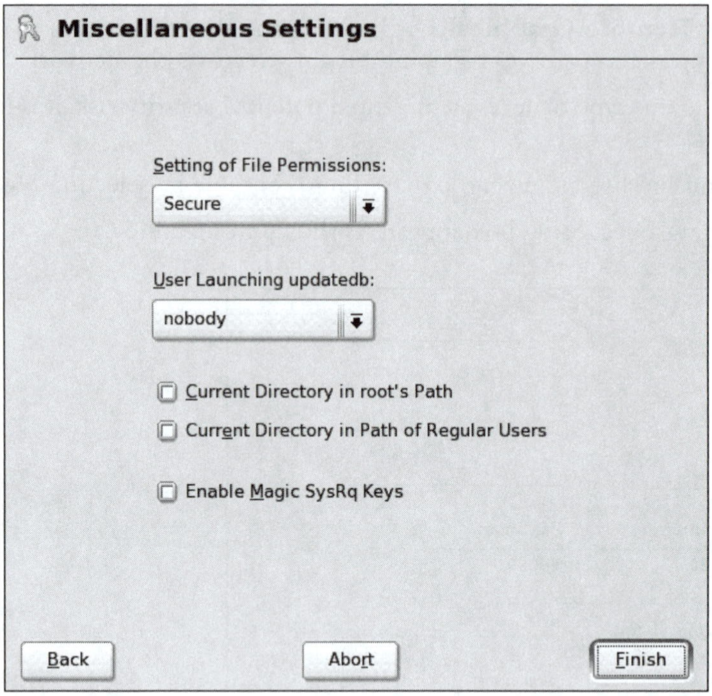

Figure 2-21

From this dialog box, you can select the following miscellaneous global settings:

- **Setting of File Permissions.** Settings for the permissions of certain system files are configured in **/etc/permissions.secure** or **/etc/permissions.easy**.

  From the drop-down list, select one of the following:

  - **Easy.** Select this option to allow read access to most of the system files by users other than root.

  - **Secure.** Select this option to make sure that certain configuration files (such as /etc/ssh/sshd_config) can only be viewed by the user root. Some programs can only be launched by root or by daemons, not by an ordinary user.

  - **Paranoid.** Select this option for an extremely secure system. All SUID/ SGID-Bits on programs have been cleared. Remember that some programs might not work or not work correctly, because users no longer have the permissions to access certain files.

Running SuSEconfig sets these permissions according to the settings in the /etc/permissions.* files. This fixes files with incorrect permissions, whether this occurred accidentally or by intruders.

- **User Launching updatedb.** If the program updatedb is installed, it automatically runs on a daily basis or after booting. It generates a database (**locatedb**) in which the location of each file on your computer is stored.

  You can search this database with the utility locate (enter **man locate** for details).

  From the drop-down list, select one of the following:

  - **nobody.** Any user can find only the paths in the database that can be seen by any other (unprivileged) user.

  - **root.** All files in the system are added into the database.

- **Current Directory in root's Path** and **Current Directory in the Path of Regular Users.** On a DOS system, DOS first searches for executable files (programs) in the current directory, and then in the current path variable. This is not the case on a Linux system.

  Some systems set up a "workaround" by adding the dot (".") to the search path, which enables files in the current path to be found and executed.

  If you deselect these options, users must always launch programs in the current directory by adding "./" (such as **./ configure**).

  If you select these options, the dot (".") is appended to the end of the search path for root and users, allowing them to enter a command in the current directory without appending "./".

  Selecting these options can be very dangerous because users can accidentally launch unknown programs in the current directory instead of the usual system-wide files.

  In addition, selecting these options allows execution of Trojan Horses, which can exploit this weakness and intrude your system.

- **Enable Magic SysRq Keys.** Selecting this option gives you some control over the system even if it crashes (such as during kernel debugging). For details, see /usr/src/linux/Documentation/sysrq.txt.

7. When you finish configuring the miscellaneous settings, save the settings and run SuSEconfig by select **Finish**.

Exercise 2-3   Configure the Password Security Settings

Do the following:

1. Open a terminal window.

2. Check the trap setting for the Ctrl+Alt+Del keystroke in the file /etc/inittab by entering **grep ctrlaltdel /etc/inittab.**

   Notice that the trap is set by default to "shutdown -r" for restart.

3. From the KDE desktop, select the **YaST** icon; then enter a password of **novell** and select **OK**.

4. Select **Security and Users > Security settings**.

   The Local Security Configuration dialog box appears.

5. Make sure **Custom Settings** is selected; then select **Next**.

   The Password Settings dialog box appears.

6. From the Password Encryption Method drop-down list, select **MD5**.

7. Continue by selecting **Next**.

   The Boot Settings dialog box appears.

8. From the Interpretation of Ctrl + Alt + Del drop-down list, select **Halt**.

9. Continue by selecting **Next**.

   The Login Settings dialog box appears.

10. Accept the default settings by selecting **Next**.

    The Adding User dialog box appears.

11. Accept the default settings by selecting **Next**.

    The Miscellaneous Settings dialog box appears.

12. Deselect the following:

    - **Current Directory in root's Path**

    - **Current Directory in Path of Regular Users**

13. Configure the system for the new settings by selecting **Finish**.

    To test the change, you must first activate the new configuration by rebooting the system or by entering (as root) **init –q** (reload the /etc/inittab file) in a terminal window.

14. From the terminal window, su to **root** (**su –**) with a password of **novell**.

15. Reboot the system by entering **init 6**.

16. When the system reboots, log in to the KDE desktop as **geeko** with a password of **N0v3ll**.

17. From a terminal window, verify that the Ctrl+Alt+Del setting has changed by entering **grep ctrlaltdel /etc/inittab**.

    Notice that the trap is now set to "shutdown –h" for halt instead of "shutdown –r" for restart.

18. Test this setting by pressing **Ctrl+Alt+F2** and log in as **root**; then press **Ctrl+Alt+Del**.

    The system shuts down instead of restarting.

19. Turn on your computer and log in to the KDE desktop as **geeko**.

20. (Optional) Use the YaST Security settings module to change the default for **Ctrl+Alt+Del** back to restart.

OBJECTIVE 4   SECURE FILES AND DIRECTORIES WITH PERMISSIONS

Although users might have access to navigate through the files and directories on a Linux system, you can limit what they can do with those files and directories by using access permissions.

To set permissions for files and directories, you need to know the following:

- Permissions and Permission Values
- How to Set Permissions from the Command Line
- How to Set Permissions from a GUI Interface
- How to Modify Default Access Permissions
- How to Configure Special File Permissions
- How to Configure Additional File Attributes for ext2

Permissions and Permission Values

You can assign the following three permissions to a file or directory:

- **Read (r).** This permission allows the file to be read or the contents of a directory to be listed.
- **Write (w).** This permission allows a file to be modified. It allows files to be created or deleted within a directory.
- **Execute (x).** This permission allows a file to be executed. It allows access to a directory.

You can use the command **ls –l** to display the contents of the current directory with the assigned permissions for each file or subdirectory.

For example, entering **ls -l** displays the permissions for myfile.txt, shown in Figure 2-22.

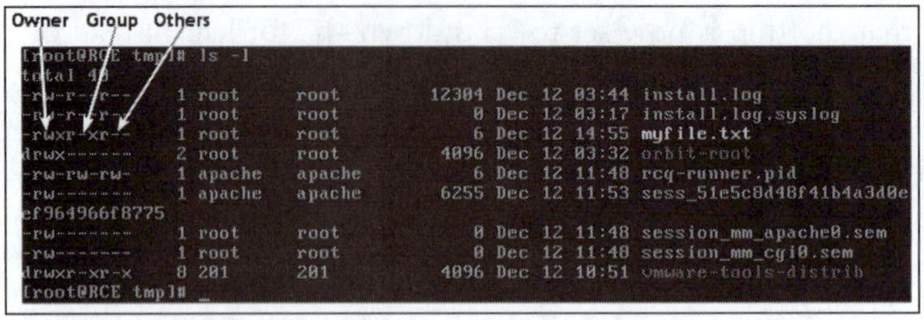
Owner Group Others
[root@RCE tmp]# ls -l
total 48
-rw-r--r-- 1 root root 12304 Dec 12 03:44 install.log
-rw-r--r-- 1 root root 0 Dec 12 03:17 install.log.syslog
-rwxr-xr-- 1 root root 6 Dec 12 14:55 myfile.txt
drwx------ 2 root root 4096 Dec 12 03:32 orbit-root
-rw-rw-rw- 1 apache apache 6 Dec 12 11:48 rcq-runner.pid
-rw------- 1 apache apache 6255 Dec 12 11:53 sess_51e5c0d48f41b4a3d0e
ef964966f8775
-rw------- 1 root root 0 Dec 12 11:48 session_mm_apache0.sem
-rw------- 1 root root 0 Dec 12 11:48 session_mm_cgi0.sem
drwxr-xr-x 8 201 201 4096 Dec 12 10:51 vmware-tools-distrib
[root@RCE tmp]# _

Figure 2-22

You can also view permissions from a file manager or browser tool.

For example, you can use the Detailed ListView in Konqueror to view permissions, owner, and group for each directory or file, as shown in Figure 2-23.

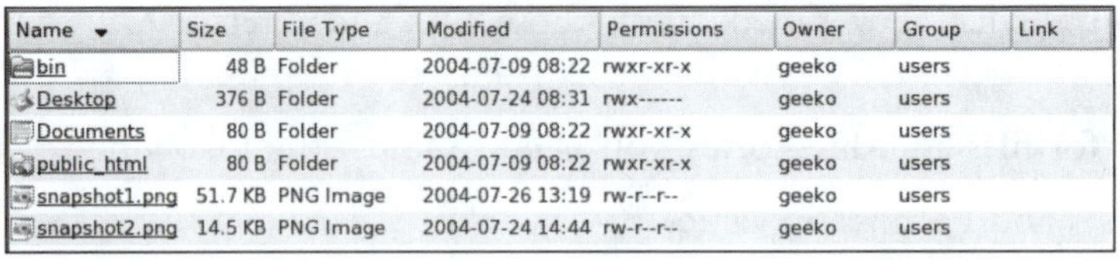
Name
Size
File Type
Modified
Permissions
Owner
Group
Link
bin 48 B Folder 2004-07-09 08:22 rwxr-xr-x geeko users
Desktop 376 B Folder 2004-07-24 08:31 rwx------ geeko users
Documents 80 B Folder 2004-07-09 08:22 rwxr-xr-x geeko users
public_html 80 B Folder 2004-07-09 08:22 rwxr-xr-x geeko users
snapshot1.png 51.7 KB PNG Image 2004-07-26 13:19 rw-r--r-- geeko users
snapshot2.png 14.5 KB PNG Image 2004-07-24 14:44 rw-r--r-- geeko users

Figure 2-23

How to Set Permissions from the Command Line

You can modify a file or directory's permissions and ownership from the command line by using the following:

- chmod
- chown and chgrp

chmod

You can use this command to add, remove, or assign permissions assigned to a file or directory. Both the owner of a file and root can use this command.

Table 2-4 shows examples of using the command chmod.

Table 2-4

chmod command	Description
chmod u+x	The owner is given permission to execute the file. The permissions r and w stay as they are.
chmod g=rw	All group members can read and write. If the members had the execute permission before, it is removed.

Table 2-4 (continued)

chmod command	Description
chmod u=rwx	The owner receives all permissions.
chmod u=rwx,g=rw,o=r	The owner has all permissions, the group has read and write permissions, and all others have read permission.
chmod +x	All users (owner, group, and others) receive executable permission, depending on umask.

For example, entering the following chmod command lets all users in the group users write to the file hello.txt:

```
geeko@earth:~ > ls -la hello.txt
-rw-r--r-- 1 geeko users 0 2007-04-06 12:40 hello.txt
geeko@earth:~ > chmod g+w hello.txt
geeko@earth:~ > ls -la hello.txt
-rw-rw-r-- 1 geeko users 0 2007-04-06 12:40 hello.txt
```

With the option –R (recursive) and a specified directory, you can change the access permissions of all files and subdirectories under the directory.

Besides using the letters rwx to indicate permissions, you can also use groups of numbers.

Every file and directory in a Linux system has a numerical permission value assigned to it. This value has three digits.

The first digit represents the permissions assigned to the file or directory owner. The second digit represents the permissions assigned to the group associated with the file or directory. The third digit represents the permissions assigned to others.

Each digit is the sum of the following three values assigned to it:

- Read: **4**
- Write: **2**
- Execute: **1**

For example, suppose a file named myfile.txt has **754** permissions assigned to it.

This means the owner of the file has read, write, and execute permissions (**4+2+1**), the group associated with the file has read and execute permissions (**4+1**), and others have read permissions (**4**).

This is illustrated in Figure 2-24.

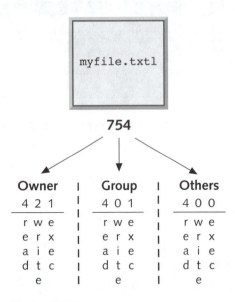

Figure 2-24

Table 2-5 shows examples of using numerical values with chmod.

Table 2-5

chmod command	Description
chmod 754 hello.txt	The owner has all permissions, the group has read and execute permissions, and all others have the read permission.
chmod 777 hello.txt	All users (user, group, and others) receive all permissions.

chown and chgrp

These commands change the owner or group assigned to a file or directory.

As user root, you can use the command chown to change the user and group affiliation of a file using the following syntax:

chown *new_user.new_group file*

For example, in the following, root changes ownership of the file hello.txt from geeko to the user newbie:

```
earth:/tmp # ls -la hello.txt
-rw-r--r-- 1 geeko users 0 2007-04-06 12:43 hello.txt
earth:/tmp # chown newbie.users hello.txt
```

```
earth:/tmp # ls -la hello.txt
-rw-r--r-- 1 newbie users 0 2007-04-06 12:43 hello.txt
earth:/tmp #
```

To change only the owner (and not the group), use the following:

chown *new_user file*

To change only the group (and not the user), use the following:

chown *.new_group file*

For example, the following command is used to limit access to the file list.txt to members of the group advanced:

```
earth:/tmp # ls -la list.txt
-rw-r----- 1 geeko users 0 2007-04-06 12:43 list.txt
earth:/tmp # chown .advanced list.txt
earth:/tmp # ls -la list.txt
-rw-r----- 1 geeko advanced 0 2007-04-06 12:43 list.txt
earth:/tmp #
```

Although the group has changed, the owner permissions remain the same (the owner and root can still access the file).

As user root, you can also change the group affiliation of a file with the command chgrp using the following syntax:

chgrp *.new_group file*

A normal user can only use the command chown to change his or her file to a new group, as in the following:

chown *.new_group file*

Of course, the user can also do the same with chgrp, as in the following:

chgrp *new_group file*

Users can change the group affiliation of their files only if they are members of the new group.

How to Set Permissions from a GUI Interface

Besides using commands (such as chmod or chown), you can modify a file or directory's permissions from a GUI interface (normally a file browser).

For example, you can use Konqueror in KDE to change permissions by doing the following:

1. Start Konqueror; then browse to the ***file*** or ***directory*** (do not open it).
2. Right-click the ***file*** or ***directory*** you want to modify; then select **Properties**.

3. Select the **Permissions** tab.

   A dialog box similar to the one shown in Figure 2-25 appears.

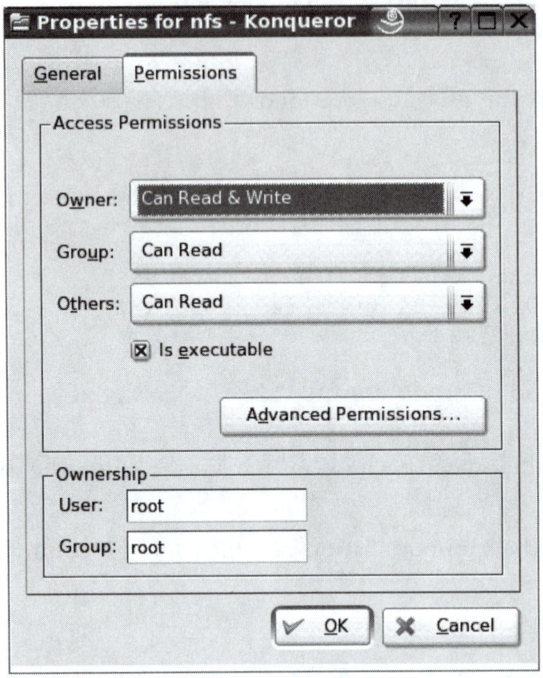

Figure 2-25

From this dialog box, you can change the Read (r) and Write (w) permissions for Owner, Group, and Others by selecting the appropriate option (**Can Read** or **Can Read & Write**) from the drop-down lists.

You can deny all permissions (equivalent to **0**) by selecting **Forbidden**.

You can also modify the user and group ownership of the file or directory by entering a user or group in the appropriate field.

4. Modify the permissions and ownership as desired.

5. (Optional) Modify individual permissions by doing the following:

a. Select **Advanced Permissions**.

The Advanced Permissions dialog box appears, as shown in Figure 2-26.

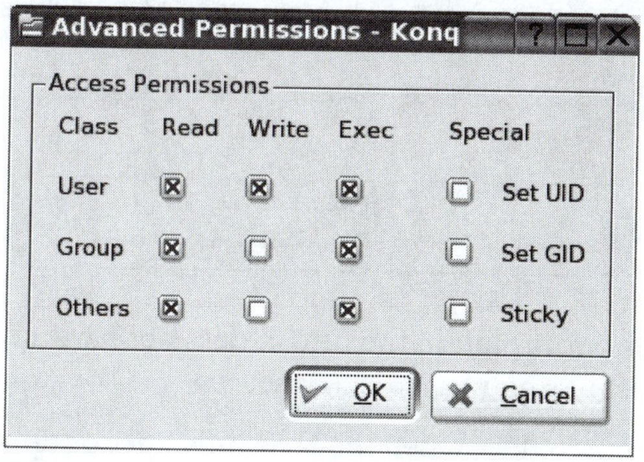

Figure 2-26

b. Select the *permissions* you want to set, and then finish by selecting **OK**.

6. When you finish configuring permissions for the file or directory, save the configuration by selecting **OK**.

How to Modify Default Access Permissions

If the default settings are not changed, files are created with the access mode **666** and directories with **777** by default.

To modify (restrict) these default access mode settings, you can use the command *umask*. You use this command with a 3-digit numerical value such as **022**.

How can you calculate the default setting for file and directory permissions from the umask value? The permissions set in the umask are removed from the default permissions.

For example, entering **umask 022** *directory_name* or **umask 022** *filename* gives the results shown in Table 2-6.

Table 2-6

	Directories			Files		
Default Permissions	rwx	rwx	rwx	rw-	rw-	rw-
	7	7	7	6	6	6
umask	---	-w-	-w-	---	-w-	-w-
	0	2	2	0	2	2
Result	rwx	r-x	r-x	rw-	r--	r--
	7	5	5	6	4	4

Entering **umask 023** *directory_name* or **umask 023** *filename* gives the results shown in Table 2-7.

Table 2-7

	Directories			Files		
Default Permissions	rwx	rwx	rwx	rw-	rw-	rw-
	7	7	7	6	6	6
umask	---	-w-	-wx	---	-w-	-wx
	0	2	3	0	2	3
Result	rwx	r-x	r--	rw-	r--	r--
	7	5	4	6	4	4

In the second example (umask 023), the **x** permission in the umask does not have any effect on the file permissions, as the x permission is missing in the default setting (rw- rw- rw-, 666).

By entering **umask 077** you restrict access to the owner and root only; the group and others do not have any access permissions.

To make the umask setting permanent, you can change the value of umask in the system-wide configuration file /etc/profile.

If you want the setting to be user-specific, enter the value of umask in the file .bashrc in the home directory of the respective user.

How to Configure Special File Permissions

The attributes shown in Table 2-8 are used for special circumstances (use the uppercase letter in the absence of the execute bit).

Table 2-8

Letter	Number	Name	Files	Directories
t or T	1	Sticky bit	Not applicable	Users can only delete files when they are the owner, or when they are root or owner of the directory. This is usually applied to the directory /tmp/.
s or S	2	SGID (set GroupID)	When a program is run, this sets the group ID of the process to that of the group of the file.	Files created in this directory belong to the group to which the directory belongs and not to the primary group of the user. New directories created in this directory inherit the SGID bit.

Table 2-8 (continued)

Letter	Number	Name	Files	Directories
s or S	4	SUID (set UserID)	Sets the user ID of the process to that of the owner of the file when the program is run.	Not applicable

You set the sticky bit with chmod, either via the permissions of others (such as **chmod o+t /tmp**) or numerically (such as **chmod 1777 /tmp**).

 NOTE The sticky bit on older Unix systems enabled the storing of an executable program in memory after it had been terminated, so it could be quickly restarted. However, with modern Unix and Linux systems, this only affects directories.

The sticky bit is listed in the permissions for Others (t), as in the following:

```
geeko@earth:~ > ls -ld /tmp
drwxrwxrwt 15 root root 608 2007-04-06 12:45 /tmp
geeko@earth:~ >
```

The following is an example for SUID:

```
geeko@earth:~ > ls -l /usr/bin/passwd\
-rwsr-xr-x 1 root shadow 79765 2007-03-24 12:19 /usr/bin/passwd
geeko@earth:~ >
```

The following is an example for SGID:

```
geeko@earth:~ > ls -l /usr/bin/wall
-rwxr-sr-x 1 root tty 10192 2007-03-22 05:24 /usr/bin/wall
geeko@earth:~ >
```

If the attributes SUID or SGID are set, the programs are carried out with the privileges the owner (in the example for SUID above: root) or the group (in the example for SGID above: tty) have.

If root is the owner of the program, the program is carried out with the permissions of root. Unfortunately, there is a certain security risk in doing this.

For example, it could be possible for a user to take advantage of an error in the program, retaining root privileges after the process has been ended.

How to Configure Additional File Attributes for ext2

The file attributes introduced so far do not cover all the possible requirements of an operating system. For that reason, the additional file permissions shown in Table 2-9 have been included in the ext2 file system (and are available in ext3).

Table 2-9

Attribute	Description
A	(atime) Controls whether an atime entry for this file is processed on the hard drive. For example, if it is set, hard drive activities for laptop computers can be reduced.
a	(append) Data can only be appended to this file. The file cannot be overwritten or deleted.
d	(no dump) If this attribute is set, the file is not saved when a backup is made with dump.
i	(immutable) The file can no longer be processed or deleted and no hard link can be set to it.
S	(synchronous update) Causes a synchronous writing to the hard drive (without saving in the buffer). This can slow down the machine, because all caching processes for this file are switched off.

You can set all these attributes as root with the command chattr (change file attributes) and display them with the command lsattr (list file attributes).

You use the syntax shown in Table 2-10 to set the attributes.

Table 2-10

Syntax	Description
+	Adds attributes to the existing ones
-	Removes attributes
=	Sets only these attributes for one file

Options for chattr and lsattr include those shown in Table 2-11.

Table 2-11

Option	Description
-R	**chattr.** Runs command in subdirectories as well **lsattr.** Lists directories and their contents
-v	**chattr.** Changes the stored version number of the file **lsattr.** Lists the version number of the file
-a	**lsattr.** Lists all files in the directory (including hidden ones)

Exercise 2-4 Set Permissions for Files and Directories from the Command Line

Do the following:

1. Open a terminal window, and su to root (**su -**) with a password of **novell**.

2. Create the directory /files/ by entering **mkdir /files**.

3. Change to the directory /files/ by entering **cd /files**.

4. Use the mkdir command to create the subdirectories **private** and **public** under /files/.

5. Change the permissions on the private directory so that only root has read, write, and execute permissions by entering the following:

   chmod 700 private

6. Change permissions on the public directory so that everyone has rights to the directory by entering the following:

   chmod 777 public

7. Verify the changes by entering **ls -l**.

8. Switch to virtual terminal 3 by pressing **Ctrl+Alt+F3**.

9. Login as **geeko** with a **N0v3ll** password.

10. Switch to the directory /files/ by entering **cd /files**.

11. Try to create a file named geeko in the private directory by entering **touch private/geeko**.

    Notice that permission is denied.

12. Try to create a file named geeko in the public directory by entering **touch public/geeko**.

13. Verify that the file is created by entering **ls public**.

14. Change to the public directory by entering **cd public**.

15. List the permissions of the file geeko by entering **ls -l geeko**.

    Notice that the group users and other have only read permission for the file.

16. Change permissions so that the users group has write permissions and other does not have any permissions by entering the following:

    chmod g+w,o-r geeko

17. Verify the change by entering **ls –l**.

18. Log out as geeko by entering **exit** (or by pressing **Ctrl+D**); then return to the KDE Desktop (**Ctrl+Alt+F7**).

19. Close the terminal window.

OBJECTIVE 5   CONFIGURE USER AUTHENTICATION WITH PAM

Linux uses PAM (Pluggable Authentication Modules) in the authentication process as a layer that communicates between users and applications.

By providing systemwide access to applications through its authentication modules, PAM lets you configure and change authentication methods between users and individual applications from centrally managed modules.

Whenever a new authentication method is needed (such as a fingerprint scan instead of a username/password) for an application, you simply reconfigure or create a PAM module for use by the application.

To understand how to configure PAM, you need to know the following:

- Location and Purpose of PAM Configuration Files
- PAM Configuration File Structure
- PAM Configuration File Examples
- PAM Documentation Resources

Location and Purpose of PAM Configuration Files

PAM provides a variety of modules—each one with a different purpose. For example, one module checks the password, another verifies the location from which the system is accessed, and another reads user-specific settings.

Every program that relies on the PAM modules has its own configuration file in the directory **/etc/pam.d/***program_name*.

These files define the PAM modules that are used for authentication, and include those shown in Figure 2-27.

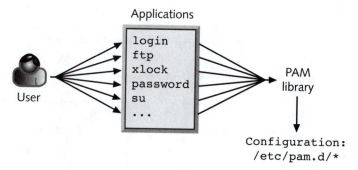

Figure 2-27

For example, the configuration file for the program passwd is called /etc/pam.d/passwd.

In addition, there are global configuration files for most PAM modules in /etc/security/, which define the exact behavior of these modules. These include modules such as pam_ env.conf, pam_pwcheck.conf, pam_unix2.conf, and time.conf.

Every application that uses a PAM module actually calls a set of PAM functions, which then process the information in the various configuration files and return the result to the calling application.

PAM Configuration File Structure

Each line in a PAM configuration file contains a maximum of four columns, as shown in Figure 2-28.

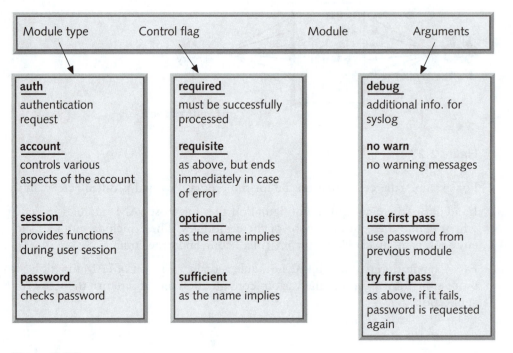

Figure 2-28

The following describes the purpose of each column:

- **Module type.** PAM recognizes four types of modules:
  - **auth.** This module type checks the user's authenticity. This is traditionally done by querying a password, but it can also be achieved with the help of a chip card or through biometrics (fingerprints or iris scan).
  - **account.** This module type verifies whether the user has general permission to use the requested service. For example, this type of check should be performed to ensure that no one can log in under the user name of an expired account.
  - **session.** This module type is responsible for managing and configuring user sessions. Sessions are started before and after authentication to register login attempts in system logs and to configure the user's specific environment (such as mail accounts, home directory, and system limits).
  - **password.** This module type is used to enable the change of an authentication token. In most cases, this is a password.

- **Control flag.** This column contains control flags that influence the behavior of PAM modules:

  - **required.** A module with this flag must be successfully processed before the authentication can proceed.

    After the failure of a module with the required flag, all other modules with the same flag are processed before the user receives a message about the failure of the authentication attempt.

  - **requisite.** A module with this flag must also be processed successfully. In case of success, other modules are subsequently processed, just like modules with the required flag.

    However, in case of failure, the module gives immediate feedback to the user and no further modules are processed.

    You can use the requisite flag as a basic filter, checking for the existence of certain conditions that are essential for a correct authentication.

  - **optional.** The failure or success of a module with this flag does not have any direct consequences.

    You can use this flag for modules that are only intended to display a message (such as telling a user that mail has arrived) without taking any further action.

  - **sufficient.** After a module with this flag has been successfully processed, the calling application receives an immediate message about the success and no further modules are processed (provided there was no preceding failure of a module with the required flag).

    The failure of a module with the sufficient flag has no direct consequences. In other words, any subsequent modules are processed in their respective order.

- **Module.** You do not need to include the module, as long as the module is located in the default directory /lib/security/.

NOTE

For all 64-bit platforms supported by SUSE Linux, the default directory is /lib64/security/.

- **Arguments (options).** You can include options in this column for the module, such as **debug** (enables debugging) or **nullok** (allows the use of empty passwords).

PAM Configuration File Examples

The following are examples of PAM configuration files for the modules pam_securetty.so and pam_nologin.so that illustrate what you can do to provide secure access to applications:

- **pam_securetty.so.** You can configure this module to determine which terminals can be regarded as secure. The user root can log in only at these terminals.

The following line in the file /etc/pam.d/login activates the module pam_securetty.so for the program login:

```
auth required pam_securetty.so
```

In the file /etc/securetty, you specify the secure terminals, as in the following:

```
earth:~ # cat /etc/securetty
#
# This file contains the device names of tty lines (one per line,
# without leading /dev/) on which root is allowed to login.
#
tty1
tty2
tty3
tty4
tty5
tty6
...
```

When this module is active, you cannot log in as root via telnet.

- **pam_nologin.so.** You can use this module to prevent users from logging into the system. This module is also listed in the configuration file /etc/pam.d/login:

```
auth required pam_nologin.so
```

If you want to use this module, then every type of login by users can be prevented by entering the following to generate the file /etc/nologin:

echo "No login possible because of maintenance work" > /etc/nologin

When a user tries to log in, the message is displayed to inform the user why the login failed.

PAM Documentation Resources

The following PAM documentation is available in the directory /usr/share/doc/packages/pam/:

- **READMEs.** In the top level of this directory, there are some general README files. The subdirectory modules/ holds README files about the available PAM modules.

- **The Linux-PAM System Administrators' Guide.** This document includes everything that a system administrator should know about PAM.

The document discusses a range of topics, from the syntax of configuration files to the security aspects of PAM. The document is available as a PDF file, in HTML format, and as plain text.

- **The Linux–PAM Module Writers' Manual.** This document summarizes the topic from the developer's point of view, with information about how to write standard-compliant PAM modules. It is available as a PDF file, in HTML format, and as plain text.

- **The Linux–PAM Application Developers' Guide.** This document includes everything needed by an application developer who wants to use the PAM libraries. It is available as a PDF file, in HTML format, and as plain text.

Thorsten Kukuk has developed a number of PAM modules for SUSE Linux and made available some information about them at *www.suse.de/~kukuk/pam*.

Exercise 2-5   Configure PAM Authentication for Digital Airlines Employees

In this exercise, you perform tests that prevent all normal users (such as geeko) from logging in to see how PAM is used by the system.

Do the following:

1. From the KDE desktop, switch to virtual console 3 (**Ctrl+Alt+F3**); then log in as **root** with a password of **novell**.

2. Create the file /etc/nologin by entering **touch /etc/nologin**.

3. Log out as root by entering **exit**.

4. Attempt to log in as **geeko** with a **N0v3ll** password.

   A Login incorrect message is displayed, indicating that you cannot log in to the system.

5. Login as **root** with a password of **novell**.

6. View the last lines of the file /var/log/messages by entering the following:

   tail /var/log/messages

   Look for the FAILED LOGIN message for geeko that indicates the failed login attempt.

7. Edit the file /etc/pam.d/login:

   a. Enter **vim /etc/pam.d/login**.

   b. Switch to the text insert mode by pressing **Insert**.

   c. Comment out the following pam_nologin.so line (add a # sign to the beginning of the line):

   #auth   required   pam_nologin.so

   This PAM module is required to be successful during system authentication. It checks to see if the file /etc/nologin exists, and if it does, this PAM module does not allow regular users to log in by returning a failed status.

Now that this line is commented out, PAM will not check for the file. This means that all users can log in, even if the file exists.

d. Return to the command mode by pressing **Esc**.

e. Save the file and exit vi by entering **:wq**.

8. Test the modified PAM configuration file:

a. Log out as root by entering **exit**.

b. Attempt to log in as **geeko** with a password of **N0v3ll**.

You are able to log in because PAM no longer checks for the file /etc/nologin.

c. Logout as geeko by entering **exit**.

9. Edit the file /etc/pam.d/login to uncomment the pam_nologin.so line:

a. Log in as **root**.

b. Enter **vim /etc/pam.d/login**.

c. Switch to the text insert mode by pressing **Insert**.

d. Uncomment the pam_nologin.so line (by removing the # sign) to look like the following:

auth   required   pam_nologin.so

e. Return to the command mode by pressing **Esc**.

f. Save the file and exit vi by entering **:wq**.

g. Log out as root by entering **exit**.

10. Try logging in as **geeko**.

This time you receive a Login incorrect message.

11. Log in as **root**; then delete the file /etc/nologin by entering **rm /etc/nologin**.

12. Log out as root by entering **exit**.

13. Log in as **geeko**.

Because the file /etc/nologin does not exist, login for normal users is enabled again.

14. Log out as geeko by entering **exit**.

15. Return to the desktop by pressing **Ctrl+Alt+F7**.

OBJECTIVE 6   IMPLEMENT AND MONITOR ENTERPRISE SECURITY POLICIES

In the previous objectives, you have learned how to perform basic administrative tasks that provide secure access to the SUSE Linux environment.

However, before implementing these features in your own enterprise network environment, you need to know the following:

- Guidelines for Implementing Security Policies
- Security Rules and Tips
- SuSE Security Information Resources
- How to Monitor Login Activity

Guidelines for Implementing Security Policies

In order to provide a secure environment for your users and data in a multiuser environment, you need to consider the following guidelines when implementing your enterprise security policies on SUSE Linux Enterprise Server:

- Local Security and User Accounts
- Linux Password Encryption
- Boot Procedure Protection
- File Permissions Configuration
- Network Security and Local Security

Local Security and User Accounts

The main goal of local security is to keep users separate from each other, so no user can assume the permissions or the identity of another.

However, the user root holds the ultimate power on the system and can log in as any other local without a password and read any locally stored file.

Linux Password Encryption

On a Linux system, passwords are, of course, not stored as plain text, and the text string entered is not simply matched with the saved pattern.

If this were the case, all accounts on your system would be compromised as soon as someone got access to the corresponding file.

Instead, the stored password is encrypted and, each time it is entered, it is encrypted again with the two encrypted strings being compared.

This only provides more security if the encrypted password cannot be reverse-computed into the original text string.

This encryption is actually achieved by a special kind of algorithm, called a *trapdoor algorithm*, because it only works in one direction. An attacker who has obtained the encrypted string is not able to get your password by simply applying the same algorithm again.

Instead, it would be necessary to test all the possible character combinations until a combination is found that looks like your password when encrypted. With passwords 8 characters long, there are quite a number of possible combinations to calculate.

Boot Procedure Protection

You should configure your Linux system so it cannot be booted from a floppy disk or from CD, either by removing the drives entirely or by setting a BIOS password and configuring the BIOS to allow booting from a hard disk only.

Normally, a Linux system is started by a boot loader, allowing you to pass additional options to the booted kernel. This is crucial to your system's security.

Not only does the kernel itself run with root permissions, but it is also the first authority to grant root permissions at system start-up.

You can prevent others from using these parameters during boot by setting an additional password in /boot/grub/menu.lst.

File Permissions Configuration

As a general rule, always work with the most restrictive privileges possible for a given task.

For example, it is definitely not necessary to be the user root to read or write email. If the mail program has a bug, this bug could be exploited for an attack that acts with exactly the permissions of the program when it was started. By following the above general rule, you can minimize the possible damage.

The permissions of the more than 200,000 files included in a SUSE Linux distribution are carefully chosen. A system administrator who installs additional software or other files should take great care when doing so, especially when setting the permission bits.

Experienced and security-conscious system administrators always use the **–l** option with the command **ls** to get an extensive file list, which allows them to detect any incorrect file permissions immediately.

An incorrect file attribute not only means that files might be changed or deleted, but that the modified files might be executed by root or, in the case of configuration files, programs could use such files with the permissions of root.

This significantly increases the possibilities of an attacker. Attacks like this are called *cuckoo eggs*, because the program (the egg) is executed (hatched) by a different user (bird), just like a cuckoo tricks other birds into hatching its eggs.

A SUSE Linux system includes the files **permissions**, **permissions.easy**, **permissions.secure**, and **permissions.paranoid**, all in the directory /etc/.

The purpose of these files is to define special permissions, such as world-writable directories or, for files, the setuser ID bit (programs with the setuser ID bit set do not run with the permissions of the user that has launched it, but with the permissions of the file owner, in most cases, root).

An administrator can use the file /etc/permissions.local to add her own settings.

NOTE

To learn more about the permissions topic, read the comments in the file /etc/permissions, refer to the manual page of chmod (**man chmod**), or see *Permissions and Permission Values*.

NOTE

For additional details on types of security breaches (such as buffer overflows and viruses, see Section 26.7, "Security and Confidentiality" in the *SLES 9 Installation and Administration Manual*.

Network Security and Local Security

Network security is important for protecting a network from an attack that is started outside. The typical login procedure requiring a user name and a password for user authentication is still a local security issue.

In the particular case of logging in over a network, you need to differentiate between these two security aspects. What happens until the actual authentication is network security and anything that happens afterward is local security.

Security Rules and Tips

The following is a list of rules and tips you might find useful in dealing with basic security concerns:

- According to the rule of using the most restrictive set of permissions possible for every job, avoid doing your regular jobs when you are logged in as root.

  This reduces the risk of getting a cuckoo egg or a virus and protects you from your own mistakes.

- If possible, always try to use encrypted connections to work on a remote machine. Using ssh (secure shell) to replace telnet, ftp, rsh, and rlogin should be standard practice.

- Avoid using authentication methods based on IP addresses alone.

- Try to keep the most important network-related packages up-to-date and subscribe to the corresponding mailing lists to receive announcements on new versions of programs such as bind, postfix, and ssh. The same should apply to software relevant to local security.

- Disable any network services you do not absolutely require for your server to work properly. This will make your system safer.

  Open ports, with the socket in state LISTEN, can be found with the program **netstat**. As for the options, we recommended that you use **netstat –ap** or **netstat –anp**. The -p option lets you see which process is occupying a port under which name.

- RPM packages from SUSE are digitally signed. You can verify the integrity of any SUSE RPM package by entering the command **rpm -- checksig package.rpm**.

  The needed public gpg-key is copied to the home directory of root upon installation and can also be found on the SLES 9 DVD.

- Check your backups of user and system files regularly. Remember that if you do not test whether the backup will work, it might actually be worthless.

- Check your log files. Whenever possible, write a small script to search for suspicious entries. Admittedly, this is not exactly a trivial task. In the end, only you can know which entries are unusual and which are not.

- Use SUSEfirewall to enhance the security provided by tcpd (tcp_-wrapper).

- Design your security measures to be redundant. A message seen twice is much better than no message at all.

SUSE Security Information Resources

To handle security competently, it is important to keep up with new developments and to stay informed about the latest security issues.

One very good way to protect your systems against problems of all kinds is to install the updated packages recommended by security announcements as quickly as possible.

SUSE security announcements are published on a mailing list to which you can subscribe by using the following link: *www.suse.de/security*.

The list suse-securityannounce@suse.de is a first-hand source of information regarding updated packages and includes members of SUSE's security team among its active contributors.

The mailing list suse-security@suse.de is a good place to discuss any security issues of interest.

The bugtraq@securityfocus.com list is one of the best-known security mailing lists worldwide. We recommend that you read this list (which receives between 15 and 20 postings per day).

NOTE

You can find more information at www.securityfocus.com.

How to Monitor Login Activity

One of the most critical tasks you have as an administrator is to make sure that there is no suspicious activity on your system that might compromise security.

Monitoring tasks include evaluating login activity for signs of security breach such as multiple failed logins.

NOTE

Reviewing files such as messages in /var/log/ also gives you information about login activity.

To monitor login activity, you can use the following commands:

- **who.** This command shows who is currently logged in to the system and information such as the time of the last login.

  You can use options such as –H (display column headings), –r (current runlevel), and –a (display information provided by most options).

  For example, entering **who –H** returns information similar to the following:

  ```
  earth: ~ # who -H
  NAME         LINE       TIME               Command
  root         0          Aug 23 05:41       (console)
  geeko        pts/2      Aug 24 02:32       (10.0.0.50)
  earth:~ #
  ```

- **w.** This command displays information about the users currently on the machine and their processes.

  The first line includes information such as the current time, how long the system has been running, how many users are currently logged on, and the system load averages for the past 1, 5, and 15 minutes.

  Below the first line is an entry for each user that displays the login name, the tty name, the remote host, login time, idle time, JCPU, PCPU, and the command line of the user's current process.

The JCPU time is the time used by all processes attached to the tty. It does not include past background jobs, but does include currently running background jobs.

The PCPU time is the time used by the current process, named in the What field.

You can use options such as –h (don't display the header), –s (don't display the login time, JCPU, and PCPU), and -V (display version information).

For example, entering **w** returns information similar to the following:

```
earth: ~ # w
USER        TTY        LOGIN@         IDLE    JCPU    PCPU  WHAT
root        0          Mon05          ?xdm?   1:48    0.02s -0
geeko       pts/2      02:32          0.00s   0.10s   0.02s  ssh: geeko [priv]
earth:~ #
```

- **finger.** This command displays information about local and remote system users. By default, the following information is displayed about each user currently logged in to the local host:

    - Login name

    - User's full name

    - Associated terminal name

    - Idle time

    - Login time (and from where)

    You can use options such as –l (long format) and –s (short format).

    For example, entering **finger –s** returns information similar to the following:

```
earth: ~ # w
Login     Name                    Tty        Idle   Login Time    Where
geeko     The SUSE Chameleon      pts/2      -      Tue 02:32     10.0.0.50
root      root                    0          54d    Mon 05:41     console
earth:~ #
```

- **last.** This command displays a listing of the last logged-in users.

    Last searches back through the file /var/log/wtmp (or the file designated by the option -f) and displays a list of all users logged in (and out) since the file was created.

    You can specify names of users and tty's to only show information for those entries.

    You can use options such as -*num* (where *num* is the number of lines to display), –a (display the hostname in the last column), and –x (display system shutdown entries and runlevel changes).

For example, entering **last -ax** returns information similar to the following:

```
earth: ~ # last -ax
geeko          pts/2      Fri Aug 24 02:32    still logged in    10.0.0.50
geeko          pts/2      Fri Aug 24 02:29 - 02:30   (00:00)     10.0.0.50
geeko          pts/2      Fri Aug 24 02:29 - 02:28   (00:07)     10.0.0.50
geeko          pts/2      Fri Aug 24 02:29 - 00:39   (00:00)     10.0.0.50
geeko          pts/2      Fri Aug 24 02:29 - 08:20   (00:07)     10.0.0.50
root           0          Thu Aug 23 05:41    still logged in    console


wtmp begins Mon Aug  6 09:04:35 2007
earth:~ #
```

- **lastlog.** This command formats and prints the contents of the last login log file (/var/log/lastlog). The login name, port, and last login time are displayed.

  Entering the command without options displays the entries sorted by numerical ID.

  You can use options such as –u *login_name* (display information for designated user only) and –h (display a one-line help message).

  If a user has never logged in, the message **Never logged in** is displayed instead of the port and time.

  For example, entering **lastlog** returns information similar to the following:

```
earth: ~ # lastlog
Username         Port        From           Latest
root             0           console        Thu Aug 23 05:41:50 -0600 2007
bin                                         **Never logged in**
daemon                                      **Never logged in**
lp                                          **Never logged in**
mail                                        **Never logged in**
...
```

- **faillog.** This command formats and displays the contents of the failure log (/var/log/faillog) and maintains failure counts and limits.

  You can use options such as –u *login_name* (display information for designated user only) and –p (display in UID order).

The command faillog only prints out users with no successful login since the last failure. To print out a user who has had a successful login since his last failure, you must explicitly request the user with the –u option.

Entering **faillog** returns information similar to the following:

```
earth: ~ # faillog
Username        Failures    Maximum    Latest
root                   0          0    Mon Aug 20 07:20:11 -0600 2007 on tty1
geeko                  0          0    Thu Aug 16 16:48:34 -0600 2007 on tty3
earth:~ #
```

 You can activate or deactivate logging activity in /var/log/lastlog and /var/log/faillog by setting options in the YaST Security settings module (see *Configure Security Settings*).

NOTE

Exercise 2-6   Change the Security Settings

As part of tightening security, SUSE provides configuration files for locking down your system. From a files perspective, there are three settings: easy, secure, and paranoid.

In this exercise, you change to the paranoid setting and observe the impact on the system.

Do the following:

1. From a terminal window, verify that SUID bit for ping is set by entering **ls -al /bin/ping**.

   Notice that the permissions are set to **–rwsr-xr-x**. The s in the fourth field indicates that the SUID is set, which means that any user can run ping, but it executes in memory as the owner of the file (root).

2. From the KDE desktop, select the **YaST** icon; then enter a password of **novell** and select **OK**.

3. Select **Security and Users > Security settings**.

   The Local Security Configuration dialog box appears.

4. Select **Level 3 (Network Server)**; then select **Details**.

   The Password Settings dialog box appears.

5. Continue by selecting **Next**.

   The Boot Settings dialog box appears.

6. Continue by selecting **Next**.

   The Login Settings dialog box appears.

7. Continue by selecting **Next**.

   The Adding User dialog box appears.

8. Continue by selecting **Next**.

   The Miscellaneous Settings dialog box appears.

9. From the Setting of File Permissions drop-down list, select **Paranoid**.

10. Configure the system for the Paranoid setting by selecting **Finish**.

11. From the terminal window, verify that SUID bit for ping is *not* set by entering **ls -al /bin/ping**.

    Notice that the permissions are now set to **-rwxr-xr-x**. The x in the fourth field indicates that the execute bit is set for root.

12. Attempt to ping DA1 by entering **/bin/ping da1**.

    You receive a ping: icmp open socket: Operation not permitted message because only root is allowed to open the socket.

13. Reset the file permissions settings to secure:

    a. From the YaST Control Center, select **Security and Users > Security settings**.

    b. Select **Level 3 (Network Server)**; then select **Details**.

       The Password Settings dialog box appears.

    c. Continue by selecting **Next**.

    d. Accept the default settings for the following dialog boxes by selecting **Next**:

       - Boot Settings

       - Login Settings

       - Adding User

       The Miscellaneous Settings dialog box appears.

    e. From the Setting of File Permissions drop-down list, select **Secure**.

    f. Configure the system for the Secure setting by selecting **Finish**.

14. From the terminal window, verify that SUID bit for ping is set by entering **ls -al /bin/ping**.

    Notice that the permissions are set back to **-rwsr-xr-x**.

15. Attempt to ping DA1 by entering **/bin/ping da1**.

    You are able to ping server DA1.

16. End the ping process by pressing **Ctrl+C**.

17. Close all open windows on the desktop.

CHAPTER SUMMARY

- Each user has a UID and a primary GID that may be viewed using the **id** and **groups** commands. Regular user accounts are used by most users to log into the system, whereas system services use system user accounts when performing tasks on the system.

- Linux systems store user information in /etc/passwd and password information in /etc/shadow. You can use the **pwck** command to check these files and **pwconv** to convert entries in /etc/passwd to /etc/shadow.

- Group information is stored in the /etc/group file on Linux systems. In SLES, each new user becomes a member of a group that is managed by the root user.

- You may use the **useradd**, **usermod**, and **userdel** commands to add, modify, and remove user accounts on your system, respectively. Similarly, you may use the **groupadd**, **groupmod**, and **groupdel commands** to add, modify, and remove group accounts on your system, respectively. YaST may be used to perform all user and group management functions.

- You can change user account passwords, lock user accounts, and control password expiry settings using the **passwd** command.

- The **su** command may be used to change your current session UID. Similarly, the **newgrp** command may be used to change your session's primary GID.

- Users can be granted rights to run certain commands as other users, using the **sudo** command via entries in the /etc/sudoers file.

- The Security Settings module in YaST can be used to configure default security-related settings on your system.

- You can assign read, write, and execute permissions to files and directories. The definitions of these permissions are separate between files and directories. In addition, there are three special file and directory permissions: SUID, SGID, and sticky bit.

- Using the **chmod** command, permissions can be set on the owner of a file (owner), members of the group of the file (group), and everyone else on the system (others). Similarly, you can change the owner and group owner for a file using the **chown** and **chgrp** commands. File and directory permissions may also be set using a desktop environment.

- New files and directories receive default permissions from the system less the value of the umask variable.

- File attributes may be used to restrict the usage of individual files and directories. The **chattr** and **lsattr** commands change and list attributes, respectively.

- ◻ PAM provides an extra layer of security between applications and system files by using modules that determine access restrictions.

- ◻ Security policies provide for standardized security within an organization. Strong passwords, encryption, boot protection, restrictive permissions, and network limitations provide the most secure systems. In addition, you should monitor login activity on a regular basis using the **who**, **w**, **last**, **lastlog**, and **faillog** commands.

KEY TERMS

/boot/grub/menu.lst — The configuration file for the GRUB boot loader in SLES.

/etc/default/passwd — A file that contains default values used when changing passwords such as encryption algorithm.

/etc/default/useradd — A file that contains default values used when creating user accounts.

/etc/group — The file that contains system groups and their members.

/etc/issue — A text file that contains a message for users that log into a command-line terminal.

/etc/login.defs — A file that contains default values used when creating user accounts.

/etc/motd — A text file that contains a message (or "message of the day") for users that log into a command-line terminal.

/etc/pam.d — The directory that stores PAM configuration information for PAM programs.

/etc/passwd — The file that contains user account information such as name, UID, primary group, home directory, and shell.

/etc/permissions.easy — A file that lists the least secure file permission restrictions for system files.

/etc/permissions.local — A file that lists user-defined file permission restrictions for system files.

/etc/permissions.paranoid — A file that lists the most secure file permission restrictions for system files.

/etc/permissions.secure — A file that lists secure file permission restrictions for system files.

/etc/security — The directory that stores PAM configuration information for PAM modules.

/etc/shadow — The file that typically contains encrypted passwords and password expiry information for user accounts on the system.

/etc/shells — A file that lists valid system shells such as /bin/bash.

/etc/skel — A directory that contains files and directories that are copied to all new users' home directories after they are created.

/etc/sudoers — A file that lists the users who are allowed to run certain commands as other users.

/home — The default directory used to store user home directories.

/root — The root user's home directory.

/var/log/faillog — A text file that lists failed login attempts.

/var/log/wtmp — A text file that lists successful login attempts.

attributes — Special flags on a file or directory that modify its usage. The read-only attribute prevents contents from being changed.

Blowfish — An encryption method used to encrypt Linux passwords.

chattr — Used to change the attributes on a file or directory.

chgrp (change group) command — Used to change the group owner of a file or directory.

chmod (change mode) command — Used to change the mode (permissions) of a file or directory.

chown (change owner) command — Used to change the owner and group owner of a file or directory.

cuckoo egg — A file that, when executed, creates a security problem.

Data Encryption Standard (DES) — The default encryption method used in SLES for passwords.

effective group — See **primary group**.

execute permission — Allows you to execute files as well as access directory contents.

Ext2 — The traditional file system used on older Linux systems.

Ext3 — A journaling version of the Ext2 file system.

faillog command — Displays the contents of /var/log/faillog.

finger command — Displays information about local user accounts.

General Electric Comprehensive Operating System (GECOS) — Represents a description of a user account stored in the comments field of /etc/passwd.

group — When referring to a long file or directory listing, it represents the group ownership of a file or directory.

Group ID (GID) — A number that uniquely identifies system groups.

groupadd command — Used to add a group to the system.

groupdel command — Used to delete a group from the system.

groupmod command — Used to modify the name, membership, or GID of a group on the system.

groups command — Displays the groups that a user is a member of.

id command — Displays the UID and GIDs associated with a user account.

last command — Displays the most recent users who have logged into the system from entries in /var/log/wtmp.

lastlog command — Displays the most recent users who have logged into the system from entries in /var/log/lastlog.

locate command — Used to search for files on the system via a pre-indexed database.

lsattr — Used to list the attributes on a file or directory.

Message Digest 5 (MD5) — An encryption method used to encrypt Linux passwords.

mkpasswd command — Used to create an encrypted password for use with user or group accounts.

2

newgrp command — Used to change the current primary group for a user account.

others — When referring to a long file or directory listing, it represents all users on the Linux system that are not the owner or a member of the group on the file or directory.

owner — The user whose name appears in a long listing of a file or directory and who typically has the most permissions to that file or directory.

passwd command — Used to modify user passwords and expiry information as well as lock and unlock user accounts.

Pluggable Authentication Modules (PAM) — A set of components that allow programs to access user account information.

primary group — The group specified for a user in the /etc/passwd file that becomes the group owner on newly created files and directories.

private scheme — A method that, during user creation, creates a new group for each user that can be managed by the user.

public scheme — A method that places new users in a common group that is managed by the root user.

pwck command — Used to check the validity of the /etc/passwd and /etc/shadow files.

pwconv command — Used to convert entries from the /etc/passwd file to the /etc/shadow file.

Read permission — Allows you to open and read files as well as list directory contents.

Red Hat Package Manager (RPM) — A format used to distribute software packages on most Linux systems.

regular users — User accounts that may be used to log in to the system interactively.

rpm command — Used to install, remove, and find information on RPM software packages.

Set Group ID (SGID) — A special permission set on executable files and directories. When you run an executable program that has the SUID permission set, you become the group owner of the executable file for the duration of the program. On a directory, the SGID sets the group that gets attached to newly created files.

Set User ID (SUID) — A special permission set on executable files. When you run an executable program that has the SUID permission set, you become the owner of the executable file for the duration of the program.

shadow passwords — Passwords that are stored in the /etc/shadow file instead of the /etc/passwd file.

sticky bit — A special permission that is set on directories that prevents users from removing files that they do not own.

su (switch user) command — Used to change the current user account.

sudo command — Used to run commands as another user via entries in /etc/sudoers.

system users — User accounts that may be used by system services and cannot be used by users to log in to the system interactively.

trapdoor algorithm — An algorithm that encrypts data but cannot be used to decrypt it.

umask — A system variable that removes permissions on all new files and directories.

umask command — Used to view and change the system umask.

updatedb command — Used to update the database used by the **locate** command.

user ID (UID) — A number that uniquely identifies each system user account.

useradd command — Used to add a user account to the system.

userdel command — Used to remove a user account from the system.

usermod command — Used to modify the properties of a user account on the system.

visudo command — Used to edit the /etc/sudoers file with the vi text editor.

w command — Displays the users currently logged in to the system and their processes.

who command — Displays the users currently logged in to the system. It also can be used to display the contents of the /var/log/wtmp file.

write permission — Allows you to open and edit files as well as add or remove directory contents.

REVIEW QUESTIONS

1. What command could you use to view your primary UID and GID?
   _____

2. Which of the following fields are stored in the /etc/passwd file? (Choose all that apply.)

   a. UID

   b. Comments

   c. Home directory

   d. Standard shell

3. What is the default group scheme used in SLES? _____

4. Which UIDs are used for special system users?

   a. 0–99

   b. 100–499

   c. 500–999

   d. 1000–4999

5. You have added information to the /etc/passwd file. What command can be used to create the appropriate lines in /etc/shadow? _____

6. Which of the following files could you edit to create groups and add members to those groups?

   a. /etc/passwd

   b. /etc/shadow

   c. /etc/groups

   d. /etc/group

2

7. Which of the following files are used to obtain default user account settings when you create a user with the **useradd** command? (Choose all that apply.)

    a. /etc/default/useradd

    b. /etc/skel

    c. /etc/login.defs

    d. /etc/useradd.default

8. What command can be used to change the UID of the user **dgrant** to **1601**?

    _____

9. What two commands below can be used to create the group **research** and add the user **dgrant** to it? (Each answer is part of the solution.)

    a. groupmod –A dgrant research

    b. groupadd –p research

    c. groupadd research

    d. groupmod –A research dgrant

10. Which of the following files contain login messages? (Choose all that apply).

    a. /etc/issue

    b. /etc/login.defs

    c. /etc/login

    d. /etc/motd

11. Which of the following lines in /etc/sudoers will give the user **bob** the right to run the **useradd** command on all computers?

    a. bob /sbin/useradd = all

    b. /sbin/useradd all = bob

    c. bob all = /sbin/useradd

    d. /sbin/useradd bob = all

12. Which YaST security level is recommended for a network server?

    a. Level 1

    b. Level 2

    c. Level 3

    d. Level 4

13. What would you type at a command prompt to execute a program called **prog1** in your current directory, if the current directory is not in your path statement?

    _____

14. Which of the following directory permissions gives the owner the ability to list the contents of the directory? (Choose all that apply).

    a. rwxr-x-r-x

    b. rwxr--r-x

    c. r-xrw-r-x

    d. -w-rw-r-x

15. What command could you use to change the owner to **dgrant** and the group owner to **research** for the file **/etc/config**? _____

16. What command could you use to change the permissions on the file **/etc/config** to rw-rw-r-- using octal notation? _____

17. What permissions does the system give to new files and directories by default prior to applying the umask?

    a. Files receive 666 and directories receive 666

    b. Files receive 666 and directories receive 777

    c. Files receive 777 and directories receive 666

    d. Files receive 777 and directories receive 777

18. What will the permission be on a new directory if the umask is set to 027?

    _____

19. Which of the following commands will set the sticky bit special permission on the directory **/public**?

    a. chmod 1777 /public

    b. chmod 2777 /public

    c. chmod 4777 /public

    d. chmod 7777 /public

20. What command will set the immutable attribute on the file **/etc/config**?

    _____

21. What are the four possible fields in a PAM configuration file?

    a. Session type, Control flag, Debug mode, Arguments

    b. PAM control, Module, Arguments, Restrictions

    c. Password, Module, Restrictions, Arguments

    d. Module type, Control flag, Module, Arguments

22. Which of the following are good security practices? (Choose all that apply.)

    a. Assigning only necessary file system permissions

    b. Using passwords that are four characters long or longer

    c. Disabling unused network services

    d. Updating network software

23. What command can you use to display failed logins? _____

Discovery Exercises

Using the Skeleton Directory

When you create new users in SLES that have a home directory, default environment files are copied to this directory during the creation process from the /etc/skel directory. In a terminal as the root user, create a file in the /etc/skel directory called **SampleNewUserFile**. Next, create a new user called **bozo** that has a home directory of /home/bozo. Following this, perform a long listing of all files in the /etc/skel and /home/bozo directories using the command **ls –l /home/bozo /etc/skel** and note the contents.

Deleting Users

In a terminal as the root user, view the UID for the **bozo** user that you created earlier. Next, remove the **bozo** user from the system without removing the home directory. Then perform another long listing of the files in the /home/bozo directory using the command **ls –al /home/bozo**, and note the owner of the files within. Next, create a new user called **bozoette** that has a home directory of **/home/bozoette** and the same UID that was previously held by the bozo user. Use the **ls –al /home/bozo** command again to verify that bozoette now owns the files in the /home/bozo directory. How can this information be useful in an enterprise environment?

Setting File Ownership and Permissions

In a terminal as the root user, perform the following actions in order. For each action, write down the command(s) that you used.

   a. Ensure that newly created files have the permissions r--r--r--.

   b. Create a **/public** directory that allows all users to add files but restricts the ability to delete other users' files.

   c. Create a **/public/test** file that gives the **geeko** user the ability to modify file contents and the **sys** group the ability to read file contents. No other user should have permission to this file.

   d. Prevent the **/public/test** file from being overwritten or deleted.

Researching PAM Modules

Using local or Internet resources, research three PAM modules that are commonly used in SLES. In a brief memo, summarize their usage, configuration, and purpose.

3

MANAGE THE LINUX FILE SYSTEM

In this section, you discover how to manage your SUSE Linux Enterprise Server file system by learning basic tasks such as implementing partitions, creating a file system, checking the file system for errors, and performing backup and restore procedures.

- ◆ Select a Linux File System
- ◆ Configure Linux File System Partitions
- ◆ Configure a File System with Logical Volume Management (LVM)
- ◆ Configure and Manage a Linux File System
- ◆ Set Up and Configure Disk Quotas
- ◆ Back Up and Restore the File System

OBJECTIVE 1 SELECT A LINUX FILE SYSTEM

One of the key roles performed by the Linux operating system is providing storage services through creating and managing a file system.

To successfully select a file system that meets your server requirements, you need to understand the following about file systems available for Linux:

- Linux File Systems
- Linux File System Formats
- Linux File System Characteristics
- File System Journaling
- Additional File System Documentation

It is very important to keep in mind that there might be no file system that best suits all kinds of applications. Each file system has its particular strengths and weaknesses, which must be taken into account.

However, even the most sophisticated file system cannot be a substitute for a reasonable backup strategy.

NOTE

For additional details on specific file systems (such as ext3 and ReiserFS), see Section 18.2 in the *SLES 9 Installation and Administration Manual*.

Also see *Additional File System Documentation* at the end of this objective.

Linux File Systems

The type of file system you select depends on several factors (including speed and journaling). The following describes the file systems and formats available on Linux:

- Traditional File Systems
- Journaling File Systems
- Virtual Filesystem Switch

All of these file system types are included in the 2.6 Linux kernel (used in SUSE Linux Enterprise Server 9).

NOTE The basic Linux 2.4 kernel includes all advanced file system types. These include XFS, ReiserFS, ext3, and non-journaling file systems.

You can enter the following command to list the file system formats the kernel currently supports:

cat /proc/filesystems

Traditional File Systems

Traditional file systems supported by Linux do not journal data or metadata. These include the following:

- **ext2.** The ext2 file system is inode-based, is designed for speed, is efficient, and does not fragment easily.

   Because of these features, ext2 continues to be used by many administrators, even though it does not provide a journaling feature.

   The ext2 file system has been available for many years, and is easily converted to an ext3 file system.

- **minix.** The minix file system is old and fairly limited (it was the first Linux file system) but is still sometimes used for floppy disks or RAM disks where minix's extremely low file system overhead allows for the storage of more data.

- **MS-DOS/VFAT.** FAT (File Allocation Table) is the primary file system for consumer versions of Microsoft Windows up to and including Windows Me.

   VFAT is the 32-bit version of FAT that includes long filenames.

- **HPFS.** HPFS (High Performance File System) is the native file system for IBM's OS/2 file system.

Journaling File Systems

The following file systems available for Linux include a journaling feature:

- **ext3.** ext3 is the version of the ext2 file system that supports journaling.

- **ReiserFS.** Originally designed by Hans Reiser, ReiserFS treats the entire disk partition as if it were a single database table, storing not only the file metadata but the file itself.

   Directories, files, and file metadata are organized in an efficient data structure called a "balanced tree," which offers significant speed improvements for many applications, especially those that use lots of small files.

- **NTFS.** NTFS (New Technology File System) is the file system used by Windows NT.

It supports multiple file systems, has file recovery for hard disk crashes, uses the Unicode character set, and provides for file names up to 255 characters long.

Although more feature-rich than MS–DOS/VFAT, only reading of the file system is currently supported under Linux.

- **JFS.** This journaling file system from IBM was released as a production version in 2001.

- **XFS.** XFS is a high-performance journaling file system from SGI. It provides quick recovery after a crash, fast transactions, high scalability, and excellent bandwidth.

  XFS combines advanced journaling technology with full 64-bit addressing and scalable structures and algorithms.

For details on XFS, see *http://oss.sgi.com/projects/xfs/*.

NOTE

- **Veritas's VxFS**. VxFS is a commercial journaling file system that first shipped for Linux during 2001 and is frequently used on Unix platforms.

Virtual Filesystem Switch

For a user or program, it does not matter which file system format is used. The same interface to the data always appears. This is implemented by the Virtual Filesystem Switch (VFS) (also referred to as the *virtual file system*).

This is an abstract level in the kernel providing defined interfaces on the part of the processes. It includes functions such as open a file, write to a file, and read a file.

A program does not have to worry about how file access is implemented technically. The VFS forwards these requests to the corresponding driver for the file system format, as illustrated in Figure 3-1.

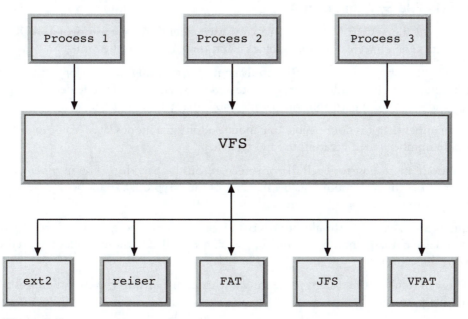

Figure 3-1

One of the features of the VFS is to display file characteristics to the user as they are known from UNIX file system formats. This includes access permissions, even if they do not exist, as is the case with VFAT.

Linux File System Formats

File system formats in Linux are characterized by the fact that data and administration information are kept separate. Each file is described by an *inode* (index node or information node).

Each of these inodes has a size of 128 bytes and contains all the information about the file apart from the filename. This includes details such as the owner, access permissions, the size, various time details (time of modification, time of access, and time of modification of the inode), and the links to the data blocks of the file.

How data organization takes place differs from one file system format to the next. To understand the basics of file system data organization on Linux, you need to know the following:

- ext2fs File System Format
- ReiserFS Format

- Directories
- Network File System Formats

ext2fs File System Format

The ext2 file system format is, in many ways, identical to traditional UNIX file system formats. The concepts of inodes, blocks, and directories are the same.

When a file system is created (the equivalent of formatting in other operating systems), the maximum number of files that can be created is specified. This inode density (together with the capacity of the partition) determines how many inodes can be created.

Remember that it is not possible to generate additional inodes later. You can only specify an inode number when creating the file system.

An inode must exist for each file or directory on the partition. The number of inodes also determines the maximum possible number of files. Typically, an inode is generated for 4096 bytes of capacity.

On average, each file should be 4 KB in size for the capacity of the partition to be used optimally. If a large number of files are smaller than 4 KB, more inodes are used compared with the capacity.

This can result in the system preventing any more file creation, even if there is still space on the file partition.

For applications that create a large number of very small files, the inode density should be increased by setting the corresponding capacity to a smaller value (such as 2048 or even 1024). However, the time needed for a file system check will increases substantially.

The space on a partition is divided into *blocks*. These have a fixed size of 1024, 2048, or 4096 bytes. You specify the block size when the file system is created; it cannot be changed later.

The block size determines how much space is reserved for a file. The larger this value is, the more space is consumed by the file, even if the actual amount of data is smaller.

In the classic file system formats (to which ext2 also belongs), data is stored in a linear chain of blocks of equal size. A specific number of blocks is grouped together in a block group (as illustrated in Figure 3-2), and each block group consists of 8192 blocks.

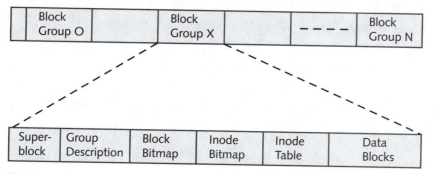

Figure 3-2

The boot sector is located at the beginning of this chain and contains static information about the file system, including where the kernel to load can be found.

Each block group contains the following components:

- **Superblock.** The superblock is read when the file system is mounted and contains the following information about the file system:

  - The number of free and occupied blocks and inodes

  - The number of blocks and inodes for each block

  - Information about file system use, such as the time of the last mount, the last write access, and the number of mounts since the last file system check

  - A valid bit, which is set to **0** when the file system is mounted and set to **1** again by umount

    When the computer is booted, the valid bit is checked. If it is set to 0 (power failure or reset), the automatic file system repair is started.

    The remains of files that can no longer be reconstructed are stored in the directory lost+found/ (in an ext2/ext3 file system).

  For reasons of security, there are copies of the superblock. Because of this, the file system can be repaired, even if the first superblock has been destroyed.

- **Group Description.** Information is stored here about where other areas are located (such as block bitmap and inode bitmap). This information is also stored a number of times for reasons of security.

- **Block Bitmap.** Information is stored here indicating which blocks in this group are free or occupied.

- **Inode Bitmap.** Information is stored here indicating which inodes are free or occupied.
- **Inode Table.** File information is stored in this table, including owners, access permissions, timestamps, and links to the data blocks in which the data is located.
- **Data Blocks.** This is where the actual data is located.

The ext2 file system format can process filenames with a length of up to 255 characters. With the path, a name can be a maximum of 4096 characters in length (slashes included).

A file can be up to 16 GB in size for a block size of 1024 bytes or 2 TB for a block size of 4096 bytes. The maximum file system size is 2 TB (with a block size of 1024 bytes) or 16 TB (with a block size of 4096 bytes).

The limitation on file size remains for the ext2 file system. However, the kernel can now handle files of almost any size.

ReiserFS Format

On a file system with ext2 and a block size of 1024 bytes, a file 8195 bytes in size occupies 8 blocks completely and a ninth block with 3 bytes.

Even though only 3 bytes are occupied, the block is no longer available. This means that approximately 11 percent of available space is wasted.

If the file is 1025 bytes in size, 2 blocks are required, 1 of which is almost completely empty. Almost 50 percent of the space is wasted.

A worst case occurs if the file is very small: even if the file is only 50 bytes in size, a whole block is used (95 percent wasted).

A solution to this problem is provided by the ReiserFS format, which organizes data in a different way. This file system format has (currently) only 1 fixed block size of 4096 bytes.

However, small files are stored more efficiently. Only as much space is reserved as is actually required—not an entire block. Small files or the ends of files are stored together in the same block.

The inodes required are not generated when the file system is created, but only when they are actually needed. This allows a more flexible solution to storage requirements, increasing efficiency in the use of hard drive space.

Another advantage of the ReiserFS is that access to files is quicker. This is done through the use of balanced binary trees in the organization of data blocks.

However, balanced trees require considerably more processing power because after every file is written, the entire tree must be rebalanced.

The current version of the ReiserFS (3.6) contained in the kernel from version 2.4 on allows a maximum partition size of 16 TB. A file also has a maximum size of 16 TB.

The same limitations exist for filenames as with the ext2 file system format.

Directories

Inodes contain all the administrative information for a file, but not the filename. This is where directories are useful.

Like a catalog, directories contain information on other files. This information includes the number of the inode for the file and its name.

Directories serve as a table in which inode numbers are assigned line-by-line to filenames. You can view the inode assigned to a filename by using the command **ls -i**, as in the following:

```
DA50:~ # ls -i /
      2 .          104002 cdrom      80045 floppy    104081 mnt    103782 sbin
      2 ..          99068 dev        99657 home       81652 opt      80044 tmp
 104005 bin        104004 dvd       102562 lib            1 proc         4 usr
      2 boot        95722 etc        95718 media       81598 root     80046 var
```

Each filename is preceded by the inode number.

On this particular SUSE Linux server there are two partitions: one configured on the root directory /, and one configured on the directory /boot/.

Because inodes are always uniquely defined on one partition only, the same inode numbers exist on each partition (at least in part).

In the example, the two entries "." (a link to the current directory—here the root directory) and "boot" (the second partition is mounted on this directory) have the same inode number (2), but they are located on different partitions.

The file "..", which is actually a link to the previous layer in the direction of the root directory, also has an inode number of 2.

Because you are already in the root directory, this link points to itself. It is another name entry for an inode number.

The table (the directory file) for the root directory can be represented as shown in Table 3-1.

Table 3-1

Inode Number	Filename
1	proc
2	
2	.
2	boot
4	usr
80044	tmp
80045	floppy
80046	var
81598	root
81652	opt
95718	media
95722	etc
99068	dev
99657	home
102562	lib
103782	sbin
104002	cdrom
104004	dvd
104005	bin
104081	mnt

Network File System Formats

In addition to the already mentioned file system formats on the local computer, Linux also understands various network file system formats. The most significant of these is the Network File System (NFS), the standard in the UNIX world.

With NFS, it does not matter which file system format is used locally on individual partitions. As soon as a computer is functioning as an NFS server, it provides its file systems in a defined format NFS clients can access.

Using additional services included on SUSE Linux Enterprise Server, Linux can also work with the network file system formats of other operating systems.

These include the Server Message Block (SMB) format used in Windows and the Netware Core Protocol (NCP) from Novell.

SMB allows Linux to mount Windows 9x/NT network shares.

Linux File System Characteristics

Linux and UNIX file systems all start from a root (/) directory and include all other physical or network file systems under the root directory.

For example, if you insert a CD or DVD into your Linux computer, it is mounted at a specific directory under root (such as /media/cdrecorder or /media/cdrom). You can then view the contents of the CD or DVD by simply changing to that directory.

This approach is unlike Windows and other operating systems where you access physical or network file systems using drive mapping (such as drive D: for a CD or DVD).

Another difference between Linux and a file system such as Windows is that filenames are case sensitive. For example, the filename **steps** is different from **STEPS** and **Steps** or **sTEPs**.

If a filename appears as STEPS, you need to enter **STEPS** at the command line or Linux will not recognize the filename.

Long filenames are supported by native Linux file systems (such as ext2 and ReiserFS), and these filenames are case sensitive.

Linux also includes support for timestamps such as ctime (inode modification time), mtime (modification time), and atime (access time).

In addition to these characteristics, you also need to know the following:

- Linux File Types
- Linux File System Directories

Linux File Types

Normal files and directories in Linux are also known to other operating systems. But there are four additional types of files that are UNIX-specific.

The following describes these file types, along with normal files and directories available in Linux:

- **Normal files.** Normal files refer to files as they are also known to other operating systems: a set of contiguous data addressed with one name. These include files such as ASCII texts, executable programs, and graphics files.

  With some limitations, you can choose the filenames. There is no association between filename and file type (for example, report.txt).

  A number of filenames still retain this structure, but these are requirements of the corresponding applications, such as a word processing program or a compiler.

- **Directories.** Directories are special files containing information about other files. In particular, they contain two entries that implement the structure of the hierarchical file system.

  One of these entries (".") points to the directory itself. The other entry ("..") points to the entry one level higher in the hierarchy.

- **Device files.** Each piece of hardware in a Linux system is represented by a device file (except for network cards). The files represent links between the hardware components or the device drivers in the kernel and the applications.

  Every program that needs to access hardware must do so through the corresponding device file. The programs write to or read from a device file. The kernel makes sure that the data finds its way to the hardware or can be read from there.

- **Links.** Links are references to files located at other points in the file system.

  Through the use of links, maintaining data becomes much simpler. Changes only need to be made to the original file. They are then automatically valid for all links.

- **Sockets.** Sockets refer to special files with which data exchange between two locally running processes can be implemented through the file system.

- **FIFOs.** *FIFO* (first in first out), or ***named pipe***, is a term used for files to exchange data between processes. However, they can only exchange data in one direction.

Linux File System Directories

The Linux file system is hierarchical, much like other operating systems you might have used. The root of the file system is named /, with the subdirectories shown in Figure 3-3.

/ bin
/ boot
/ dev
/ etc
/ home
/ lib
/ media
/ mnt
/ opt
/ proc
/ root
/ sbin
/ srv
/ suse_linux
/ sys
/ tmp
/ usr
/ var

Figure 3-3

Directories below / are referenced from the root. For example, if you have a directory named bin that is located in a directory named usr that is located right below the root directory, it would be referenced as /usr/bin/.

The directories used in a Linux system are defined by the Filesystem Hierarchy Standard (FHS) in the Linux Standard Base (LSB).

The FHS specifies which directories must be located on the first level after the root directory and what they contain, but allows for flexibility in defining your own hierarchy in other areas.

The FHS defines a two-layered hierarchy:

- The directories in the top layer (under the root directory "/")
- The directories under /usr/.

NOTE

For additional information on the Filesystem Hierarchy Standard, see *www.pathname.com/fhs/*.

Some of the important default Linux directories include the following:

- **/etc/.** This directory contains configuration files.
- **/dev/.** This directory contains special link files that reference hardware in the system. For example, /dev/fd0 references floppy disk A. The first IDE hard disk is referenced by /dev/hda.

  It also contains special links for removable devices. For example, the CD-ROM drive is referenced by /dev/cdrom; /dev/fd0 (floppy drive) is linked to /dev/floppy.
- **/usr/.** This directory contains program files.
- **/var/.** This directory contains data such as print spool directories, mail storage, log files, and other temporary files.
- **/tmp/.** This directory stores temporary files created by running applications.
- **/home/.** This directory contains user home directories.
- **/root/.** This is the root user's home directory.
- **/bin/.** This directory contains essential command-line utilities such as vi, rpm, ls, mkdir, more, mv, grep, and tar.
- **/sbin/.** This directory contains essential system executables such as fsck, grub, mkfs, arp, fdisk, and ifconfig.
- **/mnt/.** This directory is used to mount devices or remote file systems using Samba or NFS. On some Linux distributions (such as Red Hat), it is also used to mount removable devices.
- **/media/.** This directory is used to mount removable devices on some Linux distributions (such as SUSE Linux).

File System Journaling

To make an appropriate decision about which file system to choose for which partition, you need to understand the following about Linux file systems and journaling:

- Journaling and File System Transactions
- ext2 and ext3 Comparison

Journaling and File System Transactions

File systems are basically databases that store files and use file information such as the filename and timestamp (called *metadata*) to organize and locate the files on a disk.

When you modify a file, the file system performs the following transactions:

- It updates the file (the data).
- It updates the file metadata.

Because there are two separate transactions, corruption can happen when only the file data is updated (but not the metadata) or vice versa, resulting in a difference between the data and metadata.

This can happen when a large file is being downloaded from the Web and there is an interruption (such as a power outage). The data might be written first, but the metadata might not be updated.

When there is a difference between the data and metadata, the state of the file system is inconsistent and requires repair.

Although traditional file systems (such as ext2) require you to use the command fsck in a UNIX or Linux environment to check and repair the file system, you do not need to check and repair journal-based file systems such as ReiserFS.

In a journal-based file system, the journal keeps a record of all current transactions and updates the journal as transactions are completed.

For example, when you first start copying a file from a network server to your workstation, the journaled file system submits an entry to the journal indicating that a new file on the workstation is being created.

After the file data and metadata are copied to the workstation, an entry is made indicating that the file was created successfully.

While recording entries in a journal requires extra time for creating files, it makes recovering an incomplete transaction easy as the journal can be used to repair the file system.

ext2 and ext3 Comparison

The Linux file system that has been the standard file system for a long time is version 2 of the extended file system (*ext2fs* or *ext2*).

The latest version, ext3fs, has been further developed to provide journaling functionality. Logs of files that are in use or opened are continually updated. If a system crash occurs, a check of the individual partitions is made automatically.

With ext2, the complete partition (all files) must be checked because no information is available as to whether a file was open at the time of the crash.

With ext3, only the open files need to be checked. This speeds up the system check and any repairs that might be required, so the system is available more quickly.

In addition, ext3 lets you journal all file data and metadata or simply journal the metadata.

You normally use a nonjournaling system such as ext2 on a small partition (such as a /boot partition) because the administrative information overhead of a system such as ReiserFS is much larger.

Additional File System Documentation

Each of the Linux file systems maintains its own home page on which to find mailing list information, further documentation, and FAQs, as shown in Table 3-2.

Table 3-2

File System	URL
ext2	http://e2fsprogs.sourceforge.net/
ext3	http://olstrans.sourceforge.net/release/OLS2000-ext3/ OLS2000-ext3.html
ReiserFS and Reiser4	www.namesys.com/
IBM's JF	www-128.ibm.com/developerworks/linux/library/l-jfs.html
SGI's XFS	http://oss.sgi.com/projects/xfs/
Veritas's VxFS	www.veritas.com/us/products/filesystem/

A comprehensive multipart tutorial about Linux file systems can be found at IBM developerWorks at the following URL:

www-106.ibm.com/developerworks/library/l-fs.html

For a comparison of the different journaling file systems in Linux, look at Juan I. Santos Florido's article at Linuxgazette: *www.linuxgazette.com/issue55/florido.html.*

If you are interested in an in-depth analysis of Large File Support (files larger than 2 GB) in Linux, visit Andreas Jaeger's LFS site at *www.suse.de/~aj/linux_lfs.html.*

OBJECTIVE 2   CONFIGURE LINUX FILE SYSTEM PARTITIONS

A basic task of all system administrators is maintaining file system layouts. Under Linux (and UNIX), new partitions can be transparently grafted into existing file system structures using the **mount** command.

In most cases, YaST proposes a reasonable partitioning schema during installation that can be accepted without change. However, you can also use YaST to customize partitioning after installation.

To implement partitions on your SUSE Linux Enterprise Server, you need to know the following:

- Partition Types
- Linux Device and Partition Names
- Design Guidelines for Implementing Partitions
- Design Guidelines for Optimizing Partitions
- How to Manage Partitions with YaST

Partition Types

Every hard disk (on an Intel platform) has a partition table with space for four entries. An entry in the partition table can correspond to a primary partition or an extended partition. However, only one extended partition entry is allowed.

A *primary partition* consists of a continuous range of cylinders (physical disk areas) assigned to a particular operating system. If you only had primary partitions, you would be limited to four because of the four-entry limitation in the partition table.

Extended partitions are also continuous ranges of disk cylinders, but an extended partition can be subdivided into *logical partitions*. Logical partitions do not require entries in the partition table.

In other words, an extended partition is a container for logical partitions.

Because the extended partition should span the entire remaining free-cylinder range, configure your primary partitions first before configuring the extended partition.

After configuring the extended partition, create multiple logical partitions within the extended partition. The maximum number of logical partitions is 15 on SCSI disks and 63 on (E)IDE disks.

Linux Device and Partition Names

Table 3-3 shows the names of Linux devices.

Table 3-3

Device	Linux Name
Primary master IDE hard disk	/dev/hda
Primary slave IDE hard disk	/dev/hdb
Secondary master IDE hard disk	/dev/hdc
Secondary slave IDE hard disk	/dev/hdd
First SCSI hard disk	/dev/sda
Second SCSI hard disk	/dev/sdb
Third SCSI hard disk	/dev/sdc
Fourth SCSI hard disk	/dev/sdd

Partitions follow the naming convention of the device name and partition number.

For example, the first partition on the first IDE drive would be /dev/hda1 (/dev/hda + 1 as the first partition). The first logical partition defined on an IDE hard disk will always be number 5.

Table 3-4 shows the partition names corresponding to the device the partition is defined on.

Table 3-4

Partition	Linux Name
First partition on first IDE hard drive	/dev/hda1
Second partition on first IDE hard drive	/dev/hda2
First partition on first SCSI hard drive	/dev/sda1
First logical partition on first IDE hard drive	/dev/hda5
Second logical partition on first IDE hard drive	/dev/hda6

For example, if you perform a new installation of SUSE Linux on a system with two IDE drives, you might want the first drive to include a partition for swap and /. You might want to put all logs, mail, and home directories on the second hard drive.

Table 3-5 lists examples of how you might want to partition the disks (it assumes that the CD-ROM drive is the slave on the first IDE controller).

Table 3-5

Partition	Linux Name
Swap partition	/dev/hda1
/ partition	/dev/hda3
Extended partition on second disk	/dev/hdc1
/var as a logical partition on second disk	/dev/hdc5
/home as a logical partition on second disk	/dev/hdc6
/app1 as a logical partition on second disk	/dev/hdc7

NOTE

On older installations, you often find a small partition for /boot/. The reason for this is that the boot loader LILO needed the kernel within the first 1024 cylinders of the hard disk to boot the machine.

Design Guidelines for Implementing Partitions

YaST normally proposes a reasonable partitioning scheme with sufficient disk space. This is usually a swap partition (between 256 and 500 MB), with the rest of the disk space reserved for a / partition.

In addition, if there is an existing partition on the hard drive, YaST attempts to maintain that partition.

If you want to implement your own partitioning scheme, consider the following recommendations.

- **File system size.** The following are recommendations for different system types.

  - **Minimal System: 700 MB.** No graphical interface (X Window System) is installed, which means that only console applications can be used. Also, only a very basic selection of software is installed.

  - **Minimal System with Graphical Interface: 1 GB.** This includes the X Window System and some applications.

  - **Default System: 1.5 GB.** This includes a modern desktop environment, like KDE or GNOME, and also provides enough space for large application suites like Netscape or Mozilla.

  - **Full Installation: 2.5 GB.** All the packages included with SUSE Linux can be installed.

- **Disk space distribution.** Depending on the amount of space and how the computer will be used, adjust the distribution of the available disk space. The following are some basic guidelines.

  - **Up to 4 GB.** One partition for the swap space and one root partition (/). In this case, the root partition must allow for those directories that often reside on their own partitions if more space is available.

  - **4 GB or more.** A swap partition, a root partition (1 GB), and 1 partition each for the following directories as needed: /usr/ (4 GB or more), /opt/ (4 GB or more), and /var/ (1 GB). The rest of the available space can be used for /home/.

- **Boot partition.** Depending on the hardware, it might also be useful to create a boot partition (/boot) to hold the boot mechanism and the Linux kernel.

  This partition should be located at the start of the disk and should be at least 8 MB or 1 cylinder.

  As a rule of thumb, always create such a partition if it was included in YaST's original proposal. If you are unsure about this, create a boot partition to be on the safe side.

- **Software and /opt/.** Some (mostly commercial) programs install their data in /opt/. In this case, you might want to create a separate partition for /opt/ or make the root partition large enough. KDE and GNOME are also installed in /opt/.

- **Additional partitions.** If the partitioning is performed by YaST and other partitions are detected in the system, these partitions are also entered in the file /etc/fstab to enable easy access to this data.

  The following is an example:

```
/dev/sda1 /data1 auto noauto,user 0 0
/dev/sda8 /data2 auto noauto,user 0 0
```

- **Executable files.** Partitions, whether they are Linux or FAT, are specified by YaST with the options **noauto** and **user**. This allows any user to mount or unmount these partitions as needed.

  For security reasons, YaST does not automatically enter the **exec** option, which is needed for executing programs from the respective location. However, you can enter this option manually.

  Entering the exec option is necessary if you encounter system messages such as Bad interpreter or Permission denied.

Design Guidelines for Optimizing Partitions

The following guidelines are provided if you want to optimize a system for security and speed and are prepared to reinstall the entire existing system if necessary.

First, consider the following questions:

- How will the computer be used (file server, application server, compute server, stand-alone machine)?
- How many people will work with this computer (concurrent logins)?
- How many hard disks are installed? What is their size and type (EIDE, SCSI, or RAID controllers)?

Consider the following guidelines and suggestions:

- Size of the Swap Partition
- Processor Speed and Main Memory Size
- Standalone Computer Guidelines
- File Server Guidelines
- Computer Server Guidelines

Size of the Swap Partition

Many sources state the rule that the swap size should be at least twice the size of the main memory. This is an outdated guideline from the past when 8 MB RAM was considered a considerable amount of memory.

In the past, the aim was to equip the machine with about 30 to 40 MB of memory (RAM plus swap space). Modern applications require even more memory. For normal users, 256 MB of swap partition space is currently a reasonable value.

Never configure your system without any swap partition space.

Processor Speed and Main Memory Size

In Linux, the size of main memory is often more important than the processor speed. One reason for this is the ability of Linux to create dynamic buffers containing hard disk data.

For this purpose, Linux uses various techniques, such as read ahead (reading sectors in advance) and delayed write (postponing and bundling write access). Delayed write is the reason why you should not simply switch off your Linux machine.

Read ahead and delayed write contribute to the fact that the main memory seems to fill up over time and that Linux is so fast.

NOTE

For additional details, see Section 12.2.6 in the *SLES 9 Installation and Administration Manual*.

Stand-Alone Computer Guidelines

As Linux becomes more popular, it is being used as a stand-alone system. Table 3-6 provides estimated disk space requirements for home or office use.

Table 3-6

Installation	Required Disk Space
Minimum	500 MB to 750 MB
Small	750 MB to 3 GB
Medium	3 GB to 10 GB
Large	More than 10 GB

The following are examples for typical workstation installations:

- **Standard workstation (wmall)**

  To install Linux on a 2.5 GB hard disk, use 256 MB for the swap partition and the rest for / (root partition).

- **Standard workstation (average)**

  If you have 8 GB available for Linux, use 256 MB for swap, 2.5 GB for /, and the rest for a separate /home partition.

- **Standard workstation (deluxe)**

  If you have more than 10 GB available, there is no standard way to partition the disk.

File Server Guidelines

Hard disk performance is crucial on a file server. Use SCSI devices if possible. Keep in mind the performance of the disk and the controller.

Optimizing the hard disk access is vital for file servers in networks of more than 20 users.

For example, if you want to set up a Linux file server for the home directories of 25 users, and if the average user requires 2 GB for personal data, a 50 GB partition mounted under /home is probably sufficient.

For 50 users, you would need 100 GB. If possible, split /home into two 50 GB hard disks that share the load (and access time).

Web browser caches should be stored on local hard disks.

NOTE

Computer Server Guidelines

A computer server is generally a powerful machine that carries out extensive calculations in the network. Such a computer is normally equipped with a large main memory (more than 512 RAM). Fast disk throughput is only needed for the swap partitions. If possible, distribute swap partitions to multiple hard disks.

How to Manage Partitions with YaST

You can use the YaST Expert Partitioner during or after installation to customize the default or existing partition configuration.

In this part, you learn how to do the following:

- Create a Partition
- Edit a Partition
- Resize a Partition

For details on all the options available in the Expert Partitioner, see Section 1.7.5 in the **SLES 9 Installation and Administration Manual**.

NOTE

Create a Partition

The following are the basic steps for accessing the Expert Partitioner after installation to create a partition:

1. From the KDE desktop, start the YaST Expert Partitioner module by doing one of the following:

   - Select the **YaST** icon, enter the root *password*, and select **OK**; then select **System > Partitioner**.

     or

   - Open a terminal window and enter **sux –** and the root *password*; then enter **yast2 disk**.

   The warning shown in Figure 3-4 appears.

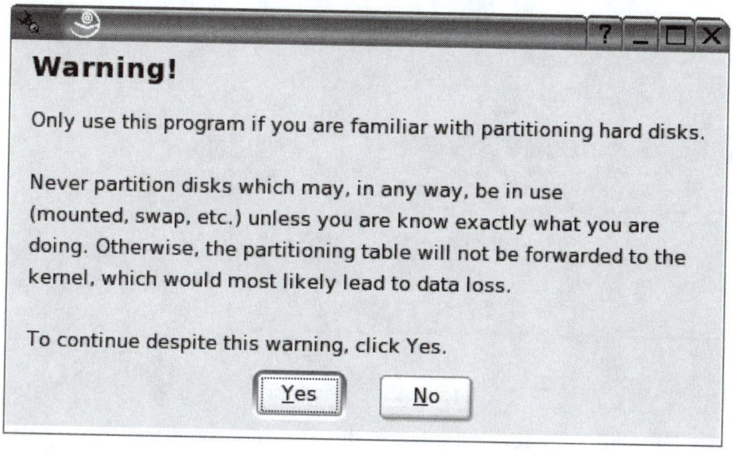

Figure 3-4

This warning gives you the opportunity to make sure you know what you are doing and the impact (data loss) it can have on your system.

2. Continue by selecting **Yes**.

The Expert Partitioner dialog box appears, as shown in Figure 3-5.

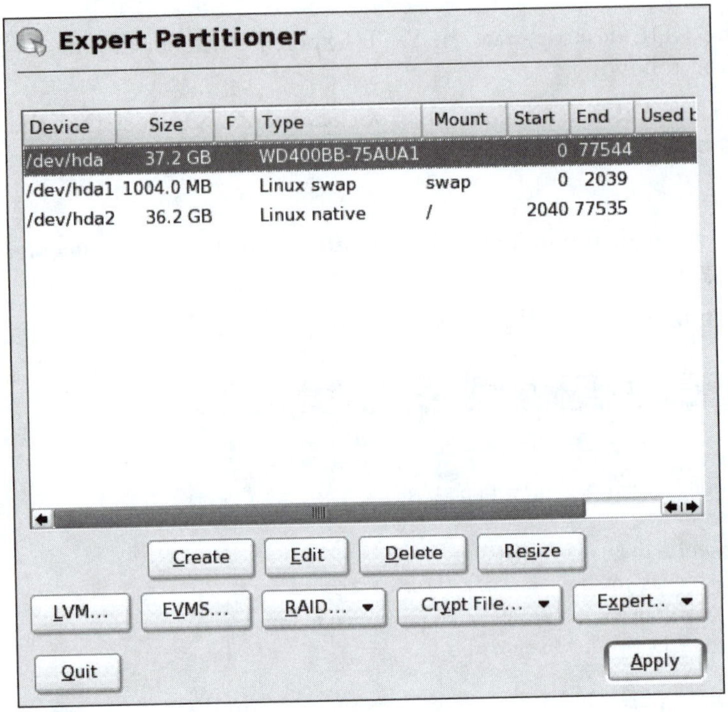

Expert Partitioner

Device	Size	F	Type	Mount	Start	End	Used b
/dev/hda	37.2 GB		WD400BB-75AUA1		0	77544	
/dev/hda1	1004.0 MB		Linux swap	swap	0	2039	
/dev/hda2	36.2 GB		Linux native	/	2040	77535	

Create   Edit   Delete   Resize

LVM...   EVMS...   RAID... ▼   Crypt File... ▼   Expert.. ▼

Quit   Apply

Figure 3-5

The Expert Partitioner lets you manually modify the partitioning of your hard disk. You can manage the list of partitions by adding (**Create**), editing (**Edit**), deleting (**Delete**), or resizing (**Resize**) partitions.

All existing or suggested partitions on all connected hard disks are displayed in the partition list. Entire hard disks are listed as devices without numbers (such as /dev/hda or /dev/sda). Partitions are listed as parts of these devices (such as /dev/hda1 or /dev/sda1).

The size, type, file system, and mount point of the hard disks and their partitions are also displayed. Any free hard disk space is also listed.

The mount point describes where the partition is mounted in the Linux file system tree.

To provide more disk space to Linux, you can free the needed space starting from the bottom toward the top of the list (starting from the last partition of a hard disk toward the first).

3. Create a partition by selecting **Create**.

If several hard disks are installed, a dialog box appears that lets you select a hard disk.

4. (Conditional) Select the hard disk for creating the partition.

The dialog box shown in Figure 3-6 appears.

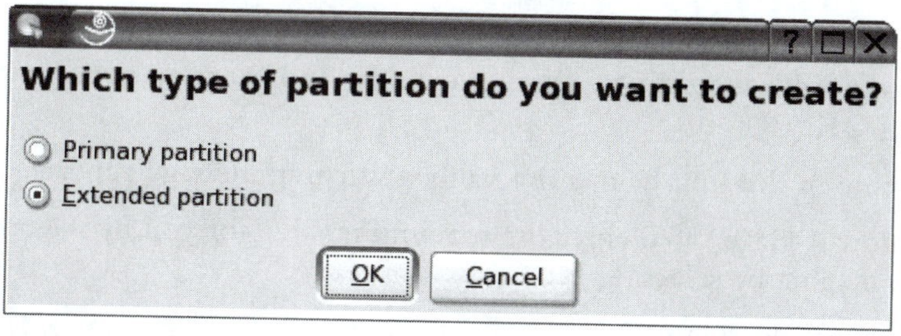

3

Which type of partition do you want to create?

○ Primary partition

◉ Extended partition

OK   Cancel

Figure 3-6

5. Select the type of partition you want to create (**Primary** or **Extended**); then select **OK**.

If you select an extended partition, the dialog box shown in Figure 3-7 appears.

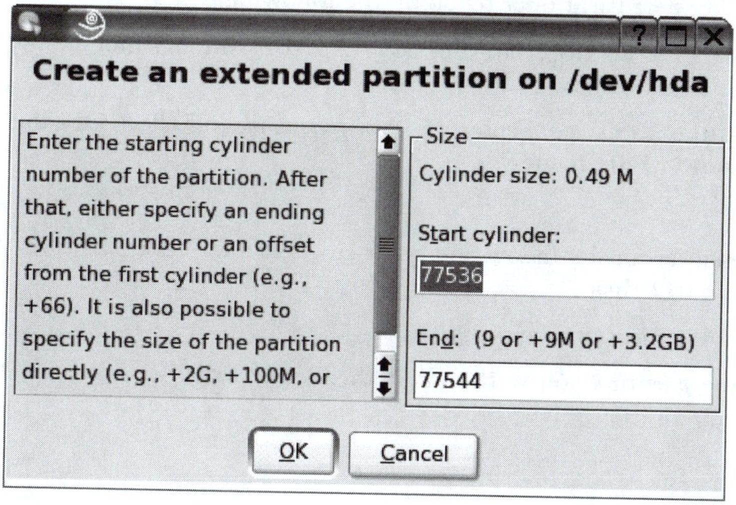

Create an extended partition on /dev/hda

Enter the starting cylinder number of the partition. After that, either specify an ending cylinder number or an offset from the first cylinder (e.g., +66). It is also possible to specify the size of the partition directly (e.g., +2G, +100M, or

Size

Cylinder size: 0.49 M

Start cylinder:

77536

End: (9 or +9M or +3.2GB)

77544

OK   Cancel

Figure 3-7

6. In the **Start cylinder** field, enter the beginning cylinder or accept the default.

7. In the **End** field, enter one of the following:

- The number of the ending cylinder (such as **77544**)

  or

- The offset from the first cylinder (such as **+66** cylinders)

  or

- A specific partition size (such as **+2G** or **+100M**)

8. When you finish indicating a starting cylinder and partition size, continue by selecting **OK**.

   If the value in the End field is not valid, a warning message appears.

9. (Conditional) Have YaST enter the maximum value for you by selecting **Yes**, or enter a value by selecting **No**.

10. Continue by selecting **OK**.

    You are returned to the Expert Partitioner with the new partition displayed in the partitions list.

Edit a Partition

After creating a partition, you can edit the partition parameters (except for start cylinder and size) with the YaST Expert Partitioner by doing the following:

1. From the KDE desktop, start the YaST Expert Partitioner module by doing one of the following:

   - Select the **YaST** icon, enter the root *password*, and select **OK**; then select **System > Partitioner**.

     or

   - Open a terminal window and enter **sux –** and the root *password*; then enter **yast2 disk**.

   The Expert Partitioner appears.

2. Select the *partition* you want to edit; then select **Edit**.

The dialog box shown in Figure 3-8 appears.

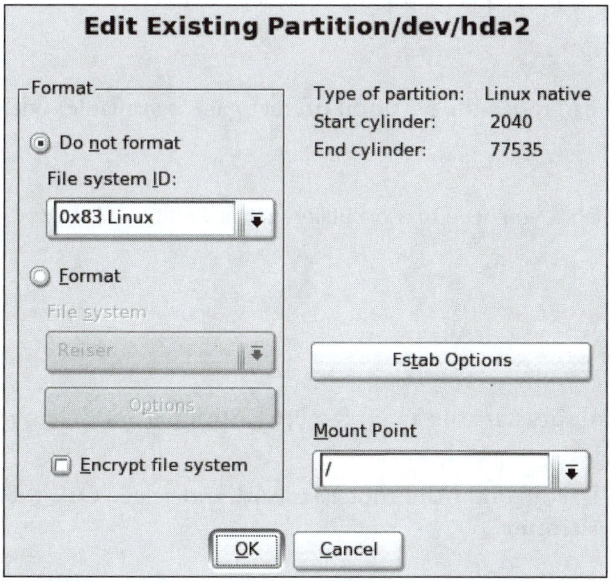

Edit Existing Partition/dev/hda2

Format

⊙ Do not format

File system ID:

| 0x83 Linux | ⬇ |

○ Format

File system

| Reiser | ⬇ |

Options

☐ Encrypt file system

Type of partition: Linux native
Start cylinder: 2040
End cylinder: 77535

Fstab Options

Mount Point

| / | ⬇ |

OK   Cancel

Figure 3-8

3. From this dialog box, you can configure the following options:

- **File system ID.** If you do not want to format the partition, select **Do not format**, and then ensure that the partition is registered correctly by selecting a *file system ID* from the drop-down list.

- **File System.** To format the partition, select **Format**, and then select a file system (such as **Ext3** or **Reiser**) for the partition from the drop-down list.

- **Options.** If you select **Format**, you can set various options, depending on the selected file system, by selecting **Options**.

- **Encrypt file system.** Select this option to have all data written to the hard disk in encrypted form.

- **Fstab Options.** Select this option to set various file system parameters in /etc/fstab. These include mounting parameters and the data journaling mode.

- **Mount Point.** Enter the directory where the partition should be mounted in the file system tree.

4. When you finish editing the options, continue by selecting **OK**.

A warning message appears, cautioning you about the changes you've made.

5. Save the changes by selecting **OK**.

You are returned to the Expert Partitioner dialog box.

Resize a Partition

After creating a partition, you can resize the partition (if free space is available) with the YaST Expert Partitioner.

 If free space is not available, you need to use a utility such as Partition Magic to resize the partition.

NOTE

Do the following:

1. From the KDE desktop, start the YaST Expert Partitioner module by doing one of the following:

   ■ Select the **YaST** icon, enter the root *password*, and select **OK**; then select **System > Partitioner**.

   or

   ■ Open a terminal window and enter **sux –** and the root *password*; then enter **yast2 disk**.

   The Expert Partitioner appears.

2. Select the *partition* you want to resize; then select **Edit**.

The dialog box shown in Figure 3-9 appears.

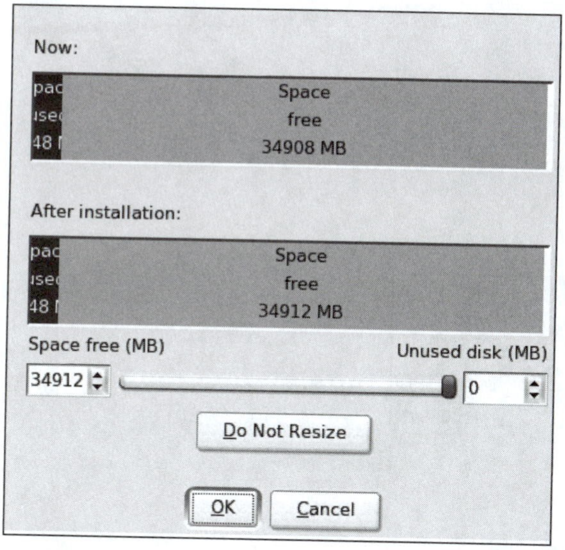

Now:

pac	Space
ise	free
48	34908 MB

After installation:

pac	Space
ise	free
48	34912 MB

Space free (MB)   Unused disk (MB)

34912 [⇅] ━━━━━━━━━━━━━━━━●━━━ 0 [⇅]

Do Not Resize

OK   Cancel

Figure 3-9

3. Resize the partition by doing one of the following:

   ■ Increase or decrease the free space on the partition by entering a value in the **Space free** field.

   or

   ■ Increase or decrease the unused disk space on the hard disk by entering a value in the **Unused disk** field.

   or

   ■ Use the slider bar to adjust the free space/unused space ratio for the partition.

The results of the new configuration appear in the lower bar graph, as shown in Figure 3-10.

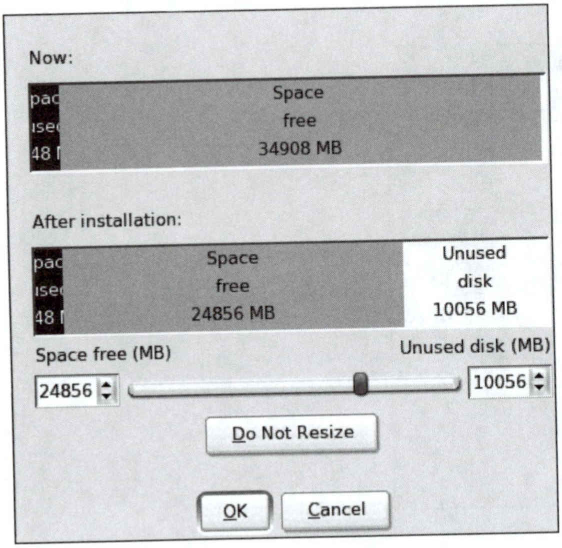

Figure 3-10

4. (Optional) If you want to reset the partition size to its original setting, select **Do Not Resize**; then select **OK**.

5. Accept the new partition size by selecting **OK**.

   If the partition is currently mounted, a warning message appears indicating that you cannot resize the partition until you unmount the file system.

6. (Conditional) Close the dialog box by selecting **OK**; then unmount the partition and try resizing it again.

   You are returned to the Expert Partitioner.

   At this point, the partition size has not been changed.

7. Change the partition size by selecting **Apply**.

Exercise 3-1   Configure Partitions on Your Hard Drive

In this exercise, you do the following:

- Part I: Use YaST to Create a Partition and File System
- Part II: Manually Partition with fdisk

Part I: Use YaST to Create a Partition and File System

In this part of the exercise, you create partitions as a prerequisite step to adding new file systems.

Do the following:

1. Create a new ext2 partition with YaST:

   a. From your KDE desktop, select the **YaST** icon; then enter a password of **novell** and select **OK**.

      The YaST Control Center appears.

   b. Select **System > Partitioner**.

      A warning message appears.

   c. Continue by selecting **Yes**.

      After a few moments, the Expert Partitioner dialog box appears.

   d. Create a new partition by selecting **Create**.

   e. Create a primary partition by making sure **Primary partition** is selected; then select **OK**.

      A Create a primary partition dialog box appears.

   f. Configure the new primary partition by entering or selecting the following:

      - File system: **Ext2**
      - End (cylinder): **+500M**
      - Mount Point: **/apps**

   g. When you finish, confirm the partition definition by selecting **OK**.

      You are returned to the Expert Partitioner dialog box, where the new partition is added to the list.

   h. Add the new partition to the hard drive by selecting **Apply**.

      A dialog box appears, asking if you really want to execute the changes.

   i. Continue by selecting **Finish**.

2. Verify creation of the new partition:

   a. Open a terminal window; then su to root (**su –**) with a password of **novell**.

   b. Verify that the new partition is mounted by entering **mount**.

      You should see the following line:

      ```
      /dev/hda3 on /apps type ext2 (rw)
      ```

c. Verify that the appropriate entry was added to the /etc/fstab for the new partition by entering the following:

cat /etc/fstab

You should see the following:

```
/dev/hda3    /apps    ext2    acl,user_xattr  1 2
```

This entry makes sure that when the system boots, the new file system is mounted.

3. Unmount the file system by entering **umount /apps**.

4. Verify that the file system is no longer mounted by entering **mount**.

The /dev/hda3 partition is not displayed.

5. Start a file system check on hda3 running in verbose mode with an automatic response of yes to prompts by entering the following:

e2fsck –f –y –v /dev/hda3

Check for any bad blocks.

6. Mount the /apps file system again by entering **mount /apps**.

7. Verify that the file system is mounted by entering **mount**.

Part II: Manually Partition with fdisk

Do the following:

1. From the command line, start the utility fdisk on the first IDE hard disk on your server by entering **fdisk /dev/hda**.

2. View the current partition table in fdisk by entering **p**.

Notice that there are three partitions (hda1, hda2, and hda3).

3. Create a new extended partition that uses the remaining space on the disk by entering **n** and then **e**; then press **Enter** twice.

4. View the updated partition table in fdisk by entering **p**.

Notice that a new hda4 partition has been added to the table.

5. Create a new 500MB Win95 FAT32 logical partition as the first partition in the extended partition by doing the following:

a. Create a new partition by entering **n**.

b. Accept the default first cylinder by pressing **Enter**.

c. Indicate the partition size by entering **+500M**.

d. Change the partition type to Win95 FAT32 by entering **t**, **5**, and then **b**.

e. Verify the new partition configuration by entering **p**.

Notice that a new hda5 partition has been added to the table.

6. Create two new logical partitions with the partition type of Linux (the default) by doing the following:

a. Create a new partition by entering **n**; then accept the default first cylinder by pressing **Enter**.

b. Indicate the partition size by entering **+1G**.

c. Create a new partition by entering **n**; then accept the default first cylinder by pressing **Enter**.

d. Indicate the partition size by entering **+2G**.

e. Verify the new partition configuration by entering **p**.

Notice that two new partitions (hda6 and hda7) have been added to the partition table.

7. Write the new partition table to your hard drive and exit fdisk by entering **w**.

8. Reboot the system by entering **reboot**.

It is important to reboot after repartitioning, especially with IDE devices. SCSI disk changes are much more forgiving.

9. When the server reboots, log in as **geeko** with a password of **N0v3ll**.

OBJECTIVE 3 CONFIGURE A FILE SYSTEM WITH LOGICAL VOLUME MANAGEMENT (LVM)

Logical volume management (LVM) provides a higher-level view of the disk storage on a computer system than the traditional view of disks and partitions. This gives you much more flexibility in allocating storage to applications and users.

When you create logical volumes with LVM, you can resize and move logical volumes while partitions are still mounted and running.

You can also use LVM to manage logical volumes with names that make sense (such as "development" and "sales") instead of physical disk names such as "sda" and "sdb."

To configure a file system with LVM, you need to know the following:

- LVM Components
- LVM Features
- How to Configure Logical Volumes with YaST

Starting from kernel version 2.6, you can use LVM version 2, which is backward-compatible with the previous LVM and enables the continued management of old volume groups.

Instead of LVM2, you can also use EVMS (Enterprise Volume Management System), which offers a uniform interface for logical volumes as well as RAID volumes. Like LVM2, EVMS makes use of the device mapper in kernel 2.6.

LVM Components

Conventional partitioning of hard disks on a Linux file system is basically inflexible. When a partition is full, you have to move the data to another medium before you can resize the partition, create a new file system, and copy the files back.

Normally, these changes cannot be implemented without changing adjacent partitions, whose contents also need to be backed up to other media and written to their original locations after the repartitioning.

Because it is difficult to modify partitions on a running system, LVM was developed. It provides a virtual pool of memory space (called a *volume group*) from which logical volumes can be generated if needed. The operating system accesses these instead of the physical partitions.

This approach lets you resize the physical media during operation without affecting the applications.

The basic structure of LVM includes the components shown in Figure 3-11.

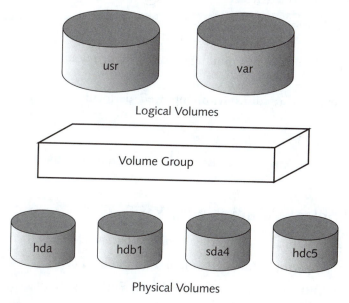

Figure 3-11

Several *physical volumes* (entire hard disks or individual partitions) are combined to a super unit referred to the *volume group*. You can add hard disks or partitions to the volume group during operation whenever necessary (no unmounting required).

The volume group can also be reduced in size by removing hard disks or partitions. The volume group, in turn, can be split into several logical volumes that can be addressed with their device names (such as /dev/system/usr), like conventional partitions with file systems.

Just as with other direct manipulations of the file system, a data backup should be made before configuring LVM.

NOTE

LVM Features

Implementing LVM makes sense for heavily used home computers as well as enterprise servers. LVM also makes sense for large data collections such as databases, MP3 archives, or user directories.

The following are features of LVM that help you implement storage solutions:

- You can combine several hard disks or partitions into a large volume group.

- Provided the configuration is suitable, you can enlarge a logical volume (such as /usr) when free space is exhausted.

- You can add hard disks to the volume group in a running system, provided you have hot-swappable hardware capable of such actions.

- You can add logical volumes in a running system, provided there is free space in the volume group.

- You can use several hard disks with improved performance in the RAID 0 (striping) mode.

- You can add up to 256 logical volumes.

- The Snapshot feature enables consistent backups (especially for servers) in the running system.

How to Configure Logical Volumes with YaST

The following are the basic steps for configuring logical volumes (LVM) with YaST:

1. Define the LVM partition (physical volume) on the hard drive:

   During (or after) the installation of SUSE Linux Enterprise Server, you need to configure the LVM partition on the hard disk.

   You can use YaST (as root) to perform this task by doing the following:

   a. Start the Expert Partitioner from the YaST Control Center (**System > Partitioner**) or from the command line (**yast2 disk**).

   b. At the warning message, select **Yes**.

      The Expert Partitioner dialog box appears.

   c. Create a new partition by selecting **Create**; then select **Primary partition** and select **OK**.

   d. Select **Do not format**; then for the File system ID, select **0x8E Linux LVM**.

   e. Accept the default setting in the **Start cylinder** field; then enter a size value in the **End** field.

   f. When you finish, select **OK**.

      The LVM partition appears in the partition list.

   g. Configure the partition by selecting **Apply**; then select **Finish**.

2. Create the volume group and logical volumes:

   a. Start the LVM module from the YaST Control Center (**System > LVM**) or from the command line (**yast2 lvm_config**).

The dialog box shown in Figure 3-12 appears.

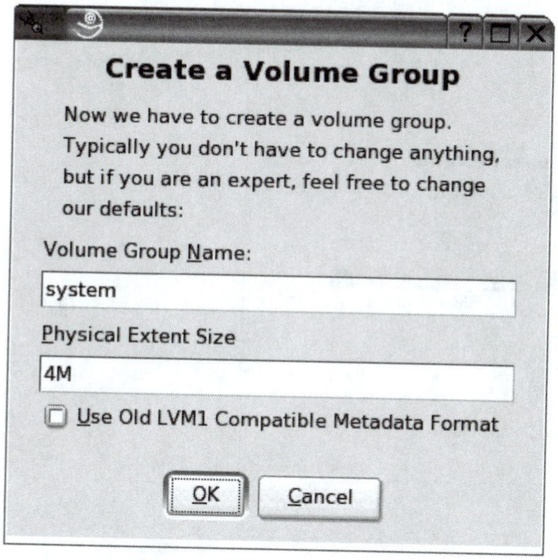

Create a Volume Group

Now we have to create a volume group. Typically you don't have to change anything, but if you are an expert, feel free to change our defaults:

Volume Group Name:

system

Physical Extent Size

4M

☐ Use Old LVM1 Compatible Metadata Format

OK   Cancel

Figure 3-12

The **Volume Group Name** is the name you want to use for selecting and managing the volume group.

The **Physical Extent Size** value is normally set to 4 MB, which allows for a maximum size of 256 GB for physical and logical volumes. You should only increase this value if you need logical volumes larger than 256 GB.

b. Accept the default *volume group name* and *physical extent size*, or enter your own settings; then select **OK**.

The dialog box shown in Figure 3-13 appears.

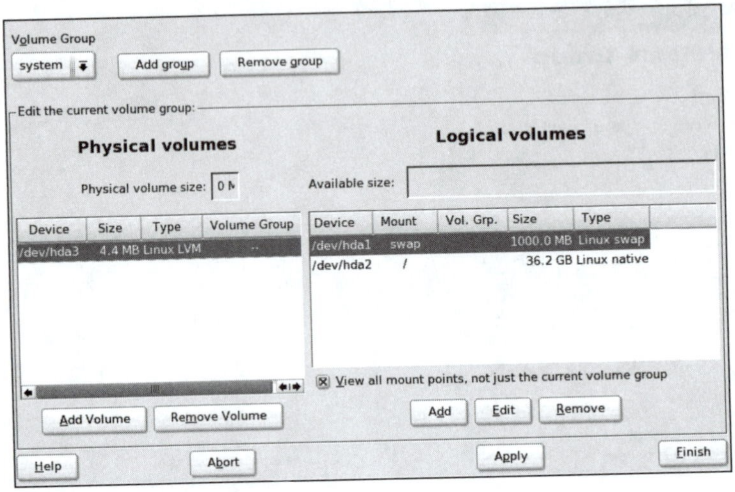

Figure 3-13

c. From the **Volume Group** drop-down list, select the *volume group* you want to configure.

You can add other volume groups (**Add group**) or delete a volume group (**Remove group**), but you can delete a volume group only if it has no partitions assigned.

> **NOTE**
>
> Only one volume group needs to be created for a normally installed SUSE Linux system.

The Physical volumes list includes all partitions with either the Linux LVM or Linux native type (no swap or DOS partitions appear).

If a partition is already assigned to a volume group, the name of the volume group is shown in the list. Unassigned partitions are indicated by "--".

d. Add an unassigned partition to the volume group by selecting the *partition*; then select **Add Volume**.

The name of the volume group is entered next to the selected partition.

The Logical volumes list includes all logical volumes defined in the volume group. In addition, you can view all mount points (including traditional file systems) by selecting **View all mount points, not just the current volume group**.

e. Create a logical volume by selecting **Add**.

The dialog box shown in Figure 3-14 appears.

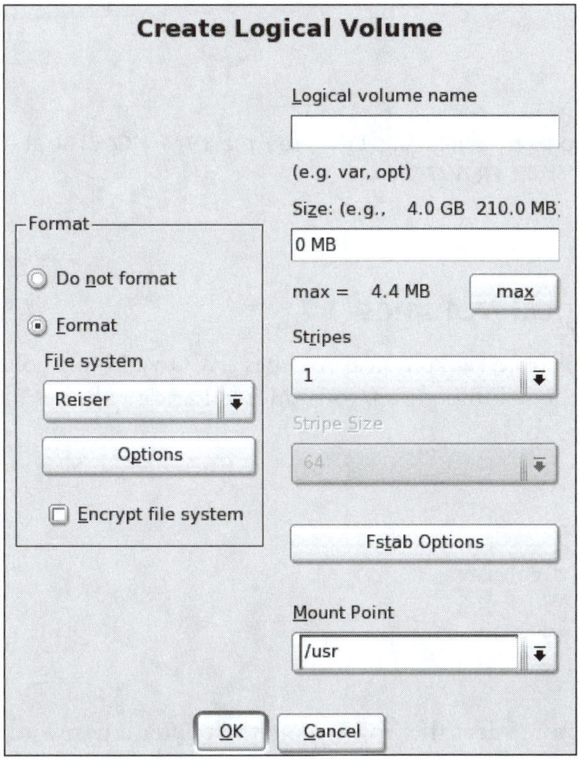

Create Logical Volume

Logical volume name

(e.g. var, opt)

Size: (e.g.,   4.0 GB 210.0 MB)

0 MB

max =   4.4 MB   max

Stripes

1

Stripe Size

64

Format

◯ Do not format

◉ Format

File system

Reiser

Options

☐ Encrypt file system

Fstab Options

Mount Point

/usr

OK   Cancel

Figure 3-14

This dialog box lets you configure a logical volume using the same options available for creating a file system (see *Create a File System from YaST*).

In addition, you can enter a logical volume name, the maximum amount of space available (by selecting **max**), the number of stripes, and the stripe size (if you configure more than one stripe).

CAUTION

You can create a logical volume with multiple stripes only if the hard disk space required by the logical volume can be distributed evenly to multiple physical volumes.

If only two physical volumes are available, a logical volume with three stripes is impossible.

   f. When you finish configuring the logical volume, select **OK**.

You are returned to the LVM configuration dialog box.

The new logical volume appears in the logical volumes list.

g. Complete the configuration by selecting **Finish**.

A dialog box appears indicating that all settings have been written and the volume is ready to use.

h. Select **OK**.

NOTE

For additional information on configuring LVM, see the LVM HOWTO at *http://tldp.org/HOWTO/LVM-HOWTO/*.

Exercise 3-2   Create Logical Volumes

In this exercise, you use YaST to create two physical volumes (PV) to add to a volume group (VG) named project1. Within the volume group, you add two logical volumes named pilot (750MB) and prod (750MB).

Do the following:

- Part I: Create LVM Volumes
- Part II: Resize an LVM Volume

Part I: Create LVM Volumes

Do the following:

1. From the KDE desktop, select the **YaST** icon; then enter a password of **novell** and select **OK**.

    The YaST Control Center appears.

2. Select **System > Partitioner**.

    A warning message appears.

3. Continue by selecting **Yes**.

    The Expert Partitioner dialog box appears.

4. Create a new LVM partition by doing the following:

    a. Select **Create**.

    b. Select **Do not format**; then select or enter the following

- File system ID: **0x8E Linux LVM**

- End (cylinder): **+1G**

    c. Save the partition definition by selecting **OK**.

5. Create another 1GB LVM partition by repeating Step 4.

    You should now have two 1GB LVM partitions.

6. Write the changes to the partition table by selecting **Apply**; then select **Finish**.

    The partitioning is configured.

7. From the YaST Control Center, start the YaST LVM module by selecting **System > LVM**.

CAUTION

If you start the LVM module through the Expert Partitioner, the following steps will not work properly.

    A Create a Volume Group dialog box appears.

8. Enter the following:

- Volume Group Name: **project1**

- Physical Extent Size: **4M**

9. Continue by selecting **OK**.

    A dialog box with lists of physical volumes and logical volumes appears. The LVM partitions you created are listed under physical volumes Linux LVM in the Type column.

10. Add each Linux LVM physical volume to the volume group project1 by selecting each physical volume (such as **/dev/hda8**) and then selecting **Add Volume**.

    Scroll to the right (if necessary) and notice that both physical volumes are listed with a volume group of project1.

11. Add a logical volume pilot from the project1 volume group:

    a. Select **Add**.

    A Create Logical Volume dialog box appears.

    b. Enter or select the following:

- Format (File system): **Reiser**

- Logical volume name: **pilot**

- Size: **750 MB**
- Mount Point: **/project1/pilot**

  c. Save the logical volume definition by selecting **OK**.

12. Add a logical volume prod from the project1 volume group:

  a. Select **Add**.

    A Create Logical Volume dialog box appears.

  b. Enter or select the following:

- Format (File system): **Reiser**
- Logical volume name: **prod**
- Size: **750 MB**
- Mount Point: **/project1/prod**

  c. Save the logical volume definition by selecting **OK**.

13. Save the changes by selecting **Finish**.

    A message appears, indicating that the process is complete.

14. Continue by selecting **OK**.

15. From a terminal window, su to root (**su –**) with a password of **novell**.

16. View the new LVM file systems by entering the following:

    df –h

    Notice the size of these new file systems.

17. View the device names and mount locations by entering **cat /etc/fstab**.

18. Change to the directory /project1/prod/ by entering **cd /project1/prod**.

19. Copy all binary files from /usr/bin to this directory by entering the following (make sure you include the period):

    cp –v /usr/bin/* .

20. View the space used and available for prod by entering **df –h**.

Part II: Resize an LVM Volume

You now require more disk space on the prod LVM file system. In the following steps, you allocate the remaining space to prod.

Doing the following:

1. From the YaST Control Center, select **System > LVM**.

   The LVM dialog box appears.

2. From the Logical volumes list, select **/dev/project1/prod**; then select **Edit**.

   The Edit Logical Volume dialog box appears.

   Notice the volume size (752.0 MB).

3. Select the **max** button.

   Notice that the size changes to the maximum space available (1.2 GB).

4. Continue by selecting **OK**.

5. Save the changes by selecting **Finish**; then select **OK**.

6. From the terminal window, view the new size of prod by entering **df -h**.

7. Close all open windows.

OBJECTIVE 4   CONFIGURE AND MANAGE A LINUX FILE SYSTEM

To perform basic Linux file system management tasks in SUSE Linux Enterprise Server, you need to know how to do the following:

- Create a File System from YaST
- Create a File System from the Command Line
- Mount a File System
- Monitor and Check a File System
- Create a Boot, Rescue, or Module Disk

Create a File System from YaST

After creating a partition (during or after installation), you can use YaST to assign the partition a file system (such as ext3 or ReiserFS) by doing the following:

1. From the KDE desktop, start the YaST Expert Partitioner module by doing one of the following:

   - Select the **YaST** icon, enter the root *password*, and select **OK**; then select **System > Partitioner**.

     or

   - Open a terminal window and enter **sux –** and the root *password*; then enter **yast2 disk**.

   The Expert Partitioner appears.

2. Select the *partition* you want to assign a file system; then select **Edit**.

   The Edit dialog box for the partition appears.

3. Format the partition with a file system by selecting **Format**; the dialog box shown in Figure 3-15 appears.

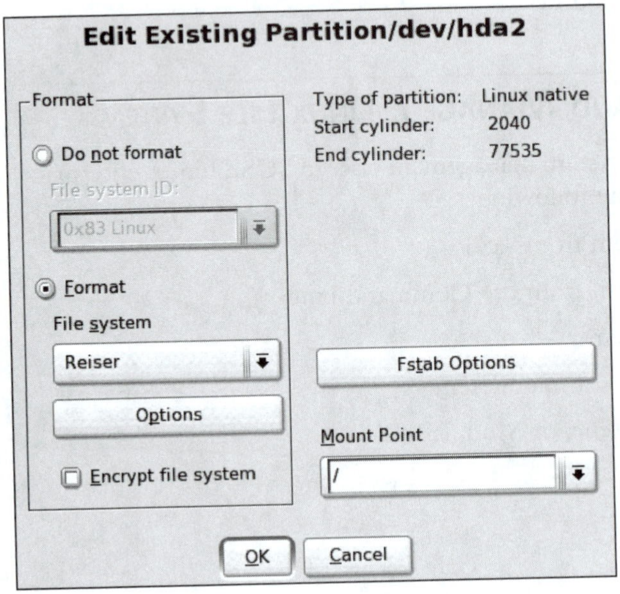

Edit Existing Partition/dev/hda2

Format
- Do not format

  File system ID:

  0x83 Linux

- Format

  File system

  Reiser

  Options

  Encrypt file system

Type of partition: Linux native
Start cylinder: 2040
End cylinder: 77535

Fstab Options

Mount Point

/

OK   Cancel

Figure 3-15

4. From the **File system** drop-down list, select an available file system (such as **Reiser** or **Ext3**).

5. View the available format options by selecting **Options**; then return to the main format menu by selecting **OK**.

These options include the hash function to use (for sorting filenames in directories) and the ReiserFS format revision to use. We recommend keeping the default settings for most implementations.

6. Encrypt all data saved to the partition by selecting **Encrypt file system**.

7. Select file system options to configure in the /etc/fstab file by selecting **Fstab Options**.

The dialog box shown in Figure 3-16 appears.

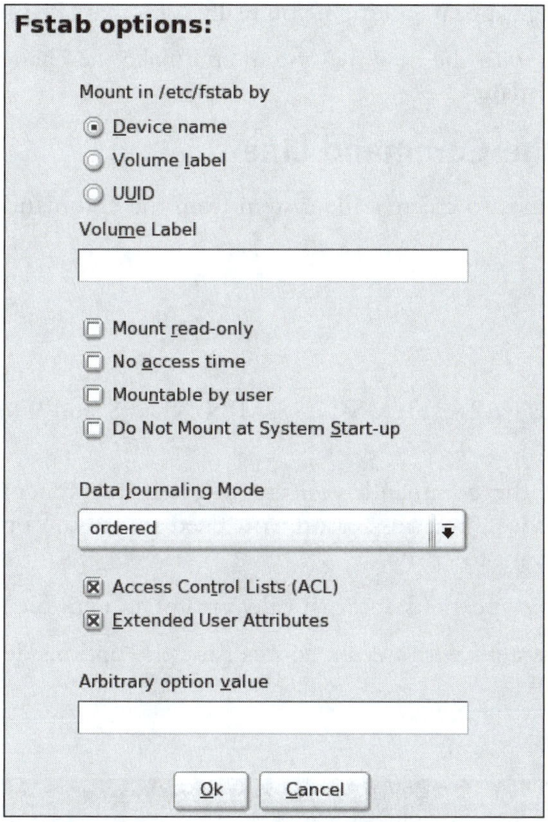

Fstab options:

Mount in /etc/fstab by
- ● Device name
- ○ Volume label
- ○ UUID

Volume Label

_____

- ☐ Mount read-only
- ☐ No access time
- ☐ Mountable by user
- ☐ Do Not Mount at System Start-up

Data Journaling Mode

| ordered | ⬇ |

- ☒ Access Control Lists (ACL)
- ☒ Extended User Attributes

Arbitrary option value

_____

| Ok | Cancel |

Figure 3-16

These options are saved in /etc/fstab and are used when mounting the file system.

A description of each option is included in the left frame of the Fstab options dialog box.

8. When you finish configuring the fstab options, select **Ok**.

9. In the **Mount Point** field, enter the *directory* where the partition should be mounted in the file system tree.

10. When you finish configuring the file system and mounting parameters, select **OK**.

    A warning message appears, cautioning you about committing the changes you've made.

11. Select **Continue**.

12. Save the changes by selecting **Apply**.

    Another warning message appears, asking if you really want to make the changes.

13. Configure the partition with the new file system and make the changes to the fstab file by selecting **Finish**.

Create a File System from the Command Line

You can use the following commands to create a file system from the command line:

- mkfs
- mkreiserfs

mkfs

You can create file systems (such as ext2, ext3, MS-DOS, MINIX, XFS, and JFS) with the command mkfs (make file system).

This command is a front end for the commands you use to create file systems (such as mkfs.ext2, mkfs.ext3, and mkfs.msdos). For this reason, you need to use the option –t to indicate the file system type you want to create.

If you do not indicate a file system type, mkfs automatically creates an ext2 file system.

If you create an ext2 or ext3 file system with mkdir, you can use the options described in Table 3-7.

Table 3-7

Option	Description
-b *blocksize*	You can use this option to indicate the size of the data blocks in the file system. Values of 1024, 2048, . . . , 16384 are allowed for the block size.

Table 3-7   (continued)

Option	Description
-i *bytes_per_inode*	You can use this option to indicate how many inodes are created on the file system. For *bytes_per_inode*, you can use the same values available for the block size. You should choose a larger value for the block size. However, it makes little sense to have a larger number of inodes than data blocks.
-j	You can use this option to create an ext3 Journal on the file system.

If you do not include options –b and –i, the data block sizes and the number of inodes is set by mkfs, depending on the size of the partitions.

The following is an example of creating a partition with an ext2 file system:

```
earth:~ # mkfs -t ext2 /dev/hdb1
mke2fs 1.34 (25-Jul-2007)
Filesystem label=
OS type: Linux
Block size=1024 (log=0)
Fragment size=1024 (log=0)
25688 inodes, 102400 blocks
5120 blocks (5.00%) reserved for the super user
First data block=1
13 block groups
8192 blocks per group, 8192 fragments per group
1976 inodes per group
Superblock backups stored on blocks:
8193, 16385, 24577, 32769, 40961, 49153, 57345, 65537,
73729, 81921, 90113, 98305
Writing inode tables: done
Writing superblocks and filesystem accounting information: done
This filesystem will be automatically checked every 31 mounts or
180 days, whichever comes first. Use tune2fs -c or -i to
override.
earth:~ #
```

This mkfs example creates a 100 MB partition formatted with the following standard values:

- **Block size=1024 (log=0)**

  The block size is 1 KB.

- **25688 inodes, 102400 blocks**

  The maximum number of files and directories is 25688. The total number of blocks is 102400.

■ **5120 blocks (5.00%) reserved for the super user**

5 percent of the entire space is reserved for the system administrator. If the hard disk is 95 percent full, then a normal user cannot use any more space.

You can also use the command mke2fs (which corresponds to mkfs.ext2 and mkfs.ext3) to create an ext2 or ext3 file system (see **man mke2fs**).

mkreiserfs

You can create a Reiser file system by using the command mkreiserfs.

Table 3-8 describes a commonly used parameter and option for mkreiserfs:

Table 3-8

Option	Description
number_of_blocks -	This parameter represents the size of the partition in number of blocks. If you do not include this parameter, mkreiserfs automatically sets the block size.
--format *format*	You can use this option to specify the format of the Reiser file system (**3.5** or **3.6**).

Mount a File System

Instead of using separate drive letters to represent different partitions in the file system (such as MS-DOS and Windows® 9*x*), Linux mounts partitions in a folder in the file system using *mount points*.

For example, to add a new hard disk to a Linux system, you would first partition and format the drive. You would then create a directory (such as /mnt/files/) in the file system and mount the drive in that directory using the command mount.

To unmount (detach) a file system, you use the umount command (for details, enter **man umount**).

You can also mount remote file systems, shared via the Network File System (NFS), to directories you create in your file system.

The directory /mnt/ is used by default for mounting local and remote file systems. All removable devices are mounted by default to /media/, such as the following:

- A CD-ROM on /dev/cdrom is mounted by default to /media/cdrom.
- A floppy disk on /dev/floppy is mounted by default to /media/floppy.

When using SLES 9 from a desktop environment such as KDE, media such as floppy disks and CDs are automatically mounted and unmounted using the defaults in /etc/fstab and the feature submount/subfs.

The file systems that automatically mount and unmount contain a subfs parameter in the line, as shown in Figure 3-17.

```
/dev/hda2       /                              reiserfs   acl,user_xattr        1 1
/dev/hda1       swap                           swap       pri=42                0 0
devpts          /dev/pts                       devpts     mode=0620,gid=5       0 0
proc            /proc                          proc       defaults              0 0
usbfs           /proc/bus/usb                  usbfs      noauto                0 0
sysfs           /sys                           sysfs      noauto                0 0
/dev/cdrom      /media/cdrom                   subfs      fs=cdfss,ro,procuid,nosuid,nodev,exec,iocharset=utf8 0 0
/dev/fd0        /media/floppy                  subfs      fs=floppyfss,procuid,nodev,nosuid,sync 0 0
```

Figure 3-17

After the media is mounted to the directory in the file system, you can access the content on the media by changing to that directory.

To understand how to manage mounting (and unmounting) file systems, you need to know the following:

- Configuration Files for Mounting
- How to View Currently Mounted File Systems
- How to Mount a File System
- How to Mount a File System in More Than One Location
- How to Unmount a File System

Configuration Files for Mounting

The file systems and their mount points in the directory tree are configured in the file /etc/fstab. This file contains one line with six fields for each mounted file system.

The lines look similar to the following:

Field 1	Field 2	Field 3	Field 4	Field 5	Field 6
/dev/hda2	/	reiserfs	acl,user_xattr	1	1
/dev/hda1	swap	swap	pri=42	0	0
devpts	/dev/pts	devpts	mode=0620,gid=5	0	0
proc	/proc	proc	defaults	0	0
usbfs	/proc/bus/usb	usbfs	noauto	0	0

```
sysfs       /sys        sysfs     noauto                                      0      0
/dev/cdrom /media/cdrom  subfs     fs=cdfss,ro,procuid,nosuid, nodev,exec      0      0
/dev/fd0   /media/floppy subfs     fs=floppyfss,procuid,nodev, nosuid,sync     0      0
```

Each field provides the following information for mounting the file system:

- **Field 1.** The name of the device file.
- **Field 2.** The mount point—the directory to which the file system should be mounted. The directory specified here must already exist.
- **Field 3.** The file system type (such as ext2 or reiserfs).
- **Field 4.** The mount options. Multiple mount options are separated by commas (such as **fs=cdfss,ro,procuid,nosuid**).

   For example, the options **ro** and **nodev** for the CD-ROM drive (/dev/cdrom) mean that the drive is read only (**ro**) and that device files on the CD are not interpreted as such by the file system (**nodev**).

- **Field 5.** Indicates whether to use the backup utility dump for the file system. **0** means no backup.
- **Field 6.** Indicates the sequence of the file system checks (with the **fsck** utility) when the system is booted:
  - **0:** file systems that are not to be checked
  - **1:** the root directory
  - **2:** all other modifiable file systems

While /etc/fstab lists the file systems and their mount points in the directory tree, the /etc/mstab file lists the file systems currently mounted and their mount points.

The mount and umount commands modify the /etc/mtab file and affect the state of mounted file systems.

The kernel also keeps information for /proc/mounts, which lists all currently mounted partitions.

For troubleshooting purposes, if there is a conflict between /proc/mounts and /etc/mstab information, the /proc/mounts data is always more current and reliable than /etc/mstab.

How to View Currently Mounted File Systems

You can view the file systems currently mounted in SUSE Linux by entering the command mount. Information similar to the following appears:

```
DA50:~ # mount
/dev/hda2 on / type reiserfs (rw,acl,user_xattr)
proc on /proc type proc (rw)
tmpfs on /dev/shm type tmpfs (rw)
```

```
devpts on /dev/pts type devpts (rw,mode=0620,gid=5)
/dev/hdc on /media/cdrom type subfs (ro,nosuid,nodev,fs=cdfss,
procuid, iocharset=utf8)
/dev/fd0 on /media/floppy type subfs (rw,nosuid,nodev,sync,
fs=floppyfss, procuid)
usbfs on /proc/bus/usb type usbfs (rw)
```

You can also view this information in the file /proc/mounts.

How to Mount a File System

You can use the command mount to manually mount a file system. The general syntax for mounting a file system with mount is

mount [-t *file_system_type***] [-o** *mount_options***]** *device mount_point_directory*

By using mount, you can override the default settings in /etc/fstab.

For example, entering the following mounts the partition /dev/hda9 on the directory /space/:

```
mount /dev/hda9 /space
```

You do not usually specify the file system type because it is recognized automatically (using magic numbers in the superblock):

The following are some of the options you can use when mounting a file system with the command mount or by entering them in /etc/fstab:

- **remount.** This option causes file systems that are already mounted to be mounted again.

  When you make a change to the options in /etc/fstab, you can use remount instead of rebooting the system to incorporate the changes.

- **rw, ro.** These options indicate whether a file system should be writable (**rw**) or only readable (**ro**).

- **sync, async.** These options set synchronous (**sync**) or asynchronous (**async**) input and output in a file system. The default setting is async.

- **atime, noatime.** These options set whether the access time of a file is updated in the inode (**atime**) or not (**noatime**). The option noatime should improve the performance.

- **nodev, dev.** The **nodev** option prevents device files from being interpreted as such in the file system.

- **noexec, exec.** You can prohibit the execution of programs on a file system with the option **noexec**.

- **nosuid, suid.** The **nosuid** option ensures that the suid and sgid bits in the file system are ignored.

Some options only make sense in the file /etc/fstab. These options include the following:

- **auto, noauto.** File systems set with the option **noauto** in the file /etc/fstab are not mounted automatically when the system is booted. These are usually floppy disk drives or CD-ROM drives.

- **user, nouser.** This option lets users mount the file system. Normally, this is a privilege of the user root.

- **defaults.** This option causes the default options rw, suid, dev, exec, auto, nouser, and async to be used.

The options **noauto** and **user** are usually combined for exchangeable media, such as floppy disk or CD-ROM drives.

How to Mount a File System in More Than One Location

Once you mount a file system, you can remount it to a new location in the file system using the --bind parameter (since Linux 2.4.0).

The syntax for using --bind is

mount --bind *old_directory new_directory*

One way to make sure the file system is not busy is to enter **cd /** at the shell prompt before using the umount command. This command takes you to the root of the file system.

For example, to mount the /home/bwayne directory to /tmp/home, you would enter the following:

mount --bind /home/bwayne /tmp/home

The mount --bind command is also useful for protecting services such as DNS by mounting them in the /chroot directory.

NOTE

To help determine the processes that are acting on a file or directory, you can use the fuser utility. For details on using the fuser utility, see *Check PID Usage (fuser)*.

How to Unmount a File System

Once a file system is mounted, you can use the **umount** command (without an "n") to unmount the file system.

You can unmount the file system by using umount with the device or the mount point.

For example, to unmount a CD file system mounted at /media/cdrecorder, you could enter one of the following:

- **umount /media/cdrecorder**

  or

- **umount /dev/cdrecorder**

In order to unmount the file system, you should not be currently at the mount point in the shell prompt. If you are at the mount point, Linux sees the file system as being "busy" and will refuse to unmount the file system.

One way to make sure the file system is not busy is to enter **cd /** at the shell prompt before using the umount command. This command takes you to the root of the file system.

However, there might be times when the system (kernel) still sees the file system as busy, no matter what you try to do.

In these cases, you can enter **umount –f** to force the file system to unmount. However, we recommend using this as a last resort, as there is probably a reason why the kernel thinks the file system is still mounted.

Exercise 3-3   Manage File Systems from the Command Line

In this exercise, you manage file systems from the command line by doing the following:

- Part I: Create File Systems
- Part II: Customize the File Systems

Part I: Create File Systems

Do the following:

1. From the KDE desktop, open a terminal window; then su to root (**su –**) with a password of **novell**.

2. Create the following file systems:

   a. Create a new FAT32 file system on /dev/hda5 by entering the following:

   mkfs.msdos –n data1 /dev/hda5

   A message such as "mkfs.msdos 2.10 (22 Sep 2006)" confirms the file system creation.

   b. Create a new ext2 file system on /dev/hda6 by entering the following:

mkfs –t ext2 –v /dev/hda6

Notice that by adding the option –v, you received extensive information about the new file system.

c. Create a new Reiser file system on /dev/hda7 that is only 625 MB by entering the following:

mkreiserfs /dev/hda7 160000

A warning message appears, indicating that all data will be lost on /dev/hda7.

d. Continue by entering **y**.

3. Add entries to the file /etc/fstab for the new file systems:

a. Make sure a directory named /export/ exists by entering **ls –ld /export**.

b. Change to the directory /export/ by entering **cd /export**.

c. Create the directories **data1** and **data3** under /export/ by using **mkdir**.

d. Verify that the directories were created by entering **ls –l**.

e. Open the file /etc/fstab in an editor by pressing **Alt+F2**, entering **kdesu kate /etc/fstab**, and selecting **Run**; then enter a password of **novell** and select **OK**.

f. At the end of the file fstab, add the following entries:

/dev/hda5 /export/data1 vfat defaults 1 2

/dev/hda6 /export/data2 ext2 defaults 1 2

/dev/hda7 /export/data3 reiserfs defaults 1 2

You must include an empty line at the end of the file, otherwise the mount command cannot read the file.

These entries make sure that the hda5, hda6, and hda7 partitions are mounted when starting or rebooting the system.

The hda4 partition is the extended partition and does not need to be mounted.

g. When you finish, select **File > Save** (keep /etc/fstab open).

4. From the terminal window, mount all of the new file systems and reread the /etc/fstab file by entering **mount –a**.

5. View the information about the mounted file systems by entering the following three commands:

mount

df –h

cat /etc/mtab

Part II: Customize the File Systems

In this part of the exercise, you convert the partition /dev/hda6 to an ext3 file system by adding a journal. You also resize the /dev/hda7 Reiser file system to consume the entire partition and not just 625 MB.

Do the following:

1. Modify the partition /dev/hda6:

   a. From the terminal window, view details about the ext2 file system on /dev/hda6 by entering the following:

      dumpe2fs /dev/hda6 | more

      Notice the block size and the file system state.

   b. Give the ext2 file system the volume name /export/data2 while the file system is mounted by entering the following:

      tune2fs –L /export/data2 /dev/hda6

      Naming a file system can be useful in system rescue situations when the /etc/fstab is not available. It is common practice to use this naming convention.

   c. Verify that the file system now has a volume name by entering **dumpe2fs / dev/hda6 | less**.

   d. Add a journal to the file system (making it an ext3 file system) by entering **tune2fs –j /dev/hda6**.

   e. Verify that the file system now contains a journal by entering **dumpe2fs / dev/hda6 | less**.

   f. View information about the mounted file systems by entering **mount**.

      Notice that the file system is still mounted as an ext2 file system.

   g. Unmount the partition /dev/hda6 by entering **umount /dev/hda6**.

   h. Verify that the file system state is clean by entering **dumpe2fs /dev/hda6 | less**.

i. From the Kate window, edit the file /etc/fstab to change the file system type from ext2 to ext3, as in the following:

/dev/hda6 /export/data2 **ext3** defaults 1 2

j. Select **File > Save**.

k. From the command line, reread /etc/fstab and mount the partition as an ext3 file system by entering **mount -a**.

l. Verify the change by entering **mount**.

m. Unmount the partition /dev/hda6 again by entering **umount /export/data2**.

n. Mount the partition as an ext2 file system manually by entering the following:

mount -t ext2 /dev/hda6 /export/data2

o. Verify that the file system is mounted without a journal (as an ext2 file system) by entering **mount**.

p. Remount /dev/hda6 as an ext3 file system and verify the change by entering the following three commands:

umount /export/data2

mount -a

mount

2. Modify the partition /dev/hda7:

a. View the size of the partition /dev/hda7 by entering **df -h**.

b. Unmount dev/hda7 so that the Reiser file system on it can be resized to fill the entire partition by entering **umount /export/data3**.

c. While the partition is unmounted, add a label to the file system of /export/data3 by entering the following:

reiserfstune -l /export/data3 /dev/hda7

d. Resize the partition to consume the entire partition by entering **resize_reiserfs /dev/hda7**.

e. Remount the partition by entering **mount -a**.

f. View the size of the partition by entering **df -h**.

The size is no longer 625 MB, but should be 1 GB or more depending on the size of your hard drive.

g. Unmount the partition to run a file system check on it by entering **umount /export/data3**.

h. Run a check on the file system on /dev/hda7 by entering the following:

reiserfsck -y /dev/hda7

i. Remount all file systems by entering **mount -a**.

3. Close all open windows.

Monitor and Check a File System

Once you set up and begin using your Linux file system, you can monitor the status and health of the system by doing the following from the command line:

- Check Partition and File Usage (df and du)
- Check Open Files (lsof)
- Check PID Usage (fuser)
- Check /lost+found (ext2 and ext3 only)
- Check and Repair Any File System (fsck)
- Check and Repair ext2/ext3 and ReiserFS (e2fsck and reiserfsck)

Check Partition and File Usage (df and du)

The following commands help you monitor usage by partitions, files, and directories:

- **df.** This command provides information on where hard drives and their partitions or other drives are mounted in the file system, and how much space they occupy.

  If you do not include a filename, the space available on all currently mounted file systems is displayed.

  If you provide the filename of a disk device node containing a mounted file system, df displays the space available on that file system rather than on the file system containing the device node (which is always the root file system).

  Some useful options include **-h** (human readable format), **-i** (list inode information instead of block usage), and **-l** (limit listing to local file systems).

  For example, to list information for all local file systems in human-readable format, you would enter **df -lh**.

- **du.** This command provides information on the space occupied by files and directories.

  Some useful options include **-c** (display a grand total), **-h** (human-readable format), **-s** (display only a total for each argument), and **--exclude=**_pattern_ (exclude files that match _**pattern**_).

For example, to display information for files in human-readable format except for files that end in ".o," you would enter the following:

du -h --exclude='*.o'

Check Open Files (lsof)

The command lsof lists open files. Entering **lsof** without any options lists all open files belonging to all active processes.

An open file can be a regular file, a directory, a block special file, a character special file, a library, and a stream or a network file (Internet socket, NFS file, or UNIX domain socket.)

In addition to producing a single output list, lsof can run in repeat mode. In repeat mode, it outputs, delays, and then repeats the output operation until stopped with an interrupt or quit signal.

Some useful options include **-c** *x* (list only files starting with *x*), **-s** (display file sizes), and **-u** *x* (list only files for users who are *x*).

For example, to list open files for the users root and geeko only and include the file sizes, you would enter **lsof -s -u root,geeko**.

Check PID Usage (fuser)

The command fuser displays the PIDs of processes using the specified files or file systems.

In the default display mode, each filename is followed by a letter that describes the type of access:

- **c:** current directory
- **e:** executable being run
- **f:** open file (omitted in default display mode)
- **r:** root directory
- **m:** mapped file or shared library

A nonzero return code is displayed if none of the specified files is accessed or in case of a fatal error. If at least one access has been found, fuser returns zero.

Some useful options include **-a** (return information for all files, even if they are not accessed by a process), **-v** (verbose mode), and **-u** (append the user name of the process owner to each PID).

For example, to check the PID information for hosts, even if no process is currently associated with the file, you would enter:

fuser -a /etc/hosts.

Check /lost+found (ext2 and ext3 only)

The directory /lost+found/ is a special feature of the ext2 and ext3 file system format. This directory is used to save files or file fragments that have "gone missing" (such as after a system crash).

After a system crash, Linux automatically carries out a check of the complete file system. Files or file fragments to which a name can no longer be allocated are not simply deleted but stored in this directory.

By reviewing the contents of this directory, you can try to reconstruct the original name and purpose of a file.

Check and Repair Any File System (fsck)

The command fsck lets you check and optionally repair one or more Linux file systems. Normally, fsck tries to run file systems on different physical disk drives in parallel to reduce the total amount of time needed to check all of the file systems.

If you do not specify a file system on the command line, and the –A option is not included, fsck defaults to checking file systems in /etc/fstab.

After checking, an exit code is returned that lists one or more of the conditions shown in Table 3-9.

Table 3-9

Exit Code	Description
0	No errors
1	File system errors corrected
2	System should be rebooted
4	File system errors left uncorrected
8	Operational error
16	Usage or syntax error
32	Fsck canceled by user request
128	Shared library error

In reality, fsck is simply a front end for the various file system checkers (**fsck.***fstype*) available on the system. The fsck utility looks for the system-specific checker in /sbin/ first, then in /etc/fs/ and /etc/, and finally in the directories listed in the PATH environment variable.

To check a specific file system, use the following syntax:

fsck *filesystem*

For example, if you wanted to check the file system /dev/hda2, you would enter **fsck /dev/hda2**.

Some options that are available with fsck include **–A** (walk through the /etc/fstab file and try to check all the file systems in one pass), **–N** (don't execute, just show what would be done), and **–V** (verbose output).

Check and Repair ext2/ext3 and ReiserFS (e2fsck and reiserfsck)

Switching off the Linux system without unmounting partitions (for example, when a power outage occurs) can lead to errors in the file system.

The next time you boot the system, the fact that the computer was not shut down correctly is detected and a file system check is performed.

If errors are found in the file system, the rescue system may need to be used. Depending on the file system type, you use either /sbin/e2fsck or /sbin/reiserfsck.

These tools check the file system for a correct superblock (the block at the beginning of the partition containing information on the structure of the file system), faulty data blocks, or faulty allocation of data blocks.

A possible problem in the ext2 (or ext3) file system is damage to the superblock. You can first view the location of all copies of the superblock in the file system using dumpe2fs.

Then, with e2fsck, you can copy one of the backup copies to the beginning of the file system, as in the following:

```
e2fsck -f -b 32768 /dev/hda1
```

In this example, the superblock located at data block 32768 in the ext2 file system of the partition/dev/hda1 is copied to the beginning of the file system.

Normally, a backup copy of the superblock is stored every 32768 blocks.

With reiserfsck, the file system is subjected to a consistency check. The journal is checked to see if certain transactions need to be repeated. With the option --fix-fixable, errors such as wrong file sizes are fixed as soon as the file system is checked.

With an error in the binary tree, it is possible to have this rebuilt by entering **reiserfsck -- rebuild-tree**.

Create a Boot, Rescue, or Module Disk

In case of a system failure (such as a corrupted file system), you normally insert CD1 (or a DVD) of the installation media and select rescue system.

CD2 also has a boot capability that works if CD1 is not available.

However, if there is no bootable CD-ROM drive, you can create a set of floppy disks to boot the machine and start a rescue system.

To create a boot disk, rescue disk, or module disk with YaST, do the following:

1. From the KDE desktop, start the YaST Create a Boot, Rescue, or Module Floppy module by doing one of the following:

    ■ Select the **YaST** icon, enter the root *password*, and select **OK**; then select **System > Create a Boot, Rescue, or Module Floppy**.

    or

    ■ Open a terminal window and enter **sux –** and the root *password*; then enter **yast2 bootfloppy**.

    The dialog box shown in Figure 3-18 appears.

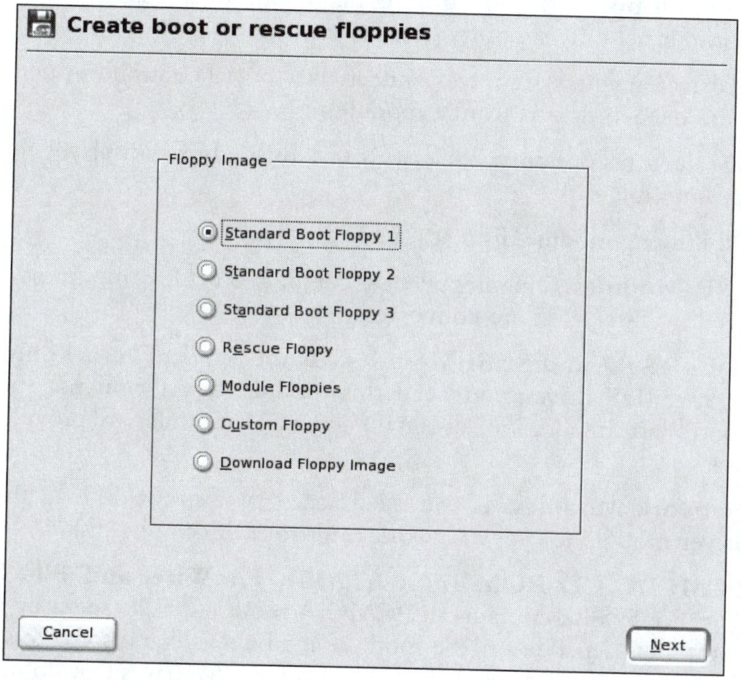

Create boot or rescue floppies

> ┌─Floppy Image──────────────────┐
> │   │
> │   ◉ Standard Boot Floppy 1   │
> │   ◯ Standard Boot Floppy 2   │
> │   ◯ Standard Boot Floppy 3   │
> │   ◯ Rescue Floppy   │
> │   ◯ Module Floppies   │
> │   ◯ Custom Floppy   │
> │   ◯ Download Floppy Image   │
> │   │
> └───────────────────────────────┘

Cancel   Next

Figure 3-18

These floppy disks are helpful if the boot configuration of your system is damaged. The rescue disk is especially necessary if the file system of the root partition is damaged.

In this case, you might also need the module disk with various drivers to be able to access the system (such as accessing a RAID system).

2. Select one of the following:

- **Standard Boot Floppy.** Select this option to create a standard boot disk with which to boot an installed system. This disk is also needed for starting the rescue system.

- **Rescue Floppy.** This disk contains a special environment that allows you to perform maintenance tasks in your installed system, such as checking and repairing the file system and updating the boot loader.

  To start the rescue system, boot with the standard boot disk, then select **Manual Installation > Start Installation or System > Rescue System**.

  You are then prompted to insert the rescue disk. If your system was configured to use special drivers (such as RAID or USB), you might need to load the respective modules from a module disk.

- **Module Floppies.** Module disks contain additional system drivers. The standard kernel only supports IDE drives.

  If the drives in your system are connected to special controllers (such as SCSI), load the needed drivers from a module disk.

  If you select this option and select **Next**, a dialog box is displayed for creating various module disks.

  The following module disks are available:

  - **USB Modules.** This floppy disk contains the USB modules you might need if USB drives are connected.

  - **IDE, RAID, and SCSI Modules.** As the standard kernel only supports normal IDE drives, you need this module disk if you use special IDE controllers. In addition, all RAID and SCSI modules are provided on this disk.

  - **Network Modules.** If you need access to a network, load the suitable driver module for your network card from this floppy disk.

  - **PCMCIA, CD-ROM (non-ATAPI), FireWire, and File Systems.** This floppy disk contains all PCMCIA modules used especially for laptop computers. In addition, the modules for FireWire and some less common file systems are available here. Older CD-ROM drives that do not comply with the ATAPI standard can also be operated with drivers from this floppy disk.

  To load drivers from a module disk to the rescue system, select **Kernel Modules (hardware drivers)** and the desired module category (such as SCSI or ethernet). You are prompted to insert the respective module disk and the contained modules are then listed. Select the desired module.

Watch the system messages carefully. For example, the message Loading module <modulename> failed indicates that the hardware could not be recognized by the module.

Some older drivers require specific parameters to be able to address the hardware correctly. In this case, refer to the documentation for your hardware.

- **Custom Floppy.** Select this option to write any existing floppy disk image from the hard disk to a floppy disk.

- **Download Floppy Image.** Select this option to enter a URL and authentication data to download a floppy disk image from the Internet.

3. After selecting a floppy disk option, continue by selecting **Next**.

4. When prompted, insert the floppy disk.

5. Create the floppy disk by selecting **Next**.

OBJECTIVE 5   SET UP AND CONFIGURE DISK QUOTAS

Drive space continues to be a problem, especially when storing data such as user files, databases, and MP3 archives. Without imposing limits, a user can easily fill up 40 GB of hard drive space with pictures, software, and music.

Linux includes a quota system that lets you specify a specific amount of storage space for each user or group, and how many files that user or group can create.

In SUSE Linux Enterprise Server, you can use the quota package to establish these limitations.

Figure 3-19 illustrates the quota architecture.

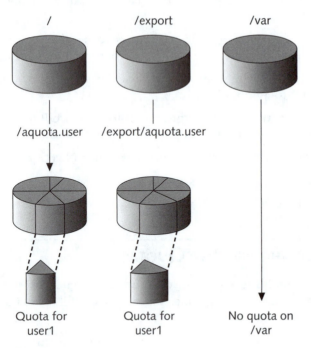

/   /export   /var

/aquota.user   /export/aquota.user

Quota for   Quota for   No quota on
user1   user1   /var

Figure 3-19

Disk quota support is already included in the kernel in SUSE Linux Enterprise Server. You can implement disk quotas for partitions configured with the ext2, ext3, or ReiserFS file systems.

Setting up and configuring the disk quota service on your server includes the following tasks (in order):

- Prepare the File System
- Initialize the Quota System
- Configure and Manage User and Group Quotas
- Start and Activate the Quota Service

Prepare the File System

When the system is started, the quotas for the file system must be activated. You can indicate which file system's quotas are to be activated by configuring entries in the file /etc/fstab.

You enter the keyword **usrquota** for quotas on the user level and the keyword **grpquota** for group quotas, as shown in Figure 3-20.

```
/dev/hda2          /              reiserfs   acl,user_xattr,usrquota,grpquota       1 1
/dev/hda1          swap           swap       pri=42                          0 0
devpts             /dev/pts       devpts     mode=0620,gid=5                 0 0
proc               /proc          proc       defaults                        0 0
usbfs              /proc/bus/usb  usbfs      noauto                          0 0
sysfs              /sys           sysfs      noauto                          0 0
/dev/cdrom         /media/cdrom   subfs      fs=cdfss,ro,procuid,nosuid,nodev,exec,iocharset=utf8 0 0
/dev/fd0           /media/floppy  subfs      fs=floppyfss,procuid,nodev,nosuid,sync 0 0
```

Figure 3-20

In this example, quotas are configured for the file system **/** (root).

If you have configured /etc/fstab without rebooting your server, you need to remount the file systems in the root partition by entering the following:

```
mount -o remount /
```

Initialize the Quota System

After remounting, you need to initialize the quota system. You can do this by using the command **quotacheck**, which is part of the package quota.

This command checks the partitions with quota keywords (in terms of already occupied data blocks and inodes) and stores the determined values in the files **aquota.user** (for user quotas) and **aquota.group** (for group quotas).

NOTE

Up to kernel version 2.4, these files were called quota.user and quota.group, and had to be created before quotacheck was run.

If you enter the command **quotacheck –avug**, all mounted file systems (**–a**) are checked for data blocks and inodes that are occupied by users (**–u**) and groups (**–g**). The option **–v** provides a detailed output.

When checking mounted file systems, you might need to use the option **–m** to force the check.

Assuming the quota entries exist for / and /export, after running **quotacheck**, the following files are created:

```
DA50:~ # ls -l /aquota*
-rw-------  1 root root 9216 Aug 27 10:06 /aquota.group
-rw-------  1 root root 9216 Aug 27 10:06 /aquota.user
```

Configure and Manage User and Group Quotas

To configure quotas for users and groups, you need to know how to do the following:

- Configure Soft and Hard Limits for Blocks and Inodes
- Configure Grace Periods for Blocks and Inodes
- Copy User Quotas
- Generate a Quota Report

Configure Soft and Hard Limits for Blocks and Inodes

With the command edquota and the following options, you can edit the current quota settings for a user or group:

- **edquota –u** *user*: for setting up user quotas.
- **edquota –g** *group*: for setting up group quotas.

The current settings are displayed in the vi editor for you to edit. You can edit the soft and hard limits; however, the blocks and inode values are for information only and cannot be edited.

For example, you can enter the following to configure quotas for the user **geeko**:

edquota –u geeko

After entering the command, the following quota information appears in vi for geeko:

```
Disk quotas for user geeko (uid 1001):
  Filesystem        blocks     soft     hard     inodes     soft     hard
  /dev/sda2           7820    10000    20000        145        0        0
```

The following describes the settings:

- **Blocks.** How much hard disk space is currently used, with soft and hard limits listed.

  The values for blocks are given in blocks of 1 KB (independent of the block size for the ext2 file system).

  For example, the value **7820** under Blocks indicates that the user geeko is currently using about 8 MB of hard drive space.

  Notice that the soft limit is set to **10** MB and the hard limit is set to **20** MB.

- **Inodes.** How many files belong to the user on the file system, with soft and hard limits listed.

  Notice that the soft and hard limits for geeko are set to **0**, which means that the user can create an unlimited number of files.

The soft limits indicate a quota that the user cannot permanently exceed. The hard limits indicate a boundary beyond which no more space or inodes can be used.

If users move beyond the soft limit, they have a fixed time available (a grace period) to free up space by deleting files or blocks.

If users exceed the grace period, they cannot create any new files until they delete enough files to move under the soft limit.

Configure Grace Periods for Blocks and Inodes

You can edit the grace periods in vi for blocks and inodes by entering **edquota -t**. A screen similar to the following appears:

```
Grace period before enforcing soft limits for users:
Time units may be: days, hours, minutes, or seconds
  Filesystem                 Block grace period      Inode grace period
  /dev/sda2                         7days                    7days
```

You can set the grace periods in days, hours, minutes, or seconds for a listed file system. However, you cannot specify a grace period for a specific user or group.

Copy User Quotas

You can copy user quotas from one user to another by using **edquota -p**.

For example, by entering **edquota -p tux geeko**, you can copy the user quotas for the user **tux** to the user **geeko**.

Generate a Quota Report

The quota system files contain information in binary format about the space occupied by users and groups, and which quotas are set up. You can display this information by using the command repquota.

For example, entering **repquota –aug** displays a report similar to the following for all users and groups:

```
*** Report for user quotas on device /dev/sda2
Block grace time: 7days; Inode grace time: 7days
                        Block limits                    File limits
User            used    soft    hard  grace    used    soft  hard  grace
----------------------------------------------------------------------------
root      -- 2646650       0       0          140161       0     0
geeko     +-   20000   10000   20000  7days       146       0     0
```

For additional details on using repquota, enter **man 8 repquota**.

Start and Activate the Quota Service

In order for the quota system to be initialized when the system is booted, the appropriate links must be made in the run-level directories by entering **insserv quota** (**innserv quotad** for NFS).

You can then start the quota system by entering

/etc/init.d/quota start.

You can also start or stop the quota system by entering the following:

/usr/sbin/quotaon *filesystem*

/usr/sbin/quotaoff *filesystem*

You can use the option **–a** to activate and deactivate all automatically mounted file systems (except NFS) with quotas.

For additional information on quotaon options, enter **man quotaon**.

Exercise 3-4   Set Up and Configure Disk Quotas

Do the following:

1. From a terminal window, su to root (**su –**) with a password of **novell**.

2. View the disk quota configuration for user geeko by entering the following:

   quota –vu geeko

   Notice that there are no quotas currently configured for geeko.

3. Add quota mount options to the partition /dev/hda6 by doing the following:

   a. Open the /etc/fstab file in the vi editor by entering **vim /etc/fstab**.

   b. Edit the /dev/hda6 entry to reflect the following:

      /dev/hda6 /export/data2 ext3 defaults,**usrquota, grpquota** 1 2

   c. When you finish, save the file and exit by entering **:wq**.

4. Remount the file system so that it reads the changes in file /etc/fstab by entering the following:

   mount –o remount /dev/hda6

NOTE If you receive the error message "/export/data2 not mounted already", or "bad option", check the contents of the /etc/fstab file. You might have misspelled the usrquota or grpquota option.

5. Run quotacheck to initialize the quota database by entering the following:

   quotacheck –mavug

   You receive several status messages about old quota files. These indicate that this is a new quota database with no previous quota database files on the system.

6. Verify that the files aquota.user and aquota.groups exist in the directory /export/data2 by entering **ls –l /export/data2**.

7. Turn quotas on for all file systems that are mounted with these options by entering the following:

   quotaon –av

8. Make the quota system persistent after reboot by entering **chkconfig quota on**.

9. View the quota report by entering the following:

   repquota –av

   The quotas are set by using the number of 1k blocks.

   Notice that root is the only user listed.

10. Determine the block size on the file system by entering the following:

    dumpe2fs /dev/hda6 | more

    Enter the block size below:

11. Set a quota for geeko of a soft limit of 20 MB and a hard limit of 30 MB on /dev/hda6 by entering the following:

    edquota –u geeko

    The quota editor appears (the vi editor).

12. Enter the required *soft limit* and *hard limit* under the Soft and Hard columns for /dev/hda6 (press **Insert** twice to replace text).

    You can calculate the soft limit and hard limit sizes you need to enter by dividing the number of bytes by the block size.

    For example, if the block size you recorded is 4096, you would divide **20,000,000** by **4096** to calculate the soft limit number you need to enter.

You can access a calculator from the KDE Menu by selecting **Utilities > Calculator**.

NOTE

13. When you finish, press **Esc**; then enter **:wq**.

14. Run repquota to view the quota information about all configured users by entering the following:

    repquota -av

    Notice that geeko is now listed with the soft limit and hard limit values you entered.

15. (Optional) If you finish early, set a quota for the users group of 100 MB for the soft limit and 150 MB for the hard limit.

16. Close all open windows.

OBJECTIVE 6   BACK UP AND RESTORE THE FILE SYSTEM

Backing up and restoring system data is one of the most critical tasks performed by a system administrator. YaST provides backup and restore modules to help you with this task.

To back up and restore a file system on SUSE Linux Enterprise Server, you need to know the following:

- Data Backup Strategies
- Back Up System Data with YaST
- Restore System Data with YaST
- Data Backup Command Line Tools

Data Backup Strategies

The following are strategies and guidelines for implementing backup on your SUSE Linux system:

- **Backup media.** Because large amounts of data are normally included in a system backup, you first need to decide which media you want to use to back up the data.

  Administrators normally use tape drives, as these have the best price-to-capacity ratio and are SCSI drives. In addition, tapes have the advantage of being relatively simple to reuse.

  Other media for data backup include writable CDs or DVDs, removable hard drives, and Magnetic-Optical (MO) drives.

Storage Area Networks (SANs) are networks that back up data from different computers on a central backup server. But even SANs often use tape-drive units to perform the backup.

3

- **Backup requirements.** When organizing data backups, you often need to compromise between the different requirements.

  For example, lost data should be reconstructed as quickly as possible. However, the amount of data to be backed up should be kept as small as possible (only data that has changed since the last backup).

- **Backup frequency.** How often a backup is performed depends on the importance of the data.

  If the data is highly sensitive, then a complete daily backup is unavoidable. With less sensitive data, you can normally perform a weekly backup.

- **Tape availability.** You need several tapes that can be overwritten in a rolling backup process.

  You should keep two sets of tapes—one for less sensitive data and one for daily backup of sensitive data.

  For a daily backup, all the tapes for a week should be kept longer, which means at least 10 to 15 sets of tapes.

  If necessary, you can carry out incremental backups at regular intervals, which back up all data that has changed since the last complete backup.

- **Tape storage.** You should always store backup tapes separately from the server. This prevents backups from being lost in a disaster (such as fire in the server room).

  This is especially true of sensitive data, which is often kept in a separate, secure room or even a secure bank vault.

Back Up System Data with YaST

The YaST System Backup module lets you create a backup of your system. The backup does not comprise the entire system, but only saves information about changed packages and copies of critical storage areas and configuration files.

To create a backup with YaST, do the following:

1. From the KDE desktop, start the YaST System Backup module by doing one of the following:

   - Select the **YaST** icon, enter the root *password*, and select **OK**; then select **System > System Backup**.

     or

   - Open a terminal window and enter **sux –** and the root *password*; then enter **yast2 backup**.

The dialog box shown in Figure 3-21 appears.

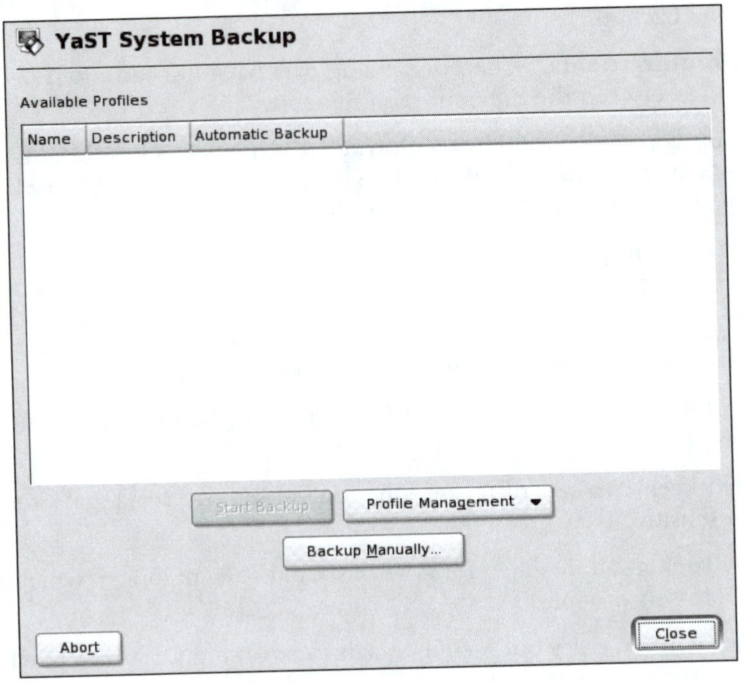

Figure 3-21

This dialog box shows the list of currently stored backup profiles. A *backup profile* is used to name a group of different settings, such as the name of an archive and how to search for files.

You can have a number of profiles, each with a unique name.

From the Profile Management drop-down list, you can add a new profile (**Add**) based on default values, duplicate an existing profile (**Duplicate**), edit the settings stored in a profile (**Change**), delete a profile (**Delete**), or configure automatic backup settings.

You can also use **Backup Manually** to configure a backup without creating a backup profile.

2. Create a profile by selecting **Profile Management > Add**.

3. Enter a *name* for the profile that will be used in the profile list; then select **OK**.

The dialog box shown in Figure 3-22 appears.

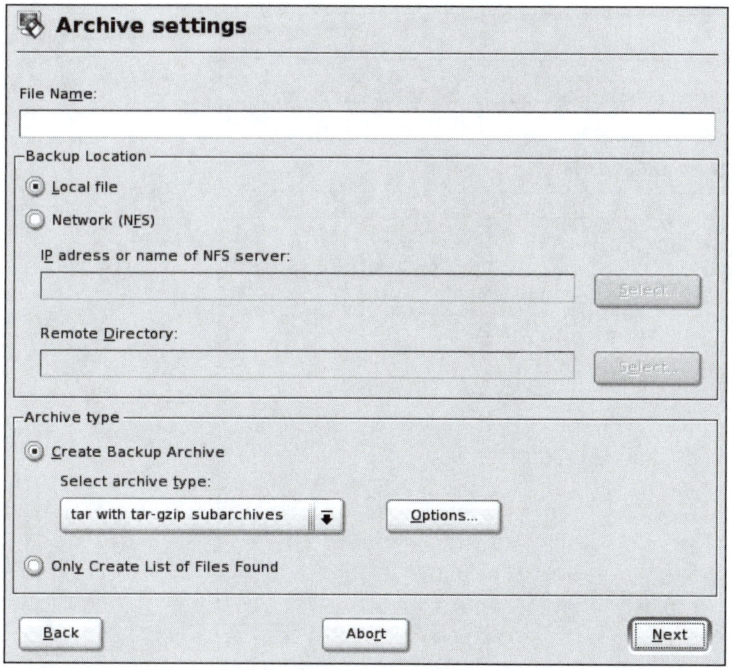

Figure 3-22

4. In the **File Name** field, enter a *filename* for the backup file.

   You need to enter a full path (absolute path) with the filename (such as **/etc/backup_1**).

5. Save the backup file to a local directory by selecting **Local file**, or save the backup file to a remote server by selecting **Network (NFS)** and entering the remote server and directory.

6. Create a backup file that contains the backup data by selecting **Create Backup Archive**, or select **Only Create List of Files Found**.

   The Create Backup Archive option lets you select an archive type (such as **tar with tar-gzip subarchives**) from a drop-down list, and configure additional options (such as multivolume archive) by selecting **Options**.

7. When you finish configuring the archive settings, continue by selecting **Next**.

The dialog box shown in Figure 3–23 appears.

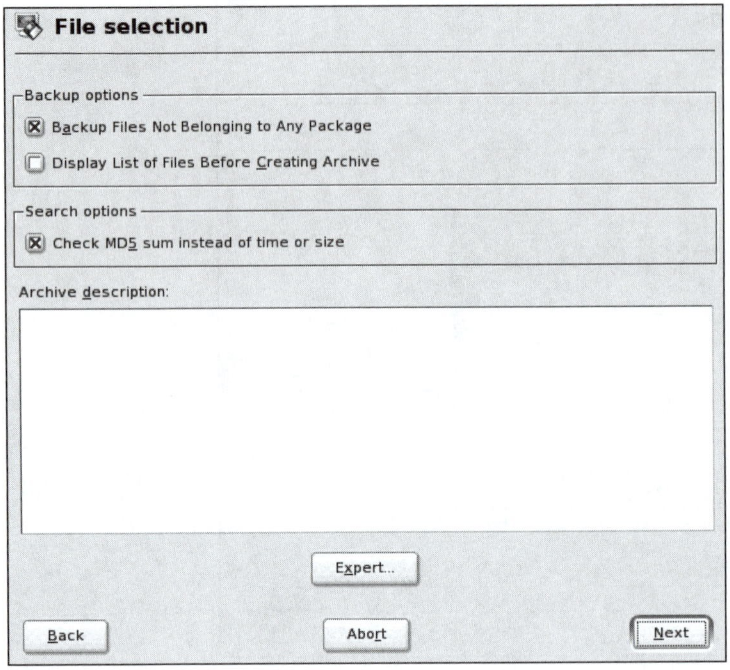

Figure 3-23

From this dialog box, you can select which parts of the system to search and back up.

The archive will contain files from packages that were changed since package installation or upgrade.

8. Select one or both of the following options:

   ■ **Backup Files Not Belonging to Any Package.** Include these files in the backup.

   ■ **Display List of Files Before Creating Archive.** Lets you show and edit a list of files found before creating the backup archive.

9. (Optional) In the **Archive description** field, enter a *description* of the backup archive.

10. Use MD5 sum checking by selecting **Check MD5 sum instead of time or size**.

    You can use MD5 sum to determine if the file was changed. It is more reliable than checking size or modification time, but it takes more time.

11. (Optional) Configure advanced options (such as adding the partition table to the backup) by selecting **Expert**.

    For most backups, you do not need to change the default Expert options.

12. When you finish configuring, continue by selecting **Next**.

    The dialog box shown in Figure 3-24 appears.

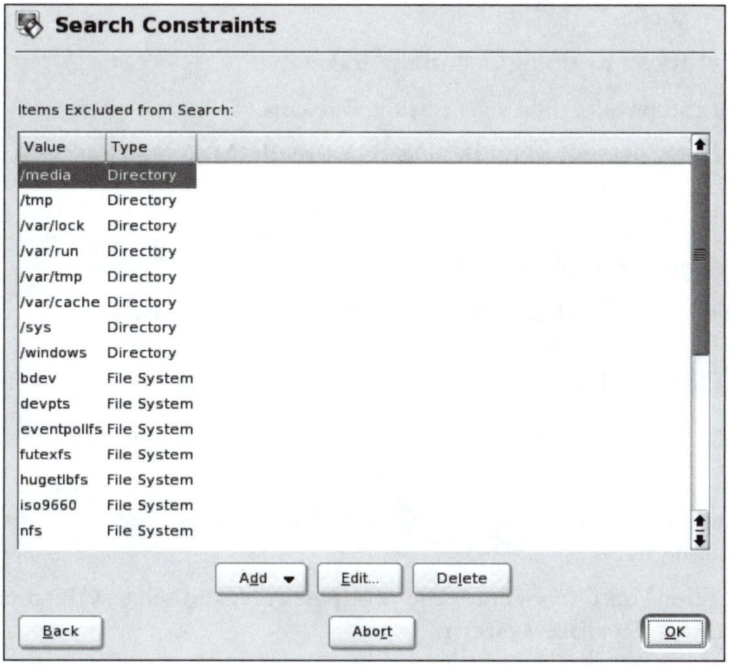

Value	Type
/media	Directory
/tmp	Directory
/var/lock	Directory
/var/run	Directory
/var/tmp	Directory
/var/cache	Directory
/sys	Directory
/windows	Directory
bdev	File System
devpts	File System
eventpollfs	File System
futexfs	File System
hugetlbfs	File System
iso9660	File System
nfs	File System

Figure 3-24

This dialog box lists all the items you want excluded from the backup, including the following exclusion types:

- **Directories.** All files located in the specified directories will not be backed up.

- **File Systems.** You can exclude all files located on a certain type of file system (such as ReiserFS or Ext2). The root directory will always be searched, even if its file system is selected.

  File systems that cannot be used on a local disk (such as network file systems) are excluded by default.

- **Regular expressions.** Any filename that matches any of the regular expressions will not be backed up. Use perl regular expressions. For example, to exclude *.bak files, add the regular expression **\.bak$**.

13. Add an item to the exclusion list by selecting **Add > exclusion type** and entering a *directory*, *file system*, or *expression*; then select **OK**.

14. Edit or remove an item from the list by selecting the *item*; then select **Edit** or **Delete**.

15. When you finish, continue by selecting **OK**.

    You are returned to the YaST System Backup dialog box, where the new profile appears in the list.

16. Start the backup by doing one of the following:

    ■ Select the profile; then select **Start Backup**.

    ■ Set an automatic backup by selecting **Profile Management > Automatic Backup**.

       You can set options such as backup frequency, backup start time, and maximum number of old backups.

17. When you finish configuring system backups, select **Close**.

Restore System Data with YaST

You can use the YaST Restore system module to restore a system backup by doing the following:

1. From the KDE desktop, start the YaST Restore system module by doing one of the following:

    ■ Select the **YaST** icon, enter the root *password*, and select **OK**; then select **System > Restore system**.

       or

    ■ Open a terminal window and enter **sux –** and the root *password*; then enter **yast2 restore**.

The dialog box shown in Figure 3-25 appears.

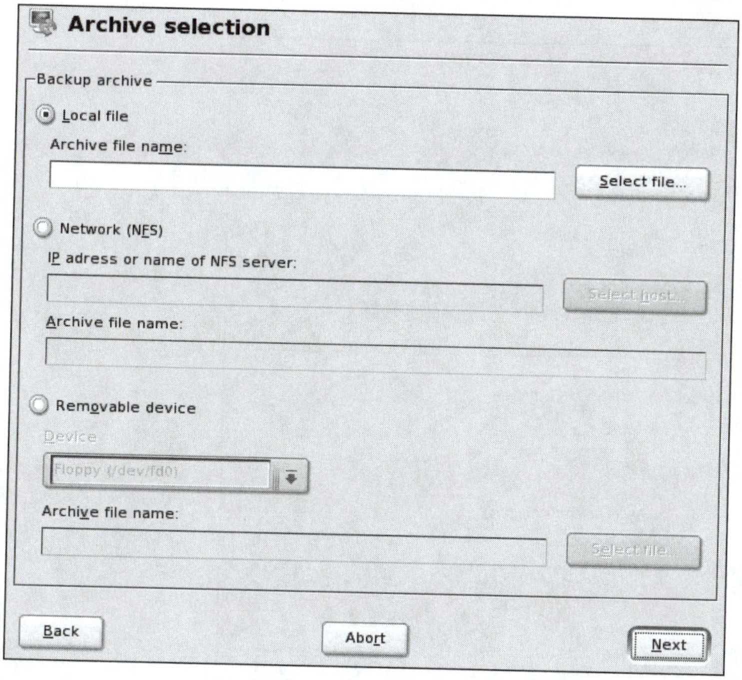

Figure 3-25

2. Do one of the following:

  - If the backup file is stored locally, select **Local file**; then enter the *archive filename* (include the full path) or locate and enter the file by selecting **Select file**.

    or

  - If the backup file is stored on a network server, select **Network (NFS)**; then enter the *remote server* and the full path of the *archive backup file*.

    or

  - If the backup file is on a removable device (such as a disk or tape drive), select **Removable device**; then select the *device* from the drop-down list and enter the full path of the *archive backup file* (or use **Select file**).

3. When you finish, continue by selecting **Next**.

YaST reads the contents of the archive file and the dialog box shown in Figure 3-26 appears.

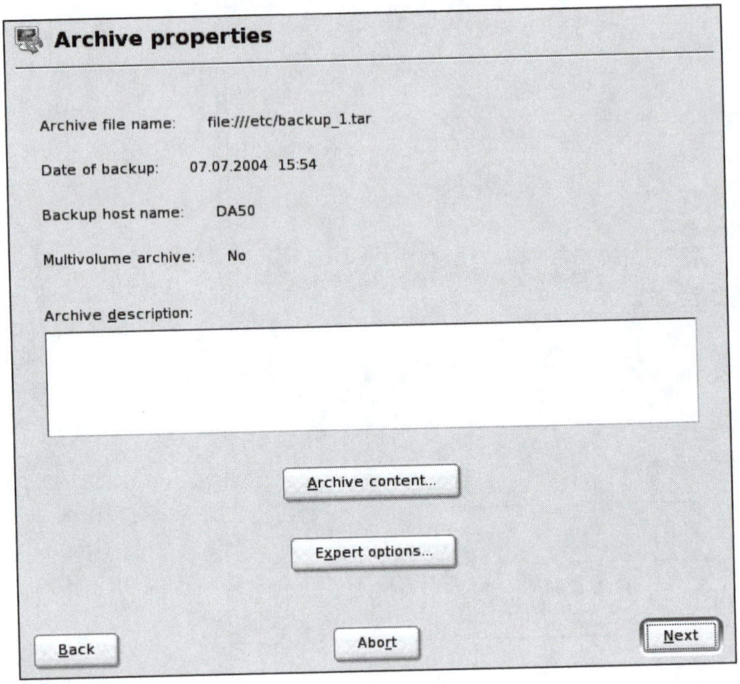

Archive properties

Archive file name: file:///etc/backup_1.tar

Date of backup: 07.07.2004 15:54

Backup host name: DA50

Multivolume archive: No

Archive description:

Archive content...

Expert options...

Back   Abort   Next

Figure 3-26

This dialog box lists the properties of the archive file.

4. View the archive contents by selecting **Archive content**.

5. Configure options such as activating the boot loader configuration after restoration and entering the target directory by selecting **Expert options**.

6. When you finish, continue by selecting **Next**.

NOTE

If this is a multivolume archive, selecting Next displays an Archive properties dialog box for each volume.

The dialog box shown in Figure 3–27 appears.

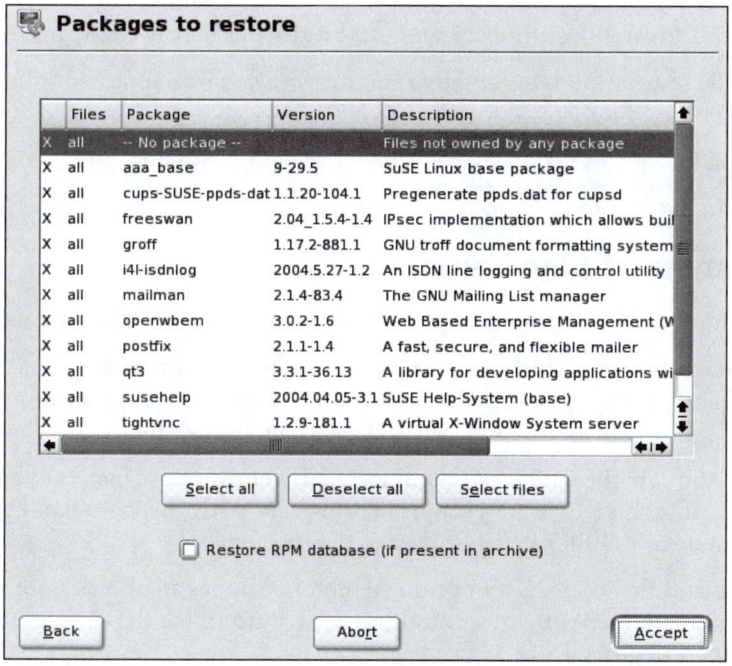

Figure 3-27

This dialog box lets you select which files you want restored from the archive (all are selected by default).

The first column in the list displays the restoration status of the package. It can be **X** (package will be restored), empty (package will not be restored), or **P** (package will be restored partially).

The number of selected files that will be restored from the archive is in the second column.

Press **Select files** to restore a package partially.

7. Do one of the following:

  - Select all packages in the list by selecting **Select all**.

    or

  - Deselect all packages in the list by selecting **Deselect all**.

    or

  - Restore particular files in a highlighted package by selecting **Select files**; then select or deselect the listed files.

8. (Optional) If the RPM database exists in the archive, restore it by selecting **Restore RPM database**.

9. When you finish selecting packages, start restoring files by selecting **Accept**.

   When the restoration is complete, a summary dialog box appears listing the status of the restored files.

10. (Optional) Save the summary to a file by selecting **Save to file**.

11. Close the dialog box by selecting **Finish**.

Data Backup Command Line Tools

Linux has several command line tools available for data backup, including the following:

- **tar (tape archiver).** This is the most commonly used tool for data backup. It archives files in a special format directly on a corresponding medium (such as magnetic tape or formatted floppy disk) or to an archive file.

  Normally, though, the data is not compressed. By convention, names of archive files end in .tar. If archive files are compressed (usually with the command gzip), then the extension of the filename is either .tar.gz or .tgz.

  The command first expects an option (which is why it can also be used without a minus sign), then the name of the archive to be written (or the device file) and the name of the directory to be backed up.

  All directories and files beneath this are also saved. Directories are typically backed up with a command similar to the following:

  tar –cvf /dev/st0 /home

NOTE

For additional details on the tar command, enter **man tar**.

- **rsync (remote synchronization).** The command rsync creates copies of complete directories across a network to a different computer.

  However, rsync can also be used to carry out local mirroring of directories. Only those files that are not already in the target directory or that only exist in older versions are copied. In fact, only the parts of a file that have changed are copied, not the entire file.

  For example, the mirroring of all home directories can be carried out by entering a command similar to the following:

  rsync –a /home /shadow

In this example, the mirroring is made to the directory **/shadow/**. There the directory **/home/** is first created, and then below it, the actual home directories of the users.

If instead, you want the home directories created directly beneath the target directory specified (such as **/shadow/geeko/**), then you would enter the following command:

rsync -a /home/. /shadow

Specifying **/.** at the end of the directory to be mirrored indicates that this directory is not included in the copy.

The option **-a** switches rsync to the archive mode. This is a combination of other options (-rlptg), which ensures that the characteristics of the files to be copied are identical to the originals.

NOTE

For additional details on rsync, enter **man rsync**, refer to the technical reference documentation in /usr/share/doc/packages/rsync/tech_report.ps, or connect to the rsync project Web site at *http://rsync.samba.org/*.

- **dd command.** With the command dd, you can convert and copy files byte-wise.

  Normally dd reads from the standard input and writes the result to the standard output. However, with the correct parameters, you can also address the files directory.

  You can copy all kinds of files with this command, including device files, which means entire partitions. Exact copies of an installed system (or just parts of it) can be created very simply.

  In the simplest case, you can copy a file with a command similar to the following:
  dd if=/etc/protocols of=protocols.org

  With the option **if=** (input file), you specify the file to be copied. With the option **of=** (output file), you specify the name of the copied file.

NOTE

For additional details on using dd to copy, convert, or format files, see **man dd**.

- **mt command.** To work with magnetic tapes, Linux provides the command **mt**.

  With this command, you can position tapes, switch compression on or off (with some SCSI-2 tape drives), and query the status of the tape.

Magnetic tape drives in Linux are always SCSI devices and can be addressed by names such as the following:

- **/dev/st0.** Refers to the first tape drive
- **/dev/nst0.** Addresses the same tape drive in the no rewind mode; in other words, after writing or reading, the tape remains at that position and is not rewound back to the beginning.

For compatibility with other Unix conversions, two symbolic links exist: **/dev/rmt0** and **/dev/nrmt0**.

You can view the status of a tape by entering a command similar to the following:

```
mt -f /dev/st0 status
```

For additional details on using the mt command, enter **man mt**.

- **cron service.** Backing up data is a task that should be carried out regularly. You can automate backup from the command line with the cron service.

  System jobs are controlled with the file /etc/crontab and the files in the directory /etc/cron.d/. Other jobs are defined with the scripts in the directories /etc/cron.hourly/, /etc/cron.daily/, /etc/cron.weekly/, and /etc/cron.monthly/.

  You specify which users can create cron jobs by using the files /var/spool/cron/allow and /var/spool/cron/deny, which are accessed in this order. If both files do not exist, then only root may define jobs.

  The jobs of individual users are stored in files in the directory /var/spool/cron/tabs/ with names matching the user names.

  You process these files by entering the command **crontab** (see **man crontab**).

The following is an example of a defined cron job:

```
0 22 * * 5 /root/bin/backup
```

The script /root/bin/backup is started every Friday at 10 o'clock in the evening. The format for the line is described in **man 5 crontab**.

Exercise 3-5   Back Up System Files on Your Server

In this exercise, you use the utilities gzip/gunzip, bzip2, and tar as archiving tools to back up files such as aafire (which displays burning flames) and user and group files.

Do the following:

1. From a terminal window, su to root (**su -**) with a password of **novell**.

2. Back up your aafire binary by copying it to root's home directory with the following command:

   cp /usr/bin/aafire ~

3. Check the size of the binary by entering **ls –lh aafire**.

   Record the size below:

4. Archive the binary file in a compressed format by entering

   gzip –1 aafire.

5. Check the size of the binary file by entering **ls –lh aafire.gz**.

   Notice that the file is smaller. Record the size:

6. Uncompress the file aafire.gz by entering **gzip –d aafire.gz**.

7. Compress aafire again, but this time use the highest compression by entering **gzip –9 aafire**.

8. Check the size of the binary by entering **ls –lh aafire.gz**.

   Record the size:

9. Uncompress the file aafire.gz by entering **gunzip aafire.gz**.

10. Compress the file aafire with bzip2 and check the file size by entering the following two commands:

    bzip2 aafire

    ls –lh aafire.bz2

11. Uncompress the file aafire.bz2 and check the file size by entering the following 2 commands:

    bzip2 –d aafire.bz2

    ls –lh aafire

12. Create a usrgrp.tar archive of /etc/passwd, /etc/shadow, /etc/group by entering the following:

    tar –cvf usrgrp.tar /etc/passwd /etc/shadow /etc/group

13. List the files in the tar archive by entering the following:

    tar tvf usrgrp.tar

14. Now create a gzip archive of the file usrgrp.tar and check the file size by entering the following two commands:

    gzip –9 usrgrp.tar

    ls –lh usrgrp.tar.gz

15. Extract the file usrgrp.tar.gz in a /tmp/ directory and check the file information by entering the following commands:

    mkdir tmp

    cd tmp/

    tar zxvf ../usrgrp.tar.gz

    ls –Rl

16. Verify you are in the directory /root/tmp by entering **pwd**.

17. (Conditional) If you are not in the directory /root/tmp, change to the directory by entering **cd /root/tmp**.

18. Delete all files in the directory tmp/ and check the results by entering the following:

    rm –rf *

    ls

19. Extract the archive again, but manually perform the same function as the command tar zxvf by entering the following:

    gzip –dc ../usrgrp.tar.gz | tar xvf –

20. Verify that the files were created by entering **ls –Rl**.

21. Close the terminal window.

CHAPTER SUMMARY

- Many file systems are available for Linux. These include the traditional nonjournaling file systems such as ext2, minix, MS-DOS/VFAT, and HPFS as well as the newer journaling file systems such as ext3, ReiserFS, NTFS, JFS, XFS, and VxFS. Applications use a VFS to support many different file systems on a single system.

- Each file system contains a superblock that stores the structure of the file system, an inode table that contains individual file and directory information, and blocks for the file data. However, different file systems have different features and use the inode and data blocks in different ways.

- The Linux file system is arranged hierarchically, using directories described by the FHS.

- Many types of files may exist on the Linux file system, such as normal files (text files, data files, executable programs), directories, device files, links, sockets, and named pipes (FIFOs). Files in Linux are case sensitive.

- Journaling file systems maintain a transaction log that is used to track changes to files and speed up the checking of file system errors related to incomplete writing of data and metadata.

- File systems on a hard disk must reside in a partition. Each hard disk can contain up to four primary partitions, or three primary partitions and an extended partition that contains logical partitions within. Device files in the /dev directory are used to identify hard disk devices and partitions.

- Prior to a SLES installation, the number and size of partitions should be carefully planned according to the workstation or server role.

- You can create, manage, check, and mount file systems and partitions using YaST. Alternatively, you can create and manage hard disk partitions using the **fdisk** command, create file systems on partitions using the **mkfs** and **mkreiserfs** commands, check file systems for errors using the **fsck**, **e2fsck**, and **reiserfsck** commands, and mount or unmount file systems using the **mount** and **umount** commands.

- Linux uses the /etc/fstab to automatically mount media as well as mount media at boot time. Removable media are typically mounted to subdirectories of /media.

- LVM logical volumes may be used as flexible file systems for use in SLES. You can create logical volumes during the installation process or afterwards.

- The **fuser**, **du**, **df**, and **lsof** commands may be used to monitor the usage of file systems.

- ext2 and ext3 file systems contain a /lost+found directory for damaged file fragments.

- It is good form to create boot disks in YaST that may be used to rescue a damaged SLES system.

❑ You can use disk quotas on a file system to restrict the number of files and directories that individual users can create as well as the amount of disk space that users can occupy. Quota entries are made using the **edquota** command. Each quota entry has a hard limit that cannot be exceeded as well as a soft limit that can be exceeded for a period of time.

❑ To prevent lost data in the event of a system crash, you should regularly back up (or archive) the data on your file systems to removable media such as DVD or tape. You can use YaST to back up and restore data and software packages on your system. Alternatively, you can use the **tar**, **rsync**, and **dd** commands to back up and restore data. The **mt** command may be used to manage tape devices and the **crontab** command may be used to schedule backups to occur in the future on a repetitive schedule.

KEY TERMS

/etc/fstab — A file used to store information used to mount file systems.

/etc/mtab — A file that contains a list of mounted file systems.

/lost+found — A directory on every ext2 and ext3 file system used to store damaged file fragments. The **fsck** command stores files that could not be repaired in this directory.

/proc/file systems — A text file that contains a list of supported file systems in SLES.

/proc/mounts — A file that contains mounted file system information from the Linux kernel.

aquota.group — A file that stores group quota information for a file system.

aquota.user — A file that stores user quota information for a file system.

block — The unit of data commonly used by a file system. Also called a **data block**.

chkconfig command — Used to set the startup status of a service in Linux.

cron — A system service that can be used to run commands on a regular schedule.

crontab command — Used to schedule commands to occur regularly using the cron service.

data block — See **block**.

dd command — Used to convert and copy files to other locations.

device file — A file used to identify hardware devices such as hard disks and serial ports.

df command — Displays disk usage by file system.

directories — Special files that are used to organize other files on the file system.

du command — Displays disk usage by directory.

dumpe2fs command — Used to obtain file system information from ext2 and ext3 file systems.

e2fsck command — Used to check ext2 and ext3 file systems for errors.

edquota command — Used to specify quota limits for users and groups.

ext2 — A traditional nonjournaling file system used on older Linux systems.

ext3 — A journaling version of the ext2 file system.

extended partition — A partition on a hard disk drive that stores logical partitions.

fdisk command — Used to create, delete, and modify hard disk partitions.

FIFOs — See named pipes.

file system — A structure used to organize blocks on a device such that they can be used by the operating system to store data.

Filesystem Hierarchy Standard (FHS) — A standard outlining the location of set files and directories on a Linux system.

fsck command — Used to check and repair file systems.

fuser command — Used to identify users and processes using a particular file or directory.

grace period — The amount of time a user can exceed a quota limit.

gzip command — A common compression utility in Linux.

hard limit — A quota limit that cannot be exceeded.

HPFS — The native OS/2 file system.

inode — That portion of a file that stores information on the file's attributes, access permissions, location, ownership, and file type.

inode table — That portion of a file system that stores the inodes for files and directories.

JFS — A journaling file system that supports large file system sizes.

journaling — A file system feature that records all file system transactions in a small transaction log on the file system for tracking and troubleshooting purposes.

links — Files that point to other files on the file system.

logical group — A virtual volume created by LVM that can be resized or manipulated following creation.

logical partition — A subpartition inside an extended partition on a hard disk drive.

logical volume management (LVM) — A set of components that allow you to create virtual or logical volumes in Linux.

lsof (list open files) command — Displays the files that processes are using.

metadata — The section of a file system that is not used to store user data.

minix — A traditional nonjournaling file system used on older Linux systems.

mkfs command — Used to create most file systems in Linux.

mkreiserfs command — Used to create ReiserFS file systems.

module disk — A floppy disk that contains additional device drivers for a SLES system.

mount command — Used to mount file systems on devices to mount point directories.

mount point — A directory to which a device is mounted.

mounting — The process of associating a device (e.g., CD-ROM) to a directory (e.g., /media/cdrom). Once a device has been mounted, it may be accessed by navigating to the appropriate directory.

MS-DOS — See **VFAT**.

mt (magnetic tape) command — Used to manage tape devices.

named pipes — Temporary connections that send information from one command or process in memory to another; they can also be represented by files on the file system. Named pipes are also called FIFO (First In First Out) files.

NetWare Core Protocol (NCP) — A file-sharing protocol used to share files on Novell Netware systems.

Network File System (NFS) — A file-sharing protocol used to share files on Linux and UNIX systems.

normal files — Commonly used files such as text files, graphic files, data files, and executable programs.

NTFS — The Windows NT file system.

partition — A physical division of a hard disk drive.

physical volume — A hard disk or hard disk partition.

primary partition — A main partition on a hard disk drive. There are four primary partitions.

quotacheck command — Used to update the quota database files.

quotaoff command — Used to deactivate disk quotas.

quotaon command — Used to activate disk quotas.

quotas — File system usage limits that may be imposed on users and groups.

ReiserFS — A journaling file system that uses dynamic inode tables and has fast data access.

reiserfsck command — Used to check and repair ReiserFS file systems.

reiserfstune command — Used to configure file system settings on ReiserFS file systems.

repquota command — Used to produce a report on quotas for a particular file system.

Rescue Disk — A floppy disk used to repair a SLES system.

resize_reiserfs command — Used to resize ReiserFS file systems.

rsync command — Used to copy files and directories to a different location on the local computer or to a remote computer across a network.

Server Message Block (SMB) — A file sharing protocol used to share files on Windows systems.

sockets — Named pipes connecting processes on two different computers; they can also be represented by files on the file system.

soft limit — A quota limit that can be exceeded for a certain period of time.

standard boot disk — A floppy disk used to start a SLES system.

superblock — The section of a file system that stores the file system structure.

tar (tape archiver) command — A command-line utility that may be used to archive files and directories.

tune2fs command — Used to configure file system settings on ext2 and ext3 file systems.

umount command — Used to unmount a device from a mount point directory.

VFAT — A Linux version of the Microsoft FAT file system.

virtual file system — See **Virtual Filesystem Switch (VFS)**.

Virtual Filesystem Switch (VFS) — A Linux component that applications write data to that is eventually written to the file system itself. It is also referred to as a virtual file system.

volume group — A system resource that logical volumes can use.

VxFS — A journaling file system that supports large data and virtual volumes.

XFS — A journaling file system that uses fast allocation groups to manage data.

REVIEW QUESTIONS

1. What command can you use to view the file systems supported by your Linux kernel? _____

2. Which of the following are journaling file systems that can be created using the **mkfs** command? (Choose all that apply.)

   a. JFS

   b. ext2

   c. ReiserFS

   d. ext3

3. What information is stored in the inode of a file? (Choose all that apply.)

   a. File ownership

   b. File timestamp

   c. File data

   d. Filename

4. What is the maximum size of the ext2, ext3, and ReiserFS file systems?

   _____

5. Which of the following are advantages of using ReiserFS instead of ext2? (Choose two answers.)

   a. Faster disk access

   b. Larger supported file size

   c. Better block utilization

   d. Dynamic inode allocation

6. What inode number is used for mount point directories? _____

7. What device file refers to the third primary partition on an IDE primary slave hard disk? _____

8. Which of the following are good practices when designing partitions for a new Linux system? (Choose all that apply.)

   a. Plan for future software additions.

   b. Create less than 256 MB of swap.

   c. Use SCSI hard disks where possible.

   d. Create a partition for the / and /boot directories at minimum.

9. How many primary partitions may be created in total on a hard disk?

   _____

10. How many partitions may be created in total on an IDE hard disk?

    _____

11. Which of the following commands could be used to create and manage partitions on the second SCSI hard disk?

    a. fdisk /dev/sdb

    b. fdisk /dev/hdb

    c. fdisk /dev/sdc

    d. fdisk /dev/hdc

12. Which command would you use to check a ReiserFS file system for errors?

    _____

13. Which of the following files could you edit to mount a new file system at system initialization?

    a. /etc/mtab

    b. /proc/mounts

    c. /etc/fstab

    d. /proc/filesystems

14. How many volume groups are typically used in a SLES system?

    _____

15. What command can you use to force the unmounting of **/dev/hda3** from the **/data** directory? _____

16. What command can you use to determine how much free space is available on mounted file systems? _____

17. You have enabled user and group quotas on the file system that is mounted to the **/var** directory. Which files contain the quota limits? (Choose two answers.)

    a. /var/aquota.group

    b. /var/aquota.user

    c. /aquota.group

    d. /aquota.user

18. What command can you use to modify the quotas for the **geeko** user?

    _____

19. What **tar** command can you use to back up all files in the /etc directory to the device /dev/nst0? _____

DISCOVERY EXERCISES

Creating Partitions and File Systems

Provided that you have free space on your hard disk that is not used by a Linux partition, log in to a terminal as the root user and use **fdisk** to create an additional partition and **mkfs** to place the Ext2 file system on it. Next, use the **tune2fs** command to convert the ext2 file system to Ext3 (use the manual pages to identify the appropriate option required). Then reformat the partition to use the ReiserFS file system, create a /**data** directory, and add a line to /**etc/fstab** that will mount the file system automatically at boot time to the /**data** directory. Reboot your computer and verify that the mount was successful. Finally, unmount and check the /**data** file system for errors.

If your system does not have free space outside a Linux partition, you can use a floppy disk to perform this exercise; the device file for your first floppy disk is /**dev/fd0** and there is no need to perform partitioning.

Configuring User Quotas

For the /**data** file system created in the previous discovery exercise, enable user quotas. Restrict the **geeko** user with a hard limit of 50000 blocks and 10000 inodes and a soft limit of 40000 blocks and 8000 inodes. The soft limit should only be exceeded for three days. When finished, test your quota entries.

Archiving Data

Use the appropriate options to the **tar** command to back up and compress (with **gzip**) the /**data** directory created in the first discovery exercise above to a file called /**root/databackup.tar.gz**. Use the **tar** command to view the contents of the archive file and perform a sample extraction of the archive file to the /**tmp** directory.

4

MANAGE SOFTWARE FOR SUSE LINUX ENTERPRISE SERVER

In this section, you learn how to manage software packages on your SUSE Linux Enterprise Server with RPM Package Manager (RPM) and YaST. You are also introduced to dynamic software libraries.

- ◆ Manage RPM Software Packages
- ◆ Verify and Update Software Library Access
- ◆ Manage Software Updates with YaST Online Update Server (YOU)

NOTE

The Novell ZENworks Linux Management product (ZLM) is now available for managing software installation and updates on Linux servers and desktops in your network.

In addition to the upgrade method of using a remote YOU server, Novell provides upgrades to licensed and registered SLES 9 servers through a channel to a Novell ZLM server.

Although not included as part of the Novell CLP curriculum (or practicum testing), the ZLM client is available in SLES 9 for installation. For details on installing the client and subscribing to the upgrade channel, see *Appendix D: Novell ZENworks Linux Management (ZLM)*.

Objective 1   Manage RPM Software Packages

While there are several software package formats available for Linux, the format used most commonly in SUSE Linux installations is the RPM Package Manager (RPM) format.

Installing software in the RPM format can be done with YaST or by using the command rpm. YaST ensures the automatic resolution of dependencies, while rpm only controls them (resolution must be performed manually).

To manage installation of RPM software packages, you need to know the following:

- RPM Components and Features
- RPM Basics
- How to Manage Software Packages with rpm
- How to Manage Software Packages with YaST

RPM Components and Features

RPM Package Manager (or RPM) is a package management system primarily intended for Linux. RPM installs, updates, uninstalls, verifies, and queries software.

The following are the basic components of RPM:

- **RPM Package Manager.** The utility that handles installing and uninstalling RPM packages.
- **RPM database.** The RPM database works in the background of the package manager and contains a list of all information for all installed RPM packages.

    The database keeps track of all files that are changed and created when a user installs a program. This helps the package manager easily remove the same files that were originally installed.

If the database becomes corrupted, double links in the database make sure that it can normally be rebuilt without any trouble.

■ **RPM package.** RPM lets you take software source code and package it into source and binary packages for end users. These are called RPM packages.

■ **Package label.** Every RPM package includes a package label that contains information such as the software name, version, and the package release number.

This information helps the package manager track the installed versions of software to make it easier to manage software installations on a Linux computer.

Some of the advantages of using RPM package manager and RPM packages include the following:

■ Provides a consistent method for users to install programs in Linux.

■ Makes it easier to uninstall programs (because of the RPM database).

■ Most software packages for Linux (including those from Novell for Linux platforms) are now formatted as RPM packages.

■ Original source archives (such as tar.gz, .tar.bz2) are included and easy to verify.

■ You can use RPM tools to enable software installations using noninteractive scripts.

■ You can use RPM tools to verify that the software installed correctly.

■ RPM can track dependent software, which means that any additional software needed is also installed.

■ RPM allows for all packaged software to use public-key technology to digitally sign the software.

RPM Basics

To manage software packages with RPM, you need to understand the following:

■ RPM Package File Format

■ RPM Configuration File

■ RPM Database

RPM Package File Format

RPM package files use the following naming format:

software_name–software_version–release_number.architecture.**rpm**

The following describes each component of the naming format:

- *software_name.* This is normally the name of the software being installed.
- *software_version.* This is the version number of the software in the RPM package and is normally a number.
- *release_number.* This is the number of times the package has been rebuilt using the same version of the software.
- *architecture.* This indicates the architecture the package was built under (such as i586, i686, athlon, ppc) or the type of package content.

  For example, if the package has an i586 architecture, you can install it on 32-bit Intel-compatible machines that are Pentium class or higher.

  If the package has a noarch extension, it does not include any binary code.

No matter what the RPM software package name, all RPM packages include a binary header.

RPM Configuration File

The global RPM configuration file of the command rpm is /usr/lib/rpm/rpmrc. However, when the rpm command is updated, all changes to this file are lost.

To prevent this from happening, write the changes to file /etc/rpmrc (for the system configuration) or to file ~/.rpmrc (for the user configuration).

RPM Database

The files of the RPM database are stored in /var/lib/rpm/. If the partition /usr/ has a size of 1 GB, this database can occupy nearly 30 MB, especially after a complete update.

If the database is much larger than expected, it is useful to rebuild the database by entering **rpm --rebuilddb**. Before doing this, make a backup of the old database.

The cron script suse.de-backup-rpmdb stored in /etc/cron.daily/ checks daily to see if there are any changes. If so, a copy of the database is made (packed with gzip) and stored in /var/adm/backup/rpmdb/.

The number of copies is controlled by the variable MAX_RPMDB_BACKUPS (default is 5) in /etc/sysconfig/backup.

The size of a single backup is approximately 5 MB for 1 GB in /usr.

How to Manage Software Packages with rpm

You can use the command rpm to manage software packages. This includes querying the RPM database for detailed information about the installed software.

The command provides the following modes for managing software packages:

- Installing, uninstalling, or updating software packages
- Rebuilding the RPM database
- Querying RPM bases or individual RPM archives
- Checking the integrity of packages

You can use the command rpmbuild to build installable RPM packages from pristine sources.

These packages contain program files to install and certain meta information used during installation by RPM to configure the software package. This same information is stored in the RPM database after installation for documentation purposes.

RPM archives normally have the extension .rpm.

To manage software packages with RPM, you need to know how to do the following:

- Verify Package Authenticity
- Install, Update, and Uninstall Packages
- Update Software with Patches
- Query Archives and the RPM Database

 For a number of packages, the components needed for software development (libraries, headers, include files, etc.) have been put into separate packages. These development packages are only needed if you want to compile software yourself (such as the most recent GNOME packages).

These packages can be identified by the name extension -devel, such as the packages alsa-devel, gimp-devel, and kdelibs-devel.

Verify Package Authenticity

All SUSE Linux RPM packages are signed with the following GnuPG key:

```
1024D/9C800ACA 2000-10-19 SuSE Package Signing Key <build@suse.de>
Key fingerprint = 79C1 79B2 E1C8 20C1 890F 9994 A84E DAE8 9C80 0ACA
```

You can enter the command **rpm --checksig** *package_name* (such as **rpm --checksig apache-1.3.12.rpm**) to verify the signature of an RPM package. This lets you determine whether the package originated from SUSE or from another trustworthy facility.

Verifying the package signature is especially recommended for update packages from the Internet.

The SUSE public package signature key is stored in the directories /root/gnupg/ and /usr/lib/rpm/gnupg/. Storing the key in /usr/lib/rpm/.gnupg/ lets normal users verify the signature of RPM packages.

Install, Update, and Uninstall Packages

To manage RPM software packages, you need to know how to do the following:

- Install an RPM Package
- Update an RPM Package
- Uninstall an RPM Package

Install an RPM Package   For most RPM packages, you use the following command to install the software:

rpm –i *package_name*.**rpm**

During installation, the RPM database ensures that no conflicts arise (such as a file belonging to more than 1 package). The package is installed only if its dependencies are fulfilled and there are no conflicts with other packages.

If there is an error, RPM requests those packages that need to be installed to meet dependency requirements.

You use other options to ignore these defaults, but this is only for experts. If you don't know what you're doing, you can risk compromising the integrity of the system and possibly jeopardizing the ability to update the system.

Update an RPM Package   You can use the options –U (or --upgrade) and –F (or --freshen) to update a package by using the following syntax:

rpm –F *package_name*.**rpm**

This command removes the files of the old version and immediately installs the new files.

The difference between the two options is that –U installs packages that previously did not exist in the system, but –F simply updates previously installed packages.

RPM updates configuration files carefully using the following guidelines:

- If a configuration file was not changed by the system administrator, RPM installs the new version of the appropriate file. No action by the system administrator is required.

- If a configuration file was changed by the system administrator before the update, RPM saves the changed file with the extension .rpmorig or .rpmsave (backup file). It then installs the version from the new package, but only if the originally installed file and the newer version are different.

If this is the case, compare the backup file (.rpmorig or .rpmsave) with the newly installed file and make your changes again in the new file. Afterward, be sure to delete all .rpmorig and .rpmsave files to avoid problems with future updates.

- A set of .rpmnew files are created if the configuration file already exists and if the noreplace label was specified in the .spec file.

After an update, you need to remove .rpmsave and .rpmnew files (after comparing them) so they do not interfere with future updates.

The .rpmorig extension is assigned if the file has not previously been recognized by the RPM database; otherwise, .rpmsave is used.

In other words, .rpmorig results from updating from a foreign format to RPM. .rpmsave results from updating from an older RPM to a newer RPM.

.rpmnew does not disclose any information as to whether the system administrator has made any changes to the configuration file.

A list of these files is available in /var/adm/ rpmconfigcheck. Some configuration files (such as /etc/httpd/httpd. conf) are not overwritten to allow continued operation.

The option -U is **not** equivalent to uninstalling with the -e option and installing with the -i option. Use -U whenever possible for updating packages.

CAUTION

Uninstall an RPM Package   To uninstall (remove) an RPM package, enter the following:

rpm -e *package_name*

RPM will delete the package only if there are no unresolved dependencies. For example, it is theoretically impossible to delete Tcl/Tk if another application requires it.

Even in this case, RPM calls for assistance from the database. If such a deletion is impossible (even if no additional dependencies exist), it might be helpful to rebuild the RPM database using the option --rebuilddb.

Update Software with Patches

To guarantee the operational security of a system, you should update packages frequently by installing patches in the packages.

When planning an update, you need to consider the following (using the package **pine** as an example):

- Is the patch RPM suitable for my system?

  To check this, first query the installed version of the package:
  ```
  rpm -q pine
  pine-4.44-188
  ```

The results indicate the currently installed version of pine. Then check if the patch RPM is suitable for this version of pine:

```
rpm -qp --basedon pine-4.44-224.i586.patch.rpm
pine = 4.44-188
pine = 4.44-195
pine = 4.44-207
```

The results indicate that the patch is suitable for 3 different versions of pine. The installed version in the example is also listed, so the patch can be installed.

- Which files are replaced by the patch?

  The files affected by a patch can easily be seen in the patch RPM. The option -P lets you select special patch features.

  You can display the list of files with the following command:

  ```
  rpm -qpPl pine-4.44-224.i586.patch.rpm
  /etc/pine.conf
  /etc/pine.conf.fixed
  /usr/bin/pine
  ```

  If the patch is already installed, use the following command:

  ```
  rpm -qPl pine
  /etc/pine.conf
  /etc/pine.conf.fixed
  /usr/bin/pine
  ```

- How can a patch RPM be installed in the system?

  Patch RPMs are used just like normal RPMs. The only difference is that a suitable RPM must already be installed.

- Which patches are already installed in the system and for which package versions?

  You can display a list of all patches installed in the system with the command **rpm -qPa**. If only one patch is installed in a new system (as with pine) the following list appears:

  ```
  rpm -qPa
  pine-4.44-224
  ```

  If at a later date you want to know which package version was originally installed, you can query the RPM database.

  For pine, this information can be displayed with the following command:

  ```
  rpm -q --basedon pine
  pine = 4.44-188
  ```

For additional details about the patch feature of RPM, enter **man rpm** or **man rpmbuild**.

NOTE

Query Archives and the RPM Database

With the -q option, you can inspect an RPM archive (by adding the option -p) and query the RPM database of installed packages.

Table 4-1 lists the most commonly used RPM query options.

Table 4-1

Option	Results
-i	List package information
-l	Display a file list
-f *file*	Find out to which package *file* belongs (the full path must be specified with *file*)
-s	Display a file list with status information (implies -l)
-d	List only documentation files (implies -l)
-c	List only configuration files (implies -l)
--dump	Display a file list with complete details (to be used with -l, -c, or -d)
--provides	List features of the package that another package can request with --requires
--requires, -R	List the capabilities the package requires
--scripts	List installation scripts (preinstall, postinstall, uninstall)

For example, entering the command **rpm –qi wget** displays the following information:

```
Name         : wget                   Relocations: (not relocatable)
Version      : 1.9.1                        Vendor: SuSE Linux AG,
Nuernberg, Germany
Release      : 45.3                     Build Date: Wed Jun 30
21:26:19 2004
Install date: Fri Jul 16 17:20:41 2004    Build Host: neumann.suse.de
Group        : Productivity/Networking/Web/Utilities    Source RPM: wget-
1.9.1-45.3.src.rpm
Size         : 1503802                     License: GPL
Signature    : DSA/SHA1, Wed Jun 30 21:32:17 2004, Key ID  a84edae89c800aca
Packager     : http://www.suse.de/feedback
URL          : http://wget.sunsite.dk/
Summary      : A tool for mirroring FTP and HTTP servers
Description :
Wget enables you to retrieve WWW documents or FTP files from a server.
This can be done in script files or via the command line.
```

```
Authors:
--------
    Hrvoje Niksic <hniksic@srce.hr>
Distribution: SuSE SLES-9 (i586)
```

The option –f only works if you specify the complete filename with a full path. You can enter several filenames, as in the following:

```
rpm -q -f /bin/rpm /usr/bin/wget
rpm-3.0.3-3
wget-1.5.3-55
```

This returns information for both /bin/rpm and /usr/bin/wget.

If you know only part of the filename, you can use a shell script to search for packages, as in the following:

```
#! /bin/sh
for i in $(rpm -q -a -l | grep $1); do
   echo "\"$i\" is in package:"
   rpm -q -f $i
   echo ""
done
```

Enter the partial filename when running the script.

Entering the command **rpm –q --changelog** *rpm_name* displays a detailed list of information (updates, configuration, modifications, etc.) about a specific package.

The following example displays information about the package rpm:

```
rpm -qp --changelog /media/dvd/suse/i586/rpm-3*.rpm
```

Only the last 5 change entries in the RPM database are listed. All entries (dating back the last two years) are included in the package itself.

The rpm package query only works if the DVD is mounted at /media/dvd/.

CAUTION

With the help of the installed RPM database, you can perform verification checks with the option –V, –y, or --verify. All files in a package that have been changed since installation are displayed.

Table 4-2 lists the character symbols RPM uses to provide hints about the changes.

Table 4-2

Character	Description
5	MD5 check sum
S	File size

Table 4-2 (continued)

Character	Description
L	Symbolic link
T	Modification time
D	Major and minor device numbers
U	Owner
G	Group
M	Mode (permissions and file type)

4

In the case of configuration files, the letter "c" is displayed. The following is an example for changes to /etc/wgetrc (wget):

```
rpm -V wget
S.5....T c /etc/wgetrc
```

Exercise 4-1   Manage Software with RPM

The package aalib is an ASCII art library that includes the file aafire which displays burning ASCII art flames.

In this exercise, you learn how to manage RPMs by working with the library aalib.

Do the following:

1. Use RPM to find out information about the package aalib:

   a. From a terminal window, determine which package installed the file /usr/bin/aafire by entering the following:

   rpm –qf /usr/bin/aafire

   Notice that the package aalib installed the file aafire.

   b. Find out information about the package aalib by entering the following:

   rpm –qi aalib

   Notice that the information includes the install date and a description.

   c. Show all the files installed by the package aalib by entering the following:

   rpm –ql aalib

   Where can you find information about the package aalib? (Notice the location of the README files.)

2. See what has changed in the files on your hard drive since the RPMs were originally installed by entering the following:

   rpm –Va

   Interpret the change information for each file listed by using Table 4-2.

3. When you finish viewing the information for a few files, stop the process by pressing **Ctrl+C**.

4. View the documentation files for the command at by entering the following:

   rpm –qd at

   Notice that some of the files are still compressed (*.gz).

5. (Optional) Try installing a package (**YaST > Software > Install and Remove Software**) from the SLES 9 Installation Server on DA1 and run **rpm –K** *package* on the package to verify the digital signature.

6. Close the terminal window.

How to Manage Software Packages with YaST

To manage software packages with YaST, you need to know the following:

- How to Manage Software Packages from the GUI Interface
- How to Install a Package from the Command Line

How to Manage Software Packages from the GUI Interface

You can install, update, and remove (uninstall) software packages on your SUSE Linux Enterprise server with YaST by doing the following:

1. From the KDE desktop, start the YaST Install and Remove Software module by doing one of the following:

   - Select the **YaST** icon, enter the root *password*, and select **OK**; then select **Software > Install and Remove Software**.

     or

   - Open a terminal window and enter **sux –** and the root *password*; then enter **yast2 sw_single**.

The dialog box shown in Figure 4-1 appears.

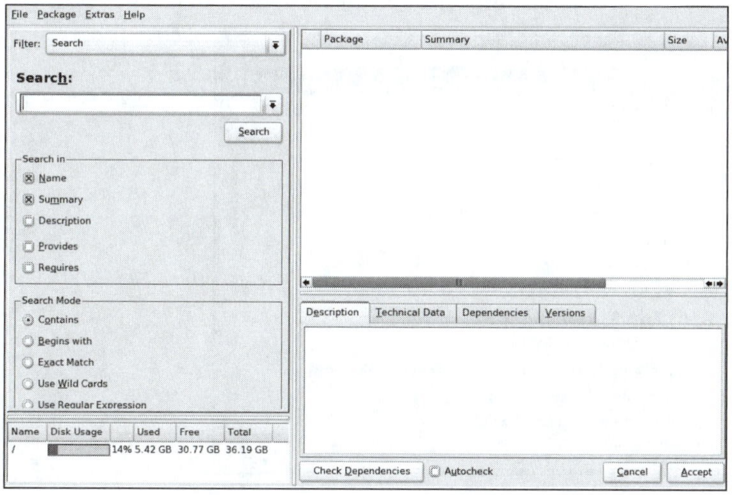

Figure 4-1

This is the same YaST package manager dialog box you use during installation to select software packages for a custom installation.

You can modify the frame sizes in the dialog box by dragging the lines separating the areas.

2. From the Filter drop-down list, select one of the following to locate the package you want to install, update, or uninstall:

- **Selections.** This filter groups the program packages according to their application purpose, such as multimedia or office applications.

- **Package Groups.** This filter provides a more technical overview of the range of packages and is suitable for users familiar with the package structure of SUSE Linux.

  The filter sorts the program packages by subjects, such as amusements, development, and hardware, in a tree structure to the left.

  To display all packages in alphabetical order, select **zzz All** in the top level.

- **Search.** The Search feature is the easiest way to find a specific package.

  Enter a search string and use the check boxes to configure where to search for this string (in the name, in the description, or in the package dependencies).

  You can even define special search patterns using wildcards and regular expressions and search the package dependencies in the Provides and Requires fields.

Once you select a package, it is displayed in the individual packages window, as shown in Figure 4-2.

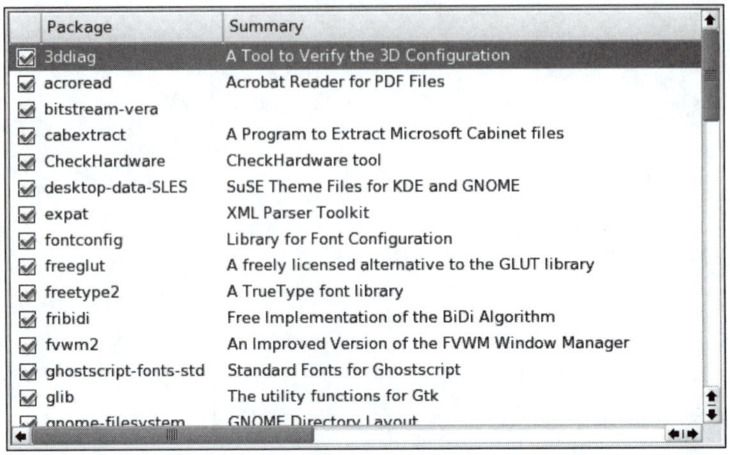

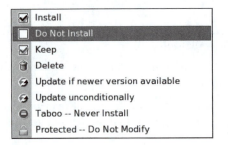

Figure 4-2

3. Right-click a *package* you want to install, update, or uninstall; then select **All in This List**.

   The menu shown in Figure 4-3 appears.

Figure 4-3

4. Select one of the following options:

   - **Install.** This package is not yet installed but will be installed.

   - **Do Not Install.** This package is not installed and will not be installed.

   - **Keep.** This package is already installed and will not be changed.

   - **Delete.** This package is already installed and will be deleted.

   - **Update if newer version available.** This package is already installed and will be replaced by the newer version on the installation medium.

- **Update unconditionally.** This package is already installed and will be replaced by the version on the installation medium, whether or not it is a new version.

- **Taboo — Never Install.** This package is not installed and will never be installed. It will be treated as if it does not exist on any of the installation media

  If a package would automatically be selected to resolve dependencies, you can prevent this by setting Taboo. However, this can cause inconsistencies that must be resolved manually (dependency check).

- **Protected — Do Not Modify.** This package is installed and should not be modified.

  Third-party packages (packages without the SUSE signature) are automatically assigned this status to prevent them from being overwritten by later versions that exist on the installation media.

  This can cause package conflicts that must be resolved manually.

5. (Optional) Locate and change the status of other packages you want to install or uninstall.

6. When you finish, from the Filter drop-down list select **Installation Summary**.

   The dialog box shown in Figure 4-4 appears.

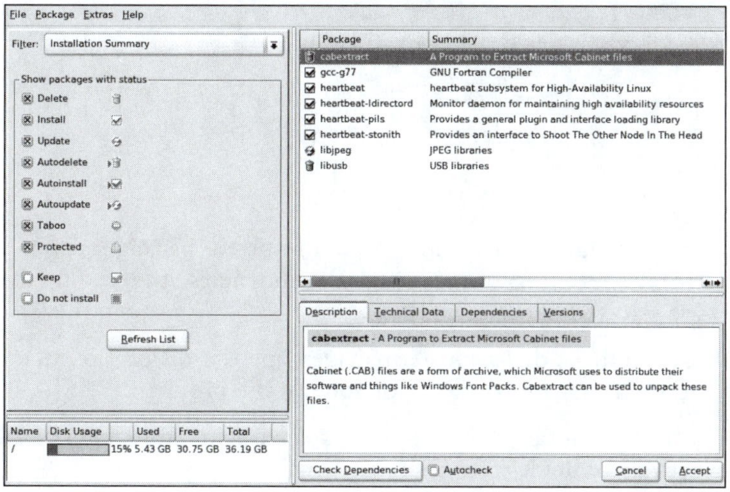

Figure 4-4

From this dialog box you can see a list of all the packages you have modified and what will happen with the packages when you select Accept.

7. (Optional) Under **Show packages with status** (on the left), display only those packages with a particular status by selecting (or deselecting) the *status*.

   Remember that only those packages displayed in the list will be processed by the package manager.

8. Display the dependencies for a particular package by selecting the package; then select Check Dependencies.

   A dialog box similar to the one shown in Figure 4–5 appears.

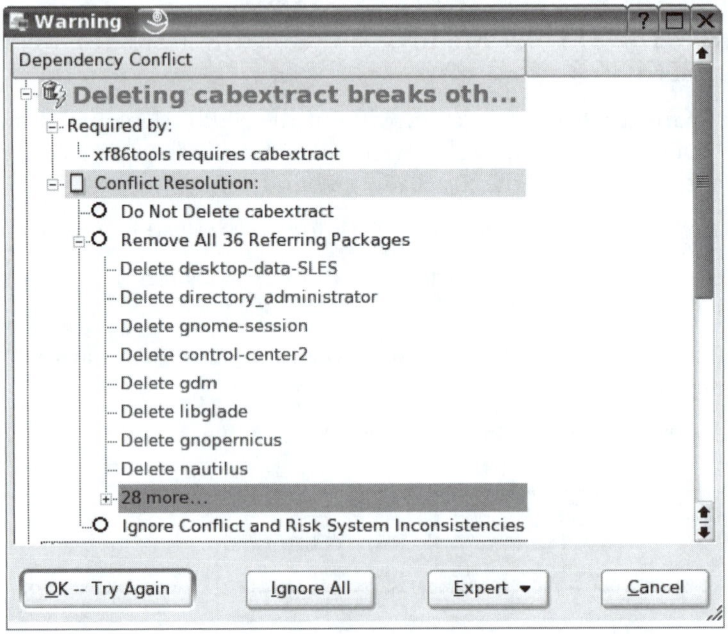

Figure 4-5

The package manger checks for any unresolved package dependencies or conflicts. In the event of unresolved dependencies, the required additional packages are selected automatically.

For package conflicts, the package manager opens a dialog box that shows the conflict and offers various options for solving the problem.

9. (Optional) If you want any change of a package status to trigger an automatic check, select **Autocheck**.

   Autocheck is a useful feature, as the consistency of the package selection is monitored permanently. However, this process consumes resources and can slow down the package manager.

   For this reason, the autocheck is not activated by default. However, a consistency check is always performed when you confirm your selection with Accept.

10. When you finish viewing the packages, start the package manager by selecting **Accept**.

    The packages are installed, updated, or uninstalled.

    You are notified when any installation medium (such as a CD) needs to be accessed.

How to Install a Package from the Command Line

One of the major functions of YaST is software installation. If you know the name of a software package, the option –i (install) is very useful.

The following is an example:

```
yast -i ethereal
```

This example installs the ethereal package plus any software package that is needed by ethereal.

Exercise 4-2   Install a Software Package with YaST

SLES 9 includes a group of graphics utilities that are not included in a full installation.

In this exercise, you install these utilities from server DA1 by doing the following:

1. Verify that the graphics utilities are not installed by selecting the **KDE menu**.

   Notice that there is no **Graphics** menu item listed.

2. From the KDE Desktop, select the **YaST** icon; then enter a password of **novell** and select **OK**.

   The YaST Control Center appears.

3. Verify that the installation source is DA1:

   a. Select **Software > Change Source of Installation**.

      A Software Source Media dialog box appears with a list of sources.

   b. Make sure that **SUSE SLES Version 9** and **SUSE CORE Version 9** sources point to 10.0.0.254 (DA1).

   c. Select the **Add** drop-down list and notice that additional installation sources are available to configure such as FTP, HTTP, and Samba.

      For example, if your installation server is not available, you can create a source that is configured for your CD-ROM drive mountpoint to install from CD.

   d. Close the dialog box by selecting **Abort**; then select **Yes**.

4. From the YaST Control Center, select **Software > Install and Remove Software**.

   A package selector dialog box appears.

5. In the Filter drop-down menu, make sure **Search** is selected.

6. In the Search field enter **graphics**; then select **Search**.

7. In the Packages list (to the right) select the following:

   ■ **kdegraphics3**

   ■ **kdegraphics3–extra**

8. Check dependencies to make sure the prerequisite packages are loaded by selecting **Check Dependencies**.

   A dialog box appears indicating that all package dependencies are OK.

9. Close the dialog box by selecting **OK**.

10. Install the packages by selecting **Accept**.

    The packages are installed and configured on your system from server DA1.

11. Verify that the graphics utilities have been installed by selecting the **KDE menu.**

    You see a new **Graphics** item on the menu.

12. From the KDE menu, select **Utilities > Desktop**.

    Graphic utilities such as KColorChooser, KColorEdit, and KSnapshot have been added to the menu.

13. Close the YaST Control Center.

14. (Optional) Find out more about the packages kdegraphics3 and kdegraphics3–extra by using the commands **rpm –qi** and **rpm –ql**.

OBJECTIVE 2   VERIFY AND UPDATE SOFTWARE LIBRARY ACCESS

In addition to checking for software package dependencies, you might also need to verify that the system is configured properly to access dynamic libraries and application uses.

Normally this is handled by the software installation, but occasionally you might need to verify software library access after installation.

For example, if an application that has been installed fails to start, try starting it from a terminal window. If the application reports that a library could not be found, then you might need to verify access to the dynamic libraries.

To verify the libraries needed for an application, you need to know the following:

■ Software Library Basics

■ How to View Shared Library Dependencies (ldd)

- How to Modify the Software Library Configuration File (/etc/ld.so.conf)
- How to Update the Library Cache (/etc/ld.so.cache)

Software Library Basics

To understand the role of software libraries in SUSE Linux, you need to know the following:

- Dynamic Software Libraries
- Static Software Libraries
- Library Naming Syntax

Dynamic Software Libraries

In a Linux environment, most programs share some code through the use of shared libraries. This provides advantages from a development and a system management standpoint.

For developers, it means their programs include only the code that is unique to the program itself, sharing functions that other programs have in common with it.

This reduces the size of the program executable, reducing the amount of disk space required for the application (an advantage for system administrators).

Unlike some other operating systems, a Linux system locates its dynamic libraries through a configuration file that points to the locations, eliminating confusion about which version of which dynamic library is used by each piece of software.

 NOTE Developers still have the ability to link everything into their executable. This can be important if the program will be used on a system that might not include all of the necessary libraries, such as an emergency rescue disk or minimal Linux installation.

Static Software Libraries

In contrast to dynamic program linking, you can link the needed libraries statically when a program is compiled.

Although static linking increases the program size, it provides independence from libraries at runtime, and is especially useful for system maintenance purposes.

Programs with statically linked libraries include sash and insmod.

Library Naming Syntax

Library filenames normally use the following syntax:

`libname.so.version`

The letters "so" indicate a shared dynamic library; the letter "a" is used for static libraries. The version indicates a major version number of the library (such as 1, 2, or 6).

For example, the library used for the ncurses screen library (version 5.3) might be named:

libncurses.so.5.3

How to View Shared Library Dependencies (*ldd*)

You can view the shared libraries required by a specific program or shared library by using the command ldd.

The following is the syntax of the command:

ldd *option filename*

For example, if you enter **ldd –v /opt/kde3/bin/suseplugger**, information similar to the following appears:

```
geeko@DA50:~> ldd -v /opt/kde3/bin/suseplugger
        linux-gate.so.1 =>  (0xffffe000)
        libhd.so.8 => /usr/lib/libhd.so.8 (0x40031000)
        libkio.so.4 => /opt/kde3/lib/libkio.so.4 (0x40158000)
        libkdeui.so.4 => /opt/kde3/lib/libkdeui.so.4 (0x40464000)
        libkdesu.so.4 => /opt/kde3/lib/libkdesu.so.4 (0x40706000)
        libkdecore.so.4 => /opt/kde3/lib/libkdecore.so.4  (0x4071f000)
        libDCOP.so.4 => /opt/kde3/lib/libDCOP.so.4 (0x4090b000)
        libresolv.so.2 => /lib/libresolv.so.2 (0x4093f000)
        libart_lgpl_2.so.2 => /usr/lib/libart_lgpl_2.so.2  (0x40951000)
        libkdefx.so.4 => /opt/kde3/lib/libkdefx.so.4 (0x40967000)
        libqt-mt.so.3 => /usr/lib/qt3/lib/libqt-mt.so.3  (0x40993000)
        libXi.so.6 => /usr/X11R6/lib/libXi.so.6 (0x4107d000)
        libXrandr.so.2 => /usr/X11R6/lib/libXrandr.so.2  (0x41085000)
        libXcursor.so.1 => /usr/X11R6/lib/libXcursor.so.1  (0x41089000)
        . . .
```

For additional information on the command ldd, from a terminal window, enter **man ldd**.

How to Modify the Software Library Configuration File (/etc/ld.so.conf)

The file /etc/ld.so.conf contains a list of paths the Linux system uses to search for libraries, as in the following:

```
/usr/X11R6/lib/Xaw95
/usr/X11R6/lib/Xaw3d
/usr/X11R6/lib
/usr/i486-linux/lib
/usr/i486-linux-libc5/lib=libc5
```

```
/usr/i486-linux-libc6/lib=libc6
/usr/i486-linuxaout/lib
/usr/i386-suse-linux/lib
/usr/local/lib
/usr/openwin/lib
/opt/kde/lib
/opt/kde2/lib
/opt/kde3/lib
/opt/gnome/lib
/opt/gnome2/lib
include /etc/ld.so.conf.d/*.conf
```

In order to modify the file /etc/ld.so.conf, you need to be authenticated as the root user. The file format for this file is simply a list of system directories containing dynamic libraries.

Typical library directories include the following: /lib/, /usr/lib/, /usr/local/lib/, and /usr/X11R6/.

As the directories /lib and /usr/lib are taken into account in all cases, they are not listed in this file. You can enter the command **/sbin/ldconfig –p** to list all libraries available in the cache that will be found by the system.

If a library is located in a directory not listed above, you can set the variable LD_LIBRARY_PATH=*path* (as in the following) to make sure that it is loaded:

export LD_LIBRARY_PATH=*path*

For a listing of variables that can be used, enter **man 8 ld.so**.

NOTE

How to Update the Library Cache (/etc/ld.so.cache)

The program ld.so or /lib/ld-linux.so.2 (this is a link to /lib/ld-2.2.3.so), referred to as the *runtime linker*, makes sure that the needed libraries are found and loaded when a program is started.

If you modify the /etc/ld.so.conf to reflect the new dynamic library paths, you need to enter the command ldconfig to update the library cache. If new libraries are installed during operation, you also need to enter ldconfig manually.

This is the same command used to update the library cache when rebooting the system.

The command sets the required links to the current shared libraries that are either located in the file /etc/ld.so.conf or in the directories /usr/lib/ and /lib/.

The library cache file is /etc/ld.so.cache and is read by the runtime linker. The cache file contains a list of all the system libraries stored in a binary format to speed the location of the libraries on the system.

If you need more information about the libraries found in each directory (such as a library is not being found when it is in one of the paths) you can run the command with the option -v to display detailed information about the libraries ldconfig has found.

The following is an example of using the option -v:

```
/lib/tls: (hwcap: 0x8000000000000000)
        libc.so.6 -> libc.so.6
        libpthread.so.0 -> libpthread.so.0
        libthread_db.so.1 -> libthread_db.so.1
        librt.so.1 -> librtkaio.so.1
        libm.so.6 -> libm.so.6
/lib/i686: (hwcap: 0x8000000000000)
        libc.so.6 -> libc.so.6
        libpthread.so.0 -> libpthread.so.0
        libm.so.6 -> libm.so.6
/usr/lib/tls: (hwcap: 0x8000000000000000)
        libdb_cxx-4.2.so -> libdb_cxx.so
        libdb-4.2.so -> libdb.so
```

Exercise 4-3 Manage Shared Libraries

In this exercise, you use some common utilities to manage the shared libraries on your SLES 9 server.

Do the following:

1. From a terminal or terminal window, su to root (**su -**) with a password of **novell**.

2. View the shared libraries:

   a. View all of the libraries linked to the SLP daemon (slpd) by entering **ldd /usr/sbin/slpd**.

   There are several libraries listed, including the file /lib/libnsl.so.1.

   b. Rename the /lib/libnsl.so.1 file to /lib/libnsl.so.1.bak by entering the following:

   mv /lib/libnsl.so.1 /lib/libnsl.so.1.bak

   c. Enter **ldd /usr/sbin/slpd** again.

   Notice that the link libnsl.so.1 indicates that the library is not found.

   By using the command ldd, you can find out if all required libraries are installed on a system for a specific program.

    d. Rename the file /lib/libnsl.so.1.bak back to /lib/libnsl.so.1 by entering the following:

    mv /lib/libnsl.so.1.bak /lib/libnsl.so.1

    e. Verify that the file can be found again by entering **ldd /usr/sbin/slpd**.

3. Rebuild the library cache:

    a. View the library cache by entering **ldconfig -p**.

    b. Rebuild the system library cache by entering **ldconfig -v**.

    The file /etc/ld.so.conf tells the Linux system where to look for libraries.

4. View the contents of the file /etc/ld.so.conf by entering **less /etc/ld.so.conf**.

5. When you finish viewing the contents, exit the display by typing **q**.

6. Close the terminal window.

OBJECTIVE 3   MANAGE SOFTWARE UPDATES WITH YaST ONLINE UPDATE SERVER (YOU)

You can use the YaST module YOU Server Configuration to create a local update server for your network. The YOU server makes current software updates available to all YOU clients in the network.

To manage software updates with a YOU server, you need to know the following:

- YOU Basics
- How to Configure a Local YOU Server
- How to Configure and Use a YOU Client

YOU Basics

This YaST feature centralizes the updating of all systems in the network. The YOU server is compared either manually or automatically with one of the update servers in the Internet authorized by SUSE.

Depending on the product, these are either the SUSE maintenance Web site (*http://sdb.suse.de/download*) or one of the mirrors of the SUSE FTP server (*ftp://ftp.suse.com/pub/suse*).

The local YOU clients start the updates via HTTP. The YOU server can be configured so that it can be recognized via SLP (Service Location Protocol) and can be recognized automatically by all clients in the network.

How to Configure a Local YOU Server

To configure a YOU server for your local network, do the following:

1. From the KDE desktop, start the YaST YOU Server Configuration module by doing one of the following:

   - Select the **YaST** icon, enter the root *password*, and select **OK**; then select **Software > YOU Server Configuration**.

   or

   - Open a terminal window and enter **sux –** and the root *password*; then enter **yast2 you_server**.

   The YaST Online Update Server Configuration dialog box appears, as shown in Figure 4-6.

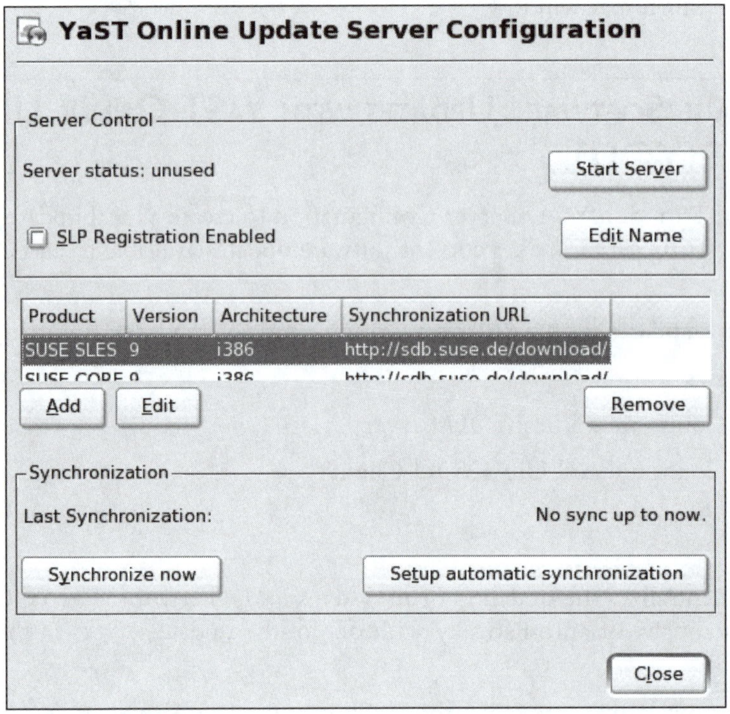

YaST Online Update Server Configuration

Server Control

Server status: unused   Start Server

☐ SLP Registration Enabled   Edit Name

Product	Version	Architecture	Synchronization URL
SUSE SLES	9	i386	http://sdb.suse.de/download/
SUSE CORE	9	i386	http://sdb.suse.de/download/

Add   Edit   Remove

Synchronization

Last Synchronization: No sync up to now.

Synchronize now   Setup automatic synchronization

                                                               Close

Figure 4-6

From this dialog box you can configure and control the YOU server.

2. Start the YOU server by selecting **Start Server**.

   The Web server (apache2) that distributes the updates to the YOU clients via HTTP is installed, configured, and started.

   The **Server status** now indicates that the server is **running**.

3. (Optional) Register the YOU server as a service on the local SLP server:

a. Name the SLP service by selecting **Edit Name**; then enter a name (such as **YOU Server**) and select **OK**.

Select **SLP Registration Enabled**.

The product list in the middle of the dialog box shows the names of all products for which the YOU server currently provides updates and indicates the URL from which the updates are derived.

The product running on the machine on which the server is set up is displayed as the default.

4. (Optional) Add or change a product in the list by doing the following:

a. Select **Add** or **Edit**.

The dialog box shown in Figure 4-7 appears.

Product Name

SUSE SLES

Version

9

Architecture

i386

Synchronization URL

http://sdb.suse.de/download/

Authentication
[X] Anonymous
User Name

Password

OK   Cancel

Figure 4-7

b. Enter or edit parameters such as the product name, hardware architecture, version, and URL of origin.

The product name, version, and architectural designation of the hardware are used internally by YOU to form the path under which the updates are searched for on the source server.

Make sure that you enter the correct information; otherwise, YOU cannot find the required updates on the source server.

c. (Conditional) In the case of update servers that require authentication (such as SUSE Maintenance Web), deselect **Anonymous**; then enter the user name and password.

d. When you finish, select **OK**.

5. Get the current patches for all products by selecting **Synchronize Now**.

When the download is complete (and the download can take a long time), the date of the synchronization process is displayed.

All updates are stored in the directory /var/lib/YaST2/you/mnt/. From here the updates are available to all associated YOU clients for installation purposes.

6. (Optional) Set up automatic synchronization by configuring a daily cron job:

a. Select **Setup automatic synchronization**; then select **Enable Automatic Update**.

The following appears:

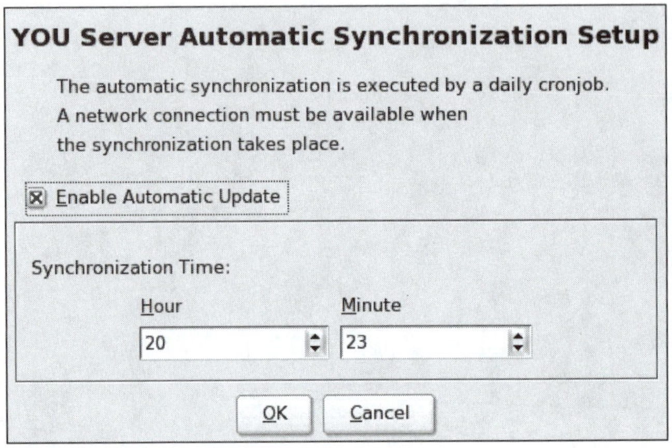

YOU Server Automatic Synchronization Setup

The automatic synchronization is executed by a daily cronjob.
A network connection must be available when
the synchronization takes place.

[x] Enable Automatic Update

Synchronization Time:

Hour	Minute
20	23

OK   Cancel

Figure 4-8

b. Enter an *hour* and *minute* when you want the synchronization to start each day.

c. Select **OK**.

7. When you finish setting up the YOU server, select **Close**.

How to Configure and Use a YOU Client

Installing software is not an absolutely static proposition. Developers find and fix bugs, security issues are resolved, and patches are created to remedy both.

To keep your SLES 9 system up-to-date and secure, you need to watch for and install relevant patches.

The solution for handling patches in SLES 9 is the YOU client. Although there is a YaST YOU module, you can also start the tool from the command line, from a script, or as a cron job.

To use YOU, you need a valid maintenance contract. As part of that contract you are issued a username and password to access the updates on SUSE servers.

To update your SLES 9 server with the YaST Online Update tool, you need to know:

- How to Install Patches from a Remote YOU Server
- How to Install Patches from a Local YOU Server
- How to Install Patches from the Command Line

How to Install Patches from a Remote YOU Server

To use YaST to update your SUSE Linux Enterprise Server system from a remote YOU server (such as the Novell SUSE Linux update server), do the following:

1. From the KDE desktop, start the YaST Online Update module by doing one of the following:

    - Select the **YaST** icon, enter the root *password*, and select **OK**; then select **Software > Online Update**.

      or

    - Open a terminal window and enter **sux –** and the root *password*; then enter **yast2 online_update**.

The Welcome to YaST Online Update dialog box appears, as shown in Figure 4-9.

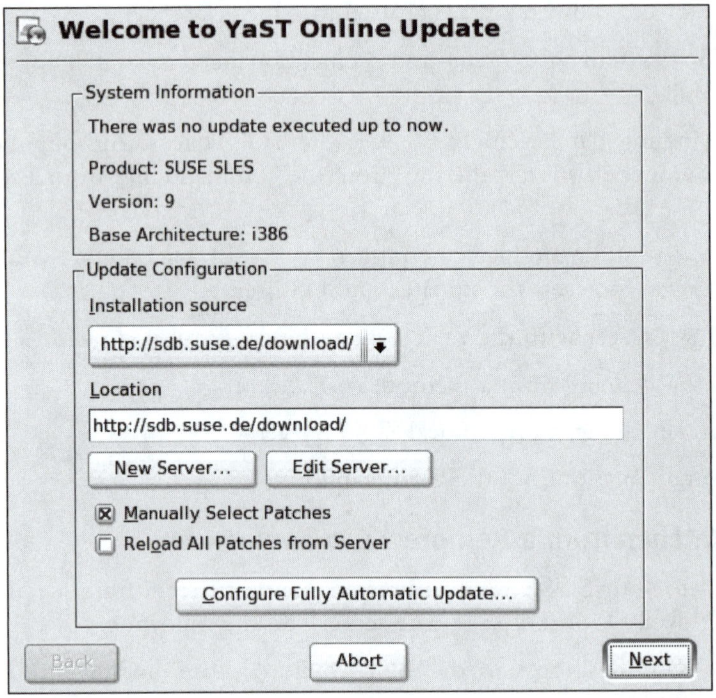

Welcome to YaST Online Update

System Information
There was no update executed up to now.

Product: SUSE SLES

Version: 9

Base Architecture: i386

Update Configuration

Installation source
http://sdb.suse.de/download/

Location
http://sdb.suse.de/download/

New Server...   Edit Server...

☒ Manually Select Patches
☐ Reload All Patches from Server

Configure Fully Automatic Update...

Back   Abort   Next

Figure 4-9

2. Accept the defaults and continue by selecting **Next**.

   The Authorization dialog box appears, as shown in Figure 4-10.

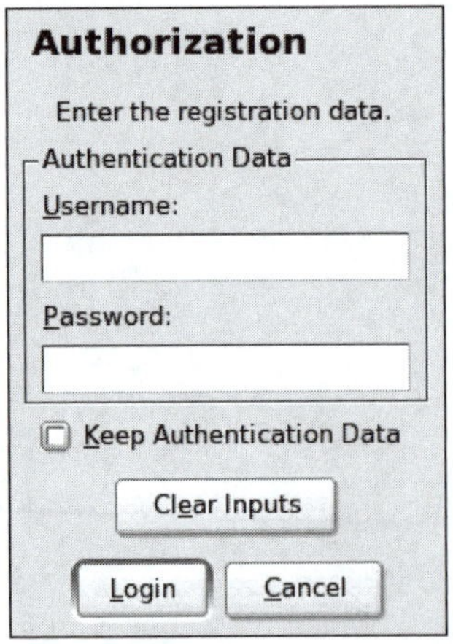

Authorization

Enter the registration data.

Authentication Data
Username:

Password:

☐ Keep Authentication Data

Clear Inputs

Login   Cancel

Figure 4-10

3. From your maintenance contract, enter your *username* and *password*; then select **Login**.

   The dialog box shown in Figure 4-11 appears.

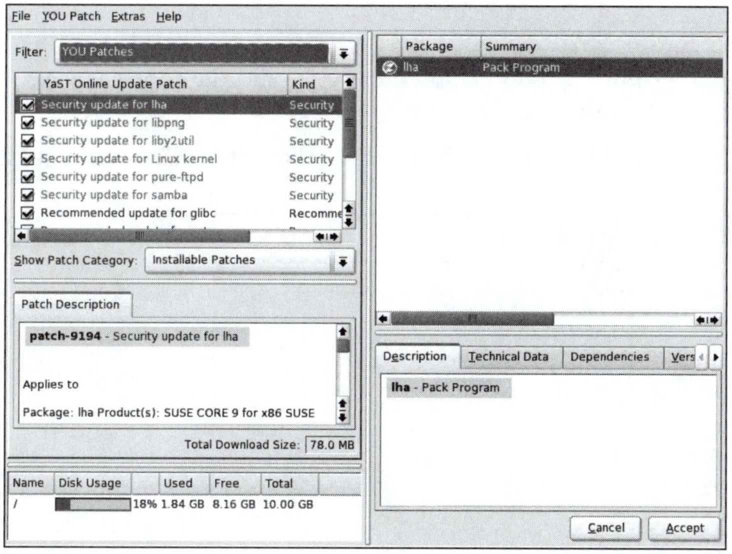

Figure 4-11

From this dialog box, you can filter the patch list view and select or deselect the patches you want to install.

4. When you finish manually selecting or deselecting patches to install, select **Accept**.

5. When the download and installation is complete, select **Remove Source Packages after Update**.

6. Update the system configuration by selecting **Finish**.

How to Install Patches from a Local YOU Server

To configure a YOU client to access the YOU server on your local network, do the following:

1. (Conditional) If you registered the YOU server as an SLP service on the local SLP server, do the following:

   a. Open the file **/etc/sysconfig/onlineupdate** in a text editor (such as Kate).

   b. Scroll down to the SLP_ENABLED variable, and activate the SLP search on your YOU client by changing the value to **yes**.

   c. Save the change.

2. From the KDE desktop, start the YaST Online Update module by doing one of the following:

- Select the **YaST** icon, enter the root *password*, and select **OK**; then select **Software > Online Update**.

  or

- Open a terminal window and enter **sux –** and the root *password*; then enter **yast2 online_update**.

The Welcome to YaST Online Update dialog box appears, as shown in Figure 4–12.

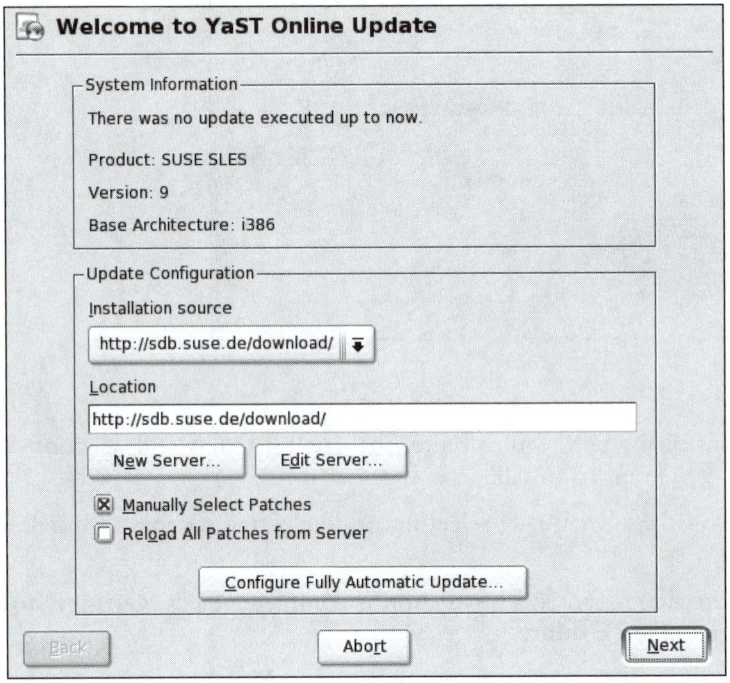

Welcome to YaST Online Update

┌─System Information──────────────────────────────────┐
│ There was no update executed up to now.   │
│   │
│ Product: SUSE SLES   │
│ Version: 9   │
│ Base Architecture: i386   │
└───┘

┌─Update Configuration────────────────────────────────┐
│ Installation source   │
│ [http://sdb.suse.de/download/ ▼]   │
│ Location   │
│ [http://sdb.suse.de/download/   ] │
│ [New Server...]   [Edit Server...]   │
│ [X] Manually Select Patches   │
│ [ ] Reload All Patches from Server   │
│   [Configure Fully Automatic Update...]   │
└───┘

[Back]   [Abort]   [Next]

Figure 4-12

From this dialog box, you can view system information about the latest update and configure your YOU client.

3. To point to the local YOU server, do one of the following:

- If you configured the YOU server as an SLP service (and completed Step 1), from the Installation source drop-down menu select the *SLP service name* (it is normally selected by default).

  or

- From the Installation source drop-down menu, select **User-defined location**, and in the Location field enter **http://*servername*/YOU** (where *servername* is the IP address or domain name of the YOU server).

NOTE

You can also edit /etc/youservers and include your YOU server in that file.

4. Select or deselect the following options:

- **Manually Select Patches.** Select this option if you want to select from a list of patches to install during the updating process.

- **Reload All Patches From Server.** Select this option if you want all patches downloaded from the YOU server, even if they are available locally on your hard drive.

5. (Optional) Set up automatic synchronization by configuring a daily cron job:

   a. Select **Configure Fully Automatic Update**; then select **Enable Automatic Update**.

      The YOU Automatic Mode Setup dialog box appears, as shown in Figure 4–13.

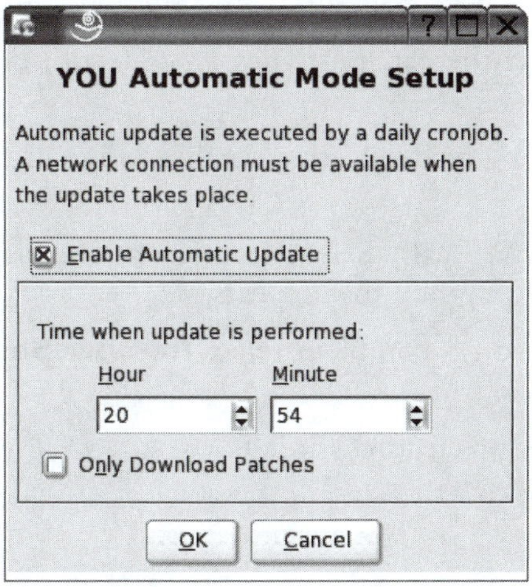

YOU Automatic Mode Setup

Automatic update is executed by a daily cronjob. A network connection must be available when the update takes place.

[X] Enable Automatic Update

Time when update is performed:

Hour	Minute
20	54

☐ Only Download Patches

OK   Cancel

Figure 4-13

b. Enter an *hour* and *minute* when you want the updating to start each day.

c. (Optional) If you only want to download patches, select **Only Download Patches**.

d. Select **OK**.

6. When you finish configuring, select **Next**.

The dialog box shown in Figure 4-14 appears.

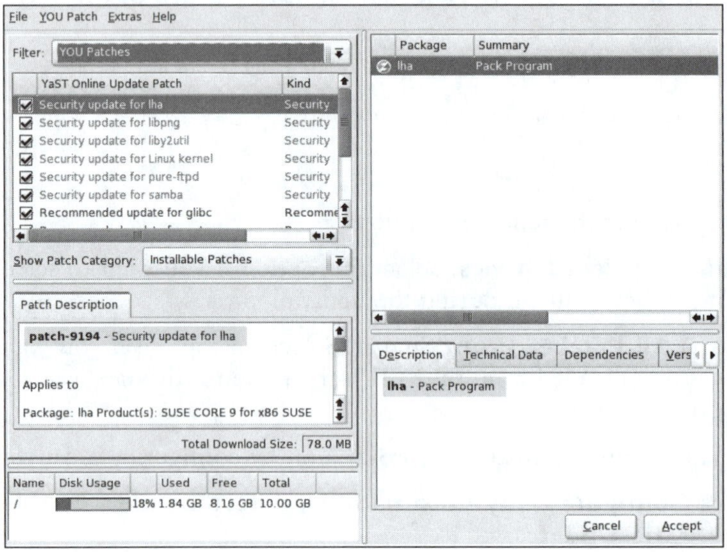

Figure 4-14

This dialog box is similar to the YaST Install and Remove Software dialog box. From this dialog box you can filter the patch list view and select or deselect the patches you want to install.

7. When you finish manually selecting or deselecting patches to install, select **Accept**.

8. (Conditional) If you selected the Manually Select Patches option, select **Install Patch** or **Skip Patch** for each dialog box that appears.

9. When the download and installation is complete, select **Remove Source Packages after Update**.

10. Update the system configuration by selecting **Finish**.

How to Install Patches from the Command Line

You can also run the YaST Online Update module from the command line. The following is the basic syntax:

online_update *parameters*

The available parameters are listed in Table 4-3.

Table 4-3

Parameter	Description
-u	Base URL of the directory tree from which the patches should be fetched.
-g	Download the patches without installing them.
-i	Install already fetched patches without downloading anything.
-k	Check for existing new patches.
-c	Show current configuration without further action.
-p	Product for which patches should be fetched.
-v	Product version for which patches should be fetched.
-a	Base architecture for which patches should be fetched.
-d	Fetch patches and simulate installation for test purposes. The system remains unchanged.
-n	No signature checking of the fetched files.
-s	Display list of available patches.
-V	Print progress messages.
-D	Debug mode for experts and for troubleshooting.

Exercise 4-4   Update SLES 9 from a Local YOU Server

As system administrator for your Digital Airlines office, you have just completed installing SUSE Linux Enterprise Server (SLES) 9 on a staging server in your lab.

As a post-installation procedure, you want to make sure you have updated your installation with the latest patches available from Novell SUSE Linux.

NOTE

The following steps are specifically designed to meet the needs of a training environment where the results of updating a server need to be controlled.

For this reason, you point to the instructor server DA1 to provide the necessary patches for updating your SLES 9 installation.

However, if you are updating SLES 9 on your own (outside of a classroom), and have a valid maintenance contract, follow the steps for installing patches from a SUSE Linux download site under *How to Install Patches From a Remote YOU Server*.

Do the following:

1. From the GUI login screen, log in as **geeko** with a password of **N0v3ll** (Uppercase **N**, zero, lowercase **v**, **3**, and two lowercase **l**'s).

2. Close any open dialog boxes or windows (such as the Welcome to SUSE Linux Enterprise Server 9 dialog box).

3. From the KDE desktop, select the **YaST** icon; then enter the root password of **novell** and select **OK**.

   The YaST Control Center appears.

4. Select **Software > Online Update**.

   The Welcome to YaST Online Update dialog box appears.

 Depending on your screen resolution, you might need to adjust the size of the dialog box to view all the text.

NOTE

5. From the Installation source drop-down list, select **User-Defined Location**.

6. In the Location field, enter **http://DA1/YOU**.

7. Continue by selecting **Next**.

   The YOU update dialog box appears with all the patches available.

   From this dialog box you can filter the patch list view and select or deselect the patches you want to install.

8. From YaST Online Update Patch list, make sure the **Optional** patches (black) are deselected.

9. Make sure all the **Security** (red) and **Recommended** (blue) patches are selected.

10. Continue by selecting **Accept**.

    One or more warning messages appear.

11. For each warning message, select **Install Patch**.

    YaST downloads and installs the patches.

12. When process is complete (or during the process), select **Remove Source Packages after Update**.

4

13. When the patches have been installed, update the system configuration by selecting **Finish**.

14. Reboot your SLES 9 server:

    a. Press **Ctrl+Alt+Del**; then select **Logout**.

       After rebooting, you are returned to the GUI login interface.

    b. Select **Menu > Shutdown**.

    c. Select **Restart computer** and enter a password of **novell**; then select **OK**.

15. After the system reboots, log back in to the KDE desktop as **geeko** with a password of **N0v3ll**.

CHAPTER SUMMARY

❏ Most Linux software is in Red Hat Package Manager (RPM) format. SLES maintains a database of all RPM-installed software in the /var/lib/rpm directory and backs up this database to the /var/adm/backup/rpmdb directory on a daily basis.

❏ You can install, remove, verify, and find information about RPM software packages using the **rpm** command in a terminal or using YaST in a desktop environment.

❏ Before installing an RPM package, you should check its digital signature with the **--checksig** option to the **rpm** command.

❏ Periodically, you should verify the contents of packages using the the **--V** option to the **rpm** command.

❏ Some programs contain static software libraries used to perform certain functions within the program. Most programs, however, use dynamic or shared software libraries that are centrally located on the file system. The runtime linker locates these libraries for programs via entries in the **/etc/ld.so.cache** file. To add shared library locations, simply add their names to the **/etc/ld.so.conf** file and run the **ldconfig** command to update the **/etc/ld.so.cache** file.

❏ You can use the Online Update tool in YaST to obtain the latest software updates for your SLES system, provided that you have a valid SUSE maintenance contract and associated login name and password.

❏ To centralize the updating of several SLES computers on your network, you can create a YOU server using YaST that contains the latest updates from Internet websites. Other computers can then use Online Update in YaST or the **online_update** command to locate your server and download the appropriate updates.

KEY TERMS

/etc/ld.so.cache — A file that contains a list of shared library locations.

/etc/ld.so.conf — A file that is used to create entries in the /etc/ld.so.cache file.

/etc/rpmrc — Contains configuration information that is written to the /usr/lib/rpm/rpmrc file.

/etc/sysconfig/backup — The configuration file that controls automatic system backups.

/etc/sysconfig/onlineupdate — The configuration file used by a YOU Client.

/etc/youservers — A text file that lists the names of YOU servers on the network.

/usr/lib/rpm/rpmrc — The main RPM configuration file.

/var/adm/backup/rpmdb — The directory that stores backup copies of the RPM database.

/var/lib/rpm — The directory that stores the RPM database.

~/.rpmrc — Contains configuration information that is written to the /usr/lib/rpm/rpmrc file.

dynamic software libraries — Files that contain software functions that are shared by several different programs. They are also called shared libraries.

ld.so — A Linux run-time linker.

ldconfig command — Updates the /etc/ld.so.cache file; it is typically run at system initialization.

ldd command — Displays the shared libraries required by a certain program.

ld–linux.so.2 — A Linux runtime linker.

LS_LIBRARY_PATH — An environment variable that may be used to add the location of a shared library.

online_update command — Used to obtain software updates from a YOU Server.

Patch RPM — An RPM package that is designed to update an existing RPM package.

Red Hat Package Manager (RPM) — A format used to distribute software packages on most Linux systems.

rpm command — Used to install, remove, and find information on RPM software packages.

runtime linker — A system component that is used to locate shared libraries when an executable program is run.

Service Location Protocol (SLP) — A protocol that may be used to locate services on other computers.

shared libraries — See **dynamic software libraries**.

static software libraries — Software functions that are contained within the software program itself after compile time and not shared with other programs.

YaST Online Update (YOU) Client — A computer that accesses software updates on a YOU Server.

YaST Online Update (YOU) Server — A computer that hosts software updates for other SUSE Linux computers.

REVIEW QUESTIONS

1. Which of the following is a valid RPM package for version 3.1.6 of the **sample** program compiled for the i686 architecture?

    a. sample–3.1.6–i686.rpm

    b. rpm.sample–i686.3.1.6

    c. sample–i686(3.1.6).rpm

    d. rpm(sample–3.1.6–i686)

2. How large can you expect an RPM database to be if the size of your /usr directory is 10 GB? _____

3. Which option to the **rpm** command may be used to uninstall an RPM package?

    a. u

    b. e

    c. r

    d. x

4. What command will display a list of all patches on your SLES computer?

    _____

5. What command will list the files in the installed **bash** RPM package?

    _____

6. Which of the following commands will install an RPM package? (Choose all that apply.)

    a. rpm –U *packagename*

    b. rpm –i *packagename*

    c. rpm –e *packagename*

    d. yast –i *packagename*

7. Which of the following is a valid Dynamic Software Library file?

    a. mylib.a.392

    b. mylib.rpm.392

    c. mylib.s.392

    d. mylib.so.392

8. You have recently added a shared library location to the /etc/ld.so.conf file. What could you do next to update your system? (Choose all that apply.)

    a. Run the **ldd** command

    b. Run the **ldconfig** command

    c. Reboot your computer

    d. Remove the /etc/ld.so.cache file

9. What file could you edit to enable the usage of SLP for finding YOU Servers?

    _____

10. What command could you use to display a list of available patches on a YOU Server?

    _____

DISCOVERY EXERCISES

Installing RPM Software Packages

Use the Internet to find an RPM package that has been compiled for use on SLES. (Some common Internet resources include *http://rpmfind.net* and *http://rpm.pbone.com*.) Next, use the appropriate command to verify that the package has not already been installed. Then download the RPM package, install it on your system, and use the appropriate commands to view the files installed and version information. When finished, use the appropriate commands to remove the software package from your system.

Installing Software Packages from Source

Although most software packages for SLES are available in RPM format, you can also download and install software from source code that is freely available on the Internet. Use the Internet to find the source code for a program that you do not have installed on your system. (The best Internet resources for source code is *http://sourceforge.net*.) Following this, download the source code (with a .tar.gz or .tgz extension) and extract it using the command **tar –zxvf** *filename*. Enter the directory that was created and run the following commands to compile and install the software on your system:

./configure

make

make install

Although these steps will work for most source code programs, additional steps may be required. Read the README and INSTALL files in the source code directory to learn more about how to compile and install the program that you have downloaded. When finished, execute your program.

Configuring a YOU Server

If you have a valid SUSE Linux maintenance contract, configure a YOU Server using YaST and download the latest updates from the Internet. Then configure another system on your network to download these updates from your YOU Server using the **online_update** command.

5

MANAGE SYSTEM INITIALIZATION

In this section, you learn how the SUSE Linux system boots and how to manage that process by setting runlevels, kernel parameters, boot loader options, and other system configurations.

- ◆ Describe the Linux Load Procedure
- ◆ Manage Runlevels
- ◆ Manage the Kernel
- ◆ Manage the GRUB Boot Loader
- ◆ Modify System Settings

Objective 1   Describe the Linux Load Procedure

The following represents the basic steps of booting a computer with a Linux system installed:

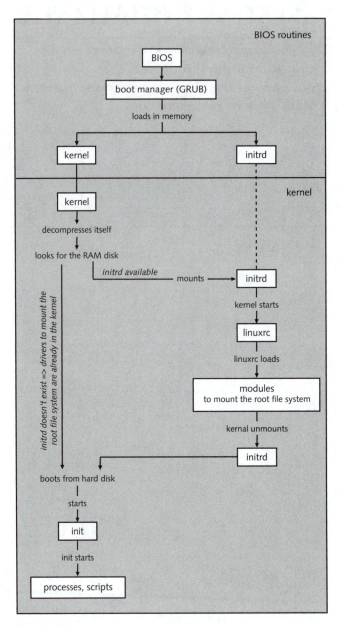

Figure 5-1

The following describes the process:

- BIOS and Boot Manager
- Kernel
- initrd and linuxrc
- init

BIOS and Boot Manager

Tasks performed by the BIOS (basic input/output system) include performing a power-on self-test, conducting the initial detection and setup of hardware, and accessing bootable devices (such as a CD or hard drive).

If the bootable device is a hard drive, BIOS also reads the MBR (Master Boot Record). Using the code in the MBR, the BIOS starts the boot manager.

The **boot manager** (such as GRUB) loads the kernel and the initrd to memory and starts the kernel.

 For details on boot managers, see *Manage the GRUB Boot Loader*.

NOTE

Kernel

The kernel uncompresses itself when you see the Uncompressing Linux... message, and then organizes and takes control of the continued booting of the system.

The kernel checks and sets the console (the BIOS registers of graphics cards and the screen output format), reads BIOS settings, and initializes basic hardware interfaces.

Next, the drivers, which are part of the kernel, probe existing hardware and initialize it accordingly.

The kernel controls the entire system, managing hardware access and allocating CPU time and memory to programs.

initrd and linuxrc

As part of the boot procedure, the kernel searches for the RAM disk, if one is available. This depends on whether the boot manager (such as GRUB) has loaded initrd.

The boot manager informs the kernel that an initrd exists and where it is located in memory. If initrd exists, it is integrated into the kernel.

If the initrd was compressed (which is typically the case), the kernel decompresses the initrd and mounts it as a temporary root file system.

A program called **linuxrc** is then started. linuxrc loads the modules required to mount the root file system.

The only requirements for the program linuxrc in the initrd are the following:

- It must have the special name linuxrc.
- It must be located in the root directory of the initrd.
- It needs to be executable by the kernel.

This means that linuxrc may be dynamically linked. In this case, the shared libraries in the directory /lib/ must be completely available in initrd.

As soon as linuxrc finishes, the initrd is unmounted and the boot process continues with the mount of the proper root file system.

 If no initrd exists, the drivers to mount the file system need to be in the kernel.

CAUTION

What is mounted as the root file system can be influenced by linuxrc; it just needs to mount the /proc file system and write the value of the real root file system in numerical form to /proc/sys/kernel/real-rootdev.

 linuxrc can also be a shell script. For this to work, a shell must exist in /bin. In other words, initrd must contain a minimal Linux system that allows the program linuxrc to be run.

NOTE

When SUSE Linux is installed, a statically linked linuxrc is used to keep initrd as small as possible. linuxrc is run with root permissions.

init

After checking the partitions and mounting the root file system, the kernel mounts from the hard drive and starts **init**, which boots the system with all its programs and configurations.

The init process is always assigned a process ID number of 1, and relies on the /etc/inittab file for configuration information on how to run the initialization process.

Once the init process starts, it begins by accessing the /etc/init.d/boot script. The /etc/init.d/boot script controls the start of services such as initializing disk quotas and mounting local file systems.

After the boot script has been completed, init starts the /etc/init.d/rc script, which uses configured runlevels to start services and daemons.

Each runlevel has its own set of services that are initiated. For example, runlevel 5 includes the X Window components that run the Linux desktop.

NOTE

For additional details on init, see *Runlevel Basics*.

5

OBJECTIVE 2   MANAGE RUNLEVELS

In this objective you continue learning about the initialization process and how to manage the runlevels associated with the services initialized during the process.

To manage runlevels, you need to understand the following:

- Runlevel Basics
- How to Change the Runlevel at Boot
- How to Manage Runlevels from the Command Line
- How to Shut Down or Halt the System
- How to Set Runlevels with YaST

Runlevel Basics

To understand the basics of runlevels, you need to know the following:

- What Runlevels Are
- init Configuration File (/etc/inittab)
- init Scripts
- Runlevel Symbolic Links
- How init Determines Which Services to Start and Stop
- Activate and Deactivate Services for a Runlevel

What Runlevels Are

In Linux, various runlevels define the state of the system. Which runlevel the system starts in when it is booted is defined in the file /etc/inittab by the entry initdefault.

The init runlevels available on SUSE Linux Enterprise Server 9 are listed in Table 5-1.

Table 5-1

Runlevel	Action
0	Shutdown Linux system
1	Single-user text mode
2	Local multiuser without remote network (such as NFS)
3	Full multiuser text mode (with networking)

Table 5-1   (continued)

Runlevel	Action
4	Not used (user-definable)
5	Full multiuser graphical mode (with an X Windows login dialog box, networking, and a desktop)
6	Reboot Linux system

You can find out the runlevel of your current environment at a command line by entering **runlevel**.

init Configuration File (/etc/inittab)

As mentioned previously, initialization of the system is done by /sbin/init, started by the kernel as the first process of the system.

The init process (or one of its child processes) starts all additional processes. This means that init controls the entire booting of the system. And because init is the last process running, it also controls the shutting down of the system, ensuring that all other processes correctly end.

NOTE

Because of this position of priority, signal 9 (SIGKILL), which you can normally use to end all processes, has no effect on init.

The basic configuration file of init is /etc/inittab. This file determines what happens on individual runlevels. Various scripts are started by init, depending on these entries. All these scripts are located in the directory /etc/init.d/.

To understand the contents of the file /etc/inittab, you need to know the following:

- inittab Syntax
- inittab Standard Entries

inittab Syntax   The following is the syntax of each line in the file /etc/inittab:

id:rl:action:process

The following describes the parameters:

- *id.* A unique name for the entry in /etc/inittab. It can be up to four characters long.

- *rl.* Refers to one or more runlevels in which this entry should be evaluated.

- *action.* Describes what init is to do.

- *process.* Is the process connected to this entry.

inittab Standard Entries The first entry in the file /etc/inittab contains the following parameters:

```
id:5:initdefault:
```

The parameter initdefault signals to the init process which level it should bring the system to. This can be overwritten at the boot prompt by entering a different level.

The following is the next entry:

```
si:bootwait:/etc/init.d/boot
```

The parameter bootwait indicates to carry out this command while booting and wait until it has finished.

The next few entries describe the actions for runlevels 0 to 6:

```
l0:0:wait:/etc/init.d/rc 0
l1:1:wait:/etc/init.d/rc 1
l2:2:wait:/etc/init.d/rc 2
l3:3:wait:/etc/init.d/rc 3
#l4:4:wait:/etc/init.d/rc 4
l5:5:wait:/etc/init.d/rc 5
l6:6:wait:/etc/init.d/rc 6
```

The parameter wait means that when the system changes to the indicated level, the appropriate command is carried out and init waits until it has been completed. The parameter also means that further entries for the level are only performed after this process is completed.

The single user mode is a special case:

```
ls:S:wait:/etc/init.d/rc S
~~:S:respawn:/sbin/sulogin
```

First, the command to initialize the level is performed. Runlevel S is used by the scripts that are run when changing to runlevel 1.

Then the command sulogin is started. sulogin is intended only for the system administrator to log in.

The parameter respawn indicates to init to wait for the end of the process, then restart it.

For those accustomed to PCs, /etc/inittab also defines the Ctrl+Alt+Del key combination for restarting:

```
ca::ctrlaltdel:/sbin/shutdown -r -t 4 now
```

The action ctrlaltdel is carried out by the init process only if these keys are pressed. If you do not want to allow this action, comment out (#) or remove the line.

The final large block of entries describe in which runlevels getty processes (login processes) are started:

```
1:2345:respawn:/sbin/mingetty --noclear tty1
2:2345:respawn:/sbin/mingetty tty2
3:2345:respawn:/sbin/mingetty tty3
4:2345:respawn:/sbin/mingetty tty4
5:2345:respawn:/sbin/mingetty tty5
6:2345:respawn:/sbin/mingetty tty6
```

The getty processes provide the login prompt and in return expect a user name as input. They are started in runlevels 2, 3, and 5.

Runlevel 4 in the above example is ignored because the line that defines the actions for the runlevel is commented out earlier in the file (**#l4:4:wait:/etc/init.d/rc 4**).

If a session ends, the processes are started again by init. If a line is disabled here, no further login is possible at the corresponding virtual console.

If /etc/inittab is damaged, the system might not boot properly. For this reason, you need to be extremely careful while editing /etc/inittab and always keep a backup of an intact version.

To repair damage, try entering **init=/bin/bash** after the kernel name at the boot prompt to boot directly into a shell. After that, replace /etc/inittab with your backup version using the command cp.

init Scripts

All the scripts used by init to start and stop services are located in the directory /etc/init.d/, as shown in Figure 5-2.

```
DA50:/etc/init.d # ls -l
total 955
drwxr-xr-x  11 root root  4896 Jul  9 08:05 .
drwxr-xr-x  92 root root  8736 Aug  6 13:05 ..
-rw-r--r--   1 root root  7000 Jun 30 12:37 README
-rwxr-xr-x   1 root root  1640 Jun 30 12:24 SuSEfirewall2_final
-rwxr-xr-x   1 root root  1628 Jun 30 12:24 SuSEfirewall2_init
-rwxr-xr-x   1 root root  1856 Jun 30 12:24 SuSEfirewall2_setup
-rwxr-xr-x   1 root root  3702 Jun 30 12:07 acct
-rwxr--r--   1 root root  4153 Jun 30 12:23 acpid
-rwxr-xr-x   1 root root  2151 Jun 30 13:04 adsl
-rwxr-xr-x   1 root root  6537 Jun 30 16:26 alsasound
-rwxr-xr-x   1 root root  2391 Jun 30 16:40 amavis
-rwxr--r--   1 root root  8630 Jun 30 16:40 apache2
-rwxr-xr-x   1 root root  3638 Jun 30 15:17 argus
-rwxr-xr-x   1 root root  3849 Jun 30 16:22 arpwatch
-rwxr-xr-x   1 root root  2792 Jun 30 13:30 atalk
-rwxr-xr-x   1 root root  3689 Jun 30 16:23 atd
-rwxr--r--   1 root root  8946 Jun 30 16:10 autofs
-rwxr-xr-x   1 root root  2954 May 26 13:22 autoyast
-rwxr-xr-x   1 root root  2694 Jun 30 12:08 avgate
-rwxr-xr-x   1 root root  3523 Jun 30 13:43 bgpd
-rwxr-xr-x   1 root root  7096 Mar 26 07:07 boot
-rwxr-xr-x   1 root root  2494 Mar  8 03:44 boot.clock
```

Figure 5-2

These scripts can be called up in the following ways:

- Directly by init when you boot the system, when the system is shut down, when you stop the system with **Ctrl+Alt+Del**, or when there is a power failure.

- Indirectly by init when you change the runlevel. In this case, it is the script /etc/init.d/rc that runs the necessary scripts in the correct order during the runlevel change.

- Directly by the /etc/init.d/ script start or stop commands.

  You can also enter **rcscript start** or **stop** if corresponding links are set in /sbin/ or /usr/sbin/.

Each of the scripts in /etc/init.d is run both as a start script and a stop script. For this reason, they must understand the parameters described in Table 5-2.

Table 5-2

Parameter	Description
start	Starts a service that is not running.
restart	Stops a running service and restarts it.
stop	Stops a running service.
reload	Rereads the configuration of the service without stopping and restarting the service itself.

Table 5-2 (continued)

Parameter	Description
force-reload	Reloads the configuration if the service supports this. Otherwise, it does the same thing as restart.
status	Displays the current status of the service.

The following describes some of the more important scripts stored in /etc/init.d:

- **boot.** This script is started directly by init when the system starts. It is run once and once only. It evaluates the directory /etc/init.d/boot.d/ and starts all the scripts linked to filenames with an "S" at the beginning of their names (see Runlevel Symbolic Links).

  These scripts perform the following tasks:

  - Starts the kernel daemon, which takes over the automatic loading of kernel modules

  - Checks the file systems

  - Deletes unnecessary files in /var/lock/

  - Sets the system time

  - Configures PnP hardware with the isapnp tools

    System extensions are activated from the script /etc/init.d/boot.local (you can add your own system extensions to this script)

- **boot.local.** This script includes additional commands to execute at boot before changing into a runlevel. It can be compared to AUTOEXEC.BAT on a DOS system.

- **boot.setup.** This script is run when changing from single user mode to any other runlevel and is responsible for a number of basic settings, such as the keyboard layout and initialization of the virtual consoles.

- **halt.** This script is run if runlevel 0 or 6 is started. It is called up either with the command halt (the system is completely shut down) or with the command reboot (the system is shut down and then rebooted).

- **rc.** This script is responsible for the correct change from one runlevel to another. It runs the stop scripts for the current runlevel, and then it runs the start scripts for the new one.

To create your own scripts, you can use the file /etc/init.d/skeleton as a template.

Runlevel Symbolic Links

For each runlevel, there is a corresponding subdirectory in /etc/init.d/. For runlevel 1, it is /etc/init.d/rc1.d/; for runlevel 2, it is /etc/init.d/rc2.d/; and so on.

When you view the files in a directory such as /etc/init.d/rc3.d/, you see two kinds of files—those that start with a "K" and those that start with an "S"—as shown in Figure 5-3.

K10sshd	3.6 KB	Shell Script	2003-03-18 06:15	rwxr-xr-x	root	root	../sshd
K12nfs	2.5 KB	Shell Script	2004-06-21 09:10	rwxr-xr-x	root	root	../nfs
K12nfsboot	1.1 KB	Shell Script	2004-06-30 12:59	rwx------	root	root	../nfsboot
K14portmap	3.5 KB	Shell Script	2004-06-30 12:49	rwxr--r--	root	root	../portmap
K14resmgr	3.4 KB	Shell Script	2004-06-30 11:56	rwxr-xr-x	root	root	../resmgr
K14smbfs	4.5 KB	Shell Script	2004-06-01 08:53	rwxr-xr-x	root	root	../smbfs
K14splash_early	617 B	Shell Script	2004-06-30 12:45	rwxr-xr-x	root	root	../splash_early
K16syslog	2.8 KB	Shell Script	2004-06-30 12:24	rwxr-xr--	root	root	../syslog
K17network	15.9 KB	Shell Script	2004-07-01 06:36	rwxr-xr-x	root	root	../network
K20coldplug	2.9 KB	Shell Script	2004-06-30 12:03	rwxr-xr-x	root	root	../coldplug
K21hotplug	2.0 KB	Shell Script	2004-06-30 12:03	rwxr-xr-x	root	root	../hotplug
K21isdn	5.4 KB	Shell Script	2004-05-03 10:24	rwxr-xr-x	root	root	../isdn
K21random	1.7 KB	Shell Script	2003-09-01 05:11	rwxr-xr-x	root	root	../random
S01hotplug	2.0 KB	Shell Script	2004-06-30 12:03	rwxr-xr-x	root	root	../hotplug
S01isdn	5.4 KB	Shell Script	2004-05-03 10:24	rwxr-xr-x	root	root	../isdn
S01random	1.7 KB	Shell Script	2003-09-01 05:11	rwxr-xr-x	root	root	../random
S02coldplug	2.9 KB	Shell Script	2004-06-30 12:03	rwxr-xr-x	root	root	../coldplug
S05network	15.9 KB	Shell Script	2004-07-01 06:36	rwxr-xr-x	root	root	../network
S06syslog	2.8 KB	Shell Script	2004-06-30 12:24	rwxr-xr--	root	root	../syslog
S08portmap	3.5 KB	Shell Script	2004-06-30 12:49	rwxr--r--	root	root	../portmap
S08resmgr	3.4 KB	Shell Script	2004-06-30 11:56	rwxr-xr-x	root	root	../resmgr
S08smbfs	4.5 KB	Shell Script	2004-06-01 08:53	rwxr-xr-x	root	root	../smbfs
S08splash_early	617 B	Shell Script	2004-06-30 12:45	rwxr-xr-x	root	root	../splash_early

Figure 5-3

The first letter is always followed by two digits and the name of a service. Whether a service is started in a specific runlevel depends on whether there are **S***xxservice* and **K***xxservice* files in the **/etc/init.d/rc***x***.d/** directory.

Entering **ls –l** in an /etc/init.d/rc*x*.d/ directory indicates that these files are actually symbolic links pointing to service scripts in /etc/ini.d/, as shown in Figure 5-4.

```
DA50:~ # cd /etc/init.d/rc3.d
DA50:/etc/init.d/rc3.d # ls -l
total 6
drwxr-xr-x   2 root root 1864 Aug  4 13:35 .
drwxr-xr-x  11 root root 4896 Jul  9 08:05 ..
lrwxrwxrwx   1 root root   14 Jul  9 07:59 K02splash_late -> ../splash_
late
lrwxrwxrwx   1 root root    7 Jul  9 07:59 K03cron -> ../cron
lrwxrwxrwx   1 root root    9 Jul 20 18:27 K03xinetd -> ../xinetd
lrwxrwxrwx   1 root root   10 Aug  4 13:35 K04apache2 -> ../apache2
lrwxrwxrwx   1 root root   12 Jul 21 13:00 K05nfsserver -> ../nfsserver
lrwxrwxrwx   1 root root   10 Jul  9 07:59 K05postfix -> ../postfix
lrwxrwxrwx   1 root root    7 Jul  9 07:59 K06nscd -> ../nscd
lrwxrwxrwx   1 root root    7 Jul  9 07:59 K07cups -> ../cups
lrwxrwxrwx   1 root root    9 Jul  9 07:59 K08hwscan -> ../hwscan
lrwxrwxrwx   1 root root    7 Jul  9 07:59 K08slpd -> ../slpd
lrwxrwxrwx   1 root root   13 Jul  9 07:51 K09powersaved -> ../powersav
ed
lrwxrwxrwx   1 root root    9 Jul  9 07:51 K09splash -> ../splash
lrwxrwxrwx   1 root root   12 Jul  9 08:26 K10alsasound -> ../alsasound
lrwxrwxrwx   1 root root    8 Jul  9 07:51 K10fbset -> ../fbset
lrwxrwxrwx   1 root root   14 Aug  3 16:45 K10powertweakd -> ../powertw
eakd
lrwxrwxrwx   1 root root   17 Jul  9 07:58 K10running-kernel -> ../runn
```

Figure 5-4

Some services point to the same script. For example, if you enter

ls –l *network in the /etc/init.d/rc3.d/ directory, you see that two network services both point to the script /etc/init.d/network, as shown in Figure 5-5.

```
DA50:/etc/init.d/rc3.d # ls -l *network
lrwxrwxrwx  1 root root 10 Jul  9 08:20 K17network -> ../network
lrwxrwxrwx  1 root root 10 Jul  9 08:20 S05network -> ../network
DA50:/etc/init.d/rc3.d # █
```

Figure 5-5

By using symbolic links in subdirectories, only the script in /etc/init.d/ needs to be modified.

 Sometimes K*xx* links are referred to as *kill scripts*, while S*xx* links are referred to as *start scripts*. In fact, there are no separate scripts for starting and stopping services—just the parameters stop and start.

How init Determines Which Services to Start and Stop

You already know that a service is started with the parameter start, and stopped with the parameter stop. The same parameters are also used when changing from one runlevel to another.

The script /etc/init.d/rc examines the directories /etc/init.d/rccurrentrl.d/ and /etc/init.d/rcnewrl.d/ and determines what to do. The following are three possibilities:

- There is a **K*xx*** link for a certain service in /etc/init.d/rccurrentrl.d/, and there is an **S*xx*** link in /etc/init.d/rcnewrl.d/ for the same service.

  In this case, the service is neither started nor stopped; the corresponding script in /etc/init.d/ is not called at all.

- There is a **K*xx*** link for a certain service in /etc/init.d/rccurrentrl.d/, and there is no corresponding **S*xx*** link in /etc/init.d/rcnewrl.d/.

  In this case, the script in /etc/init.d/service is called with the parameter stop, and the service is stopped.

- There is an **S*xx*** link in /etc/init.d/rcnewrl.d/ and there is no corresponding **K*xx*** link for the service in /etc/init.d/rccurrentrl.d/.

  In this case, the script in /etc/init.d/service is called with the parameter start, and the service is started.

The number after the K or S determines the sequence in which the scripts are called.

For example, script K10serviceA is called before script K20serviceB, which means that serviceA is shut down before serviceB.

Script S15serviceC is called before S23serviceD, which means that serviceC starts before serviceD. This is important if serviceD depends on a running serviceC.

For example, the following happens when you change from runlevel 3 to runlevel 5:

1. You tell init to change to a different runlevel by entering (as root) **init 5**.

2. init checks its configuration file (/etc/inittab) and determines it should start /etc/init.d/rc with the new runlevel (**5**) as a parameter.

3. rc calls the stop scripts (**K**_xx_) of the current runlevel for those services for which there is no start script (**S**_xx_) in the new runlevel.

4. The start scripts in the new runlevel for those services for which there was no kill script in the old runlevel are launched.

When changing to the same runlevel as the current runlevel, init only checks /etc/inittab for changes and starts the appropriate steps (such as starting a getty on another interface).

Activate and Deactivate Services for a Runlevel

The services in a runlevel can be activated and deactivated from the command line with the command insserv or by using YaST.

Although you could create symbolic links in the runlevel subdirectories yourself to modify services that are stopped and started, an easier way is to edit the header of a script.

The INIT INFO block at the beginning of the script determines in which runlevel the service that the script controls should start or stop:

```
### BEGIN INIT INFO
# Provides: syslog
# Required-Start: network
# Required-Stop: network
# Default-Start: 2 3 5
# Default-Stop:
# Description: Start the system logging daemons
### END INIT INFO
```

The INIT INFO block is used by the program insserv to determine in which runlevel subdirectories links need to be placed and what numbers need to be put after K and S.

NOTE

For details on the program insserv, enter **man 8 insserv**.

The entry Default-Start determines in which runlevel directories links are to be placed. The entry Required-Start determines which services have to be started before the one being considered.

After editing the INIT INFO block, enter **insserv** to create the needed links and renumber the existing ones as needed.

To remove all links for a service (disabling the service), stop the service (if it is running) by entering **/etc/init.d/***service* **stop**, and then enter **insserv -r** *service*.

You can also use the YaST runlevel editor to set these links. We recommend that you choose one method or the other. Switching between methods can lead to errors.

How to Change the Runlevel at Boot

The standard runlevel is 3 or 5. However, you can boot to another runlevel. By default, at system start-up, GRUB offers the following three choices:

- Linux
- Floppy
- Failsafe

When you select one of these entries, additional options are displayed in the field boot options (you might need to press additional keystrokes to display the options).

For the entry Linux, this is the option starting root=/dev/hd, which tells the kernel the location of the root partition of the system.

In addition, the option vga=, with the resolution for the framebuffer device, is specified in most cases.

At this point, you can indicate the runlevel at which you want the system to start. This parameter is passed to init.

The following is an example entry at boot options:

```
root=/dev/hda4 vga=791 1
```

As root partition, /dev/hda4 is transmitted to the kernel. The framebuffer is configured, and the system boots to runlevel 1 (single-user mode for administration), with a resolution for the framebuffer set at 791.

How to Manage Runlevels from the Command Line

You can change to another runlevel after the system is running by using the command init. For example, you can change to runlevel 1 from a command line by entering **init 1**.

In the same way, you can change back to the standard runlevel where all programs needed for operation are run and where individual users can log in to the system.

For example, you can return to a full GUI desktop and network interface (runlevel 5) by entering **init 5**.

If the partition /usr of a system is mounted through NFS, you should not use runlevel 2 because NFS file systems are not available in this runlevel.

CAUTION

You stop the system by entering **init 0**; you restart the system by entering **init 6**.

Runlevels are useful if you encounter problems caused by a particular service (X or network) in a higher runlevel. In this case, you can switch the system to a lower runlevel to repair the service.

Many servers operate without a graphical user interface and must be booted in a runlevel without X Windows (such as runlevel 3).

If the graphical user interface freezes at any time, press **Ctrl+Alt+Backspace** to restart the X Window system.

You can also restart the X Window system by switching to a text console with **Ctrl+Alt+F1**, logging in as root, and switching to runlevel 3 with the command **init 3**.

This shuts down your X Window system, leaving you with a text console. To restart the graphical system, enter **init 5**.

Sometimes a remote login is required to enter **init 3**.

NOTE

How to Shut Down or Halt the System

Like most modern operating systems, Linux reacts sensitively to being switched off without warning. If this happens, the file systems need to be checked and corrected before the system can be used again.

For this reason, the system should always be shut down properly. With the appropriate hardware, Linux can also switch off the machine as the last stage of shutting down.

Although you can halt the system by changing to runlevel 0 and restarting in runlevel 6, Table 5-3 lists some other useful commands for properly shutting down the system or restarting it.

Table 5-3

Command	Description
halt	This command ensures an immediate, controlled system halt. All processes are stopped, and the system no longer reacts to any input.
	You can now switch off the computer if it is not configured to switch off automatically.

Table 5-3 (continued)

Command	Description
poweroff	This command has the same effect as halt except that the machine is switched off automatically (if the hardware allows it).
reboot	This command reboots the system.
shutdown -h *time*	This command shuts down the system after the specified *time*: +m (number of minutes from now), hh:mm (time in hours:minutes, when Linux should shut down), and now (system is stopped immediately). If you use the option -r instead of -h, the system is rebooted (runlevel 6). Without options, it changes to runlevel 1 (single-user mode).

The command shutdown controls the shutdown of the system in a special way, compared with the other stop commands. The command informs all users that the system will be shut down and does not allow other users to log in before it shuts down.

The command shutdown can also be supplied with a warning message, such as the following:

```
shutdown +5 The new hard drive has arrived
```

If a shutdown planned for a later time should not be carried out after all, you can revoke the shutdown by entering **shutdown -c**.

How to Set Runlevels with YaST

To set runlevels with YaST, do the following:

1. From the KDE desktop, start the YaST Runlevel Editor module by doing one of the following:

   - Select the **YaST** icon, enter the root *password*, and select **OK**; then select **System > Runlevel Editor**.

     or

   - Open a terminal window and enter **sux -** and the root *password*; then enter **yast2 runlevel**.

The dialog box shown in Figure 5-6 appears.

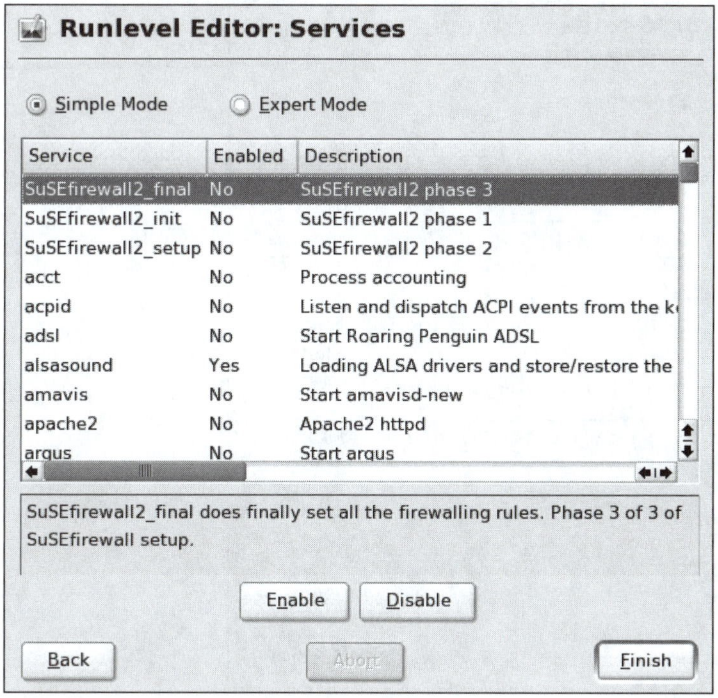

Runlevel Editor: Services

○ Simple Mode   ○ Expert Mode

Service	Enabled	Description
SuSEfirewall2_final	No	SuSEfirewall2 phase 3
SuSEfirewall2_init	No	SuSEfirewall2 phase 1
SuSEfirewall2_setup	No	SuSEfirewall2 phase 2
acct	No	Process accounting
acpid	No	Listen and dispatch ACPI events from the k
adsl	No	Start Roaring Penguin ADSL
alsasound	Yes	Loading ALSA drivers and store/restore the
amavis	No	Start amavisd-new
apache2	No	Apache2 httpd
argus	No	Start argus

SuSEfirewall2_final does finally set all the firewalling rules. Phase 3 of 3 of SuSEfirewall setup.

Enable   Disable

Back   Abort   Finish

Figure 5-6

From this dialog box, you can select from the following modes:

- **Simple Mode.** This mode displays a list of all available services and the current status of each service.

  You can select a service, and then select **Enable** or **Disable**.

  Selecting Enable starts the service—and other services it depends on—and enables them to start at system boot time. Selecting Disable stops dependent services and the service itself, and disables their start at system boot time.

- **Expert Mode.** This mode gives you control over the runlevels in which a service is started or stopped, and lets you change the default runlevel.

2. Switch to the Expert mode by selecting **Expert Mode**.

The dialog box shown in Figure 5-7 appears.

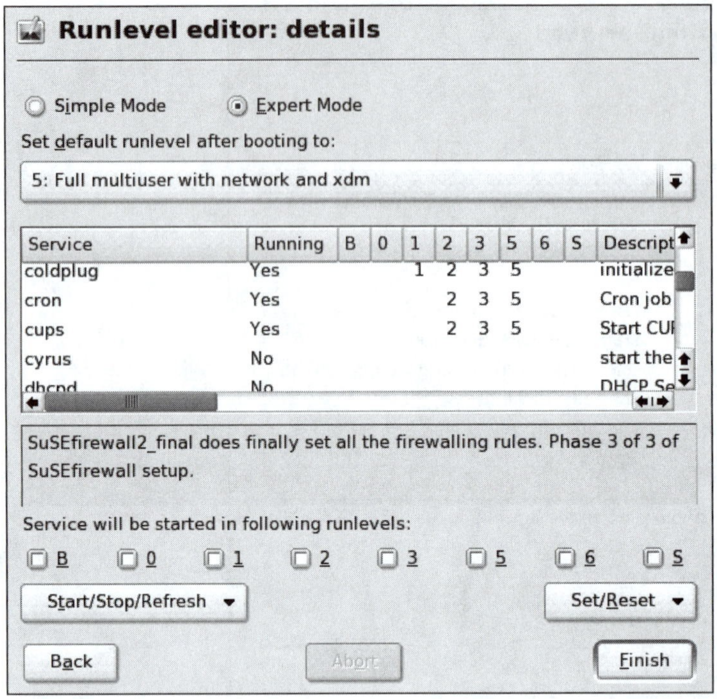

Runlevel editor: details

◯ Simple Mode   ⦿ Expert Mode

Set default runlevel after booting to:

5: Full multiuser with network and xdm

Service	Running	B	0	1	2	3	5	6	S	Descript
coldplug	Yes			1	2	3	5			initialize
cron	Yes				2	3	5			Cron job
cups	Yes				2	3	5			Start CUP
cyrus	No									start the
dhcpd	No									DHCP Se

SuSEfirewall2_final does finally set all the firewalling rules. Phase 3 of 3 of SuSEfirewall setup.

Service will be started in following runlevels:

☐ B   ☐ 0   ☐ 1   ☐ 2   ☐ 3   ☐ 5   ☐ 6   ☐ S

[Start/Stop/Refresh ▾]   [Set/Reset ▾]

[Back]   [Abort]   [Finish]

Figure 5-7

In this mode, the dialog box displays the current default runlevel at the top.

3. (Optional) From the default runlevel drop-down list, select a new ***default runlevel***.

Normally, the default runlevel of a SUSE Linux system is runlevel 5 (full multiuser with network and xdm). A suitable alternative might be runlevel 3 (full multiuser with network).

Changes to the default runlevel take effect the next time you boot your computer.

4. From the list of services, select a **service**; then, from the options below the list, select the ***runlevels*** you want associated with the service.

The list includes the services and daemons available, indicates whether they are currently enabled on your system, and lists the runlevels currently assigned.

Runlevel 4 is initially undefined to allow creation of a custom runlevel.

5. (Optional) If you want a service activated after editing the runlevels, from the drop-down list select **Start now**, **Stop now**, or **Refresh status**.

   You can use Refresh status to check the current status (if this has not been done automatically).

6. From the Set/Reset drop-down list, select one of the following:

   ▪ **Enable the service:** activates the service in the standard runlevels.

   ▪ **Disable the service:** deactivates the service.

   ▪ **Enable all services:** Activates all services in their standard runlevels.

7. When you finish configuring the runlevels, save the configuration by selecting **Finish**.

Remember that faulty runlevel settings can make a system unusable. Before applying your changes, make absolutely sure you know about the impact of the changes.

Exercise 5-1   Manage Run Levels

Do the following:

1. From the KDE desktop, open a terminal window; then su to root (**su –**) with a password of **novell**.

2. Check the previous and current runlevels by entering **runlevel**.

   List the runlevels in Table 5-4.

Table 5-4

Previous	Current

Notice that the previous runlevel is listed as N, which means that there was no previous runlevel set.

3. Change to runlevel 3 by entering **telinit 3**.

   The KDE desktop (X Windows) is terminated, and you are left at a terminal login prompt.

4. Log in as **root** with a password of **novell**.

5. Check the previous and current runlevels by entering **runlevel**.

   List the runlevels in Table 5-5.

Table 5-5

Previous	Current

6. Switch to runlevel 5 by entering **init 5**.

   The GUI login screen appears.

7. Log in as **geeko** with a password of **N0v3ll**.

Objective 3   Manage the Kernel

The primary function of the Linux kernel is to manage the system hardware resources, making them available to various system processes.

To manage the kernel, you need to understand the following:

- Kernel Module Basics
- How to Find Hardware Driver Information
- How to Manage Modules from the Command Line
- modprobe Configuration File (/etc/modprobe.conf)
- Kernel Module Loader (kmod)

NOTE

For the latest kernel documentation, see /usr/src/linux/Documentation.

Kernel Module Basics

The kernel that is installed in the directory /boot/ is configured for a wide range of hardware. It is not necessary to compile a custom kernel, unless you want to test experimental features and drivers.

Drivers and features of the Linux kernel can either be compiled into the kernel or be loaded as kernel modules. These modules can be loaded later, while the system is running, without having to reboot the computer.

This is especially true of kernel modules that are not required to boot the system. By loading them as components after the system boots, the kernel can be kept relatively small.

The kernel modules are located in the directory

/lib/modules/***version***/kernel/.

For example, the modules for the 2.6 kernel can be found in the following directory:

/lib/modules/2.6.5-7.79-default/kernel/

The following are files and directories related to the kernel:

- **/boot/initrd.** A link to the initrd module.
- **/boot/vmlinuz.** A link to the kernel of the SUSE Linux Enterprise Server.
- **/proc/sys/kernel/.** The directory with information about the kernel.
- **/proc/version.** Features the version of the current kernel.
- **/usr/src/linux/.** The directory containing the source files of the kernel.

How to Find Hardware Driver Information

You can use the command *hwinfo* to detect the hardware of your system and select the drivers needed to run this hardware.

For a short introduction to this command, enter **hwinfo --help**. For specific hardware information, enter **hwinfo --hardware_type** (such as **hwinfo --scsi**).

All this information is also available in YaST in the Hardware Information module (**Hardware > Hardware Information**).

Exercise 5-2   View Information about the Hardware System

In this exercise, you do the following:

- Part I: View General Information about the Hardware System
- Part II: View Information about Specific Hardware

Part I: View General Information about the Hardware System

Do the following:

1. View hardware information from the command line:

    a. Open a terminal window and su to root (**su -**) with a password of **novell**.

    b. View the devices used on your Linux system listed in /proc/devices by entering **less /proc/devices**.

    c. Return to the command line by typing **q**.

    d. View the system devices on your SLES 9 server by entering **hwinfo | less**.

    It takes a few moments for the information to be gathered and displayed.

    e. Scroll through the information by pressing the **Spacebar**.

    f. Exit the information screen by typing **q**.

2. View and save hardware information from YaST:

   a. From the KDE desktop, select the **YaST** icon; then enter a password of **novell** and select **OK**.

      The YaST Control Center appears.

   b. Select **Hardware > Hardware Information**.

      After a few moments of gathering information, the Hardware info dialog box appears.

   c. Try expanding several entries (such as **Display** or **Network Card**) to view information about your server.

   d. Save the hardware information by selecting **Save to File**; then save the information as **server_hwinfo** in the directory **/files/private**.

   e. When you finish, close the Hardware info dialog box by selecting **Close**; then close the YaST Control Center.

   f. Open the File Manager in superuser mode (root) by pressing **Alt+F2** and entering **kdesu konqueror**; then select **Run**.

   g. Enter a password of **novell**; then select **OK**.

   h. In the Location field, view the file server_hwinfo by entering **/files/private/server_hwinfo**.

   i. Scroll through the file and note the available information.

   j. Close the Konqueror window.

3. View and configure hardware from suseplugger:

   a. From the KDE desktop, view hardware information using suseplugger by selecting the **SUSE Hardware Tool** icon in the system tray (at the bottom right of the screen).

      The suseplugger dialog box appears.

   b. Expand the **Network Controller** hardware category.

   c. Select a *network card* under the category.

      Notice that the Configure and Details buttons become active.

   d. Select **Configure**; then enter a password of **novell** and select **OK**.

      The YaST Network cards configuration dialog box appears.

      By using suseplugger, you can directly access the YaST module you need to configure the hardware you selected.

   e. Close the dialog box by selecting **Abort**; then select **Yes**.

   f. From the suseplugger dialog box, select **Details**.

      A dialog box appears with three tabs: General, Resources, and Driver.

g. Select each tab to view the information.

h. When you finish, close the dialog box by selecting **OK**.

i. Close the suseplugger dialog box by selecting **Close**.

NOTE

You can also start suseplugger from a command line by logging in as root (**sux -**), and then entering **suseplugger**.

5

Part II: View Information about Specific Hardware

Do the following:

1. View CPU information from the command line:

   a. From the terminal window, change to the directory /proc/ by entering **cd /proc**.

   b. View the contents of the file /proc/cpuinfo by entering

   cat cpuinfo.

   c. Monitor only CPU utilization at 5 second intervals 10 times by entering **iostat –c –t 5 10**.

   d. When you finish viewing the information, exit the display by pressing **Ctrl+C**.

   e. View CPU utilization every second by entering **top –d 1**.

   Note the headings at the top of the list (primarily the %CPU column).

   f. Try sorting the processes by % Memory (type **F**, then enter **n**), by % CPU (type **F**, then enter **k**), and by user (type **F**, then enter **e**).

   g. When you finish, exit the top display by typing **q**.

   h. View the CPU utilization for each process by entering

   ps –aux | less.

   i. Page through the processes by pressing the **Spacebar**; then exit the display by typing **q**.

2. From the KDE menu, view current CPU statistics from Xosview by selecting **System > Monitor > X osview**.

   Close the display when you finish monitoring the CPU.

3. View CPU information from KDE System Guard:

   a. From the KDE Menu, select **System > Monitor > KDE System Guard**.

   The KDE System Guard dialog box appears with the System Load tab selected.

   From this tab, you can view updated information about the CPU load, load average (1 minute), physical memory, and swap memory.

   Besides the preconfigured tabs, you can also create your own worksheet of specific system information.

   b. Select **File > New**.

   A Worksheet Properties dialog box appears.

   c. Enter the following properties:

   - Title: **CPU Information**

   - Rows: **2**

   - Columns: **2**

   d. Continue by selecting **OK**.

   A CPU Information tab appears with four areas for dropping sensors.

   e. From the Sensor Browser panel (on the left), expand **localhost > CPU Load**.

   f. Select and drag the following to the four sensor areas (with the indicated display styles):

   - **Idle Load** (Signal Plotter)

   - **Load Average (1 minute)** (Multimeter)

   - **System Load** (Bar Graph)

   - **User Load** (Signal Plotter)

   g. Maximize the KDE System Guard window.

   h. (Optional) Right-click a sensor area; then select **Properties** and change the properties of the display (such as the grid background color).

   i. When you finish using KDE System Guard, select **File > Quit**; then select **No**.

4. View device information using /proc:

   a. Make sure you are su'd to root from a terminal window.

   b. From the command line, view the I/O ports used on your Linux system by entering **cat /proc/ioports**.

c. View the IRQs used on your Linux system by entering
cat /proc/interrupts.

d. View the DMA channels used on your Linux system by entering **cat /proc/dma**.

e. View the PCI devices used on your Linux system by entering
cat /proc/bus/pci/devices | less or by entering **lspci**.

5. View hard disk information:

a. View the geometry of the first IDE disk on your Linux system by entering **fdisk –l /dev/hda**.

Using fdisk, you can see the number of cylinders on your disk.

b. View the hard disk settings by entering **hdparm –a /dev/hda**.

6. View SCSI information:

You can find SCSI information by checking the files in /proc/scsi/ or an information summary in /proc/scsi/scsi.

a. View the SCSI summary information by entering
cat /proc/scsi/scsi.

You can find detailed information about the configuration in the files in /proc/scsi/sg/.

b. Change to the directory /proc/scsi/sg/ by entering
cd /proc/scsi/sg.

c. List the files by entering **ls –l**.

d. View one or more files in the directory by entering
cat *filename* (such as **cat version**).

e. Run a scan of the SCSI bus by entering **sg_scan**.

f. Check for SCSI devices on your system by entering
scsiinfo –l.

7. View ISA devices by entering **pnpdump | less**.

8. View USB information:

a. View the USB devices by entering **lsusb**.

b. View detailed information about USB devices and drivers from the /proc file system by entering the following commands:

cat /proc/bus/usb/devices

cat /proc/bus/usb/drivers

NOTE

If there are no USB drivers on your server, the directory /proc/bus/usb/drivers does not exist.

    c. Determine the kernel modules available for the USB plugged-in device in /proc/bus/usb/001/001 by entering the following:

    usbmodules --device /proc/bus/usb/001/001

9. Close the terminal window.

How to Manage Modules from the Command Line

The following are commands you can use from a command line when working with modules:

- **lsmod.** This command lists the currently loaded modules in the kernel.

  The following is an example:

```
DA50:~ # lsmod
Module                   Size  Used by
quota_v2                12928  2
edd                     13720  0
joydev                  14528  0
sg                      41632  0
st                      44956  0
sr_mod                  21028  0
ide_cd                  42628  0
cdrom                   42780  2 sr_mod,ide_cd
nvram                   13448  0
usbserial               35952  0
parport_pc              41024  1
lp                      15364  0
parport                 44232  2 parport_pc,lp
ipv6                   276348  44
uhci_hcd                35728  0
intel_agp               22812  1
agpgart                 36140  1 intel_agp
evdev                   13952  0
usbcore                116572  4 usbserial,uhci_hcd
```

  The list includes information about the module name, size of the module, how often the module is used, and which other modules use it.

- **insmod** *module.* This command loads the indicated *module* into the kernel.

  The module must be stored in the directory /lib/modules/*version_number*/. However, it is recommended to use modprobe for loading modules.

- **rmmod** *module.* This command removes the indicated *module* from the kernel. However, it can only be removed if no processes are accessing hardware connected to it or corresponding services.

  We recommend that you use **modprobe –r** for removing modules.

- **modprobe** *module.* This command loads the indicated *module* into the kernel or removes it (with option –r).

  Dependencies of other modules are taken into account when using modprobe. In addition, modprobe reads in the file /etc/modprobe.conf for any configuration settings.

  This command can only be used if the file /lib/modules/*version*/modules.dep created by the command depmod exists. This file is used to add or remove dependencies.

  The kernel daemon (kmod since kernel version 2.2.x) ensures that modules needed in the running operation are automatically loaded using modprobe (such as accessing the CD-ROM drive).

NOTE

For more detailed information, enter **man modprobe**.

- **depmod.** This command creates the file /lib/modules/*version*/modules.dep. This file contains the dependencies of individual modules on each other.

  When a module is loaded (such as with modprobe), modules.dep ensures that all modules it depends on are also loaded.

  If the file modules.dep does not exist, it is created automatically when the system starts by the start script /etc/init.d/boot. For this reason, you do not need to create the file manually.

- **modinfo** *option module.* This command displays information (such as license, author, and description) about the module indicated on the command line.

  The following is an example:

```
DA50:~ # modinfo isdn
license:        GPL
author:         Fritz Elfert
description:    ISDN4Linux: link layer
depends:        slhc
supported:      yes
vermagic:       2.6.5-7.21-default 586 REGPARM gcc-3.3
```

For more detailed information, enter **man modinfo**.

modprobe Configuration File (/etc/modprobe.conf)

The file /etc/modprobe.conf is the configuration file for the kernel modules. For example, it contains parameters for the modules that access hardware directly.

The file plays an important role in loading modules. Various command types can be found in the file, such as the following:

- **install.** These instructions let modprobe execute commands when loading a specific module into the kernel.

  The following is an example:
  ```
  install    eth0    /bin/true
  ```

- **alias.** These instructions determine which kernel module will be loaded for a specific device file.

  The following is an example:
  ```
  alias    eth0    nvnet
  ```

- **options.** These instructions are options for loading a module.

  The following is an example:
  ```
  options    ne    io=0x300 irq=5
  ```

For more detailed information, enter **man 5 modprobe.conf**.

Kernel Module Loader (kmod)

The kernel module loader (kmod) is the most elegant way to use modules. Kmod performs background monitoring and makes sure the required modules are loaded by modprobe as soon as the respective functionality is needed in the kernel.

To activate kmod, the option Kernel module loader (CONFIG_KMOD) needs to be set to "y" (yes) in the kernel configuration. This is the default setting for SLES 9.

Kmod is not designed to unload modules automatically; compared with today's RAM capacities, the potential memory savings would be marginal.

For performance reasons, monolithic kernels might be more suitable for servers that are used for special tasks and need only a few drivers.

Exercise 5-3   Manage the Linux Kernel

In this exercise, you view information about your kernel, and load and unload kernel modules.

Do the following:

1. From a terminal window, su to root (**su -**) with a password of **novell**.

2. View the currently loaded kernel modules by entering **lsmod**.

3. Scroll through the modules to see if the joystick module (**joydev**) is loaded.

    The 0 in the Used column indicates that the module is not in use.

4. Remove the joystick module from the kernel memory by entering **rmmod joydev**.

5. Verify that the joydev kernel module was removed from memory by entering **lsmod**.

    Notice that the module joydev is no longer listed.

6. Load the joystick kernel module by entering **modprobe joydev**.

7. Verify that the joydev kernel module is loaded in memory by entering **lsmod**.

8. View the kernel modules configuration by entering the following:

    modprobe -c | less

9. Scroll through the configuration information by pressing the **Spacebar**.

10. When you finish, return to the command line by typing **q**.

11. Create a list of kernel module dependencies by entering

    depmod -v | less.

    It takes a few moments for the information to be generated.

12. Scroll through the dependency information by pressing the **Spacebar**.

13. When you finish, return to the command line by typing **q**.

14. Close the terminal window by entering **exit** twice.

OBJECTIVE 4   MANAGE THE GRUB BOOT LOADER

To manage the GRUB boot loader, you need to know the following:

- What a Boot Manager Is
- Boot Managers in SUSE Linux
- How to Start the GRUB Shell

- How to Modify the GRUB Configuration File
- How to Configure GRUB with YaST

What a Boot Manager Is

To boot a system, you need a program that can boot the respective operating system. This program, called the **boot loader**, loads the operating system kernel, which then loads the system.

After running the Power-On Self Test (POST), the PC BIOS searches the boot sector on the first hard drive for a boot loader. If it finds one, it turns control of the boot process over to the boot loader.

The boot loader then locates the operating system files on the hard drive and starts the operating system.

A **boot manager** is also a boot loader, but it can handle several operating systems. If there is more than one operating system present, the boot manager presents a menu allowing you to select a specific operating system to be loaded.

After selecting an operating system, the boot manager loads the operating system files and specifies the kernel parameters.

Linux boot managers can be used to load Linux or other operating systems, such as Microsoft Windows, Windows NT, Windows 2000, or Windows XP.

A boot manager is designed with the following two-stage architecture:

- **Stage 1.** The first stage of a boot manager is usually installed in the Master Boot Record (MBR) of the hard disk (first stage boot loader).

  As the space in the MBR is limited to 446 bytes, this program code merely contains the information for loading the next stage.

  Stage 1 can be installed in the MBR, in the boot sectors of partitions, or on a floppy disk.

- **Stage 2.** This stage usually contains the actual boot manager. The files of the boot manager are located in the directory /boot/.

Boot Managers in SUSE Linux

SUSE Linux Enterprise Server provides two boot managers for the Linux environment: GRUB (GRand Unified Boot loader) and LILO (LInux LOader).

To understand something about these boot managers, you need to know the following:

- GRUB Boot Manager
- LILO Boot Manager

- Map Files, GRUB, and LILO
- Additional Information

GRUB Boot Manager

GRUB is the standard boot manager in SUSE Linux Enterprise Server. The following are some special features of GRUB:

- **File system support.** Stage 2 includes file system drivers for ReiserFS, ext2, ext3, Minix, JFS, XFS, FAT, and FFS (BSD). For this reason, the boot manager can access files through filenames even before the operating system is loaded.

  For example, this feature is useful for searching for the kernel and loading it if the boot manager configuration is faulty.

- **Interactive control.** GRUB has its own shell that enables interactive control of the boot manager.

LILO Boot Manager

Because LILO is not the default boot manager of SUSE Linux Enterprise Server, it is only covered briefly in this objective.

The LILO configuration file is /etc/lilo.conf. Its structure is similar to that of the GRUB configuration file.

When you modify the configuration file /etc/lilo.conf, you need to enter the command **lilo** for the changes to be applied.

CAUTION

You also need to use the command lilo when moving the kernel or the initrd on your hard disk.

Map Files, GRUB, and LILO

The main obstacle for booting an operating system is that the kernel is usually a file within a file system on a partition on a disk. These concepts are unknown to the BIOS. To circumvent this, maps and map files were introduced.

These maps simply note the physical block numbers on the disk that comprise the logical files. When such a map is processed, the BIOS loads all the physical blocks in sequence as noted in the map, building the logical file in memory.

In contrast to LILO, which relies entirely on maps, GRUB tries to become independent from the fixed maps at an early stage. GRUB achieves this by means of the file system code, which enables access to files by using the path specification instead of the block numbers.

Additional Information

You can refer to the following sources for additional information on GRUB and LILO:

- **Linux system.** The following are available from your Linux system:
  - Enter the following for manual pages and info files:
    - info grub
    - man grub
    - man grub-install
    - man grub-md5-crypt
    - man lilo
    - man 5 lilo.conf
  - Check the following README files:
    - In the directory /usr/share/doc/packages/grub/
    - In the directory /usr/share/doc/packages/lilo/
- **Internet sites.** Check the following site on the Internet:
  - *www.gnu.org/software/grub/*

How to Start the GRUB Shell

Because GRUB has its own shell, you can boot the system manually if the Linux system does not start due to an error in the boot manager.

There are two ways to start the GRUB shell:

- From a Running System
- From the Boot Prompt

From a Running System

To start the GRUB shell during operation, enter the command grub as root. The following appears:

```
GNU GRUB  version 0.94  (640K lower / 3072K upper memory)

[ Minimal BASH-like line editing is supported.  For the first
  word, TAB lists possible command completions.  Anywhere else
  TAB lists the possible completions of a device/filename. ]


grub>
```

As in a Bash shell, you can complete GRUB shell commands with the Tab key. To find out which partition contains the kernel, enter the command find, as in the following:

```
grub> find /boot/vmlinuz
  (hd0,2)

grub>
```

In this example, the kernel (/boot/vmlinuz) is located in the third partition of the first hard disk (hd0,2).

5

You can close the GRUB shell by entering **quit**.

From the Boot Prompt

You can start the GRUB shell at the boot prompt by doing the following:

1. From the graphical boot selection menu, press **Esc**.

   A text-based menu appears.

2. Start the GRUB shell by typing **c** (U.S. keyboard layout).

How to Modify the GRUB Configuration File

You can configure GRUB by editing the file /boot/grub/menu.lst. The following is the general structure of the file:

- First, general options (such as the background color of the boot manager menu) are listed:

  ```
  color white/blue black/light-gray
  ```

- The general options are followed by options for the various operating systems that can be booted with the GRUB.

  Each entry for an operating system begins with the command title:

  ```
  title linux
        kernel (hd0,0)/boot/vmlinuz root=/dev/hda1
        initrd (hd0,0)/boot/initrd
  ```

The following is a simple example of the configuration file /boot/grub/menu.lst:

```
default 0
timeout 8

title Linux
    kernel (hd0,0)/boot/vmlinuz root=/dev/hda1
    initrd (hd0,0)/boot/initrd
```

The following describe the settings:

- **default 0.** The first entry (numbering from 0) is the default boot entry that is started automatically if no other entry is selected with the keyboard.

- **timeout 8.** The default boot entry is started automatically after 8 seconds.

How to Configure GRUB with YaST

While you can use the YaST Boot Loader Configuration module to simplify the configuration of the boot loader, you should not experiment with this module unless you understand the concepts behind it.

To configure GRUB with YaST, do the following:

1. From the KDE desktop, start the YaST Boot Loader Configuration module by doing one of the following:

   - Select the **YaST** icon, enter the root *password*, and select **OK**; then select **System > Boot Loader Configuration**.

     or

   - Open a terminal window and enter **sux –** and the root *password*; then enter **yast2 bootloader**.

The dialog box shown in Figure 5-8 appears.

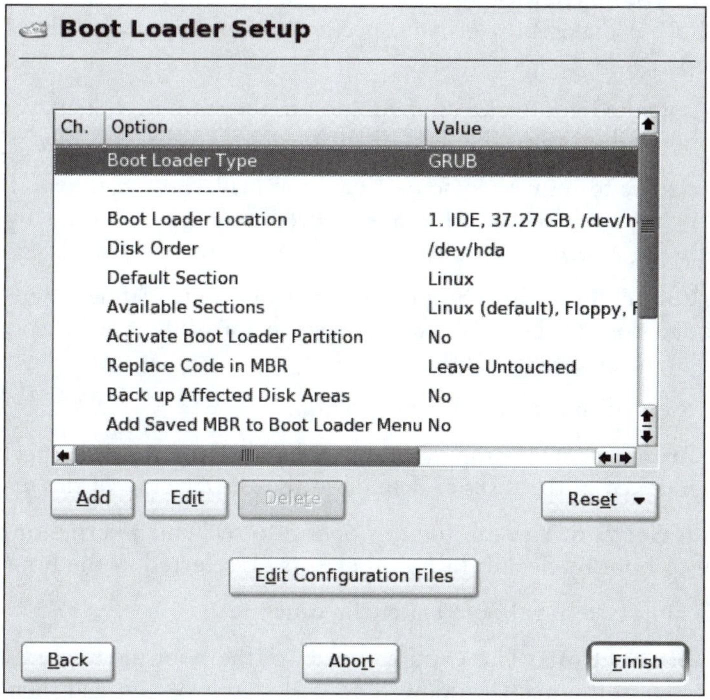

Boot Loader Setup

Ch.	Option	Value
	Boot Loader Type	GRUB

	Boot Loader Location	1. IDE, 37.27 GB, /dev/h
	Disk Order	/dev/hda
	Default Section	Linux
	Available Sections	Linux (default), Floppy, F
	Activate Boot Loader Partition	No
	Replace Code in MBR	Leave Untouched
	Back up Affected Disk Areas	No
	Add Saved MBR to Boot Loader Menu	No

Add   Edit   Delete   Reset ▾

Edit Configuration Files

Back   Abort   Finish

Figure 5-8

These are the current GRUB settings for your system, including a **Ch** (changed) column that indicates which default settings you have changed.

2. Do one of the following:

   - Add an option to the list by selecting **Add**, selecting an *option* from the drop-down list, and then selecting **OK**.

     or

   - Edit an option by selecting the *option*, selecting **Edit**, and then changing the parameters in the displayed dialog box.

     or

   - Delete an option by selecting the *option* and selecting **Delete**.

The following describes some of the more commonly used GRUB options:

- **Boot Loader Type.** You can use this option to switch between GRUB and LILO. A dialog box lets you specify the way this change should be performed.

  If you start the boot loader configuration in the running system, you can load the configuration from the hard disk.

  If you decide to return to the original boot loader, you can load its configuration by means of the last option. However, this is possible only if you do not close the boot loader module.

- **Boot Loader Location.** You can use this option to define where to install the boot loader in the MBR, in the boot sector of the boot partition (if available), or on a floppy disk.

  Use Others to specify a different location.

- **Disk Order.** If your computer has more than one hard disk, specify the boot sequence of the disks as defined in the BIOS setup of the machine.

- **Default Section.** You can use this option to set which kernel or operating system to boot by default (if no other entry is selected in the boot menu).

  The default system is booted after the timeout.

- **Available Sections.** The existing entries of the boot menu are listed under this option in the main window. If you select this option and then select **Edit**, a dialog box opens that is identical to the Default Entry dialog box.

- **Make Boot Loader Partition Active.** You can use this option to activate the partition whose boot sector holds the boot loader, independently from the partition that the directory with the helper files of the boot loader holds (the /boot/ or root directory /).

- **Replace Code in MBR.** You can use this option to specify whether to overwrite the MBR, which may be necessary if you have changed the location of the boot loader.

- **Backing up Files and Parts of Hard Disks.** This option backs up the changed hard disk areas.

- **Add Saved MBR to Boot Loader Menu.** This option adds the saved MBR to the boot loader menu.

3. (Optional) Display and edit the configuration files (such as /boot/grub/menu.lst or /boot/grub.conf) by selecting **Edit Configuration Files**.

4. (Optional) You can select from the following options by selecting one of the following from the **Reset** drop-down list:

- **Propose New Configuration.** This option generates a new configuration suggestion. Older Linux versions or other operating systems found on other partitions are included in the boot menu, enabling you to boot Linux or its old boot loader. The latter takes you to a second boot menu.

- **Start from Scratch.** This option lets you create the entire configuration from scratch. No suggestions are generated.

- **Reread Configuration from Disk.** If you already performed some changes and are not satisfied with the result, you can reload your current configuration with this option.

- **Propose and Merge with Existing GRUB Menus.** If another operating system and an older Linux version are installed in other partitions, the menu is generated from an entry for the new SUSE Linux, an entry for the other system, and all entries of the old boot loader menu.

  This procedure might take some time and is only available with GRUB.

- **Restore MBR from Hard Disk.** The MBR saved on the hard disk is restored.

5. When you finish configuring the boot loader, save the configuration changes by selecting **Finish**.

Remember that the sequence of the options or commands is very important in GRUB. If the specified sequence is not followed, the machine might not boot.

Exercise 5-4   Manage the Boot Loader

In this exercise, you do the following:

- Part I: Pass Kernel Parameters to the Boot Loader
- Part II: Configure Boot Managers

Part I: Pass Kernel Parameters to the Boot Loader

Do the following:

1. Reboot the system to runlevel 1, set the VGA mode to normal, and disable the SUSE splash screen by doing the following:

   a. From a terminal window on the KDE desktop, su to root

   (**su -**) with a password of **novell**.

b. Switch to runlevel 6 by entering **init 6**.

The system shuts down and reboots to a GUI menu that includes the options Linux and Failsafe.

c. Stop the timer for the GUI menu by pressing the **Spacebar**.

d. Exit the GUI menu by pressing **Esc**; then select **OK**.

A TUI (Text User Interface) menu for GRUB appears with the same options (Linux and Failsafe).

e. Make sure **Linux** is selected; then edit the boot commands by typing **e**.

A menu with two boot commands (kernel and initrd) appears.

f. Make sure that the command **kernel** is selected; then edit the command options by typing **e**.

The command is displayed in a command line editor.

g. Move to the beginning of the command by pressing **Home**.

h. Edit the command line to match the following:

kernel (hd0,1)/boot/vmlinuz root=/dev/hda2

vga=normal selinux=0 splash=0 resume=/dev/hda1 showopts 1

i. Save the edited command options by pressing **Enter**.

You are returned to the TUI menu for GRUB.

j. Boot the system to runlevel 1 by typing **b**.

NOTE

To boot from the graphical screen, you could enter the options **1 vga=normal** (with a space before the "1") in the Boot Options field.

2. Log in by entering the root password of **novell**.

3. Check the previous and current runlevels by entering **runlevel**.

List the runlevels in Table 5-6.

Table 5-6

Previous	Current

Note that both "1" and "S" indicate a single–user mode.

4. Change to runlevel 3 by entering **init 3**.

5. Log in as **root** with a password of **novell**.

6. Check the previous and current runlevels by entering **runlevel**.

List the runlevels in Figure 5-7.

Table 5-7

Previous	Current

7. Change the default runlevel to 3 for the system in the file /etc/inittab:

   a. From the command line, enter **vim /etc/inittab**.

   b. Press the **Insert** key.

   c. Scroll down to the line id:5:initdefault: and make the following change:

      id:**3**:initdefault:

   d. Press **Esc**; then save the change and exit vim by entering **:wq**.

8. Reboot the system by entering **shutdown -r now**.

9. When the login prompt appears, log in as **root** with a password of **novell**.

10. Check to make sure your system booted to runlevel 3 by entering **runlevel**.

11. Change the default runlevel back to runlevel 5 using YaST:

   a. From the command line, enter **yast2 runlevel**.

      The Runlevel Editor appears.

   b. Select the Expert Mode by pressing **Alt+E**.

      The Runlevel Editor switches to the Expert Mode.

   c. Press **Alt+D**; then from the drop-down list select **5: Full multiuser with network and xdm**.

   d. Save the changes by pressing **Alt+F** (to select **Finish**).

      You are returned to the command line.

12. Reboot the system with a one minute warning and an alert message to users by entering the following:

    shutdown -r 1 "==========> Log off now <=========="

    The message appears on your screen and the system reboots to the GUI login screen.

13. Log in as **geeko** with a password of **N0v3ll**.

Part II: Configure Boot Managers

Although GRUB is newer and was the first to overcome the 1024th cylinder problem, LILO still has many features that make it an attractive option.

You decide to test LILO by doing the following:

1. Change the boot manager to LILO:

    a. From the KDE desktop, start YaST by selecting the **YaST** icon.

    b. Enter a password of **novell**; then select **OK**.

       The YaST Control Center appears.

    c. Select **System > Boot Loader Configuration**.

       The Boot Loader Setup dialog box appears.

    d. From the list of boot loader parameters, make sure that **Boot Loader Type** is selected; then select **Edit**.

       A boot loader type dialog box appears.

    e. From the Boot Loader Type drop-down list, select **LILO**; then select **OK**.

       A warning dialog box appears about changing your boot loader.

    f. Make sure **Convert Current Configuration** is selected; then select **OK**.

    g. Save the changes by selecting **Finish**.

2. Customize the LILO configuration (/etc/lilo.conf) to enhance video settings and secure LILO with a boot password:

    a. Open the file /etc/lilo.conf in an editor by pressing **Alt+F2** and entering **kdesu kate /etc/lilo.conf**; then enter a password of **novell** and select **OK**.

    b. (Conditional) If the parameter **vga = 791** does not exist at the top of the file under "boot = /dev/hda," add the parameter.

       This is a VESA frame buffer code in decimal format indicating that the screen should be set to 1024 x 768 and a 16-bit color depth.

    c. Under the "root = /dev/hda2" line in the image section with "label = Linux," add the parameter **password = novell**.

       This parameter password protects this image at boot.

    d. Save the changes by selecting **File > Save**.

       Keep the file lilo.conf open in the Kate window.

3. Open a terminal window; then su to root (**su -**) with a password of **novell**.

4. Update the LILO configuration by entering **lilo**.

Now that the LILO configuration is updated with the new parameters, you should remove the password parameter to prevent others from viewing the password in the file /etc/lilo.conf.

5. From the Kate window, edit the file /etc/lilo.conf by deleting **password = novell**.

6. Save the change and close Kate by selecting **File > Quit**; then select **Save**.

7. From the terminal window, reboot the system by entering **reboot**.

When the system boots to the LILO startup screen, you are asked for a password.

8. Enter a password of **novell**; then select **OK**.

The system begins booting.

The GUI login screen appears.

9. Log in as **geeko** with a password of **N0v3ll**.

10. Test your KDE desktop (X Windows) by starting and closing a few applications.

Now that you've tested LILO, you decide to return to using GRUB as your boot loader.

11. Reinstall GRUB as the boot loader for your SLES 9 server by editing the file /etc/sysconfig/bootloader:

   a. Open the file /etc/sysconfig/bootloader in an editor by pressing **Alt+F2** and entering **kdesu kate /etc/sysconfig/bootloader**; then enter a password of **novell** and select **OK**.

   b. Locate the parameter LOADER_TYPE="lilo" and change it to the following:

   LOADER_TYPE=**"grub"**

   c. Save the change and close the Kate window by selecting **File > Quit**; then select **Save**.

   d. Open a terminal window and su to root (**su -**) with a password of **novell**.

   e. Reinstall the GRUB boot loader by entering

   grub-install /dev/hda.

12. Reboot the server by entering **init 6**.

13. From the GUI login screen, log in as **geeko** with a password of **N0v3ll**.

14. (Optional) If you have time, add a GRUB password using YaST (**System > Boot Loader Configuration**); then reboot and test the configuration.

5

OBJECTIVE 5   MODIFY SYSTEM SETTINGS

To tune your SUSE Linux Enterprise Server system to meet your specific requirements, you need to know how to do the following:

- View and Change System Settings (/proc/sys/)
- Modify Kernel and Hardware Parameters with Powertweak
- Configure /etc/sysconfig/ Files with YaST

View and Change System Settings (/proc/sys/)

The files and directories under the directory /proc/ contain a wealth of information about various aspects of the running system. This includes the files under /proc/sys/, which you can view and modify during operation to change the system settings.

The files in /proc/ and /proc/sys/ are not kept on the hard disk but are created by the kernel in memory when the system starts up. Changes to these files are lost after a reboot.

To manage these settings, you need to know how to do the following:

- View the Current Configuration
- Edit the Current Configuration

View the Current Configuration

The individual configuration files in the directory /proc/sys/ are text files that you can view with commands such as cat and less.

For example, entering **cat /proc/sys/dev/cdrom/info** displays the following information about the CD-ROM drive:

```
geeko@DA50:~> cat /proc/sys/dev/cdrom/info
CD-ROM information, Id: cdrom.c 3.20 2003/12/17

drive name:             hdc
drive speed:            0
drive # of slots:       1
Can close tray:         0
Can open tray:          0
Can lock tray:          1
Can change speed:       1
Can select disk:        0
Can read multisession:  1
Can read MCN:           1
Reports media changed:  1
Can play audio:         1
Can write CD-R:         0
Can write CD-RW:        0
Can read DVD:           1
```

```
Can write DVD-R:        0
Can write DVD-RAM:      0
Can read MRW:           0
Can write MRW:          0
Can write RAM:          0
```

You can also use the command sysctl to view all or specific modifiable values below /proc/sys/, as in the following:

```
geeko@DA50:~> /sbin/sysctl net.ipv4.ip_forward
net.ipv4.ip_forward = 0

geeko@DA50:~> /sbin/sysctl -a
sunrpc.tcp_slot_table_entries = 16
sunrpc.udp_slot_table_entries = 16
sunrpc. nlm_debug = 0
sunrpc.nfsd_debug = 0
sunrpc. nfs_debug = 0
sunrpc.rpc_debug = 0
abi.fake_utsname = 0
abi.trace = 0
abi.defhandler_libcso = 68157441
...
```

Edit the Current Configuration

You can use the command echo to edit individual configuration values. For example, entering the following command activates routing:

echo 1 > /proc/sys/net/ipv4/ip_forward

You can also do the same thing by using the command sysctl:

sysctl –w net.ipv4.ip_forward=1

Another example is deploying an Oracle database. This requires a number of kernel parameters to be set, as in the following:

```
DA50:~ # echo 65535 > /proc/sys/fs/file-max
DA50:~ # echo 2147483648 > cat /proc/sys/kernel/shmmax
```

The same is true of using sysctl to deploy an Oracle database:

```
DA50:~ # sysctl -w fs.file-max=65535
DA50:~ # sysctl -w kernel.shmmax=2147483648
```

If you want to load a number of kernel parameters when the system is booted, you can use the command sysctl. You enter the parameters in the file /etc/sysconfig/sysctl. The following are some sample settings:

```
net.ipv4.ip_forward = 1
net.ipv4.icmp_echo_ignore_broadcasts = 1
```

```
fs.file-max = 65535
kernel.shmmax = 2147483648
```

Once you finish editing the configuration file, you set the parameters by entering **sysctl -p** or **/etc/init.d/boot.sysctl start**.

To execute the script /etc/init.d/boot.sysctl when the system is booted, activate it by entering **insserv -d boot.sysctl**.

Modify Kernel and Hardware Parameters with Powertweak

SUSE Linux Enterprise Server offers a special tool for configuring kernel and hardware parameters called *Powertweak*. This tool includes the daemon powertweakd and a graphical YaST front end.

A significant advantage of using Powertweak to set kernel and hardware parameters is that a short description is provided for every parameter.

To start Powertweak, do the following:

1. From the KDE desktop, start the YaST Powertweak Configuration module by doing one of the following:

   ■ Select the **YaST** icon, enter the root *password*, and select **OK**; then select **System > Powertweak Configuration**.

   or

   ■ Open a terminal window and enter **sux -** and the root *password*; then enter **yast2 powertweak**.

   The first time you start Powertweak, the dialog box shown in Figure 5-9 appears.

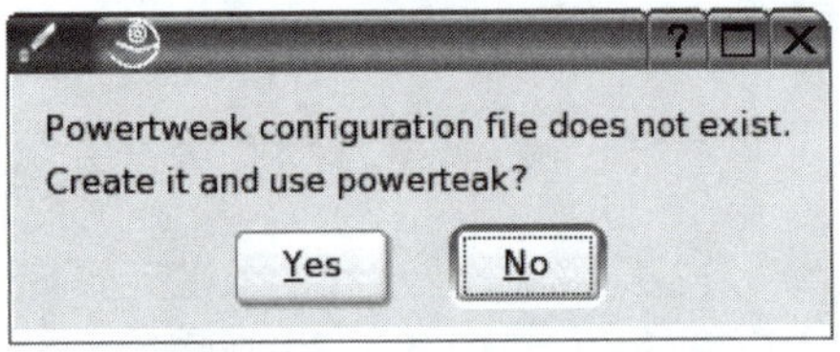

Figure 5-9

2. Create the Powertweak configuration file by selecting **Yes**.

   The configuration file /etc/powertweak/tweaks is created and the daemon is started. From this point on, the daemon is started every time the system is booted

   The links to the start script /etc/init.d/powertweakd are also set in the respective runlevel directories under /etc/init.d/.

The dialog box shown in Figure 5-10 appears.

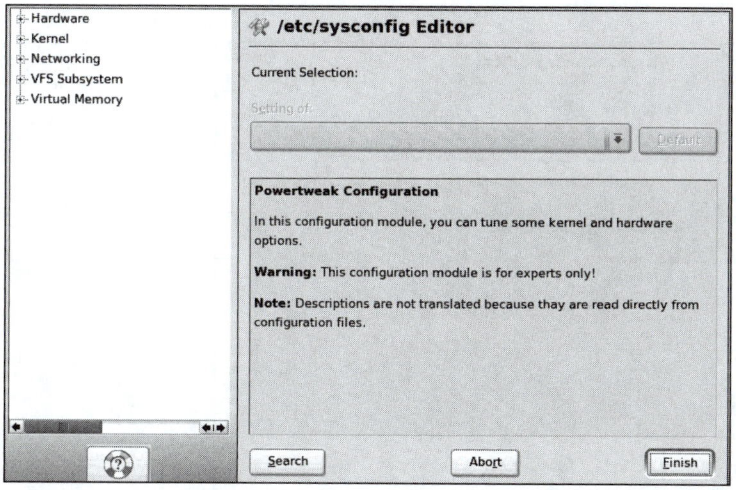

Figure 5-10

3. To find a parameter, do one of the following:

   ■ From the left frame, expand a category and subcategories until you find the parameter you want to change; then select the *setting*.

   or

   ■ Select **Search** and enter a *keyword*; then select **OK**.

   Once you select a parameter, information appears in the right frame.

For example, if you find and select **Networking > IP > net/ipv4/ ip_forward**, the dialog box shown in Figure 5-11 appears.

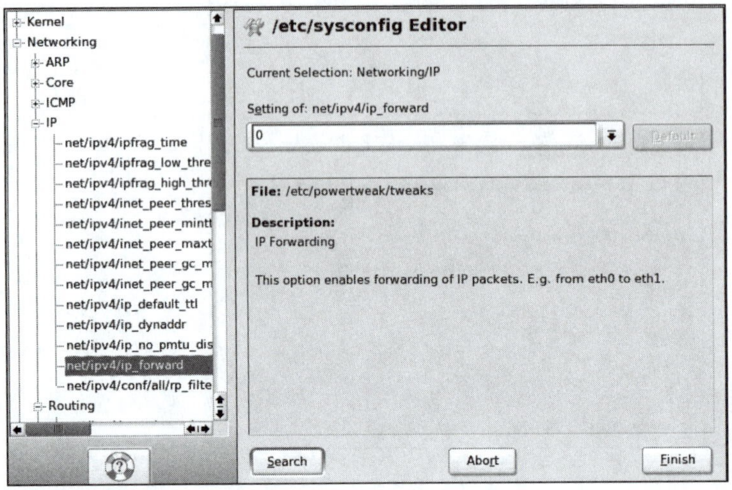

Figure 5-11

4. From the right frame, read the information (file, possible values, default value, and description); then select or enter the *setting*.

   For example, you can activate routing by entering **1**.

5. (Optional) Find and configure other settings.

   If you want to return a setting to its default value, select **Default**.

6. When you finish, select **Finish**.

The dialog box shown in Figure 5-12 appears.

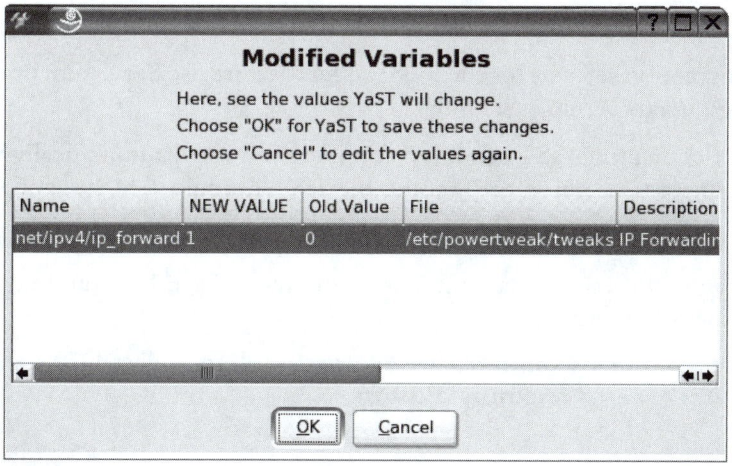

Figure 5-12

This dialog box lists a summary of all the changes you have indicated that you want made.

7. When you finish reviewing the list, save the changes by selecting **OK**.

The changes are saved and activated by SUSEConfig.

Configure /etc/sysconfig/ Files with YaST

All changes to the system configuration you make with YaST happen in one of the following ways:

- **Direct modification of configuration files.** The following are some examples:
  - Installation of software resulting in changes to the RPM database
  - Printer configuration is written directly to the configuration files of the CUPS print system (in /etc/cups/)
  - Using the Runlevel Editor modifies /etc/inittab and the links in the runlevel directories in /etc/init.d
- **YaST modifies the configuration files in /etc/sysconfig/.** The following are some examples:
  - The network configuration is saved in files in the directory /etc/sysconfig/network/.

- The mail configuration is saved in /etc/sysconfig/mail and /etc/sysconfig/postfix.

- The DMA mode for hard disks is saved in /etc/sysconfig/hardware.

A majority of configuration settings for the SUSE Linux Enterprise Server environment are saved in files in the directory /etc/sysconfig/.

You can edit these files by using YaST modules (configuration saved automatically when you select Finish), by using a text editor, or by using the YaST module /etc/sysconfig Editor.

To configure the files in /etc/sysconfig/ and its subdirectories with YaST, do the following:

1. From the KDE desktop, start the YaST /etc/sysconfig Editor module by doing one of the following:

   - Select the **YaST** icon, enter the root *password*, and select **OK**; then select **System > /etc/sysconfig Editor**.

     or

   - Open a terminal window and enter **sux –** and the root *password*; then enter **yast2 sysconfig**.

   The dialog box shown in Figure 5-13 appears.

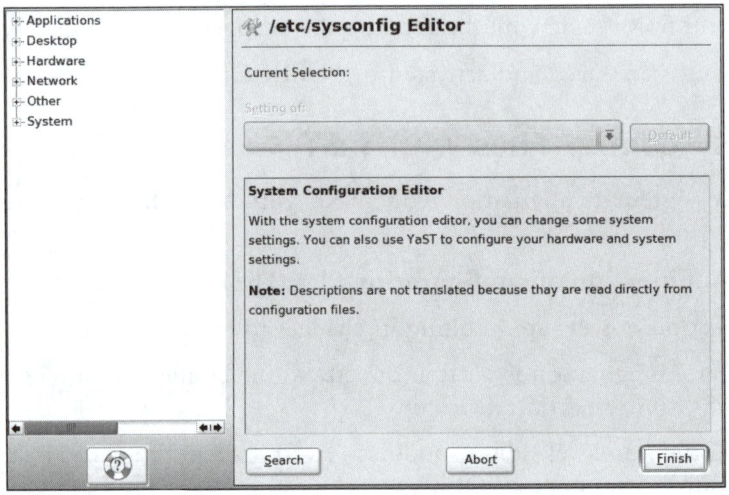

/etc/sysconfig Editor

Current Selection:

Setting of:

▼   Default

System Configuration Editor

With the system configuration editor, you can change some system settings. You can also use YaST to configure your hardware and system settings.

Note: Descriptions are not translated because thay are read directly from configuration files.

Applications
Desktop
Hardware
Network
Other
System

Search   Abort   Finish

Figure 5-13

From this dialog box, you can change the system settings stored in the directory /etc/sysconfig/.

2. To find a setting, do one of the following:

   ▪ From the left frame, expand a category and subcategories until you find the setting you want to change; then select the **setting**.

   or

   ▪ Select **Search** and enter a **keyword**; then select **OK**.

   Once you select a setting, information appears in the right frame.

   For example, if you find and select **System > Bootloader > LOADER_ TYPE**, the dialog box shown in Figure 5-14 appears.

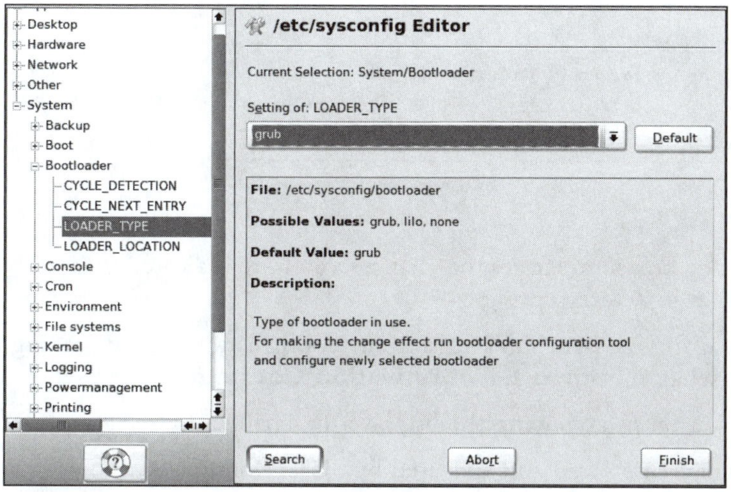

Figure 5-14

3. From the right frame, read the information (file, possible values, default value, and description); then select or enter the **setting**.

4. (Optional) Find and configure other settings.

   If you want to return a setting to its default value, select **Default**.

5. When you finish, select **Finish**.

The dialog box shown in Figure 5-15 appears.

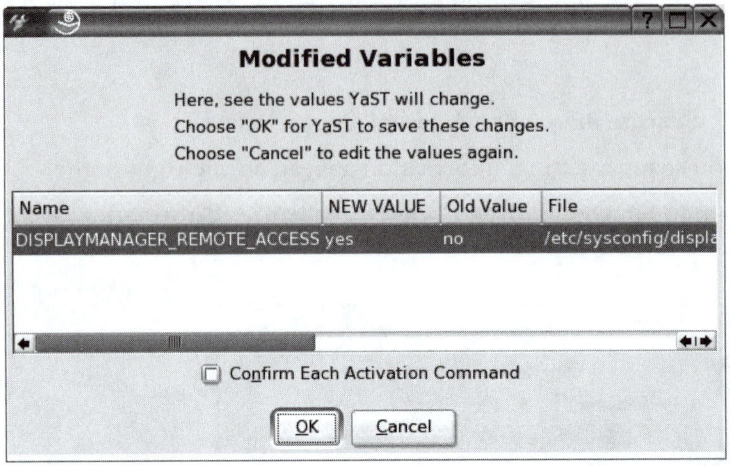

Modified Variables

Here, see the values YaST will change.
Choose "OK" for YaST to save these changes.
Choose "Cancel" to edit the values again.

Name	NEW VALUE	Old Value	File
DISPLAYMANAGER_REMOTE_ACCESS	yes	no	/etc/sysconfig/displa

☐ Confirm Each Activation Command

[OK]   [Cancel]

Figure 5-15

This dialog box summarizes the changes you have indicated that you want made to the files in /etc/sysconfig/.

6. (Optional) If you want YaST to stop for confirmation before making each change, select **Confirm Each Activation Command**.

7. When you finish reviewing the list, save the changes by selecting **OK**.

The changes are saved and activated by SUSEConfig.

Exercise 5-5   Change the Power Setting with YaST

Do the following:

1. From a terminal window, check the currently running CPU MHz speed by entering **cat /proc/cpuinfo**.

The model name indicates the installed CPU and supported maximum processing speed (on most newer computers). The CPU MHz parameter indicates the current running speed.

If there is a significant discrepancy between the maximum process speed and the CPU MHz value, then your CPU supports dynamic frequency scaling.

This is controlled by the SLES 9 Power Management scheme and can be reconfigured to Maximum Performance.

NOTE If you do not see a supported maximum processing speed with the model name, or do not notice a significant discrepancy, you can still complete the exercise to learn how to adjust the power settings.

2. From the KDE desktop, select the **YaST** icon; then enter a password of **novell** and select **OK**.

   The YaST Control Center appears.

3. Select **System > /etc/sysconfig Editor**.

   The /etc/sysconfig Editor appears.

4. From the list on the left, expand **System > Powermanagement > Scheme > Performance**; then select **POWERSAVE_CPUFREQUENCY**.

5. From the Setting of POWERSAVE_CPUFREQUENCY drop-down list (on the right), select **performance**.

6. Save the setting by selecting **Finish**; then select **OK**.

7. From the terminal window, su to root (**su -**) and enter a password of **novell**.

8. Restart the powersave daemon by entering

   rcpowersaved restart.

9. Check the currently running CPU MHz speed by entering

   cat /proc/cpuinfo.

   If they did not before, both the supported maximum processing speed and the CPU MHz value now closely match each other.

10. Close all windows.

Chapter Summary

- After performing a POST, the BIOS typically loads the boot manager from the MBR. The boot manager starts the Linux kernel and usually loads an initrd file that contains device drivers for system devices such as hard disks. Next, the Linux kernel loads the init daemon that starts all other processes on the system to bring it to a usable state.

- A Linux system is categorized using runlevels. There are seven standard runlevels based on the number and type of daemons loaded in memory.

- The init daemon is responsible for loading and unloading daemons using its configuration file /etc/inittab.

- The /etc/inittab file runs scripts that start with S (start) or K (kill) in the /etc/init.d/ rc*runlevel*.d directory when changing runlevels; these scripts are shortcuts to the scripts in the /etc/init.d directory used to start and stop daemons. You may edit these files to control the daemons that start in a particular runlevel. Alternatively, you can use the YaST Runlevel Editor to edit the appropriate runlevel files.

❑ You can view your current runlevel using the **runlevel** command, and force the init daemon to change runlevels using the **init** command.

❑ Individual daemons may be started by running the appropriate script in the /etc/init.d directory with the **start** argument, or by using the **rcdaemonname start** command.

❑ Device drivers are either compiled into the Linux kernel or loaded into the kernel as modules. Kernel modules are loaded by the kmod process from the /lib/modules/version/kernel directory via entries in the /etc/modprobe.conf file during system initialization. Drivers may be found and managed following system initialization using the **lsmod, insmod, rmmod, modprobe, depmod, modinfo**, and **hwinfo** commands.

❑ The Linux kernel is loaded into memory during system initialization by a boot loader or boot manager. The traditional Linux boot manager is LILO. The GRUB boot loader is used by default in SLES and offers file system support and an interactive shell.

❑ To manage LILO, you can edit the /etc/lilo.conf file and run the **lilo** command. To manage GRUB, you can edit the /boot/grub/menu.lst and /etc/grub.conf files. Alternatively, LILO and GRUB can be managed with the Boot Loader Configuration module of YaST.

❑ The /proc/sys directory exists in memory and contains information and settings for a running system. You can edit these settings directly by using the **sysctl** command or by using the Powertweak utility in YaST.

❑ Most configuration information set in YaST is written to the /etc/sysconfig directory. You can edit the files in /etc/sysconfig using a text editor to change system configuration, or you can use the **/etc/sysconfig Editor** module of YaST.

KEY TERMS

/boot/grub.conf — The file that contains information about GRUB components.

/boot/grub/menu.lst — The GRUB configuration file in SLES.

/etc/init.d — The directory that contains the scripts used to start and stop most daemons.

/etc/init.d/boot — The script used to activate file systems and swap during system initialization.

/etc/init.d/rc — The script used to start and stop daemons based on runlevel.

/etc/init.d/skeleton — A sample script that may be copied to create scripts used to start a daemon.

/etc/inittab — The configuration file for the init daemon.

/etc/lilo.conf — The LILO configuration file.

/etc/modprobe.conf — Used at system initialization to load kernel modules.

/etc/powertweak/tweaks — The configuration file for the Powertweak daemon.

5

/etc/rc.d/rc*runlevel*.d — The directories used by the init daemon to start and kill daemons in each *runlevel*.

/etc/sysconfig — The directory that stores most system configuration settings.

/etc/sysconfig Editor — A YaST utility that may be used to change system configuration settings in the /etc/sysconfig directory.

/lib/modules/*version*/kernel — The directory that stores most kernel modules in SLES.

/proc — A virtual directory in memory that stores kernel-exported system information.

/proc/sys — A virtual directory in memory that stores running system settings.

/var/log/boot.msg — The log file that stores information about daemon start up at system initialization.

basic input/output system (BIOS) — The program located in mainboard ROM that is used to perform the POST and locate a boot loader or boot manager.

boot loader — The program used to load and start the operating system kernel at system startup.

boot manager — A program used to load and start one of several different operating systems at system start-up.

depmod command — Used to create and update the module dependency database.

fdisk command — Used to view and manage hard disk partitions.

getty — A program used to display a login prompt on a character-based terminal.

Grand Unified Boot Loader (GRUB) — The default boot manager in SLES.

halt command — Used to quickly bring a system to runlevel 0.

hdparm command — Used to view and manage hard disk settings.

hwinfo command — Generates a report for various hardware devices in your computer.

init — The first daemon started by the Linux kernel; it is responsible for starting and stopping other daemons.

init command — Used to change the system runlevel.

initrd — A ramdisk image that contains device drivers that are loaded during system initialization.

insmod command — Used to insert a module into the Linux kernel.

insserv command — Used to enable scripts used to start daemons.

iostat command — Displays input and output statistics for the system and system devices.

KDE System Guard — A graphical application that may be used to view CPU and system statistics.

kdesu command — A KDE version of the **su** command that may be used to start a graphical program as another user.

kernel — The core component of the Linux operating system.

kmod — The process used to load and unload kernel modules.

lilo command — Used to reinstall the LILO boot manager after configuration changes.

Linux Loader (LILO) — The traditional boot manager used on Linux systems.

linuxrc — A program used to load device drivers within the initrd during system initialization.

lsmod command — Used to list modules loaded into the Linux kernel.

map files — Used by a boot manager or boot loader to locate physical data on the hard disk.

Master Boot Record (MBR) — The first area of a hard disk that stores the partition table and bootable partition.

modinfo command — Used to list information about specific modules.

modprobe command — Used to insert a module and its dependent modules into the Linux kernel.

Plug and Play (PnP) — A system used by the BIOS, hardware devices, and the operating system to automatically configure hardware resources for hardware devices in the computer.

pnpdump command — Displays information about PnP devices and their configuration.

Power On Self Test (POST) — A simple hardware test performed by the BIOS at system initialization.

poweroff command — Used to quickly bring a system to runlevel 0 and power off the system.

Powertweak — A system that consists of a daemon and YaST utility that may be used to change running system settings.

Powertweak Configuration — A YaST utility that may be used to change running system settings.

reboot command — Used to quickly bring a system to runlevel 6.

rmmod command — Used to remove a module from the Linux kernel.

runlevel — A category that describes the number and type of daemons on a Linux system.

runlevel command — Used to display the current and most recent runlevel.

scsiinfo command — Used to view information about SCSI devices on your system.

shutdown command — Used to change to runlevel 0 at a certain time.

sulogin — A runlevel 1 program used to display a login prompt on a character-based terminal for the root user only.

sysctl command — Used to change running system settings.

usbmodules command — Displays information about the USB device modules used on the system.

Xosview — A graphical application that may be used to view CPU and system statistics.

YaST Boot Loader Configuration — A graphical program that may be used to configure LILO and GRUB.

YaST Runlevel Editor — A graphical program that may be used to configure the daemons that start in each runlevel.

REVIEW QUESTIONS

1. What script is executed at boot time to activate and mount file system devices?

   a. linuxrc

   b. initrd

   c. /etc/init.d/rc

   d. /etc/init.d/boot.d

2. What is the PID of the init daemon? _____

3. What action in the /etc/inittab file is used to determine the default runlevel at system initialization? _____

4. What is the default runlevel in SLES? _____

5. Which runlevel loads all networking daemons (including NFS) but does not start a display manager?

   a. 1

   b. 2

   c. 3

   d. 5

6. Which runlevel is used to shut down the system?

   a. 0

   b. 1

   c. 5

   d. 6

7. What command can you type to change your runlevel to single-user mode?

   _____

8. Which of the following commands may be used to stop the SSH daemon (sshd)? (Choose all that apply.)

   a. rcsshd stop

   b. kstopsys sshd

   c. /etc/init.d/sshd stop

   d. /etc/rc/stopsshd

9. Which of the following methods can you use to start the SSH daemon (sshd) upon entering runlevel 3? (Choose all that apply.)

   a. Create a shortcut to the /etc/init.d/sshd script called /etc/init.d/rc3.d/S88sshd

   b. Create a shortcut to the /etc/init.d/sshd script called /etc/init.d/rc3.d/K88sshd

   c. Change the INIT INFO section of the /etc/init.d/sshd script and run the **insserv** command

   d. Run the YaST Runlevel Editor Ext3

10. What template can you copy to create a script that is used to start or stop daemons in the /etc/init.d directory? _____

11. Which of the following commands will force your system to reboot? (Choose all that apply.)

    a. init 0

    b. reboot

    c. powerwait

    d. init 6

12. What command can you use to load the module **testmod** and its dependant modules into the Linux kernel? _____

13. Which of the following lines in /etc/modprobe.conf will load the **tulip** module for your first Ethernet network card (eth0)?

    a. options eth0 tulip

    b. alias eth0 tulip

    c. options tulip eth0

    d. alias tulip eth0

14. You have made changes to your /etc/lilo.conf file. When you reboot your system, you notice that these changes have not taken effect. What should you do to correct the problem? _____

15. Which of the following are benefits of the GRUB boot manager as compared to LILO? (Choose all that apply.)

    a. GRUB has an interactive shell.

    b. GRUB can boot multiple operating systems.

    c. GRUB can read files on the file system.

    d. GRUB can be installed on the MBR.

16. Which of the following methods may be used to change running system settings? (Choose all that apply.)

    a. Changing the contents of files within /proc/sys

    b. Changing the contents of files within /etc/sysconfig

    c. Using the **sysctl** command

    d. Using the Powertweak Configuration utility in YaST

Discovery Exercises

Starting a Daemon in a Runlevel

Log in to tty1 as the root user and create a file called /etc/init.d/sampledaemon that has the permissions 755. Next, edit this file with the **vi** editor and add a line that reads **echo My daemon has started**. Then, create a soft link to this file called /etc/init.d/rc3.d/ S90sampledaemon. In which runlevel will this script be run? Finally, change to runlevel 3 (press Enter to receive your prompt). Did your daemon start in this runlevel? When finished, log out of tty1.

Enabling Runlevel 4

Runlevel 4 is typically reserved for custom use on a Linux system. Using the information in this section, edit the appropriate files on your system to enable the use of runlevel 4. Ensure that runlevel 4 starts all daemons that are started in runlevel 3 as well as the **sampledaemon** used in the previous Discovery Exercise. Test your configuration by switching to runlevel 4. How can runlevel 4 be useful in a corporate environment?

Using the GRUB Shell

One of the most useful features of the GRUB boot loader over other boot loaders is its interactive shell, which can run several functions and search files on the file system. The GRUB shell also can be run after the Linux kernel has been executed and your system is in full functional mode. Log in to tty1 as the root user and type **grub** to start the GRUB shell. Next, run the **help** command to see a list of commands that are available to you in this shell. Which command can display memory statistics? Execute this command. Next, type **find /boot/vmlinuz** to determine which drive and partition your kernel resides on. Explain the results. Then, type **cat hd(0,0)/boot/grub/menu.lst** to list the contents of the GRUB configuration file. (If your kernel is not on **hd(0,0)**, supply the appropriate hard disk and partition instead.) Finally, run the **quit** command to exit the GRUB shell and log out of tty1.

6

MANAGE LINUX PROCESSES AND SERVICES

In this section, you learn how to manage processes, schedule jobs, use system logging services, and understand the purpose and architecture of startup shell scripts and services.

- ◆ Manage Processes
- ◆ Describe Startup Shell Scripts and Services
- ◆ Schedule Jobs
- ◆ Use System Logging Services

OBJECTIVE 1   MANAGE PROCESSES

To manage processes on your SUSE Linux Enterprise Server, you need to know the following:

- Process Definitions
- Jobs and Processes
- How to Manage Foreground and Background Processes
- How to Prioritize Processes
- How to End a Process
- Processes and Services (Daemons)
- How to Manage a Daemon Process

Process Definitions

The following terms are used to describe Linux processes:

- **Program.** A structured set of commands stored in an executable file on a Linux file system. A program can be executed to create a process.
- **Process.** A program that is running in memory and on the CPU.
- **User Process.** A process launched by a user that runs from a terminal.
- **Daemon Process.** A system process that is not associated with a terminal.

Figure 6-1 illustrates the relationship between daemon processes and user processes.

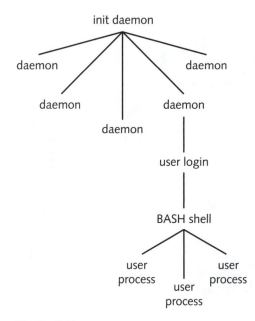

Figure 6-1

In this example, during the boot process of a Linux system, the init daemon launches several other daemons (***daemon processes***), including a daemon for user login.

After the user logs in, the user can start a terminal window or virtual terminal with a BASH shell that lets the user start processes manually (***user processes***).

- **Process ID (PID).** A unique identifier assigned to every process as it begins.

- **Child Process.** A process that is started by another process (the parent process).

- **Parent Process.** A process that starts other processes (child processes).

- **Parent Process ID (PPID).** The PID of the parent process that created the current process.

Figure 6-2 illustrates the relationship between parent and child process ID numbers.

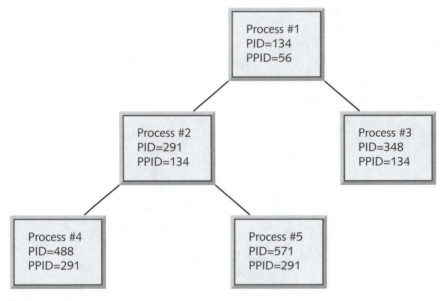

Figure 6-2

For example, Process #1 is assigned a PID of 134. This process also launches Process #2 with a PID of 291 and Process #3 with a PID of 348.

Because Process #1 launched Process #2 and Process #3, the second and third processes are considered *child processes* of Process #1 (the *parent process*).

Jobs and Processes

In Linux, you use a *job identifier* (commonly called a *job ID*) to refer to processes when using commands. The job identifier is a shell-specific numeric value that identifies the running program uniquely within that shell.

On the other hand, each process (independent of a shell) is identified using a *process ID* (commonly called a *PID*) that is unique across the entire system. All jobs have a PID, but not all processes have a usable job identifier.

PID 1 always belongs to the init process. This is the first process started on the system and it creates a number of other processes, which in turn can generate additional processes.

If PID 1 has been reached, the next process is allocated the lowest available number (such as PID 17494). Processes run for different lengths of time. After one process has ended, its number again becomes available.

When performing tasks such as changing the priority level of a running program, you use the PID instead of the job ID.

When you want to switch a process from the background to the foreground (and the process was started from a terminal), you use the job ID.

How to Manage Foreground and Background Processes

The Linux shell environment allows processes to run in either the *foreground* or the *background*.

Processes executed in the foreground are started in a terminal window and run until the process completes; the terminal window does not return to a prompt until the program's execution is complete.

Background process execution occurs when a process is started and the terminal window returns to a prompt before the process finishes executing.

Existing processes can be switched from foreground to background execution under the following circumstances:

- The process must be started in a terminal window or console shell.
- The process does not require input from the terminal window.

If the process meets this criteria, it can be moved to the background.

NOTE

Processes that require input within the terminal can be moved to the background as well, but when input is requested, the process will be suspended until it is brought to the foreground and the requested input is provided.

Commands in a shell can be started in the foreground or in the background. Processes in the foreground can directly receive transmitted signals.

For example, if you enter **xeyes** to start the XEYES program, it is running in the foreground. If you press **Ctrl+Z**, the process stops:

```
[1]+  Stopped                 xeyes
geeko@DA50:~>
```

You can continue running a stopped process in the background by entering **bg**, as in the following:

```
geeko@DA50:~> bg
[1]+ xeyes &
geeko@DA50:~>
```

The ampersand (**&**) displayed in the output means that the process is now running in the background.

Appending an ampersand to a command starts the process in the background (instead of the foreground), as in the following:

```
geeko@DA50:~> xeyes &
[2] 4351
geeko@DA50:~>
```

This makes the shell from which you started the program still available for user input.

In the above example, both the job ID (**[2]**) and the process ID of the program (**10982**) are returned.

Each process started from the shell is assigned a *job ID* by the job control of the shell. The command jobs lists the contents of job control, as in the following:

```
geeko@DA50:~> jobs
[1]+  Stopped                   xeyes
[2]   Running                   xeyes &
[4]-  Running                   sleep 99 &
geeko@DA50:~>
```

In this example, the process with job ID 3 is already terminated. The processes 2 and 4 are running in the background (notice the ampersand), and process 1 is stopped.

The next background process will be assigned the job ID of 5 (highest number + 1).

Not only can you continue running a stopped process in the background by using the command bg, you can also switch a process to the foreground by entering **fg *job_ID***, as in the following:

```
geeko@DA50:~> fg 1
xeyes
```

The shell also informs you about the termination of a process running in the background:

```
[4]-  Done                      sleep 99
```

The job ID is displayed in square brackets. **Done** means the process terminated properly. If you see **Terminated** instead, it means that the process was requested to terminate. **Killed** indicates a forceful termination of the process.

How to Prioritize Processes

In addition to running jobs in the foreground or the background, you can view information about the processes and assign priorities by using the following tools:

- ps
- pstree
- nice and renice
- top

NOTE You can use the command lsof (list open files) in /usr/bin/ to view which files are opened by processes. For a description of the command and possible options, enter **man lsof**.

ps

You can view all running processes by using the command ps (process status). With the option x, you can also view terminal-independent processes, as in the following:

```
geeko@DA50:~> ps x
  PID TTY       STAT    TIME COMMAND
 4170 pts/0     Ss      0:00 -bash
 4354 pts/0     S       0:00 sleep 99
 4355 pts/0     R+      0:00 ps x
geeko@DA50:~>
```

In the above example, the process with PID 4354 is a terminal-independent process. If you do not include the option x with ps, the process does not appear (as in the following):

```
geeko@DA50:~> ps x
  PID TTY       STAT    TIME COMMAND
 4170 pts/0     Ss      0:00 -bash
 4357 pts/0     R+      0:00 ps
geeko@DA50:~>
```

Table 6-1 lists some commonly used options with the command ps.

Table 6-1

Option	Description
x	Select processes without controlling ttys.
a	Select all processes on a terminal, including those of other users. (**Note:** "a" is not the same as "-a".)
-w, w	Provides detailed, wide output.
u	Display user-oriented format.
f	List processes hierarchically (in a tree format).

For example, the output of entering **ps axl** is similar to the following:

```
geeko@DA50:~> ps axl
F   UID   PID  PPID  PRI NI  VSZ   RSS   WCHAN STAT   TTY      TIME COMMAND
...
0  1013  4170  4169   15  0  3840  1760  wait4  Ss    pts/0    0:00 -bash
0  1013  4332  4170   15  0  4452  1812  finish T     pts/0    0:00 xeyes
0  1013  4351  4170   15  0  4452  1812  schedu S     pts/0    0:01 xeyes
0  1013  4356  4170   17  0  2156  652   -      R+    pts/0    0:00 ps axl
```

However, the output of entering **ps aux** looks like the following:

```
geeko@DA50:~> ps aux
USER    PID %CPU %MEM   VSZ  RSS TTY       STAT START    TIME COMMAND
geeko 4170  0.0  0.3  3840 1760 pts/0     Ss   12:10    0:00 -bash
geeko 4332  0.0  0.3  4452 1812 pts/0     T    12:59    0:00 xeyes
geeko 4351  0.3  0.3  4452 1812 pts/0     S    13:01    0:03 xeyes
geeko 4375  0.0  0.1  2156  680 pts/0     R+   13:19    0:00 ps aux
```

The basic difference is that with the option –l, you see the process ID of the father process (**PPID**), the process priority (**PRI**), and the nice value (**NI**) of the individual processes.

With the –u option, the load percentage is shown (**%CPU, %MEM**).

Table 6-2 describes each field (column) in the process list.

Table 6-2

Field	Description
UID	User ID
PID	Process ID
PPID	Parent process ID
TTY	Number of the controlling terminal
PRI	Priority number (the lower it is, the more computer time is allocated to the process)
NI (nice)	Influences the dynamic priority adjustment
STAT	Current process status (see Table 6-3)
TIME	Computer time used
COMMAND	Name of the command

The process state **STAT** can be one of those listed in Table 6-3.

Table 6-3

Code	Description
R (Runnable)	Process can be run
S (Sleeping)	Process is waiting for an external event (such as data arriving)
D (Uninterruptable sleep)	Comparable to "S" (the process cannot be terminated at the moment)
T (Traced or Stopped)	Process is suspended
X	Process is dead
Z (Zombie)	Process has terminated itself, but its return value has not yet been requested

You can format the output of ps to present the information you need:

```
geeko@DA50:~ > ps ax --format 'cputime %C, nice %n, name %c'
cputime %CPU, nice  NI, name COMMAND
cputime  0.0, nice   0, name bash
cputime  0.0, nice   0, name xeyes
cputime  0.3, nice   0, name xeyes
cputime  0.0, nice   0, name ps
```

For detailed information about using the command ps, enter **man ps**.

pstree

With the command pstree, you can view a list of processes in the form of a tree structure. This gives you an overview of the hierarchy of a process.

To end a series of processes, find the appropriate parent process and end that instead. The option –p displays the PID of the processes. The option –u displays the user ID if the owner has changed.

Because the list of processes is often long, you can enter **pstree –up | less** to view part of the processes at a time.

nice and renice

Linux always tries to distribute the available computing time equitably to all processes. However, you might want to assign a process more or less computing time.

You can do this with the command nice, as in the following:

```
nice -n +5 sleep 99
```

This command assigns a process a specific nice value that affects the calculation of the process priority (which is increased or decreased). If you do not enter a nice value, the process is started with the value +10.

The NI column in the top list (see Figure 6-3) contains the nice value of the process. The default value 0 is regarded as neutral. You can assign the nice level using a numeric value of –20 to 19.

The lower the value of the nice level, the higher the priority of the process. A process with a nice level of –20 runs at the highest priority; a process with a nice level of 19 runs at the lowest priority.

The nice level is used by the scheduler to determine how frequently to service a running process.

Only root is permitted to start a process with a negative nice value (such as **nice –n –3 sleep 99**). If a normal user attempts to do this, an error message is returned.

You can use the command renice to change the nice value of a running process, increasing or reducing its priority, such as

renice 5 1712

In this example, the command assigns the process with the PID 1712 the new nice value 5. This can also be done in top by entering **r**.

Only root can reduce the nice value of a running process (such as from 10 to 9 or from 3 to –2). All other users can only increase the nice value (such as from 10 to 11).

For example, if the user geeko attempts to assign the process 28056 that currently has a nice value of 3 to a nice value of 1, a Permission denied message is returned.

top

The command top combines the functionality of the command ps and the command renice in a single utility that provides a real-time view of a running system.

The information displayed in top can be filtered by a specific user, and can be sorted on any displayed field. By typing **r**, you can adjust the priority of a process, provided the you have sufficient privileges to do so.

As with the command renice, the same restrictions apply when changing process nice levels using top. Non-root users can lower the nice level, but they cannot raise it.

NOTE

When you enter **top**, a list similar to the one in Figure 6-3 appears.

```
top - 12:40:25 up 6 days,  1:11,  1 user,  load average: 1.03, 1.03, 1.00
Tasks:  92 total,   1 running,  91 sleeping,   0 stopped,   0 zombie
Cpu(s): 97.0% us,  2.7% sy,  0.0% ni,  0.0% id,  0.0% wa,  0.3% hi,  0.0% si
Mem:    514712k total,   501004k used,    13628k free,   109896k buffers
Swap:  1028120k total,       0k used,  1028112k free,   140464k cached

  PID USER      PR  NI  VIRT  RES  SHR S %CPU %MEM    TIME+  COMMAND
 3539 root      15   0 84800  16m  68m S 10.6  3.3  4:19.51 X
 7182 root      15   0 26276  13m  17m S  2.7  2.7 215:38.19 y2base
 3657 geeko     15   0 26448  14m  23m S  1.7  2.8  0:29.64 kdeinit
 3665 geeko     15   0 28816  17m  24m S  1.3  3.4  0:25.69 kdeinit
 3757 geeko     15   0 27296  17m  23m S  0.7  3.5  0:25.57 ksnapshot
22908 geeko     15   0 27616  14m  24m S  0.7  3.0  0:01.10 kdeinit
    1 root      16   0   588  244  444 S  0.0  0.0  0:05.00 init
    2 root      34  19     0    0    0 S  0.0  0.0  0:00.06 ksoftirqd/0
    3 root       5 -10     0    0    0 S  0.0  0.0  0:00.07 events/0
    4 root      13 -10     0    0    0 S  0.0  0.0  0:00.00 kacpid
    5 root       5 -10     0    0    0 S  0.0  0.0  0:00.00 kblockd/0
    6 root       5 -10     0    0    0 S  0.0  0.0  0:00.00 khelper
    7 root      15   0     0    0    0 S  0.0  0.0  0:05.37 pdflush
    8 root      15   0     0    0    0 S  0.0  0.0  0:04.74 pdflush
   10 root      10 -10     0    0    0 S  0.0  0.0  0:00.00 aio/0
    9 root      15   0     0    0    0 S  0.0  0.0  0:09.68 kswapd0
  163 root      23   0     0    0    0 S  0.0  0.0  0:00.00 kseriod
```

Figure 6-3

The displayed list is sorted by computing time and is updated every 5 seconds. You can terminate the display typing **q**.

Table 6-4 describes the default columns.

Table 6-4

Command	Description
PID	Process ID
USER	User name
PR	Priority
NI	Nice value
VIRT	Virtual Image (in KB)
RES	Resident Size (in KB)
SHR	Shared Mem Size (in KB)
S	Process Status
%CPU	CPU Usage
%MEM	Memory Usage (RES)
TIME+	CPU time
COMMAND	Command name/line

You can view the process management commands available in top by entering **?** or **h**. Table 6-5 lists some of the more commonly used commands.

Table 6-5

Command	Description
r	Assign a new nice value to a running process
k	Send a running process the termination signal (same as kill or killall)
N	Sort by process ID
P	Sort by CPU load

How to End a Process

If a process loses the connection to the terminal controlling it (so it can no longer be controlled by keyboard input such as Ctrl+Z), you can use the following to end the process:

- kill and killall
- KDE System Guard

NOTE

You can also send a signal to end the process in top using the command k.

kill and killall

You can use the commands kill and killall to terminate a process. The command killall kills all processes with an indicated command name; the command kill kills only the indicated process.

The command kill requires the PID of the process (use ps or top to find the PID). The command killall needs the command name of the process.

For example, if you enter xeyes at the command line to start the XEYES program (and the PID is 18734), you can enter **kill 18734** or **killall xeyes** to end the process.

A process can do one of the following when receiving a signal:

- Capture the signal and react to it (if it has a corresponding function available). For example, an editor can close a file properly before it is terminated.

 or

- Ignore the signal if no function exists for handling that signal.

However, the process does not have control over the following two signals as they are handled by the kernel:

- **kill –SIGKILL** or **kill –9**
- **kill –STOP** or **kill –19**

These signals cause the process to be ended immediately (**SIGKILL**) or to be stopped (**STOP**).

You should use SIGKILL with caution. Although the operating system closes all files that are still open, data in buffers is no longer processed. This means that some processes might leave the service in an undefined state, so it cannot easily be started again.

NOTE

For a complete list of signals generated by kill and what their numbers stand for, enter **kill -l** or **man 7 signal**.

The more commonly-used signals are listed in Table 6-6.

Table 6-6

Number	Name	Description
1	SIGHUP	Reload configuration file
2	SIGINT	Interrupt from keyboard (**Ctrl+C**)
9	SIGKILL	Kill process
15	SIGTERM	End process immediately (terminate process in a controlled manner so clean-up is possible)
18	SIGCONT	Continue process stopped with STOP
19	STOP	Stop process

For the kernel to forward the signal to the process, it must be sent by the owner of the process or by root. By default (without options), kill and killall send signal 15 (SIGTERM).

The following is the recommended way of ending an unwanted process:

1. Send SIGTERM by entering one of the following:

   - **kill –SIGTERM** *PID*

     or

   - **kill –15** *PID*

     or

   - **kill** *PID*

   You can use killall instead of kill and the command name of the process instead of the PID.

2. Wait a few moments for the process to be cleaned up.

3. If the process is still there, send a SIGKILL signal by entering one of the following:

   - **kill –SIGKILL** *PID*

     or

   - **kill –9** *PID*

   You can use killall instead of kill and the command name of the process instead of the PID.

If a process has been started from the bash shell, you can also use the job ID instead of the process number (such as **kill %4**).

KDE System Guard

From the KDE desktop, you can start the utility KDE System Guard (**System > Monitor > KDE System Guard**) to view and kill processes, as shown in Figure 6-4.

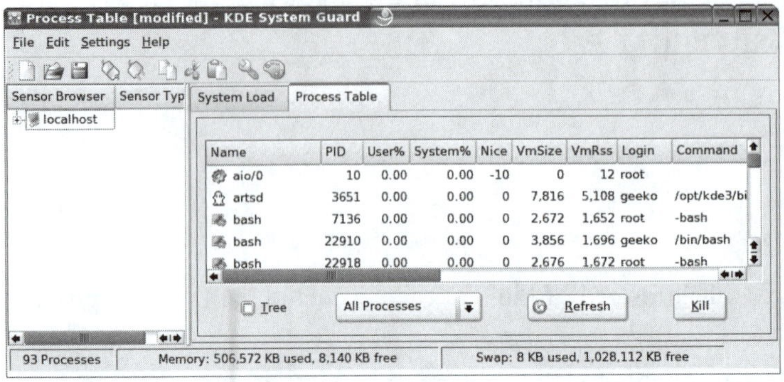
Process Table [modified] - KDE System Guard
File Edit Settings Help
Sensor Browser
Sensor Typ
System Load
Process Table
localhost
Name
PID
User%
System%
Nice
VmSize
VmRss
Login
Command
aio/0 10 0.00 0.00 -10 0 12 root
artsd 3651 0.00 0.00 0 7,816 5,108 geeko /opt/kde3/bi
bash 7136 0.00 0.00 0 2,672 1,652 root -bash
bash 22910 0.00 0.00 0 3,856 1,696 geeko /bin/bash
bash 22918 0.00 0.00 0 2,676 1,672 root -bash
Tree
All Processes
Refresh
Kill
93 Processes
Memory: 506,572 KB used, 8,140 KB free
Swap: 8 KB used, 1,028,112 KB free

Figure 6-4

If you encounter a misbehaving or hung process, you can kill it with KDE System Guard by selecting the ***process*** from the Process Table and selecting **Kill**.

Processes and Services (Daemons)

On a Linux system, the terms process and service are used to describe different pieces of software that run on the system.

A ***service*** is also called a ***daemon*** (Disk And Execution MONitor) and is a process or collection of processes that wait for an external event to trigger an action on the part of the program. Examples of common services are the Apache Web Server, the OpenLDAP server, and the xinetd service.

In each of these network-based services (during system startup) a script runs to start a ***listener*** on a TCP or UDP port. This listener waits for network traffic to appear on the designated port, and when traffic is detected, the program processes the traffic as input and generates output that is sent back to the requester.

For example, when a Web browser connects to a Web server, the traffic seen by the Apache httpd service might look similar to the following:

```
GET /
```

The result that is sent back by the Apache httpd daemon might look something like the following:

```
<!DOCTYPE html PUBLIC "-//W3C//DTD XHTML 1.0 Transitional//
EN" "http://www.w3.org/TR/xhtml1/DTD/xhtml1-transitional.dtd">

<html xmlns="http://www.w3.org/1999/xhtml">
```

```
<head><title>Test Page for Apache Installation</title></head>

<!-- Background white, links blue (unvisited), navy (visited),
red (active) -->

<body bgcolor="#FFFFFF" text="#000000" link="#0000FF"

vlink="#000080" alink="#FF0000">

<p>If you can see this, it means that the installation of the
<a href="http://www. apache.org/foundation/preFAQ.html">Apache
web server</a> software on this system was successful. You may
now add content to this directory and replace this page.</p>

<hr width="50%" size="8" />

<h2 align="center">Seeing this instead of the website you
expected?</h2>

<p>This page is here because the site administrator has changed
the configuration of this web server. Please <strong>contact the
person responsible for maintaining this server with questions.
</strong>

The Apache Software Foundation, which wrote the web server
software this site administrator is using, has nothing to do with
maintaining this site and cannot help resolve configuration
issues.</p>

<hr width="50%" size="8" />

<p>The Apache <a href="manual/">documentation</a> has been
included with this distribution.</p>

<p>You are free to use the image below on an Apache-powered
web server. Thanks for using Apache!</p>

<div align="center"><img src="apache_pb.gif" alt="" />
</div></body></html>
```

This response is then handled by the software that made the request. In this example, that would typically be a Web browser, which would make the page human-readable.

Most network-based services work in a similar way. The data is not always clear text data (such as httpd), but the service is a request/reply pair that comes into a process listening on a port for something that is valid input to the process.

How to Manage a Daemon Process

Daemons run in the background and are usually started when the system is booted. Daemons make a number of services available.

For this reason, daemons are terminal-independent processes and are indicated in the **ps x** TTY column by a "?."

In most cases, you can recognize a daemon by the ending "d" (such as syslogd or sshd). However, there are also a number of services where this is not the case (such as cron or portmap).

There are 2 types of daemons available:

- **Signal-controlled daemons.** These are always activated when a corresponding task exists (such as cupsd).

- **Interval-controlled daemons.** These are always activated at certain intervals (such as cron or atd).

For each daemon, there is a script in /etc/init.d/. Each script can be controlled and run with the parameters shown in Table 6-7.

Table 6-7

Parameter	Description
start	Starts the service.
stop	Stops the service.
reload (or restart)	Reloads the configuration file of the service, or stops the service and starts it again.

For many scripts, there is a symbolic link in the directory /usr/sbin/ or in the directory /sbin/, such as the following:

```
DA50:~ # ls -l /usr/sbin/rcsshd
lrwxrwxrwx  1 root root 16 Jul 16 17:26 /usr/sbin/rcsshd ->
/etc/init.d/sshd
```

You can start the service from the directory /etc/init.d/ (such as **/etc/init.d/sshd start**). If a link exists in the /usr/sbin/ or /sbin/, you can use rc (such as **rcsshd start**).

You can find configuration files for daemons in the directory /etc/ or in a subdirectory of /etc/.

The executable programs (the actual daemons) are located either in the directory /sbin/ or in the directory /usr/sbin/.

NOTE   For documentation on most daemons, see /usr/share/doc/packages/.

Some important daemons include the following:

- **cron.** Starts other processes at specified times (system-wide files: /etc/crontab and in /etc/cron.*; user-specific files are in /var/spool/cron/tabs/).

- **cupsd.** The printing daemon. When the system is booted, printing is started by the script /etc/init.d/cups.

- **httpd.** The daemon of the Apache2 Web Server (start script is /etc/init.d/apache2; configuration files are in /etc/apache2/; main configuration file is /etc/apache2/httpd.conf; log files are in /var/log/apache2/).

- **sshd.** Enables secure communication by way of insecure networks (secure shell). The start script is /etc/init.d/sshd.

- **syslogd.** Logs system messages in the directory /var/log/ (start script is /etc/init.d/syslog; configuration file is /etc/syslog.conf).

Exercise 6-1   Manage Linux Processes and Services

In this exercise, you do the following:

- Part I: Move Processes in the Background
- Part II: Modify Process Priorities
- Part III: Enable Services
- Part IV: Enable Services Using YaST

Part I: Move Processes in the Background

Do the following:

1. Make sure you are logged in as **geeko** to the KDE desktop.

2. Open a terminal window.

3. From the command line, display the processes that are currently owned by geeko by entering **ps -lU geeko**.

4. Display the processes that are currently owned by root by entering **ps -lU root**.

5. Start the program Xosview by entering **xosview**.

   Notice that the terminal is not available to receive new commands (no command is line displayed) because the Xosview program is running in the foreground.

6. Move the **xosview** window below the **Konsole** window; then select the **Konsole** window to activate it.

7. Suspend the Xosview program by pressing **Ctl+Z**.

   Notice that the data is no longer being updated in Xosview.

8. View the job in the background by entering **jobs**.

9. View the Xosview process running from the current terminal by entering **ps –l**.

   The process shows a status of T, which means that it is being traced or stopped.

10. Resume the Xosview program running in the background by entering **bg %1**.

    The program Xosview is running again (notice the data being updated).

    Because it is running in the background, you can use the terminal window to enter other commands.

11. Verify that the job status is running by entering **jobs**.

12. View the Xosview branch in the process tree by entering

    pstree –p | grep xosview.

    Xosview is listed as part of the tree.

13. Bring the Xosview process into the foreground by entering **fg %1**.

14. Close the terminal window.

    Notice that the Xosview program ends as well.

15. Open a new terminal window.

16. Start Xosview in the background so that it runs when the terminal window closes by entering **nohup xosview&**.

17. Close the terminal window.

    The Xosview program is still running.

18. Open a new terminal window.

19. Start the top program by entering **top**.

20. View only the processes started by geeko by typing **u**; then enter **geeko**.

21. Check for the Xosview program (**xosview.bin**) listed in top.

22. (Conditional) If you cannot find the Xosview program, try maximizing the Konsole window.

23. Record the PID of the Xosview process:_____

24. Exit top by typing **q**.

25. View information about the Xosview process by entering **ps** *PID_of_xosview_process*.

26. Stop the Xosview program and check the status by entering the following commands:

    kill *PID_of_xosview_process*

    ps aux | grep xosview

27. Start the program xeyes in the background by entering **xeyes&**.

28. Kill the program xeyes by entering **killall xeyes**.

Part II: Modify Process Priorities

Do the following:

1. Start the program Xosview in the background by entering **xosview&**.

2. Record the PID for Xosview (displayed in the terminal window):

    _____

3. View the process running by entering **ps lf**.

    Notice that the nice value (NI) is currently at 0.

4. Increase the priority of the process to a nice value of –5 by entering the following:

    renice –5 –p *PID_of_xosview_process*

    Notice that a regular user cannot change the nice value below 0, only 0–20.

5. Su to root (**su –**) with a password of **novell**.

6. Try setting the nice value to –5 again by entering the following:

    renice –5 –p *PID_of_xosview_process*

7. Check that the setting is effective by entering **ps lf**.

    Notice that the process is not displayed because ps lf only displays processes started by the current user. The program Xosview was started by geeko (not root).

8. View all processes by entering **ps alf**.

    The Xosview process is now displayed.

9. Change the nice value for the Xosview process to a higher priority by entering the following:

    renice –10 –p *PID_of_xosview_process*

10. Verify that the Xosview process nice value is set to –10 by entering **ps alf**.

11. Exit the shell running as root by entering **exit**.

    You should now be user geeko again.

12. Start the program xeyes in the background with the nice value of +10 by entering **nice xeyes&**.

13. Verify that the xeyes process nice value is set to +10 by entering **ps lf**.

14. Kill the xosview and xeyes processes by entering the following commands:

    kill *PID_of_xosview_process*

    killall xeyes

Part III: Enable Services

In this part of the exercise, you enable the system service at to run at system boot at runlevels 2, 3, and 5.

The service at allows commands to be scheduled at a future point in time. You use it later in this section.

Do the following:

1. From the terminal window, su to root (**su -**) with a password of **novell**.

2. View the current runlevel configuration for atd by entering **chkconfig atd -l**.

    Notice that configuration is off for all runlevels.

3. Install the service to its predefined runlevels by entering **insserv -d atd**.

4. Check the modified runlevel configuration for at by entering **chkconfig atd -l**.

    Notice that the default configuration for at sets runlevels 2, 3, and 5 to on.

5. Change to the directory /etc/rc.d/rc3.d by entering **cd /etc/rc.d/rc3.d**.

6. List the atd files in the directory by entering **ls -l *atd**.

    Notice that there are two atd links—one is used to start and one is used to kill the service atd.

7. Start the service at by entering **rcatd start**.

8. Verify that the service is running by entering **rcatd status**.

9. Switch to virtual terminal 1 by pressing **Ctrl+Alt+F1**; then log in as **root**.

10. Switch to runlevel 1 by entering **telinit 1**.

11. Enter a root password of **novell**.

12. Check to see if the service is running by entering **rcatd status**.

    The service is listed as unused because it is not configured to start at runlevel 1.

13. Switch back to your previous runlevel (5) by entering **init 5**.

    The GUI login screen appears.

14. Log in as **geeko** with a password of **N0v3ll**.

15. From the KDE desktop, open a terminal window and su to root (**su -**) with a password of **novell**.

16. From the command line, remove the service at from system startup runlevels by entering **chkconfig atd off**.

17. View the current runlevel configuration for at by entering **chkconfig atd -l**.

    Notice that the service is off for all runlevels.

18. Re-enable the service to start at the default runlevels by entering **chkconfig atd on**.

Part IV: Enable Services Using YaST

Do the following:

1. From the KDE desktop, select the **YaST** icon; then enter a password of **novell** and select **OK**.

    The YaST Control Center appears.

2. Select **System > Runlevel Editor**.

    The Runlevel Editor: Services dialog appears.

3. Switch to a more detailed view (with additional options) by selecting **Expert Mode**.

4. Scroll down the Services list and select **rsyncd**.

5. Below the list, configure this service to start at runlevels 3 and 5 by selecting **3** and **5**.

6. From the Set/Reset drop-down list select **Enable the service**.

7. Start the service rsyncd from the Start/Stop/Refresh drop-down list by selecting **Start now**.

    A status message appears indicating that the service started successfully.

8. Close the status message by selecting **OK**.

9. Stop the service rsyncd from the Start/Stop/Refresh drop-down list by selecting **Stop now**.

    A status message appears indicating that the service stopped successfully.

10. Close the status message by selecting **OK**.

11. Change the configuration so that rsyncd does not run at any runlevel from the Set/Reset drop-down list by selecting **Disable the service**.

12. Save the changes by selecting **Finish**; then select **Yes**.

13. Close the YaST Control Center and the terminal window.

OBJECTIVE 2   DESCRIBE STARTUP SHELL SCRIPTS AND SERVICES

You can start services selectively by selecting a default runlevel (defined in /etc/inittab) or by changing the runlevel of the system using the command init.

To describe the relationship between startup shell scripts and services, you need to understand the following:

- Startup Scripts
- Startup Script Directory Structure
- Startup Script Structure

Startup Scripts

Startup scripts are run as soon as the system is switched to a new runlevel. This runlevel is usually a multiuser runlevel (such as 3 or 5), but the scripts can be initiated in any runlevel as long as their dependencies are met.

The scripts listed in Table 6-8 are called during system startup.

Table 6-8

Startup Script	Description
/etc/init.d/network	This script handles the configuration of the network hardware and software when the system is booted.
/etc/init.d/inetd	Starts xinetd. xinetd makes server services available on the system. For example, it can start vsftpd whenever an FTP connection is initiated.
/etc/init.d/portmap	Starts the portmapper needed for the RPC (Remote Procedure Call)-based services (such as an NFS server).
/etc/init.d/nfsserver	Starts the NFS server.
/etc/init.d/sendmail	Controls the sendmail process.
/etc/init.d/ypserv	Starts the NIS server.
/etc/init.d/ypbind	Starts the NIS client.

Scripts for network-based services need to run after the network script is run. Because the network script is not run in runlevel 1, you cannot use network-based services scripts in runlevel 1.

Startup Script Directory Structure

The following are the directories for the startup scripts in a SUSE Linux Enterprise Server 9 environment:

- **/etc/init.d/.** This is the directory where the startup scripts are stored.
- **/etc/init.d/rcn.d/.** These are the directories that store the links for each runlevel to the startup scripts in /etc/init.d/. For example, the directory for runlevel 5 is /etc/init.d/rc5.d.

The symbolic links inside the rc*n*.d directories look similar to those shown in Figure 6-5.

```
lrwxrwxrwx  1 root root   6 Jul  9 07:47 K12nfs -> ../nfs
lrwxrwxrwx  1 root root  10 Jul  9 07:47 K12nfsboot -> ../nfsboot
lrwxrwxrwx  1 root root  10 Jul 21 13:00 K13nfslock -> ../nfslock
lrwxrwxrwx  1 root root  10 Jul  9 07:47 K14portmap -> ../portmap
lrwxrwxrwx  1 root root   9 Jul  9 07:46 K14resmgr -> ../resmgr
lrwxrwxrwx  1 root root   8 Jul  9 08:01 K14smbfs -> ../smbfs
lrwxrwxrwx  1 root root  15 Jul  9 07:46 K14splash_early -> ../splash_early
lrwxrwxrwx  1 root root   9 Jul  9 07:46 K16syslog -> ../syslog
lrwxrwxrwx  1 root root  10 Jul  9 08:20 K17network -> ../network
lrwxrwxrwx  1 root root  11 Jul  9 07:46 K20coldplug -> ../coldplug
lrwxrwxrwx  1 root root  10 Jul  9 07:46 K21hotplug -> ../hotplug
lrwxrwxrwx  1 root root   7 Jul  9 07:48 K21isdn -> ../isdn
lrwxrwxrwx  1 root root   9 Jul  9 07:44 K21random -> ../random
lrwxrwxrwx  1 root root  10 Jul  9 07:46 S01hotplug -> ../hotplug
lrwxrwxrwx  1 root root   7 Jul  9 07:48 S01isdn -> ../isdn
lrwxrwxrwx  1 root root   9 Jul  9 07:44 S01random -> ../random
lrwxrwxrwx  1 root root  11 Jul  9 07:46 S02coldplug -> ../coldplug
lrwxrwxrwx  1 root root  10 Jul  9 08:20 S05network -> ../network
lrwxrwxrwx  1 root root   9 Jul  9 07:46 S06syslog -> ../syslog
lrwxrwxrwx  1 root root  10 Jul  9 07:47 S08portmap -> ../portmap
lrwxrwxrwx  1 root root   9 Jul  9 07:46 S08resmgr -> ../resmgr
lrwxrwxrwx  1 root root   8 Jul  9 08:01 S08smbfs -> ../smbfs
lrwxrwxrwx  1 root root  15 Jul  9 07:46 S08splash_early -> ../splash_early
lrwxrwxrwx  1 root root  10 Jul 21 13:00 S09nfslock -> ../nfslock
```

Figure 6-5

The name of the link is prefixed with **S** (Start) or **K** (Kill) and a two-digit numeric value.

During system startup, the links with an S in front of them are accessed in numeric order (and alphabetically for scripts at the same priority). As each link is accessed, the corresponding script has the parameter start passed to it.

During a clean system shutdown, the scripts with a K in front of them are accessed in sequence with a parameter of stop passed to the corresponding script.

This shuts down the services in a predefined sequence and ensures that the services are all shut down cleanly before the system is powered off.

Startup Script Structure

The following script is the file skeleton stored in /etc/init.d/. You can use skeleton to create your own startup scripts:

```
#! /bin/sh
# Copyright (c) 1995-2004 SUSE Linux AG, Nuernberg, Germany.
# All rights reserved.
#
# Author: Kurt Garloff
# Please send feedback to http://www.suse.de/feedback/
#
# /etc/init.d/FOO
#    and its symbolic link
# /(usr/)sbin/rcFOO
#
# Template system startup script for some example service/daemon FOO
#
# LSB compatible service control script;
# see http://www.linuxbase.org/spec/
#
# Note: This template uses functions rc_XXX defined in /etc/rc.status on
# UnitedLinux (UL) based Linux distributions. If you want to base your
# script on this template and ensure that it works on non UL based LSB
# compliant Linux distributions, you either have to provide the rc.status
# functions from UL or change the script to work without them.
#
### BEGIN INIT INFO
# Provides:          FOO
# Required-Start:    $syslog $remote_fs
# Should-Start:      $time ypbind sendmail
```

You can view the contents of this file (which is several pages long) by entering **less /etc/init.d/skeleton**, or edit the file in any text editor.

If you are at a SLES 9 server, we recommend displaying the file skeleton as you review the following information.

NOTE

The following are some of the more important parts of the template for building a startup script:

- General Section
- Start Section
- Stop Section
- Restart Section
- Force-Reload Section
- Reload Section
- Status Section
- Last Option (*)

NOTE For additional details on init, the /etc/init.d scripts, and runlevels, see *Runlevel Basics* in Section 5.

General Section

Before checking the parameter passed to the script, there are commands in the **general** section that are executed regardless of the parameter passed to the script.

These commands test the existence of certain files and executables, set variables, and define functions or read configuration files (as in the following):

```
# Check for missing binaries (stale symlinks should not happen)
# Note: Special treatment of stop for LSB conformance
FOO_BIN=/usr/sbin/FOO
test -x $FOO_BIN || { echo "$FOO_BIN not installed";
        if [ "$1" = "stop" ]; then exit 0;
        else exit 5; fi; }

# Check for existence of needed config file and read it
FOO_CONFIG=/etc/sysconfig/FOO
test -r $FOO_CONFIG || { echo "$FOO_CONFIG not existing";
        if [ "$1" = "stop" ]; then exit 0;
        else exit 6; fi; }

# Read config
. $FOO_CONFIG
```

After this general section, there is a section for each valid parameter passed to the script. If a wrong parameter is passed to the script, a short help text message is displayed showing the valid parameters.

Start Section

The parameters passed to the script are evaluated using a case statement within the script, such as the following:

```
case "$1" in
```

In this example, the command line extracts the first parameter (**$1**) to perform comparisons for the following lines:

```
case "$1" in
    start)
        echo -n "Starting FOO "
        ## Start daemon with startproc(8). If this fails
        ## the return value is set appropriately by startproc.
        startproc $FOO_BIN

        # Remember status and be verbose
        rc_status -v
        ;;
```

This section compares the first parameter to the value **start** and executes the lines through the **;;** if the comparison is true.

Stop Section

As with the start section, the stop section compares the first parameter to the value **stop** and shuts down the process by sending the **SIGTERM** signal, which is typically used to shut a process down cleanly:

```
 stop)
        echo -n "Shutting down FOO "
        ## Stop daemon with killproc(8) and if this fails
        ## killproc sets the return value according to LSB.

        killproc -TERM $FOO_BIN

        # Remember status and be verbose
        rc_status -v
        ;;
    try-restart|condrestart)
        ## Do a restart only if the service was active before.
        ## Note: try-restart is now part of LSB (as of 1.9).
        ## RH has a similar command named condrestart.
        if test "$1" = "condrestart"; then
                echo "${attn} Use try-restart ${done}(LSB) ${attn} \
                        rather than condrestart ${warn}(RH) ${norm}"
        fi
        $0 status
        if test $? = 0; then
```

```
            $0 restart
    else
            rc_reset          # Not running is not a failure.
    fi
    # Remember status and be quiet
    rc_status
    ;;
```

In this example, the **try-restart** and **condrestart** parameters are used to restart the service only if it has already been running.

A value of try-restart is now considered in compliance with the Linux Standards Base (LSB), and condrestart is no longer used.

Notice that the script includes code to check for the use of condrestart in order to inform the user that condrestart is decremented usage.

Restart Section

The **restart** section in the script is used to unconditionally restart the service:

```
restart)
        ## Stop the service and regardless of whether it was
        ## running or not, start it again.
        $0 stop
        $0 start

        # Remember status and be quiet
        rc_status
        ;;
```

If the service was not running previously, there might be some error on the stop part, but the start is executed anyway.

With the try-restart and restart parameters, the commands pass $0. This calls the script with a different parameter to cause this behavior.

Nesting of a script in itself is something that is common in startup scripts in order to reduce duplication of code in the script.

Force-Reload Section

The **force-reload** section is commonly used to cause a service to reload its configuration files:

```
force-reload)
        ## Signal the daemon to reload its config. Most daemons
        ## do this on signal 1 (SIGHUP).
        ## If it does not support it, restart.

        echo -n "Reload service FOO "
        ## if it supports it:
```

```
killproc -HUP $FOO_BIN
#touch /var/run/FOO.pid
rc_status -v

## Otherwise:
#$0 try-restart
#rc_status
;;
```

Not all services support this, so check with the service you are working with to see if it has this functionality. Typically, the hangup signal (**SIGHUP**) is used to force processes to reload their configuration files.

While commented out in the above section of script, it is not uncommon to use the touch command to update the time stamp on the process' pid file (a file used to track what process ID is in use by the service itself).

Reload Section

The **reload** section is like the force-reload parameter except that if the service does not support the **HUP** signal, it does nothing:

```
reload)
        ## Like force-reload, but if daemon does not support
        ## signaling, do nothing (!)

        # If it supports signaling:
        echo -n "Reload service FOO "
        killproc -HUP $FOO_BIN
        #touch /var/run/FOO.pid
        rc_status -v

        ## Otherwise if it does not support reload:
        #rc_failed 3
        #rc_status -v
        ;;
```

Status Section

The **status** section is used to verify the service is running:

```
status)
        echo -n "Checking for service FOO "
        ## Check status with checkproc(8), if process is running
        ## checkproc will return with exit status 0.

        # Return value is slightly different for the status command:
        # 0 - service up and running
        # 1 - service dead, but /var/run/  pid  file exists
        # 2 - service dead, but /var/lock/ lock file exists
```

```
# 3 - service not running (unused)
# 4 - service status unknown :-(
# 5--199 reserved (5--99 LSB, 100--149 distro, 150--199 appl.)

# NOTE: checkproc returns LSB compliant status values.
checkproc $FOO_BIN
# NOTE: rc_status knows that we called this init script with
# "status" option and adapts its messages accordingly.
rc_status -v
;;
```

In some cases, all you want to do is check that the service is active rather than take the action of reloading; this is commonly done when troubleshooting a service.

Last Option (*)

The last option (*) is used for anything that has not been matched up to this point:

```
*)
        echo "Usage: $0 {start|stop|status|try-restart|restart|\
                        force-reload|reload|probe}"
        exit 1
        ;;
```

Anything else is considered invalid, and a help message is displayed to provide instructions on how to use the script.

The **exit 1** line tells the script to exit with an error. This can be used by a script that calls the startup script to perform actions based on the return value being an error.

OBJECTIVE 3   SCHEDULE JOBS

Most SUSE Linux Enterprise Server administrators and regular users find that they need to carry out certain tasks regularly on a running system (such as updating a database or backing up data).

You can automate these jobs in Linux by doing the following:

- Schedule a Job (cron)
- Run a Job One Time Only (at)

Schedule a Job (cron)

You can schedule jobs to be carried out on a regular basis by using the service cron (/usr/sbin/cron).

6

The service runs as a daemon and checks once a minute to see if jobs have been defined for the current time. By default, the service should be activated.

The file that contains the list of jobs is called a ***crontab***. A crontab exists for the entire system as well as for each user defined on the system.

The file /etc/sysconfig/cron contains variables for the configuration of some scripts started by cron.

There are two types of jobs that can be defined with cron:

- System Jobs
- User Jobs

System Jobs

You control system jobs with the file /etc/crontab. The cron jobs that are defined here after installation run the scripts contained in the directories listed in Table 6-9.

Table 6-9

Directory	Interval
/etc/cron.hourly	Jobs are run on an hourly basis.
/etc/cron.daily	Jobs are run on a daily basis.
/etc/cron.weekly	Jobs are run on a weekly basis.
/etc/cron.monthly	Jobs are run on a monthly basis.

You can add lines to /etc/crontab, but you should not delete the lines added at installation.

NOTE

For a detailed description of the syntax for /etc/crontab, enter **man 5 crontab**.

The scripts called from the file /etc/crontab not only ensure that the scripts are run at the prescribed intervals (handled by the script /usr/lib/cron/run-crons), but also that jobs are run later if they could not be run at the specified time.

For example, if a script could not be run at the specified time because the computer was turned off overnight, the script is automatically run later using the settings in /etc/crontab.

This is only valid for jobs defined in a script in cron.hourly, cron.daily, cron.weekly, or cron.monthly.

Information about the last time the jobs were run is kept in the directory /var/spool/cron/lastrun/ in a file such as cron.daily.

The time stamp of the file is evaluated by the script /usr/lib/cron/run-crons to determine if scripts have to be run or not.

In a standard installation, only the directory /etc/cron.daily/ contains scripts, such as the ones shown in Figure 6-6.

cron.d	96 B	Folder	2004-07-09 07:59	rwxr-xr-x	root	root
cron.daily	448 B	Folder	2004-07-09 08:02	rwxr-xr-x	root	root
clean_catman	924 B	Unknown	2004-06-30 15:31	rwx------	root	root
clean_core	1.7 KB	Unknown	2004-06-30 12:12	rwx------	root	root
cyrus	646 B	Plain Text Document	2004-06-30 15:38	rwxr-xr-x	root	root
do_mandb	1.1 KB	Unknown	2004-06-30 15:31	rwx------	root	root
logrotate	176 B	Shell Script	2004-06-30 12:07	rwxr-xr-x	root	root
suse.de-backup-rc.config	1.8 KB	Shell Script	2003-09-01 05:10	rwxr-xr-x	root	root
suse.de-backup-rpmdb	2.0 KB	Shell Script	2003-09-08 07:50	rwxr-xr-x	root	root
suse.de-check-battery	566 B	Shell Script	2003-10-06 09:36	rwxr-xr-x	root	root
suse.de-clean-tmp	1.1 KB	Shell Script	2003-09-01 05:10	rwxr-xr-x	root	root
suse.de-clean-vi	472 B	Shell Script	2003-09-01 05:10	rwxr-xr-x	root	root
suse.de-cron-local	371 B	Shell Script	2003-09-01 05:10	rwxr-xr-x	root	root
updatedb	1.5 KB	Unknown	2004-06-30 12:12	rwx------	root	root
cron.hourly	48 B	Folder	2004-06-30 12:43	rwxr-xr-x	root	root
cron.monthly	48 B	Folder	2004-06-30 12:43	rwxr-xr-x	root	root
cron.weekly	72 B	Folder	2004-07-09 08:00	rwxr-xr-x	root	root

Figure 6-6

These scripts are standard shell scripts set up to use a designated shell. These scripts are overwritten when you update your system.

For this reason, you should store any modifications to these scripts the script /root/bin/cron.daily.local, because this script is not overwritten when you update your system.

Other files for system jobs can be stored in the directory /etc/cron.d/. These files must have the same format as /etc/crontab. Jobs defined in /etc/cron.d are not run automatically at a later time.

User Jobs

You can set up cron to allow individual users (including root) the right to configure their own cron jobs by using the following 2 files:

- **/var/spool/cron/allow** (users entered here can define jobs)
- **/var/spool/cron/deny** (users who are not listed in this file can define jobs)

These files are text files you can modify or create.

By default, the file /var/spool/cron/deny already exists with its own entries, such as the following:

```
guest
gast
```

If the file /var/spool/cron/allow exists, only the file is evaluated. If neither of these files exist, only the user root can define jobs.

The jobs of individual users are stored in the directory /var/spool/cron/tabs/ in files matching the user names. These files always belong to the user root. You can use the command crontab to edit them.

Table 6-10 lists options for the command crontab.

Table 6-10

Option	Description
crontab -e	Creates or edits jobs. The vi editor is used.
crontab *file*	The specified *file* contains a list of jobs.
crontab -l	Displays current jobs.
crontab -r	Deletes all jobs.

Each line in a file defines a job. There are six fields in a line.

The first five fields define the time, the final field contains the command to run. This can be any type of command or shell script. However, no user interaction is available when the command or shell script is run.

Table 6-11 shows the format for the first five fields.

Table 6-11

Field	Range
Minutes	0–59
Hours	0–23
Day of the Month	1–31
Month	0–12
Weekday	0–7

The guidelines for configuring these fields are:

- If you want a job to run on every date, enter an asterisk (*) in the corresponding field.
- You can include several entries in a field, separated by commas.
- You can specify a range with start and end values separated by a hyphen.
- You can configure time steps with */n* (where *n* stands for the size of the step).
- You can specify months and weekdays by their first three letters (not case-sensitive). However, when you use letters, you cannot use ranges or lists.
- Numbers representing the weekdays start a 0 for Sunday and run through the entire week consecutively, with 7 representing Sunday again.

  For example, 3 is Wednesday and 6 is Saturday.

The following is an example of a cron job entry:

```
*/10 8-17 * * 1-5 fetchmail mailserver
```

In this example, from Monday to Friday (**1-5**) every 10 minutes (***/10**) between 8.00 and 17.00 (**8-17**), the command **fetchmail** is run to fetch incoming emails from the computer **mailserver**.

For system jobs, the user who has the permissions to run the command must be specified in the file /etc/crontab, by entering the user name between the time details (the first 5 fields) and the name of the command (which now becomes the seventh field).

Run a Job One Time Only (at)

If you want to run a job one time only (instead of scheduling it on a regular basis with cron) you can use the command at. To use at, you must make sure the service atd is started.

There are two files that determine which users can run this command (in the same way as cron):

- **/etc/at.allow** (users entered here can define jobs)
- **/etc/at.deny** (users who are not listed in this file can define jobs)

These files are text files you can modify or create.

By default, the file /etc/at.deny already exists with its own entries, such as the following:

```
alias
backup
bin
daemon
ftp
games...
```

If the file /etc/at.allow exists, only the file is evaluated. If neither of these files exist, only the user root can define jobs with at.

You define a job from a command prompt by entering

at *launch_time* (where *launch_time* is when you want the job to begin).

At this point you are placed in a special environment where you enter commands 1 line at a time. When you finish entering commands, you save the job by pressing **Ctrl+D**.

The following is an example of creating a job with the command at:

```
geeko@DA50:~> at 21:00
warning: commands will be executed using /bin/sh
at> /home/geeko/bin/doit
at> mail -s "Results file of geeko" geeko@DA50 < /home/geeko/
results
at> <EOT>
job 4 at 2007-08-27 21:00
```

If the commands you want executed are contained in a text file, you need to enter **at -f** *file launch_time* (where *file* is the pathname of the file).

Table 6-12 shows some other commonly used commands and options for at.

Table 6-12

Command	Description
atq	Display defined jobs (including job numbers, which are needed to delete a job)
atrm *job_number*	Delete a job (using the job number)

Exercise 6-2   Schedule Jobs With cron and at

In this exercise, you do the following:

- Part I: Schedule Jobs with at
- Part II: Schedule Jobs with cron

Part I: Schedule Jobs with at

Do the following:

1. From a terminal window on your KDE desktop, su to root (**su –**) with a password of **novell**.

2. Verify that the service at is running by entering **rcatd status**.

3. (Conditional) If the at service is not running, start the service by entering **rcatd start**.

4. Verify that the service is running in your current runlevel by entering **chkconfig atd –l**.

5. Display the current date and time by entering **date**.

6. Three minutes from now, log to /var/log/messages who is logged in by entering the following commands:

    at *hh*:*mm*

    finger >> /var/log/messages

7. Exit the at editor by pressing **Ctrl+D**.

8. View the scheduled at jobs by entering **atq** (or **at –l**).

    Notice that the job number is listed as 1.

9. Wait for the 3 minutes to pass; then check the file /var/log/messages for the finger information by entering **tail /var/log/messages**.

    Login information for geeko is listed at the end of the file.

6

10. Schedule the same job to run tomorrow at noon by entering the following:

    at noon tomorrow

    finger >> /var/log/messages

    Ctl+D

11. Schedule the date to be logged tomorrow at 2:00 P.M. to the file /var/log/ messages by entering the following:

    at 14:00 tomorrow

    date >> /var/log/messages

    Ctl+D

12. View the scheduled at jobs by entering **atq** (or **at –l**).

    Notice that the two jobs are listed, each with an individual job number.

13. Remove the job scheduled for tomorrow at 2:00 P.M. by entering the following:

    atrm *job_number*

14. View the scheduled at jobs by entering **atq** (or **at –l**).

    Only the job scheduled for 12:00 P.M. is still listed.

15. Restrict the user dba1 from submitting at jobs by adding the account name to the file /etc/at.deny:

    a. Open the file /etc/at.deny in the vi editor by entering **vim /etc/at.deny**.

    b. Press **Insert**; then scroll to the bottom of the file.

    c. Start a new line by pressing **Enter** and type **dba1**.

    d. Return to command mode by pressing **Esc**.

    e. Save the changes and close the vi editor by entering **:wq**.

16. Test the deny restriction by logging in as **dba1** and attempting to submit an at job:

    a. From the KDE Desktop, restart X windows by pressing **Ctrl+Alt+Backspace**.

    The GUI login screen appears.

    b. Log in as **dba1** with a password of **suse1**.

    c. Open a terminal window.

    d. Display the current date and time by entering **date**.

    e. Try entering the following for three minutes from the current time:

       at *hh*:*mm*

       A message appears indicating that you do not have permission to use at.

17. (Optional) If you have time, try restoring the right to create an at job to dba1, and then create an at job as dba1.

18. Log in to the KDE desktop as geeko by pressing **Ctrl+Alt+Backspace**; then log in as **geeko** with a password of **N0v3ll**.

Part II: Schedule Jobs with cron

Do the following:

1. Change to the Level 2 (Networked Workstation) security level:

   Before using cron as a normal user, you need to make sure that the security settings on your server are set to the correct level, or you cannot use the utility.

    a. From the KDE desktop, select the **YaST** icon; then enter a password of **novell** and select **OK**.

       The YaST Control Center appears.

    b. From the YaST Control Center, select **Security and Users > Security settings**.

    c. Select **Level 2 (Networked Workstation)**; then select **Finish**.

2. Open a terminal window.

3. Schedule a cron job as geeko:

    a. Enter **crontab -e**.

       The vi editor is displayed for a cron table file (such as /tmp/crontab.11743).

    b. Press **Insert**.

    c. Add a job that runs at 2:00 a.m. every Tuesday and creates a tarball of /etc that is saved in /export/data2/backup by entering the following:

       0 2 * * 2 tar czvf /export/data2/backup/etc.tgz /etc

    d. Press **Esc**.

    e. Save the file and exit the vi editor by entering **:wq**.

    f. Verify that the job is in the crontab file for geeko by entering **crontab -l**.

4. Schedule a cron job as root:

    a. Su to root (**su -**) with a password of **novell**.

    b. Enter **crontab -e**.

c. Schedule a job to run every minute that uses finger to record to the file ~/users.log who is logged in by entering the following:

* * * * * finger >> ~/users.log

d. Press **Esc**.

e. Save the file and exit the vi editor by entering **:wq**.

f. Watch the file users.log for a few minutes to validate that it is being updated by entering the following:

tail –f /root/users.log

g. When you finish watching the file update, press **Ctrl+C**.

5. Remove root's crontab file by entering **crontab –r**.

6. Verify that the crontab file no longer exists by entering **crontab –l**.

7. Verify that the crontab file is no longer active by entering **tail –f ~/users.log**. Notice that entries to users.log are no longer being added.

8. Press **Ctrl+C**.

9. Log out as root by entering **exit**.

10. Remove geeko's crontab file by entering **crontab –r**.

11. Verify that the crontab file no longer exists by entering **crontab –l**.

12. Change to the security level back to Level 3 (Network Server):

a. From the YaST Control Center, select **Security and Users > Security settings**.

b. Select **Level 3 (Network Server)**; then select **Finish**.

13. Close all open windows.

Objective 4 Use System Logging Services

In a Linux system, there are many logs that track various aspects of system operation. Many services log their activities to their own log files, and the level of detail can be set on a per-service basis. In addition, system logs in /var/log/ track system-level events.

The information logged in these log files is typically used to assist in troubleshooting and security auditing. However, you will probably want to review the logs from time to time as a preventative measure.

To use system logging services, you need to understand the following:

- The syslog Daemon
- Important Log Files
- How to View Log Files with YaST
- How to Archive Log Files (logrotate)
- How to Monitor Hard Drive Space

The syslog Daemon

The syslog daemon syslogd is used by many services to log system events. The advantage in using a single service for logging is that all logging can be managed from one configuration file.

The daemon syslogd in Linux is based on the BSD syslogd service. While it conforms to standard behavior, it has been extended for use in Linux as well. This means that syslogd is compatible with non-Linux systems that conform to the documented BSD interfaces.

The syslog daemon accepts messages from system services and logs them based on settings in the configuration file /etc/syslog.conf.

For details on the syslog.conf file, enter **man syslog.conf**.

The following is an example of the syslogd configuration file:

```
# /etc/syslog.conf - Configuration file for syslogd(8)
#
# For info about the format of this file, see "man syslog.conf".
#

#
# print most on tty10 and on the xconsole pipe
#
kern.warning;*.err;authpriv.none          /dev/tty10
kern.warning;*.err;authpriv.none          |/dev/xconsole
*.emerg                                   *

# enable this, if you want that root is informed
# immediately, e.g. of logins
#*.alert                                  root
...
```

The file /etc/syslog.conf contains one rule per line. Each rule consists of two fields separated by spaces or tabs.

The category is given in the first field, which is always allocated a priority, separated by a dot (such as **kern.warn**). The second field specifies what should be done with the corresponding system messages (such as **/dev/xconsole**).

To understand how syslog.conf works, you need to know about the following components:

- Categories
- Priorities
- Second Field Options
- Additional Priority Parameters

Categories

The category refers to the subsystem that provides the corresponding message. Each program that uses syslog for logging is assigned such a category.

Table 6-13 lists these categories.

Table 6-13

Category	Description
authpriv	Used by all services that have anything to do with system security or authorization. All PAM messages use this category. The ssh daemon uses the auth category.
cron	Accepts messages from the cron and at daemons.
daemon	Used by various daemons that do not have their own category, such as the ppp daemon.
kern	A category for all kernel messages.
lpr	This category handles messages from the printer system.
news	This category is for messages from the news system. As with the mail system, many messages might need to be logged in a short time.
mail	This category is for messages from the mail system. This is important because many messages can arrive very quickly.
syslog	This category is for internal messages of the syslog daemon.
user	This is a general category for messages on a user level. For example, It is used by login to log failed login attempts.
uucp	This category handles messages from the uucp system.
local0 – local7	These 8 categories are available for your own configuration. All of the local categories can be used in your own programs. By configuring one of these categories, messages from your own programs can be administered individually through entries in the file /etc/syslog.conf.

Priorities

The priority gives details about the urgency of the message. The priorities shown in Table 6-14 are available (listed in increasing degree of urgency).

Table 6-14

Priority	Description
debug	This priority should only be used for debugging purposes, since all messages of this category and higher are logged.
info	This priority is for messages that are purely informative.
notice	This priority is for messages that describe normal system states that should be noted.
warning	This priority is for messages displaying deviations from the normal state.
err	This priority displays the occurrence of an error.
crit	This priority informs you of critical conditions for the specified program.
alert	This priority level informs the system administrator that immediate action is needed to keep the system functioning.
emerg	This priority warns you that the system is no longer usable.

Second Field Options

As already mentioned, the second field for each entry determines what will be done with the corresponding message.

The following options are available:

- **Output of a file.** Adding a - before the filename specifies that the file is not synchronized for each entry.

  The following is an example:
  ```
  mail.*              -/var/log/mail
  ```

- **Specifying the device file for a text console.** All corresponding messages are sent to the console specified.

  The following is an example:
  ```
  kern.warn;*.err;authpriv.none /dev/tty10
  ```

- **Specifying a FIFO file (named pipe) by putting the pipe character (|) in front of the file name.** All corresponding messages are written into the FIFO file.

  The following is an example:
  ```
  kern.warn;*.err;authpriv.none        |/dev/xconsole
  ```

- **Specifying a user list.** All users mentioned who are logged in receive a message on their text terminal (this does not work on all terminal types).

  The following is an example:
  ```
  *.alert              root,geeko
  ```

- **Specifying a computer name with a prefixed @.** Messages are forwarded to the computer specified and logged there by syslog, depending on the configuration on that computer.

  The following is an example:
  ```
  *.*              @mars.example.com
  ```

- **Using an asterisk (*).** All users logged in receive a message through the **wall** (write all) command.

  The following is an example:
  ```
  *.crit              *
  ```

Additional Priority Parameters

The rules listed are always valid for the specified priority and all higher priorities. The following are additional parameters you can use for defining the priority in a rule:

- **An equal sign (=) before the priority.** By entering an equal sign, the rule is set only for messages of this priority.

  The following is an example:
  ```
  *.=warn;*.=err          -/var/log/warn
  ```

- **An exclamation mark (!) before the priority.** By entering an exclamation mark, this and all higher priorities are excluded from logging.

  The following is an example:
  ```
  mail.*;mail.!=info          /var/adm/mail
  ```

- **Add an asterisk (*).** If you enter an asterisk, it stands for "all categories" or "all priorities."

- **Set none as the priority.** You can exclude a category from logging by setting none as the priority.

  The following is an example:
  ```
  *.*;mail.none;news.none          -/var/log/messages
  ```

You can specify parameters for the syslog daemon in the file /etc/sysconfig/syslog.

The variable KERNEL_LOGLEVEL determines the logging level for the kernel log daemon (klogd). You can use the variable SYSLOGD_PARAMS to pass start parameters to the daemon.

For example, if you want a host to log messages of other hosts, the syslog daemon of the host that should accept the messages from a remote syslog must be started with the option -r.

In this case, the entry in the file /etc/sysconfig/syslog looks like the following:

```
## Type:              string
## Default:           ""
## Config:            ""
## ServiceRestart:    syslog
#
# if not empty: parameters for syslogd
# for example SYSLOGD_PARAMS="-r -s my.dom.ain"
#
SYSLOGD_PARAMS="-r"
```

Important Log Files

The log file to which most messages are written is the file /var/log/messages. Often hints can be found here about problems such as why a service does not function properly when it starts.

The entry **-- MARK --** is written to the file by the syslog daemon every 20 minutes if no other messages to log exist. This makes it easy to check whether the syslog daemon has been running the entire time or if the daemon has been stopped (the entries -- MARK -- are missing).

The best approach for reading the log files from the command line is to use the command tail (**tail /var/log/messages**). This displays the last 10 lines of the file, which are also the most current entries.

By using **tail -n** (such as **tail -n 30**) you can specify the number of lines to display.

If you want to have new messages displayed immediately, use the interactive mode with **tail -f**.

For example, entering **tail -20f /var/log/messages** switches tail to interactive mode. The last 20 lines of the file /var/log/messages are displayed. If new messages are added these are displayed immediately.

You can close the display by pressing **Ctrl+C**.

Important log files stored in the directory /var/log/ are shown in Table 6-15.

Table 6-15

Log File	Description
/var/log/cups	This directory stores the log files for the printing system CUPS.
/var/log/news	This directory stores messages for the news system.
/var/log/YaST2	This directory stores log files for YaST.

Table 6-15   (continued)

Log File	Description
/var/log/boot.msg	When the system boots, all boot script messages are displayed on the first virtual console. This often happens so fast that you cannot read all the messages. You can, however, read the boot messages in this file. You can display the messages from the kernel during the boot procedure with the command **dmesg** (/bin/dmesg).
/var/log/mail	Messages from the mail system are written to this file. Because this system often generates a lot of messages, there are additional log files: • /var/log/mail.err • /var/log/mail.info • /var/log/mail.warn
/var/log/wtmp	This file contains information about which user was logged in from where and for how long (since the file was created). The file contents are in binary form and can only be displayed with the command **last** (/usr/bin/last). Because of the binary format, it is difficult to manipulate entries in this file.
/var/log/lastlog	This file contains information about which user was last logged in, from where, and for how long. You can only view the contents with the command **lastlog** (/usr/bin/lastlog).

How to View Log Files with YaST

You can view startup or system logs with YaST by doing the following:

1. From the KDE desktop, start the YaST View Start-up Log or View System Log module by doing one of the following:

   ■ Select the **YaST** icon, enter the root *password*, and select **OK**; then select **Misc > View Start–up Log** or **Misc > View System Log**.

   or

   ■ Open a terminal window and enter **sux –** and the root *password*; then enter **yast2 view_anymsg**.

Figure 6-7 appears.

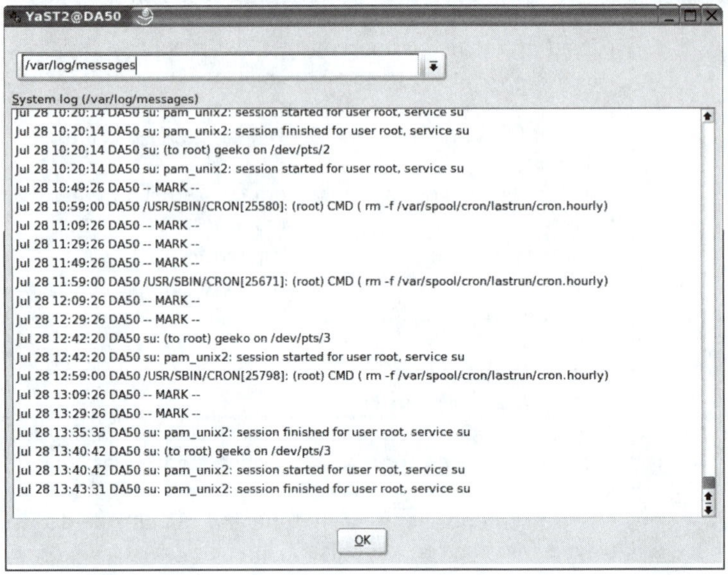

Figure 6-7

The same dialog is used for both YaST modules; the only difference is the default log displayed (messages for System Log and boot.msg for Start-up Log).

2. Select a *log* to view from the drop-down list.

3. When you finish viewing logs, close the dialog by selecting **OK**.

How to Archive Log Files (logrotate)

It is important to ensure that log files do not get too large or too complex, or require too much space inside the system. For this reason, the size and age of log files are monitored automatically by the program logrotate (/usr/sbin/logrotate).

The program is run daily by the cron daemon (/etc/cron.daily/logrotate). The program checks all log files listed in its configuration files (based on the parameters given).

You can configure the settings in the files to indicate whether files should be compressed or deleted in regular intervals or when a determined size is reached.

You can also configure how many compressed versions of a log file are kept over a specified period of time, and the forwarding of log files through email.

The configuration file of logrotate is /etc/logrotate.conf, which contains general configuration settings. The following is an example of logrotate.conf:

```
# see "man logrotate" for details
# rotate log files weekly
weekly

# keep 4 weeks worth of backlogs
rotate 4

# create new (empty) log files after rotating old ones
create

# uncomment this if you want your log files compressed
#compress

# uncomment these to switch compression to bzip2
#compresscmd /usr/bin/bzip2
#uncompresscmd /usr/bin/bunzip2

# RPM packages drop log rotation information into this directory
include /etc/logrotate.d
...
```

Table 6-16 describes the options in the file.

Table 6-16

Option	Description
weekly	The log files are created or replaced once a week.
rotate 4	Unless the option rotate is specified, the old files are deleted. In this example, the last 4 versions of the log file are kept (rotate 4).
create	The old file is saved under a new name and a new, empty log file is created.
compress	If the option compress is activated, the copies are stored in a compressed form.

Many RPM packages contain preconfigured files for evaluation by logrotate, which are stored in /etc/logrotate.d/. The files contained in that directory are read by logrotate through the **include /etc/logrotate.d** entry in /etc/logrotate.conf.

Any settings in the logrotate.d files supersede the general settings in logrotate.conf.

All the files to monitor must be listed. This is done through the entries in /etc/logrotate.conf (such as **/var/log/wtmp [*options*]**) or in separate configuration files.

The following is an example of the file syslogd in /etc/logrotate.d/:

```
/var/log/warn /var/log/messages /var/log/allmessages\
    /var/log/localmessages /var/log/firewall {
    compress
    dateext
    maxage 365
    rotate 99
    missingok
    notifempty
    size +4096k
    create 640 root root
    sharedscripts
    postrotate
        /etc/init.d/syslog reload
    endscript
}

/var/log/mail /var/log/mail.info /var/log/mail.warn /var/log/
mail.err {
    compress
    dateext
    maxage 365
    rotate 99
    missingok
    notifempty
    size +4096k
    create 640 root root
    sharedscripts
    postrotate
        /etc/init.d/syslog reload
    endscript
}
```

The file syslogd contains settings for configuring how the log files written by the daemon syslog will be treated.

Table 6-17 describes the options in the file.

Table 6-17

Option	Description
size +4096k	Files will not be rotated weekly, but as soon as they reach a size of 4096 KB.
rotate 99	Ninety-nine versions of each of the files will be kept.
compress	The old log files will be stored compressed.
maxage 365	As soon as a compressed file is older than 365 days, it is deleted.
notifempty	If a log file is empty, no rotation takes place.

Table 6-17 (continued)

Option	Description
create 640 root root	New log files are created after the rotation and owner, group, and permissions are specified.
postrotate . . . endscript	Scripts can be called after the rotation. For example, some services have to be restarted after log files have been changed. In this example, the syslog daemon will reread its configuration files after the rotation (/etc/init.d/syslog reload).

6

Most of the services whose log files should be monitored come with preconfigured files, so only minor adjustments are normally needed.

For a complete list of all possible options, enter **man logrotate**.

NOTE

How to Monitor Hard Drive Space

You can use the command /bin/df (disk free) to monitor hard drive space. For all mounted partitions, the command displays how much space is still occupied and available.

With the option –h (for human-readable) the output is given in units of GB or MB, which is easier to interpret, as in the following:

```
DA50:~ # df -h
Filesystem      Size  Used  Avail Use% Mounted on
/dev/hda1       500M  152M  348M  31% /
/dev/hda2       2.0G  551M  1.4G  27% /opt
/dev/hda3       7.0G  1.3G  5.7G  18% /rest
/dev/hda5       500M  141M  359M  29% /tmp
/dev/hda6       3.0G  2.5G  521M  84% /usr
/dev/hda7       2.0G  119M  1.8G   6% /var
tmpfs           374M     0  373M   1% /dev/shm
/dev/hda8      19:0G 5:4G   13G  29% /home
```

To find out how large individual files or directories are, use the command /usr/bin/du (disk usage). Without any options, it displays, for each subdirectory and the current directory, how large the current directory and subdirectories are in 1KB units.

Table 6-18 shows some commonly used options with the command du.

Table 6-18

Option	Description
-a	Displays the size of directories and files.
-c	Displays the total as the final value. This option is useful to determine how much space is taken up by all files with a specific extension (such as .tex)
-h	Displays the sizes (in KB and MB) in a human-readable format.
-s	Shows only the total amount. This option is useful to find out how much space is taken up by directories.

The following are some examples of using the command du:

```
geeko@DA50:~ > du
4          ./Letters
400        .
geeko@DA50:~ > du -h
4.0k       ./Letters
400k       .
geeko@DA50:~ > du -ha
4.0k       ./Letters
4.0k       ./file1
4.0k       ./file2
308k       ./file3
76k        ./file4
400k       .
```

If you enter a command such as **du –h –c /home/geeko**, first the size of the directories in the home directory of the user geeko is given, and then (with total), the total size of the directory (with the size of files included).

For a high-level view of disk space usage, you can run utilities from the KDE desktop such as Info Center (Storage Devices) or KDiskFree.

You can access the Info Center from the Start menu by selecting **System > Monitor > Info Center** (or by entering **kinfocenter**).

You can access the KDiskFree from the Start menu by selecting **System > File System > KDiskFree** (or by entering **kdf**).

Figure 6-8 shows an example of a KDiskFree display.

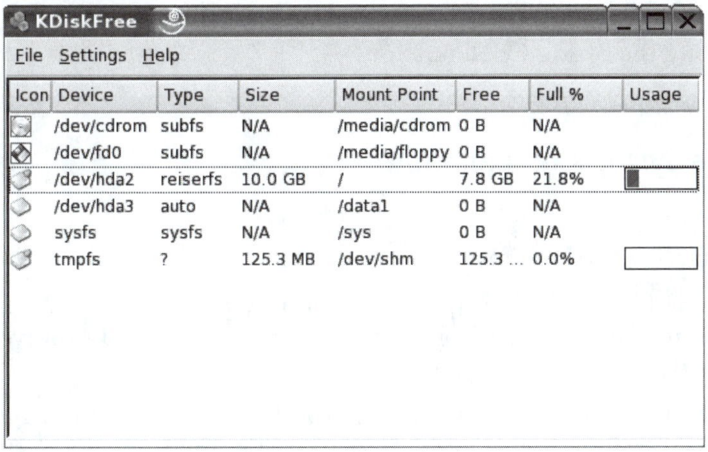

Icon	Device	Type	Size	Mount Point	Free	Full %	Usage
	/dev/cdrom	subfs	N/A	/media/cdrom	0 B	N/A	
	/dev/fd0	subfs	N/A	/media/floppy	0 B	N/A	
	/dev/hda2	reiserfs	10.0 GB	/	7.8 GB	21.8%	
	/dev/hda3	auto	N/A	/data1	0 B	N/A	
	sysfs	sysfs	N/A	/sys	0 B	N/A	
	tmpfs	?	125.3 MB	/dev/shm	125.3 ...	0.0%	

Figure 6-8

You can also monitor disk space usage by directory or file when using views such as Tree View or Detailed List View in Konqueror, as in Figure 6-9.

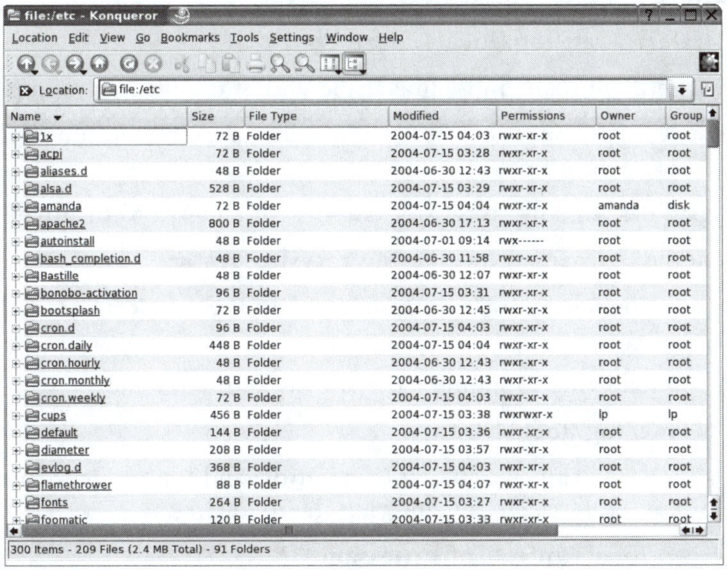

Figure 6-9

However, you can only view individual directory and file sizes. You cannot automatically determine total amounts for a group of files (such as all the files in a directory).

Exercise 6-3   Manage System Logging

In this exercise, you do the following:

- Part I: Modify the Syslog Configuration
- Part II: Configure Logrotate

Part I: Modify the Syslog Configuration

Do the following:

1. Edit the file /etc/syslog.conf:

    a. Open the file /etc/syslog.conf in an editor by pressing **Alt+F2** and enter-
       ing **kdesu kate /etc/syslog.conf**; then enter a password of **novell** and
       select **OK**.

    b. Add the following lines at the bottom of the file to allow for logging of
       the local4 facility on the levels of debug, notice, info, err, and alert:

    local4. debug /var/log/local4.debug

    local4.notice /var/log/local4.notice

    local4.info /var/log/local4.info

    local4.err /var/log/local4.err

    local4.alert /var/log/local4.alert

    c. Make sure there is an empty line at the end of the file by pressing **Enter**.

    d. Save the changes but keep the Kate window open by selecting **File >
       Close**; then select **Save**.

2. From a terminal window, su to root (**su –**) with a password of **novell**.

3. Restart the syslog daemon by entering **rcsyslog restart**.

4. Check the configuration by logging an entry to the info level in the local4
   facility:

    a. Enter the following to monitor the activity of the log file:

    tail –f /var/log/local4.info

    b. Open another terminal window (su to **root**) and log an entry to the info
       level in the local4 facility by entering the following:

    logger –p local4.info "Info message 1"

c. Check the results in the second terminal window.

The message is logged in the file /var/log/local4.info.

The message should also be logged in the file /var/log/localmessages because of other entries in /etc/syslog.conf.

d. In the terminal window where the log activity is being monitored with tail –f, stop the monitoring by pressing **Ctrl+C**.

5. Repeat step 4 to send a message at each of the log levels (such as **logger –p local4. debug "Info message 2"**) and monitor the messages with tail –f for the associated log file (such as **tail –f /var/log/local4. debug**).

Notice that at certain levels messages from other levels are also recorded.

Only those log level files with entries will be compressed in Part II of the exercise during log rotation.

Part II: Configure Logrotate

Now that the local4 facility is being logged to separate files, you can use the program logrotate to manage the files for the system by creating a file /etc/logrotate.d/local4 that does the following:

- Compresses the old logs in gzip format
- Saves the old logs with a date extension
- Limits the oldest log to one day
- Limits the rotated logs saved to 5
- Limits the maximum size of the file to 20 bytes
- Proceeds without error if a log file is missing
- Logs the date in the local4.info file each time a new log file is generated

Do the following:

1. From the Kate window in a new document, enter the following:

   /var/log/local4.err /var/log/local4.info

   /var/log/local4.alert /var/log/local4. debug /var/log/local4.notice

   {

   compress

   dateext

> **maxage 1**
>
> **rotate 5**
>
> **size=20**
>
> **postrotate**
>
>> **date >> /var/log/local4.info**
>
> **endscript**
>
> **}**

Make sure the directories are separated with spaces.

2. Save the file by selecting **File > Save**; then enter **/etc/logrotate.d/local4** and select **Save**.

3. Close the Kate window by selecting **File > Quit**.

4. Switch to virtual terminal 1 by pressing **Ctrl+Alt+F1**.

5. Log in as **root** with a password of **novell**.

6. Rotate the logs manually by entering the following:

   logrotate /etc/logrotate.conf

7. Check the directory /var/log for the zipped local4 log files by entering **ls –l /var/log | less**.

   You see files such as the following:

   ■ local4.info-*current_date*.gz

   ■ local4.notice-*current_date*.gz

   For example, if the current date is July 15, 2007, then the zipped file for local4.info would be **local4.info-20070715**.

Only those log files with entries are zipped.

8. Exit the list by typing **q**.

9. Check the contents of the local4.info zipped archive by entering the following commands:

   less /var/log/local4.info-*current_date*.gz

   zcat /var/log/local4.info-*current_date*.gz

10. Log out as root by entering **exit**.

11. Return to the KDE desktop by pressing **Ctrl+Alt+F7**.

12. Close all open windows.

Chapter Summary

□ Processes are programs that are executing on the system. User processes run on a terminal and are executed by users, whereas daemon processes are system services that do not run on a terminal.

□ Every process has a PID and a PPID and can possibly start an unlimited number of child processes.

□ The first process loaded by the kernel during system initialization is the init daemon, which always has a PID of 1.

□ In addition to a PID, background processes have a job ID that you can use to control their execution. You can start any program in the background by appending the & character to the program command. This program can then be viewed using the **jobs** command or manipulated using the **fg** and **bg** commands.

□ You can view processes within a desktop environment using the KDE System Guard, or at a command prompt by using the **ps**, **pstree**, and **top** commands.

□ The KDE System Guard as well as the **kill**, **killall**, and **top** commands can be used to stop processes by sending them signals. Although there are many available signals, the default signal used by these commands is SIGTERM.

□ You can affect the priority of a process by changing its nice value. All processes are started with a 0 nice value, which can be decreased to –20 (high priority) or increased to +19 (low priority). Only the root user may increase the priority of a process.

□ To change the nice value of a program, you use the **nice** command. To change the nice value of a process, you must use the **renice** command.

□ Daemon process names typically end with d and contain a ? in the TTY column of **ps** command output. Signal-controlled daemons execute when a certain event occurs, whereas interval-controlled daemons run periodically on the system.

□ You can start daemons by running the appropriate script in the /etc/init.d directory with the **start** argument, or by using the **rc*daemonname* start** command.

□ The init daemon loads daemons during system startup according to runlevels defined in the /etc/inittab file. The /etc/inittab file runs scripts in the /etc/init.d/ and /etc/init.d/ rc*.d directories to start and stop various system components.

□ Commands may be scheduled to run at a later time using the at daemon.

□ To schedule tasks to occur regularly in the future, you must use the cron daemon and create a crontab (cron table). System tasks are scheduled to run using the /etc/crontab file. User tasks may be scheduled using the **crontab** command and are stored in the /var/spool/cron/tabs directory.

□ Most log files are stored in the /var/log directory and created by the syslog daemon (syslogd) via entries in the /etc/syslog.conf file. The last entries of these files may be viewed using a text program such as **tail** or by using YaST.

□ The **logrotate** program is run daily to archive log files, using entries in the /etc/logrotate. conf file and application-specific information in the /etc/logrotate.d directory.

□ The **df** command, **du** command, KDE Info Center, and KDiskFree utility can be used to monitor disk usage.

Key Terms

& — A special character used to start a program in the background.

/etc/at.allow — A file that lists users who can use the **at** command.

/etc/at.deny — A file that lists users who cannot use the **at** command.

/etc/cron.d — A directory that contains additional system cron tables.

/etc/crontab — The system cron table.

/etc/init.d — The directory that contains the scripts used to start and stop most daemons.

/etc/init.d/skeleton — A sample script that may be copied to create scripts used to start a daemon.

/etc/inittab — The configuration file for the init daemon.

/etc/logrotate.conf — The configuration file for the **logrotate** command. It typically uses parameters listed in the /etc/logrotate.d directory for each log file.

/etc/logrotate.d — The directory that stores log file-specific information for use by the **logrotate** command.

/etc/rc.d/rc*n*.d — The directories used by the init daemon to start and kill daemons in each runlevel (*n*).

/etc/sysconfig/cron — A file that contains parameters for the cron daemon.

/var/spool/cron/allow — A file that lists users who can use the **crontab** command.

/var/spool/cron/deny — A file that lists users who cannot use the **crontab** command.

/var/spool/cron/lastrun — The directory used to store information about system cron jobs run in the past.

at command — Used to schedule commands to run at a certain time in the future and manipulate at jobs.

atq command — Used to view scheduled at jobs.

atrm command — Used to remove a scheduled at job.

background process — A process that runs unnoticed in your terminal and does not interfere with your command-line interface.

bg command — Used to start a process in the background.

child process — A process that is started by another process.

cron — The system service that executes commands regularly in the future, based on information in crontabs.

crontab (cron table) — A file specifying the commands to be run by the cron daemon and the schedule to run them.

crontab command — Used to view and edit user cron tables.

daemon process — A system process that is not associated with a terminal. It stands for Disk and Execution Monitor.

df command — Displays disk usage by file system.

du command — Displays disk usage by directory.

fg command — Used to force a background process to run in the foreground.

foreground process — A process that runs in your terminal and must finish execution before you receive your shell prompt.

init — The first daemon started by the Linux kernel; it is responsible for starting and stopping other daemons.

interval–controlled daemon — A daemon that is started at a certain time on a regular basis.

job identifier (job ID) — The ID given to a background process that may be used in commands that manipulate the process during exection.

jobs command — Used to view background processes in your terminal.

KDE Info Center — A graphical utility that displays system information.

KDE System Guard — A graphical utility that may be used to view and control processes.

kdf command — Starts the KDiskFree utility.

KDiskFree — A graphical utility that displays free space by filesystem.

kill command — Used to send a signal to a process by PID or job ID.

killall command — Used to send a signal to a process by name.

kinfocenter command — Starts the KDE Info Center utility.

listener — A process that listens for network traffic on a port and forwards that traffic to a daemon.

nice command — Used to change the priority of a process as it is started.

nice value — Represents the priority of a process. A higher nice value reduces the priority of the process.

nohup command — Used to prevent a process from stopping when the shell that started it has exited.

parent process — A process that has started another process.

Parent Process ID (PPID) — The PID of the parent process of a process.

poweroff command — Used to quickly bring a system to runlevel 0 and power off the system.

process — A program currently loaded into memory and running on the CPU.

Process ID (PID) — A unique identifier assigned to every process.

program — A file that may be executed to create a process.

ps command — Used to list processes that are running on the system.

pstree command — Used to list processes that are running on the system as well as their parent and child relationships.

reboot command — Used to quickly bring a system to runlevel 6.

renice command — Used to change the priority of a running process.

runlevel — A category that describes the number and type of daemons on a Linux system.

runlevel command — Used to display the current and most recent runlevel.

service — See **Daemon Process**.

shutdown command — Used to change to runlevel 0 at a certain time.

signal — A termination request that is sent to a process.

signal-controlled daemon — A daemon that is started when an event occurs on the system.

sulogin — A runlevel 1 program used to display a login prompt on a character-based terminal for the root user only.

top command — Used to view, renice, and kill the processes on the system that are using the most CPU time.

user process — A process begun by a user that runs on a terminal.

YaST Runlevel Editor — A graphical program that may be used to configure the daemons that start in each runlevel.

Review Questions

1. Which of the following terms refers to a system service that does not run on a terminal?

   a. Program

   b. User Process

   c. Daemon Process

   d. Child Process

2. Which of the following statements are true? (Choose all that apply.)

   a. A parent process may only have one child process.

   b. Each process is given a PPID that is used to uniquely identify it on the system.

   c. A child process may have only one parent process.

   d. All background processes have a PID and a job ID.

3. Which of the following commands can quickly identify the child processes started by a particular daemon?

   a. top

   b. lsof

   c. ps

   d. pstree

4. What processes are regular users allowed to send kill signals to?
   _____

5. You have just run the **ps aux** command and notice that most daemons have an S in the STAT column. What does this mean? _____

6. What key can you press in the **top** command to send the process a signal?

   a. s

   b. k

   c. R

   d. N

7. What can you type at a command prompt to run the **updatedb** command in the background? _____

8. Which of the following key combinations can you use to pause a foreground process such that it may be sent to the background with the **bg** command?

   a. Ctrl+c

   b. Ctrl+p

   c. Ctrl+z

   d. Ctrl+r

9. Which of the following kill commands may be used to send the second background job a SIGINT?

   a. kill –2 %2

   b. kill –1 –b 2

   c. kill –9 %2

   d. kill –15 2

10. If you do not specify the type of signal when using the **kill** or **killall** commands, which signal is used by default?

    a. SIGHUP

    b. SIGINT

    c. SIGKILL

    d. SIGTERM

11. What command could you use change the priority of a process (PID=592) to run with the highest priority? _____

12. What startup script is used to start the services associated with the network in SLES?

    _____

13. Which directory stores links to the startup scripts for daemons that should be started in runlevel 3?

    a. /etc/init.d

    b. /etc/init.d/rc3.d

    c. /etc/init3.d

    d. /etc/init.d/skeleton

6

14. You have a script that is used to remove temporary files and would like this script to run on a daily basis. What directory could you place this script in to have the cron daemon execute it each day? _____

15. What command could a regular user use to edit their crontab? _____

16. What lines would you add to your crontab to schedule the /bin/false command to run at 10:30 a.m. and 2:50 p.m. from Monday to Friday? _____

17. What command can you use to run the contents of the file **cleanup** at noon? _____

18. Which command can you use to view **at** jobs that have been scheduled on your system?
    a. at --view
    b. atq
    c. atrm
    d. cron --view

19. Which line can you add to the **/etc/syslog.conf** file to log messages of priority **crit** from the Linux kernel to **/var/log/kernlog**?
    a. kern.crit /var/log/kernlog
    b. kern.=crit /var/log/kernlog
    c. kern.crit -/var/log/kernlog
    d. kern.crit |/var/log/kernlog

20. You have added the following lines to the /etc/logrotate.d/mylog file:

/var/log/mylog {

maxage 44

rotate 5

notifempty

compress

}

Which of the following statements are true about the rotation of the /var/log/mylog file? (Choose all that apply.)

    a. A maximum of 5 archive logs will be kept.
    b. A maximum of 44 archive logs will be kept.
    c. The log file will be rotated if the file is empty.
    d. The log file will be compressed after being rotated.

DISCOVERY EXERCISES

Viewing Processes Using ps

There are two main types of options that are used with the **ps** command: those that require a dash and those that do not. We have examined options that do not require a dash in this chapter (e.g., **ps aux**); these options have traditionally been used on BSD UNIX systems. Options that require a dash are taken from AT&T System V UNIX systems. Using the man or info pages, research four more options to the ps command that require a dash character. What processes does each option display? What information is given about each process?

Using Kill Signals

Login to tty1 as the root user and perform the following actions in order. For each action, write the command(s) that you used.

1. Run the **ps** command to view processes in your current shell. Record the PID for your bash shell.

2. Send the PID of your bash shell as SIGINT. What happened and why?

3. Send the PID of your bash shell as SIGTERM. What happened and why?

4. Send the PID of your bash shell as SIGCONT. What happened and why?

5. Send the PID of your bash shell as SIGKILL. What happened and why?

Process Priorities

Log in to tty1 as the root user and perform the following actions in order. For each action, write the command(s) that you used. When finished, log out of tty1.

1. Start the **ps –l** command with the default nice value. What nice value is shown in the output?

2. Start the **ps –l** command with a nice value of –20 and verify the correct nice value in the output. Did this command run with high or low priority? Which users can run this command?

3. Start the **ps –l** command with a nice value of –19 and verify the correct nice value in the output. Did this command run with high or low priority? Which users can run this command?

Scheduling Processes Using the at Daemon

The **at** command is versatile in that it can understand nearly any time format. Log in to tty1 as the root user, ensure that the **at** daemon is running, and schedule the **date** and **who** commands to run at teatime (use the **at teatime** command). When you have finished scheduling the at job, note the time that the two commands will be scheduled. Next, remove your at job and use the manual or info pages to research other time formats that may be used with the **at** command. When finished, log out of tty1.

Cron Tables

Write the lines that you could use in your crontab to schedule the /bin/sample command to run:

1. every Friday at 1:30 a.m.

2. at 4:30 p.m. on May 15th only

3. at 4:00 p.m. and 4:30 p.m. on the first Sunday of every month

4. every 10 minutes from 9:00 a.m. to 5:00 p.m. on Monday

5. at 8:15 a.m. and 6:30 p.m., Monday to Friday

The /etc/syslog.conf File

Write the lines that you could use in your /etc/syslog.conf file to:

1. log all PAM messages of level warning and more serious to /var/log/pamlog.

2. log all daemon messages of level notice to /var/log/pamlog.

3. log all kernel messages to /var/log/pamlog without synchronization.

4. send all cron messages of level warning and more serious to the /bin/false program.

CONNECT THE SUSE LINUX ENTERPRISE SERVER TO THE NETWORK

In this section, you learn how to configure and manage your SUSE Linux Enterprise Server network connection.

♦ Configure Your Network Connection

♦ Configure and Manage Routes

♦ Test the Network Interface

OBJECTIVE 1   CONFIGURE YOUR NETWORK CONNECTION

Linux offers all the necessary networking tools and features for integration into all types of network structures.

To configure your server to connect with the network, you need to know the following:

- TCP/IP Fundamentals
- Network Interfaces in Linux
- Network Interface Requirements
- How to Configure a Network Card with YaST
- How to Modify a Network Card Manually

NOTE

Only information relevant to connecting a SUSE Linux Enterprise Server to the network is covered in this objective.

For a primer on networking, see *Appendix B: Network Components and Architecture.*

TCP/IP Fundamentals

In order to connect your SLES 9 server to a network that uses Transmission Control Protocol/Internet Protocol (TCP/IP), you need to understand the following:

- TCP/IP Network Components
- IP Address Structure
- Network Classes and IP Addresses
- Special IP Addresses

TCP/IP Network Components

The following are the basic components used to build the Internet delivery architecture:

- **Host.** A computer (server or client) that receives requests for information from the Internet and passes them to installed server applications (such as a Web server).

  After a server application fulfills the request, the host sends the data back to the Internet.

- **TCP/IP.** This protocol suite defines how packets of information should be structured for successful transmission over a TCP/IP network (such as an intranet or the Internet).

  TCP allows two hosts (or a host and a client) to establish a connection and exchange packets of data. TCP guarantees the delivery of data and guarantees that packets are delivered in the same order in which they were sent.

- **IP packet.** An electronic package of data sent over the Internet. The packet is labeled with information such as the sender's address, the receiver's address, and the type of packet.

  Packet types include TCP packets for delivering requests and content, and Internet Control Message Protocol (ICMP) Ping packets for testing an Internet connection between computers.

- **Router.** A hardware device (or sometimes software) that forwards an IP packet to the next network point on its way to a destination. A router is often included as part of a network switch.

  A packet normally travels through a number of network points with routers before arriving at its destination.

- **Firewall.** A set of related programs (often installed on a network gateway server or other hardware) that protects the resources of a private intranet or network from unauthorized access by users from other networks.

  A company with an intranet that allows its employees to access the Internet can install a firewall to prevent outsiders from accessing its own private data resources and to control what outside resources its employees can access.

  There are several firewall filtering (screening) methods. A simple one is to filter requests to make sure they come from acceptable (previously identified) domain names and IP addresses.

  A firewall can also enforce company policies that prevent access to specific Internet sites (such as streaming media or pornographic sites).

IP Address Structure

Every protocol suite defines some type of addressing that identifies computers and networks. An Internet address uses 32 bits and includes both a network ID and a host ID.

A *host* refers to either a workstation or a server. A host is also referred to as a *node* or *station*. Routers locate hosts on the Internet based on their assigned IP addresses.

An IP address of a host consists of four bytes divided into two parts:

- A network address (from 1 to 3 bytes)
- A node or station address (from 1 to 3 bytes)

 The IPv6 addressing scheme allows IP addresses to be 16 bytes long.

In Figure 7-1, an IP network has been assigned the network address of 132.132.

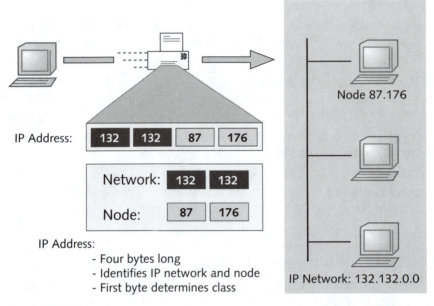

IP Address:
- Four bytes long
- Identifies IP network and node
- First byte determines class

Figure 7-1

The 132.132 network address uniquely identifies the network from all other networks on the internetwork.

Each host or node on this network must have an IP address such as 132.132.*x.x*, where the last two bytes of the address need to be unique on the network.

In the above example, a node that is assigned the last two octets of 87.176 is uniquely identified on the internetwork by the IP address of 132.132.87.176.

Each byte of a node address falls in the range of 0 to 255, but 0 and 255 are usually not used in addressing. Not all systems support a node address of 0, and 255 is reserved for broadcast packets.

IP addresses take the form of a dotted octet; that is, each byte (8 bits in an octet) is separated by a dot. In binary format, an IP address looks like that shown in Figure 7-2, with each *x* representing a binary bit with the value of 0 or 1.

Figure 7-2

A complete IP address in binary format looks like the following:

`10101100.00010000.00000100.00000010`

When you convert the binary bits to decimal numbers, an IP address takes a readable form. Converting the binary example above to decimal numbers results in the IP address 172.16.4.2.

One easy way to convert from binary to decimal numbers is to create a binary table such as the one shown in Figure 7–3, with columns for each power of 2 with its decimal equivalent.

Binary	2^7	2^6	2^5	2^4	2^3	2^2	2^1	2^0	Decimal Equivalent
Decimal	128	64	32	16	8	4	2	1	
	1	0	1	0	1	1	0	0	(1x128)+ (1x32)+ (1x8)+ (1x4)=172
	0	0	0	1	0	0	0	0	(1x16)=16
	0	0	0	0	0	1	0	0	(1x4)=4
	0	0	0	0	0	0	1	0	(1x2)=2

Figure 7-3

Correspond each of the 8 bits in a byte to a column and add the decimal values for each bit with a value of 1 in a single row. The result is the decimal equivalent of the byte.

Network Classes and IP Addresses

Figure 7-4 illustrates the five address classes that exist in the Internet Protocol addressing scheme, classes A through E.

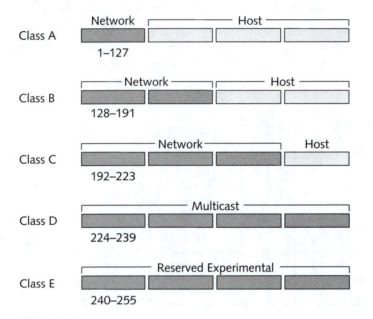

Figure 7-4

Classes A through C can be assigned; classes D and E are reserved for specific uses and are not assigned to hosts.

Your network class determines how the four-byte IP address is divided between network and node portions, as shown in Figure 7–5.

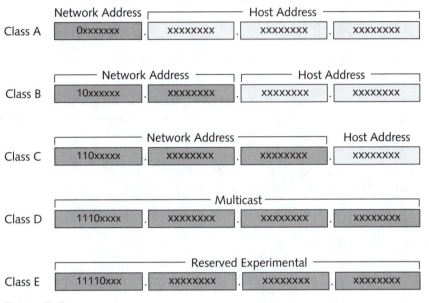

Figure 7-5

Notice that the first bits of the first byte in the address identify the network class.

The following describes the addresses available in each class:

- **Class A addresses.** In a class A address, the first byte is in the 0 to 127 range and also identifies the network; the final three bytes identify the node. The first bit must be zero.

  There are 126 possible class A networks, each having up to 16,777,216 hosts. Virtually all class A addresses have been assigned.

- **Class B addresses.** In a class B address, the first byte is in the 128 to 191 range (the first two bits of the first byte are 1 and 0). The first two bytes identify the network, and the last two bytes identify the node on the network.

  There are 16,384 possible class B networks. Each class B network can have up to 65,534 hosts. Relatively few class B addresses remain available.

- **Class C addresses.** In a class C address, the first byte is in the 192 to 223 range (the first three bits of the first byte are 1, 1, and 0). The first three bytes identify the network and the last byte identifies the node.

  There are 2,097,152 possible class C networks. Each class C network can have up to 255 hosts. Organizations that request a registered class B address can receive one or more class C addresses instead.

- **Class D addresses.** In a class D address, the first byte is in the 224 to 239 range (the first four bits of the first byte are 1, 1, 1, and 0).

  Class D addresses are used for multicast packets. Multicast packets are used by a host to transmit messages to a specified group of hosts on the network.

  Multicasts are packets typically exchanged between routers only.

- **Class E addresses.** In a class E address, the first byte is in the 240 to 255 range (the first five bits of the byte are 1,1,1,1, and 0).

  Class E addresses are reserved for experimental use and potential future addressing modes. Class E addresses are typically used for broadcasts. (A broadcast message is one that is transmitted to every host on the network.)

  One particular class E address, 255.255.255.255, is used to identify a broadcast message. When the destination IP address is 255.255.255.255, the message is directed to all hosts on the network from which the broadcast originated.

  Routers do not typically forward broadcast messages to other networks.

Special IP Addresses

Table 7–1 lists addresses that have special meaning within the TCP/IP protocol suite and should not be used when assigning IP addresses.

Table 7-1

IP Address	Purpose
Network 0.0.0.0	Refers to the default route; this route is used to simplify routing tables used by IP. On some older (BSD 4.2) networks, the 0.0.0.0 address is used for broadcasts.
Address with all network bits set to 0	Reserved for loopback; the address 127.0.0.1 is often used to refer to the local host. Using this address, applications can address a local host as if it were a remote host without relying on any configuration information.
Address with all host bits set to 0	Refers to a host on "this" network For example, 0.0.0.34 would address node 34 on the local class A network.
Network or node address with all bits set to 1	Refers to the network itself For example, the address 145.67.0.0 can be used to refer to network 145.67. This notation is used within routing tables.

Table 7-1 (continued)

IP Address	Purpose
Network 127.0.0.0	Refers to all hosts
255.255.255.255	Refers to a limited broadcast meant for hosts on this network only

Network Interfaces in Linux

In Linux, network interfaces are always referred to with a fixed name. The name depends on the type and position of the network card in the computer.

The first card is called eth0, the second is eth1, and so on. Similarly, the designations for token ring cards are tr0, tr1, and so on.

Linux supports a range of network cards and supports all well-known network protocols. This support is in the form of corresponding drivers, which must be available for the interfaces on the Linux computer.

SUSE Linux Enterprise Server already contains the drivers for all common network cards. These drivers are kernel modules that can be loaded if and when required.

Network Interface Requirements

Your computer must have a supported network card. Normally the network card is detected during installation and a suitable driver is loaded.

To see if your network card has been integrated correctly with the appropriate driver, enter the command **ifstatus** *device* (such as **ifstatus eth0**). The output should list all information about the network device or display an error message.

If the kernel support for the network card is implemented as a module, which is done by default for the SUSE kernel, the name of the module is entered by YaST in a file in /etc/sysconfig/hardware/ (such as **hwcfg-id-*MACAddress***).

This is done automatically when the driver support for the network card is loaded in linuxrc during the first installation. This task can also be done after installation with YaST.

If you are using a hotplug network card (such as PCMCIA or USB), the drivers are autodetected when the card is plugged in. No configuration is necessary.

How to Configure a Network Card with YaST

In SUSE Linux Enterprise Server, the easiest way to configure network interfaces is to use YaST. You can also configure the network card manually.

To configure your network card with YaST, do the following:

1. From the KDE desktop, start the YaST Network Card module by doing one of the following:

   - Select the **YaST** icon, enter the root *password*, and select **OK**; then select **Network Devices > Network Card**.

     or

   - Open a terminal window and enter **sux –** and the root *password*; then enter **yast2 network** and select **Network Card > Launch**.

   The dialog box shown in Figure 7-6 appears.

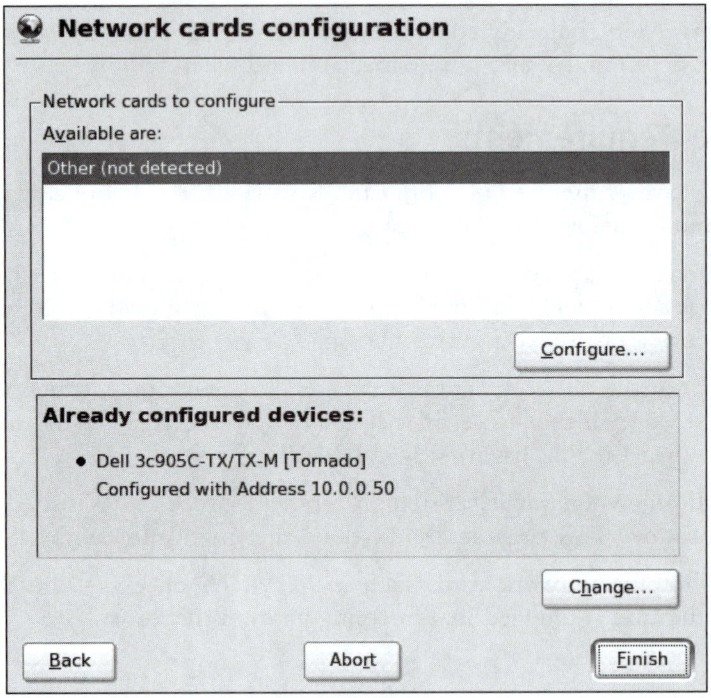

Network cards configuration

Network cards to configure
A̲vailable are:

Other (not detected)

Configure...

Already configured devices:

- Dell 3c905C-TX/TX-M [Tornado]
  Configured with Address 10.0.0.50

Change...

| Back | Abort | Finish |

Figure 7-6

This dialog box displays any unconfigured network cards (**Network cards to configure**) and currently configured network cards (**Already configured devices**).

2. (Conditional) If you have not yet configured a network card, select one of the following from the Network cards to configure list:

- **Configure an undetected card.** If there are no cards listed to configure, select **Other > Configure**; then enter the requested information.

  or

- **Configure an autodetected card.** From the list, select the *network card*; then select **Configure**.

Normally the network card is autodetected by YaST, the correct kernel module is used, and the card is listed for configuration.

If the card is not autodetected by YaST and you select **Other > Configure** to configure it manually, the dialog box shown in Figure 7-7 appears.

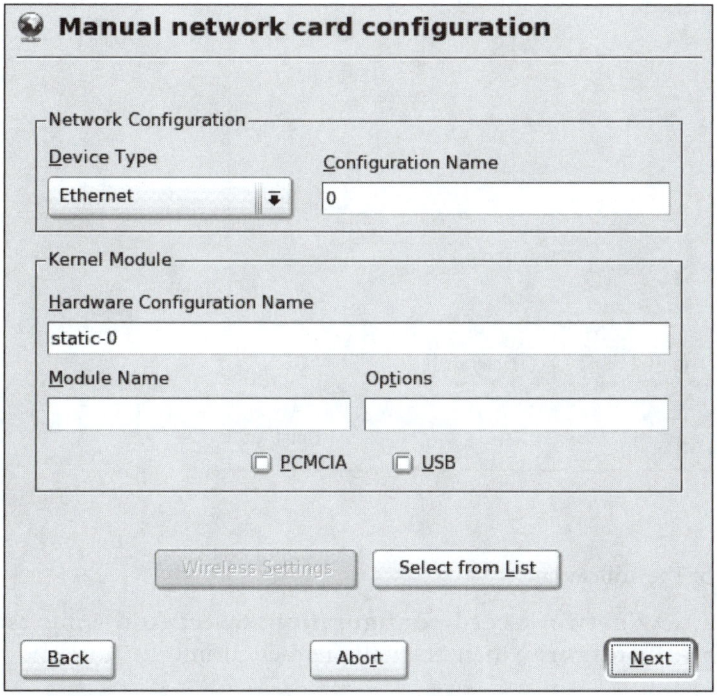

Figure 7-7

From this dialog box, you select a device type (such as Ethernet) and enter a hardware configuration name (such as **eth1**).

Under Kernel Module, enter a hardware configuration name and module name. You can configure some kernel modules more precisely by adding options or parameters (see the kernel documentation).

If you want to use an existing network card as a template, select **Select from List**. When you finish, add the network card to the list for configuration by selecting **Next**.

3. (Conditional) If you have already configured a network card (such as during installation), modify the settings by selecting **Change**. The dialog box shown in Figure 7-8 appears.

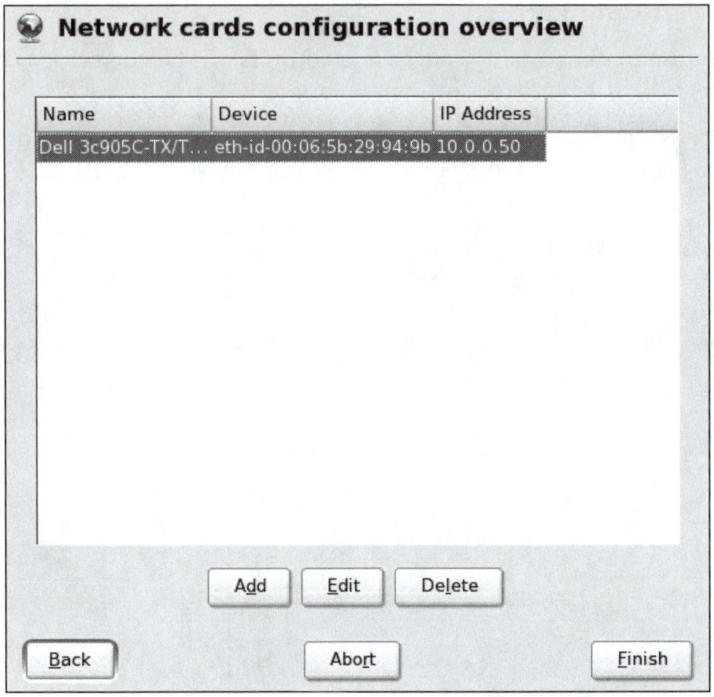

Figure 7-8

4. Do one of the following:

 ■ **Add a new network card configuration.** Select **Add** (same as selecting **Other > Configure**); then enter the requested information.

 or

 ■ **Modify an existing configuration.** Select the *network card*; then select **Edit**.

 or

 ■ **Delete a listed configuration.** Select the *network card*; then select **Delete**.

If you select Edit (or selected *network card* > **Configure** from the previous dialog box), the dialog box shown in Figure 7-9 appears.

```
⬤ Network address setup
─────────────────────────────────────────────

  Network device │ eth-id-00:06:5b:29:94:9b

 ┌Choose the setup method──────────────────────────┐
 │                                                  │
 │  ◯ Automatic address setup (via DHCP)            │
 │                                                  │
 │  ◉ Static address setup                          │
 │  IP Address                Subnet mask           │
 │  ┌──────────────┐          ┌──────────────────┐  │
 │  │10.0.0.50     │          │255.255.255.0     │  │
 │  └──────────────┘          └──────────────────┘  │
 │                                                  │
 └──────────────────────────────────────────────────┘

 ┌Detailed settings────────────────────────────────┐
 │                                                  │
 │        ┌────────────────────────────────┐        │
 │        │   Host name and name server    │        │
 │        └────────────────────────────────┘        │
 │        ┌────────────────────────────────┐        │
 │        │            Routing             │        │
 │        └────────────────────────────────┘        │
 │        ┌────────────────────────────┬───┐        │
 │        │         Advanced...        │ ▼ │        │
 │        └────────────────────────────┴───┘        │
 │                                                  │
 └──────────────────────────────────────────────────┘

  ┌────────┐         ┌────────┐        ┌────────┐
  │  Back  │         │ Abort  │        │  Next  │
  └────────┘         └────────┘        └────────┘
```

Figure 7-9

In this dialog box, you can enter or select the following to integrate the network card into the network:

- **Setup method.** First decide if the network card should receive an IP address from a DHCP server; if so, select **Automatic address setup** (via DHCP). Alternatively, if a permanent address should be used, select **Static address setup**.

  If you chose to set up a static address, enter the *IP address* of the network interface (such as **10.0.0.50**) in the IP Address field, and enter the *subnet mask* (such as **255.255.255.0**) in the Subnet mask field.

  The network mask (referred to as subnet mask in YaST) determines in which network an IP address is located.

CAUTION

If the computer will be connected directly to the Internet, you must use an officially assigned IP address.

- **Host name and name server.** Computers in the network can be addressed directly through their IP addresses or with a unique name.

  In addition, a name server must exist to resolve names into IP addresses and vice versa.

  When you select **Host name and name server**, the dialog box shown in Figure 7-10 appears.

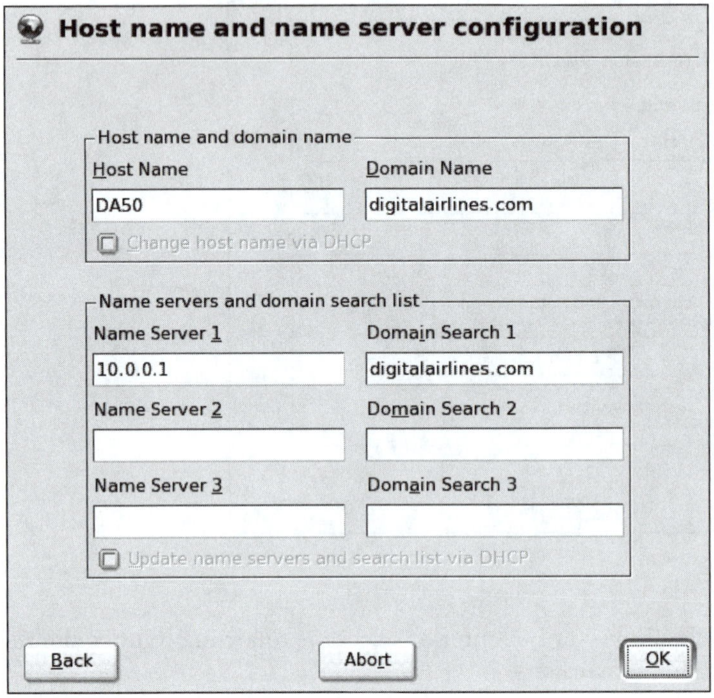

Host name and name server configuration

Host name and domain name

Host Name	Domain Name
DA50	digitalairlines.com

☐ Change host name via DHCP

Name servers and domain search list

Name Server 1	Domain Search 1
10.0.0.1	digitalairlines.com

Name Server 2	Domain Search 2

Name Server 3	Domain Search 3

☐ Update name servers and search list via DHCP

Back	Abort	OK

Figure 7-10

You enter a **Host Name** (a unique name to identify the server on the network) and a **Domain Name** (the name of the DNS to which the computer belongs).

A computer can be addressed uniquely by giving its FQDN (Fully Qualified Domain Name), which is a combination of the hostname and the domain name (such as **DA50.digitalairlines.com**).

To address other computers in the network with their hostnames, you need to enter at least one *name server* in the list of name servers.

In the local network, it is more appropriate to address other hosts not with their FQDN but with their hostnames. In the domain search list, you can enter up to three *domain names* with which the system can expand the host name to the FQDN.

If the search list contains several domains, the resulting FQDN will be passed to the name server until an entry returns an associated IP address.

■ **Routing.** If you want the server to access hosts in other networks (subnets), define the routes by selecting **Routing**.

The dialog box shown in Figure 7–11 appears.

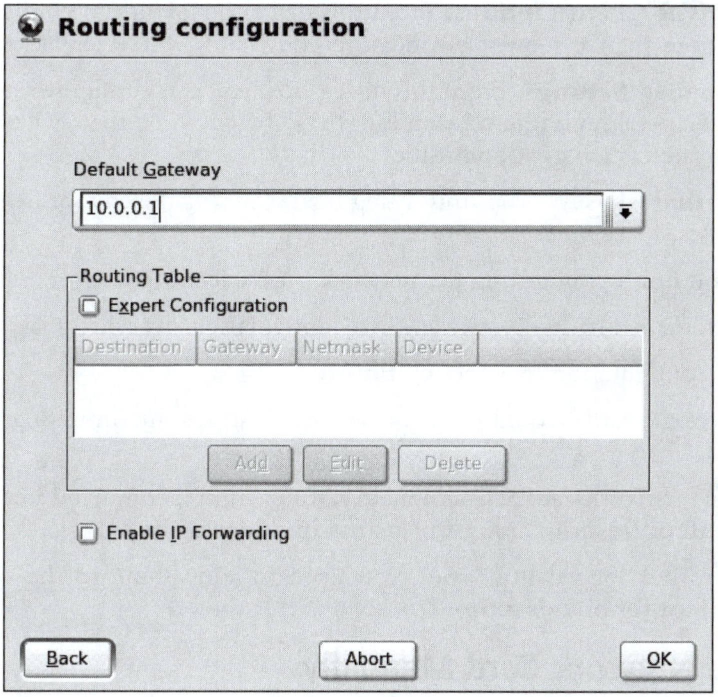

7

Routing configuration

Default Gateway

| 10.0.0.1 | |

Routing Table
☐ Expert Configuration

Destination	Gateway	Netmask	Device	

Add	Edit	Delete

☐ Enable IP Forwarding

Back	Abort	OK

Figure 7-11

You enter or select an IP address to point to a **Default Gateway** (a server that forwards information from a network to another network).

All data not addressed to the local network is forwarded directly to the gateway.

You can create entries in the **Routing Table** by selecting **Expert Configuration**; then select **Add**. You need to provide a Destination, Gateway, and Netmask for each entry.

If your system is a router, then select **Enable IP Forwarding**.

- **Advanced settings.** From the **Advanced** drop-down list, you can configure the following:

  - **Hardware Details.** From this dialog box, you can configure kernel module settings such as hardware configuration name and module name. These settings are saved in the file corresponding to the interface in /etc/sysconfig/hardware/.

  - **DHCP Client Options.** From this dialog box, you can configure client options such as request broadcast response and DHCP client identifier.

  - **Detailed Settings.** From this dialog box, you can configure settings such as the maximum transmission unit (MTU) and when the device should be activated (such as at boot time).

  - **Virtual Aliases.** From this dialog box, you can add, edit, or delete virtual aliases.

5. When you finish configuring the network card, select **Next**.

   You are returned to the Network cards configuration overview dialog box.

6. Save the configuration by selecting **Finish**.

   The network card should now be activated and communicating with the network.

7. Check the network card activation and settings from a command line by entering **ifconfig** or by using **ip** (such as **ip address show**).

   If you are not logged in as root, you need to add /sbin/ to the commands (**/sbin/ifconfig** or **/sbin/ip**).

How to Modify a Network Card Manually

Once you have configured a network card with YaST, you can make temporary modifications to the network card settings from the command line at any time by using the command ifconfig. This type of modification is especially useful for testing purposes.

To make permanent configuration changes, you need to modify and save the configuration file manually, or use YaST to make the modifications.

To manually modify network card settings, you need to know how to do the following:

- Configure the Network Interface with ifconfig
- Configure IP Aliases with ifconfig
- Modify Network Interface Configuration Files
- Configure Host and Domain Names

Configure the Network Interface with ifconfig

You can use the command ifconfig (/sbin/ifconfig) for manually configuring network card interfaces. You can also view all information about the status of network interfaces.

The command also displays the MAC address (hardware address), which is unique for every network card.

For this reason, you should be familiar with the basic syntax of the command, even though it has now been replaced in the network scripts of SUSE Linux Enterprise Server by the command ip.

If you change a configuration setting with ifconfig, the change is temporary. The new data is not written to any configuration file, so the original configuration is again used when the network is restarted.

The following is the syntax for the command ifconfig:

ifconfig [*interface*] [*address*] [*options*]

interface is the symbolic name of the network device to configure (such as eth0). *address* is the IP address to assign to the network card. The most commonly used *options* are listed in Table 7-2.

Table 7-2

Option	Description
netmask *mask*	Assigns *mask* as the subnet mask
broadcast *address*	Sets the broadcast address
pointtopoint *address*	Sets the IP address of the other end for a ppp (point-to-point) connection
mtu *bytes*	Sets the maximum transmission unit (MTU); this is the maximum size for a data packet in bytes.
up or down	Activates or deactivates the network card interface
hw ether *MAC_address*	Sets the MAC address of an Ethernet network card to *MAC_address*

For example, if you enter **ifconfig eth0 192.168.0.1**, the network card eth0 is assigned the IP address 192.168.0.1.

If you do not specify the network mask and the broadcast address (as in the following), they are set according to the association of the IP address with a network class:

```
eth0      Link encap:Ethernet  HWaddr 00:00:1C:B0:A2:85
          inet addr:192.168.0.1  Bcast:192.168.0.255  Mask:255.255.255.0
          inet6 addr: fe80::200:1cff:feb0:a285/64 Scope:Link
          UP BROADCAST RUNNING MULTICAST  MTU:1500  Metric:1
. . .
```

By allocating an IP address, the interface is also activated (UP in the output of ifconfig).

If you enter **ifconfig eth0 up**, eth0 is activated. This works only if values have previously been assigned to the interface.

The command ifconfig does not read any values from configuration files but only values from memory. If an interface has not yet been activated after a reboot, it cannot be activated directly by the option up.

This works only by assigning explicit values with the commands ifconfig or ip (as in the start-up scripts). The same applies if the respective module is unloaded with the command rmmod.

Entering **ifconfig** lists all defined network interfaces together with their corresponding parameters, as in the following:

```
DA50:~ # ifconfig
eth0       Link encap:Ethernet  HWaddr 00:00:1C:B0:A2:85
           inet addr:192.168.0.1  Bcast:192.168.0.255  Mask:255.255.255.0
           inet6 addr: fe80::200:1cff:feb0:a285/64 Scope:Link
           UP BROADCAST RUNNING MULTICAST  MTU:1500  Metric:1
           RX packets:87618 errors:2 dropped:0 overruns:0 frame:0
           TX packets:93583 errors:30 dropped:0 overruns:0 carrier:30
           collisions:0 txqueuelen:1000
           RX bytes:12102862 (11.5 Mb)  TX bytes:18062074 (17.2 Mb)
           Interrupt:17 Base address:0xb400

lo         Link encap:Local Loopback
           inet addr:127.0.0.1  Mask:255.0.0.0
           inet6 addr: ::1/128 Scope:Host
           UP LOOPBACK RUNNING  MTU:16436  Metric:1
           RX packets:167574 errors:0 dropped:0 overruns:0 frame:0
           TX packets:167574 errors:0 dropped:0 overruns:0 carrier:0
           collisions:0 txqueuelen:0
           RX bytes:21117134 (20.1 Mb)  TX bytes:21117134 (20.1 Mb)
```

This includes information such as address and network masks, packages received (RX, received) and sent (TX, transmitted), and collisions that might have occurred.

Entering **ifconfig -a** (as in the following) lists all network interfaces, including those that have not been configured:

```
DA50:~ # ifconfig -a
eth0       Link encap:Ethernet  HWaddr 00:00:1C:B0:A2:85
           inet addr:192.168.0.1  Bcast:192.168.0.255  Mask:255.255.255.0
           inet6 addr: fe80::200:1cff:feb0:a285/64 Scope:Link
           UP BROADCAST RUNNING MULTICAST  MTU:1500  Metric:1
```

```
              RX packets:87618 errors:2 dropped:0 overruns:0 frame:0
              TX packets:93583 errors:30 dropped:0 overruns:0 carrier:30
              collisions:0 txqueuelen:1000
              RX bytes:12102862 (11.5 Mb)  TX bytes:18062074 (17.2 Mb)
              Interrupt:17 Base address:0xb400
eth1          Link encap:Ethernet  HWaddr 00:00:1C:B5:58:94
              BROADCAST MULTICAST  MTU:1500  Metric:1
              RX packets:0 errors:0 dropped:0 overruns:0 frame:0
              TX packets:0 errors:0 dropped:0 overruns:0 carrier:0
              collisions:0 txqueuelen:1000
              RX bytes:0 (0.0 b)  TX bytes:0 (0.0 b)
              Interrupt:16 Base address:0xb000
```

Configure IP Aliases with ifconfig

With ifconfig, you can define more than one IP address for a network card by using **IP aliases**. There is virtually no limit for the number of possible IP aliases you can define.

For example, if a host has only one network card but needs to be addressed directly from several different subnets, you can use IP aliases to interface with these subnets.

However, it is always better to use a number of interfaces with genuine addresses (instead of IP aliases). This is because a host can only send or receive packets via one address on an interface at any given time.

You can configure an IP alias with ifconfig or YaST. The following is an example of configuring an IP alias with ifconfig:

```
DA50:~ # ifconfig eth0:1 10.10.0.69 broadcast 10.10.255.255 \
                                netmask 255.255.0.0
DA50:~ # ifconfig
eth0          Link encap:Ethernet  HWaddr 00:00:1C:B0:A2:85
              inet addr:192.168.0.1  Bcast:192.168.0.255  Mask:255.255.255.0
              inet6 addr: fe80::200:1cff:feb0:a285/64 Scope:Link
              UP BROADCAST RUNNING MULTICAST  MTU:1500  Metric:1
              RX packets:87618 errors:2 dropped:0 overruns:0 frame:0
              TX packets:93583 errors:30 dropped:0 overruns:0 carrier:30
              collisions:0 txqueuelen:1000
              RX bytes:12102862 (11.5 Mb)  TX bytes:18062074 (17.2 Mb)
              Interrupt:17 Base address:0xb400

eth0:1        Link encap:Ethernet  HWaddr 00:00:1C:B0:A2:85
              inet addr:10.10.0.69  Bcast:10.10.255.255  Mask:255.255.0.0
              UP BROADCAST RUNNING MULTICAST  MTU:1500  Metric:1
              Interrupt:17 Base address:0xb400
```

You can use both letters and numbers for IP aliases (such as **eth0:100**, **eth0:a1**, or **eth1:B42**). Remember that IP alias letters are case sensitive.

You can configure an IP alias with ifconfig, but you cannot view aliases with it. To view IP aliases, enter **ip address show**.

Modify Network Interface Configuration Files

In order to save the network configuration settings permanently, you need to manually edit and save the appropriate configuration files.

You can find all relevant network configuration files in the directory /etc/sysconfig/network/. This directory contains a configuration file for each configured network adapter, including details of the device.

For example, /etc/sysconfig/network/ifcfg-eth-id-00:00:1c:b5:55:74 is the configuration file for the network card with the hardware address 00:00:1c:b5:55:74, and /etc/sysconfig/network/ifcfg-lo is the configuration file for the loopback device.

To understand the structure of the configuration files, you need to know something about the activation of the network device when booting.

All network interfaces (as well as configured routes) are activated at boot by the script /etc/init.d/network, which is run in runlevels 2, 3, and 5.

By accessing the settings of the existing configuration files in /etc/sysconfig/network/, the script knows which interfaces need to be activated at boot or deactivated when the computer is shut down.

The file /etc/sysconfig/network/config contains a number of general variables that influence the behavior of the script, such as whether a search should be made for existing connections when the interface is deactivated and if these should be automatically terminated.

The directory /etc/sysconfig/network/scripts/ contains additional scripts that are run by /etc/init.d/network (depending on the type of interface).

Activating or deactivating network interfaces is performed by running the script /sbin/ifup from the script /etc/init.d/network. With this script, the configuration files for the interface are evaluated, and the network cards are activated with the command ip.

The scripts /sbin/ifdown (deactivating network interfaces) and /sbin/ifstatus (displaying the status of network interfaces) are only symbolic links to the script /etc/sbin/ifup.

If the start script /etc/init.d/network is used, all configured network interfaces are activated or deactivated, or the status of all configured network interfaces is given.

To activate just a single interface with the preconfigured values, to find out the status of the single interface, or to deactivate only one interface, you have to add the interface name after start, stop, or status (such as **/etc/init.d/network stop eth0** or **/etc/init.d/network start ippp0**).

You can also enter the commands ifup, ifstatus, and ifdown directly from the command line.

For example, entering **ifup eth0** activates the first Ethernet network card, and entering **ifup eth1** activates the second Ethernet network card or network device.

Entering **ifstatus eth0** displays information similar to the following:

```
DA50:~ # ifstatus eth0
    eth0  device: Digital Equipment Corporation DECchip 21142/43 (rev 41)
    eth0  configuration: eth-id-00:00:1c:b0:a2:85
eth0 is up
2: eth0: <BROADCAST,MULTICAST,UP> mtu 1500 qdisc pfifo_fast qlen 1000
    link/ether 00:00:1c:b0:a2:85 brd ff:ff:ff:ff:ff:ff
    inet 192.168.0.1/24 brd 192.168.0.255 scope global eth0
    inet6 fe80::200:1cff:feb0:a285/64 scope link
        valid_lft forever preferred_lft forever
    eth0      IP address: 192.168.0.1/24
Configured routes for interface eth0:
  default 192.168.0.254 - -
  169.254.0.0 - 255.255.0.0 eth0
Active routes for interface eth0:
  192.168.0.0/24  proto kernel  scope link  src 192.168.0.1
  default via 192.168.0.254
1 of 2 configured routes for interface eth0 up
```

When the interfaces are activated through the script /etc/init.d/network or ifup, the settings are read from the configuration file for that particular network adapter.

The following are example settings in the configuration file /etc/sysconfig/network/ifcfg-eth-id-00:00:1c:b5:55:74:

```
BOOTPROTO='static'
BROADCAST='10.10.255.255'
IPADDR='10.10.0.69'
MTU=''
NETMASK='255.255.0.0'
NETWORK='10.10.0.0'
REMOTE_IPADDR=''
STARTMODE='onboot'
UNIQUE='gZD2.+xOL8ZCSAQC'
_nm_name='bus-pci-0000:00:0b.0'
```

These settings are evaluated by /sbin/ifup (enter **man 8 ifup** for a detailed description). The script calls up /sbin/ip with the evaluated settings both to assign address, network mask, and so on, for that particular network interface, and to set routes.

The parameter UNIQUE contains a unique hash value that is required by YaST for identifying which network card to activate.

In the example, a static address is assigned (BOOTPROTO='static'). In a configuration for DHCP, the value dhcp would appear.

The STARTMODE='onboot' setting specifies that this interface should be activated when the script /etc/init.d/network is run.

The values IPADDR='10.10.0.69', NETMASK='255.255.0.0', and NETWORK='10.10.0.0' specify the IP address, network mask, and network address for the network card.

If the configuration is implemented through DHCP, these entries remain empty or are deleted entirely.

NOTE

For additional documentation about network configuration, see /usr/share/doc/packages/sysconfig/ or refer to the man pages for the individual commands.

To configure IP aliases permanently, you need to enter them in the respective configuration file of the network card. For an example, see the template file /etc/sysconfig/network/ifcfg.template.

When the network script /etc/init.d/network is executed, this interface will also be activated.

Configure Host and Domain Names

In order to provide a hostname and domain name for a server whose network settings are configured manually, you need to modify the following two files:

- **/etc/HOSTNAME.** The entry for the FQDN of the host is located in this file and looks like the following:

```
earth.example.com
```

- **/etc/resolv.conf.** Information about the name servers to query and the domain search list are stored in this file, and look like the following:

```
nameserver 192.168.0.200
nameserver 192.168.0.213
search example.com
```

You can list a maximum of three name server entries. To enter several domains in the search list, keep them in the same line separated by blank spaces.

OBJECTIVE 2 CONFIGURE AND MANAGE ROUTES

For IP packets to reach their destination, TCP/IP networks use routes. For packets that are not addressed to a host in the local network, routes show the way to a router that forwards the packets to their respective destinations.

In a running system, the routes are read from the kernel routing table. This table does not exist as an actual file but is generated in memory by the kernel.

If you need to configure routes permanently, you need to create a corresponding configuration file. This file is read by the script /etc/init.d/network, and the routes listed are activated (they are included in the kernel routing table).

To configure and manage routes, you need to know the following:

- Route Types
- How to Manage Routes with route
- How to Modify Route Configuration Files
- How to Activate Routing
- How to Manage the Network Interface and Routes with ip

Route Types

There are three basic types of routes:

- Host Routes
- Network and Gateway Routes
- Default Route

Host Routes

A host route defines the path that a data packet can take for exactly one destination host. For example, you need host routes when using ISDN cards to define the point-to-point connection on the provider connection.

The following from a routing table shows typical host routes:

```
Kernel IP routing table
Destination     Gateway         Genmask          Flags Metric Ref   Use Iface
[...]
192.168.1.2     0.0.0.0         255.255.255.255  UH    0      0     0 ippp0
192.168.15.7    192.168.0.3     255.255.255.255  UGH   0      0     0 eth0
```

The defined target with the IP address **192.168.1.2** appears, which represents one host. The corresponding netmask **255.255.255.255** is always set for host routes.

The set flags **U** and **H** specify that the route is up (U) and that this involves a host route (H).

The name of the network interface tells a correspondingly addressed data packet through which interface the packet should leave the Linux machine.

In this case, an outgoing data packet is leaving through the network interface **ippp0** (the first ISDN interface) toward 192.168.1.2. The gateway address **0.0.0.0** indicates that no routing gateway is needed to reach the destination. This represents a point-to-point connection to the provider's dial-in server.

In the second line, a host route is defined for the host **192.168.15.7**. This host can only be accessed by way of the router (gateway) **192.168.0.3**, which is marked with the flag **G** (Gateway).

Network and Gateway Routes

A network route defines the path a data packet can take for an entire destination network. Network routes are most frequently used because they define the path into your own network and into remote networks.

The following from a routing table shows two typical network routes:

```
Kernel IP routing table
Destination    Gateway         Genmask           Flags Metric Ref    Use Iface
192.168.0.0    0.0.0.0         255.255.255.0     U     0      0        0 eth0
192.168.15.0   192.168.0.254   255.255.255.0     UG    0      0        0 eth0
```

In the above example, the network route for your own network appears first (**eth0**).

The network address for your own network is **192.168.0.0** with a netmask of **255.255.255.0**. This results in a total addressable range of 256 IP addresses (192.168.0.0–192.168.0.255).

All data packets from this Linux machine addressed to an address in this range leave the Linux machine via the interface eth0.

The route to network **192.168.15.0** also addresses a total of 256 IP addresses (192.168.15.0–192.168.15.255). The set flag **G** indicates that this network is a special case.

This route represents a gateway route—a route to the destination network via a defined gateway.

The corresponding gateway is defined with the IP address **192.168.0.254** and must be located in a network directly connected to the Linux machine.

Data packets to the defined destination network 192.168.15.0 are forwarded directly by the Linux machine to the specified gateway.

The gateway in turn has its own routes and forwards the data packets received depending on the rules defined in its own routing table.

Default Route

A default route is a special gateway route. It defines the route a data packet can take if no previous host, network, or gateway route matched the destination of the packet.

The following from a routing table shows a typical default route in the last line:

```
Kernel IP routing table
Destination    Gateway          Genmask          Flags Metric Ref    Use Iface
192.168.0.0    0.0.0.0          255.255.255.0    U     0      0        0 eth0
192.168.15.0   192.168.0.254    255.255.255.0    UG    0      0        0 eth0
0.0.0.0        192.168.0.253    0.0.0.0          UG    0      0        0 eth0
```

The destination of the default route is defined by the IP address **0.0.0.0** and the network mask **0.0.0.0**. This definition includes all existing IP addresses in the range from 0.0.0. 0–255.255.255.255.

If a data packet is generated on the Linux computer that cannot be delivered to the networks **192.168.0.0** and **192.168.15.0** over one of the first two routes, the data packet will always be delivered over the default route to the configured default gateway.

A Linux computer that is connected to an Internet provider through an ISDN point-to-point connection will always have a default route defined on the IP address of the opposite point of the provider (on the provider's gateway), so all computers on the Internet can be reached via this gateway.

A corresponding routing table with just one installed network interface could be configured as follows:

```
Kernel IP routing table
Destination    Gateway          Genmask          Flags Metric Ref    Use Iface
192.168.1.2    0.0.0.0          255.255.255.255  UH    0      0        0 ippp0
0.0.0.0        192.168.1.2      0.0.0.0          UG    0      0        0 ippp0
```

How to Manage Routes with route

You can use the command route (/sbin/route) to check and edit the routing table.

For example, the command **route –n** returns a table of activated routes with the listed addresses in numerical form (no name server query).

Although the functions of the command route are covered by the command ip in the script for starting the network, because route is a standard tool in all Linux distributions, it is important that you are familiar with the command.

CAUTION

Routes defined with the command route are entered directly in the kernel routing table and no longer exist after restarting the server. To define permanent routes, you need to modify the respective configuration files.

To manage routes with the command route, you need to know how to do the following:

- Create a Route
- Delete a Route

Create a Route

The following is the syntax for creating new routes:

route add [-net | –host *destination***] [netmask** *mask***] [gw** *gateway***] [metric** *n***] [dev** *interface***]**

For example, to set up a new route for the directly connected network 192.168.0.0/255.255.255.0 on the network interface eth0, you would enter the following:

route add –net 192.168.0.0 netmask 255.255.255.0 dev eth0

To set up a new network route for a network lying behind the gateway with the IP address 192.168.0.254 using the address range 192.168.3.0/255.255.255.240, you would enter the following:

route add –net 192.168.3.0 netmask 255.255.255.240 gw 192.168.0.254 dev eth0

Static routing is set up by default. It is also possible to implement dynamic routing by installing and configuring a routing daemon.

If you want to use dynamic routing, you need to add the option **metric** *n*, where *n* is a value greater than or equal to zero and is used to define the distance to the destination host or network.

The higher the value, the more costly the connection to the destination network is estimated to be by the routing daemon.

In this way, several routes to a destination network can be defined.

When a data packet is sent, the system will first try to deliver it over the most convenient route. The system will deliver the data packet through the next most favorable route only if the path is closed due to overload or failure of the targeted transmission route.

Delete a Route

You can remove an existing route from the routing table with the command route. The following is the syntax for deleting a route:

route del [-net | –host *destination***] [gw** *gateway***] [netmask** *mask***] [dev** *interface***]**

For example, you can remove the previously configured routes from the routing table by entering the following:

route del –net 192.168.3.0 netmask 255.255.255.240

You can delete the default route with the following command:

route del default

To delete a network route, you need to specify the target address and the network mask.

7

How to Modify Route Configuration Files

An entry is generated in the kernel routing table for all active network interfaces. This means that all hosts in the local network can be addressed without defining any further routes.

For example, if you assign the following parameters to the network interface eth0

```
ifconfig eth0 192.168.0.1 netmask 255.255.255.0
```

the output of the existing routes will be as follows:

```
DA50:~ # route -n
Kernel IP routing table
Destination    Gateway        Genmask         Flags Metric Ref   Use Iface
192.168.0.0    0.0.0.0        255.255.255.0   U     0      0       0 eth0
```

Notice that a route was generated to the local network, which is defined by the network mask.

Additional static routes are defined by entries in the respective configuration files and activated when the network is started.

As long as the system is up, these routes will not be modified by any dynamic processes and will be kept until they are deleted. For this reason, they are referred to as *static routes*.

All static routes are configured in the files /etc/sysconfig/network/routes and /etc/sysconfig/network/ifroute-Interface.

These files are read when the network is started, and the routes are written to the routing table.

The script /etc/init.d/network is responsible for transferring the entries from /etc/sysconfig/network/routes to the routing table and is executed automatically when the machine is booted to the runlevels 2, 3, or 5.

When you use the YaST module Network Services Routing, the entries in these files are automatically updated. You can also define your own static routes in these files with any editor.

The structure of the files is largely based on the output of **route –n**. The entries include the following fields (in the order of their appearance):

- Destination network/destination host
- The gateway to use
- The network mask
- The network interface over which the packets are to be sent (this field can remain empty)

The following is an example of typical entries in the file /etc/sysconfig/network/routes:

```
192.168.0.0       0.0.0.0         255.255.255.0
192.168.15.0      192.168.0.254   255.255.255.0
192.168.17.12     192.168.0.251   255.255.255.255
default           192.168.0.251   0.0.0.0             eth0
```

A typical example for a routing file for a special interface is /etc/sysconfig/network/ifroute-ippp0. This route is only set when a dial-in connection is established with the provider by way of the ISDN card. Normally, the default route is set (such as **default 192.168.1.2 0.0.0.0 ippp0**).

For the default route, do not enter **0.0.0.0** as a destination in the file; instead, use the keyword **default**.

How to Activate Routing

A Linux host can also serve as a router itself. However, this property is deactivated by default. An entry in the process file system activates routing in the kernel:

echo 1 > /proc/sys/net/ipv4/ip_forward

If a 0 is entered in this file, the routing will be deactivated. To activate routing permanently, set the following variable in the file /etc/sysconfig/sysctl:

IP_FORWARD="yes"

How to Manage the Network Interface and Routes with ip

In SUSE Linux Enterprise Server, the commands ifconfig and route have been replaced (as far as possible) in the scripts for network configuration by the command ip.

You can use the command ip to perform the following common administrative tasks:

- Assign addresses to network interfaces
- Assign parameters to network interfaces

- Set routes

- Define simple filter rules

- Display the current configuration

Because of the many tasks you can perform with ip, the command syntax is relatively complex. The following is the general syntax for the command:

ip [*options*] *object* [*command* [*parameters*]]

object specifies what should be changed with the command. Table 7–3 lists some possible values for *object*.

Table 7-3

Object	Description
link	Allocates parameters for a network interface
addr or address	Determines an address for a network device
route	Configures routes

Depending on the objects, various options and commands are available. You can also significantly abbreviate command parameters (such as entering **ip a s** instead of **ip address show**).

As with ifconfig, all modifications made with the command ip are temporary and are no longer valid after restarting the network script /etc/init.d/network.

For configuration changes to be permanent, you need to make them with YaST or directly edit the appropriate configuration files.

You can perform the following common tasks with the command ip:

- Assign Parameters for Network Interfaces (ip link)

- Assign IP Addresses (ip address)

- Set Up Routes (ip route)

NOTE

Many other configuration options are available for the command ip, such as setting simple filter rules or adding other types of routes.

For detailed information on the command ip, see /usr/share/doc/packages/iproute2/ip-cref.pdf.

Assign Parameters for Network Interfaces (ip link)

The only commands you can use when you assign parameters to network devices with ip are set (for setting values) and show (for displaying set parameters).

Table 7-4 lists some commonly used parameters for set.

Table 7-4

Parameter	Description
dev *interface*	Name of the interface to address (standard parameter)
up or down	Activates or deactivates the interface
mtu	Sets the maximum transmission unit (MTU), which is the maximum size of a data packet in bytes
address *MAC_address*	Overwrites the MAC address of the interfaces

For example, entering **ip link set eth0 mtu 1492** sets the MTU value for the network card eth0 to 1492 bytes.

The parameter dev (normally in front of eth0) does not have to be given, since this is the default parameter.

Entering **ip link set eth0 down** deactivates network card eth0.

Entering **ip link show** displays parameters for all configured network interfaces, as in the following:

```
DA50:~ # ip link show
1: lo: <LOOPBACK,UP> mtu 16436 qdisc noqueue
    link/loopback 00:00:00:00:00:00 brd 00:00:00:00:00:00
2: eth0: <BROADCAST,MULTICAST,UP> mtu 1500 qdisc pfifo_fast qlen 1000
    link/ether 00:00:1c:b0:a2:85 brd ff:ff:ff:ff:ff:ff
3: eth1: <BROADCAST,MULTICAST> mtu 1500 qdisc noop qlen 1000
    link/ether 00:00:1c:b5:58:94 brd ff:ff:ff:ff:ff:ff
4: sit0: <NOARP> mtu 1480 qdisc noqueue
    link/sit 0.0.0.0 brd 0.0.0.0
```

Assign IP Addresses (ip address)

When configuring IP addresses, the most important commands are add (assign an address), del (delete an address), and show (display addresses).

Table 7-5 lists some commonly used parameters for add.

Table 7-5

Parameter	Description
dev *interface*	Name of the interface to address
local *address/mask*	IP address and netmask of the interface (default parameter)
peer *address*	IP address of the other end of a PPP connection
broadcast *address*	Broadcast address (must be given explicitly)
label *name*	Generates an IP alias with the *name*

The following example uses the parameter dev:

```
ip address add 192.168.0.1/24 dev eth0 broadcast +
```

In this example, the network card eth0 is given the IP address 192.168.0.1. In contrast to the command ifconfig, you need to specify a netmask when using ip; otherwise, the netmask is set to 255.255.255.255 by default.

For the same reason, you need to specify a broadcast address. In this example, entering broadcast + sets a broadcast address calculated from the given netmask.

You do not need to enter the parameter local (before the IP address) because this is the default parameter for ip. You can also abbreviate the parameter broadcast to brd.

The following example uses parameters dev and label:

```
ip address add 192.168.1.1/24 broadcast 192.168.1.255 dev eth0
 label eth0:1
```

In this example, the IP alias eth0:1 is activated with the given values. Assigned IP aliases are listed with the network interface, as in the following:

```
DA50:~ # ip address show
1: lo: <LOOPBACK,UP> mtu 16436 qdisc noqueue
    link/loopback 00:00:00:00:00:00 brd 00:00:00:00:00:00
    inet 127.0.0.1/8 brd 127.255.255.255 scope host lo
    inet6 ::1/128 scope host
       valid_lft forever preferred_lft forever
2: eth0: <BROADCAST,MULTICAST,UP> mtu 1500 qdisc pfifo_fast qlen 1000
    link/ether 00:00:1c:b0:a2:85 brd ff:ff:ff:ff:ff:ff
    inet 192.168.0.1/24 brd 192.168.0.255 scope global eth0
    inet 192.168.1.1/24 brd 192.168.0.255 scope global eth0:1
    inet6 fe80::200:1cff:feb0:a285/64 scope link
       valid_lft forever preferred_lft forever
3: eth1: <BROADCAST,MULTICAST> mtu 1500 qdisc noop qlen 1000
    link/ether 00:00:1c:b5:58:94 brd ff:ff:ff:ff:ff:ff
4: sit0: <NOARP> mtu 1480 qdisc noqueue
    link/sit 0.0.0.0 brd 0.0.0.0
```

In the following example, the IP alias with the address 192.168.1.1 is deleted:

```
ip address delete 192.168.1.1 dev eth0
```

Set Up Routes (ip route)

When you set up routes using ip route, you can add routes (add), modify routes (change), delete routes (delete), and display routes (show).

Table 7-6 lists some commonly used parameters for adding routes.

Table 7-6

Parameter	Description
default	Add a default route
via *address*	Specify the IP address of a gateway
dev *interface*	Name of the interface to which packets should be sent

The following is an example of using the parameter via:

```
ip route add 192.168.1.1/24 via 192.168.0.254
```

The route to the network 192.168.1.1/24 is added through the gateway host 192.168.0.254.

The following is an example of how to delete the default route:

```
ip route delete default
```

OBJECTIVE 3   TEST THE NETWORK INTERFACE

In this objective, you learn how to perform the following tasks to check the health of your TCP/IP network interface connection (and the network in general):

- Check a Network Connection between Hosts (ping)
- Check the Routing (traceroute)
- Analyze Network Traffic (tcpdump and ethereal)
- Determine the Status of All Network Connections (netstat)
- Check for Service Availability (netcat)

Check a Network Connection between Hosts (ping)

The command ping (/bin/ping) is a simple tool for checking network connections. It is normally available on all hosts that contain a TCP/IP stack, and should always be used first to test network connectivity.

With ping, you can check network connections between two hosts that are in the same or remote networks. If the ping works, then both the physical and logical connection (on an IP basis) is correctly set up between the hosts.

To use the command ping effectively, you need to know the following:

- How the Command Tests a Connection
- Command Options
- Troubleshooting Suggestions

How the Command Tests a Connection

When you enter **ping** *host*, your server sends an ICMP datagram to the target host with the message echo request. If datagram can be received, the target host answers with an ICMP datagram containing the message echo reply.

Sending the message using the ICMP protocol means that no higher level protocols (such as TCP or UDP) are involved. This has the advantage of ensuring that wrong configurations within the higher protocols do not automatically lead to a reply failure.

The following is a typical result of entering the command **ping** *host*:

```
DA50:~ # ping DA10
PING DA10.example.com (192.168.0.10) 56(84) bytes of data.
64 bytes from DA10.example.com (192.168.0.10): icmp_
seq=1 ttl=64 time=0.215 ms
64 bytes from DA10.example.com (192.168.0.10): icmp_
seq=2 ttl=64 time=0.187 ms
64 bytes from DA10.example.com (192.168.0.10): icmp_
seq=3 ttl=64 time=0.190 ms

--- DA10.example.com ping statistics ---
3 packets transmitted, 3 received, 0% packet loss, time 3000ms
rtt min/avg/max/mdev = 0.182/0.193/0.215/0.018 ms
```

In the above example, a total of three ICMP datagrams were sent to the host DA10.example.com (echo request), which were answered with a message (echo reply).

The following information is displayed:

- The IP address of the target host (DA10 is resolved to DA10.example.com and DA10.example.com is resolved to 192.168.0.10)

- The size of the ICMP datagram (dates, ICMP header, and IP header) as 56(84) bytes of data

- The sequence number of the reply datagram (icmp_seq starting with 1 and increasing by 1 each time)

- The TTL (Time To Live) of the datagram

  When the packet is created, the TTL value is usually set to 64, 128, or 255, depending on the operating system and its configuration.

  Every time the packet passes through a router, it is decreased by 1. If the TTL reaches the value 0, the packet is discarded.

  By means of the TTL, you can often figure out how many routers a datagram has passed through from the destination host.

  In the example, the TTL is still 64, which means that no router was encountered.

- The time (time) each round-trip needs

  This is the amount of time that passes between the transmission of an echo request datagram and the corresponding echo reply datagram received.

- A statistical output of the round-trip times (rtt min/avg/max/mdev), which includes the minimum, average, maximum, and medium deviation in milliseconds

The following is a typical output of the command ping when a network connection fails:

```
DA50:~ # ping DA90
PING DA90.example.com (192.168.0.90) 56(84) bytes of data.
From DA50.example.com (192.168.0.50): icmp_seq=2 Destination Host
Unreachable
From DA50.example.com (192.168.0.50): icmp_seq=2 Destination Host
Unreachable
From DA50.example.com (192.168.0.50): icmp_seq=3 Destination Host
Unreachable

--- DA90.example.com ping statistics ---
3 packets transmitted, 0 received, +3 errors, 100% packet loss,
time 2010ms, pipe 3
```

In the above example, an attempt was made to send three ICMP datagrams (echo request) to the target host DA90.example.com, but the sending host received no answer from the target host within a set period of time.

Command Options

The command ping provides a variety of options for checking a network connection. Table 7-7 lists some of the more commonly used options.

Table 7-7

Parameter	Description
-c *count*	Specifies the exact count of how many echo request data-grams are sent before ping terminates
-I *interface_addr*	Specifies the interface to be used on a server with several network interfaces
-i *wait*	Specifies the number of seconds (*wait*) between individual data shipments (default: 1 second)
-f (flood ping)	Sends datagrams one after another at the same rate as the respective replies arrive, or one hundred times per second (whichever is greater)
	Only root can use this option. For normal users, the minimum time is 200 milliseconds
-l *preload*	Causes ping to send *preload* datagrams without waiting for a reply

Table 7-7 (continued)

Parameter	Description
-n	Forces a numerical output of the IP address; address resolutions to hostnames are not carried out
-t *ttl*	Specifies the TTF value for echo request datagrams
-w *maxwait*	Specifies a time-out (in seconds) before ping exits, regardless of how many packets have been sent or received
-b	Sends echo request datagrams to the broadcast address of the network

NOTE

For details on all parameters available for the command ping, enter **man 8 ping**.

Troubleshooting Suggestions

When using the command ping to check the communication between two hosts, start by checking the host-internal network (**ping *localhost***). Then check the network interface connected to your own host (**ping *interface_addr***).

If checking the host-internal network and the connected network interface is successful, then check the network segment to the next closest network element (such as a router) in the direction of the target host, followed by the network section containing the next segment (and so on) until the check ends at the target host.

By doing this, you check increasingly large partial sections (both physical and logical) from your own host toward the target host, narrowing the search for a possible error source to a minimum.

During this check, if no reply datagram is returned at a defined point, you can assume that at least one error is located in the last segment checked. That error could be in a cable, hub, switch, router, or configuration.

Check the Routing (*traceroute*)

You can use the command traceroute (/usr/sbin/traceroute) to help you follow the route taken by an IP datagram to the specified target host.

This tool is primarily used to check routings between different networks and to illustrate the routings involved between the various TCP/IP-based networks.

To use the command traceroute effectively, you need to know the following:

- How a Route Is Traced
- Command Options
- Troubleshooting Suggestions

How a Route Is Traced

traceroute traces a route by sending three UDP datagrams with the same TTL value, and then increasing the value for the next three datagrams.

First, three packets with a TTL of 1 are sent to the host. The second time, three packets with a TTL of 2 are sent (and so on).

Because the TTL is reduced by 1 when the UDP datagram passes through a router (hop) and the datagram is discarded at TTL=0, a gateway at TTL=0 sends an ICMP datagram with the message "TTL exceeded" back to the sender.

If the UDP datagram reaches the target host, the host replies with an ICMP datagram Port Unreachable, as the target port for the UDP datagrams is set to values in which normally no services from the target host are offered.

From the ICMP message Port Unreachable, the sender recognizes that the target host has now been reached. traceroute evaluates the information collected and then provides some statistical information.

You can perform a simple check of the routing to a target host by entering **traceroute** *host*, as in the following:

```
DA50:~ # traceroute pluto.example.com
traceroute to pluto.example.com (192.168.2.1), 30 hops max,
40 byte packets
 1 sun.example.com (192.168.0.254) 1.148 ms   1.503 ms   1.466 ms
 2 antares.example.com (192.168.1.254)  4.953 ms   5.905 ms   6.762 ms
 3 pluto.example.com (192.168.2.1) 9.428 ms   *   8.166 ms
```

In the above example, a total of three nodes were detected in the network across which the datagrams were routed to the target host.

The following information is displayed:

- The IP address of the target host (pluto is resolved to pluto.example.com, and pluto.example.com is resolved to 192.168.2.1)

- The maximum TTL of a UDP packet is 30 (30 hops max), which means that a maximum of 30 steps over routers/gateways can be detected on the path to the destination host

- A UDP datagram has a length of 40 bytes

- The time for a round-trip for three packets sent in succession by each router/recipient is displayed in milliseconds (ms).

- The second UDP datagram to reach pluto.example.com directly was not answered within the given time-out of three seconds (*).

Command Options

The command traceroute provides a variety of options for tracing a route over a network. Table 7-8 lists some of the more commonly used options.

Table 7-8

Parameter	Description
-m *max_ttl*	Sets the TTL (maximum number of hops) to *max_ttl* (default: 30 hops)
-n	Only outputs the IP addresses of the hops being surveyed (does not resolve any addresses)
-p *port*	Sets the target port for the UDP datagrams to *port* (default: port 33434); this is increased by 1 for each datagram
-q *nqueries*	Sets the number of UDP datagrams for each hop to *nqueries* (default: 3 datagrams)
-r	Sends a UDP datagram directly to a host in the local network without taking the routing table into account
-S *src_addr*	Sets the sender address to *src_addr* if the sending host has multiple interfaces; the parameter *src_addr* must be valid for this host
-w *waittime*	Sets the time (in seconds) to wait for a response to a probe

NOTE

For details on all parameters available for the command traceroute, enter **man traceroute**.

Troubleshooting Suggestions

A common reason for defective communication between two networks is that the transport path between these networks contains errors.

The command traceroute is an excellent tool for checking routers that are located on this transport path.

It also provides detailed information on the path that a datagram must take to the target network and information on the availability of the routers installed on this path.

If you enter **traceroute** *target_host*, you can immediately see at which hop a data package can move along the transport path without a problem, and at which point the transport path is faulty.

Analyze Network Traffic (tcpdump and ethereal)

You can use the tools tcpdump and ethereal in networks for troubleshooting a variety of problems, from analyzing the causes of simple broadcasts to analyzing complex data connections between two or more hosts.

To effectively use tcpdump and ethereal, you need to know the following:

- How to Use tcpdump
- How to Use ethereal
- Command Options (tcpdump)
- Troubleshooting Suggestions

How to Use tcpdump

The command tcpdump (/usr/sbin/tcpdump) is a diagnosis tool that lets you analyze data packets through a network interface connected to the network.

The simplest way to use tcpdump is to enter **tcpdump –i** *interface*. This command puts the network interface into promiscuous mode (the interface evaluates all data packets received) and displays some information about the data reaching the network interface.

When you enter this command, information similar to the following is displayed:

```
DA50:~ # tcpdump -i eth0
tcpdump: listening on eth0

12:15:43.666301 earth.example.com.1023 > venus.example.com.ssh:
 S 4057372301:4057372301 (0)
win 32120 <mss 1460,sackOK,timestamp 359463 0,nop,wscale 0> (DF)

12:15:43.666836 venus.example.com.ssh > earth.example.com.1023:
 S 4047727479:4947727479 (0)
ack 4057372302 win 32120 <mss 1460,sackOK,timestamp 327365500 359
nop,wscale 0> (DF)

12:15:43.666943 earth.example.com.1023 > venus.example.com.ssh:
. 1:
1(0) ack 1 win 32120 <nop,nop,timestamp 359463 327365500> (DF)

...
```

In the above example, the following information is displayed:

- The network interface over which the information is collected (listening on eth0)
- Each of the information blocks represents one sent packet and contains the following data:
  - The time for each datagram (such as 12:15:43.666301)
  - The sender, sender port, destination, and destination port (such as earth.example.com.1023 > venus.example.com.ssh)
- The flags set in the protocol header—possible flags are S (SYN), F (FIN), P (PUSH), R (RST)
- Data sequence number, such as 4057372301:4057372301(0).

- An ACK bit that might have been set with the sequence number of the next data packet to be expected (such as ack 4057372302)

- The size of the receive buffer for data packets in the opposite direction (such as win 32120)

- Additional TCP options (such as mss 1460,sackOK,timestamp 359463 0,nop, wscale 0)

How to Use ethereal

The program ethereal is a graphical tool that provides the same functionality as tcpdump. It can be configured entirely through menus and provides a direct way of displaying all data at once, which is sent over a TCP connection.

The ethereal utility is located in the ethereal package and must first be installed with YaST. The dialog box shown in Figure 7-12 appears when you select **Capture > Start**.

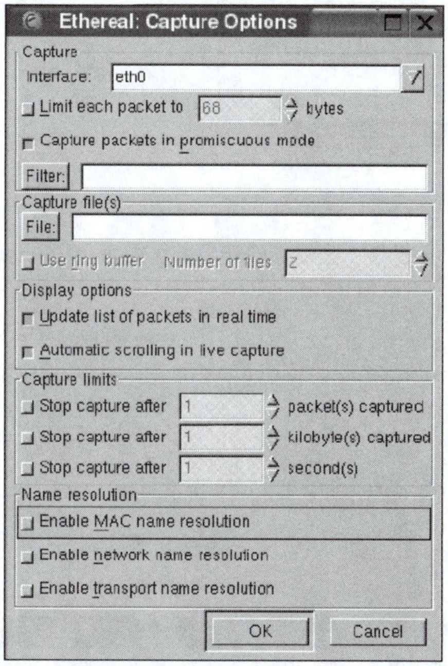

Figure 7-12

You can configure settings for monitoring network traffic, such as the following:

- **Interface.** Enter or select the interface on which you want to listen
- **Capture limits.** Enter the scope and duration of the data capture
- **Name resolution.** Specify whether or not to perform name resolutions

When you finish, you can start monitoring network traffic by selecting **OK**.

The program window shown in Figure 7-13 appears.

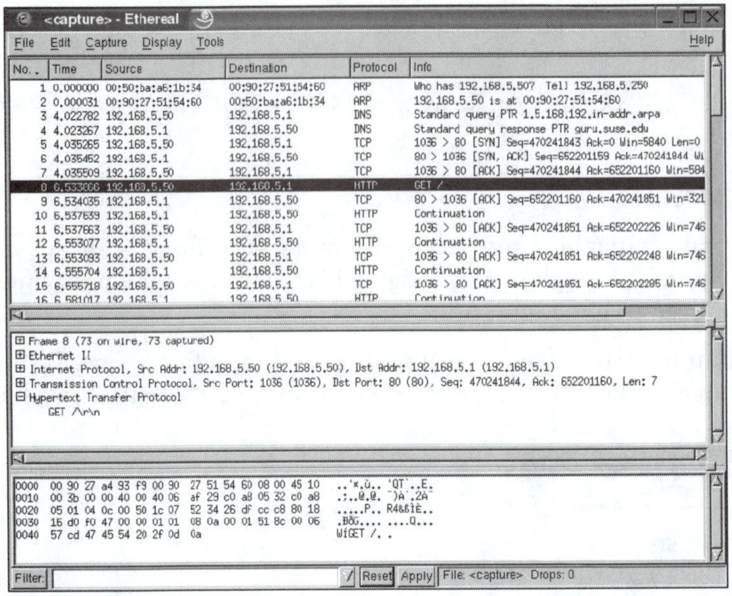

Figure 7-13

Individual packets are listed in the upper large window. You can select a packet to view details and contents of the packet in the two lower windows.

You can right-click a TCP packet to access a context menu. If you select **Follow TCP Stream**, the entire content of the TCP connection is displayed in a new window.

Command Options (tcpdump)

The command tcpdump provides a variety of options for analyzing data packets. Table 7-9 lists some of the more commonly used options.

Table 7-9

Parameter	Description
-l	Buffers the output to the standard output
-e	Prints the link-level header on each dump line
-n	Does not convert addresses (host, port) to names
-q	Displays a brief output with less information (less verbose)
-v, -vv, or -vvv	Displays more detailed information
-x	Displays the output in hexadecimal format
-c *count*	Ends when *count* packets have been received

Table 7-9   (continued)

Parameter	Description
-i *interface*	Uses the network interface (*interface*); if unspecified, tcpdump searches the system interface list for the lowest-numbered interface (such as eth0)
-r *file*	Reads the data packets from *file*
-w *file*	Writes data packets to *file*
expression	Acts as a filter for the packets you want to display; if you do not specify a filter, all packets in the network are displayed The options for *expression* are described in the man pages of tcpdump (enter **man tcpdump**).

7

The following are examples of using tcpdump:

- **tcpdump –nv –i eth0 –c 64 –w /tmp/tcpdump.net192 net 192**

  64 packets are written to the file /tmp/tcpdump.net192 (-w). Addresses are not converted to names (-n), and the output contains detailed information (-v).

  This information is gathered by the interface eth0 (–i eth0) and is shown only if the sender or recipient addresses are located in the network 192.0.0.0/255.0.0.0 (net 192).

- **tcpdump –r /tmp/tcpdump.net192**

  tcpdump gathers data from the file /tmp/tcpdump.net192 and displays this to the standard output.

- **tcpdump –e –i eth0 src 192.168.0.1 and dst 192.168.0.2 or host 192.168.0.3**

  All packets are shown that are sent from the IP address 192.168.0.1 to the IP address 192.168.0.2. In addition, all data packets are shown that contain the IP address 192.168.0.3 as sender or recipient.

Troubleshooting Suggestions

If communication in the network is faulty or nontransparent and you have used tools such as ping and traceroute without success, try using tcpdump or ethereal to analyze details of network traffic.

These tools can help you find which packets are exchanged by which applications in the network. They are also very useful when networks are frequently overloaded and no physical errors are detected.

Using tcpdump and ethereal are especially recommended for security–critical environments (such as firewalls) to more precisely analyze data traffic passing through and to design a more secure environment.

NOTE For details on all parameters available for the command tcpdump, enter **man tcpdump**.

Determine the Status of All Network Connections (*netstat*)

The command netstat (/bin/netstat) is a tool that can help you determine the status of all network connections, routes, and interfaces on a host.

To use the command netstat effectively, you need to know the following:

- How to Use netstat
- Command Options
- Troubleshooting Suggestions

How to Use netstat

The command netstat displays the status of all open sockets (network connections) and lets you analyze all network connections on the host.

When you enter **netstat**, information similar to the following appears:

```
DA50:~ # netstat
Active Internet connections (w/o servers)
Proto Recv-Q Send-Q Local Address      Foreign Address        State
tcp    0      0 DA50.example.com:604 venus.example.com:966 TIME_WAIT
tcp    0      0 DA50.example.com:1023 venus.example.com:ssh ESTABLISHED
Active UNIX domain sockets (w/o servers)
Proto RefCnt Flags   Type     State     I-Node Path
unix  2      [ ]     DGRAM              2814   /var/lib/ntp/dev/log
unix  10     [ ]     DGRAM              2809   /dev/log
unix  2      [ ]     DGRAM              11474
unix  2      [ ]     DGRAM              9983
unix  3      [ ]     STREAM CONNECTED   9179
unix  3      [ ]     STREAM CONNECTED   9178
...
```

In the example, information is displayed in the following two blocks:

- **First block.** In the first block, each socket is listed on a separate line, and includes the following:

  - The first line involves a socket between the hosts DA50.example.com (Local Address) and venus.example.com (Foreign Address) through the TCP protocol (Proto).

    The connection was established between the ports 604 (DA50) and 966 (venus).

  - The information below Recv-Q and Send-Q shows that in the receive queue for this host, no data is waiting to be collected by the process and that in the send queue, no data is waiting for the host venus.example.com.

    At this point, all data has been processed.

  - Finally, the information under State provides details about what condition the corresponding socket is in. TIME_WAIT indicates that the socket still needs to be cleared up but is almost closed.

    An active socket is referred to as ESTABLISHED.

- **Second block.** The second block contains information on the UNIX domain sockets active on this host. Every line stands for one socket and includes the following information:

  - unix is always specified as the protocol (Proto).

  - The reference counter (RefCnt) shows the number of active processes that are connected to the matching socket.

  - Special flags (Flags) in this example are not set (possible flags: SO_ACCEPTION = ACC, SO_WAITDATA = W, SO_NOSPACE = N).

  - The type for all sockets listed is DGRAM or STREAM (a connection-oriented socket).

  - All sockets listed are connected (State, CONNECTED).

  - Finally, the inodes (I-Node) of the sockets and the pathname (Path) of the process connected to them are listed.

Command Options

The command netstat provides a variety of options for viewing the connection status of all open sockets. Table 7-10 lists some of the more commonly used options.

Table 7-10

Parameter	Description
-a	Lists all active and passive sockets
-e	Displays additional information

Table 7-10 (continued)

Parameter	Description
-i *interface*	Displays information for *interface*; without a specified interface, a table of all network interfaces is displayed
-p	Shows the PID and name of the program to which each socket belongs
-rn	Lists the entries of the routing table; there is no resolution of addresses to names
-t	Lists only sockets for TCP packets
-u	Lists only sockets for UDP datagrams

NOTE

For details on all parameters available for the command netstat, enter **man 8 netstat**.

Troubleshooting Suggestions

netstat is an ideal tool for monitoring the resources for network sockets on a host.

In some cases, resources on a server are sized too low. If a number of clients access this server simultaneously, the number of sockets available or the resources for these might not be sufficient.

In these cases, netstat provides detailed information on existing and available network sockets or resources.

Check for Service Availability (netcat)

The command /usr/bin/netcat (called *nc* on other systems) is a UNIX tool that uses the TCP and UDP protocols to read and write data through network connections.

You can use netcat for establishing connections of any kind, and you can control it with scripts.

To use the command effectively, you need to know the following:

- How to Use netcat
- Advanced Use of netcat
- Command Options

How to Use netcat

You can establish a connection to another host with netcat by entering **netcat *host port***, as in the following:

```
DA50:~ # netcat DA10 80
GET /
<html>
```

```
<head>
<title>Web server on DA10.example.com</title>
</head>
<frameset cols=21%,79%>
<frame src="content.html" name="content">
<frame src="start.html" name="main">
</frameset>
</html>
```

In this example, all entries to the standard input (GET /) are sent to the specified host and all responses from that host are displayed in the standard output (the <html> lines). This procedure is also possible with a telnet client.

However, netcat offers even more possibilities, such as the use of the UDP protocol or deployment as a server waiting for a connection.

For example, entering **netcat –v –l –p 2000** means that if a client connects to port 2000 (possibly also using netcat), everything that is entered in the associated terminal window will be transmitted to the client. The same takes place in the opposite direction.

Advanced Use of netcat

You can use netcat to query a number of ports and display the responses of the services, as in the following examples:

```
geeko@DA50:~> netcat -v -w 2 -z DA10 20-80
DA10.example.com [192.168.0.10] 80 (http) open
DA10.example.com [192.168.0.10] 22 (ssh) open

geeko@DA50:~> echo QUIT | netcat -v 192.168.0.10 22
DA10.example.com [192.168.0.10] 22 (ssh) open
SSH-1.99-OpenSSH_3.8p1
Protocol mismatch.
```

For a simple port scan, the program nmap is more suitable. However, you can enter the command (in the second part of the example) to quickly obtain information about a service.

The command shown in the first part of the example (on port 80) can also be used to check a connection to a host that does not respond to ping queries (possibly because they are blocked by a packet filter).

If a response is received as in the first example, the host is accessible.

Another use of netcat is to transmit files between hosts. For example, if no FTP server is available, start netcat on the server side with the following command:

netcat –l –p 2000 < file

On the client side, fetch the file with the following command:

netcat host 2000 > file

This connection remains intact until you terminate it with Ctrl+C.

Command Options

There is no man page for netcat. However, you can display a list of available options with the command netcat –h. Table 7-11 lists some commonly used netcat options.

Table 7-11

Option	Description
-l	netcat starts in listen mode; this option can only be used together with the option -p
-p	Specifies the local port netcat should use
-u	Prompts netcat to use the UDP protocol
-v	Controls the verbosity level of the output of netcat; the option -vv produces even more information
-w	Limits time spent trying to make a connection
-z	Shows which ports are open

NOTE

For detailed documentation of netcat, see /usr/share/doc/packages/netcat/README.

This text describes additional usage possibilities as well as security issues that netcat can cause when it's used by malicious individuals.

Exercise 7-1   Configure and Test Your Network Connection

Although your SLES 9 server is already connected to the network with an IP address assigned by the DHCP service, in this exercise you reconfigure your network connection for a static IP address by doing the following:

- Part I: View and Record Network Configuration
- Part II: Configure a Static Network with YaST
- Part III: Test the Network Card Configuration

Part I: View and Record Network Configuration

In this part of the exercise, you fill in Table 7-12 by entering commands at a shell prompt.

Table 7-12

Item	Network Setting
Host Name	
Domain Name	
IP Address	
Subnet Mask	
Default Gateway	
DNS Server	

Do the following to find the information you need to fill in the table:

1. From a terminal window, su to root (**su –**) with a password of **novell**.
2. View information about the network interfaces by entering **ifconfig –a**.
3. View information about the loopback network interface by entering **ifstatus lo**.
4. View information about the eth0 network interface by entering **ifstatus eth0**.
5. Change to the directory /etc/sysconfig/network by entering

   cd /etc/sysconfig/network.
6. List the configuration file for the eth0 network interface by entering **ls –l ifcfg-eth-id***.

   Note the ID number associated with the filename.
7. View the contents of the configuration file by entering

   cat ifcfg-eth-id-*number*.
8. View network interface statistics by entering **netstat –i**.
9. View the routing in numeric format by entering **netstat –nr**.
10. Remove the default route by entering **route del default**.
11. View the routing in numeric format by entering **route –n**.
12. Add a default route with a gateway of 10.0.0.254 by entering the following:

    route add default gw 10.0.0.254 dev eth0
13. View the routing in numeric format by entering **route –n**.
14. Shut down eth0 by entering **ifdown eth0**.
15. Bring up eth0 by entering **ifup eth0**.
16. View the system hostname by entering **hostname**.
17. View the system DNS domain name by entering **dnsdomainname**.
18. View the DNS configuration by entering **cat /etc/resolv.conf**.
19. Verify that the default route is accessible by pinging the default gateway (**ping –c 3 10.0.0.254**).

Part II: Configure a Static Network Configuration with YaST

In this part of the exercise, you use YaST to configure a static network configuration with the information you gathered from Part I of this exercise.

Do the following:

1. From the KDE desktop, select the **YaST** icon; then enter a password of **novell** and select **OK**.

   The YaST Control Center appears.

2. Select **Network Devices > Network Card**.

   The Network cards configuration dialog box appears.

3. Change the configuration of your already configured network card by selecting **Change**.

4. Make sure your network card for eth0 is selected (check the **eth-id-*number***); then select **Edit**.

5. Select **Static address setup**.

6. Enter the following from Table 7-12:

   ■ **IP Address**

   ■ **Subnet mask**

7. Under Detailed settings, select **Host name and name server**.

8. (Conditional) If prompted, modify the host and name server configuration by selecting **Modify**.

9. Enter the following from Table 7-12:

   ■ **Host Name**

   ■ **Domain Name**

   ■ **Name Server 1** (DNS Server)

   ■ **Domain Search 1** (Domain Name)

10. Save the host and DNS configuration changes by selecting **OK**.

    You are returned to the Network address setup dialog box.

11. Under Detailed settings, select **Routing**.

12. In the Default Gateway field, enter the *default gateway* from Table .

13. Save the routing configuration changes by selecting **OK**.

14. Save these changes to the system by selecting **Next**; then select **Finish**.

Part III: Test the Network Card Configuration

Do the following:

1. From the terminal window, perform a DNS lookup on www.novell.com by entering **host www.novell.com**.

2. View the name servers for www.theonion.com by entering the following:

   dig www.theonion.com NS

3. Show the contact information for the domain novell.com by entering **whois novell.com**.

4. Verify that the file /etc/HOSTNAME contains the correct hostname by entering **cat /etc/HOSTNAME**.

5. Check the arp cache by entering **arp –v –a**.

6. Check the listening sockets on your server, and the PID and name of the program to which each socket belongs by entering

   netstat –lp.

7. Query the ports 20-80 on DA1 to display the service responses by entering the following:

   netcat –v –w 2 –z DA1 20–80

8. Try querying another student's computer with the same netcat command and compare the results.

9. Work with another student in the class by opening a new terminal window (su to **root**) and running a port scan on each other's computers by entering the following:

   watch nmap –sS *other_student_IP*

10. In the original terminal window, capture packets exchanged from the port scan by entering **tcpdump –i eth0**.

11. Open a Konqueror browser window; then enter **www.novell.com**.

12. When you are finished viewing the traffic from the tcpdump screen, press **Ctrl+C** to kill the trace.

13. View the contents of file /etc/nsswitch.conf to verify that DNS is being used for hostname resolution by entering

    cat /etc/nsswitch.conf.

14. When you finish, close all open windows.

CHAPTER SUMMARY

❑ Each host that communicates on a TCP/IP network has an IP address and subnet mask (or netmask) that identifies the network that the host is on as well as the host itself.

❑ Three classes of IP networks are normally used for IP addressing: Class A, Class B, and Class C. Each class uses a different number of bits for identifying the network and host. The 127.0.0.0 network is used for testing the local computer.

❑ You can view and change your TCP/IP configuration using the **ifconfig** and **ip** commands; you can also create IP aliases. Alternatively, you can manage your TCP/IP configuration in a desktop environment using the Network Card utility of YaST.

❑ Network interface and TCP/IP information is stored in the /etc/sysconfig/network directory and started by the /etc/init.d/network script at system initialization. After system initialization, you can use the **netstat** command to view network interface statistics, or the **ip**, **ifup**, **ifdown**, and **ifstatus** commands to manage the status of your network interfaces.

❑ Each host contains a hostname that is stored in the /etc/HOSTNAME file.

❑ To connect to network hosts by name, the /etc/resolv.conf file contains the addresses of up to three DNS servers. Hosts contact these DNS servers to resolve remote hostnames to their respective IP addresses.

❑ Different TCP/IP networks are connected to one another via routers. A host has a routing table that typically contains a default gateway route that identifies the router on the local network used to relay messages to remote TCP/IP networks. You can view and change the routing table using the **route** and **ip** commands.

❑ The **ping** and **traceroute** commands can be used to test network communication and routing, respectively. Similarly, the **netcat** command may be used to test TCP and UDP connections to other computers.

❑ To capture and analyze network traffic, you can use the **tcpdump** and **ethereal** utilities.

KEY TERMS

/etc/HOSTNAME — A file that contains the name of the host.

/etc/init.d/network — The script that activates network interfaces at system initialization.

/etc/resolv.conf — A file that lists up to three DNS servers that may be contacted to resolve a remote hostname to an IP address.

/etc/sysconfig/hardware — The directory that contains hardware device information for system devices, such as network interfaces used to load and initialize devices by the Linux kernel.

/etc/sysconfig/network — The directory that contains most network configuration information.

/etc/sysconfig/network/ifcfg.template — A template file that may be used to create the TCP/IP configuration for a network interface.

/etc/sysconfig/network/ifroute-*interface* — A file that stores static routes for a specific interface.

/etc/sysconfig/network/routes — A file that stores static routes for use on the system.

/proc/sys/net/ipv4/ip_forward — A file that is used to enable routing on a router.

broadcast — A message destined for all computers on a TCP/IP network.

Class A address — An IP address that uses the first byte to identify the TCP/IP network.

Class B address — An IP address that uses the first two bytes to identify the TCP/IP network.

Class C address — An IP address that uses the first three bytes to identify the TCP/IP network.

Class D address — An IP address that is used for communicating to several hosts simultaneously using multicast packets.

Class E address — An IP address that should not be used on a TCP/IP network and is intended for research purposes only.

default gateway — The router that connects a network to other networks. Hosts send packets destined for remote networks to this default gateway router.

default route — See **default gateway**.

domain name — A name that identifies the portion of DNS that your host belongs to.

Domain Name System (DNS) — The naming system used on the Internet. Each host is identified by a hostname and domain name.

Dynamic Host Configuration Protocol (DHCP) — A protocol that is used to assign TCP/IP configuration information to a host on the network.

Ethereal — A graphical program used to capture and examine IP packets on the network.

Ethernet — The standard method used to access network media today. Most network adapters on networks use Ethernet.

firewall — A software feature that allows a host to drop IP packets that meet a certain criteria or are harmful.

gateway route — See **network route**.

host — A computer that can communicate on a network.

host ID — The part of an IP address that uniquely identifies the host on a network.

host route — A route that specifies the router that must be sent packets destined for a particular host.

ifconfig command — Used to view, configure, and manage IP addresses on a network interface.

ifdown command — Used to deactivate a network interface.

ifstatus command — Used to display the status of a network interface.

ifup command — Used to activate a network interface.

Internet Control Message Protocol (ICMP) — A TCP/IP core protocol used to notify hosts of network error conditions. It is also used for network diagnostics by programs such as ping.

Internet Protocol (IP) address — A unique address used to identify a computer on a TCP/IP network.

Internet Protocol (IP) packet — A unit of information sent on a TCP/IP network.

IP aliases — Additional IP addresses that are assigned to a network interface.

ip command — Used to view, configure, and manage network interfaces and the routing table.

loopback — An IP address that is used to test the local host.

name server — A server that contains records for hosts on a network. It may be queried to resolve a hostname to an IP address.

netcat command — Used to test communication among hosts using TCP or UDP.

network ID — The part of an IP address that identifies the network a host is on.

network mask — See **subnet mask**.

network route — A route that specifies the router that must be sent packets destined for a particular network.

node — See **host**.

ping command — Used to test network connectivity using ICMP.

route command — Used to view and modify the routing table.

router — A device that is used to relay IP packets from one TCP/IP network to another.

routing — The process of sending IP packets from one IP network to another.

routing table — A table that is stored on each host and that contains a list of local and remote networks and routers.

socket — An established network connection between two hosts. TCP uses STREAM sockets, whereas UDP uses DGRAM sockets.

static route — Identifies a remote network and the router that must be used to forward packets to it.

station — See **host**.

subnet mask — A number used to determine which portions of an IP address are the network ID and host ID.

tcpdump command — Used to capture and examine IP packets on the network.

traceroute command — Used to identify the route an IP packet takes to a remote host.

Transmission Control Protocol (TCP) — A part of the TCP/IP protocol suite that provides reliable communication between hosts on a network.

Transmission Control Protocol/Internet Protocol (TCP/IP) — A suite of protocols that are used to communicate with other computers on a network.

User Datagram Protocol (UDP) — A part of the TCP/IP protocol suite that provides fast but unreliable communication between hosts on a network.

REVIEW QUESTIONS

1. What must each computer have in order to participate on a TCP/IP network as well as contact hosts on remote networks by name? (Choose all that apply.)

   a. IP address

   b. netmask

   c. DNS server

   d. default gateway

2. How long is the host ID by default in a Class A network?

   a. 1 byte

   b. 2 bytes

   c. 3 bytes

   d. 4 bytes

3. Which of the following are Class B IP addresses? (Choose all that apply.)

   a. 192.168.1.1

   b. 177.16.41.10

   c. 127.0.0.1

   d. 133.1.1.2

4. What network address is reserved for loopback? _____

5. What name is used to identify the first Ethernet network interface in Linux?

   _____

6. What file stores the list of DNS servers that your computer can contact to resolve hostnames into IP addresses?

   a. /etc/resolv.conf

   b. /etc/sysconfig/network/scripts

   c. /etc/dns.sysconfig

   d. /etc/sysconfig/network/ifcfg-dns

7. What command can you use to configure the IP address 192.168.1.1 and default subnet mask on your first Ethernet network interface? _____

8. What command can you use to configure an additional IP address of 192.168.1.2 and default subnet mask on the same network interface configured in Question 7?

   _____

7

9. Which of the following commands may be used to view IP configuration? (Choose all that apply.)

   a. ifshow eth0

   b. ip address show

   c. ifconfig –a

   d. ifstatus eth0

10. What file contains the information used to configure your second Ethernet network interface at boot time? _____

11. What line would you configure in the file described in Question 10 to obtain an IP configuration from a DHCP server? _____

12. How many DNS servers may be listed in /etc/resolv.conf?

   a. one

   b. three

   c. ten

   d. unlimited

13. Which two commands could you type at a command prompt to add a route to the 188.16.0.0 network via the router 192.168.1.254?

   a. ip route add 188.16.0.0/16 via 192.168.1.254

   b. route add 188.16.0.0 via 192.168.1.254

   c. ip route add gw 192.168.1.254 via 188.16.0.0/16

   d. route add –net 188.16.0.0 netmask 255.255.0.0 gw 192.168.1.254

14. What file could you use to configure the static route configured in Question 13 for use with all network interfaces on your system? _____

15. What command could you use to send five ICMP echo requests to the host 192.168.1.254? _____

16. What command could you use to listen to all traffic sent to port 1433 on your computer? _____

17. What option(s) to the **netstat** command could you use to display the routing table? _____

18. What command could you use to listen to all packets received on your first Ethernet network interface? _____

DISCOVERY EXERCISES

Network Interface Commands

Log in to tty1 as the root user and perform the following actions in order. For each action, write the command(s) that you used. When finished, log out of tty1.

1. Configure your first Ethernet adapter such that your IP address is 10.10.10.*x* (where *x* is a unique student number assigned by your instructor).

2. View your IP configuration.

3. Deactivate and reactivate your first Ethernet adapter.

4. View your IP configuration. What file does this configuration come from?

Configuring IP Aliases

Log in to tty1 as the root user and perform the following actions in order. For each action, write the command(s) that you used. When finished, log out of tty1.

1. Configure an IP alias for your first Ethernet adapter such that your first virtual IP address is 10.10.10.*x* (where *x* is a unique student number assigned by your instructor).

2. View your IP configuration.

3. Use the **ping** command to verify both virtual IP addresses.

4. Deactivate and reactivate your first Ethernet adapter.

Routing Commands

Log in to tty1 as the root user and perform the following actions in order. For each action, write the command(s) that you used. When finished, log out of tty1.

1. Create a route to the 42.0.0.0 network via the gateway 10.18.11.88 using the **route** command.

2. Create a route to the 43.0.0.0 network via the gateway 10.68.1.9 using the **ip** command.

3. View the routing table.

4. Remove all routes from your system.

ENABLE INFRASTRUCTURE SERVICES

In this section you learn the basics of enabling some of the more commonly used network infrastructure services available in SUSE Linux Enterprise Server 9.

◆ Configure and Manage Network Printing Services

◆ Configure Network File Systems

◆ Manage Resources on the Network

OBJECTIVE 1   CONFIGURE AND MANAGE NETWORK PRINTING SERVICES

To configure network printing services in SUSE Linux Enterprise Server, you need to understand the following:

- Printers and Linux Support
- CUPS and SUSE Linux Enterprise Server
- How to Configure a SUSE Linux Enterprise Server Network Printer
- How to Modify a SUSE Linux Enterprise Server Network Printer
- How to Manage Printing from the Command Line
- How to Access the CUPS Web Administration Tools
- How to Troubleshoot the CUPS Print System

Printers and Linux Support

If you want to find out if your printer is supported by Linux (or before buying a new printer), check the following sources to see how well the printer is supported by Linux:

- http://cdb.suse.de/ or http://hardwaredb.suse.de/. This is the SUSE Linux Enterprise Server printer database.
- www.linuxprinting.org/. This contains the printer database on linuxprinting.org.
- www.cs.wisc.edu/~ghost/. This is the Ghostscript Web page.
- file:/usr/share/doc/packages/ghostscript/catalog.devices. This lists included drivers.

The online databases always show the latest Linux support status. However, a Linux distribution can only integrate the drivers available at the production time.

For this reason, a printer currently rated as Perfectly Supported might not have had this status when the latest SUSE Linux Enterprise Server version was released.

CUPS and SUSE Linux Enterprise Server

CUPS (Common Unix Printing System) is the default printing system of the SUSE Linux Enterprise Server.

To understand how CUPS works with SUSE Linux Enterprise Server, you need to know the following:

- How CUPS Handles Print Jobs
- How the cupsd Printer Daemon Works

How CUPS Handles Print Jobs

The following is the sequence of events that happens between submitting a print job and getting the actual printout on the printer:

- The print job is created by a user or a program.

- The file to print is saved in a queue.

  This creates two files for the print job in the directory /var/spool/cups/. One of the files contains the data to print, and the other contains information about the print job (such as who submitted the print job and which printer is addressed).

- The printer daemon cupsd collects the file to print from the queue, determines the type of the data to print, and converts it to the printer-specific format.

  After the conversion, the data is transmitted to the printer.

- The printer receives the data and prints it.

- When the print job has been transmitted completely to the printer, it is removed from the queue.

This sequence of events ensures that you can submit print jobs at any time. It also ensures that the print jobs are processed one after the other without losing any print jobs.

How the cupsd Printer Daemon Works

The printer daemon cupsd is a background process and is launched at system start-up by the script /etc/init.d/cups. Its configuration file is /etc/cups/cupsd.conf.

The cupsd daemon administers the local queues and filters or converts data to print to a printer-specific format.

The following describes how cupsd handles print jobs:

- cupsd gets the submitted print jobs from the queue and sends them to the printer.

- cupsd then executes the print jobs in the queue in order.

  It controls the state of the queues and displays information about it, if queried.

Figure 8-1 illustrates and describes how cupsd filters or converts data to print.

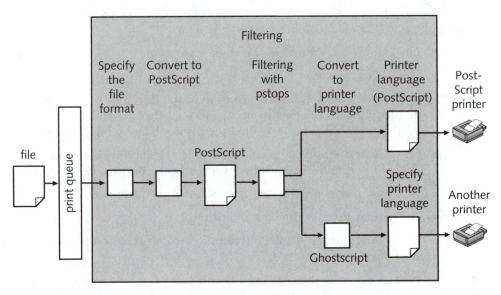

Figure 8-1

- First, the data type is determined with the help of /etc/cups/mime.types.

- Next, the data is converted to PostScript by using the tool specified in /etc/cups/mime.convs.

- After that, the number of pages is determined with the tool pstops (/usr/lib/cups/filter/pstops). The number of pages is written into the file /var/log/cups/page_log.

  If necessary, further pstop filtering functions are enabled, depending on which options were chosen for the printing. These include options such as selected pages (the psselect option of pstops) or multiple pages should print on one sheet of paper (the ps-n-up option of pstops).

- If data is printed on a non–PostScript printer, a filter that converts the data into the printer-specific format starts (such as /usr/lib/cups/filter/cupsomatic which calls Ghostscript).

  The filter processes all device-dependent print options, such as resolution and paper size.

- To print the data on the printer itself, an additional filter (stored in /usr/lib/cups/backend) is started, depending on how the printer is connected.

As the root user, you can start or stop cupsd manually with the following commands:

- **/etc/init.d/cups start** *or* **rccups start**
- **/etc/init.d/cups stop** *or* **rccups stop**

If you make changes manually to the file /etc/cups/cupsd.conf, you need to restart the daemon by entering **/etc/init.d/cups restart** or **rccups restart**.

How to Configure a SUSE Linux Enterprise Server Network Printer

After connecting a printer to the network and installing the software, you need to install the printer in the SUSE Linux Enterprise Server operating system.

If at all possible, you should use the command line and YaST tools delivered with SUSE Linux Enterprise Server. Because SUSE Linux puts great emphasis on security, third-party tools often have difficulties with the security restrictions and end up causing more problems than solutions or benefits.

To configure a network printer for SUSE Linux Enterprise Server, you need to know the following:

- SUSE Linux Enterprise Server and Supported Printing Protocols
- SUSE Linux Enterprise Server and Postscript Printers
- How to Configure a Network Printer with YaST
- How to Configure a Network Printer from the Command Line

SUSE Linux Enterprise Server and Supported Printing Protocols

A network printer can support various protocols.

Although most of the supported protocols are standardized, some manufacturers modify the standard protocol to test systems that have not implemented the standard correctly or to provide certain functions that are not available in the standard protocol.

In addition, some manufacturers believe that they can integrate these extensions and test them on Microsoft Windows without causing any difficulties for other operating systems.

Unfortunately, these extensions that run well on Windows can causes problems in Linux. For this reason, you cannot assume that that every protocol works properly in Linux. You might have to experiment with various options to achieve a functional configuration.

CUPS supports the socket, LPD, IPP, and smb protocols. The following describes these protocols:

- **socket.** This refers to a connection in which data is sent to an Internet socket without first performing a data handshake. Some of the socket port numbers that are commonly used are 9100 or 35.

  Device URI example: **socket://*host-printer*:9100/**

- **LPD (Line Printer Daemon).** The LPD protocol is described in RFC 1179. Under this protocol, some job-related data such as the printer queue is sent before the actual print data.

  This means that a printer queue must be specified when configuring the LPD protocol for the data transmission.

  The implementations of most printer manufacturers are flexible enough to accept any name as the printer queue. If necessary, the printer manual might indicate which name to use (such as LPT, LPT1, or LP1).

  Of course, an LPD queue can also be configured on a different Linux or UNIX host in a network that uses the CUPS system. The port number for an LPD service is 515.

  Device URI example: **lpd://*host-printer*/LPT1**

- **IPP (Internet Printing Protocol).** IPP is a relatively new protocol (since 1999) that is based on the HTTP protocol. Under IPP, much more job-related data can be transmitted than in the other protocols.

  CUPS uses IPP for the internal data transmission. This is the preferred protocol for a forwarding queue between CUPS servers.

  You need the name of the printer queue to configure IPP correctly. The port number for IPP is 631.

  Device URI examples:

  ipp://*host-printer*/psoder:

  ipp://host-cupsserver/printers/ps

- **SMB (Standard Message Block).** CUPS also supports printing on printers connected to Windows shares. The protocol used for this purpose is SMB.

  SMB uses port numbers 137, 138, and 139.

  Device URI examples:

  smb://*user:password@workgroup/server/printer*

  smb://*user:password@host/printer*

  smb:// *server/printer*

The protocol supported by the printer must be determined prior to the configuration. If the manufacturer does not provide the needed information, you can use the command nmap (**nmap** *package*) to guess the protocol. The command checks a host for open ports.

Example: **nmap –p 35,137–139,515,631,9100–10000**

SUSE Linux Enterprise Server and PostScript Printers

PPD (PostScript Printer Description) is the computer language that describes the properties (such as resolution) and options (such as duplex unit) of PostScript printers.

These descriptions are necessary to use the various printer options in CUPS. Without a PPD file, the print data would be forwarded to the printer in a raw state, which is usually not desired.

During the installation of SUSE Linux Enterprise Server, a lot of PPD files are preinstalled. In this way, even printers that do not have built-in PostScript support can be used.

If a PostScript printer is configured, the best approach is to get a suitable PPD file and store it in the directory /usr/share/cups/model/ or add it to the print system with YaST (preferred approach). You can then select the PPD file during the installation.

Be careful if a printer manufacturer wants you to install entire software packages. This kind of installation results in the loss of the support provided by SUSE Linux.

In addition, print commands might work in a different way than before, and the system might not be able to address devices from other manufacturers.

How to Configure a Network Printer with YaST

The following are the basic steps for configuring a network printer with YaST:

1. From the KDE desktop, start the YaST Printer module by doing one of the following:

    ■ Select the **YaST** icon, enter the root *password*, and select **OK**; then select **Hardware > Printer**.

    or

    ■ Open a terminal window and enter **sux –** and the root *password*; then enter **yast2 printer**.

The Printer Configuration dialog box in Figure 8-2 appears.

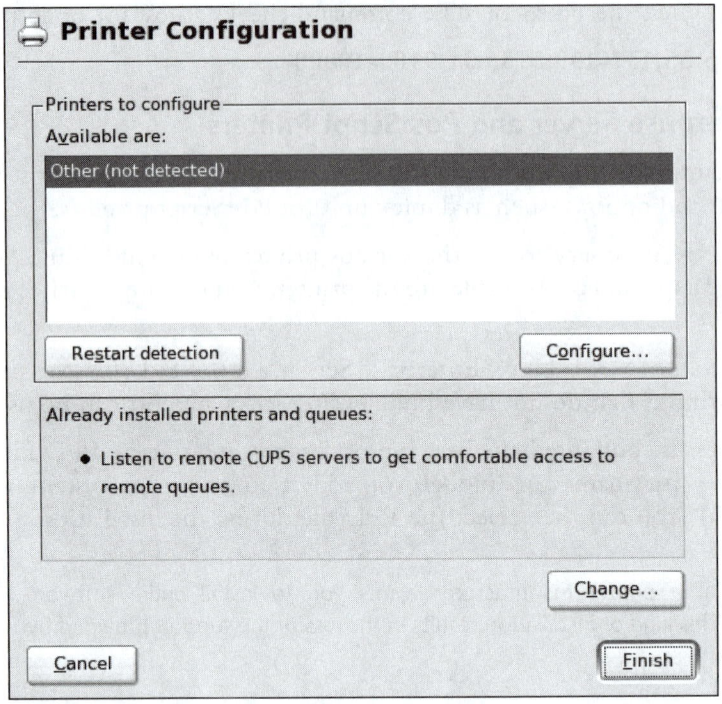

Figure 8-2

You can do one of three basic tasks:

- If your printer was detected and is listed, create a configuration for the printer by selecting it from the list; then select **Configure**.

  or

- If your printer was *not* detected, set up a printer configuration manually by selecting **Other**; then select **Configure**.

  You can try automatically detecting your printer by selecting **Restart detection**.

  or

- Edit a configured printer queue by selecting **Change**.

  To add a printer manually, continue with Step 2.

2. Add a new printer manually to the system by selecting **Other**; then select **Configure**.

The list of printer types shown in Figure 8-3 appears.

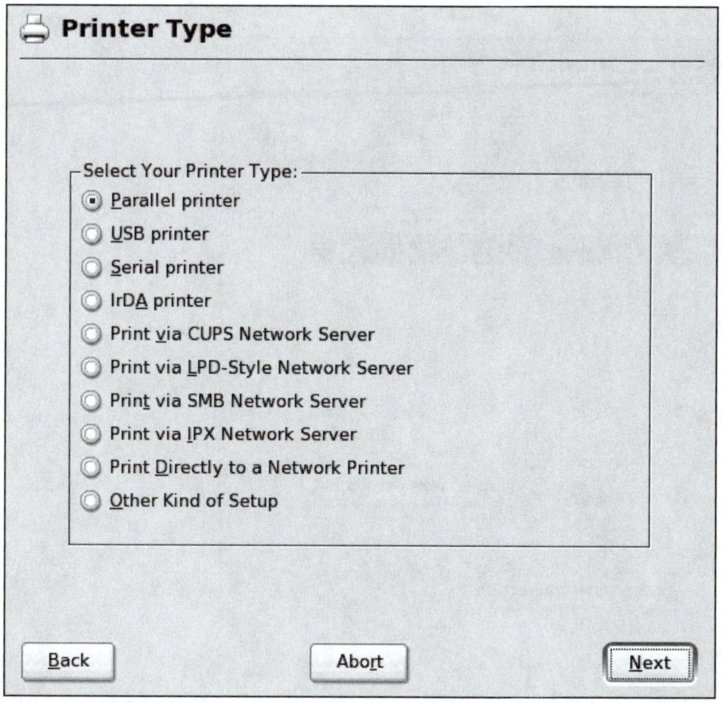

🖨 **Printer Type**

┌─ Select Your Printer Type: ─────────────────────┐
○ Parallel printer
○ USB printer
○ Serial printer
○ IrDA printer
○ Print via CUPS Network Server
○ Print via LPD-Style Network Server
○ Print via SMB Network Server
○ Print via IPX Network Server
○ Print Directly to a Network Printer
○ Other Kind of Setup

[Back]   [Abort]   [Next]

Figure 8-3

3. Select the *printer type* you want to configure (such as **Parallel printer**); then select **Next**.

   The configuration screens that appear depend on the type of printer you select.

For example, if you select **Parallel printer**, the dialog box shown in Figure 8-4 appears.

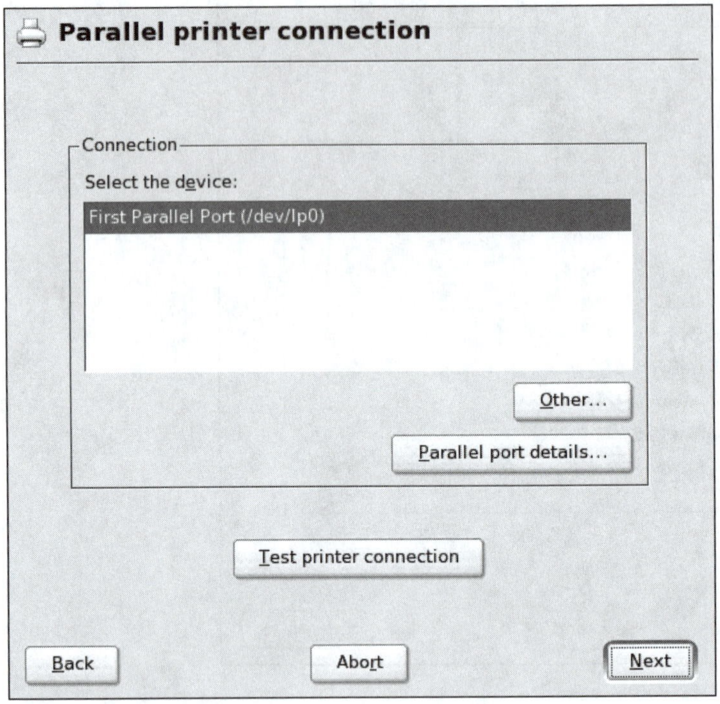

Figure 8-4

From this dialog box, you can configure the parallel port (one or more ports). By selecting **Next**, you move through a series of configuration screens that let you enter printer information such as the queue name and printer manufacturer and model.

If you select a printer type such as **Print via CUPS Network Server**, the dialog box shown in Figure 8-5 appears.

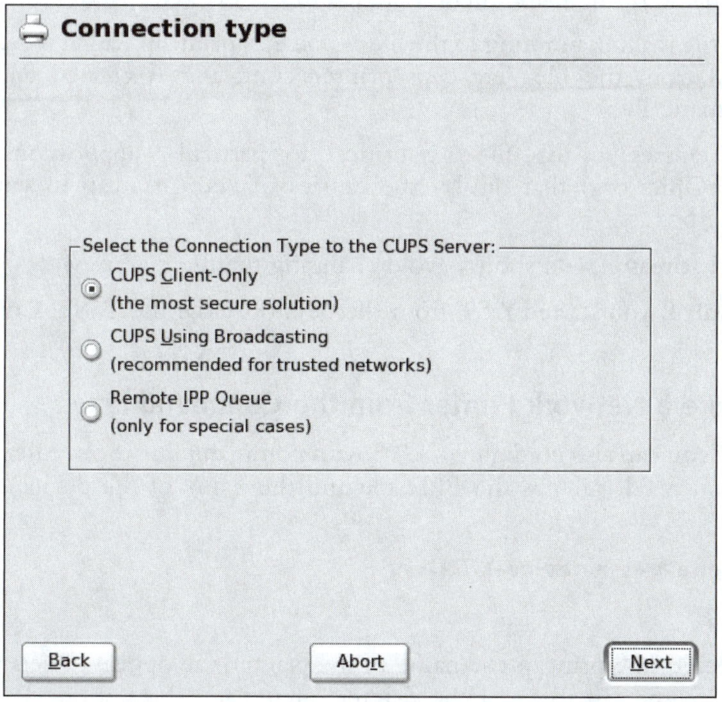

🖨 **Connection type**

Select the Connection Type to the CUPS Server:
- ⦿ CUPS Client-Only
  (the most secure solution)
- ○ CUPS Using Broadcasting
  (recommended for trusted networks)
- ○ Remote IPP Queue
  (only for special cases)

| Back | Abort | Next |

Figure 8-5

From this dialog box, you can select one of three connection types for CUPS printing. What you configure next depends on the type of connection you select.

NOTE

For additional information about configuring a printer type, use the Help screens available with each configuration screen.

4. When you finish selecting a printer type and configuring it, save the configuration by selecting **Finish**.

   You are returned to the YaST Control Center.

   After configuring the printer (print queue), the following happens:

   ■ The print queue is added to the file /etc/cups/printers.conf with default queue settings.

- A ppd file for the printer is created in /etc/cups/ppd which includes settings such as paper size and paper type.

- The name of the print queue is added to the file /etc/printcap.

  This file is a link pointing to the file /etc/cups/printcap which is generated by cupsd from the file /etc/cups/printers.conf, and is created and updated automatically.

  The entries in this file are critical to particular applications (such as OpenOffice.org) that display the entries of /etc/printcap in your printer dialog box.

  For that reason, you should avoid changing the file manually.

5. (Optional) If you started YaST from the desktop, close the **YaST Control Center**.

How to Configure a Network Printer from the Command Line

Besides using YaST, you can also configure CUPS with command line tools. After collecting the information you need (such as the PPD file and the name of the device), enter the following:

**lpadmin -p <queue> -v <device-URI> **

-P <PPD-file> -E

The option **-p** specifies the print queue name of the printer, the option **-v** sets the device URI (such as a filename) attribute of the printer queue, and the option **-P** specifies a PostScript printer.

Do not use **-E** as the first option. For all CUPS commands, –E as the first argument implies the use of an encrypted connection and –E at the end enables the printer to accept print jobs.

For example, to enable a parallel printer, enter a command similar to the following:

**lpadmin -p ps -v parallel:/dev/lp0 -P **

/usr/share/cups/model/Postscript.ppd.gz -E

To enable a network printer, enter a command similar to the following:

**lpadmin -p ps -v socket://192.168.1.0:9100/ -P **

/usr/share/cups/model/Postscript-level1.ppd.gz -E

How to Modify a SUSE Linux Enterprise Server Network Printer

During installation of SUSE Linux Enterprise Server, YaST allows certain print options to be activated by default. You can modify these options for every print job (depending on the print tool that is used) or modify them later with YaST or from the command line.

To modify the network printer options, you need to know the following:

- How to Modify a Network Printer with YaST
- How to Modify a Network Printer from the Command Line
- How to Modify Printer from KDE

How to Modify a Network Printer with YaST

The following are the basic steps for modifying a network printer with YaST:

1. From the KDE desktop, start the YaST Printer module by doing one of the following:

   - Select the **YaST** icon, enter the root *password*, and select **OK**; then select **Hardware > Printer**.

     or

   - Open a terminal window and enter **sux –** and the root *password*; then enter **yast2 printer**.

   The Printer Configuration dialog box appears.

2. Select **Change**.

8

A Printer administration for CUPS dialog box appears with a list of configured printers, as shown in Figure 8-6.

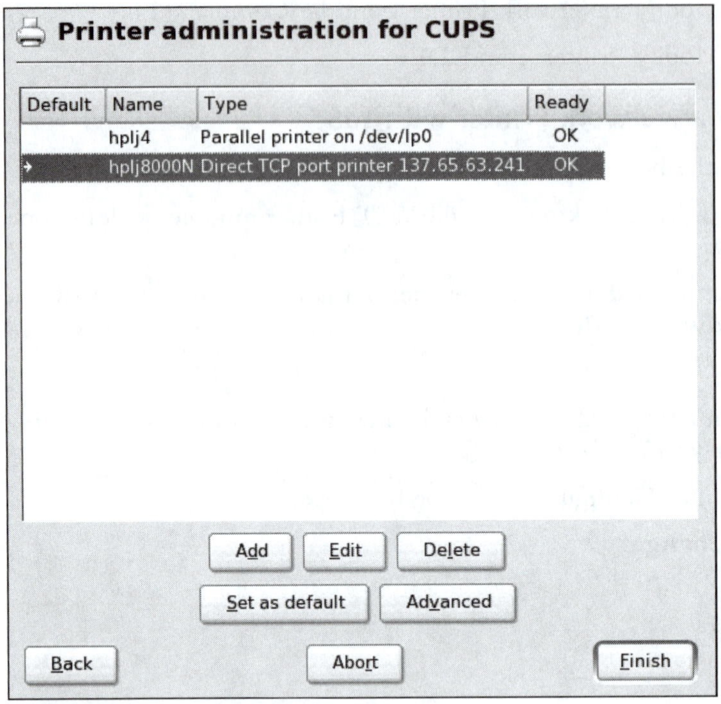

Figure 8-6

From this dialog box you can perform the following tasks:

- Create a printer configuration by selecting **Add**.

  This is the same as adding a printer configuration from the main Printer Configuration screen by selecting **Configure**.

- Edit configuration settings for a printer in the list by selecting **Edit**.

- Delete a printer in the list by selecting **Delete**.

- Select a printer and make it the default printer by selecting **Set as default**.

- Perform additional configuration (such as switching from a CUPS server installation to a CUPS client configuration) by selecting **Advanced**.

3. Edit an existing network printer configuration by selecting the *network printer* from the list; then select **Edit**.

The list shown in Figure 8-7 appears.

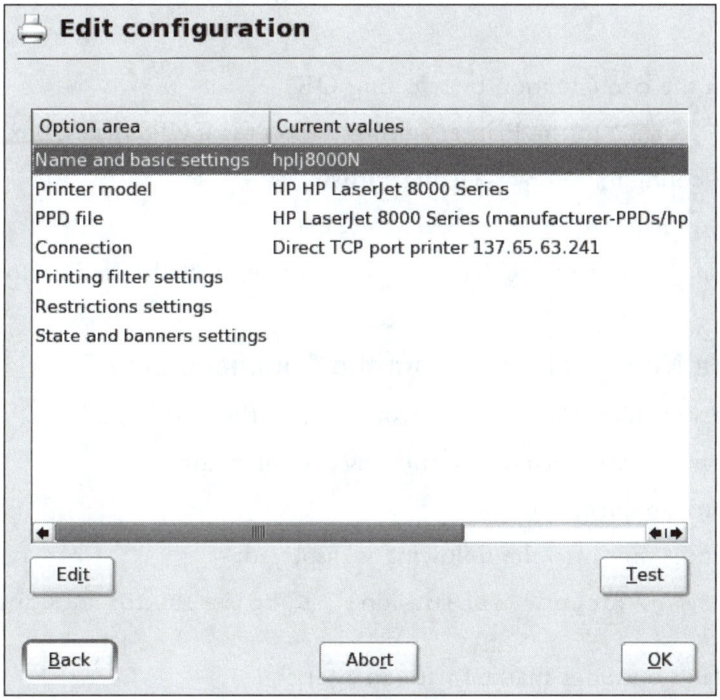

Figure 8-7

From this list you can modify settings such as the PPD file, filter settings, and restriction settings.

These settings are stored in the file /etc/cups/printers.conf which contains the printing queues that have been configured by YaST.

4. Select an *option area*; then select **Edit**.

A configuration dialog box appears.

You can use the Help information on the left to complete or select settings that meet your needs.

5. When you finish making configuration changes, select **Next**.

You are returned to the Edit configuration dialog box.

6. Do one of the following:

   ■ Select another *option area* to configure; then select **Edit**.

      or

   ■ Finish the configuration by selecting **OK**.

   You are returned to the Printer administration for CUPS dialog box.

7. Save the configuration by selecting **Finish**.

   You are returned to the YaST Control Center.

8. (Optional) If you started YaST from the desktop, close the **YaST Control Center**.

How to Modify a Network Printer from the Command Line

To modify a network printer from the command line, do the following:

1. List all options for a printer by entering the following:

   lpoptions -p *queue-name* **-l**

   Information similar to the following is displayed:

   ```
   Resolution/Output Resolution: 150dpi *300dpi 600dpi
   1200dpi
   ```

   The default option is marked with an asterisk (*).

2. Change an option using the **lpadmin** command.

   For example, to change the default resolution to 600dpi, enter the following:

   lpadmin -p *queue-name* **-o Resolution=600dpi**

3. Check the new setting by entering the following:

   lpoptions -p queue-name -l

How to Modify Printer Settings from KDE

The KDE desktop environment provides a *kprinter* utility for changing the properties of a printer (print queue) stored in its ppd file (/etc/cups/ppd/ directory).

This kprinter dialog box is available when you print from a desktop application, or you can start it from the command line.

To change print queue settings using kprinter, do the following:

1. Start kprinter from an application (by selecting a menu option such as **Print**), or from the command line by entering **kprinter**.

The dialog box shown in Figure 8-8 appears.

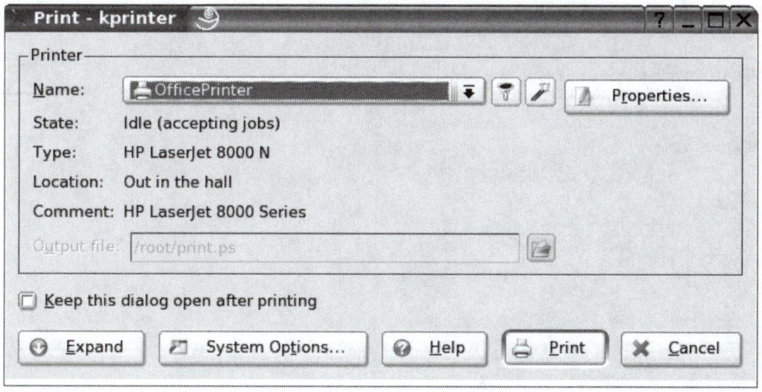

Figure 8-8

2. From the Name drop-down list, select the *printer* (print queue) you want to modify; then select **Properties**.

The dialog box shown in Figure 8-9 appears.

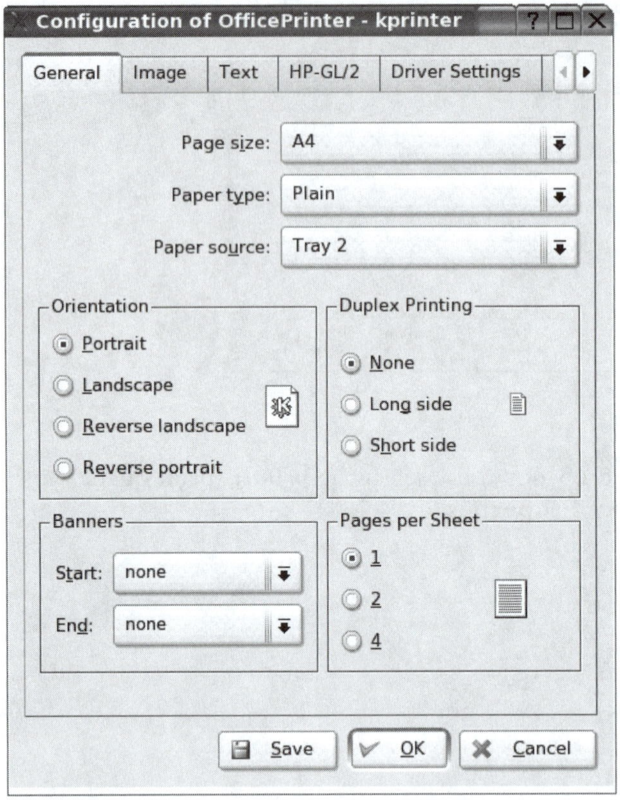

Figure 8-9

From this dialog box you can change settings such as page size and paper type.

3. When you finish modifying the settings, select **Save**.

   If you start kprinter as root, the changes are saved to the file /etc/cups/lpoptions and affect all users.

   If you start kprinter as a normal user, the changes are saved to the user's home directory in .lpoptions and affect only the print jobs for that user.

How to Manage Printing from the Command Line

You can manage print jobs from the command line by using the following command:

- Basic Printer Management
- CUPS Printer Commands
- SUSE Linux Enterprise Server Printer Commands

Basic Printer Management

You can use the following commands to perform basic printer management tasks:

- **/usr/bin/enable** *printer.* You can use this command to start a printer queue for the indicated *printer*.

    If there are any queued print jobs, they are printed after the printer is enabled.

- **/usr/bin/disable** *printer.* You can use this command to stop a printer queue for the indicated *printer*.

    Disabling a printer is useful if the printer malfunctions and you need time to correct the problem.

    Printers that are disabled can still accept jobs for printing but won't actually print any files until they are restarted.

- **/usr/sbin/reject** *printer.* You can use this command to reject print jobs for the indicated *printer*.

    While the command /usr/sbin/stop stops the printer from printing, the print queue continues to accept submitted print jobs.

    With the command /usr/sbin/reject, the printer finishes the print jobs in the queue but rejects any new print jobs.

    This command is useful for times when you need to perform maintenance on a printer and the printer will not be available for a significant period of time.

- **/usr/sbin/accept** *printer.* You can use this command to accept print jobs for the indicated *printer*.

    By using this command, you can reset the print queue to begin accepting and printing new print jobs.

CUPS Printer Commands

CUPS provides two kinds of commands: Berkeley3 and System V. The System V commands can also be used to configure queues.

The following are print management tasks you can perform using CUPS printer commands:

- **Submit a print job (lpr, lp)**. The following is the syntax for these commands:
    - Berkeley: **lpr –P** *queue file*
    - System V: **lp –d** *queue file*

The following are examples:

lpr -P color chart.ps

or

lp -d color chart.ps

In this example, the file **chart.ps** is printed over the queue color.

You can use the **-o** option to specify options regarding the printout, such as the following:

lpr -P lp -o duplex=none order.ps

or

lp -d lp -o duplex=none order.ps

In this example, the file **order.ps** is submitted to the queue lp and the duplex function of the printer is disabled for the printout (duplex=none).

For additional information about these commands, enter **man lpr** or **man lp**, or enter http://localhost:631 in a Web browser and select **On-Line Help**.

- **Display print jobs (lpq, lpstat)**. The following is the syntax for these commands:

  - Berkeley: **lpq -P** *queue*

  - System V: **lpstat -o** *queue* **-p** *queue*

If you do not specify a queue, all queues are displayed. lpstat -o displays the active print jobs in the following format:

queue-jobnumber

You can display more information by entering **lpstat -l -o** *queue* **-p** *queue* and all available information by entering **lpstat -t** or **lpstat -l -t**.

For additional information about these commands, enter **man lpq** or **man lpstat**, or enter http://localhost:631 in a Web browser and select **On-Line Help**.

- **Cancel print jobs (lprm, cancel)**. The following is the syntax for these commands:

  - Berkeley: **lprm -P** *queue jobnumber*

  - System V: **cancel** *queue-jobnumber*

For additional information about these commands, enter **man lprm** or **man cancel**, or enter http://localhost:631 in a Web browser and select **On-Line Help**.

- **Configure a queue (lpoptions)**. You can find the printer-specific options to determine the kind of printout for a printer in the PPD file (/etc/cups/ppd/ directory) that belongs to a queue.

  All users can display the options with the following command:

  lpoptions -p *queue* **-l**

  The following are some examples of what might be displayed:

  ```
  PageSize/Page Size: A3 *A4 A5 Legal Letter
  Resolution/Resolution: 150 *300 600
  ```

  The asterisk (*) in front of an option indicates the current setting. In the example above, the paper format is set to A4 and the resolution to 300 dpi.

  You can change the options of a queue with the following command:

  lpoptions -p *queue* **-o option=***value*

  For example, to change the paper format for the queue lp to letter, you would enter the following:

  lpoptions -p lp -o PageSize=Letter

  The users who are affected by these new settings depends on the following:

  - If a normal user (such as **geeko**) enters the command, the change only affects that user. The setting is saved in the file **.lpoptions** in the user's home directory.

  - If **root** enters the command, the settings become preferences for every user on the local computer and are saved in the file /etc/cups/lpoptions. The corresponding PPD file will remain unchanged.

For information about hardware-independent standard options for printout types, read the file /usr/share/doc/packages/cups/sum.html#USING_SYSTEM.

For information about saving options, read the file /usr/share/doc/packages/ cups/ sum.html#SAVING_OPTIONS.

SUSE Linux Enterprise Server Printer Commands

You can perform the following basic print management tasks using SUSE Linux Enterprise server printer commands:

- **Disable a print queue (/usr/bin/disable).** To disable printing on a print queue, use the command **/usr/bin/disable** *queue* (such as **/usr/bin/disable lj4050**).

  After entering the command, all subsequent print jobs are accepted, but not printed.

- **Enable a print queue (/usr/bin/enable).** To enable printing on a print queue, use the command **/usr/bin/enable** *queue*.

  You need to enter the path with the queue name, as enable is also a Bash built-in command.

- **Reject print jobs (/usr/bin/reject).** If you do not want the printer available for an extended period of time (such as for repairs), you can reject print jobs for the queue with the command **/usr/bin/reject** *queue*.

- **Accept print jobs (/usr/bin/accept).** To activate accepting print jobs for a printer, use the command **/usr/bin/accept** *queue*.

How to Access the CUPS Web Administration Tools

CUPS provides a Web page for administering printers. You can access this interface by entering the following:

http://localhost:631

The Web page shown in Figure 8-10 appears.

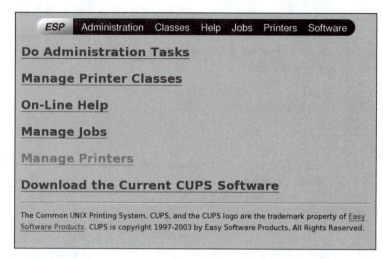

Figure 8-10

From this Web page you can perform tasks such as managing printer classes, jobs, and printers.

To use the management options on this Web page (or the printer administration tool in KDE), **root** must be set up as a CUPS administrator with the CUPS administration group sys and a CUPS password.

You can do this as the root user by entering the following command:

lppasswd –g sys –a root

For information on setting up another user as a CUPS administrator, see Section 13.6.2 in the **SLES 9 Installation and Administration Manual**.

NOTE

How to Troubleshoot the CUPS Print System

The following are basic tasks for troubleshooting the CUPS print system:

- Set the Log Level to Record Errors
- Check the Access Log
- Perform Basic Troubleshooting

Set the Log Level to Record Errors

Messages from cupsd are written to the file /var/log/cups/error_log. By default, only inquiries and status changes are logged to the file.

If you want errors recorded, you need to change the LogLevel option in the cupsd configuration file /etc/cups/cupsd.conf:

```
# LogLevel: controls the number of messages logged to the   ErrorLog
# file and can be one of the following:
#
#       debug2      Log everything.
#       debug       Log almost everything.
#       info        Log all requests and state changes.
#       warn        Log errors and warnings.
#       error       Log only errors.
#       none        Log nothing.
#
```

```
LogLevel debug2
```

For debugging and troubleshooting, set the log level to **debug2**. After changing the configuration, restart CUPS by entering **rccups restart**.

Check the Access Log

The file /var/log/cups/access_log logs every access to the CUPS daemon from a browser or a CUPS/IPP client. Each line includes the fields shown in Table 8-1.

Table 8-1

Field	Description
host	DNS name or IP number
group	The group name (always "−" for CUPS)
user	User name if the user identified himself with a login and password (otherwise "−")
date	The current date
method	The HTTP method (such as GET or POST)
resource	The requested resource
version	The HTTP version (with CUPS always HTTP/1.1)
status	The HTTP result status (normally 200, but other codes are also possible)
bytes	The number of transmitted bytes

Perform Basic Troubleshooting

To perform basic troubleshooting on the CUPS print system, do the following:

1. Set the LogLevel to **debug** in the **/etc/cups/cupsd.conf** file.

2. Stop cupsd by entering **rccupsd stop**.

3. Avoid searching through large log files by renaming the file /var/log/cups/error_log (such as the following):

   mv /var/log/cups/error_log /var/log/cups/error_log-*yyyymmdd*

4. Start cupsd by entering **rccupsd start**.

5. Repeat the action that led to the problem.

6. Check the messages in **/var/log/cups/error_log** to identify the cause of the problem.

Exercise 8-1   Configure CUPS Network Printing Services

In this exercise you set up and manage a CUPS printing environment on your SLES 9 server by doing the following:

- Part I: Add a Printer to the Network with YaST
- Part II: Manage the Printer from the Command Line
- Part III: Manage the Printer with YaST
- Part IV: Provide Access to the CUPS Administrator
- Part V: Print to a Remote CUPS Printer

Part I: Add a Printer to the Network with YaST

The first task in setting up a CUPS printing environment on your SLES 9 server is to add the network printer.

Do the following:

1. From the KDE desktop, select the **YaST** icon; then enter a password of **novell** and select **OK**.

   The YaST Control Center appears.

2. Select **Hardware > Printer**.

   After initializing the printer configuration, the Printer Configuration dialog box appears.

3. Add a new printer by selecting **Configure**.

4. Make sure **Parallel printer** is selected; then continue by selecting **Next**.

   A Printer connection dialog box appears with a list of connection devices.

   The device for the first parallel port is /dev/lp0.

5. Make sure the device **/dev/lp0** is selected; then continue by selecting **Next**.

   A Queue name dialog box appears.

6. In the Name for printing field enter **hplj4**.

7. Make sure that **Do Local Filtering** is selected; then continue by selecting **Next**.

   A Printer model dialog box appears with two lists—manufacturer and model.

8. From the Select manufacturer list, select **HP**.

9. From the Select model list, select **LaserJet 4**.

10. Continue by selecting **Next**.

    An Edit configuration dialog box appears that lets you view and edit the configuration settings.

11. Continue by selecting **OK**.

    You are returned to the Printer Configuration dialog box where the HP LaserJet 4 printer is listed at the bottom with a status of "changed, not yet saved."

12. Save the printer configuration by selecting **Finish**.

    Leave the YaST Control Center open. You use it later in the exercise.

13. Open the Konqueror browser and enter the following URL:

    http://localhost:631

    A CUPS printer management page appears.

14. At the top of the page, select **Printers**.

    A Printer page appears with the HP LaserJet 4 printer listed.

15. Submit a test print job by selecting **Print Test Page**.

16. From the top of the Web page, view the print job by selecting **Jobs**.

    The CUPS jobs page appears with the test page job listed.

Part II: Manage the Printer from the Command Line

Do the following:

1. Open a terminal window.

2. Send a print job to the HP LaserJet 4 printer using the Berkeley printer commands:

    a. Send the file /etc/hosts to be printed by entering the following:

       lpr –P hplj4 /etc/hosts

    b. View the print queue for hplj4 by entering the following Berkeley command:

       lpq –P hplj4

       There are two jobs listed—the test page and the hosts file.

3. Send a print job to the HP LaserJet 4 printer using the System V printer commands:

    a. Send the file **/etc/hosts** to the printer by entering the following:

       lp –d hplj4 /etc/hosts

    b. View the print queue for hplj4 by entering the following Berkeley command:

       lpstat hplj4

       There are three jobs listed—the test page and the two hosts file jobs.

4. From the Konqueror window, reload the CUPS job page by selecting **Jobs** to see the new jobs in the Web interface.

5. From the terminal window, cancel the test page job (Job 1) by entering the following Berkeley command:

   lprm –P hplj4 1

   An error message appears indicating that you don't own Job 1.

   Notice that the first job in the list has no owner listed.

6. Su to root (**su –**) with a password of **novell**.

7. Enter **lprm –P hplj4 1** again; then enter **lpstat hplj4**.

   The first print job has been deleted.

8. Check the status of the printer by entering **lpc status**.

9. Reload the CUPS jobs page to verify that Job 1 has been removed.

10. From the terminal window, view the contents of the file /etc/printcap by entering **cat /etc/printcap**.

Part III: Manage the Printer with YaST

In this part of the exercise, you perform some basic printer management tasks with YaST.

Do the following:

1. Change basic settings for the HP LaserJet 4 printer:

   a. From the YaST Control Center select **Hardware > Printer**.

      The Printer Configuration dialog box appears.

   b. Modify an existing printer by selecting **Change**.

   c. Make sure the **hplj4** printer is selected; then select **Edit**.

      A list of option areas to edit appears.

   d. Make sure **Name and basic settings** is selected; then select **Edit**.

   e. Enter the following:

      ■ Description of Printer: **LaserJet 4 on DA*xx*** (where *xx* is your host number)

      ■ Location of Printer: **DA*xx* computer**

   f. Return to the Edit configuration dialog box by selecting **Next**.

   g. Save the changes and close the YaST module by selecting **OK**; then select **Finish**.

   h. From the Konqueror browser, view the changes by selecting **Printers**.

2. Change the filter settings for the HP LaserJet 4 printer:

   a. From the YaST Control Center select **Hardware > Printer**.

      The Printer Configuration dialog box appears.

   b. Modify the existing printers by selecting **Change**.

   c. Make sure the **hplj4** printer is selected; then select **Edit**.

      A list of option areas to edit appears.

   d. Select **Printing filter settings**; then select **Edit**.

      A list of options appears at the top of the screen with a list of values for each option at the bottom of the screen.

   e. Scroll down the list of options and select **Page Size**.

      Notice that the page size is set to **A4**.

   f. Change the page size to US Letter by selecting **Letter**; then select **Next**.

   g. Save the changes and close the YaST module by selecting **OK**; then select **Finish**.

h. From the terminal window, verify that the new default page size is set to US Letter by entering the following:

grep DefaultPageSize /etc/cups/ppd/hplj4.ppd

Part IV: Provide Access to the CUPS Administrator

Before printers can be administered through a Web browser, you need to create a CUPS password for each authorized user.

Do the following:

1. Make sure you are su'd to root in the terminal window.

2. Enter the following to create a CUPS digest password for the root user:

   lppasswd –a root

3. Enter a password of **N0v3ll** twice.

4. From the Konqueror Web browser, enter the following URL:

   http://localhost:631/admin.

5. Log in by entering the following:

   ■ Username: **root**

   ■ Password: **N0v3ll**.

   The CUPS administrator page appears.

Part V: Print to a Remote CUPS Printer

The HP LaserJet 4 printer is configured to print locally through your parallel port. However, a CUPS network printer is also available on the Digital Airlines office network that you would like to access.

NOTE

In a classroom environment, this printer has already been set up for students on the DA1 server. If there is no CUPs printer configured on another server, you can use your own server and print queue for this part of the exercise.

Do the following:

1. From the YaST Control Center select **Hardware > Printer**.

   The Printer Configuration dialog box appears.

2. Add a new CUPS printer by selecting **Configure**.

3. Select **Print via CUPS Network Server**; then select **Next**.

4. Select **Remote IPP Queue**; then select **Next**.

8

5. Next to the Host name of the printer server field, select **Lookup**; then select **Scan for IPP Servers**.

6. From the drop-down list, select **DA1.digitalairlines.com**.

7. (Conditional) If DA1.digitalairlines.com does not appear in the drop-down list, enter **DA1.digitalairlines.com** in the field.

8. Next to the Name of the remote queue field, select **Lookup** to select the default queue configured on DA1.

9. Test connectivity to the printer server by selecting **Test remote IPP access**.

10. When a success message appears, select **OK**.

11. Continue by selecting **Next**.

    A Queue name dialog box appears.

    Notice that Do Local Filtering is not selected because filtering is being done on the remote CUPS printer server.

12. From the Name for printing field, record the name of the printer queue on the instructor's server:

13. Accept the default settings by selecting **Next**.

14. Save the configuration changes by selecting **Finish**.

15. From the terminal window, test printing to the instructor's server by entering the following:

    lpr –P *queue_name* **/etc/hosts** (where *queue_name* is the name instructor's printer)

16. From the Konqueror Web browser, check your print job on the instructor's computer by selecting **jobs**.

17. The job is displayed in the Jobs list.

18. Try monitoring your print job from the instructor server by entering the following:

    http://10.0.0.254:631/printers

19. Select the *printer link* for the instructor's printer or select **Jobs**.

20. (Conditional) If you do not see your print job, try selecting **Show Completed Jobs**.

21. When you finish, close all windows.

OBJECTIVE 2   CONFIGURE NETWORK FILE SYSTEMS

To configure network file systems on SUSE Linux Enterprise Server, you need to understand the following:

- Network File System (NFS)
- Samba (CIFS)

Network File System (NFS)

Network File System (NFS) lets you configure an NFS file server that gives users transparent access to programs, files, or storage space on the server.

To configure NFS for your network, you need to know the following:

- Network File System Basics
- How NFS Works
- NFS Configuration Overview
- How to Configure an NFS Server with YaST
- How to Configure an NFS Server Manually
- How to Configure NFS Client Access with YaST
- How to Configure and Mount NFS Directories
- How to Monitor the NFS System

Network File System Basics

NFS is designed for sharing files and directories over a network, and requires configuration of an NFS server (where the files and directories are located) and NFS clients (user computers that access the files and directories remotely).

File systems are exported by an NFS server, and appear and behave on a NFS client as if they were located on a local machine.

For example, with NFS each user's home directory can be exported by an NFS server and imported to a client, so the same home directories are accessible from every workstation on the network.

Directories like /home/, /opt/, /usr/, and /var/spool/mail/ are good candidates for export via NFS. However, others, including /bin/, /boot/, /dev/, /etc/, /lib/, /root/, /sbin/, /tmp/, and (parts of) /var/, should be available on the local disk only.

NFS is frequently used with Network Information Service (NIS) to provide centralized user management on a network.

Figure 8-11 shows an example of mounting the directory /home/ (exported by the NFS server sun) on the host computer earth.

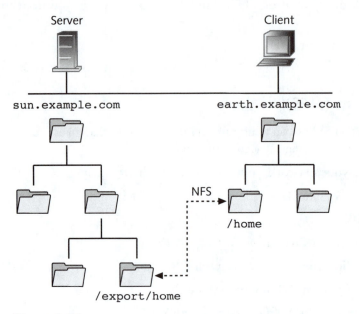

Figure 8-11

A computer can be both a NFS server and an NFS client. It can supply file systems over the network (export) and mount file systems from other hosts (import).

A computer that hosts an NFS server generally has a very large hard disk capacity. Its file systems are mounted by other clients.

The NFS daemon is part of the kernel and only needs to be configured, then activated. The start script is /etc/init.d/nfsserver.

A number of additional tools are included in the package nfs-utils, which is part of the standard installation.

The kernel NFS daemon includes file locking, which means that only one user at a time has write access to files.

How NFS Works

Both NFS and NIS are Remote Procedure Call (RPC) services. An essential component for RPC services is the *portmapper* that manages these services and needs to be started first.

When an RPC service starts up, it binds to a port in the system (as any other network service), but also communicates this port and the service it offers (such as NFS) to the portmapper.

Because every RPC program must be registered by the portmapper when it is started, RPC programs must be restarted each time you restart the portmapper.

Table 8-2 lists the services required on an NFS server.

Table 8-2

Service	Program (daemon)	Start Script
Port mapper	/sbin/portmap	/etc/init.d/portmap
NFS locking daemon	/sbin/rpc.lockd	/etc/init.d/nfslock (started automatically with nfsserver)
NFS server	/usr/sbin/rpc.nfsd /usr/sbin/rpc.mountd	/etc/init.d/nfsserver

8

File locking is activated through the script /etc/init.d/nfslock. The script controls the daemon /sbin/rpc.lockd.

You can use the command /etc/init.d/nfsserver to start the NFS server. The script nfsserver passes the list of exported directories to the kernel, and then starts or stops the daemons rpc.nfsd and rpc.mountd.

The NFS service daemon (/usr/sbin/rpc.nfsd) starts the required kernel threads.

The mount daemon (/usr/sbin/rpc.mountd) accepts each mount request and compares it with the entries in the configuration file /etc/exports. If access is allowed, the data is delivered to the client.

Because daemon rpc.nfsd can be started directly with several kernel threads, the start script interprets the variable USE_KERNEL_NFSD_NUMBER in the file /etc/sysconfig/nfs.

This variable determines the number of threads to start. By default, four server threads are started.

NFS Configuration Overview

All configuration settings for the NFS server are stored in the file /etc/exports (enter **man 5 exports**). These settings include information such as which directories should be exported over the network with which options, and which computers can access them.

Client-side configuration takes place using the file /etc/fstab (enter **man 5 nfs**).

Both the NFS server and the clients can be configured with YaST modules. You can also modify the configuration files directly.

For the NFS server to start automatically when the computer is booted, the corresponding soft links in the runlevel directories must first be generated.

If you configure the NFS server with YaST, this is done automatically; otherwise, you need to generate the soft links with insserv.

How to Configure an NFS Server with YaST

To use YaST to configure the NFS server, do the following:

1. From the KDE desktop, start the YaST NFS Server module by doing one of the following:

   - Select the **YaST** icon, enter the root *password*, and select **OK**; then select **Network Services > NFS Server**.

   or

   - Open a terminal window and enter **sux –** and the root *password*; then enter **yast2 nfs-server**.

   The dialog box shown in Figure 8-12 appears.

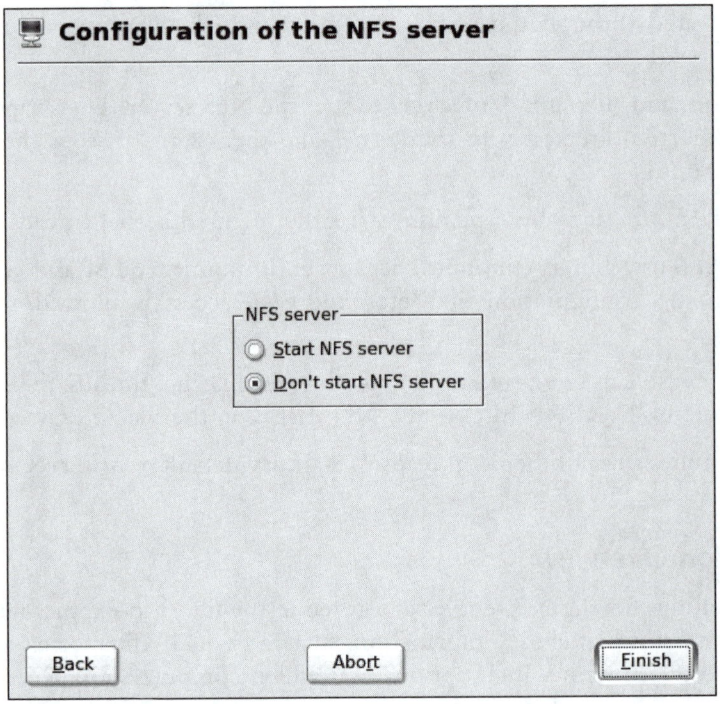

Figure 8-12

2. Select **Start NFS Server**; then select **Next**.

The Directories to export to the others dialog box appears, as shown in Figure 8-13.

Figure 8-13

3. Add a directory for export by selecting **Add directory**; then enter or browse to and select a *directory*.

The dialog box shown in Figure 8-14 appears.

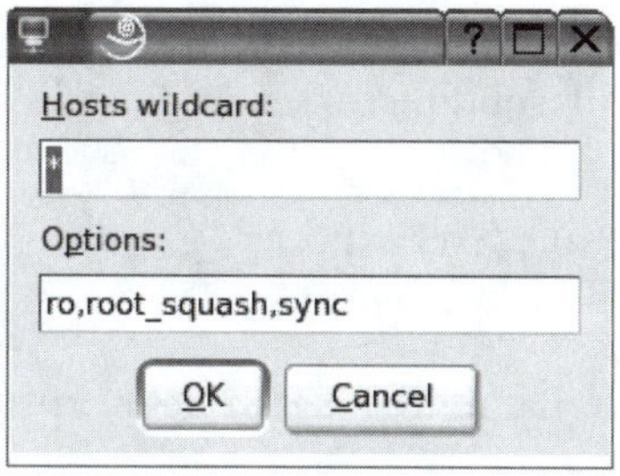

Figure 8-14

This dialog box lets you configure the hosts that should have access to the directory. There are four options that can be set for each host: single host, netgroups, wildcards, and IP networks.

For details on configuring the host settings, see *How to Configure an NFS Server Manually*.

4. Add other directories by selecting **Add directory**.

 You can also edit a directory or delete it by selecting the directory and selecting **Edit** or **Delete**.

5. Add, edit, or delete a host for a directory by selecting the directory; then select **Add host**, **Edit**, or **Delete**.

6. When you finish, save the configuration by selecting **Finish**.

How to Configure an NFS Server Manually

If you do not want to use YaST to set up an NFS server, you can configure the server from the command line by doing the following:

- **Check for service (daemon) availability.** Make sure the following are available on your NFS server:

  - RPC portmapper (portmap)

  - RPC mount daemon (rpc.mountd)

  - RPC NFS daemon (rpc.nfsd)

- **Configure the services to be available at bootup.** For these services to be started by the scripts /etc/init.d/portmap and /etc/init.d/nfsserver when the system is booted, enter the following commands:

 insserv /etc/init.d/nfsserver

 insserv /etc/init.d/portmap

- **Define exported directories (file systems) in /etc/exports.** You also need to define which file systems should be exported to which host in the configuration file /etc/exports.

 For each directory to export, one line is needed to set which computers can access that directory with what permissions. All subdirectories of this directory are automatically exported as well.

 The following is the general syntax of the file /etc/exports:

 directory **[***host*[**(***option1***,***option2***,***option3***,...)]]** ...

 Do not put any spaces between the host name, the parentheses enclosing the options, and the option strings themselves.

 A *host* can be one of the following:

  - A standalone computer with its name in short form (it must be possible to resolve this with name resolution), with its Fully Qualified Domain Name (FQDN), or with its IP address.

- A network, specified by an address with a netmask or by the domain name with a prefixed placeholder (such as ***.example.com**).

Authorized computers are usually specified with their full names (including domain name), but you can use wildcards like * or ?.

If you do not specify a host, any computer can import the file system with the given permissions.

- **Set permissions for exported directories (file systems) in /etc/exports.** You need to set permission options for the file system to export in brackets after the computer name. The most commonly used options include those shown in Table 8-3.

Table 8-3

Option	Meaning
ro	File system is exported with read-only permission (default).
rw	File system is exported with read-write permission.
root_squash	This ensures that the user root of the given machine does not have root permissions on this file system. This is achieved by assigning user ID 65534 to users with user ID 0 (root). This user ID should be set to nobody (which is the default).
no_root_squash	Does not assign user ID 65534 to user ID 0, keeping the root permissions valid.
link_relative	Converts absolute links (those beginning with /) to a sequence of ../. This is only useful if the entire file system of a machine is mounted (default).
link_absolute	Symbolic links remain untouched.
map_identity	User IDs are exactly the same on both client and server (default).
map_daemon	Client and server do not have matching user IDs. This tells nfsd to create a conversion table for user IDs. The ugidd daemon is required for this to work.

The following is an example of an edited /etc/exports file that includes permissions:

```
#
# /etc/exports
#
/home           sun(rw)  venus(rw)
/usr/X11        sun(ro)  venus(ro)
/usr/lib/texmf  sun(ro)  venus(rw)
/               earth(ro,root_squash)
/home/ftp       +(ro,sync)
# End of exports
```

Whenever you want an additional directory (such as /home/geeko/pictures/) exported to form part of an already exported directory (such as /home/geeko/), the additional directory needs its own separate entry in /etc/exports (such as the following):

```
/home/geeko/picturesearth(rw,all_squash,anonuid=150,
anongid=100,sync)
```

- **Restart mountd and nfsd.** The /etc/exports is read by mountd and nfsd. If you change anything in this file, you need to restart mountd and nfsd for your changes to take effect. You can do this by entering **rcnfsserver restart**.

How to Temporarily Export a Directory

You can export a directory temporarily (without editing the file /etc/exports) by using the command exportfs.

For example, to export the directory software to all hosts in the network 192.168.0.0/24, you would enter the following command:

exportfs –o ro,root_squash,sync 192.168.0.0/24:/ software

To restore the original state, all you need to do is enter the command **exportfs –r**. The file /etc/exports is reloaded and the directory software is no longer exported.

The directories that are currently exported are listed in the file /var/lib/nfs/etab. The content of this file is updated when you use the command exportfs.

How to Configure NFS Client Access with YaST

Users authorized to do so can mount NFS directories from an NFS server into their own file tree. The easiest way to do this is to use the YaST NFS Client module.

Do the following:

1. Start the YaST NFS Client module by doing one of the following:

   - From the desktop, start the YaST Control Center by selecting **Start Applications > System > YaST**; then select **Network Services > NFS Client**.

     or

   - From a terminal window, enter **yast2 nfs-client**.

The NFS client configuration dialog box shown in Figure 8-15 appears.

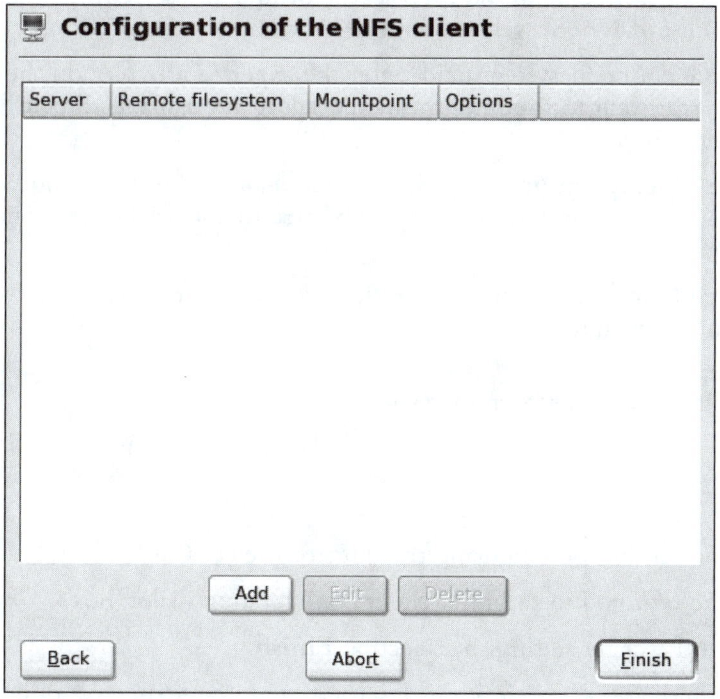

Figure 8-15

A list in the dialog box lets you add, edit, or delete NFS server directories in your file tree.

2. Add a directory to the list by selecting **Add**.

The dialog box shown in Figure 8-16 appears.

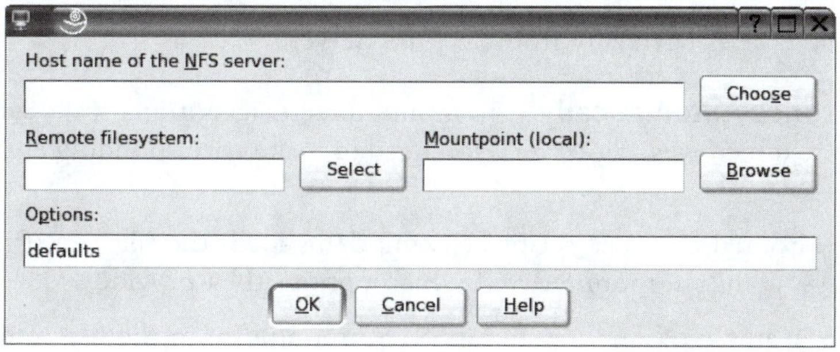

Figure 8-16

From this dialog box, you can configure the directory to mount in your file tree.

3. Configure the directory by doing the following:

   a. Enter the *host name* of the NFS server, or find and select the NFS server from a list of NFS servers on your network by selecting **Choose**.

   b. In the Remote filesystem field, enter the *exported directory* on the NFS server you want to mount, or find and select the available directory by selecting **Select**.

   c. In the Mountpoint (local) field, enter the *mountpoint* in your local file tree to mount the exported directory, or browse to and select the mountpoint by selecting **Browse**.

   d. In the Options field, enter any *options* you would normally use with the mount command.

For a list of these options, enter **man mount**.

   e. When you finish configuring the directory, select **OK**.

   You are returned to the NFS client configuration dialog box.

4. Save the NFS client settings by selecting **Finish**.

   The settings are saved, services restarted, and the exported directories are mounted in your local file tree.

5. (Optional) If you started YaST from the desktop, close the **YaST Control Center**.

How to Configure and Mount NFS Directories

To configure and mount NFS directories, you need to know how to do the following:

- Mount NFS Directories Automatically
- Import Directories Manually from an NFS Server

Mount NFS Directories Automatically   To mount directories automatically when booting (such as the home directories of a server), you need to make corresponding entries in the file /etc/fstab.

When the system is booted, the start script /etc/init.d/nfs loads the file /etc/fstab, which indicates where file systems are mounted and which options they provide.

The following is an example of an entry for an NFS mountpoint in the file /etc/fstab:

```
sun:/training/home /home nfs soft,rsize=8192,wsize=8192 0 0
```

In this entry, the first value indicates the host name of the NFS server (**sun**) and the directory it exports (**/training/home/**).

The second value indicates the mountpoint, which is the directory in the local file system where the exported directory should be attached (**/home/**).

The third value indicates the file system type (**nfs**). The comma-separated values following the file system type provide NFS-specific mounting options.

At the end of the line, there are two numbers (**0 0**) that indicate whether to back up the file system with the help of dump (first number) and whether to perform a file system check on the mounted volume with fsck (second number).

In the example, the system does neither, as both options are set to 0.

After modifying the file /etc/fstab, you can have the system read the changes by entering **mount -a**. All new entries that do not contain the option noauto are evaluated and the corresponding directories or partitions are mounted.

You also need to activate the start script of the NFS client by entering **insserv nfs** (which sets the symbolic links in the respective runlevel directories).

Import Directories Manually from an NFS Server   You can import a directory (file system) manually from an NFS server by using the command mount. The only prerequisite is a running RPC port mapper, which you can start by entering (as root) the command **rcportmap start**.

The command mount automatically tries to recognize the file system (such as ext2, ext3, or ReiserFS). However, if you are using a file system like Linux SMB (Samba), you must use the mount option -t to indicate the file system type.

In the following example, /sbin/mount.smb is specified:

mount -t smbfs -o *options device directory*

If you do not want to mount a directory permanently or if it should not be imported automatically when the computer is booted, you can mount a directory exported by NFS like a local partition with the mount option **-o**.

The following is an example:

mount -o soft sun:/training/home /home

Instead of a device file, you can also pass the name of the NFS server together with the directories to import to the mount command.

8

The following are the most important -o options:

- **soft (opposite: hard).** If the attempt to access the NFS server extends beyond the preset time frame (major timeout is 60 seconds), the mount attempt will be aborted.

    Otherwise, the client attempts to mount the exported directory until it receives feedback from the server that the attempt was successful.

    This can cause the boot process to hang because the process will stop at this point when it attempts to mount the NFS directory.

    For directories that are not essential for the system to function, you can use the option soft. For directories that must be mounted (such as home directories), you can use the option hard.

- **bg (default: fg).** If you use this option, and the first attempt is unsuccessful, all further mount attempts are run in the background.

    This prevents the boot process from hanging when NFS exports are automatically mounted, with attempts to mount the directories continuing in the background.

- **rsize=*n*.** This option lets you set the number of bytes (*n*) that NFS reads from the NFS server at one time.

    Because older NFS versions have a limitation of 1024 bytes, this is the default value. The current version (NFSv3) can process larger amounts of data.

    For quicker access, we recommend resetting the rsize to **8192**.

- **wsize=*n*.** This option lets you set the number of bytes (*n*) that can be written to the NFS server.

    The default value is set to 1024. For faster write access, we recommend setting wsize to **8192**.

- **retry=*n*.** This option lets you set the number of minutes (**n**) an attempt can take to mount a directory through NFS. The default value is **10000** minutes (approximately 1 week).

- **nosuid.** This option lets you disable any evaluation of the SUID and SGID bits on the corresponding file system.

    For security reasons, always use this option for any file system that might be susceptible to tampering.

    If you do not use this option, there is a possibility that a user can obtain root access to the local file system by putting a SUID root executable on the imported file system.

- **nodev.** This option lets you disable any interpretation of device files in the imported file system. We recommend that you use this option for security reasons.

    Without setting this option, someone could create a device such as /dev/hda on the NFS export, then use it to obtain write permissions for the hard disk as soon as the file can be accessed from the client side.

You can use the command umount (enter **man umount**) to unmount a file system. However, you can only do this if the file system is currently not being accessed.

For additional information on nfs, mount options, and on the file /etc/fstab, enter **man 5 nfs**, **man 8 mount**, or **man 5 fstab**.

How to Monitor the NFS System

Some tools are available to help you monitor the NFS system.

For example, you can enter **rpcinfo –p** to display information about the portmapper. The option **–p** displays all the programs registered with the portmapper, similar to the following:

```
DA50:~ # rpcinfo -p
  program vers proto    port
   100000    2   tcp     111   portmapper
   100000    2   udp     111   portmapper
   100003    2   udp    2049   nfs
   100003    3   udp    2049   nfs
   100227    3   udp    2049   nfs_acl
   100003    2   tcp    2049   nfs
   100003    3   tcp    2049   nfs
   100227    3   tcp    2049   nfs_acl
   100021    1   udp   32773   nlockmgr
   100021    3   udp   32773   nlockmgr
   100021    4   udp   32773   nlockmgr
   100024    1   udp   32773   status
   100021    1   tcp   32872   nlockmgr
   100021    3   tcp   32872   nlockmgr
   100021    4   tcp   32872   nlockmgr
   100024    1   tcp   32872   status
   100005    1   udp     693   mountd
. . .
```

The NFS server daemon registers itself to the port mapper with the name nfs. The NFS mount daemon uses the name mountd.

You can use the command showmount to display information about the exported directories of an NFS server.

For example, **showmount –e sun** displays the exported directories of the machine sun. The option –a shows which computers have mounted which directories.

Exercise 8-2   Set Up and Manage Network File System (NFS)

In this exercise, you use NFS as a server and a client to share files between Linux hosts.

Do the following:

- Part I: Add a Remote File System to the NFS Client
- Part II: Set Up an NFS Server

Part I: Add a Remote File System to the NFS Client

In this part of the exercise you access a remote file system (/export/sles9) on the instructor's server.

Do the following:

1. From your KDE desktop, open a terminal window and su to root (**su –**) with a password of **novell**.

2. Create a mountpoint named /mnt/sles9 for the instructor's remote file system to be mounted on your server by entering the following:

   mkdir –p /mnt/sles9

3. Add a remote file system to the NFS client configuration:

   a. From your KDE desktop, select the **YaST** icon; then enter a password of **novell** and select **OK**.

      The YaST Control Center appears.

   b. Select **Network Services > NFS Client**.

      The Configuration of the NFS client dialog box appears.

   c. Mount a remote file system by selecting **Add**.

      A dialog box appears for adding the remote file system.

   d. Enter the following:

      - Host name of the NFS Server: **10.0.0.254** (this is the address of the instructor's server)
      - Remote filesystem: **/export/sles9/**
      - Mountpoint (local): **/mnt/sles9/**
      - Options field: **defaults,rsize=8192,wsize=8192,soft**

   e. Save the configuration by selecting **OK**.

      You are returned to the Configuration of the NFS client dialog box where the remote file system is listed.

4. Save the changes to the system by selecting **Finish**.

5. From the terminal window, verify that the file system is mounted by entering **mount**.

   You see the remote host mounted on /mnt/sles9.

6. List the files in the mounted file system by entering

   ls -l /mnt/sles9.

7. Check the entry entered by YaST in the file /etc/fstab by entering **cat /etc/fstab.**

   This entry ensures that the file system is mounted each time the server boots.

8. Check for any other exports on the instructor's SLES9 server by entering the following:

   showmount -e 10.0.0.254

Part II: Set Up an NFS Server

Do the following:

1. From the YaST Control Center, configure an NFS server on your computer by selecting **Network Services > NFS Server**.

   A Configuration of the NFS server dialog box appears.

2. Select **Start NFS server**; then continue by selecting **Next**.

   A Directories to export to the others dialog box appears.

3. Add the directory /export/data2 to the list for export:

   a. Select **Add directory**.

      A dialog box appears, requesting the directory to export.

   b. Enter **/export/data2/**; then select **OK**.

      A dialog box appears with fields for entering a wildcard and options.

   c. Enter the following:

      - Hosts wildcard: *****

      - Options: **rw,no_root_squash,sync** (make sure you replace "ro" with "rw")

   d. Continue by selecting **OK**.

      The directory is added to the list.

4. Save the changes to the system by selecting **Finish**.

5. From the terminal window, verify that the file system was exported by entering the following:

   showmount -e localhost

6. View the entry made by YaST to the file /etc/exports by entering **cat /etc/exports**.

   These are the settings you entered in YaST.

7. Work with a partner to access the directory /export/data2 directly from the partner's server by doing the following:

   a. Create a mountpoint /mnt/share on your server by entering **mkdir –p /mnt/share**.

   b. Mount your partner's directory doing one of the following:

      - Enter **mount –t nfs** *partner_IP***:/ export/data2 /mnt/share**

      - Use the YaST NFS Client module to mount the directory

8. Verify that your partner's directory is mounted by entering **mount**.

9. Start Konqueror in the Super User Mode by pressing **Alt+F2** and entering **kdesu konqueror**; then select **Run**.

10. Enter a password of **novell** and select **OK**.

11. View your NFS export by entering the following URL:

    nfs://localhost

12. View your partner's NFS export by entering the following URL:

    nfs://*partner_server_IP_address*

13. (Optional) If you finish early, try changing the entry in the **/etc/exports** file so that only you or your partner can write to the file system, and only one of you can read from it.

14. When you finish, close all open windows and dialog boxes.

Samba (CIFS)

Samba is a software package that implements the following Microsoft networking protocols on Linux:

- **Server Message Block (SMB).** SMB is a protocol for sharing resources between networked computers. SMB can be implemented over a number of protocols including TCP/IP, NetBEUI (often called NetBIOS), or IPX/SPX.

NOTE

For more information about SMB, see www.samba.org/cifs/docs/what-is-smb.html.

- **Common Internet File System (CIFS).** CIFS is an implementation of SMB over native TCP/IP that does not require NetBIOS.

CIFS is a client/server protocol and is used by Microsoft Windows operating systems. It is also implemented on many other platforms (such as DOS, NetWare, UNIX, Linux, and VMSTM).

With Samba installed, a Linux computer can function as the following:

- **Windows server.** Samba enables a server to provide Windows file and print services to users.

- **Windows client.** Samba enables a workstation to access and use Windows file and print services, whether they originate on a Windows server or on a Linux server with Samba installed.

To configure Samba on your SUSE Linux Enterprise Server, you need to know the following:

- Samba Features and Version

- Samba Client Support on Linux

- Samba Services and Configuration File

- How to Configure a Samba Server with YaST

- How to Configure a Samba Client with YaST

- How to Monitor and Test Samba

NOTE

For additional information on Samba, enter **man samba** at the command line or browse the directory /usr/share/doc/packages/samba/. If the documentation is not installed, use the YaST Install and Remove Software module to install the documents.

Samba Features and Version

SLES 9 provides version 3 of the Samba suite, which includes the following new important features:

- Support for Active Directory

- Much improved Unicode support

- Complete revision of the internal authentication mechanisms

- Improved support for the Windows 200x/XP printing system

- The ability to set up servers as member servers in Active Directory domains

- Adoption of an NT4 domain, enabling the migration from an NT4 domain to a Samba domain

Samba Client Support on Linux

All common operating systems, such as Mac OS X, Windows, and OS/2, support the SMB protocol. For the SMB protocol to operate, the TCP/IP protocol must be installed on all computers.

 Clients can only access the Samba server via TCP/IP. NetBEUI and NetBIOS via IPX cannot be used with Samba.

Samba provides a client for the different UNIX versions. For Linux, there is a file system kernel module for SMB that allows for the integration of SMB resources on the Linux system level.

SMB servers use shares to provide hard disk space to their clients. A share includes a directory and its subdirectories on the server. It is exported by means of a name and can be accessed by its name.

The share name can be set to any name—it does not have to be the name of the export directory.

A printer is also assigned a name. Clients can access the printer by its name.

Samba Services and Configuration File

The services required for Samba can be started by entering the following:

rcnmb start && rcsmb start

You can stop the Samba services by entering the following:

rcsmb stop && rcnmb stop

The main configuration file of Samba is /etc/samba/smb.conf. This file can be divided into two logical sections:

- **[global] section.** Contains the central and global settings
- **[share] sections.** Contain the individual file and printer shares

By using two logical sections, configuration of shares can be set individually or by using global settings included in the [global] section.

The following helps you understand how the smb.conf file is configured:

- [global] Section Configuration
- [cdrom] and [homes] Shares Configuration Examples
- Share Password Protection

You can configure the file manually or by using the YaST Samba Server module.

You can find a commented example configuration file (**smb.conf.SuSE**) in the directory /usr/share/doc/packages/samba/examples.

[global] Section Configuration   The following parameters of the [global] section need some adjustment to match the requirements of your network setup (manually or through YaST) so other machines can access your Samba server via SMB in a Windows environment:

- **workgroup = TUX-NET.** This line assigns the Samba server to a workgroup. Replace TUX-NET with an appropriate workgroup of your networking environment.

- **netbiosname = MYNAME.** Your Samba server appears under its DNS name unless this name has been assigned to any other machine in the net. If the DNS name is not available, set the server name using netbiosname=MYNAME.

For more details about this parameter, see **man smb.conf**.

- **os level = 2.** This parameter triggers whether your Samba server tries to become LMB (Local Master Browser) for its work group.

  Choose a very low value to protect the existing Windows network from any disturbances caused by a misconfigured Samba server.

For more information about this important topic, see the file /usr/share/doc/packages/samba/htmldocs/howto/NetworkBrowsing.html.

- **wins support and wins server.** To integrate your Samba server into an existing Windows network with an active WINS server, enable the **wins server** option and set its value to the IP address of that WINS server.

  If your Windows computers are connected to separate subnets and should still be aware of each other, you need to set up a WINS server.

  To turn a Samba server into a WINS server, set the wins support option to **Yes** (**wins support = Yes**). Make sure that only one Samba server of the network has this setting enabled.

  The options **wins server** and **wins support** must never be enabled at the same time in the file smb.conf.

[cdrom] and [homes] Shares Configuration Examples   The following examples illustrate how a CD-ROM drive and user directories (homes) can be made available to SMB clients by configuring shares in the file smb.conf:

- **[cdrom].** The following lines make the CD-ROM drive on your Linux server available to the clients:

```
[cdrom]
        comment = Linux CD-ROM
        path    = /media/cdrom
        locking = No
```

You can configure the following:

- **[cdrom].** This is the name of the share that can be seen by all SMB clients on the network.

- **comment.** Use this to an additional comment that describes the share.

- **path.** This is the path for exporting the cdrom directory (such as **path = /media/cdrom**).

By means of a very restrictive default configuration, this kind of share is only made available to the users present on this system.

If this share should be made available to everybody, add a

guest ok = yes line to the configuration. This setting gives read permissions to anyone on the network.

You need to handle this parameter with great care, especially when using it in the [global] section.

- **[homes].** If a user has a valid account and password for the Linux file server and his own home directory, he can be connected to it through the [homes] share.

The following is an example of a configured [homes] share:

```
[homes]
        comment = Home Directories
        valid users = %S
        browseable = No
        read only = No
        create mask = 0640
        directory mask = 750
        inherit permissions = Yes
```

Configure the following:

- **[homes].** As long as there is no other share using the share name of the user connecting to the SMB server, a share is dynamically generated using the [homes] share directives. The resulting name of the share is identical to the user name.

- **valid users = %S.** %S is replaced with the actual name of the share as soon as a connection has been successfully established.

  For a [homes] share, this is always identical to the user's name. As a consequence, access rights to a user's share are restricted exclusively to the user.

- **browseable = No.** This setting enables the share to be invisible in the network environment.

- **read only = No.** By default, Samba prohibits write access to any exported share by means of this parameter.

  To make a share writable, set the value **read only = No**, which is synonymous with writeable = Yes.

- **create mask = 0640.** Systems that are based on Windows NT do not understand the concept of UNIX permissions, so they cannot assign permissions when creating a file.

  This parameter defines the access permissions assigned to newly-created files. This only applies to writable shares.

  In this example, the owner has read and write permissions and the members of the owner's primary group have read permissions.

NOTE The parameter **valid users = %S** prevents read access even if the group has read permissions. If you want the group to have read or write access, you need to deactivate the line valid users = %S.

Share Password Protection The SMB protocol comes from the DOS and Windows environment and directly considers the problem of security.

Each share access can be protected with a password. SMB has three possible ways of checking the permissions:

- **Share Level Security (security = share).** A password is firmly assigned to a share. Everyone who knows this password has access to that share.

- **User Level Security (security = user).** All users must register with the server with their own password. After registering, the server can grant access to individual exported shares dependent on user names.

- **Server Level Security (security = server).** To its clients, Samba pretends to be working in User Level Mode. However, it passes all password queries to another User Level Mode Server, which takes care of authentication. This setting expects an additional parameter (**password server =**).

Setting share, user, and server level security applies to the entire server. It is not possible to offer individual shares of a server configuration with share level security and others with user level security. However, you can run a separate Samba server for each configured IP address on a system.

NOTE

> For additional information about password security, check the Samba HOWTO Collection.

How to Configure a Samba Server with YaST

To configure a Samba server with YaST, do the following:

1. From the KDE desktop, start the YaST Samba Server module by doing one of the following:

   - Select the **YaST** icon, enter the root *password*, and select **OK**; then select **Network Services > Samba Server**.

     or

   - Open a terminal window and enter **sux –** and the root *password*; then enter **yast2 samba-server**.

The dialog box shown in Figure 8–17 appears.

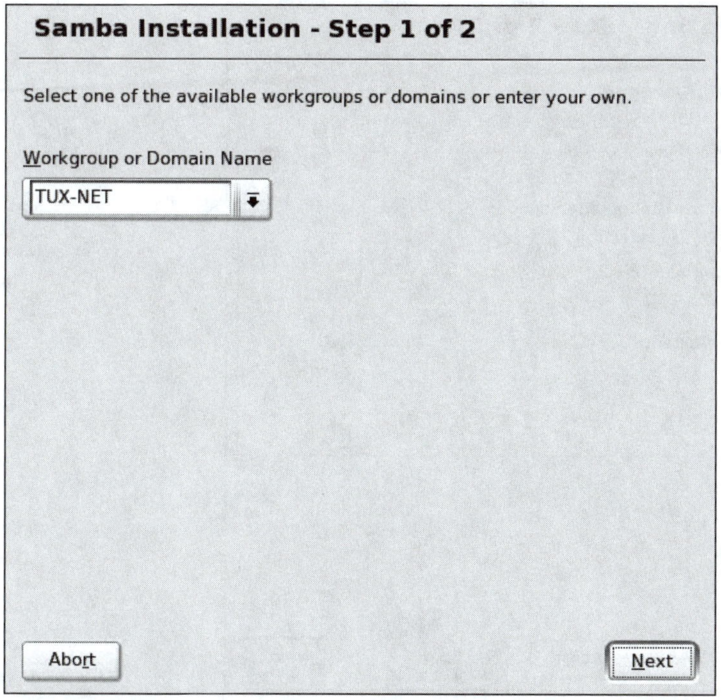

Samba Installation - Step 1 of 2

Select one of the available workgroups or domains or enter your own.

Workgroup or Domain Name

| TUX-NET | ⬇ |

| Abort | | Next |

Figure 8-17

2. From the drop–down list, select an available **_workgroup_** or **_domain_** on the network (detected by YaST), or enter a name.

3. Continue by selecting **Next**.

The dialog box shown in Figure 8-18 appears.

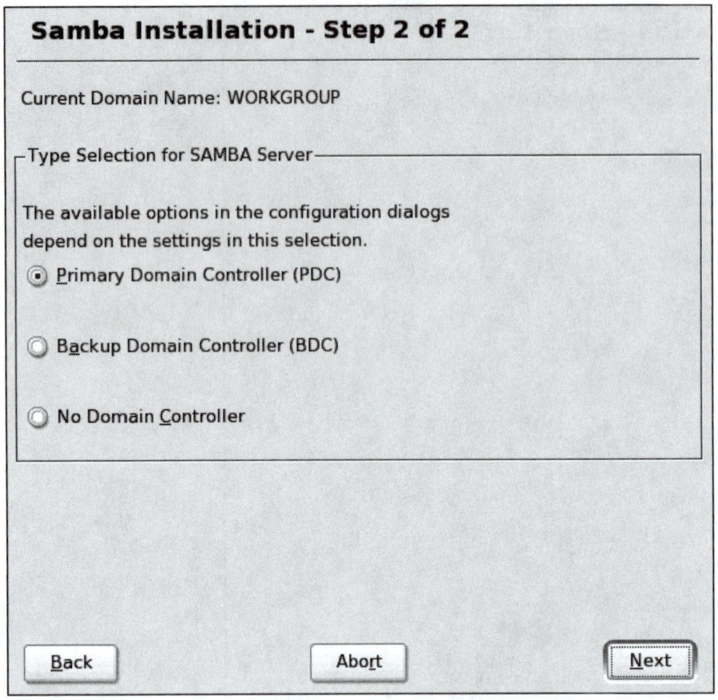

Samba Installation - Step 2 of 2

Current Domain Name: WORKGROUP

┌─Type Selection for SAMBA Server───────────────────────────┐

The available options in the configuration dialogs
depend on the settings in this selection.

⦿ <u>P</u>rimary Domain Controller (PDC)

◯ <u>B</u>ackup Domain Controller (BDC)

◯ No Domain <u>C</u>ontroller

└──┘

[<u>B</u>ack]   [Abort]   [<u>N</u>ext]

Figure 8-18

4. Select a *domain controller* type for your Samba server; then select **Next**.

   Normally, you will want to select **Primary Domain Controller** to use the locally-defined users and passwords for security purposes.

The dialog box shown in Figure 8-19 appears.

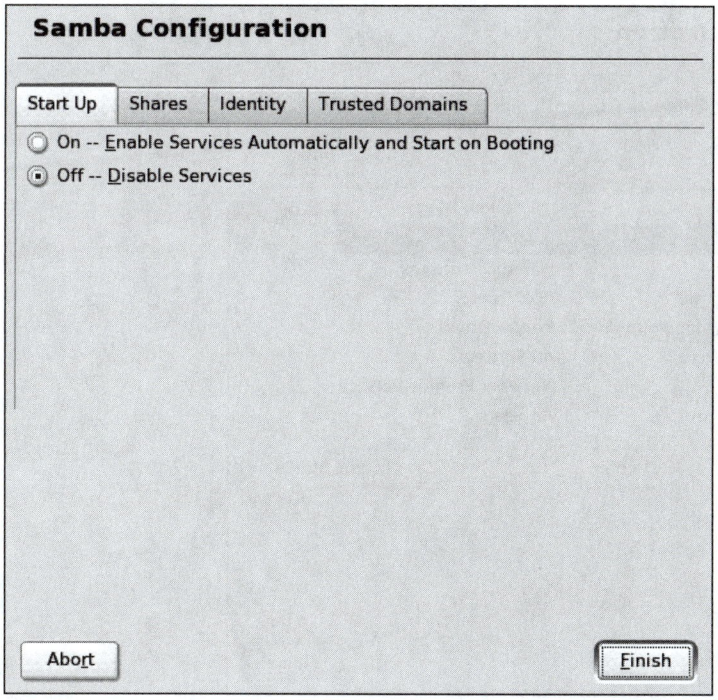

Samba Configuration

| Start Up | Shares | Identity | Trusted Domains |

○ On -- Enable Services Automatically and Start on Booting
◉ Off -- Disable Services

Abort   Finish

Figure 8-19

The four tabs on the dialog box let you configure startup, shares, identity, and trusted domains for your Samba server.

5. Configure the system services to start on bootup by selecting **On**.

6. Display a list of configured shares by selecting **Shares**.

The list of available shares appears, as shown in Figure 8-20.

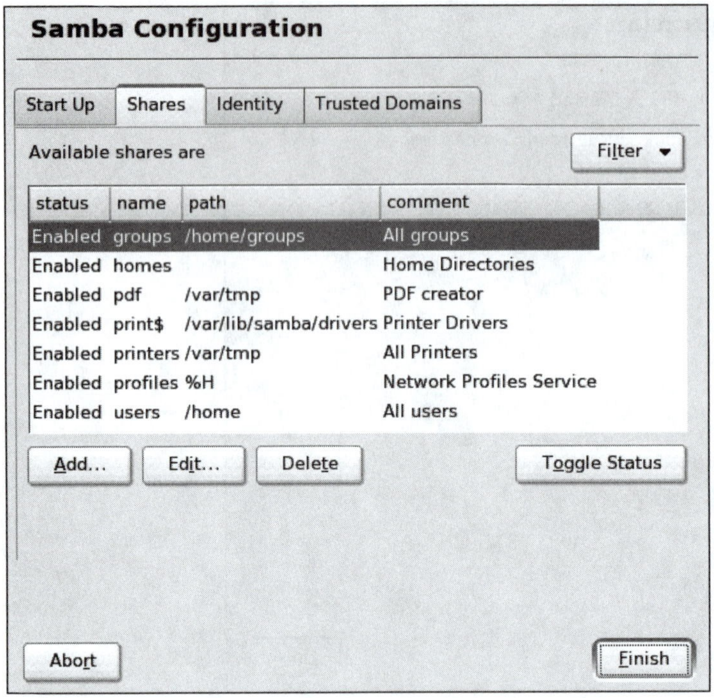

Samba Configuration

| Start Up | Shares | Identity | Trusted Domains |

Available shares are   Filter ▾

status	name	path	comment
Enabled	groups	/home/groups	All groups
Enabled	homes		Home Directories
Enabled	pdf	/var/tmp	PDF creator
Enabled	print$	/var/lib/samba/drivers	Printer Drivers
Enabled	printers	/var/tmp	All Printers
Enabled	profiles	%H	Network Profiles Service
Enabled	users	/home	All users

Add...   Edit...   Delete   Toggle Status

Abort   Finish

Figure 8-20

You can manage the available shares list by adding (**Add**), editing (**Edit**), or deleting (**Delete**) shares.

You can also enable or disable a selected share by selecting **Toggle Status**. Disabled indicates that the share will not be activated when you boot the server.

7. Display options for configuring the Samba server identity by selecting **Identity**.

The Identity tab appears, as shown in Figure 8-21.

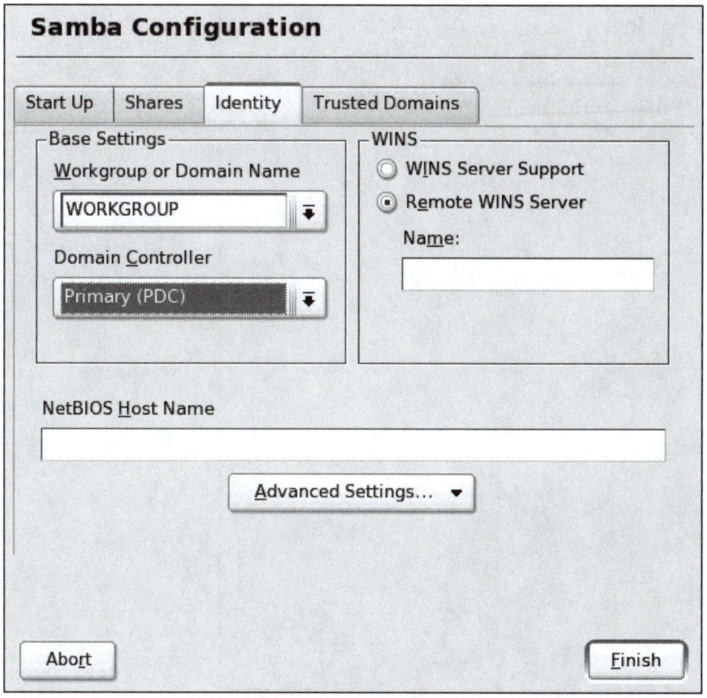

Samba Configuration

| Start Up | Shares | Identity | Trusted Domains |

Base Settings

Workgroup or Domain Name

WORKGROUP

Domain Controller

Primary (PDC)

WINS

○ WINS Server Support

● Remote WINS Server

Name:

NetBIOS Host Name

Advanced Settings... ▾

Abort   Finish

Figure 8-21

You can change the base settings you configured during installation (**Workgroup or Domain Name** and **Domain Controller**).

You can also configure the host as a WINS server, or enter the IP address of a WINS server on the network. If you enter an asterisk (*), YaST will automatically find the WINS server.

In addition, you can determine whether to use an alternative host name in the network by entering the name in the **NetBIOS Host Name** field.

8. Display a list of trusted domains by selecting Trusted Domains.

The Trusted Domains List appears, as shown in Figure 8-22.

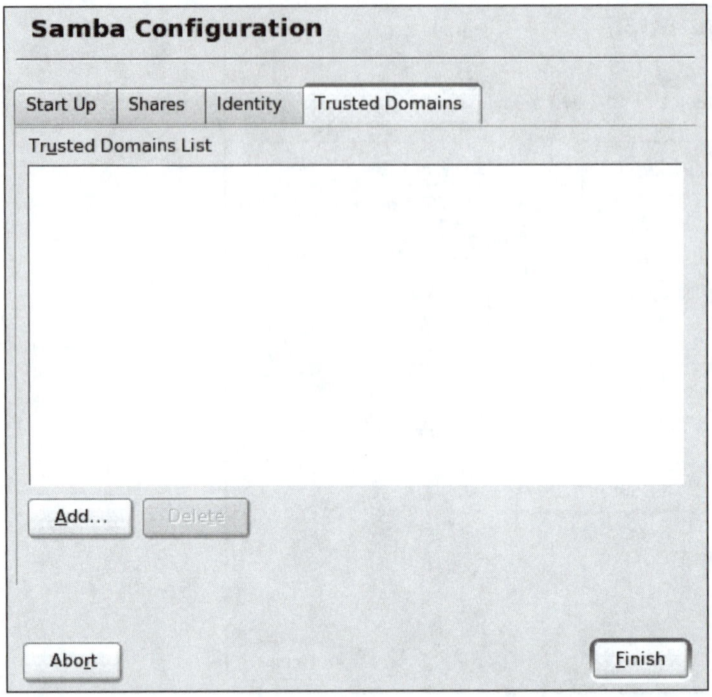

Figure 8-22

You can manage the list of which domains the host can trust by adding (**Add**) or deleting (**Delete**) domains.

Remember that adding a trusted domain means that you adopt the respective settings of that domain.

9. When you finish configuring the Samba server, save the settings by selecting **Finish**.

10. (Optional) If you started YaST from the desktop, close the **YaST Control Center**.

How to Configure a Samba Client with YaST

To configure a Samba client with YaST, do the following:

1. Start the YaST Samba Client module by doing one of the following:

   - From the desktop, start the YaST Control Center by selecting **Start Applications > System > YaST**; then select **Network Services > Samba Client**.

     or

   - From a terminal window, enter **yast2 samba-client**.

   The SAMBA Workgroup dialog box appears, as shown in Figure 8-23.

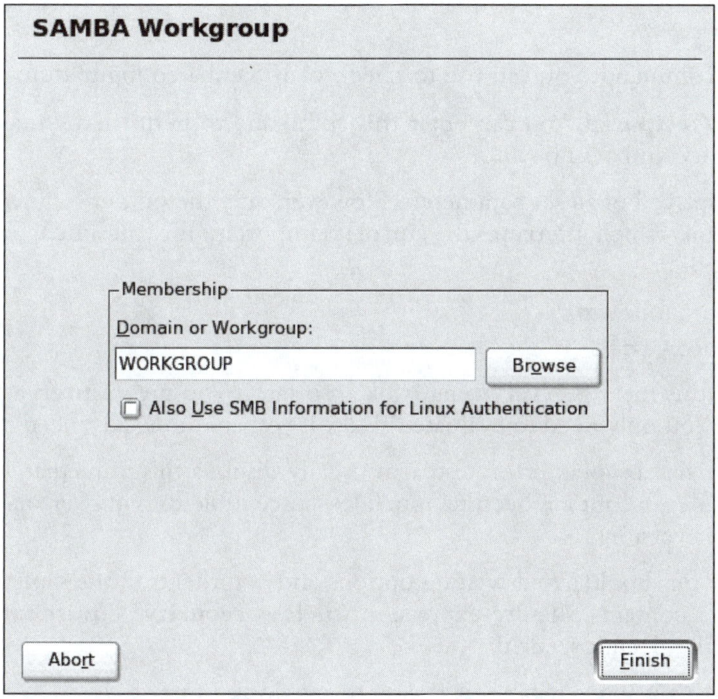

8

SAMBA Workgroup

Membership
Domain or Workgroup:

WORKGROUP   [Browse]

☐ Also Use SMB Information for Linux Authentication

[Abort]   [Finish]

Figure 8-23

2. Enter the name of a **workgroup** or NT **domain** for the Samba client membership, or find and select an available workgroup or domain by selecting **Browse**.

3. Allow for verification of passwords against an NT server by selecting **Also Use SMB Information for Linux Authentication**.

4. When you finish, save the Samba client configuration settings by selecting **Finish**.

5. (Optional) If you started YaST from the desktop, close the **YaST Control Center**.

How to Monitor and Test Samba

After configuring Samba, you need to know the following to monitor and test your configuration:

- Diagnosis Tools
- How to Start and Test Samba

Diagnosis Tools

The following are commands you can use to check your Samba configuration:

- **/usr/bin/testparm.** You can enter this command to perform a syntax check of the file /etc/samba/smb.conf.

  A list is displayed of all set parameters. However, only the output following the last listed section (which interrupts the cursor) is important for your initial check of the configuration.

  Look for the following:

  ```
  Loaded services file OK.
  ```

  If you see this message, everything is okay so far. If you press **Enter**, a long list is displayed. You only need to evaluate this list if you are doing advanced debugging.

  If a service has a syntax error, testparm usually displays this immediately. The file /etc/samba/smb.conf has become much less susceptible to syntax errors compared with earlier versions.

  However, you should avoid writing options and comments in the same line. If the option line contains a faulty expression (such as **security = purchase**), Samba reverts to the default security = user.

  Although this is more reliable, it is easy to overlook in practice.

- **/usr/bin/nmblookup.** You can enter this command to display the registered local or remote names of a host, regardless of the operating system with which NetBIOS is run. (The Microsoft counterpart is nbtstat.)

  You can review the variety of features available with this command by entering **nmblookup –help**.

  The command nmblookup is a bit more verbose with the options –A and –S. When you use the option –S, nmblookup first displays the IP number of the queried host then all names under which they are registered, including all aliases.

However, using the option –A limits the output to the unique entries bearing the same name and the group entries. Both options display the status of the registrations.

When you use the option –M, you can display the local master browser of each workgroup.

- **/usr/bin/smbclient.** You can use this command for checking network resources as well as for establishing connections. The following is a recommended command syntax:

  smbclient –L // *hostname* [–I *IP_address* –U *username*]

  This provides a list of all shares on the specific host as well as the member and group names of the host.

  Occasionally, the host address of the target host must be specified with **–I *IP_address*.** If there are special shares linked to a user authentication, the login name must be included using

  –U *username*.

- **/usr/bin/smbstatus.** You can use this command to list all currently existing connections to the Samba server.

How to Start and Test Samba

All the Samba server really needs is the file /etc/samba/smb.conf with an entry about the workgroup. Entering the following lines in the configuration file is enough to start the server:

```
[global]
   workgroup = TUX-NET
   encrypt passwords = yes
   guest account = nobody
```

Entering **rcsmb start** at the command line is enough to make the host visible with its host name in a Windows environment.

You can use nmblookup to see whether the new Samba host is already visible in the network environment (such as **nmblookup earth**).

NOTE

If nmb does not run, nmblookup does not seem to come up with a sensible response. Try entering **rcnmb start && rcsmb start** instead of rcsmb start.

Exercise 8-3   Configure a Basic Samba Server

In this exercise, you do the following:

- Part I: Configure the Samba Client
- Part II: Configure the Samba Server

Part I: Configure the Samba Client

In this part of the exercise, you connect to the instructor's Samba server by doing the following:

1. From the KDE desktop, select the **YaST** icon; then enter a password of **novell** and select **OK**.

   The YaST Control Center appears.

2. Select **Network Services > Samba Client**.

   A Samba Workgroup dialog box appears.

3. In the Domain or Workgroup field, browse to and select or enter **SUSE-CLASS**.

4. Save the changes by selecting **Finish**.

5. Open a terminal window and su to root (**su –**) with a password of **novell**.

6. Connect the instructor's Samba server by entering the following:

   smbclient //10.0.0.254/sles9 –U geeko

7. Enter a password of **N0v3ll**.

   You are logged in to an smbclient session.

8. View the files on the share by entering **dir**.

9. Copy the file manual.pdf to the local directory /tmp by entering the following:

   lcd /tmp

   cd SUSE-SLES-Version-9/CD1/docu/en

   get manual.pdf

10. End the smbclient session by entering **quit**.

11. Create the directory /mnt/sles9-2 by entering

    mkdir –p /mnt/sles9–2.

12. Mount the remote CIFS filesystem to the local host by entering the following:

    mount -t smbfs -o username=geeko,password=N0v3ll //10.0.0.254/ sles9 /mnt/sles9-2

    Now the files on the instructor's system are accessible through the NFS and CIFS protocols.

13. Verify that the file system mounted by entering **mount**.

14. View the files in the directory by entering **ls -l /mnt/sles9-2**.

Part II: Configure the Samba Server

In this part of the exercise you configure a basic CIFS server using YaST to configure Samba.

Do the following:

1. From the terminal window, create the user account geeko for the Samba server by entering **smbpasswd -a geeko**.

2. Enter a password of **N0v3ll** twice.

3. Verify that the user geeko was added to the Samba user database by entering **cat /etc/samba/smbpasswd**.

4. From the YaST Control Center, select **Network Services > Samba Server**.

    A Samba Configuration dialog box appears.

5. Select the **Startup** tab; then select **On - Enable Service Automatically and Start on Booting**.

6. Select the **Shares** tab.

7. Add a share by selecting **Add**.

    An Add New Share dialog box appears.

8. Enter the following:

    - Share Name: **data2**
    - Description: **DBA data**
    - Share Type: **Directory**
    - Share Path: **/export/data2/**

9. When you finish, select **OK**.

    You are returned to the Samba Configuration dialog box, and the share data2 is added to the list.

10. Save the changes to the system by selecting **Finish**.

    A dialog box appears requesting a root password.

11. Enter **novell** twice; then select **OK**.

12. From the terminal window, view the CIFS shares enabled in the Samba configuration by entering the following:

    smbclient -L localhost -U geeko

13. Enter a password of **N0v3ll**.

14. Open a Konqueror browser window; then enter the following URI:

    smb://geeko@*your_IP_address*/data2

    An authentication dialog box appears.

15. Authenticate as **geeko** with a password of **N0v3ll**; then select **OK**.

16. From Konqueror, access a partner's /export/data2 directory by entering the following:

    smb://geeko:N0v3ll@*your_partner's_IP_address*/data2

    An authentication dialog box appears.

17. When you finish, close all open windows.

OBJECTIVE 3   MANAGE RESOURCES ON THE NETWORK

To manage resources on the network, you need to understand the following:

- Network Information Service (NIS)
- LDAP

Network Information Service (NIS)

When multiple Linux/UNIX systems in a network are configured to access common resources, it becomes important that all user and group identities are the same for all computers in that network.

In other words, the network should be transparent to the user. No matter which machine a user logs in to, that user should always see exactly the same environment.

You can meet this requirement by using Network Information Service (NIS) and Network File System (NFS) services. NFS distributes file systems over a network and is discussed in *Network File System*.

To configure NIS for your network, you need to know the following:

- Network Information Service Basics
- NIS Domain Components
- NIS Configuration Overview
- How to Configure a NIS Master Server with YaST

- How to Configure an NFS Server Manually
- How to Configure Maps Manually
- How to Configure a Slave Server
- How to Configure a NIS Client with YaST
- How to Configure MIS Users with YaST
- NIS Security Considerations
- NIS Utilities

Network Information Service Basics

NIS is a database system that allows the centralized administration of configuration files. NIS enables centralized user management and printer administration as well.

In addition, NIS makes administration of large networks easier by distributing configuration files to individual workstations. NIS is usually installed with the network file system (NFS)—the user's configuration files and home directories are administered centrally on one or more servers.

Linux administrators originally referred to NIS as "YP," which simply stands for the idea of the network's "yellow pages." The names of specific components of NIS still use the YP (such as ypbind, ypserv, and yppasswd).

The NIS server stores the files to distribute over the whole network in maps. The files are stored in a special database format with the corresponding keys.

For example, the file /etc/passwd can be converted to a database using the UID or user name as the key. The respective database files are then called passwd.byuid or passwd. byname.

Other files that are often converted to map databases for distribution across a network include /etc/passwd, /etc/shadow, /etc/group, /etc/hosts, and /etc/services.

NIS Domain Components

In a NIS domain, there are three types of computers:

- **Master server.** All important configuration files distributed across the network are stored on the master server. These configuration files are converted to NIS maps (files in DBM format) and distributed to slave servers.

  Daemons run on the master server and are responsible for processing the NIS clients' requests. The NIS server program is ypserv.

- **Slave servers.** Slave servers help the master server process requests. For example, they can process NIS requests if the master server cannot be accessed.

  After the maps on the master server have been updated, they are automatically passed to the slave servers. Either a master server or a slave server can respond to requests. The first response that arrives is used.

- **NIS clients.** NIS clients retrieve the configuration files (stored as maps) from the NIS server. You can configure a client to completely ignore local configuration files and to use only the NIS maps.

  You can also configure a client to use both local configuration files and NIS maps in any order. The NIS client program is ypbind.

The NIS servers, together with their clients, form a NIS domain, that works as illustrated in Figure 8-24.

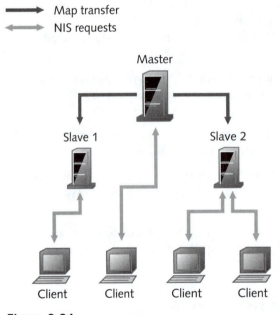

Figure 8-24

You can configure these components with YaST or manually.

NIS Configuration Overview

The name of the NIS domain is stored in the file /etc/defaultdomain and the server to address is written to the file /etc/yp.conf.

If several NIS servers are in the domain (such as a master server and a number of slave servers), it makes sense to enter the slave servers first then the master server in yp.conf.

On a slave server, first the local NIS server should be addressed, then any other existing slave servers, and finally the master server.

The following is an example:

```
DA50:~ # cat /etc/yp.conf
ypserver 127.0.0.1
ypserver 192.168.0.20
ypserver 192.168.0.1
```

On the slave server, first the local host is queried (127.0.0.1). If this is not available, another slave server (192.168.0.20) is queried. If this does not respond, the master server (192.168.0.1) is contacted.

The NIS client must be configured so it uses the NIS maps instead of or in addition to the local configuration files. The configuration file you need to modify is /etc/nsswitch.conf.

The order of queries is also determined by this configuration file. This file contains an entry for almost every configuration file that can be administered across the network.

The following is an example:

```
passwd:         compat
group:          compat

hosts:          files nis dns
services:       files
protocols:      files
```

In this example, the entry for name resolution (**hosts: files nis dns**) means that first the local file /etc/hosts is queried, then the corresponding NIS map, and finally the DNS server.

The entry **compat** for passwd and group means that a compatibility mode should be used for programs linked to older versions of the GNU C Library.

To achieve this, an entry is added automatically by YaST as a last entry in the files /etc/passwd and /etc/group.

This entry specifies that the contents of the NIS maps should be regarded as an extension of the files and should be evaluated after the local files.

If only the NIS maps should be used, you need to modify the entries for passwd and shadow in the file /etc/nsswitch.conf as follows:

```
passwd: nis
group: nis
```

For additional information on nsswitch.conf, enter **man nsswitch.conf**.

NOTE

How to Configure a NIS Master Server with YaST

To use YaST to configure your host as a NIS server, do the following:

1. From the KDE desktop, start the YaST NIS Server module by doing one of the following:

   - Select the **YaST** icon, enter the root *password*, and select **OK**; then select **Network Services > NIS Server**.

     or

   - Open a terminal window and enter **sux –** and the root *password*; then enter **yast2 nis_server**.

   The NIS Server Setup dialog box appears, as shown in Figure 8-25.

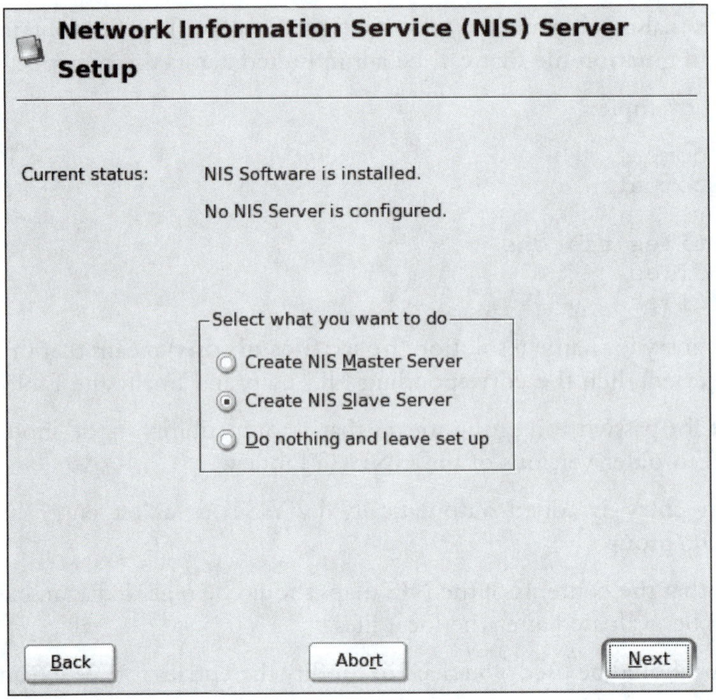

Network Information Service (NIS) Server Setup

Current status: NIS Software is installed.

No NIS Server is configured.

┌─ Select what you want to do ─────────────┐
│ ○ Create NIS Master Server   │
│ ⦿ Create NIS Slave Server   │
│ ○ Do nothing and leave set up   │
└──┘

[Back]   [Abort]   [Next]

Figure 8-25

This initial NIS server configuration dialog box lets you create a master NIS server or a slave NIS server.

2. Do one of the following:

   - If no NIS server exists so far in your network, select **Create NIS Master Server**.

- If you already have a NIS master server in the network (as indicated under Current status), you can add a NIS slave server by selecting **Create NIS Slave Server**.

  For example, you might want to create a slave server if you want to configure a new subnetwork.

- If you want to quit the NIS server setup, select **Do nothing and leave set up**.

3. Create a NIS Master Server by doing the following:

   a. Select **Create NIS Master Server**.

      The dialog box shown in Figure 8-26 appears.

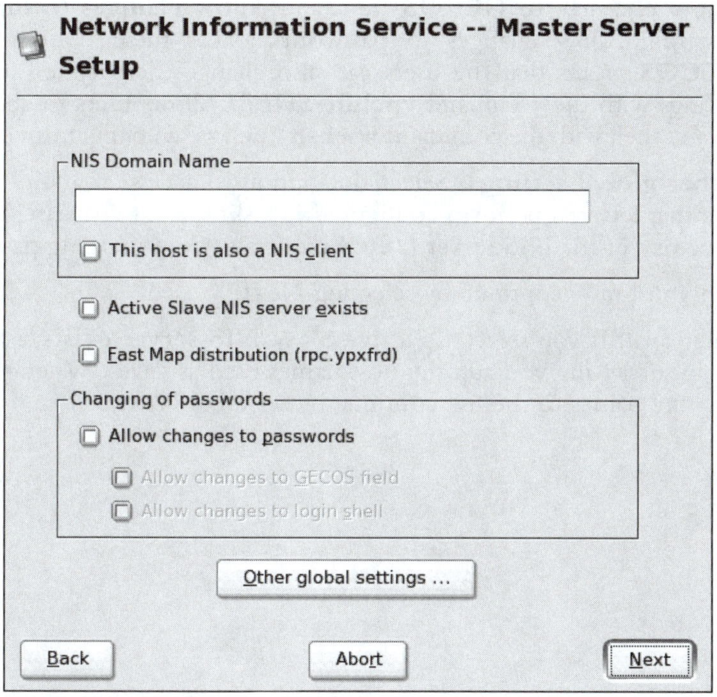

8

Network Information Service -- Master Server Setup

NIS Domain Name

☐ This host is also a NIS client

☐ Active Slave NIS server exists

☐ Fast Map distribution (rpc.ypxfrd)

Changing of passwords

☐ Allow changes to passwords

   ☐ Allow changes to GECOS field

   ☐ Allow changes to login shell

Other global settings ...

Back   Abort   Next

Figure 8-26

   b. Enter the NIS server *domain name* in the **NIS Domain Name** field.

c. Select from the following options:

- **This host is also a NIS client.** Select this option to indicate that the host should also be a NIS client, enabling users to log in and access data from the NIS server.

- **Active Slave NIS server exists.** Select this option to configure additional NIS servers (slave servers) in your network later.

- **Fast Map distribution.** Select this option to set fast transfer of the database entries from the master to the slave server.

- **Allow changes to passwords.** Select this option to let users in your network (both local users and those managed through the NIS server) to change their passwords on the NIS server (with the command **yppasswd**).

- **Allow changes to GECOS field** and **Allow changes to login shell**. Selecting Allow changes to passwords makes these options available. *GECOS* means that the users can also change their names and address settings with the command **ypchfn**. *SHELL* allows users to change their default shell with the command **ypchsh** (such as switching from bash to sh).

- **Other global settings.** Select this option to access an additional dialog box that lets you perform configuration tasks such as changing the source directory of the NIS server (**/etc/** by default) and merging passwords.

d. When you finish, continue by selecting **Next**.

e. (Conditional) If you selected **Active Slave NIS server exists**, a dialog box appears letting you add the host names used as slaves. When you finish adding the names to the list, continue by selecting **Next**.

The NIS Server Maps Setup dialog box appears, as shown in Figure 8-27.

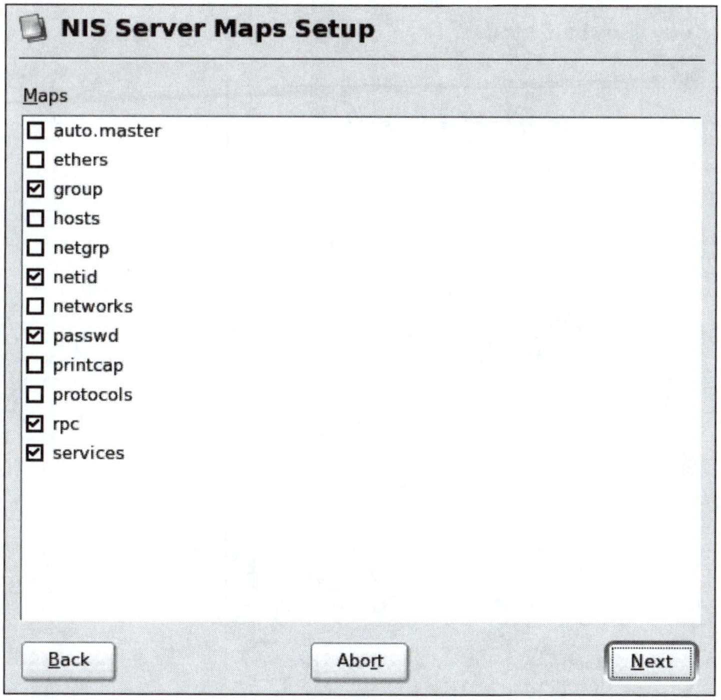

NIS Server Maps Setup

Maps

☐ auto.master
☐ ethers
☑ group
☐ hosts
☐ netgrp
☑ netid
☐ networks
☑ passwd
☐ printcap
☐ protocols
☑ rpc
☑ services

[<u>B</u>ack]   [Abor<u>t</u>]   [<u>N</u>ext]

Figure 8-27

    f. Select the maps (the partial databases) to transfer from the NIS server to the client; then continue by selecting **Next**.

NOTE

The default settings are usually adequate, so you should normally leave them unchanged.

The NIS Server Query Hosts Setup dialog box appears, as shown in Figure 8-28.

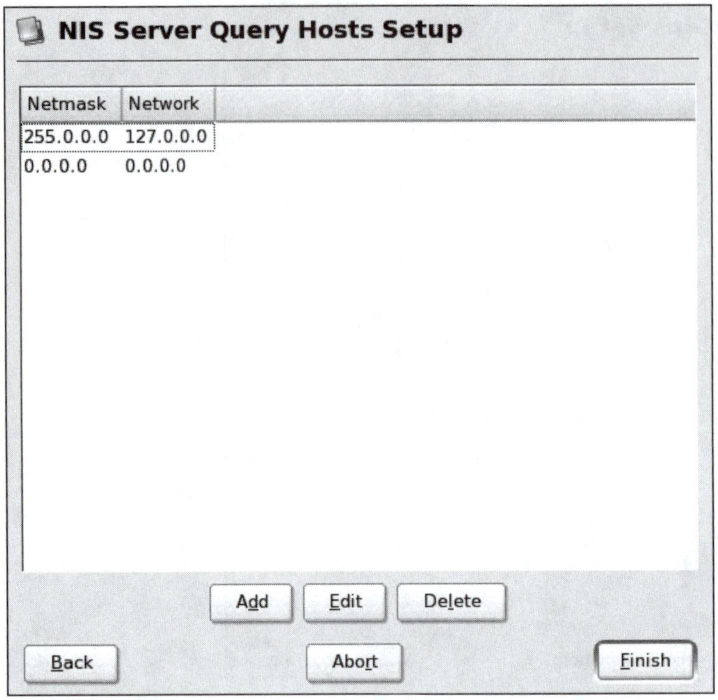

Figure 8-28

This is the last dialog box in the NIS server configuration. It lets you specify from which networks requests can be sent to the NIS server. You can add, edit, or delete networks from the list.

Normally, requests will be sent from your internal network. For example, if this is the case, and your network is **192.168.1.0/24**, you only need the following 2 entries:

255.0.0.0 127.0.0.0

255.255.255.0 192.168.1.0

The entry 127.0.0.0 enables connections from your own host, which is the NIS server. The entry 192.168.1.0 allows all hosts from the network 192.168.1.0/24 to send requests to the server.

g. NIS S(Optional) If you need to change the entry 0.0.0.0, highlight the entry, select **Edit**, make the appropriate changes, and then select **OK**.

h. Add all networks you want to recognize requests from; then save the NIS server configuration settings by selecting **Finish**.

i. (Optional) If you started YaST from the desktop, close the **YaST Control Center**.

How to Configure a NIS Master Server Manually

If you want to configure a NIS server manually, do the following:

- Make sure that the following software packages are installed on the NIS server:

    - **ypserv** (on the NIS server)

    - **ypbind** (on the clients and server)

    - **yp-tools** (contains the NIS utilities)

    - **portmap** (RPC port mapper)

    Because NIS is an RPC service, the port mapper must be started on the server and on the clients. This is done by default in the standard installation of SUSE Linux Enterprise Server.

    You can display the RPC services registered with the port mapper by entering **rpcinfo -p**.

- If you want the NIS server to be started automatically when the system is booted, you need to generate the symbolic links in the respective runlevel directories by entering the following:

    insserv portmap

    insserv yppasswdd

    insserv ypserv

- You also need to set the NIS domain name by using the command ypdomain-name, similar to the following:

    ypdomainname planets

    To make sure the domain name is set correctly the next time the system is booted, you need to include it in the file /etc/defaultdomain.

- Most configuration files for the NIS server are located in the directory /var/yp/. In addition, a number of variables are set in /etc/sysconfig/ypserv.

    Check the following configuration files:

    - **/etc/yp.conf.** This file only exists on the server if it has also been configured as a client. It contains the NIS server for the client to address.

    - **/etc/ypserv.conf.** This file is involved with security aspects of the NIS server daemon ypserv and the transfer daemon ypxfrd.

- **/etc/sysconfig/ypserv.** The following values are stored in this file:

  - **YPPWD_SRCDIR.** The NIS source directory.

  - **YPPWD_CHFN.** Indicates if users can change the GECOS field (Yes or No).

  - **YPPWD_CHSH.** Indicates if users can change their login shell (Yes or No).

- Information about the YP source directory is required to generate the NIS maps.

  You create the NIS maps with the command make, which creates the database files based on information in the Makefile (/var/yp/Makefile).

  You need to edit the following options in the Makefile /var/yp/Makefile:

  - **NOPUSH.** If you are using slave servers, you must set this option to **false**. This makes sure that after NIS maps are generated, they are transferred (pushed) to the slaves.

  - **MINUID and MINGID.** With these options, you can set the lowest UID and GID numbers that are accepted by the NIS maps (such as **MINUID=500** and **MINGID=100**).

  - **all.** After the keyword all, list all the configuration files that should be presented by the NIS server as maps (such as

    all: group netid passwd rpc services).

- There are additional configuration files in the directory /var/yp/ that include the following:

  - **securenets.** This file contains the networks from which the server can be queried.

  - **ypservers.** This file lists the slave servers to which the maps should be transferred if they are modified.

  - **nicknames.** This is a preconfigured file providing an allocation of "nicknames" to existing NIS maps. For example, it is evaluated by ypcat.

How to Configure Maps Manually

To create NIS maps, the Makefile (/var/yp/Makefile) is evaluated. To generate maps using the Makefile, the NIS domain name must be set.

You can display the domain name by entering **ypdomainname**; you can set the domain name by entering

ypdomainnam *domain_name*.

Once you set the NIS domain name, you can create the NIS maps with the command make.

You can run the command from directory where the Makefile is located, or use the option –C followed by the directory where the Makefile is located (such as **make –C /var/yp**).

If the daemon ypserv is not running or if slave servers were entered that are not yet active, the command make gives a series of error messages that you can safely ignore.

The Makefile evaluates the NIS domain names and creates a directory in /var/yp/ with the name of the NIS domain. All NIS maps are stored in DBM format in this directory.

If you want to set up a cron job to regularly regenerate the NIS maps, the option –s (silent) is useful. It ensures that make does not generate any output.

If you make changes to the server configuration with YaST, the NIS maps are regenerated automatically. Changing password data with yppasswd also causes the NIS maps to be updated immediately.

After creating a new user account, you need to run the command make (such as **make –C /var/yp –s**) to include the new user in the NIS maps (see the steps under *How to Configure a NIS Client with YaST*).

How to Configure a Slave Server

Theoretically, a master server and an unlimited number of slave servers can run in a NIS domain. To spread the load evenly, we recommend using slave servers in networks with a large number of NIS clients.

Only copies of the NIS maps exist on the slave server. The copies are automatically updated if changes are made to the maps on the master server.

To copy the maps from the master server to the slave server, you use the program /usr/sbin/yppush.

To configure a slave server, you need to know how to do the following:

- How to Configure a Slave Server on the Master Server
- How to Configure a Slave Server

How to Configure a Slave Server on the Master Server   On the master server, the required settings can be made when you configure the master server with YaST.

By selecting **Active Slave NIS server exists**, the entry for pushing the maps is activated in the Makefile on the server (the option NOPUSH is set to false).

By selecting **Fast Map distribution** on the master, rpc.ypxfrd (the YP transfer daemon) is started, which ensures a quicker transfer of the NIS maps to the slave servers.

The slave servers entered in YaST are written to the file /var/yp/ypservers. Only the slave servers listed there are sent the NIS maps by the master server.

How to Configure a Slave Server Only   You can also configure a slave server by itself with YaST.

After starting the NIS Server module (**Network Services > NIS Server**), select the option **Create NIS Slave Server > Next** and follow the prompts.

As with the master server, the package ypserv is needed on the slave server (installed by default). The symbolic links for starting in the corresponding runlevels are also set automatically by YaST.

The slave server is given the name of the NIS domain for which it should be responsible as well as the IP address of the NIS master server. You also need to decide if the slave server should function as a NIS client and which access permission should be configured.

The Makefile (/var/yp/Makefile) on a slave server does not need to be adjusted, because the maps are only collected from the server and are never generated on the slave.

When the configuration with YaST is finished, the command **/usr/lib/yp/ypinit -s *master-server*** is run once in the background. This causes the slave server to request the maps from the master server.

On the slave server, the maps are also stored in the directory **/var/yp/*NIS-domain-name***. As soon as the maps have been generated on the master server, the slave will automatically receive the new files.

How to Configure a NIS Client with YaST

To use YaST to configure your host as a NIS client, do the following:

1. From the KDE desktop, start the YaST NIS Client module by doing one of the following:

   - Select the **YaST** icon, enter the root *password*, and select **OK**; then select **Network Services > NIS Client**.

     or

   - Open a terminal window and enter **sux –** and the root *password*; then enter **yast2 nis–client**.

The Configuration of NIS client dialog box appears, as shown in Figure 8-29.

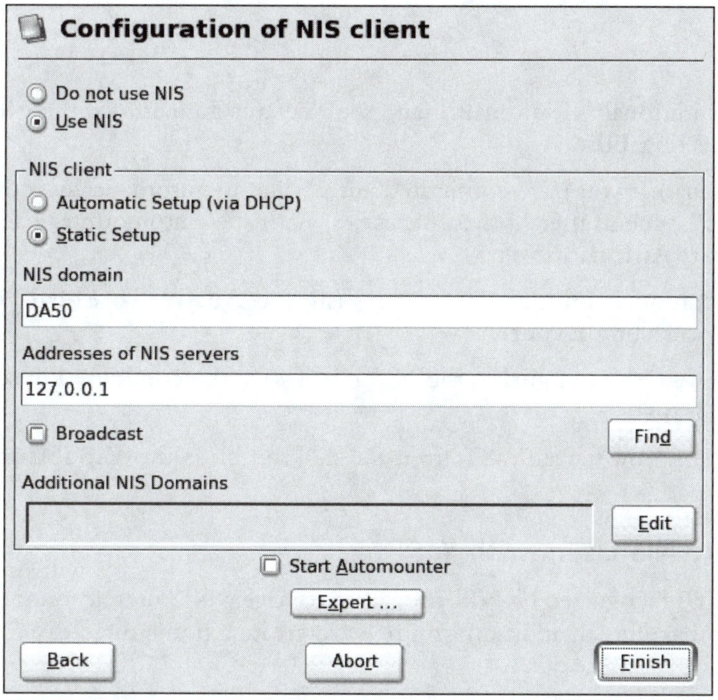

Figure 8-29

2. Make sure **Use NIS** is selected.

3. Do one of the following:

   ■ If the host gets an IP address through DHCP, select **Automatic Setup (via DHCP)**.

   or

   ■ If the host has a static (fixed) IP address, select **Static Setup**.

4. (Conditional) If you select Static Setup, do the following:

   a. In the **NIS domain** field, enter the *NIS domain name*.

   b. In the **Addresses of NIS servers** field, enter the *NIS server IP address*.

      You can also search for and select NIS servers broadcasting in the network by selecting **Find**. Multiple servers in the field need to be separated with spaces.

   c. If you want NIS to search for additional servers in the local network if the configured servers fail to respond, select **Broadcast**.

Selecting this option is not normally recommended due to security risks.

   d. Add additional NIS domains (and set a default domain) for the NIS client by selecting **Edit**.

5. (Conditional) If you have configured auto.* files to automatically mount directories (such as user home directories) with the Automounter daemon, select **Start Automounter**.

6. Access additional configuration options (such as **Answer to Local Host Only**) by selecting **Expert**.

7. When you finish configuring the NIS client, save the configuration settings by selecting **Finish**.

8. (Optional) If you started YaST from the desktop, close the **YaST Control Center**.

How to Configure NIS Users with YaST

In order for users to be recognized by NIS, they need to have a NIS user account created on the NIS server host machine. In addition, you need to create a home directory for the NIS network users.

To configure NIS users on the NIS server host machine, do the following:

1. Create a directory for NIS network users.

   For example, enter the following:

   mkdir -p /export/nis-*hostname*/home

2. From the KDE desktop, start the YaST Edit and create users module by doing one of the following:

   ■ Select the **YaST** icon, enter the root *password*, and select **OK**; then select **Security and Users > Edit and create users**.

   or

   ■ Open a terminal window and enter **sux -** and the root *password*; then enter **yast2 users**.

The User and Group Administration dialog box appears, as shown in Figure 8-30.

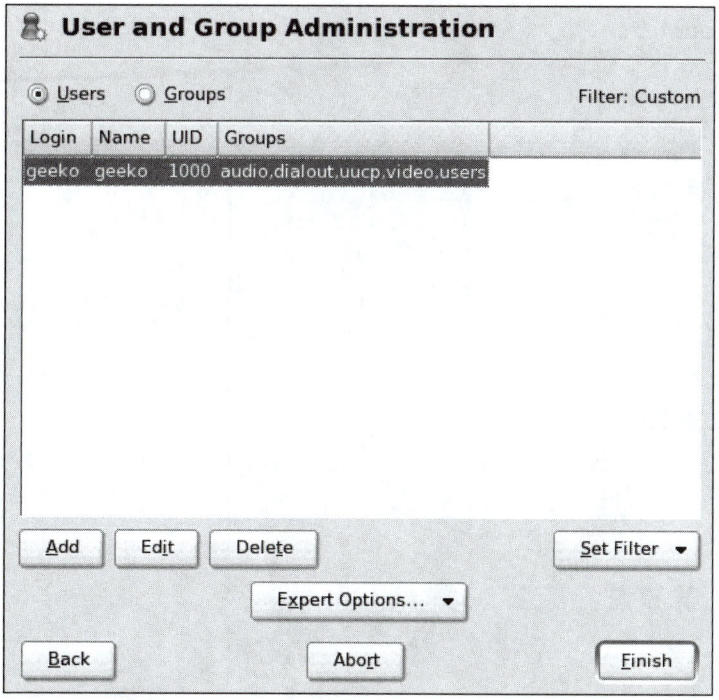

Figure 8-30

3. Select **Set Filter**; then select **Local Users**.
4. Create a new user by selecting **Add**.

The Add a New Local User dialog box appears, as shown in Figure 8-31.

Figure 8-31

5. Enter a *full user name*, *user login ID*, and *password* (twice).
6. Select **Details**.

The dialog box shown in Figure 8-32 appears.

Figure 8-32

7. In the **Home Directory** field, enter the *home directory* for the user based on the directory you created for the NIS network users (such as **/export/nis-hostname/home/joe/**).

   You can also edit user properties such as the default login shell and the default group (see the Help information in the dialog box).

8. When you finish configuring the additional user properties, continue by selecting **Next**.

   You are returned to the Add a New Local User dialog box.

9. Add the user by selecting **Create**.

   You are returned to the User and Group Administration dialog box.

10. With the *new user* selected in the list, select **Set Filter**; then select **NIS Users**.

    Notice that the user has not been added as a NIS account.

11. Save the changes by selecting **Finish**.

    Although you have created the user account, users do not show up in NIS until the maps are updated. Accounts need to be created in the file /etc/passwd and then ported to NIS.

12. Open a terminal window.

13. Change to the directory /var/yp/ by entering **cd /var/yp**.

14. Update the NIS maps by entering **make**.

15. From the Yast Control Center, select **Security and Users > Edit and Create Users** (or enter **yast2 users**).

16. Select **Set Filter > NIS Users**.

    The new user account is now displayed.

17. Close the **User and Group Administration** dialog box and the **YaST Control Center**.

NIS Security Considerations

An important question when implementing NIS is that of access protection. How can you restrict access to a NIS domain and the information stored there to computers that can be trusted?

You can configure this type of restriction in the file /var/yp/securenets. All networks that require access to the NIS server must be listed in this file.

For example, the following securenets file provides for the NIS server to be accessible from the network 192.168.0.0/24, from the computer 192.l68.1.1, and from itself (with access refused to all other computers):

```
255.0.0.0 127.0.0.0
255.255.255.0 192.168.0.0
255.255.255.255 192.168.1.1
```

Entries for individual computers can also be made with the keyword host (such as **host 192.168.1.1**). Although not accepted by YaST, this option can be used when editing the file manually.

For additional information on the structure of the file /var/yp/securenets, enter **man 8 ypserv**.

NOTE

Only IP addresses are valid in /var/yp/securenets; you cannot use host or network names.

If you are using a version of ypserv in which TCP wrapper support is still included, the files /etc/hosts.allow and /etc/hosts.deny must be modified accordingly.

For details, enter **man 5 hosts_access** or **man 5 hosts_options**.

NIS Utilities

There are many utilities available for NIS. Some are for diagnostic purposes, but others are normal user programs (such as such as yppasswd for changing the NIS password).

These utilities are in the package yp-tools. The following are some of the more commonly used utilities:

- **/bin/ypdomainname.** If you enter **ypdomainname** without options, the command displays the name of the current NIS domain.

  To set a new domain name, use the command ypdomainname. For example, to set the current domain name to planets, enter **ypdomainname planets**.

- **/usr/bin/ypwhich.** You can use this utility to display the NIS server used by the client.

  You can also query the NIS client on other machines for the server addressed by it (as in the following):

  ```
  DA50:~ # ypwhich
  sun.example.com
  DA50:~ # ypwhich sun.example.com
  localhost
  ```

  In this example, entering ypwhich displays which NIS server the local computer is using (**sun.exmaple.com**). By entering ypwhich sun.example.com you find out which NIS server sun.example.com is using (**localhost**).

  By using the option -m, you can display all NIS maps with the NIS master server to which they belong (as in the following):

  ```
  DA50:~ # ypwhich -m
  passwd.byname sun.example.com
  passwd.byuid sun.example.com
  services.byname sun.example.com
  services.byservicename sun.example.com
  rpc.byname sun.example.com
  rpc.bynumber sun.example.com
  group.byname sun.example.com
  group.bygid sun.example.com
  ypservers sun.example.com
  netid.byname sun.example.com
  ```

- **/usr/bin/ypcat.** You can use this utility to display the contents of a NIS database file (map). Include either the nickname (such as passwd) or the name of the map itself (such as passwd.byuid).

- **/usr/bin/ypmatch.** You can use this utility to query the key field of a NIS map such as passwd.byname or passwd.byuid, and have the corresponding entry for the field displayed.

  For example, to search in the map passwd.byuid for the user with a UID of 500, you would enter

  ypmatch 500 passwd.byuid.

- **/usr/bin/yppasswd.** You can use this utility to change the password of the user on the NIS server.

  This command requires that rpc.yppasswdd (the YP password daemon) is running on the NIS master server.

  When you use this command, the password in the file /etc/shadow on the NIS server is changed and the corresponding NIS maps are automatically regenerated.

  If slave servers exist, the modified maps are also transferred to them automatically.

  The same applies for the commands ypchfn and ypchsh, which users can use to change their description field and their standard shell.

  If the user has changed her password, it is valid immediately. However, if she logs in again immediately, the old password might still be expected.

  This is because the nscd (Name Service Cache Daemon) saves various information in its cache for a certain length of time. What information is stored and for how long is defined in the configuration file /etc/nscd.conf.

  The contents of the file passwd are stored for 10 minutes (600s) by default.

  You can shorten the time for which the old password is still valid by changing this value, or you can turn off nscd by entering **rcnscd stop** or restart it by entering **rcnscd restart**.

- **/usr/sbin/yppoll.** You can use this utility to display the ID number of a NIS map used by the NIS server.

  This ID number is assigned by the system. It changes whenever a map is updated. Use the command whenever you want to make sure your servers are using the most current version of a NIS map.

  The syntax of yppoll is

  yppoll [-h *host*] [-d *domain*] *mapname*

  Replace *mapname* with the full name of the NIS map. The command cannot handle nicknames. Table 8-4 describes the options.

Table 8-4

Option	Description
-h *host*	This option enables you to specify a server other than the default server. To find out which server the command defaults to, use the command ypwhich. If a host is not specified, the server polled is the default server.
-d *domain*	This option enables you to specify a domain other than the default domain. To find out which domain the command defaults to, use the command ypdomainname. If domain is not specified, the domain polled is the default domain.

Exercise 8-4   Enable Network Information Service (NIS) on Your Network

In this exercise, you do the following:

- Part 1: Configure a NIS Server YaST
- Part II: Create a NIS User
- Part III: Update the NIS Maps
- Part IV: Verify a Local NIS Configuration
- Part V: Prepare for NIS Network Users
- Part VI: Configure the NIS Client Using YaST

In this exercise, you work with a partner in class with one of you acting as the NIS server, and the other as the NIS client.

 IMPORTANT: For this exercise to work properly, all the steps need to be done in sequence.

CAUTION

For example, in Part V complete the steps on the NFS server computer before completing the steps on the NFS client computer.

Part I: Configure a NIS Server with YaST

From the NIS server computer, do the following:

1. From the KDE desktop, select the **YaST** icon; then enter a password of **novell** and select **OK**.

   The YaST Control Center appears.

2. Select **Network Services > NIS Server**.

   The Network Information Service (NIS) Server Setup dialog box appears.

3. Select **Create NIS Master Server**; then continue by selecting **Next**.

   The Master Server Setup dialog box appears.

4. In the NIS Domain Name field enter **NIS-DA***xx* (where *xx* is the host number of your server).

   For example, if your server hostname is DA50, you would enter **NIS-DA50**.

5. Select the following options:

   - **This host is also a NIS client**
   - **Fast Map distribution (rpc.ypxfrd)**
   - **Allow changes to passwords**
   - **Allow changes to GECOS field**
   - **Allow changes to login shell**

6. Continue by selecting **Next**.

   A NIS Server Maps Setup dialog box appears.

7. From the list of server maps, deselect **netid**; then make sure that **group**, **passwd**, **rpc**, and **services** are selected.

8. Continue by selecting **Next**.

   The NIS Server Query Hosts Setup dialog box appears.

9. Accept the default settings and complete the NIS server setup by selecting **Finish**.

Part II: Create a NIS User

Before testing the NIS configuration, you need to create a NIS user on the computer where the NIS server is configured.

From the NIS server computer, do the following:

1. From a terminal window, su to root (**su -**) with a password of **novell**.

2. Create the directory /export/nis-xx/home for NIS network users by entering the following:

   mkdir -p /export/nis-*xx***/home** (where *xx* is the host number of your server)

3. From the YaST Control Center, select **Security and Users > Edit and create users**.

   The User and Group Administration dialog box appears.

4. Select **Set Filter**; then select **NIS Users**.

   Notice that when you create new users are added as NIS users by default.

5. Select **Set Filter**; then select **Local Users**.

6. Create a new user by selecting **Add**.

   The Add a New Local User dialog box appears.

7. Enter the following (where **xx** is the host number of your server):

   - Full User Name: **dbaxx**

   - User Login: **dbaxx**

   - Password: **N0v3ll**

   - Verify password: **N0v3ll**

8. Select **Details**.

   A Details dialog box appears.

9. In the Home Directory field, enter **/export/nis-xx/home/dbaxx**; then select **Next**.

10. Continue by selecting **Create**.

    Notice that the user dba**xx** is listed with the other users.

11. Select **Set Filter**; then select **NIS Users**.

    The maps have not been updated, so the user dba**xx** is not listed as a NIS user.

12. Save the changes by selecting **Finish**.

13. From the terminal window, enter **ls -l /export/nis-xx/home/**.

    Check to make sure that the owner of the directory **dbaxx** is the user dba**xx**.

14. (Conditional) If dba**xx** is not the owner, then enter the following:

    chown -R dbaxx.users /export/nis-xx/home/dbaxx

Part III: Update the NIS Maps

From the NIS server computer, update the NIS maps by doing the following:

1. From the terminal window, make sure that the yp services are running by entering the following;

   rcypserv restart

2. Change to the directory /var/yp by entering **cd /var/yp**.

3. Update the NIS maps by entering **make**.

Part IV: Verify a Local NIS Configuration

From the NIS server computer, do the following:

1. Switch to a virtual console by entering **Ctrl+Alt+F2**.

2. Log in as **dba**xx with a password of **N0v3ll**.

   You are now ready to test the configuration.

3. Check the NIS domain by entering **domainname**.

   You see NIS-DA**xx** listed.

4. Change the GECOS field by entering **chfn**; then enter a password of **N0v3ll**.

5. Enter the following values:

   - Room Number: **Classroom**
   - Work Phone: **555-1212**
   - Home Phone: **444-1212**

6. Su to root (**su -**) with a password of **novell**.

7. Update the NIS maps by changing to the directory /var/yp

   (**cd /var/yp**) and entering **make**.

8. Verify that the NIS map was updated by entering the following:

   ypcat passwd

9. Return to the KDE desktop by pressing **Ctrl+Alt+F7**.

Part V: Prepare for NIS Network Users

A NIS user needs a home directory on the NIS client computer.

In this part of the exercise, you work with a partner to create an NFS export of the NIS home directory path and then mount this exported file system on the NIS client computer.

On the NIS server computer, do the following:

1. Configure the directory /export/nis-**xx** as an NFS export:

   a. From the YaST Control Center, configure the NFS server by selecting **Network Services > NFS Server**.

      A Configuration of the NFS server dialog box appears.

   b. Make sure **Start NFS server** is selected; then continue by selecting **Next**.

      A Directories to export to the others dialog box appears.

   c. Select **Add directory**.

      A dialog box appears requesting the directory to export.

   d. Browse to and select or enter **/export/nis-xx/**; then select **OK**.

      A dialog box appears with fields for entering a wildcard and options.

e. Enter the following:

   - Hosts wildcard: *****

   - Options: **rw,no_root_squash,sync**

   Make sure you replace the "ro" with "rw" or you will not be able to log in remotely to the KDE desktop as dba*xx*.

f. Continue by selecting **OK**.

   The directory is added to the list.

g. Save the changes to the system by selecting **Finish**.

h. From the terminal window, verify that the file system was exported by entering the following:

   showmount -e localhost

i. View the entry made by YaST to the file /etc/exports by entering **cat /etc/exports**.

2. On the NIS client computer, do the following:

a. From a terminal window, su to root (**su -**) with a password of **novell**.

b. Create a directory /export/nis-*xx* (where *xx* is the host number of the NIS server computer) by entering the following:

   mkdir -p /export/nis-*xx*

   For example if your NIS server is DA50, you would enter

   mkdir -p /export/nis-50

c. From the KDE desktop, select the **YaST** icon; then enter a password of **novell** and select **OK**.

   The YaST Control Center appears.

d. From the YaST Control Center, select **Network Services > NFS Client**.

   The Configuration of the NFS client dialog box appears.

e. Mount a remote file system by selecting **Add**.

   A dialog box appears for adding the remote file system.

f. Enter the following:

   - Host name of the NFS Server: **10.0.0.*rr*** (where *rr* is the host number of the NIS server computer)

   - Remote file system: **/export/nis-*xx***

8

- Mountpoint (local): **/export/nis-*xx*/** (where *rr* is the host number of the remote NFS server)

- Options field: **defaults,rsize=8192,wsize=8192,soft**

g. Save the configuration by selecting **OK**.

You are returned to the Configuration of the NFS client dialog box where the remote file system is listed.

h. Save the changes to the system by selecting **Finish**.

i. From the terminal window, verify that the file system is mounted by entering **mount**.

j. Verify that an entry exists in /etc/fstab by entering

cat /etc/fstab.

Part VI: Configure the NIS Client Using YaST

From the NIS client computer, do the following:

1. From the YaST Control Center, select **Network Services > NIS Client**.

   The Configuration of NIS client dialog box appears.

2. Make sure **Use NIS** is selected.

3. In the NIS domain field, enter **NIS-DA*rr*** (where *rr* is the host number of your NIS server computer).

4. In the Addresses of NIS servers field, enter **10.0.0.*rr*** (where *rr* is the host number of your NIS server computer).

5. Save the changes to the system by selecting **Finish**.

6. Test the NIS remote access:

   a. Log out of the KDE desktop by selecting **KDE Menu > Logout > Logout**.

   The GUI login screen appears.

   Scroll through the list of users and notice that the **dba*xx*** user appears, even though it is not a local user account.

   b. Log in as the user **dba*xx*** with a password of **N0v3ll**.

   c. When you finish, log out as **dba*xx***; then log back in as **geeko**.

LDAP

It is crucial within a networked environment to keep important information structured and quickly available. In the ideal case, a central server keeps the data in a directory and distributes it to all clients using a certain protocol.

An open and standardized protocol like LDAP (Lightweight Directory Access Protocol) ensures that as many different client applications as possible can access such information.

LDAP is an Internet communications protocol that lets client applications access Directory information. It is based on the X.500 Directory Access Protocol (DAP) but is less complex and can be used with any directory service following X.500.

The use of TCP/IP by LDAP makes it easy to establish interfaces between an application and the LDAP service.

The OpenLDAP package (openldap2) included in SLES 9 consists of the following:

- **slapd.** A standalone LDAPv3 server that administers object information in a BerkeleyDB-based database.

- **slurpd.** This program enables the replication of modifications to data on the local LDAP server to other LDAP servers installed on the network.

- **slapcat, slapadd, slapindex.** These are additional tools for system maintenance.

One of the most common uses of LDAP is user authentication. To set up OpenLDAP for user authentication, you need to know the following:

- LDAP Versus NIS

- Structure of an LDAP Directory Tree

- How to Configure an LDAP Server with YaST

- How to Configure the LDAP Client with YaST

- How to Configure Users for LDAP Authentication

LDAP Versus NIS

System administrators for Linux/UNIX have traditionally used NIS service for name resolution and data distribution in a network. The configuration data contained in the files in /etc/ (group, hosts, netgroup, networks, passwd, printcap, protocols, rpc, and services) are distributed by clients all over the network.

However, NIS is only designed for Linux/UNIX platforms, which makes using it as a central data administrator in a multiplatform network impossible.

Unlike NIS, the LDAP service is not restricted to pure Linux/UNIX networks. Windows servers (since Windows 2000) support LDAP as a directory service. Novell NetWare also offers an LDAP service. Application tasks mentioned above are additionally supported in non–Linux/UNIX systems.

LDAP can be applied to any data structure that should be centrally administered, including

- Replacement for NIS

- Mail routing (postfix, sendmail)

- Address books for mail clients like Mozilla, Evolution, and Outlook
- Administration of zone descriptions for a BIND9 name server

This list can be extended because LDAP is extensible as opposed to NIS. In addition, the hierarchical structure of LDAP helps when performing administrative tasks such as searching through large amounts of data.

Structure of an LDAP Directory Tree

An LDAP directory has a tree structure. All entries (called *objects*) of the directory have a defined position within the tree. This hierarchy is called the *directory information tree* (DIT).

A complete path to a desired entry is called the *distinguished name* or DN. The single nodes along the path to this entry are called the *relative distinguished name* or RDN. You can generally assign objects to 1 of 2 types:

- **container.** These objects can contain other objects. Such object classes are *root* (the root element of the directory tree, which does not really exist), *c* (country), *ou* (organizational unit), and *dc* (domain component).

    This model is similar to the directories (folders) in a file system.

- **leaf.** These objects sit at the end of a branch and have no subordinate objects. Examples are *person*, *InetOrgPerson*, or *groupofNames*.

An example of an LDAP tree hierarchy is shown in Figure 8-33.

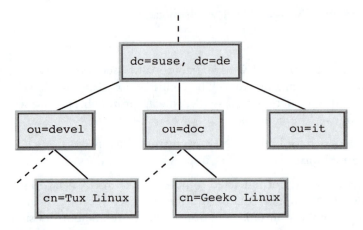

Figure 8-33

In this example, the complete, valid distinguished name for the SUSE employee Geeko Linux is

```
cn=Geeko Linux,ou=doc,dc=suse,dc=de
```

It is created by adding the RDN **cn=Geeko Linux** to the DN **ou=doc,dc=suse,dc=de**.

The definition of which types of objects can be stored in the DIT is is called the *schema*, which includes object classes. An *object class* defines what attributes the object must or can be assigned.

While there are a few common schemas (see RFC 2252 and 2256), it is possible to create custom schemas or to use multiple schemas complementing each other if this is required by the environment in which the LDAP server operates.

 For a good introduction to the use of schemes, see the OpenLDAP documentation (it may need to be installed) in /usr/share/doc/packages/openldap2/admin-guide/index.html.

NOTE

How to Configure an LDAP Server with YaST

Typically, an LDAP server handles user account data, but with SUSE Linux Enterprise Server it can also be used for mail, DHCP, and DNS-related data. By default, an LDAP server is set up during the installation.

To set up an LDAP server for user authentication, you can use YaST by doing the following:

1. From the KDE desktop, start the YaST LDAP Server module by doing one of the following:

   ■ Select the **YaST** icon, enter the root *password*, and select **OK**; then select **Network Services > LDAP Server**.

   or

   ■ Open a terminal window and enter **sux –** and the root *password*; then enter **yast2 ldap-server**.

The LDAP Server Configuration dialog box appears, as shown in Figure 8-34.

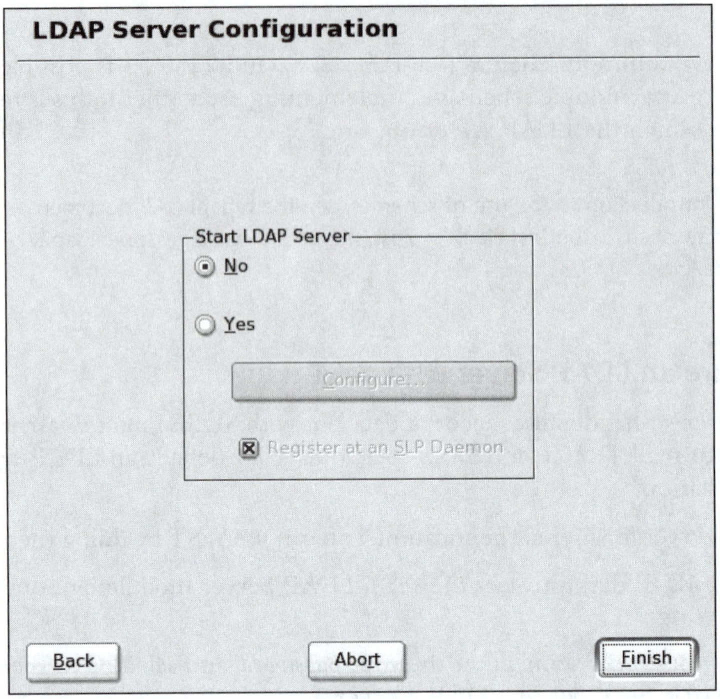

LDAP Server Configuration

Start LDAP Server

◉ No

○ Yes

Configure...

☒ Register at an SLP Daemon

Back   Abort   Finish

Figure 8-34

2. Start the LDAP server by selecting **Yes**.

3. Configure the LDAP server by selecting **Configure**.

4. At the left, view the configuration settings by expanding **Global Settings**; then select a *category*.

For example, if you select **Log Level Settings**, the dialog box shown in Figure 8-35 appears.

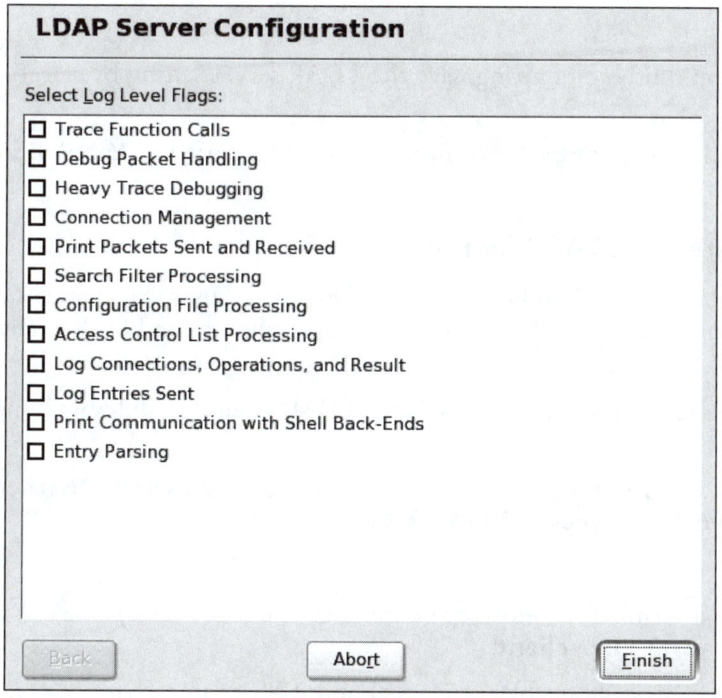

LDAP Server Configuration

Select Log Level Flags:

☐ Trace Function Calls
☐ Debug Packet Handling
☐ Heavy Trace Debugging
☐ Connection Management
☐ Print Packets Sent and Received
☐ Search Filter Processing
☐ Configuration File Processing
☐ Access Control List Processing
☐ Log Connections, Operations, and Result
☐ Log Entries Sent
☐ Print Communication with Shell Back-Ends
☐ Entry Parsing

Back   Abort   Finish

Figure 8-35

5. The following describes each LDAP settings category:

 ■ **Schema Files.** Selecting this category lets you manage a list of schema files used by the LDAP server, including the order in which the schema files are accessed.

 ■ **Log Level Settings.** Selecting this category lets you configure the degree of logging activity (verbosity) of the LDAP server.

    From the predefined list, select or deselect logging options. The more options you enable, the larger your log files will grow.

 ■ **Allow Settings.** Selecting this category lets you define which connection types should be allowed by the LDAP server.

 ■ **TLS Settings.** Selecting this category lets you define how the data traffic between server and client should be secured.

 ■ **Databases.** Selecting this option lets you select the databases to be managed by the server by selecting **Add Database**.

NOTE

For details on configuring the LDAP server from the LDAP Server Configuration dialog box, see Section 21.8.5 in the *SLES 9 Installation and Administration Manual.*

6. When you finish configuring, save the LDAP server setting by selecting **Finish**.

7. (Optional) If you started YaST from the desktop, close the **YaST Control Center**.

How to Configure the LDAP Client with YaST

YaST includes an LDAP Client module to set up LDAP-based user management. If you did not enable this feature during the installation, you can configure the LDAP client by doing the following:

1. From the KDE desktop, start the YaST LDAP Client module by doing one of the following:

   ■ Select the **YaST** icon, enter the root *password*, and select **OK**; then select **Network Services > LDAP Client**.

   or

   ■ Open a terminal window and enter **sux –** and the root *password*; then enter **yast2 ldap-client**.

   YaST automatically enables any PAM and NSS-related changes as required by LDAP and installs the necessary files.

The LDAP Client Configuration dialog box appears, as shown in Figure 8-36.

```
┌─────────────────────────────────────────────────────────────┐
│  🐧 LDAP Client Configuration                                 │
│  ─────────────────────────────────────────────────────────   │
│                                                               │
│  ┌─User Authentication──────────────────────────────────┐    │
│  │  ⦿ Do N̲o̲t Use LDAP                                    │    │
│  │  ○ U̲se LDAP                                            │    │
│  └──────────────────────────────────────────────────────┘    │
│                                                               │
│  ┌─LDAP client──────────────────────────────────────────┐    │
│  │  LDAP base D̲N                                          │    │
│  │  ┌─────────────────────────────────────────────────┐ │    │
│  │  │ dc=example,dc=com                               │ │    │
│  │  └─────────────────────────────────────────────────┘ │    │
│  │  Addresses of LDAP S̲ervers                            │    │
│  │  ┌─────────────────────────────────────────────────┐ │    │
│  │  │ 127.0.0.1                                       │ │    │
│  │  └─────────────────────────────────────────────────┘ │    │
│  │  ☒ LDAP T̲LS/SSL                                       │    │
│  │  ☐ LDAP V̲ersion 2                                     │    │
│  └──────────────────────────────────────────────────────┘    │
│                                                               │
│              ☐ Start Auto̲mounter                              │
│                                                               │
│            ┌────────────────────────────────┐                 │
│            │  A̲dvanced Configuration...      │                 │
│            └────────────────────────────────┘                 │
│  ┌────────┐      ┌────────┐        ┌──────────┐               │
│  │ B̲ack   │      │ Abo̲rt  │        │ F̲inish   │               │
│  └────────┘      └────────┘        └──────────┘               │
└─────────────────────────────────────────────────────────────┘
```

Figure 8-36

2. Enable user authentication with an LDAP server by selecting **Use LDAP**.

3. In the **LDAP base DN** field, enter the distinguished name of the search base.

4. In the **Addresses of LDAP Servers**, enter the *IP address* of the LDAP server.

    You can enter multiple IP addresses by separating them with spaces. You can also specify the port on which the LDAP service is running (*IP address: port*).

5. (Conditional) If your LDAP server is configured and supports TLS/SSL, select **LDAP TLS/SSL**.

6. (Conditional) If the LDAP server is using version 2 protocol, select **LDAP Version 2**.

7. Configure advanced LDAP settings by selecting **Advanced Configuration**.

NOTE   For details on configuring advanced LDAP client settings, see Section 21.8.6 in the *SLES 9 Installation and Administration Manual.*

8. Automatically mount directories on remote hosts by selecting **Start Automounter**.

9. When you finish configuring the LDAP client, save the settings by selecting **Finish**.

10. (Optional) If you started YaST from the desktop, close the **YaST Control Center**.

How to Configure Users for LDAP Authentication

To configure user accounts for LDAP authentication, do the following:

1. From the KDE desktop, start the YaST Edit and create users module by doing one of the following:

    ■ Select the **YaST** icon, enter the root *password*, and select **OK**; then select **Security and User > Edit and create users**.

    or

    ■ Open a terminal window and enter **sux –** and the root *password*; then enter **yast2 users**.

2. Select **Set Filter > Local Users**.

3. From the user list, select a *user*; then select **Edit**.

    The Edit an Existing Local User dialog box appears.

4. Select **Details**.

The dialog box shown in Figure 8-37 appears.

Figure 8-37

From this dialog box you can configure settings such as group membership, login shell, and the home directory.

5. Continue by selecting **Next**.

If LDAP authentication has been configured, the dialog box shown in Figure 8-38 appears.

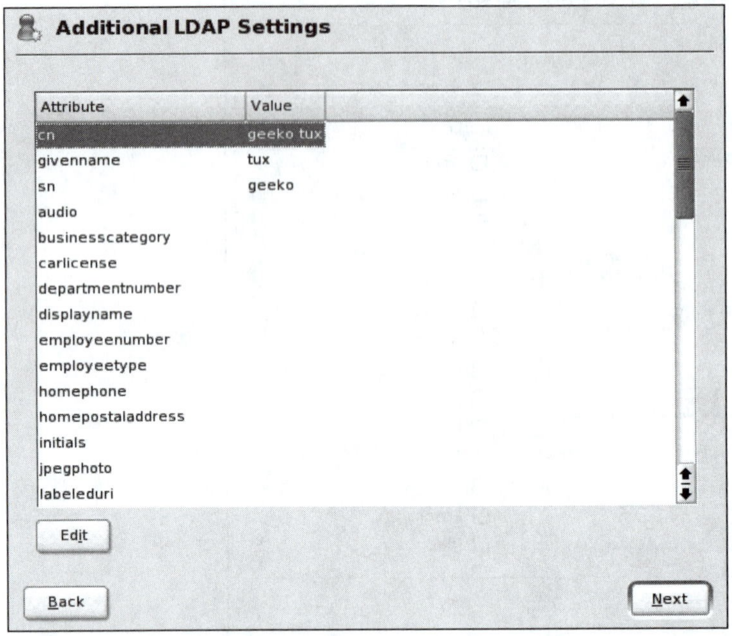

Additional LDAP Settings

Attribute	Value
cn	geeko tux
givenname	tux
sn	geeko
audio	
businesscategory	
carlicense	
departmentnumber	
displayname	
employeenumber	
employeetype	
homephone	
homepostaladdress	
initials	
jpegphoto	
labeleduri	

Edit

Back   Next

Figure 8-38

A list of attributes appears with values for each attribute.

6. Edit an attribute value by selecting the attribute; then select **Edit**.

7. When you finish, continue by selecting **Next**.

You are returned to the User and Group Administration dialog box.

NOTE

For more information on OpenLDAP, see Section 21.8.7 in the *SLES 9 Installation and Administration Manual*.

CHAPTER SUMMARY

❏ SLES uses the CUPS printing system, which supports the socket, LPD, IPP, and SMB printing protocols.

❏ You can configure CUPS using YaST, the **lpadmin** command line utility, the CUPS Web Administration Tool (http://hostname:631), or by editing the appropriate configuration files in the /etc/cups directory and restarting the cups daemon.

◻ The CUPS daemon writes logging information to the /var/log/cups/error_log and /var/log/cups/access_log files. You can control the level of logging by editing the /etc/cups/cupsd.conf file.

◻ Print jobs are sent to a queue directory before being sent to the printer itself. You can use the **enable**, **disable**, **accept**, and **reject** commands to control this process.

◻ The **lp** and **lpr** commands may be used to create print jobs within a command-line terminal. Similarly, the kprinter utility may be used to print from graphical applications.

◻ You can view print jobs in the print queue using the **lpstat** or **lpq** commands, and remove print jobs from the print queue using the **cancel** or **lprm** commands.

◻ Users can modify print options using the **lpoptions** command, or by using the kprinter utility in a desktop environment. System-wide print options are stored in the /etc/cups/lpoptions file and user-specific print options are stored in the ~/.lpoptions file.

◻ On TCP/IP networks, NFS is typically used to share files amongst Linux and UNIX computers using RPCs, whereas Samba is used to share files between Linux, UNIX, and Windows computers using the SMB/CIFS protocol.

◻ An NFS server shares directories to NFS clients using the **exportfs** command or entries in the /etc/exports file. NFS clients mount shared NFS directories on remote computers to local directories using the **mount** command or entries in the /etc/fstab file. YaST may also be used to configure an NFS server or client.

◻ The **showmount** and **rpcinfo** commands may be used to troubleshoot NFS servers and clients.

◻ To become a Samba server, you must start the Samba and NetBIOS daemons, configure entries in the /etc/samba/smb.conf file, and configure Samba user accounts. YaST may be used to configure a Samba server. In addition, the **testparm**, **nmblookup**, and **smbstatus** commands may be used to troubleshoot a Samba server.

◻ You can connect to a Windows or Samba file server using the **mount** and **smbclient** commands.

◻ NIS is unique to UNIX and Linux operating systems. It has traditionally been used to distribute configuration and authentication data on a network, provide central resource access, and resolve names.

◻ NIS clients obtain information from a NIS master server or NIS slave servers for a particular NIS domain. NIS slave servers are additional NIS servers that may be used to aid in distributing data to NIS clients.

◻ To create a NIS server, you must create NIS maps of various system components and start the **ypserv**, **ypbind**, and RPM portmapper daemons. NIS clients need to start the **ypbind** daemon and typically forward information requests to NIS servers based on entries in the /etc/nsswitch.conf file. YaST may be used to configure a NIS master server, NIS slave server, or NIS client.

8

❏ The LDAP service provides the same functionality as NIS but is supported by nearly all operating systems.

❏ LDAP resources are organized into a directory information tree. Each resource (leaf object) is stored in a series of container objects and can be accessed using a DN or RDN.

❏ YaST may be used to configure LDAP servers and clients as well as LDAP authentication for local user accounts.

Key Terms

/etc/cups/cupsd.conf — The main CUPS configuration file.

/etc/cups/lpoptions — The file that stores system-wide print options set by the root user.

/etc/cups/ppd — The directory that stores the active PPD files used for a particular printer.

/etc/cups/printers.conf — Contains CUPS printer definitions.

/etc/defaultdomain — A file that stores the default NIS domain name.

/etc/exports — The file that lists exported directories on an NFS server.

/etc/fstab — A file that may be used to mount NFS file systems automatically at boot time.

/etc/hosts — A file used for local name resolution.

/etc/nsswitch.conf — A file that determines when NIS maps are used to configure system information.

/etc/samba/smb.conf — The main Samba configuration file.

/etc/sysconfig/ypserv — Stores NIS server options.

/etc/yp.conf — A file that stores the location of NIS servers.

/etc/ypserv.conf — The main NIS server configuration file.

/usr/share/cups/model — The directory that stores sample PPD files used for a particular printer.

/var/lib/named — The directory that stores zone files in SLES.

/var/lib/nfs/etab — A file that lists currently exported directories on an NFS server.

/var/log/cups/access_log — A CUPS log file that stores information about network print requests.

/var/log/cups/error_log — A CUPS log file that stores information about the CUPS daemon.

/var/spool/cups — The default print queue directory in SLES.

/var/yp/Makefile — A file whose settings are used to create NIS maps.

/var/yp/nicknames — A file that contains aliases for NIS maps.

/var/yp/securenets — A file on a NIS server that lists valid networks for NIS clients.

/var/yp/ypservers — A file on a NIS master server that lists NIS slave servers.

~/.lpoptions — The file that stores user-defined print options.

accept command — Allows print jobs to enter the print queue.

cancel command — Used to remove a print job from the print queue.

Common Internet File System (CIFS) — A file- and printer-sharing protocol used by Windows systems.

Common Unix Printing System (CUPS) — The default printing system in SLES.

container — An LDAP object used to organize leaf objects.

CUPS Web Administration Tools — A series of CUPS administration utilities that may be accessed using a Web browser on port 631.

Directory Information Tree (DIT) — The hierarchical structure of an LDAP database.

disable command — Prevents print jobs in the print queue from being sent to the printer.

Distinguished Name (DN) — A full pathname to an LDAP leaf object.

enable command — Allows print jobs in the print queue to be sent to the printer.

exportfs command — Used to temporarily export directories on an NFS server.

Internet Printing Protocol (IPP) — A printing protocol that allows print jobs to be sent across the Internet using a Web browser.

kprinter — A graphical utility that is invoked when a graphical application creates a print job. It may also be used to change printing options such as resolution.

leaf — An LDAP object that represents a network resource.

Lightweight Directory Access Protocol (LDAP) — A protocol used to provide central authentication and distribute information to network computers.

Line Printer Daemon (LPD) — A common printing protocol used on older Linux and UNIX computers.

lp command — Used to create a print job.

lpadmin command — Used to create and manage CUPS printers.

lpoptions command — Used to create or change printing options such as resolution.

lppasswd — Used to create CUPS passwords and configure access to the CUPS Web Administration Tools.

lpq command — Used to view print jobs in the print queue.

lpr command — Used to create a print job.

lprm command — Used to remove a print job from the print queue.

lpstat command — Used to view print jobs in the print queue.

make command — Used to generate NIS maps using the Makefile.

maps — NIS database files containing information that is central to the network, such as user accounts and host names.

master server — A NIS server that contains the maps used to configure NIS clients.

NetBIOS — A Windows protocol that uses unique 15-character computer names to identify network hosts. Short for *Network Basic Input Output System*.

Network File System (NFS) — A file sharing protocol used by UNIX and Linux systems.

Network Information Service (NIS) — A service that allows the centralization of Linux and UNIX configuration.

NFS client — A computer that accesses exported files on an NFS server using the NFS protocol.

NFS server — A computer that hosts (exports) files using the NFS protocol.

8

NIS client — A computer that authenticates or obtains its configuration information from a master or slave NIS server.

nmblookup command — Displays NetBIOS computer names for hosts.

object — A component of an LDAP database. The two main object types are container objects and leaf objects.

object class — A type of object within an LDAP database.

portmapper — The service that provides for RPCs in Linux.

PostScript — A printing format that is widely used by many printers and printing systems.

GhostScript — A system used to format information for non-PostScript printers in SLES.

PostScript Printer Description (PPD) — A file that stores PostScript printing instructions for a printer.

queue — A directory used to store print jobs before they are sent to the physical printer.

reject command — Prevents print jobs from entering the print queue.

Relative Distinguished Name (RDN) — The simple name of an object in LDAP.

Remote Procedure Call (RPC) — A routine that is executed on a remote computer.

rpcinfo command — Displays information regarding the RPM portmapper daemon.

rpcinfo command — Displays RPC ports and their associated services.

Samba — A set of services in Linux that provides the SMB and CIFS protocols for file and printer sharing with Windows computers.

schema — The list of object and object properties for an LDAP database.

Server Level Security — A Samba share security level that requires a valid login to another server in order to access a shared directory or printer.

Server Message Block (SMB) — A file- and printer-sharing protocol used by Windows systems.

Share Level Security — A Samba share security level that requires a password in order to access a shared directory.

showmount command — Displays exported directories on an NFS server.

slave server — A NIS server that contains a copy of the maps from the master server and uses them to configure NIS clients.

smbclient command — Used to view and access Windows file and printer shares.

smbpasswd command — Sets a Windows-formatted password for Linux user accounts.

smbstatus command — Displays current Samba server connections.

socket — An established network connection between two hosts that uses a port. CUPS can use sockets to print to a remote system, and remote systems can use sockets to print to a CUPS printer.

testparm command — Checks the syntax of /etc/samba/smb.conf.

User Level Security — A Samba share security level that requires a valid Linux login in order to access a shared directory.

Windows Internet Naming Service (WINS) — A Windows service that is used to resolve NetBIOS names to IP addresses. Samba can be configured as a WINS server or client.

workgroup — A name that identifies a group of computers in a Windows network that are not part of a domain.

ypbind — The NIS client program. This program also runs on NIS servers.

ypcat command — Displays the contents of NIS maps.

ypchfn command — Used to change user account descriptions on a NIS server.

ypchsh command — Used to change the default user account shell on a NIS server.

ypdomainname command — Used to set the NIS domain name for a computer.

ypinit command — The NIS slave server program.

ypmatch command — Used to query NIS maps for specific information.

yppasswd command — Used to change a user password on a NIS server.

yppoll command — Displays NIS map ID numbers.

yppush command — Copies NIS maps from master servers to slave servers.

ypserv — The NIS server program.

ypwhich command — Displays the NIS server used by a host.

8

REVIEW QUESTIONS

1. What command may be used to create printers?

   a. cupsadmin

   b. lpadmin

   c. lpstat

   d. cupsd

2. When you try to send a print job to the printer **p1**, you receive an error message stating that the print queue is unavailable. What command can you use to allow print jobs to enter the print queue for **p1**? _____

3. What address would you use in your Web browser to administer your local CUPS server? _____

4. When you save print options in the kprinter utility as the root user, what file are these options saved to? _____

5. What CUPS log stores remote printing requests? _____

6. What line in the /etc/exports file will export the /home directory to the host **arfa** as read-write, while ensuring that the root user does not have administrative rights to the exported directory? _____

7. What three services need to be started on an NFS server?

   a. RPC mount daemon

   b. RPC portmapper

   c. RPC NFS daemon

   d. RPC exporter

8. What command may be used to mount the /home directory on a remote computer called **server2** using the NFS protocol to the local /mnt directory?
   _____

9. What command may be used to display the NFS ports registered by the RPM port-mapper daemon? _____

10. What two commands can you run to activate changes made to the /etc/samba/smb.conf file?
    a. smbclient --restart
    b. rcsmb restart
    c. nmbclient --restart
    d. rcnmb restart

11. What command can you use to check the /etc/samba/smb.conf file for errors?
    _____

12. What command may be used to mount the **acctg** shared directory on the server **arfa** to the local /mnt directory using SMB? _____

13. Which of the following daemons is started on a NIS server? (Choose all that apply.)
    a. ypbind
    b. ypwhich
    c. ypserv
    d. RPC portmapper

14. What command may be used to generate NIS maps on the command line using entries on the /var/yp/Makefile? _____

15. You have configured your system to authenticate to a NIS server. When you use the **passwd** command to change your password, it does not change as expected. What command must you use to change your NIS password for it to take effect on the NIS server? _____

16. Which of the following is a valid DN for an LDAP object?
    a. cn=joe
    b. cn=joe.ou=acctg.
    c. cn=joe.ou=acctg.dc=suse
    d. cn=joe.ou=acctg.dc=suse.dc=com

17. What package is used to implement LDAP in SLES 9? _____

DISCOVERY EXERCISES

Configuring a Samba Domain Controller

Use the Internet to research the steps required to use your Samba server as a Windows domain controller. Next, log in to tty1 as the root user and configure your Samba service as a domain controller by editing your /etc/samba/smb.conf file. The minimum lines required in this file are:

[global]

        domain logons = yes

        security = user

        encrypt passwords = yes

        wins support = yes

        netbios name = _____

        workgroup = _____ (put your domain name here)

[netlogon]

        path=/netlogon (create this directory with permissions 777)

        public = no

        writable = no

        locking = no

Next, create a new user on the system (**useradd −m testuser**) and give the user an encrypted password in the samba database (**smbpasswd testuser**). Then, add computer accounts for each Windows XP computer that will be joining the domain on your Linux computer by adding a line to /etc/passwd and /etc/shadow that lists the computer name followed by a $ character as shown below:

/etc/passwd sample line:

        clientcomputername$:x:5000:5000::/dev/null:/bin/false

/etc/shadow sample line:

        clientcomputername$:*:6445::::::

When finished, test your configuration by joining a Windows client to the domain and testing domain logon. Log out of tty1 on your Samba server when finished.

Researching File and Printer Sharing Protocols

Use the Internet to find three organizations that use SLES. Summarize the file and sharing protocols that each company uses in its network infrastructure and the configuration. For each organization, provide a rationale for the use of each technology.

Configuring LDAP

As the root user, configure your system to be an LDAP server using YaST. On a partner's computer, use YaST to configure their computer as an LDAP client and set the properties of user accounts on their system to authenticate to your LDAP server. Test your configuration. When finished, remove the LDAP configuration from both systems.

ENABLE INTERNET SERVICES

In this section, you learn the basics of enabling some of the more commonly used network Internet services available in SUSE Linux Enterprise Server 9.

- Configure SUSE Linux Enterprise Server Time
- Enable a Web Server (Apache)
- Enable the Extended Internet Daemon (xinetd)
- Enable an FTP Server

OBJECTIVE 1   CONFIGURE SUSE LINUX ENTERPRISE SERVER TIME

In order to implement a unified time on all computers in a network, all computers must be able to access at least one time server so that times will synchronize.

There are two ways of synchronizing the time on a SUSE Linux Enterprise Server: netdate and NTP. To configure and synchronize the time, you need to understand:

- SUSE Linux Enterprise Server Time Overview
- How to Synchronize Time with hwclock and netdate
- What Network Time Protocol (NTP) Is
- How to Synchronize Time with NTP

SUSE Linux Enterprise Server Time Overview

In order to configure and synchronize time on a SUSE Linux Enterprise Server, you need to understand the following fundamental concepts:

- Hardware Clock and System Clock
- GMT (UTC) and Local Time
- Time Configuration Files

Hardware Clock and System Clock

There are two main clocks in a Linux system:

- **Hardware clock.** This is a clock that runs independently of any control program running in the CPU. It even runs when you turn off the server.

    This clock is part of the ISA standard and is commonly called the ***hardware clock***. It is also called the time clock, the RTC, the BIOS clock, or the CMOS clock.

    The term "hardware clock" is used on Linux systems to indicate the time set by the hwclock utility.

- **System time.** This is the time kept by a clock inside the Linux kernel and is driven by a ***timer interrupt*** (another ISA standard).

    System time is meaningful while Linux is running on the server. System time is the number of seconds since 00:00:00 January 1, 1970, UTC (or the number of seconds since 1969).

On a Linux server, it's the system time that is important. The hardware clock's basic purpose is to keep time when Linux is not running.

The system time is synchronized to the hardware clock when Linux first starts. After that, Linux only uses the system time.

In DOS (for which ISA was designed), the hardware clock is the only real time clock.

Once the system time is set on the Linux server, it's important that you do not use commands such as **date** to adjust the system time without considering the impact on applications and network connections.

For a Linux server connected to the Internet (or equipped with a precision oscillator or radio clock), the best way to regulate the system clock is with **ntpd**.

For a stand-alone or intermittently connected machine, you can use **adjtimex** instead to correct systematic drift.

If your computer can be connected to the Internet, you can run **ntpd** for at least several hours and use adjtimex --print to learn what values of tick and freq it settled on.

You can set the hardware clock (with a command such as **hwclock**) while the system is running. The next time you start Linux, it will synchronize with the adjusted time from the hardware clock.

The Linux kernel maintains a concept of a local time zone for the system.

Some programs and parts of the Linux kernel (such as file systems) use the kernel time-zone value. An example is the vfat file system. If the kernel time-zone value is wrong, the vfat file system reports and sets the wrong timestamps on files.

However, programs that care about the time zone (perhaps because they want to display a local time for you) almost always use a more traditional method of determining the time zone, such as the file /usr/lib/zoneinfo/localtime (which is a link pointing to /etc/localtime) and the files in the directory /usr/share/zoneinfo/.

GMT (UTC) and Local Time

On start-up, Linux reads the time from the computer's local hardware (CMOS clock) and takes control of the time. The hardware clock can be set using one of the following:

- **UTC (Universal Time Coordinated).** This time is also referred to as GMT (Greenwich mean time). For this setting, the variable HWCLOCK in the file /etc/sysconfig/clock has the value **-u**.

- **Local time.** If the hardware clock is set to the local time, the variable HWCLOCK in the file /etc/sysconfig/clock has the value **--localtime**.

Choosing GMT as the hardware time makes it easier to coordinate a large number of computers in different places (especially if the computers are located in different time zones.)

Time Configuration Files

The current time (system time) is calculated with the help of the variable TIMEZONE in the file /etc/sysconfig/clock, which also handles the required changes between daylight saving time and standard time.

The following is an example of the settings in /etc/sysconfig/clock:

```
HWCLOCK="--localtime"
TIMEZONE="Europe/Berlin"
DEFAULT_TIMEZONE="Europe/Berlin"
```

By means of the variable TIMEZONE, the time configured on the local host (=system time) is set in the file /usr/lib/zoneinfo/localtime (a symbolic link to /etc/localtime).

The directory /usr/share/zoneinfo/ is a database of all time zones.

You can view the hardware clock time by entering

cat /proc/driver/rtc.

How to Synchronize Time with hwclock and netdate

To synchronize time between network servers with hwclock and netdate, you need to know the following:

- How to Use hwclock
- How to Use netdate

How to Use hwclock

hwclock is a tool for accessing the hardware clock. You can display the current time, set the hardware clock to a specified time, set the hardware clock to the system time, and set the system time from the hardware clock.

You can also run hwclock periodically to insert or remove time from the hardware clock to compensate for systematic drift (where the clock consistently gains or loses time at a certain rate if left to run).

hwclock uses several methods to get and set hardware clock values. The normal way is to initialize an I/O process to the device special file /dev/rtc, which is maintained by the rtc device driver.

However, this method is not always available. The rtc driver is a relatively recent addition to Linux and is not available on older systems.

On older systems, the method of accessing the hardware clock depends on the system hardware.

 For additional details on how the system accesses the hardware clock and other hwclock options, see the man pages for hwclock (**man hwclock**).

NOTE

Some of the more commonly used options with hwclock are listed in Table 9-1.

Table 9-1

Option	Description
-r or **--show**	This options displays the current time of the hardware clock. The time is always shown in local time, even if you keep your hardware clock set to UTC time.
-w or **--systohc**	This option sets the hardware clock to the current system time.
-s or **--hctosys**	This option sets the system time to the current hardware clock time. It also sets the kernel's time-zone value to the local time zone as indicated by the TZ variable.
-a or **--adjust**	This option adds or subtracts time from the hardware clock to account for system drift (enter **man hwclock** for details).
-v or **--version**	This option displays the version of hwclock.
--set --date=newdate	This option sets the hardware clock to the date given by the --date option. For example: **hwclock --set --date="9/22/07 16:45:05"**

How to Use netdate

To set up the system time once only, you can use the command netdate as follows:

netdate *timeserver1 timeserver2. . .*

where *timeserver* represents a time server on the network or on the Internet.

After querying the time servers, the netdate client compares their times with its own time.

Time differences are then sorted into groups to determine which is the largest group of servers with an identical time (within certain limits). The first computer in the group is then used to update the time on the local server.

To synchronize the time to a specific external time source, you enter **netdate** *time_source*, as in the following:

netdate ptbtime1.ptb.de

In this case, the client queries the time server at the Physikalisch-Technische Bundesanstalt (PTB) in Braunschweig, Germany.

You then need to set the hardware clock to the system clock time by entering **hwclock --systohc** or **hwclock -w**.

The simplest way to implement time synchronization with netdate and hwclock is to use a script that is run regularly by cron.

NOTE

What Network Time Protocol (NTP) Is

As the networking environment continues to expand to include mixed operating system environments, time synchronization is becoming more dependent on NTP.

To configure NTP on SUSE Linux Enterprise Server, you need to understand the following:

- NTP
- Stratum
- NTP Daemon (xntpd)
- NTP Terms
- How the NTP Daemon Works

This section is designed to teach you some of the basic concepts of NTP. For more information on NTP, visit www.ntp.org.

NOTE

NTP

NTP is an industry standard protocol that uses UDP on port 123 to communicate between time providers and time consumers.

The UDP suite is part of the TCP/IP suite. Therefore, a computer using NTP needs the TCP/IP suite loaded.

An NTP time provider is a server that understands NTP and provides NTP time to other servers or to workstations on the network. The NTP time provider gives time to operating systems that are NTP-compliant.

An NTP time consumer is a server that understands NTP and seeks NTP time from an NTP time provider. A time consumer can also, in turn, act as a time provider for other servers and client workstations on the network.

The NTP time consumer can work with operating systems that are NTP-compliant.

Any computers on your network with Internet access can get time from NTP servers on the Internet. NTP synchronizes clocks to the UTC standard, which is the international time standard.

NTP not only corrects the time but keeps track of consistent time variations and automatically adjusts for system time drift on the client. It allows for less network traffic and keeps the client clocks more stable, even when the network is down.

Stratum

NTP introduces the concept of a stratum. Stratum x is used as a designation of the location of the servers in NTP tree hierarchy.

Stratum 1 is the first (highest) level in the hierarchy. It denotes servers that adjust their time by means of some external reference time source (such as a GPS, an atomic clock, or a radio).

Servers that synchronize their time to stratum 1 servers are denoted as stratum 2, and those that use stratum 2 servers to synchronize their time are denoted as stratum 3, and so on until you reach a stratum level of 15 (the maximum allowed).

Differences between stratum 2 and stratum 1 servers are normally very small and, for the majority of users, unnoticeable.

Figure 9-1 depicts the stratum hierarchy.

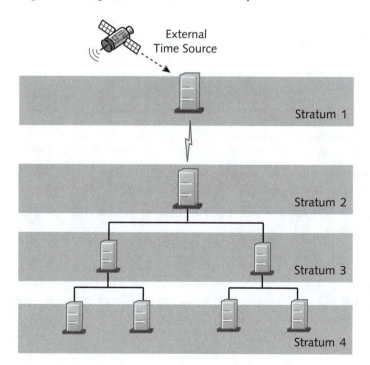

Figure 9-1

Generally only one server in a network communicates with an external time provider. This reduces network traffic across geographical locations and minimizes traffic across routers and WANs.

NTP Daemon (xntpd)

The NTP distribution includes xntpd, the NTP daemon. This daemon is used by the time provider (server) and the time consumer (client) to give and obtain time, respectively.

The xntpd process is designed to adjust time continuously, making the time adjustments very small.

xntpd can also limit the wander of the local clock based on historical data, even when a time provider is unavailable.

The xntpd process requires little resource overhead. This allows NTP to be easily deployed on servers hosting other services, even if the servers are heavily loaded.

The hardware clock can easily be corrected with ntpdate from time to time. However, this causes a sudden time difference that might not be tolerated by all applications.

xntpd uses an interesting approach for solving this problem by:

- regularly correcting the local computer clock on the basis of collected correction data.
- continuously correcting the local time with the help of time servers in the network.
- enabling the management of local reference clocks, such as radio-controlled clocks.

NTP Terms

To configure and adjust NTP, you need to understand the following terms:

- **Drift.** During operation, ntpd (and xntpd) measures and corrects for incidental clock frequency error and writes the current value to a file /etc/ntp/drift.

  If you start and stop ntpd (and xntpd), the daemon initializes the frequency from this file. This helps prevent a potentially long interval to relearn the frequency error.

- **Jitter.** This is the estimated time error of the peer clock (the delta between the client and server since the last poll.)

How the NTP Daemon Works

After starting the xntpd daemon, it automatically synchronizes the system time with a time server on an ongoing basis. The correction takes place in small increments by expanding or compressing the system time—not abruptly—as when netdate and hwclock are used.

Transactions between the client and the server occur about once per minute, increasing gradually to once per 17 minutes under normal conditions. Poorly synchronized clients will tend to poll more often than well-synchronized clients.

The client uses the information it gets from the server or servers to calibrate its clock. This consists of the client determining how far its clock is off and adjusting its time to match that of the server.

To allow clocks to quickly achieve high accuracy yet avoid overshooting the time with large time adjustments, NTP uses a system in which large adjustments occur quickly and small adjustments occur over time.

For small time differences (less than 128 milliseconds), NTP uses a gradual adjustment. This is called *slewing*. For larger time differences, the adjustment is immediate. This is called *stepping*.

If the accuracy of a clock becomes too insufficient (off by more than about 17 minutes), NTP aborts the NTP daemon, with the assumption that something has gone wrong with either the client or the server. This is referred to as an *insane* time source.

NOTE   An NTP article found at http://developer.novell.com/research/appnotes/1999/ july/03/apv.htm explains that an insane time source is one that is more than 1000 seconds (or about 17 minutes) off.

Because NTP averages the results of several time exchanges in order to reduce the effects of variable latency, it might take several minutes for NTP to even reach consensus on what the average latency is.

It often takes several adjustments (and several minutes) for NTP to reach synchronization.

In the long run, NTP tries to decrease the amount of polling it does by making the clock on each system more accurate.

Because of the algorithm that the NTP daemon uses, it is best to synchronize with multiple servers to help protect the client from an incorrect or downed server. In many environments, it is unlikely that an NTP server failure will be noticed quickly.

9

How to Synchronize Time with NTP

To synchronize network time with NTP, you need to know how to do the following:

- Start NTP from the Command Line
- Adjust the Time with ntpdate
- Configure the NTP Server (/etc/ntp.conf)
- Configure an NTP Client with YaST
- Trace the Time Source with ntptrace

Start NTP from the Command Line

In SUSE Linux Enterprise Server, the time server daemon xntpd is contained in the package xntp, which is installed by default. Its start script is /etc/init.d/xntpd, and its central configuration file is /etc/ntp.conf.

By starting the NTP daemon, you configure the host server to run as an NTP server.

You can start the NTP daemon by entering **rcxntpd start**. You can check the status of NTP by entering **rcxntpd status**.

To start NTP automatically when the system is booted, you need to set the symbolic links in the respective runlevel directories by entering **insserv /etc/init.d/xntpd**.

If you make any changes to the ntp.conf file, you need to start and restart xntpd in order to update the configuration without rebooting. Do the following:

- To stop xntpd when logged in as root, enter **rcxntpd stop**.
- To start xntpd when logged in as root, enter **rcxntpd start**.
- To restart xntpd when logged in as root, enter **rcxntpd restart**.

After the ntp.conf file has been read by xntpd, the client sends a request to the server and the server sends back a timestamped response, along with information such as its accuracy and stratum.

Adjust the Time with ntpdate

If the difference between the system time and the time server is too great, the synchronization of the system time in small increments might take too long.

In this case, you can set the system time manually using the NTP program ntpdate.

To perform a one-time update of the client to the server, enter the following at the console prompt:

rcxntpd stop

ntpdate *timeserver*

hwclock --systohc

rcxntpd start

Notice that you need to stop the NTP daemon before updating with ntpdate.

Because the ntpdate synchronization only occurs once, the system time will eventually stray from the time on the time provider's clock. Therefore, ntpdate is not the best long-term solution for time synchronization.

Configure the NTP Server (/etc/ntp.conf)

As soon as you start xntpd on a host, it serves as an NTP server and can be queried via NTP. You configure the NTP server by editing the configuration file /etc/ntp.conf.

For example, you can configure a network host as a server that synchronizes the time with a time server on the Internet. The other network hosts can access the time server on the Intranet.

First you need to make sure that the following entries exist in the file /etc/ntp.conf for the local clock, which is used if the time server is not available:

```
server 127.127.1.0            # local clock (LCL)
fudge 127.127.1.0 stratum 10  # LCL is unsynchronized
```

The value after "stratum" indicates the divergence of a server from the atomic clock, showing how precise the time server is.

The value **1** means that the server is connected directly to the atomic clock and is very reliable. A server with the value **2** gets the time from a server with the stratum value 1, and so on. A value of **16** indicates that the server is very unreliable.

The next entry in /etc/ntp.conf is for the time servers that are to be asked for the current time:

```
## Outside source of synchronized time
server ptbtime1.ptb.de
server ptbtime2.ptb.de
```

There are two possible methods of synchronization between the time server and the client:

- **Polling.** With polling, the client asks the server for the current time.

  Polling starts at one-minute intervals. If the time interval is determined to be trustworthy, the interval is reset to once every 1024 seconds.

  You can set the minimum and maximum limits of the polling in /etc/ntp.conf, as in the following:
  ```
  server ptbtime1.ptb.de minpoll 4 maxpoll 12
  ```
  The minpoll and maxpoll values are interpreted as powers of 2 (in seconds). The default settings are 6 (26 = 64 seconds) or 10 (210 = 1024 seconds). Values between 4 and 17 are permitted.

- **Broadcasting.** By means of broadcasting, the server sends the current time to all clients, and the clients receive the signal through the option broadcaseclient.

In large networks, traffic caused by polling of the time can be significant. In this case, you might want to configure the time server to distribute time information by sending broadcast packets.

To do this, you need to enter the following in /etc/ntp.conf (where the IP address is that of the time server):

```
broadcast 192.168.0.255
```

For reasons of security, broadcast-based synchronization should always be used together with an authentication key so that the client only accepts information from trustworthy time servers.

You also need to include the name for the drift file and log file in /etc/ntp.conf, as in the following:

```
driftfile /var/lib/ntp/drift/ntp.drift
logfile /var/log/ntp
```

The drift file contains information that describes how the hardware clock drifts. When the daemon xntpd is started for the first time, this file does not exist. It takes about 15 minutes for the daemon to gather enough information to create the file.

You edit and save the file /etc/ntp.conf, and the daemon xntpd updates it about once an hour. However, you can manually update the configuration by entering **rcxntpd restart**.

For time requests of other kinds (such as time servers for netdate) to be processed, the services must be made available by means of inetd or xinetd.

For this reason, the prepared entries for daytime and time must be enabled for UDP and TCP in the configuration file of inetd or xinetd.

Configure an NTP Client with YaST

YaST provides an NTP Client module for configuring an NTP client on your SUSE Linux Enterprise Server so it can synchronize with an existing NTP server.

To configure the NTP client with YaST, do the following:

1. From the KDE desktop, start the YaST NTP Client module by doing one of the following:

   - Select the **YaST** icon, enter the root *password*, and select **OK**; then select **Network Services > NTP Client**.

     or

   - Open a terminal window and enter **sux –** and the root *password*; then enter **yast2 ntp-client**.

   The NTP Client Configuration dialog box appears.

2. Configure the NTP client to start each time you boot your system by selecting **When Booting System**.

The NTP Server field becomes active, as illustrated in Figure 9-2.

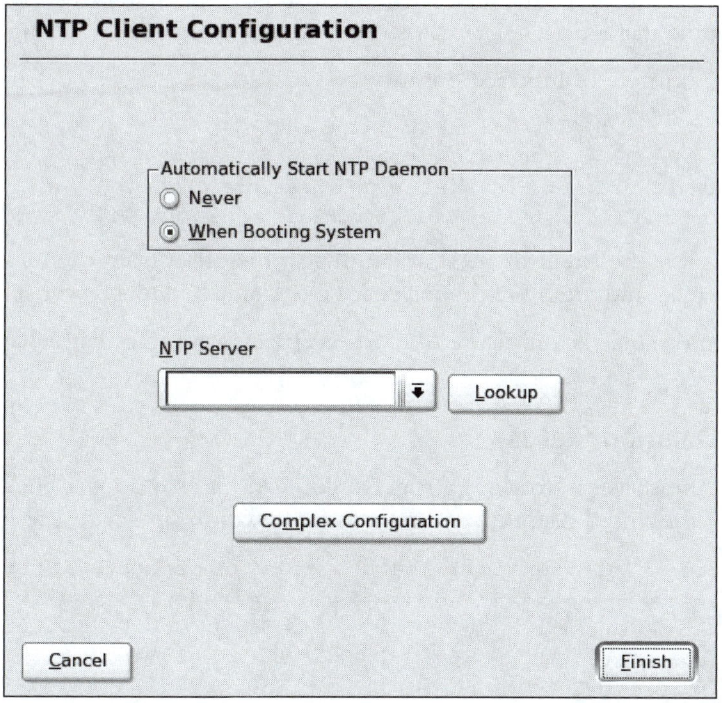

NTP Client Configuration

Automatically Start NTP Daemon
- ○ Never
- ◉ When Booting System

NTP Server

[   ] ⬇ [Lookup]

[Complex Configuration]

[Cancel]   [Finish]

Figure 9-2

3. Enter an NTP server by doing one of the following:

- Use SLP to select a local NTP server on your network by selecting **Lookup**; then select the *server*.

  or

- In the NTP Server field, enter or select (from the drop-down list) the *IP address* of an NTP server.

4. (Optional) Configure your server to synchronize against multiple remote hosts or against a locally connected clock by selecting **Complex Configuration**.

5. When you finish, configure the NTP client by selecting **Finish**.

6. (Optional) If you started YaST from the desktop, close the **YaST Control Center**.

Trace the Time Source with ntptrace

The NTP distribution also includes the ntptrace program. ntptrace is an informational tool that traces the source of time that a time consumer is receiving. It can be a useful debugging tool.

The following is an example of ntptrace output:

```
DA50:~ # ntptrace
localhost: stratum 3, offset 0.000723, synch distance 1.18225
tick.east.ca: stratum 2, offset 1.601143, synch distance 0.06713
tock.usask.ca: stratum 1, offset 1.712003, synch distance  0.00723, refid 'TRUE'
```

The ntptrace output lists the client name, its stratum, its time offset from the local host, the synchronization distance, and the ID of the reference clock attached to a server, if one exists.

The synchronization distance is a measure of clock accuracy, assuming that it has a correct time source.

Query the NTP Daemon Status

To verify that the time server is working properly, you can enter ntpq -p. The command queries the status of the xntpd daemon, and returns information similar to the following:

```
remote        refid     st when poll reach   delay   offset  jitter
==============================================================================
LOCAL(0)     LOCAL(0) 10   15   64    1     0.000   0.000   0.008
*ptb1.ptb.de .PTB.     1   14   64    1    27.165   2.348   0.001
ntp2.ptb.de .PTB.     1   13   64    1    26.159   0.726   0.001
```

Displayed information includes the following:

- **remote.** Hostname or IP address of the time server

- **refid.** Type of reference source (0.0.0.0 = unknown)

- **st.** Stratum value for the server

- **when.** Number of seconds since the last poll

- **poll.** Number of seconds between two polls

- **reach.** Indicates if the time server was reached in the last poll attempt; reach begins with the value 0 when you start xntpd

  For every successful attempt, a 1 is added to the binary register on the right. The maximum value of 377 means that the server was reachable in the last eight requests.

- **delay.** Time between the xntpd request and the arrival of the answer (in milliseconds)

- **offset.** Difference between the reference time and the system time (in milliseconds)
- **jitter.** Size of the discrepancies between individual time comparisons (in milliseconds)

An asterisk (*) in front of a server name means that this server is the current reference server with which system time is compared. If this server cannot be reached, then the server that is marked with a preceding plus sign (+) is used.

Exercise 9-1   Configure Linux Time with NTP

In this exercise, you configure your server to get time from server DA1.

Do the following:

- Part I: Check System Time and Hardware Clock Time
- Part II: Enable NTP Client with YaST

Part I: Check System Time and Hardware Clock Time

Do the following:

1. From a terminal window, su to root (**su -**) with a password of **novell**.

2. View the system date and time by entering **date**.

3. View the hardware clock time by entering **hwclock**.

Part II: Enable NTP Client with YaST

In this part of the exercise, you configure the system to get time from another NTP time source (DA1).

Do the following:

1. Check the current system time by entering **date**.

   Record the time:

2. Manually set the system time with the time from the instructor's computer by entering the following:

   ntpdate 10.0.0.254

   If the offset is large, try entering the command again to reduce the size of the offset.

3. Check the time adjustment for the system date by entering **date**.

4. Configure the NTP client for your server with YaST:

   a. From your KDE desktop, select the **YaST** icon; then enter a password of **novell** and select **OK**.

   The YaST Control Center appears.

   b. Select **Network Services > NTP Client**.

   The NTP Client Configuration dialog box appears.

   c. Under Automatically Start NTP Daemon, select **When Booting System**.

   d. Scan for NTP servers on the network by selecting **Lookup**.

   e. (Conditional) If YaST finds more than one NTP server, select **DA1.digitalairlines.com** as the NTP server; if YaST does not find the NTP server, enter **DA1.digitalairlines.com**.

   f. Save the configuration by selecting **Finish**.

5. From the terminal window, view the status of the NTP time synchronization by entering **ntpq -p**.

6. View the changes made to the file /etc/ntp.conf by entering

   less /etc/ntp.conf.

   Notice that the NTP server is da1.digitalairlines.com.

7. View the hardware clock time by entering **hwclock**.

8. Set the hardware clock from the system time by entering the following:

   hwclock --systohc

9. Check the new hardware clock time by entering **hwclock**.

10. Close all open windows.

OBJECTIVE 2   ENABLE A WEB SERVER (APACHE)

Web servers play a critical role in delivering content over the Internet. Each Web page you see in your browser is delivered from a Web server installed on a host computer that stores the page and its objects.

Apache is the standard Web server in SUSE Linux Enterprise Server. To enable the Apache Web server on SLES 9, you need to know:

- How a Web Server Works
- Apache and SUSE Linux Enterprise Server
- How to Configure an Apache HTTP Server with YaST

For examples of Web documents you can use with Apache Web server, install the package apache2-example-pages and see the documents available in /srv/www/htdocs/.

How a Web Server Works

To understand how a Web server works, you need to know the following:

- What a Web Server Is
- How a Web Server Labels Content Types
- URL Components
- How a Web Server Delivers Content

What a Web Server Is

A Web server is a software program that runs on a host computer (such as a NetWare, Linux, or Windows server) and delivers files over the Internet that are stored on the host computer.

Web servers let you publish Hypertext Markup Language (HTML) documents over the Internet. HTML is the primary language used to create content pages on the Web.

Web servers can also distribute many other types of files, such as programs, videos, audio, graphics, and compressed Zip files.

Because the delivery of content is over the Internet or intranet, the host computer running the Web server must be physically connected to a TCP/IP-based network.

How a Web Server Labels Content Types

Web servers were developed to deliver simple HTML documents and images to a client (such as a Web browser). However, Web servers can now deliver more than HTML pages.

To correctly identify and display other types of documents, a Web browser relies on a Multipurpose Internet Mail Extension (MIME) header sent by the Web server.

The MIME header tells the Web browser what type of document is being sent and what program or plug-in is required to display it. These types include hundreds of different kinds of documents.

For example, more than 360 MIME types are included with the Apache Web server in the MIME.TYPES configuration file. The configuration file also includes variations on file extensions (such as MPEG, MPG, or MPE for files containing MPEG video content).

URL Components

Clients use URLs (such as *www.suse.com/index_us.html*) to request pages from a Web server. A URL consists of the following:

- **A protocol.** The following are frequently used protocols:
  - **http://** — Hypertext Transfer Protocol
  - **https://** — Secure, encrypted version of HTTP
  - **ftp://** — File Transfer Protocol for uploading and downloading files
- **A domain.** The domain can be divided into two parts. The first part (such as **www**) points to a computer. The second part (such as **suse.com**) is the actual domain. Together, they are referred to as FQDN (fully qualified domain name).
- **A resource**. This part of the URL specifies the full path to the resource. The resource can be a file (such as index.html). It can also be a CGI script, a Java server page, or some other resource.

How a Web Server Delivers Content

A Web server works in a client-server relationship with client programs. Client programs are usually Web browsers, such as Konqueror or Mozilla.

The client program requests information (such as an HTML page), and the Web server program supplies it.

Apache then delivers the actual resource (such as index.html) from its file directory. The file can be located in the top level of the directory (*www.suse.com/index.html*) or in a subdirectory (*www.suse.com/us/business/services/support/index.html*).

 The file path is relative to the DocumentRoot setting, which can be changed in the Apache configuration file (http.conf).

NOTE

HTML pages can be stored in a directory (passive or static pages) or generated in response to a query (active contents).

These requests and transfers use HTTP, which is part of the TCP/IP suite of protocols. The current version, HTTP 1.1, is documented in RFC 2068 and in the update RFC 2616. These RFCs are available at *www.w3.org*.

Commands and data are passed as plain text to port 80 (the default Web server port) through a TCP connection. Web browsers submit HTTP requests; Web servers use HTTP to respond by sending the requested file through port 80.

Apache and SUSE Linux Enterprise Server

To manage Apache Web server on SLES 9, you need to know the following:

- Installation of Apache Packages
- Activating Apache

- Storing Web Resource Files for Apache
- Expanding Apache Functionality
- Security Guidelines for Apache Web Server

Installation of Apache Packages

The following are recommendations for installing Apache software packages:

- **Basic installation.** For a basic installation, select the Apache package **apache2**.

- **Multiprocessing.** For multiprocessing, you can install one of the MPM (multiprocessing module) packages, such as **apache2-prefork** or **apache2-worker**.

  When choosing an MPM, remember that the thread-based worker MPM cannot be used with mod_php4, as some of the libraries of mod_php4 are not yet thread-safe.

  Newer versions of php (such as php5) are compatible with the thread-based worker MPM.

- **Documentation.** It is recommended that you install the extensive documentation provided in **apache2-doc**. An alias is available for the documentation, enabling you to access it with http://localhost/manual following the installation.

- **Development and compilation.** To develop modules for Apache or compile third-party modules, install **apache2-devel** and the needed development tools. These include the apxs tools, which are described in Section 22.6.5 of the **SLES 9 Installation and Administration Manual**.

Activating Apache

After installation, Apache is not started automatically. To start Apache, activate it in the runlevel editor. To start it permanently when the system is booted, select runlevels **3** and **5** in the runlevel editor.

To test whether Apache is running, enter **http://localhost/** in a Web browser. If Apache is active, you will see an example page (if **apache2-example-pages** is installed).

Storing Web Resource Files for Apache

The following are some basic SUSE Linux Enterprise Server directories you use to store resource files for the Apache Web server:

- **Static Web pages.** To display static Web pages with Apache, place your files in /srv/www/htdocs/.

  A few small example pages might already be installed there. Use these pages to check if Apache was installed correctly and is currently active. You can overwrite or uninstall these pages.

- **Custom CGI scripts.** Store custom CGI scripts in /srv/www/cgi-bin/.

■ **Log files.** During operation, Apache writes log messages to the file /var/log/ apache2/access_log.

These messages show which resources were requested, the time they were delivered, and what method was used (such as GET or POST).

Error messages are logged to /var/log/apache2/error_log.

Expanding Apache Functionality

By means of modules, Apache can be expanded with a wide range of functions. For example, Apache can execute CGI scripts in diverse programming languages by means of modules. Besides Perl and PHP, additional scripting languages, such as Python or Ruby, are also available.

Furthermore, there are modules for secure data transmission (Secure Sockets Layer [SSL]), user authentication, expanded logging, and other functions.

The modularization in Apache 2 has reached an advanced level, where almost everything except some minor tasks is handled by means of modules.

In Apache 2, even HTTP is processed by modules. For this reason, Apache 2 does not necessarily need to be a Web server. It can also be used for completely different purposes with other modules.

For example, there is a proof-of-concept POP3 server module based on Apache.

For additional information, see Section 22.13.4 in the *SLES 9 Installation and Administration Manual*.

Security Guidelines for Apache Web Server

The following are security guidelines for working with Apache Web server:

■ **Limit unneeded servers.** If you do not need a Web server on a machine, deactivate Apache in the runlevel editor, uninstall it, or do not install it.

To minimize the risk, deactivate all unneeded servers. This especially applies to hosts used as firewalls. If possible, do not run any servers on these hosts.

■ **Limit access to DocumentRoot.** By default, the DocumentRoot directory (/srv/www/htdocs/) and the CGI directory belong to the user **root**. You should not change this setting.

Apache should not have any write permissions for the data and scripts it delivers. If these directories are writable for all users, any user can place files into them. These files might then be executed by Apache with the permissions of user **wwwrun**.

- **Specify subdirectories for user Web content.** If users need to place files in the document directory of Apache, do not make it writable for all. Instead, create a subdirectory that is writable for all (such as /srv/www/htdocs/miscellaneous).

  Another possibility is to specify a subdirectory in users' home directories in the configuration file (http.conf). Users can then place any files for Web presentations in this directory (such as ~/public_html). By default, this is activated in SUSE Linux Enterprise Server.

  These Web pages can be accessed by specifying the user in the URL. The URL contains the element **~username** as a shortcut for the respective directory in the user's home directory.

  For example, enter **http://localhost/~geeko** in a browser to list the files in the directory public_ html in the home directory of the user geeko.

- **Keep updated on vulnerabilities.** If you operate a Web server—especially if this Web server is publicly accessible—stay informed about bugs and potentially vulnerable spots.

How to Configure an Apache HTTP Server with YaST

To configure an Apache HTTP Web server with YaST, do the following:

1. From the KDE desktop, start the YaST HTTP Server module by doing one of the following:

   - Select the **YaST** icon, enter the root *password*, and select **OK**; then select **Network Services > HTTP Server**.

     or

   - Open a terminal window and enter **sux -** and the root password; then enter **yast2 http-server**.

   The dialog box shown in Figure 9-3 appears.

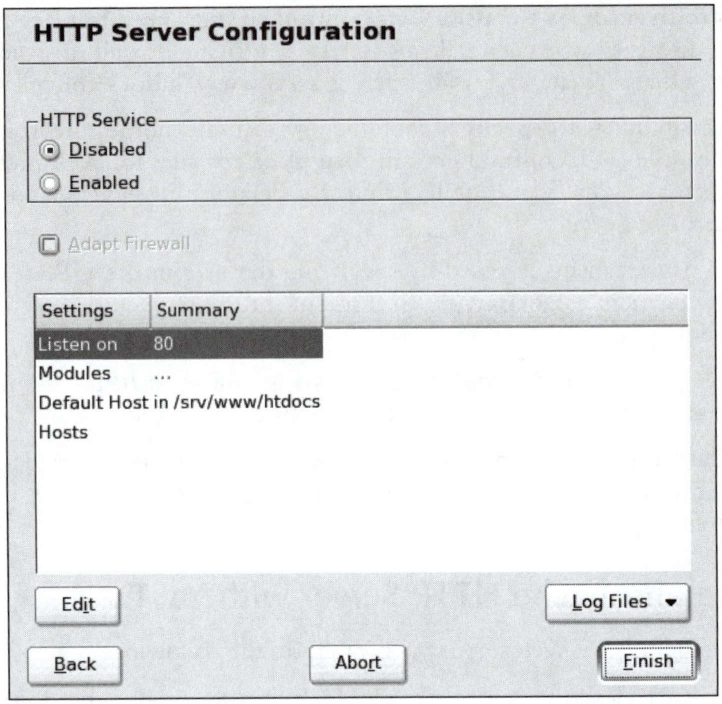

HTTP Server Configuration

HTTP Service
- ⊙ Disabled
- ○ Enabled

☐ Adapt Firewall

Settings	Summary
Listen on	80
Modules	...
Default Host in /srv/www/htdocs	
Hosts	

Edit   Log Files ▾

Back   Abort   Finish

Figure 9-3

2. Enable the HTTP server by selecting **Enabled**.

3. (Optional) Adapt the firewall to the ports where Apache2 listens by selecting **Adapt Firewall**.

   This option is available only if you have enabled the firewall.

4. Edit the following settings to meet your HTTP server needs by selecting a setting and selecting **Edit**:

   - **Listen on.** This is a list of ports and network IP addresses on which the server should listen for incoming requests. The default setting is port **80**.

   - **Modules.** This is a list of available modules (such as **cgi** and **mime**) available to the server. You can toggle the status of each module between **enabled** and **disabled**. You can also install additional modules.

   - **Default Host.** This is the server name of a host used as a default (fallback) host.

     If the server name of the default host is not specified, a path to the document root of the default host is displayed. The default setting is **/srv/www/htdocs**.

- **Hosts.** This is a list of hosts available to the Web server. You can add, edit, or delete hosts in the list.

  You can select one of the hosts in the list as a default host by selecting the host, and then selecting **Set as Default**. The default host is used if no other host matches an incoming request.

5. View existing HTTP server logs by selecting **Log Files > Show Access Log** or **Log Files > Show Error Log**.

6. When you finish configuring the HTTP server, save the settings by selecting **Finish**.

7. (Optional) If you started YaST from the desktop, close the **YaST Control Center**.

Exercise 9-2   Enable a Basic Apache Web Server

In this exercise, you do the following:

- Part I: Configure an Apache Server
- Part II: Test the Apache Server Configuration

Part I: Configure an Apache Server

Do the following:

1. Create a symbolic link under the Web server document directory dba that links back to /export/data2:

   a. From the KDE desktop, open a terminal window and su to root (**su -**) with a password of **novell**.

   b. Create the symbolic link by entering the following:

      ln -s /export/data2 /srv/www/htdocs/data2

      You will use this link later in the exercise.

2. From the KDE desktop, select the **YaST** icon; then enter a password of **novell** and select **OK**.

   The YaST Control Center appears.

3. Select **Network Services > HTTP Server**.

   The HTTP Server Configuration dialog box appears.

4. Select **Enabled**.

5. From the list of settings, select **Default Host**; then select **Edit**.

   A Host 'default' Configuration dialog box appears with a list of default configurations you can edit.

6. Select **Server Name**; then select **Edit**.

7. Enter **da***xx***.digitalairlines.com** (where **da***xx* is the hostname of your server); then select **OK**.

8. Select **Server Administrator E-Mail**; then select **Edit**.

9. For the e-mail address, enter **geeko@***your host*; then select **OK**.

10. Select the **Directory /srv/www/htdocs** option; then select **Edit**.

11. Change the Options parameter from Options None to the following:

    Options Indexes FollowSymLinks

    This makes the project files available via the Web server.

12. When you finish, save the change by selecting **OK**.

13. Return to the HTTP Server Configuration dialog box by selecting **OK**.

14. Save the changes to the system by selecting **Finish**.

Part II: Test the Apache Server Configuration

Do the following:

1. Open the Konqueror browser and enter the ***IP address*** (or ***DNS name***) of your server.

   A Web page appears indicating that the Apache Web server was successfully installed.

2. Test the symbolic line configuration by entering **http://***your_IP_address*/**data2**.

   The files in data2 are listed in the browser.

   By default, each user has his or her own Web page.

3. Access geeko's Web page by entering **http://***your_IP_address*/**~geeko**.

   The home page for geeko appears.

4. Manage the Apache service from the command line:

   a. From the terminal window, stop the HTTP server by entering **rcapache2 stop**.

   b. Start the service again by entering **rcapache2 start**.

   c. Check to see if the process is running by entering the following:

      ps auxf | grep httpd

5. (Optional) If you have time, return to YaST and try disabling user home directory access through the Web server.

6. When you finish, close all open windows.

OBJECTIVE 3   ENABLE THE EXTENDED INTERNET DAEMON (XINETD)

In this objective, you learn how to enable the extended internet daemon (xinetd) by reviewing:

- What inetd Is
- How to Configure xinetd with YaST
- How to Manage xinetd Manually
- How to Configure the TCP Wrapper

What inetd Is

Many services on a server are administered and started through the super daemon package inetd or xinetd. The package xinetd is the default used on SLES 9.

The super daemon acts as a mediator of connection requests for a series of services. It accepts the connection requests directly, starts the required service, and passes the request to the newly started server.

If the connection between the client and the server is terminated, the server started by inetd is removed from memory.

Starting services through inetd has both advantages and disadvantages. The most significant advantage is saving resources (especially memory), since a server is only started when it is needed. A disadvantage, however, is that a delay occurs while the required service is loaded, started, and connected.

As a rule, you only want to use inetd for services that are occasionally (not permanently) needed on the server. Some of the services run traditionally by inetd include Telnet and FTP.

 For detailed information about xinetd, enter **man 8 xinetd**.

NOTE

How to Configure xinetd with YaST

To configure the services mediated by xinetd, you can use the YaST Network Services (inetd) module.

Do the following:

1. From the KDE desktop, start the YaST Network Services (inetd) module by doing one of the following:

   - Select the **YaST** icon, enter the root *password*, and select **OK**; then select **Network Services > Network Services (inetd)**.

or

- Open a terminal window and enter **sux –** and the root *password*; then enter **yast2 inetd**.

The dialog box shown in Figure 9-4 appears.

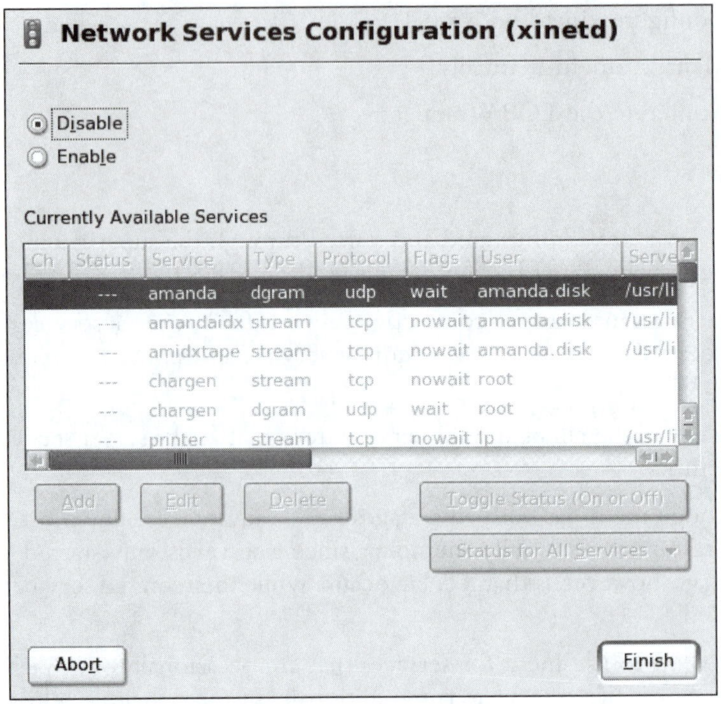

Network Services Configuration (xinetd)

◉ Di̱sable
◯ Enab̲le

Currently Available Services

Ch	Status	Service	Type	Protocol	Flags	User	Serve
	---	amanda	dgram	udp	wait	amanda.disk	/usr/li
	---	amandaidx	stream	tcp	nowait	amanda.disk	/usr/li
	---	amidxtape	stream	tcp	nowait	amanda.disk	/usr/li
	---	chargen	stream	tcp	nowait	root	
	---	chargen	dgram	udp	wait	root	
	---	printer	stream	tcp	nowait	lp	/usr/li

[Add]   [Edit]   [Delete]   [Toggle Status (On or Off)]

[Status for All Services ▾]

[Abo̱rt]   [F̲inish]

Figure 9-4

2. Enable the inetd super daemon by selecting **Enable**.

   This enables inetd or xinetd, depending on what you have installed (the default for SLES 9 is xinetd).

   The Currently Available Services list is activated. You can add, edit, or delete services in the list.

> **NOTE** Managing the services available through inetd (except for enabling services such as Telnet or FTP) requires a skill set beyond the objectives of this course. This is especially true of configuring services with **Edit**.

Notice that some services are off (---), while others are not installed (NI) and cannot be configured.

3. Configure a service to be administered by inetd by selecting the service; then select **Toggle Status (On or Off)**.

   The word "On" appears in the Status column. An "X" appears in the Changed (Ch) column to indicate that the service has been edited and will be changed in the system configuration.

4. (Optional) Change the status of all installed services to on or off by selecting **Status for All Services > Activate All Services** or **Status for All Services > Deactivate All Services**.

5. When you finish configuring the services, save the configuration setting and start the inetd (or xinetd) daemon by selecting **Finish**.

6. (Optional) If you started YaST from the desktop, close the **YaST Control Center**.

How to Manage xinetd Manually

To manage xinetd manually, you need to know how to do the following:

- Start, Stop, and Restart xinetd
- Configure xinetd
- Configure Access Control
- Configure Log Files

Start, Stop, and Restart xinetd

Xinetd (/etc/init.d/xinetd) is a script that starts xinetd. To provide services through xinetd, you need to install and start the daemon on your SUSE Linux Enterprise Server.

To have the daemon automatically activated at boot, enter

insserv xinetd. You can find out whether the daemon is activated or not by entering **rcxinetd status**. You can also start and stop the daemon by entering **rcxinetd start** or **rcxinetd stop**.

Configure xinetd

To configure xinetd, you need to know the following:

- How to Edit the File /etc/xinetd.conf
- The Directory /etc/xinetd.d
- Internal Services

How to Edit the File /etc/xinetd.conf   You can configure xinetd manually by editing the configuration file /etc/xinetd.conf. With more than two dozen keywords recognized by /etc/xinetd.conf, it can be difficult to modify the file (despite the good documentation).

The following is the syntax of /etc/xinetd.conf for the default configuration parameters of xinetd:

```
defaults
     {
            key operator parameter parameter. . .
     }
```

The following is the syntax for configuring each network service in the file:

```
service service_name
     {
            key operator parameter parameter. . .
     }
```

Operators include =, -=, and +=. Most attributes (keys) only support the operator =, but you can include additional values to some attributes by entering += or remove them by entering -=.

The first entry in the configuration file is optional and enables default configurations such as the following to be made:

```
defaults
{
          log_type        = FILE /var/log/xinetd.log
          log_on_success  = HOST EXIT DURATION
          log_on_failure  = HOST ATTEMPT
#          only_from        = localhost
          instances       = 30
          cps             = 50 10
```

The configurations for log_type and instances will be overwritten if something else has been defined in the individual service entries. For all other attributes, the default configurations are combined with the values set in the services.

The log_type statement can define whether (as in the example) the output is written directly to a log file (/var/log/xinetd.log) or forwarded to the daemon syslog (such as **log_type = SYSLOG authpriv**).

If there are high security demands, you might want to consider leaving logging up to the syslog daemon in order to prevent potential unwanted access to the xinetd log file.

The keywords log_on_success and log_on_failure configure what should be recorded in the log file, depending on whether the network service runs successfully or fails.

The value for instances can be used to limit the maximum possible number of daemons for each service, which protects the machine from either intentional or accidental overload due to too many simultaneous connections (denial-of-service attempts).

The cps is the connections per second. The first value (50) is the maximum number of connections per second that can be handled; the second value (10) is the wait period before accepting new connections after the maximum has been exceeded (helpful in preventing denial-of-service attacks).

All other entries look similar to the default entry but only contain the configuration for the respective network service, such as the following example for finger:

```
# default: off
# description: The finger server answers finger requests.
 Finger is \
#        a protocol that allows remote users to see information such \
#        as login name and login time for currently logged in users.
service finger
{
        socket_type      = stream
        protocol         = tcp
        wait             = no
        user             = nobody
        server           = /usr/sbin/in.fingerd
        server_args      = -w
#        disable          = yes
}
```

Table 9-2 describes the keywords in the example.

Table 9-2

Keyword	Description
socket_type	Refers to the type of socket (stream, dgram, raw, or seqpacket)
protocol	Refers to the protocol (usually tcp or udp) used by the corresponding network service; the protocol must be entered in the file /etc/protocols
wait	Specifies whether xinetd must wait for the daemon to release the port before it can process further connection requests for the same port (Yes: single-threaded) or not (No: multithreaded)
user	Indicates under which user ID the daemon will start; the user name must be listed in the file /etc/passwd
server	Specifies the absolute path name of the daemon to start
server_args	Specifies which parameters to pass to the daemon when it starts

NOTE

For a description of all possible parameters, enter **man xinetd.conf**.

The Directory /etc/xinetd.d/   Besides the configuration of services in the file /etc/ xinetd.conf, you can create a separate configuration file for every service in the directory /etc/xinetd.d/.

The directive includedir /etc/xinetd.d in the file /etc/xinetd.conf prompts xinetd to interpret all files in the directory /etc/xinetd.d/ for the configuration of the services. The same attributes and the same syntax can be used as in xinetd.conf.

The main advantage of splitting the configuration into several files is improved transparency.

Internal Services   The daemon xinetd contains internal services (such as echo, time, daytime, chargen, and discard) that can be labeled in the configuration as follows:

```
type = INTERNAL
```

Otherwise, xinetd assumes that external services are involved. With services such as echo, which is both TCP- and UDP-based, you not only need to specify the respective socket_ type but also need to identify the service in the id field in such a way that it is properly distinguished from other services.

The following is an example for echo:

```
# /etc/xinet.d/echo
# default: off
# description: An echo server. This is the tcp version.

service echo
{
        type            = INTERNAL
        id              = echo-stream
        socket_type     = stream
        protocol        = tcp
        user            = root
        wait            = no
        disable         = yes
}
# /etc/xinet.d/echo-udp
# default: off
# description: An echo server. This is the udp version.

service echo
{
        type            = INTERNAL UNLISTED
        id              = echo-dgram
        socket_type     = dgram
        protocol        = udp
        user            = root
        wait            = yes
        disable         = yes
        port            = 7
}
```

Table 9–3 lists signals for checking xinetd.

Table 9-3

Signal	Number	Description
SIGUSR1	10	Causes an internal state dump (the default dump file is /var/run/xinetd.dump)
SIGQUIT	3	Causes xinetd termination
SIGTERM	15	Terminates all running services before terminating xinetd
SIGHUP	1	xinetd rereads the configuration file and terminates the servers for services that are no longer available
SIGIO	29	Causes an internal consistency check to verify that the data structures used by the program have not been corrupted

Configure Access Control

The daemon xinetd recognizes the following four parameters used to control access monitoring:

- **only_from.** With this parameter, you define which hosts can use which service. You can specify complete IP addresses from hosts or networks or just the network or hostnames.

  You can define this parameter in the defaults section or in the service section.

- **no_access.** With this parameter, you define which hosts can be excluded from access. You can specify complete IP addresses from hosts or networks or just the network or hostnames.

  You can define this parameter in the defaults section or in the service section.

- **access_time.** You can use this parameter to define at which times the service is available (in 24-hour format).

  You can define this parameter in the defaults section or in the service section.

- **disabled.** You can use this parameter to completely shut off a server. This also applies to logging access attempts.

  The parameter disabled can only be used in the defaults section.

The following is an example for the Telnet service:

```
# default: off
# description:
# Telnet is the old login server which is INSECURE and should
#   therefore not be used. Use secure shell (openssh).
#   If you need telnetd not to "keep-alives" (e.g.
#   if it runs over an ISDN \
```

```
#    uplink), add "-n".  See 'man telnetd' for more details.
service telnet
{
          socket_type        = stream
          protocol           = tcp
          wait               = no
          user               = root
          server             = /usr/sbin/in.telnetd
          server_args        = -n
          only-from          = 192.168.0.3   192.168.0.7   192.168.0.9
          only-from         += 192.168.0.10 192.168.0.12
          no_access          = 192.168.1.0
          flags              = IDONLY
          access_times       = 07:00-21:00
#          disable = yes
}
```

These settings result in the following:

- Access is permitted for machines with the following IP addresses:

  192.168.0.3

  192.168.0.7

  192.168.0.9

  192.168.0.10

  192.168.0.12

- Access is denied to the network with the IP address 192.168.1.0.

- The service is available from 7:00 a.m. to 9:00 p.m.

The following is an example for the attribute disabled:

`disabled = finger`

With this setting, the service finger is switched off completely. If a computer tries to access the service, the attempt is not even logged.

If you place high demands on access monitoring, you can tighten the security level even more by using the parameters INTERCEPT and IDONLY in the flags entry.

If the parameter USERID was set in the log_on_access and log_on_failure entries, IDONLY then makes sure that a connection to the network service is permitted only when the user identification service (such as identd) of the host requesting the network service issues the user ID.

If the parameter INTERCEPT has been entered as well, xinetd also attempts to make sure that an authorized host is on the other end of already existing connections that the connection has not been intercepted.

However, connection monitoring only functions if a multithreaded or an internal xinetd service is not involved. In addition, it puts a heavy burden on the network connection and the performance of the network service.

Configure Log Files

Almost every hacker has to make several attempts and needs some time before achieving success. To protect your server, you not only need hacker-resistant software but also need log files that the software can use to detect unauthorized login attempts.

Because of this, it does not make sense to deter only unauthorized access attempts. To maintain optimal system security, you need to record failed and unauthorized connection attempts.

To shut off a service but still retain its logging functions, configure only_from without using any additional parameters, as in the following:

```
only_from      =
```

Logging through xinetd is controlled by the log_type statement along with the attributes log_on_success and log_on_failure.

These let you record from which host and for how long an access attempt was made, and which user was using the service (if the remote host supports this feature).

In addition, you can also log the circumstances of how and why the network service was used. However, even the best log does not mean much if you do not check it on a regular basis for failed connection attempts.

How to Configure the TCP Wrapper

Every computer connected to a network can be accessed from the network as long as the connection exists.

If the computer is not protected by software (such as a firewall), anyone on the Internet can attempt to use the network services on an unprotected computer without being noticed.

You can use the ***TCP wrapper*** to restrict access to individual network services.

For stand-alone services, TCP wrapper support must be compiled into the daemon, service, or application. For services started via inetd, TCP wrapper support is controlled by inetd.conf.

To configure TCP wrappers, you need to understand:

- The Role of the tcpd Daemon
- How to Configure Access Controls
- How to Check the TCP Wrapper

The Role of the tcpd Daemon

The standard inetd does not let you regulate access to the services on your own computer. inetd uses a separate application, the TCP wrapper /usr/sbin/tcpd, to regulate that access.

The TCP wrapper acts as a filter, and is placed between inetd and the service daemons. Inetd starts the wrapper instead of directly starting the service.

The wrapper writes the name and address of the host requesting the connection to a log file, verifies if the request is permitted, then starts the corresponding daemon.

This is reflected in /etc/inetd.conf, which uses /usr/sbin/tcpd instead of the service daemon (such as /usr/sbin/vsftpd for ftp) to start the service.

The following is an example:

```
ftp      stream  tcp     nowait  root    /usr/sbin/tcpd  vsftpd
telnet   stream  tcp     nowait  root    /usr/sbin/tcpd  in.telnetd
finger   stream  tcp     nowait  nobody  /usr/sbin/tcpd  in.fingerd -w
```

Because the wrapper is not integrated with the client or with the server program, its existence cannot be perceived from the outside. This also guarantees that the wrapper can remain independent of the programs it is supposed to monitor.

When the connection between the client and the server program is established, the wrapper is deleted from memory and does not create any additional load for the current connection.

However, after an authorized server has started, it can accept additional connections on its own without consulting the wrapper about whether additional connections should take place.

For example, some UDP services remain in memory for a while after the connection has already been closed in order to receive additional connection requests.

You can recognize these UDP-based services in inetd.conf because they include the wait option.

How to Configure Access Controls

You can configure access controls for the TCP wrapper by editing /etc/hosts.allow (to permit requests) and /etc/hosts.deny (to deny requests).

When receiving a request, tcpd first reads /etc/hosts.allow. If no matching pattern is found, then tcpd reads /etc/hosts.deny.

NOTE

If you allow access in /etc/hosts.allow, it cannot be restricted again in /etc/hosts.deny.

If tcpd does not find a pattern that matches the request in either of the configuration files, the connection is permitted. The same is true if one or both configuration files are empty or do not exist.

The syntax of both configuration files is the same and consists of the following three fields:

daemon: *host* [: *option* : *option* ...]

- *daemon*. A list of services from /etc/inetd.conf
- *host*. A list of hostnames or IP addresses separated by commas
- *option*. A list of options

In addition, tcpd recognizes the keywords ALL and EXCEPT for both fields, and LOCAL, KNOWN, UNKNOWN, and PARANOID for the host field.

Table 9-4 provides a description of these keywords.

9

Table 9-4

Keyword	Description
ALL	All services and all hosts from which exceptions can be defined by EXCEPT
LOCAL	All hostnames that do not have a dot in the name—usually all the hostnames defined in /etc/hosts
UNKNOWN	All hosts whose names tcpd cannot distinguish
KNOWN	All hosts in which the hostname matches the given IP address and vice versa
PARANOID	All hosts in which the hostname does not match the given IP address and vice versa

The following example shows configurations for hosts.allow and hosts.deny that permit the use of all network services in the local network but deny external computers access to Telnet, finger, and FTP:

- **/etc/hosts.allow:**
  ```
  ALL: LOCAL
  ```

- **/etc/hosts.deny:**
  ```
  in.telnetd, in.fingerd, vsftpd: ALL
  ```

The following is an example of a more complex configuration:

- **/etc/hosts.allow:**
  ```
  ALL: pluto.example.com
  ALL EXCEPT vsftpd: mars.example.com
  vsftpd: andromeda.example.com
  ```

- **/etc/hosts.deny:**
  ```
  ALL: ALL
  ```

The first line in /etc/hosts.allow ensures that all network services can be accessed from pluto.example.com. In the second line, all network services other than FTP are made available for mars.example.com.

The third line ensures that only FTP transfers are possible from the host andromeda. example.com.

In /etc/hosts.deny, all other hosts are denied all services. "All services" also includes services that are not started via inetd but run as independent services, and whose access control is also implemented via the files /etc/hosts.allow and /etc/hosts.deny.

Since this might apply to the portmapper, NFS would also be involved in the above configuration—a possibly unwanted effect, which, if you do not consider, could lead to a long search for the cause of errors.

If you require more specific control functions, Table 9-5 lists some of the more commonly used keywords for monitoring access.

Table 9-5

Keyword	Description
ALLOW and DENY	You can use these keywords to summarize all the access rules in the file /etc/hosts.allow. Both of these options either allow or refuse access.
spawn	This runs the given shell script after the placeholders shown in Table 9-6 are replaced.
twist	The given command is started instead of the running process. Existing placeholders are replaced first.
rfc931 [*timeout*]	This option identifies users attempting to establish a connection. For this, a client-side RFC931-compatible daemon is required. If the daemon is not present, it can lead to delays in setting up the connection. If no value is given for *timeout*, the default value (10 seconds) is used.
banners */directory*	Searches in */directory* for a file whose name matches the daemon to be started. If such a file is found, its contents will be sent to the client after the placeholders have been expanded.
nice [*number*]	The server process is started with the corresponding nice value. This can be useful to make more resources available to other server processes.
setenv *name value*	This option defines environment variables for the server process. Here, too, a placeholder expansion is executed.

The following example in /etc/hosts.allow allows Telnet access from anywhere:

```
in.telnetd: ALL: banners /etc/tcpd: ALLOW
```

If a file in .telnetd is located in the /etc/tcpd directory, its contents will be sent to the client before the Telnet service is started.

In the following example, finger is only allowed in the local network:

```
in.fingerd: ALL EXCEPT LOCAL: banners /etc/tcpd:
spawn ( echo "finger request from %h"| mail -s "finger!!" root ) & : DENY
```

Clients outside the local network can obtain information from the /etc/tcpd/in.fingerd file. An e-mail to root is generated, which contains the hostname or IP address of the machine making this request.

The following example starts the FTP daemons with a nice value of 15:

```
vsftpd: ALL: nice 15
```

This enables you to influence the load on a server, for instance, by allocating more resources to other services.

In the following example, the command **echo "No one logged in"** is started instead of the finger daemon:

```
in.fingerd: ALL: twist ( echo "No one logged in" )
```

The client is informed that no one is logged in.

 For additional information about these and other options, enter **man hosts_options**.

NOTE

How to Check the TCP Wrapper

Since a command's flexibility can easily lead to configuration errors, you cannot just hope that your network services are secure without reviewing them first.

Fortunately, the TCP wrapper package offers some tools for troubleshooting as well as for analyzing errors.

You can review the configuration of tcpd using the **tcpdchk** command. This program reports a multitude of possible problems; these can be network services listed in /etc/inetd. conf that do not really exist, syntax errors in the configuration files, or unknown hostnames.

However, there are some configurations in which tcpdchk does not find any errors but where tcpd still does not act as expected. In such cases, you can use **tcpdmatch** to provide information about how tcpd would handle various types of access attempts.

Moles and Trappers   You can enter shell commands in the configuration files, which will be executed when the request matches one of the patterns defined in the daemon and host fields.

Because tcpd recognizes the placeholders in Table 9-6, which can be used in shell scripts, attempts at accessing certain services can be monitored.

Table 9-6

Placeholder	Description
%a	Address of the host making the request
%c	Information about the host making the request (such as user@host and user@address), depending on the information available
%d	Name of the daemon
%h	Either the name of the host making the request or the address, if the name cannot be ascertained
%n	Name of the host making the request, unknown, or paranoid
%p	The process ID of the daemon
%s	Information about the server (such as daemon@host and daemon@ address), depending on the information available
%u	User name of the host making the request or unknown if the remote host does not possess a user ID as recognized by RFC931

The following example shows a script in the configuration file /etc/hosts.allow that records all successful access attempts to the network services in a log file:

```
ALL: ALL: spawn echo "Access of %u@%h to %d" >> /var/log/net.log
```

A finger client (/usr/sbin/safe_finger) is also included in the TCP wrapper to provide better protection against defense measures that other machines might put in place when their finger daemons are queried.

The idea behind safe_finger is to entrap (using simple methods) possible intruders by uncovering their identities with a **fingerd** query.

In the following example, all query results of access attempts to any network service taking place outside the network, other than finger, are stored in a log file:

```
ALL EXCEPT in.fingerd : ALL EXCEPT LOCAL : \
twist /usr/sbin/safe_finger -l @%h >> /var/log/unknown.net.log
```

Excluding finger itself from this screening process is a measure of caution. If such a trap including finger were likewise set up remotely, an endless loop could result, in which the finger query of one machine would result in a finger query of the other in an endless cycle.

Exercise 9-3   Configure the Internet Daemon (xinetd) and TCP Wrappers

In this exercise, you do the following:

- Part I: Enable xinetd Services with YaST
- Part II: Enable xinetd Services Manually
- Part III: Configure TCP Wrappers

Part I: Enable xinetd Services with YaST

Do the following:

1. From your KDE desktop, select the **YaST** icon; then enter a password of **novell** and select **OK**.

   The YaST Control Center appears.

2. Select **Network Services > Network Services (inetd)**.

   The Network Services Configuration (xinetd) dialog box appears.

3. Select **Enable**.

   A list of currently available services becomes active.

4. Scroll down and select the service **telnet**; then set the service to On by selecting **Toggle Status (On or Off)**.

5. Save the configuration to the system by selecting **Finish**.

6. Test the configuration:

   a. Open a terminal window and su to root (**su –**) with a password of **novell**.

   b. Telnet to localhost by entering **telnet localhost**.

   c. Log in as **geeko** with a password of **N0v3ll**.

   d. Log out by entering **exit**.

   e. Log in to a partner's server as geeko by entering

   telnet *partner_server_IP_address*.

   You'll need to wait until the neighbor completes enabling inetd and Telnet.

   f. Log out by entering **exit**.

9

Part II: Enable xinetd Services Manually

Enable the FTP server by doing the following:

1. From the terminal window, edit the file /etc/xinetd.d/vsftpd by entering **vim /etc/xinetd.d/vsftpd**.

2. At the bottom of the file, change the disable = yes setting to the following:

   disable = **no**

3. Exit vi and save the changes by entering **:wq**.

4. Restart the service xinetd by entering **rcxinetd restart**.

5. Test the FTP service by doing the following:

   a. Enter **ftp localhost**.

   b. Log in anonymously by entering the following:

   - Name: **ftp**
   - Password: *your e-mail address*

   c. Exit FTP by entering **exit**.

   d. Log in to a partner's server anonymously by entering

   ftp *partner_server_IP_address*.

   e. Log out by entering **exit**.

Part III: Configure TCP Wrappers

Do the following:

1. Secure the Telnet service so that everyone in the classroom except your part-ner can Telnet to your system:

   a. Edit the file /etc/hosts.deny by entering **vim /etc/hosts.deny**.

   b. Add the following to the end of the file:

   in.telnetd : *partner_server_IP_address*

   Make sure there is an empty line at the end of the file or the configuration will not work.

   c. Exit vi and save the file by entering **:wq**.

   d. Have the partner attempt to Telnet to your host; then have another student in the classroom attempt to Telnet to your host.

   The connection for your partner is closed. However, others can Telnet to your server.

If the results are not what you expect, check the file /var/log/messages by entering **tail -f /var/log/messages**.

   e. Edit the file /etc/hosts.deny again by entering **vim /etc/hosts.deny**.

   f. Place a comment character (#) in front of the line you just added to the file /etc/hosts.deny; then add the following line.

   ALL : ALL

   g. Exit vi and save the file by entering **:wq**.

   Apply the same security restriction by editing the file /etc/hosts.allow.

   h. Edit the file /etc/hosts.allow by entering **vim /etc/hosts.allow**.

   i. Add the following to the end of the file:

   in.telnetd : ALL EXCEPT *partner_server_IP_address*

   j. Exit vi and save the file by entering **:wq**.

   k. Have your partner attempt to Telnet to the system; then have another student in the classroom attempt to Telnet to your host.

   The results are the same as with the file hosts.deny.

2. Perform a twist by editing ALL : ALL in the file /etc/hosts.deny:

   a. Edit the file /etc/hosts.deny by entering **vim /etc/hosts.deny**.

   b. Edit the ALL : ALL line to reflect the following:

   ALL: ALL: twist echo "This service is not accessible from %a!"

   c. Exit vi and save the file by entering **:wq**.

   d. Have your partner attempt to Telnet to the system to verify that the message is sent.

   e. When you finish testing the twist, edit the file /etc/hosts.deny by entering **vim /etc/hosts.deny**.

   f. Comment out (#) the ALL: ALL: ... line.

   g. Exit vi and save the file by entering **:wq**.

   Commenting out the line makes sure that exercises later in the course work properly.

3. Make sure that all users that Telnet or FTP to your server are logged by IP address to the file /tmp/service-access.log:

   a. Edit the file /etc/hosts.allow by entering

   vim /etc/hosts.allow.

9

b. At the bottom of the file, change the line in.telnetd to reflect the following:

in.telnetd,vsftpd : ALL EXCEPT
partner_server_IP_address **:**
spawn (echo "%a accessed %s" >> /tmp/service–access.log)

c. Exit vi and save the file by entering **:wq**.

d. Have someone in the class other than your partner attempt to Telnet to your system to verify that the entry is logged.

e. Verify that all of the activity to the services under xinetd have been logged in /var/log/xinetd.log by entering

cat /var/log/xinetd.log.

4. Disable the vsftpd service:

To be able to complete the exercise successfully, you need to disable vsftpd.

a. Edit the file /etc/xinetd.d/vsftpd by entering **vim /etc/xinetd.d/vsftpd**.

disable = **yes**.

b. Exit vi and save the file by entering **:wq**.

c. Restart the service xinetd by entering **rcxinetd restart**.

5. Close all open windows.

OBJECTIVE 4 ENABLE AN FTP SERVER

To enable an FTP server on SLES 9, you need to understand the following:

- The Role of an FTP Server
- How FTP Works
- Advantages of PureFTPd Server
- How to Install and Run PureFTPd Server
- How to Configure PureFTPd Server

The Role of an FTP Server

As the name indicates, the File Transfer Protocol (FTP) enables the transfer of files from one computer to another. Today, FTP is used mainly for file transfer on the Internet.

The basic features supported by FTP and available to the user are:

- Sending, receiving, deleting, and renaming files
- Creating, deleting, and changing directories
- Transferring data in binary or ASCII mode

An FTP server allows accesses after authentication against a password database. As a rule, these are the files /etc/passwd and /etc/shadow. Other authentication systems, such as NIS or LDAP, are possible.

An FTP server such as PureFTPd also supports authentication against its own password database, which is independent from the files /etc/passwd and /etc/shadow.

In addition, guest access can be set up as anonymous FTP (**aFTP**). Generally, users logging in to an FTP use **anonymous** or **ftp** as their user name and their e-mail address as the password.

The address is not normally checked for correctness, although some servers check the syntax and require an entry in the format *user@hostname.domain*. An anonymous user is normally given access to a restricted directory tree (a chroot environment).

How FTP Works

FTP uses the TCP transport protocol. FTP basically uses two TCP connections between the client and the server.

The first of these connections sends FTP commands from the client to the server. By default, this command channel is port 21 on the server.

To begin an FTP session, the client addresses the FTP command channel on port 21 of the server. The client then sends the desired commands to the FTP server.

For the actual file transfer, or in response to certain commands like **ls**, FTP uses the second TCP connection, which is only created when a file is ready for transfer (for example, by a GET or PUT command).

There are two different types of data transfer:

- **Active data transfer.** The FTP client offers the FTP server an unprivileged TCP port for the data channel connection. The server then initializes the data channel from port 20 to the port offered by the client.

- **Passive data transfer.** The FTP client informs the FTP server that it wants to use a passive data transfer using the PASV command.

  The FTP server then offers the FTP client an unprivileged TCP port for a data channel connection, and the client initializes the data channel on the port offered by the server.

Passive FTP transfer avoids the need of an initializing connection from the server to the client for allowing firewall administrators to establish a secure configuration.

Advantages of PureFTPd Server

A number of FTP servers for Linux are available, such as the standard FTP server in.ftpd, the FTP server from Washington University (wu.ftpd), proftpd, or the PureFTPd FTP server (pure-ftpd).

Although you can use other FTP servers to provide FTP network services, PureFTPd has several features that make it stand out from other FTP servers:

- Consistent use of chroot environments
- Uncomplicated configuration of virtual FTP servers
- Virtual users independent of the system users listed in the file /etc/passwd
- Configuration via command-line parameters or with a configuration file

How to Install and Run PureFTPd Server

You can install the PureFTPd server with the YaST Install and Remove Software module by selecting the package pure-ftpd.

After installation, you configure the FTP server manually by editing the configuration file /etc/pure-ftpd/pure-ftpd.conf.

You can run PureFTPd server using one of the following methods:

- **From the command line.** To start PureFTPd from the command line, enter **pure-ftpd** *options* (such as **pure-ftpd –B –e**). If you start pure-ftpd this way, no configuration file is used.

NOTE

For details on the possible pure-ftpd options, enter **man pure-ftpd**.

- **From a start script.** To start PureFTPd, enter **/etc/init.d/pure-ftpd start** (or **rcpure-ftpd start**). To stop the PureFTPd service, enter **rcpure-ftpd stop**.

  The configuration file /etc/pure-ftpd/pure-ftpd.conf is parsed by the Perl script /usr/sbin/pure-config-args to translate the parameters in the configuration file to command-line options.

  These options are then passed to the daemon /usr/sbin/pure-ftpd.

  If you want pure-ftpd to be initialized upon start-up, you need to set symbolic links by entering the following:

  insserv /etc/init.d/pure-ftpd

- **From inetd.** If you want to start PureFTPd via inetd, you need to add a corresponding entry to the file /etc/inetd.conf with the required options, as in the following example:

```
ftp stream tcp nowait root /usr/sbin/tcpd pure-ftpd -A -i
```

In this example, PureFTPd is started by the TCP wrapper (/usr/sbin/tcpd), allowing access restriction through /etc/hosts.allow or /etc/hosts.deny.

Because the configuration file pure-ftpd.conf is not parsed or evaluated when PureFTPd is started via inetd, all the required options must be given in the file /etc/inetd.conf.

For details on all command-line options for PureFTPd, enter **pure-ftpd --help**.

9

How to Configure PureFTPd Server

To perform basic configuration tasks for PureFTPd server, you need to know the following:

- How to Configure Anonymous FTP
- How to Configure FTP with Virtual Hosts for Anonymous FTP
- How to Configure FTP for Authorized Users
- How to Configure FTP with Virtual Users Not Included in /etc/passwd

How to Configure Anonymous FTP

To configure anonymous FTP for PureFTPd, you need to have an FTP user and home directory (such as /srv/ftp/) in the file /etc/passwd (exists by default in SLES 9).

However, unlike other FTP servers, you do not need to create any subdirectories (such as bin) in the home directory.

The following is an example of a simple pure-ftpd.conf file:

```
# Cage in every user in his home directory
ChrootEveryone          yes

# Don't allow authenticated users - have a public anonymous FTP only.
AnonymousOnly           yes

# Disallow anonymous users to upload new files (no = upload is allowed)
AnonymousCantUpload     yes

# Disallow downloading of files owned by "ftp", i.e.
# files that were uploaded but not validated by a local admin.
```

```
AntiWarez                        yes

# Never overwrite files. When a file whose name already exists is
# uploaded, it gets automatically renamed to file.1, file.2, file.3, ...
AutoRename                       yes
```

In this configuration file, it is only possible to log in as an anonymous user, regardless of what user name is given. It is not possible to change to a directory above /srv/ftp/, and no files can be uploaded to the server—only downloads are possible.

The equivalent command on the command line would be

pure-ftpd -A -e -i.

If you want anonymous users to upload files to the server, the configuration file would look like the following:

```
# Cage in every user in his home directory
ChrootEveryone                   yes

# Don't allow authenticated users - have a public anonymous FTP only.
AnonymousOnly                    yes

# Allow anonymous users to upload new files
AnonymousCantUpload              no

# Disallow downloading of files owned by "ftp", i.e.
# files that were uploaded but not validated by a local admin.
AntiWarez                        yes

# Never overwrite files. When a file whose name already exists is
# uploaded, it gets automatically renamed to file.1, file.2, file.3, ...
AutoRename                       yes
```

The AntiWarez option is recommended because the server could otherwise be misused to handle undesirable (or even illegal) data.

Files uploaded to the server belong to the user ftp, but files of the user ftp cannot be downloaded from the server because of this option. The administrator must change the owner of the file using the command /bin/chown before this is possible.

The last line ensures that a file that might already exist is not overwritten. Instead, a new file is created with a number on the end (such as **file.1**).

The equivalent command on the command line would be

pure-ftpd -A -e -s -r.

How to Configure FTP with Virtual Hosts for Anonymous FTP

Virtual FTP hosts allow a number of FTP sites to be hosted on one machine (such as ftp.planets.dom and ftp.moons.dom). Each of these FTP sites requires its own IP address because the FTP protocol cannot handle hostnames.

For this reason, you need to assign multiple IP addresses to your network card. In addition, you need to configure a service such as DNS that guarantees that an IP address is matched correctly to a domain.

Instead of using the command line or the file pure-ftpd.conf, you configure a virtual host through the directory /etc/pure-ftpd/. The configuration is a very simple two-step process:

1. From the command line, use ifconfig to create virtual network devices, as in the following example:

   ifconfig eth0:0 192.168.5.80

   ifconfig eth0:1 192.168.5.81

2. Create a symbolic link in /etc/pure-ftpd/ with this IP address, which is linked to the directory with the files to offer over anonymous FTP at this address.

   The following is an example:

   cd /etc/pure-ftpd

   ln –s /ftp/directory/of/ftp.planets.dom 192.168.5.80

   ln –s /ftp/directory/of/ftp.moons.dom 192.168.5.81

To prevent these anonymous areas from being filled with undesired files, start PureFTPd with the option **–i**. This makes it impossible for anonymous users to upload files.

Virtual FTP servers only handle anonymous FTP users and not authorized users.

How to Configure FTP for Authorized Users

Configuring an FTP server for authorized users is important for those who are hosting Web sites. Individual customers maintain their own pages in directories to which they alone have access.

The following is an example configuration in which no anonymous FTP access is allowed and all users are limited to their home directory:

```
# Cage in every user in his home directory
ChrootEveryone          yes

# Disallow anonymous connections. Only allow authenticated users.
NoAnonymous             yes
```

The equivalent command on the command line would be

pure-ftpd -A -E.

If you want to modify the previous configuration so that certain users are not held in a chroot environment (for example, members of a group ftpadmin with the GID 500), you could enter the following:

```
# Cage in every user in his home directory
ChrootEveryone            no

# If the previous option is set to "no", members of the following group
# won't be caged. Others will be. If you don't want chroot()ing anyone,
# just comment out ChrootEveryone and TrustedGID.
TrustedGID                500

# Disallow anonymous connections. Only allow authenticated users.
NoAnonymous               yes
```

The equivalent command on the command line would be

pure–ftpd –a 500 –E.

How to Configure FTP with Virtual Users Not Included in /etc/passwd

PureFTPd provides a way of administering FTP users in its own file, similar in structure to the file /etc/passwd.

The advantages are that pure FTP users are separated from system users and can only access the system by FTP. A normal login is not possible if there are no matching entries in the file /etc/passwd.

To administer PureFTPd users in a separate user database, you need to create a system user with whose UID the FTP users appear in the system.

Once you complete this step, you can then create the FTP users with **pure–pw** (in the file /etc/pure-ftpd/pureftpd.passwd) by entering the following (using user **joe** as an example):

useradd –m ftpusers

pure–pw useradd joe –u ftpusers –d /home/ftpusers/joe

You are requested to enter a password (twice) for the user.

With the help of command-line options, you can specify user options such as quotas for the number of files, size limits in MB, or the times when users can log in.

PureFTPd does not use the ASCII file /etc/pure-ftpd/pureftpd.passwd directly but the binary file /etc/pure-ftpd/pureftpd.pdb. This file must be regenerated every time changes are made by entering **pure–pw mkdb**.

To access the special user database, you need to start PureFTPd with **–j** to ensure that the home directory is created as soon as the user logs in and, after the –l option, the password database file.

The following is an example:

pure-ftpd –j –l puredb:/etc/pureftpd.pdb

You can modify FTP users by entering **pure-pw usermod** and delete users by entering **pure-pw userdel**.

> For additional details on using the pure-pw syntax, enter **man 8 pure-pw** or **pure-pw --help**.
>
> **NOTE**

How to Manage PureFTPd Logs

PureFTPd sends its messages to the syslog daemon, so these messages appear in the usual log files.

It is also possible for PureFTPd to write its own log files in various formats. The option for this is **–O** *format:logfile*, where *format* can be **clf** (a similar format to the Apache Web server), **stats**, or **w3c**.

Suitable entries already exist in the configuration file /etc/pure-ftpd/pure-ftpd.conf. However, you might need to remove the comment symbol (#) to activate the entry.

The following is an example entry:

```
AltLog              clf:/var/log/pureftpd.log
```

Exercise 9-4   Configure Anonymous PureFTPd Access

Do the following:

1. From the KDE desktop, open the file /etc/pure-ftpd/pure-ftpd.conf in an editor by pressing **Alt+F2** and entering **kdesu kate /etc/pure-ftpd/pure-ftpd.conf**.

2. Enter a password of **novell** and select **OK**.

   The configuration file for PureFTPd appears:

```
############################################################
#                                                          #
#          Configuration file for pure-ftpd wrappers       #
#                                                          #
############################################################

# If you want to run Pure-FTPd with this configuration
# instead of command-line options, please run the
# following command:
#
# /usr/sbin/pure-config.pl /usr/etc/pure-ftpd.conf
#
# Please don't forget to have a look at documentation at
```

```
# http://www.pureftpd.org/documentation.html for a complete list of
# options.

# Cage in every user in his home directory

ChrootEveryone               yes
```

3. Allow anonymous users to upload files to the FTP server by changing the AnonymousCantUpload parameter to **no**, as in the following:

   AnonymousCantUpload no

4. When you finish, select **File > Quit**; then save the change by selecting **Save**.

5. From a terminal window, su to root (**su –**) and enter a password of **novell**.

6. Restart the PureFTPd server by entering **rcpure–ftpd restart**.

7. Change the ownership of the directory /srv/ftp to the user ftp by entering **chown ftp /srv/ftp**.

8. Change to the directory /tmp by entering **cd /tmp**.

9. Log in by entering **ftp localhost**; then log in by entering a name of **ftp**.

10. Verify that you can upload files as the anonymous ftp user:

    a. Change to binary transfer mode by entering **bin**.

    b. Turn hash marks on by entering **hash**.

    c. Upload the file manual.pdf by entering the following:

       put manual.pdf.

    d. Exit the FTP session by entering **bye**.

    e. Verify that the file was uploaded by entering **cd /srv/ftp**; then enter **ls –al**. The file is listed.

11. Close the terminal window.

Chapter Summary

❑ The system time in SLES is maintained by the interrupt timer and obtained from the computer hardware clock during system initialization by default. You can use the **date** command to view and set the system time. The **hwclock** command can view and set the hardware clock or update the system time from the hardware clock.

❑ The **netdate** utility may be used to synchronize your system time with that of another computer on the network. This utility does not automatically adjust for time drift.

❏ You may implement NTP to accurately coordinate system time on your network. NTP time consumers obtain system times from NTP time providers that synchronize their time with reliable time sources. The distance from a reliable time source is called the stratum.

❏ NTP automatically adjusts for local time drift and is more accurate when NTP time consumers obtain system times from several NTP time providers.

❏ To configure NTP, you may use YaST or edit the /etc/ntp.conf file and start the NTP daemon. The **ntpdate** command may be used to manually obtain time from an NTP time provider. In addition, you may use the **ntpq** command to query the status of the NTP daemon or the **ntptrace** command to troubleshoot NTP.

❏ The Apache Web server (httpd) is the most common Web server on Linux systems. By default, Apache hands out Web content in the /srv/www/htdocs directory to client Web browsers.

❏ Some network daemons are started by the Internet Super Daemon (inetd) or Extended Internet Super Daemon (xinetd). SLES uses xinetd by default to start network daemons via entries in the /etc/xinetd.d directory.

❏ The TCP wrapper daemon (tcpd) may be used with inetd or xinetd to provide additional security for network daemons via lines in the /etc/hosts.allow and /etc/hosts.deny files.

❏ The main TCP/IP protocol used to transfer files across the Internet today is FTP. You may log into an FTP server to obtain files or interact with the server anonymously.

❏ The PureFTPd server may be installed and used on SLES to provide FTP services to clients. You can use the **pure-ftpd** command or entries in the /etc/pure-ftpd/pure-ftpd. conf file to configure PureFTPd.

KEY TERMS

/etc/hosts.allow — A text file used by tcpd listing hosts that are allowed to connect to network daemons.

/etc/hosts.deny — A text file used by tcpd listing hosts that are not allowed to connect to network daemons.

/etc/inetd.conf — The main configuration file for inetd.

/etc/localtime — A file that specifies the time zone used by a SLES system.

/etc/ntp.conf — The NTP configuration file.

/etc/ntp/drift — A file that contains a value for time drift that was detected by the NTP daemon.

/etc/pure-ftpd/pure-ftpd.conf — The main PureFTPd configuration file.

/etc/sysconfig/clock — A file that stores time and time-zone configuration information.

/etc/xinetd.conf — The main configuration file for xinetd. It loads configuration files from the /etc/xinetd.d directory.

/etc/xinetd.d — The directory that stores most xinetd configuration.

/proc/driver/rtc — A file that stores the current hardware clock time in SLES.

/srv/www/cgi-bin — The default location for CGI scripts in SLES.

/srv/www/htdocs — The default DocumentRoot in SLES.

/usr/lib/zoneinfo/localtime — A link to /etc/localtime.

/usr/share/zoneinfo/ — The directory that stores time-zone definitions.

/var/log/apache2/access_log — A file that stores information about every access attempt for the Apache Web server.

/var/log/apache2/error_log — A file that stores information from the Apache daemon.

adjtimex command — Used to change the algorithm in the Linux kernel to count system time in order to adjust for time drift.

Apache — The default Web server software in SLES.

broadcasting — The process whereby an NTP time provider broadcasts time to NTP time consumers.

Common Gateway Interface (CGI) — A standard used to define programs that interface with a Web server.

date command — Used to view and set the system time.

DocumentRoot — A directory that stores HTTP content on a Web server.

drift — The deviance that system time or a hardware clock experiences over time.

File Transfer Protocol (FTP) — A part of the TCP/IP suite that is used for Internet file transfer.

Greenwich mean time (GMT) — See **Universal Time Coordinated (UTC)**.

hardware clock — The device that maintains time within the system BIOS on a computer mainboard.

hwclock command — Used to view and set the hardware clock.

Hypertext Markup Language (HTML) — The format used by documents on the Internet.

Hypertext Transfer Protocol (HTTP) — The TCP/IP protocol used to send documents to Web browsers on the Internet.

inetd — The Internet Super Daemon used to start other network daemons on Linux systems.

insane time source — An NTP time provider that has a time difference of more than 17 minutes with the NTP time consumer.

jitter — The deviance between system times on an NTP time provider and an NTP time consumer.

local time — A time that is set on the local computer and not synchronized from other computers.

Multipurpose Internet Mail Extensions (MIME) — A standard used to identify content sent across the Internet.

netdate command — Used to obtain and set the system time from a remote computer.

Network Time Protocol (NTP) — A standard protocol in the TCP/IP suite used to maintain consistent time on a network.

ntpd — The NTP daemon on older Linux systems.

ntpdate command — Used to obtain and set the system time from a remote computer using NTP.

ntpq command — Displays NTP daemon statistics.

ntptrace command — Identifies the servers in each stratum that are used to provide time information to an NTP time consumer.

polling — The process whereby an NTP time consumer polls its NTP time provider for time information.

PureFTPd — An advanced FTP server for Linux systems.

pure-ftpd command — Used to configure PureFTPd.

pure-pw command — Used to configure PureFTPd user accounts.

slewing — A gradual adjustment of system time from an NTP time provider. It is used to adjust smaller time differences.

stepping — A fast adjustment of system time from an NTP time provider. It is used to adjust larger time differences.

stratum — A measurement of distance from a reliable NTP time source. A stratum of 1 is the most reliable.

system time — The time used by an operating system after system initialization.

TCP wrapper (tcpd) — A small program that is used to start network daemons via inetd or xinetd. It provides additional security by using the /etc/hosts.allow and /etc/hosts.deny files to control access.

tcpdchk command — Used to report on the configuration of the tcpd program.

tcpdmatch command — Used to test the behavior of the tcpd program.

time consumer — A computer that obtains NTP time information from other computers.

time provider — A computer that provides NTP time information to other computers.

timer interrupt — The interrupt used to maintain time by the Linux kernel.

Uniform Resource Locator (URL) — The address of a resource on the Internet. It consists of a protocol, domain, and resource name.

Universal Time Coordinated (UTC) — A standard time system used to coordinate time across the world by referring to the difference in time from Greenwich, England.

xinetd — The Extended Internet Super Daemon used to start other network daemons on Linux systems. It is the default Internet Super Daemon used in SLES.

xntpd — The NTP daemon in SLES.

REVIEW QUESTIONS

1. Which of the following options to the **hwclock** command may be used to set the hardware clock to the system time? (Choose two answers.)

   a. --systohc

   b. -x

   c. -w

   d. --settime

2. What command could you use to set your system time from the system time of a remote computer without using NTP? _____

3. Using NTP, what command could you use to set your system time from the system time of a remote computer? _____

4. What NTP stratum is considered the most accurate time source?

   a. 1

   b. 10

   c. 15

   d. 16

5. What command could you use to see all NTP time providers from which you received time information?

   a. ntpq

   b. ntpd

   c. ntpdate

   d. ntptrace

6. What mode should you use in /etc/ntp.conf to improve NTP performance if there are several NTP servers on the network?

   a. polling

   b. drift

   c. multicast

   d. broadcast

7. Which directory on a SLES system contains the default Web page for the Apache Web server? _____

8. Which of the following URLs would specify the Web page in the public_html subdirectory of a user's home directory on a Web server?

   a. www.course.com/bob

   b. www.course.com/~bob

   c. www.course.com.bob

   d. www.course.com/home/bob

9. What line in /etc/xinetd/telnet could you modify to enable the Telnet service for use with xinetd?

   a. type = disabled

   b. protocol = tcp

   c. user = nobody

   d. disable = yes

10. What lines could you add to the /etc/hosts.allow and /etc/hosts.deny files to allow only the host **arfa** the ability to use the **telnet** utility to connect to your server? (Choose two answers.)

   a. /etc/hosts.allow: in.telnetd: arfa

   b. /etc/hosts.allow: in.telnetd: ALL

   c. /etc/hosts.deny: in.telnetd: arfa

   d. /etc/hosts.deny: in.telnetd: ALL

11. What command could you use to check the syntax of your TCP wrappers?
   _____

12. What login names could you provide to access an FTP server anonymously? (Choose two answers.)

   a. anonymous

   b. guest

   c. your e-mail address

   d. ftp

13. What line in /etc/pure-ftpd/pure-ftpd.conf can you use to prevent your FTP server from spreading potentially illegal data?

   a. AutoRename yes

   b. AntiWarez yes

   c. ChrootEveryone yes

   d. AnonymousOnly yes

14. What command could you use to perform the same function described in Question 13? _____

15. Where does the PureFTPd log its information by default? _____

DISCOVERY EXERCISES

Configuring an NTP Time Provider

In Exercise 9-1, you configured your system as an NTP time consumer and synchronized your computer with DA1.digitalairlines.com. Configure NTP on your computer to act as an NTP time provider in broadcast mode. Next, configure another SLES computer in your LAN as an NTP time consumer to your NTP time provider. Finally, verify the configuration using the **ntptrace** command on the NTP time consumer.

Researching the Apache Web Server

The Apache Web server has many features that have allowed it to become the most commonly used Web server software today. Examine the /etc/httpd/conf/httpd.conf file and use the Internet to learn about the following features. For each feature, prepare a short memo about its configuration.

❏ Virtual directories/server

❏ URL redirection

❏ Directory security (host and user–based)

Exploring FTP Server Software

There are several FTP server software packages available for Linux in addition to PureFTPd discussed in this section. Use the Internet to research some available FTP server packages. Download and install an FTP server package of your choice. Next, configure and test your FTP server. When finished, prepare a short memo comparing your FTP server package to PureFTPd.

10

Manage Remote Access

In this section you learn how to configure your SUSE Linux Enterprise Server to provide remote access for users and to perform administrative tasks.

- Provide Secure Remote Access with OpenSSH
- Enable Remote Administration with YaST
- Configure a Network Installation

Objective 1   Provide Secure Remote Access with OpenSSH

In the past, remote connections were established with Telnet, which offers no guards against eavesdropping in the form of encryption or other security mechanisms. There are also other traditional communication channels (such as FTP and some remote copying programs) that provide unencrypted transmission.

The SSH suite was developed to provide secure transmission by encrypting the authentication strings (usually a login name and a password) and all the other data exchanged between the hosts.

With SSH, the data flow can still be recorded by a third party, but the contents are encrypted and cannot be reverted to plain text unless the encryption key is known.

SUSE Linux installs the package OpenSSH by default, which includes programs such as ssh, scp, and sftp as alternatives to Telnet, rlogin, rsh, rcp, and FTP.

To provide secure remote access on a network with the OpenSSH version of SSH, you need to know the following:

- Cryptography Basics
- SSH Features and Architecture
- How to Configure the SSH Client
- SSH Client Commands
- How to Configure the SSH Server
- SSH Server Commands
- Public Key Authentication Management

Cryptography Basics

Cryptography deals with procedures and techniques used to encrypt data and prove the authenticity of data. The information required to encrypt and decrypt data is referred to as a *key*.

There are basically two types of encryption procedures for using keys:

- Symmetric Encryption
- Asymmetric Encryption

Symmetric Encryption

With symmetric encryption, the same key is used for encryption and decryption.

While symmetric encryption helps with high-speed transmission when encrypting and decrypting, only one key is used to encrypt data. If this key is known, then all data can be decrypted.

An important feature of an encryption procedure is the length of the key. A key with a length of 40 bits (1099511627776 possibilities) can be broken with brute-force methods in a short time.

In other words, the longer the key length, the more secure the data transmission.

The following are some of the more important symmetric encryption technologies:

- **DES (Data Encryption Standard).** DES was standardized in 1977 and is the foundation of many encryption procedures (such as UNIX/Linux passwords). The key length is 56 bits.

  However, even with a 56-bit key length, in January 1999 the EFF (Electronic Frontier Foundation) decrypted a text encrypted with DES in 22 hours.

- **3DES (Triple-DES).** 3DES is an extension of DES and has a key length of 112 or 168 bits.

- **IDEA.** IDEA is an algorithm with a key length of 128 bits. This algorithm has been patented in the USA and Europe (its noncommercial use is free).

- **Blowfish.** This algorithm has a variable key length of up to 448 bits.

- **AES (Advanced Encryption Standard).** AES is the successor to DES.

  In 1993 the National Institute of Standards and Technology (NIST) decided that DES no longer met today's security requirements, and organized a competition for a new standard encryption algorithm.

  The winner of this competition was announced on October 2, 2000, and is the Rijndael algorithm that supports key lengths of 128, 192, or 256 bits (see *http:// rijndael.com/*).

Asymmetric Encryption

The main concern with symmetric algorithms is how to securely transmit a secret key to a communication partner. This problem is solved by the asymmetric encryption procedure.

In an asymmetric encryption there are two keys—a private key and a public key. Data that is encrypted with the private key can only be decrypted with the public key, and data encrypted with the public key can only be decrypted with the private key.

However, a disadvantage of asymmetric procedures is a low-speed data transmission. Symmetric procedures are much faster.

Symmetric and asymmetric procedures are often combined. For example, a key for symmetric encryption is transmitted through a channel encrypted asymmetrically. SSH uses a combination of both procedures.

Some important asymmetric encryption procedures are RSA, DSA, and Diffie-Hellman.

SSH Features and Architecture

To understand what SSH can offer as a secure, remote transmission protocol, you need to know the following:

- SSH Features
- SSH Protocol Versions
- SSH Authentication Mechanism Configuration

SSH Features

In most cases, a secure shell not only provides all the functionality of Telnet, rlogin, rsh, and rcp, but even includes some features of FTP.

SSH supports the protection of X11 and any TCP connections, by routing them through a cryptographically secure channel.

The following lists the basic functionality provided by SSH:

- Login from a remote host
- Interactive or noninteractive command execution on remote hosts
- Copying files between different network hosts
- High-performance authentication and cryptographically secured communication on nonsecure networks
- Automatic and transparent encryption of all communication
- Complete substitution of the "r" utilities: rlogin, rsh, and rcp
- Port forwarding
- Tunneling

In addition to the basic SSH functionality, the following are special features of the secure shell:

- Through RSA-based server authentication you can prevent security loopholes through IP, routing, and DNS spoofing.
- You can control the client by using system-wide and user-based configuration files. With these settings, you can simplify work for the average user.
- You can transmit any type of binary data between hosts. Optional support for compressing data is also available.
- There are up to six procedures available from the client for server authentication.

In SUSE Linux Enterprise Server the Open Source implementation of SSH (OpenSSH) is used. OpenSSH is available as open source because it does not use any patented algorithms.

By default, the OpenSSH server is already activated when you install SUSE Linux Enterprise Server.

For more details on OpenSSH functionality, see *www.openssh.org.*

SSH Protocol Versions

The following are the versions currently available for the SSH protocol:

- Protocol Version 1 (SSH1)
- Protocol Version 2 (SSH2)

SSH1 and SSH2 are used for convenience in referencing the protocol versions in this section. They are not official designations of the protocol versions.

10

Protocol Version 1 (SSH1)   Figure 10-1 illustrates the process SSH1 uses to transmit data over a secure connection.

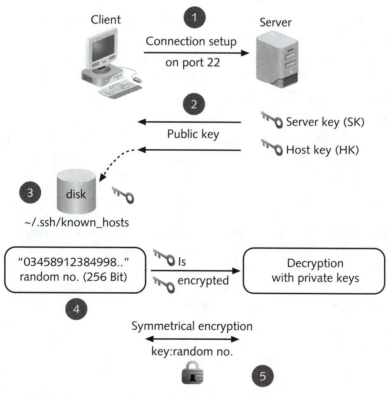

Figure 10-1

The following describes the steps in this process:

1. The client establishes a connection to the server (port 22).

   In this, phase the SSH client and the server agree on the protocol version and other communication parameters.

2. The SSH server works with the following two RSA key pairs and transmits the public keys to the client:

   - **Long-life host key pair (HK).** This key pair consists of a public host key (/etc/ssh/ssh_host_key.pub) and a private host key (/etc/ssh/ssh_host_key) that identify the computer.

     This long-life key pair is identical for all SSH processes running on the host.

   - **Server process key pair (SK).** This key pair is created at the start of each server process that includes a public server key and a private server key that are changed at specific intervals (normally once an hour).

     This pair is never stored in a file. These dynamic keys help prevent an attacker from being able to decrypt recorded sessions, even if the attacker can break into the server and steal the long-life key pair.

3. The client checks to see if the public host key is correct.

   To do this, it compares the host key with keys in the file /etc/ssh/ssh_known_hosts or ~/.ssh/known_hosts.

4. The client generates a 256-bit random number, encrypts this using the public keys of the SSH server and sends it to the server.

5. The server is now in a position to decrypt the random number, because it possesses the secret key.

6. This random number is the key for the symmetric encryption that now follows.

   The random number is also referred to as the *session key*.

The client can now authenticate itself to the server.

Protocol Version 2 (SSH2)   SSH protocol version 1 does not have a mechanism to ensure the integrity of a connection. This allows attackers to insert data packets into an existing connection (an insertion attack).

SSH2 provides features to avoid such attacks. These are referred to as HMAC (Keyed-Hash Message Authentication Code) and are described in detail in RFC 2104.

You should only use SSH1 if SSH2 is not available.

Figure 10-2 illustrates the process SSH2 uses to transmit data over a secure connection.

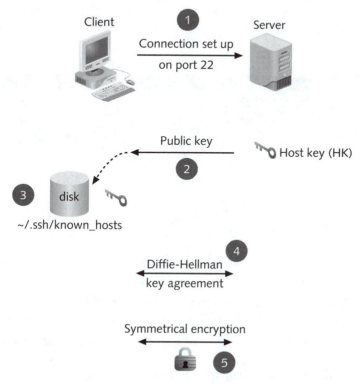

Figure 10-2

The following describes the steps in this process:

1. A connection is established between the server and client as described for SSH1.

2. The server now contains a key pair (DSA or RSA), the public and private host key.

   The corresponding files are called /etc/ssh/ssh_host_rsa_key (RSA) and /etc/ssh/ssh_host_dsa_key (DSA).

3. As with SSH1, the host key is compared with the keys in the files /etc/ssh/ssh_known_hosts and ~/.ssh/known_hosts.

4. A Diffie–Hellman key agreement then follows, through which client and server agree on a secret session key.

5. As with SSH1, communication is ultimately encrypted symmetrically.

The basic difference between SSH1 and SSH2 are mechanisms that guarantee the integrity of the connection (HMAC), and the mechanism for the session key agreement (Diffie-Hellman).

To see which SSH version an SSH server supports, you can log on to port 22 with Telnet. Table 10-1 shows the potential responses from the server.

Table 10-1

Protocol	Server Response
SSH1 only	SSH-1.5-OpenSSH...
SSH1 and SSH2	SSH 1.99-OpenSSH...
SSH2 only	SSH-2.0-OpenSSH...

The following is an example of a Telnet connection on port 22:

```
DA50:~ # telnet DA10 22
Trying 192.168.0.10...
Connected to DA10.
Escape character is '^]'.
SSH-1.99-OpenSSH_3.8p1
```

In the server configuration file /etc/ssh/sshd_config, the Protocol parameter defines which protocol versions are supported.

For example, **Protocol 2,1** in the configuration file means that SSH2 and SSH1 are both supported, but preference is given to SSH2. If SSH2 is not available, then SSH1 is used.

You can also specify the version to use when starting the clients (such as **ssh –1** for SSH1).

SSH Authentication Mechanism Configuration

The SSH server can discover the session key generated and encrypted by the client only if it also has the private key. If the server does not manage to do this, the communication ends at that point.

An absolute condition for the security of this procedure is that the client can check if the public host key of the server really belongs to the server.

SSH currently does not use any directory services (such as LDAP) or any certificates (such as with SSL) when distributing the public keys.

This means that a random key pair can be easily created by anyone, even potential attackers, and included in the authentication dialog box.

It is possible, when first contacting an unknown server, to automatically "learn" its host key. In this case, the SSH client then writes this key to the local key database.

The following is an example of an SSH connection to a computer whose host key is unknown:

```
geeko@DA50:~ > ssh geeko@DA10
The authenticity of host 'DA10 (192.168.0.10)' can't be
established.
```

```
RSA key fingerprint is ea:79:90:9a:d4:bf:b6:a2:40:ee:72:56:f8:d9:
e5:76.
Are you sure you want to continue connecting (yes/no)? yes
Warning: Permanently added 'DA10,192.168.0.10' (RSA) to the list
of known hosts.
```

If you answer the question with "yes," the host key is saved in the file ~/.ssh/known_hosts.

Four mechanisms are available on the server side to authenticate clients. The mechanisms allowed by the server are specified in its configuration file /etc/ssh/sshd_config.

The following describes these mechanisms with the appropriate configuration parameters for /etc/ssh/sshd_config in parentheses:

- **Host-based authentication**

  (sshd_config: RhostsAuthentication)

  Authentication is based on configuration of the files /etc/hosts.equiv or /etc/shosts.equiv, and/or ~/.rhosts or ~/.shosts.

  This procedure corresponds to authentication with rlogin and rsh. Because it is insecure, it is normally not supported by the server. For this reason, newer versions of SSH no longer accept this option.

- **Host-based RSA authentication**

  (sshd_config: RhostsRSAAuthentication   for   SSH1)   (sshd_config: HostbasedAuthentication for SSH2)

  A combination of host-based authentication with RSA-based host authentication (also known as Rhosts-RSA authentication), this procedure is only supported in protocol version 1 and is normally not activated.

  The known public keys of the clients are saved on the server in the files ~/.ssh/known_hosts and /etc/ssh/ssh_known_hosts.

  After the public keys are stored on the server, the client must prove that it has the corresponding private key. The private key of a host is stored in the file /etc/ssh/ssh_host_key, which must only be readable by root.

- **Public key (RSA/DSA) authentication**

  (sshd_config: RSAAuthentication for SSH1)

  (sshd_config: PubkeyAuthentication for SSH2)

  Authentication through a public key procedure is the most secure method. In this case, the user proves knowledge of his private key (and thus her identity) through a challenge-response procedure, which can be run automatically using the SSH agent.

- **Password authentication**

  (ssh_config: PasswordAuthentication)

10

This authentication procedure takes place through a UNIX user password. The transfer of the password is encrypted.

After successful authentication, a work environment is created on the server. For this purpose, environment variables are set (TERM and DISPLAY), and X11 connections and any possible TCP connections are redirected.

Before access is granted to the home directory of the user on the server host, the initialization routines defined in the file /etc/ssh/sshrc2 or ~/.ssh/rc are processed.

When the user logs in, the commands in this file are executed by SSH even before the shell of the user is started, and user data can be exchanged.

The redirection of the X11 connections only works if the DISPLAY variable set by SSH is not subsequently changed by the user. The SSH daemon must appear to the X11 applications as a local X11 server, which requires a corresponding setting of DISPLAY.

In addition, the program xauth must exist. This program is in the package xf86.

The parameter X11Forwarding in the configuration file of the SSH server (/etc/ssh/sshd_config) determines whether or not the graphical output is forwarded by default.

If you want to configure X forwarding, you must set the parameter to Yes, or you must start the SSH client with the option –X.

How to Configure the SSH Client

You configure the SSH client by editing the file /etc/ssh/ssh_config. Each user can edit his individual settings in the file ~/.ssh/config.

If a user wants to ensure (in general) that only servers are accepted that have been previously entered, then the option StrictHostKeyChecking in the client configuration file (~/.ssh/config) needs to be set to **yes** (on).

This prevents the client from simply entering new keys from unknown servers without checking. This is only entered on the first connection.

From SSH version 1.2.20 on, 3 values are allowed for StrictHostKeyChecking: yes, no, and ask. The default setting is ask, which means that before a new key is entered, the user is asked for permission.

For additional information on SSH server configuration options, enter **man ssh**.

SSH Client Commands

Table 10-2 lists commonly used SSH client commands.

Table 10-2

Command	Description
scp	This command copies files securely between two computers using ssh, and replaces rcp and FTP (for pure file transfer).
ssh	This is the SSH client. SSH can be a replacement for rlogin, rsh. and Telnet. An alternative name for the client is slogin. Every user should use ssh consistently instead of Telnet.
ssh-add	This command registers new keys with the ssh-agent.
ssh-agent	This command can handle private RSA keys, responding to challenges (challenge response) from the server. This simplifies authentication.
ssh-keygen	This command generates RSA keys.

10

The following are some examples of using the SSH client commands:

- geeko@mars:~ > **ssh earth.example.com**

  In this example, the user geeko logs in to the computer **earth.example.com**.

- geeko@mars:~ > **ssh –l tux earth.example.com**

  or

  geeko@mars:~ > **ssh tux@earth.example.com**

  In these examples, the user geeko on the computer mars logs in as the user tux on the computer earth.example.com.

- **geeko@mars:~ > ssh root@earth.example.com shutdown –h now**

  In this example, the user geeko shuts down the computer earth.example.com.

- **geeko@mars:~ > scp earth.example.com:/ etc/HOSTNAME ~**

  In this example, the user geeko copies the file /etc/HOSTNAME from the computer earth.example.com to his local home directory.

- **geeko@mars:~ > scp /etc/motd earth.example.com:**

  In this example, the user geeko copies the local file /etc/motd to his home directory on the computer earth.example.com.

- **geeko@mars:~ > ssh –X earth.example.com**

  In this example, the user geeko logs on to the host earth from mars via SSH. The connection is established with a graphical X11 tunnel, allowing X11 applications started on earth to be displayed on mars.

- **geeko@mars:~ > ssh –L 4242:earth.example.com:110 geeko@earth.example.com**

In this example, the user geeko forwards the connection coming in on port 4242 of his local host mars to port 110 (POP3) of the remote host earth via an SSH tunnel (port forwarding).

By using port forwarding through an SSH tunnel, you can set up an additional secure channel for connections between the local host and a remote host.

Privileged ports (0–1024) can only be forwarded by root.

In addition, you can forward port queries addressed to a port of a remote host to the port of the local host (reverse port forwarding) by entering a command similar to the following:

- **geeko@mars:~ > ssh –R 4242:mars.example.com:110 geeko@earth.example.com**

In this example, queries coming in on port 4242 of the remote host earth are reverse-tunneled via SSH to port 110 of the local host mars.

If the host you want to forward to cannot be reached directly through SSH (for example, because it is located behind a firewall), you can establish a tunnel to another host running SSH, as in the following:

- **geeko@mars:~ > ssh –L 4242:earth.example.com:110 geeko@jupiter.example.com**

In this example, the user geeko forwards incoming connections on port 4242 of her local host mars to the remote host jupiter by way of an SSH tunnel.

This host then forwards the packets to port 110 (POP3) of the host earth by using an unencrypted connection.

How to Configure the SSH Server

The configuration file for the server is /etc/ssh/sshd_config. Table 10-3 lists some of the more commonly used options.

Table 10-3

Option	Description
AllowUsers	Allows an SSH login for selected users
DenyUsers	Denies an SSH login for selected users
Protocol	Specifies the protocol versions supported. (Default: 2,1)

> **NOTE**
>
> For additional information on SSH server configuration options, enter **man sshd**.

SSH Server Commands

The programs and commands in Table 10–3 are important to running an SSH server.

Table 10-4

Program/Command	Description
/usr/sbin/sshd	This is the SSH daemon (controlled via the script /etc/init.d/sshd). In a standard SLES 9 installation, the SSH daemon is started automatically in runlevels 3 and 5.
ssh-keyscan	This command collects public host keys from SSH servers. It finds the public host key of an SSH server and displays this on the standard output. This output can then be compared with the key in the file /etc/ssh/ssh_known_hosts and be included in the file.

In the following ssh-keyscan example, the host key is read from the computer **DA10**:

```
geeko@DA50:~> ssh-keyscan DA10
# DA10 SSH-1.99-OpenSSH_3.8p1
DA10 1024 35 147116390451437464467351275310861709847606158603563071800818865787706191767856017132785636399973349166063879859678369401026625347604794392506620950228716583686336203594892096896374927305879210188934164336947706584743066290431167188190984198742641974982665121723726610710391613190438605447841958842149740620127
```

Public Key Authentication Management

Instead of password authentication, a user can also authenticate using a public key procedure. Protocol version 1 only supports RSA keys. Protocol version 2 provides authentication through RSA and DSA keys.

To manage public key authentication, you need to know the following:

- Public Key Authentication Process
- How to Create a Key Pair
- How to Configure and Use Public Key Authentication

Public Key Authentication Process

The public key of the user is stored on the server (usually in the user's home directory); the private key must be stored on the client computer.

With the keys stored in the appropriate places, the following occurs in the public key authentication process:

1. The client informs the server of which public key is being used for authentication.

2. The server checks to see if the public key is known.

3. The server encrypts a random number using the public key and transfers this to the client.

4. Only the client is able to decrypt the random number with its private key.

5. The client sends the server an MD5 checksum that has calculated from the number.

6. The server also calculates a checksum and, if they are identical, the user has authenticated successfully.

The secret key should be protected by a passphrase. Without passphrase protection, simply owning the file with the private key is sufficient for a successful authentication.

However, if the key is additionally protected with a passphrase, the file is useless if you do not know the passphrase.

How to Create a Key Pair

You create a key pair with the command ssh-keygen. A different key is required for SSH1 than for SSH2. For this reason, you need to create a separate key pair for each version.

You use the option **–t** *keytype* to specify the type of key. For example, **sshkeygen –t rsa1** generates a key pair for SSH1.

The keys are stored in the files ~/.ssh/identity (private key) and ~/.ssh/identity.pub (public key).

The following shows how a key pair for the protocol version 2 is generated using option -t (required) so that a DSA key pair is to be generated:

```
geeko@DA50:~> ssh-keygen -t dsa
Generating public/private dsa key pair.
Enter file in which to save the key (/export/home/geeko/.ssh/id_
dsa):
Enter passphrase (empty for no passphrase):
Enter same passphrase again:
Your identification has been saved in /export/home/geeko/.ssh/id_
dsa.
Your public key has been saved in /export/home/geeko/.ssh/id_dsa.
pub.
The key fingerprint is:
ef:73:c6:f6:8a:ff:9d:d1:50:01:cf:07:65:c5:54:8b geeko@DA50
```

In this example, the private DSA key is stored in ~/.ssh/id_dsa and the public key is stored in ~/.ssh/id_dsa.pub.

You can generate an RSA key pair with the command **ssh-keygen -t rsa**. The keys are stored in the files ~/.ssh/id_rsa and ~/.ssh/id_rsa.pub.

How to Configure and Use Public Key Authentication

For authentication using RSA or DSA keys, you need to copy the public key to the server, and then append the public key to the file ~/.ssh/authorized_keys.

For example, you can copy the key to the server with the command scp, as in the following:

scp .ssh/id_dsa.pub sun:geeko-pubkey

The key is stored in the file ~/.ssh/authorized_keys in such a way that the existing key is not overwritten, as in the following:

```
cat geeko-pubkey >> ~/.ssh/authorized_keys
```

You can now launch the client to see if authentication with the DSA key works properly, as in the following:

```
geeko@DA50:~ > ssh DA10
Enter passphrase for key '/export/home/geeko/.ssh/id_dsa':
Last login: Mon Aug 30 13:55:12 2004 from DA50.example.com
```

You can use the option -i to enter the file name for the private key.

When authentication is done with keys, a password is still required when logging in to the server or when copying with scp. This password can be conveniently entered by the ssh-agent, which serves as a wrapper for any other process (such as for a shell or the X server).

When you first start the ssh-agent, you need to enter the password with the command ssh-add. After that, the ssh-agent monitors all SSH requests and provides the required password (if necessary).

The following example shows the start of a bash shell through the ssh-agent:

```
geeko@DA50:~> ssh-agent bash
geeko@DA50:~> ssh-add .ssh/id_dsa
Enter passphrase for .ssh/id_dsa:
Identity added: .ssh/id_dsa (.ssh/id_dsa)
```

For all ssh or scp commands entered from this shell (for which a key authentication is configured), the agent will automatically provide the password.

You can also use the ssh-agent with a graphical login. When you log in to the graphical interface, an X server is started. If you log in by using a display manager, the X server loads the file /etc/X11/xdm/sys.xsession.

For the ssh-agent to start automatically when an X server starts, you simply enter the following parameter in the file sys.xsession:

usessh="yes"

This entry is already set by default in SUSE Linux Enterprise Server.

After entering the Yes parameter, the ssh-agent starts automatically the next time the user logs in to the graphical interface.

As with logging from a console, the agent running in the background must be given the password once, as in the following:

```
geeko@DA50:~> ssh-add .ssh/id_dsa
Enter passphrase for .ssh/id_dsa:
Identity added: .ssh/id_dsa (.ssh/id_dsa)
```

For subsequent connections in which authentication takes place with the public key procedure, a password now no longer has to be given. This is handled by the ssh-agent.

When the X server is terminated, the ssh-agent is also closed. The password is never stored in the file, but only stored in memory by the ssh-agent until the user has logged out again.

Exercise 10-1   Manage Remote Connections with OpenSSH

In this exercise you do the following:

- Part I: Use SSH Utilities
- Part II: Create a Trusted Connection Between Servers

Part I: Use SSH Utilities

In this part of the exercise, you need to work with a partner to practice using the SSH suite of utilities.

Do the following:

1. From the KDE desktop, open a terminal window and su to root (**su –**) with a password of **novell**.

   During Exercise 9-3, you modified the file /etc/hosts.allow and /etc/hosts.deny to allow all but your partner to Telnet to your server.

   To perform this exercise, you need to make sure that the file /etc/hosts.deny has the ALL : ALL ... line commented out.

   a. Edit the file in vi by entering **vim /etc/hosts.deny**.

   b. Make sure that the following line at the bottom of file is removed or commented out (#):

      ALL : ALL: twist (echo "This service is not accessible from %a!")

   c. Save the file and exit vi by entering **:wq**.

2. From the terminal window, log in to your partner's computer as geeko:

   a. From the command line, enter the following:

      ssh –l geeko *partner_server_IP_address*

   b. (Conditional) If you receive a warning about the authenticity of the remote host, continue by entering **yes**.

   c. Enter a password of **N0v3ll**.

      You are now logged in as geeko to your partner's server.

   d. Log out by entering **exit**.

3. Check who is logged into your partner's system by entering the following (password of **novell**):

   ssh –l root *partner_server_IP_address* **ps aux**

   A list of all processes currently running on your partner's server is displayed.

4. Copy your partner's /etc/hosts file to your /tmp directory by entering the following (password of **N0v3ll**):

   scp geeko@*partner_server_IP_address***:/etc/hosts /tmp/**

5. Copy your /etc/hosts file to geeko's directory on your partner's server by entering the following (password of **N0v3ll**):

   scp /etc/hosts geeko@*partner_server_IP_address***:/tmp/**

6. Use sftp to connect to your partner's computer as geeko by entering the following:

   sftp geeko@*partner_server_IP_address*

7. Copy the program /bin/date to geeko's directory on your computer by entering the following:

   get /bin/date /home/geeko/

8. Quit sftp by entering **exit**.

9. Create the file **/etc/nologin** on your system by entering **touch /etc/nologin**.

10. Have your partner attempt to ssh or Telnet to your server as geeko (such as **ssh –l geeko** *partner_server_IP_address*).

    The file /etc/nologin does not allow geeko or any normal user access.

11. Remove the file /etc/nologin by entering **rm /etc/nologin**.

10

Part II: Create a Trusted Connection Between Servers

In this part of the exercise, you create a trusted connection between your server and a partner's server.

So that keys are not accidentally overwritten, one of you needs to perform the steps as geeko, and the other needs to perform the steps as dba1. To perform the steps as dba1, just replace geeko with **dba1**, N0v3ll with **suse1**, and /home/geeko with **/export/home/dba1**.

Do the following:

1. Generate an RSA key pair:

   a. From the terminal window (make sure you are root) enter **ssh-keygen -t rsa**.

   b. Accept the default location for the key (/root/.ssh/id_rsa) by pressing **Enter**.

   c. Enter a passphrase of **novell**.

      Information about your key pair is displayed, such as the location of your identification and the public key.

2. Copy the RSA public key to your partner's geeko .ssh directory by entering the following (password of **N0v3ll**):

   scp .ssh/id_rsa.pub geeko@*partner_server_IP_address*:/home/geeko/

Remember that the home directory for dba1 is /export/home/dba1.

NOTE

3. SSH as geeko to your partner's computer by entering **ssh -l geeko *partner_server_IP_address***.

4. Enter **ls -al**.

   Look for an .ssh directory.

5. (Conditional) If a directory .ssh does not exist then create it by entering **mkdir .ssh**.

6. Change to the **.ssh** directory by entering **cd .ssh**.

7. Copy the public key to the file ~/.ssh/authorized_keys by entering the following:

   cat ../id_rsa.pub >> authorized_keys

8. Change the permissions on the file authorized_keys so that only the owner can write to the file, and the group and other can only read by entering the following:

   chmod 644 authorized_keys

9. Log out from the partner's server by entering **exit**.

10. SSH as geeko to your partner's computer by entering **ssh -l geeko** *partner_server_IP_address*.

    You are prompted for a passphrase, not a password.

11. Log in by entering **novell**; then log out by entering **exit**.

12. Start the ssh-agent to track authentication by entering **ssh-agent bash**.

13. Add your private key to the agent for authentication by entering **ssh-add .ssh/id_rsa**; then enter a passphrase of **novell**.

14. SSH as geeko to your partner's server by entering **ssh -l geeko** *partner_server_IP_address*.

    This time you are not prompted for a password or a passphrase.

15. Log out by entering **exit**; then close the terminal window.

OBJECTIVE 2   ENABLE REMOTE ADMINISTRATION WITH YaST

You can enable remote administration of your SUSE Linux Enterprise Server by using the YaST Remote Administration module.

To implement and use this remote connection, you need to know the following:

- VNC and YaST Remote Administration
- How to Confiure Your Server for Remote Administration
- How to Access Your Server for Remote Administration

VNC and YaST Remote Administration

VNC (virtual network computing) is a client-server solution that allows a remote X server to be managed through a lightweight and easy-to-use client from anywhere on the Internet.

The two computers don't even have to be the same type. For example, you can use VNC to view an office Linux machine on your Windows computer at home.

The server and client are available for a variety of operating systems, including Microsoft Windows, Apple MacOS, and Linux.

You can use the YaST Remote Administration module to configure your SUSE Linux Enterprise Server for remote access through VNC from any network computer (or over the Internet).

When you activate Remote Administration, xinetd offers a connection that exports the X login through VNC.

With the Remote Administration activated, you connect to the server through a VNC client such as krdc (connect to *hostname*:**5901**), through a VNC connection in Konqueror (**vnc://***hostname*:**5901**), or through a Java-capable Web browser (**http://***hostname*:**5801**).

The hostname parameter can be the actual host name (such as **http://suse.linux.com:5801**) or the host IP address (such as **http://192.168.1.1:5801**).

A Remote Administration connection is less secure than SSH, which encrypts all data transmitted (including the password). For this reason, we recommend using the remote connection only when necessary for performing administrative tasks.

NOTE

For additional information on VNC, enter **man vncviewer** or see *www.realvnc. com*. Also refer to the documentation in */etc/xinet.d/vnc* or enter **netstat -patune** for a list of Internet connections to the server.

How to Configure Your Server for Remote Administration

To configure your SUSE Linux Enterprise Server for remote administration, do the following:

1. From the KDE desktop, start the YaST Remote Administration module by doing one of the following:

   - Select the **YaST** icon, enter the root *password*, and select **OK**; then select **Network Services > Remote Administration**.

     or

   - Open a terminal window and enter **sux –** and the root *password*; then enter **yast2 remote**.

   The dialog box in Figure 10–3 appears.

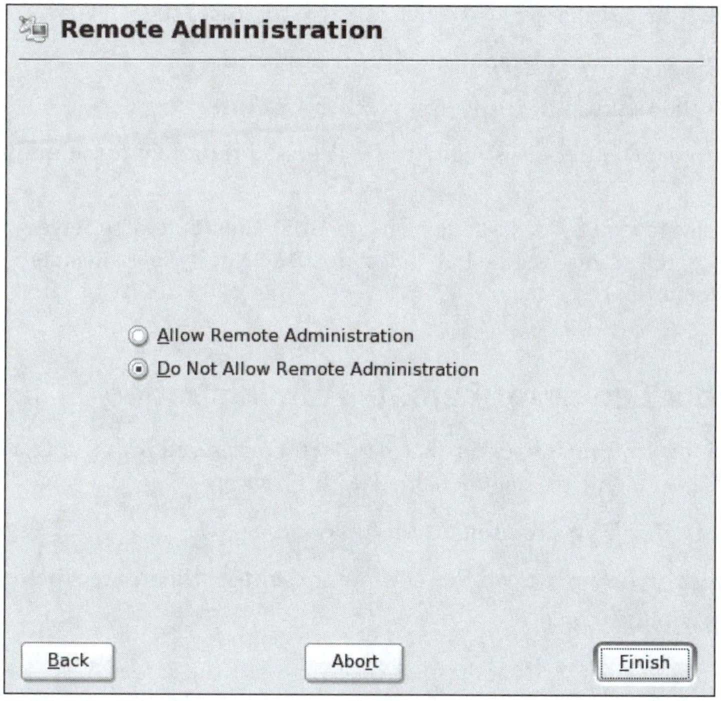

Figure 10-3

2. Select **Allow Remote Administration**; then select **Finish**.

   The message shown in Figure 10-4 appears.

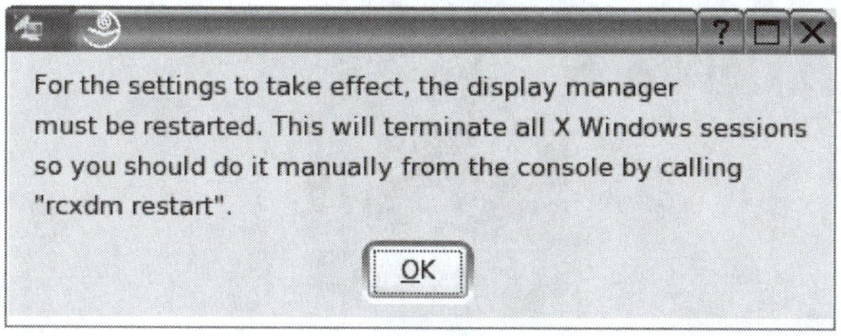

Figure 10-4

You need to restart the display manager to activate the remote administration settings.

3. Close the dialog box by selecting **OK**.

4. Close any open applications; then display a console pressing **Ctrl+Alt+F2**.

5. Log in as **root** with the appropriate *password*.

6. Restart the display manager by entering **rcxdm restart**.

    After a few moments, a graphical login is displayed.

7. Log in to the desktop as **root** or any other *local user*.

Your SUSE Linux Enterprise Server is ready to be accessed remotely for administration.

You can deactivate remote administration on your SUSE Linux Enterprise Server by following the same steps but selecting **Do Not Allow Remote Administration**.

NOTE

How to Access Your Server for Remote Administration

To access a SUSE Linux Enterprise Server that has been configured for remote administration, you can use a VNC client or a Java-enabled Web browser.

To access the server from a Web browser, do the following:

1. Open the Web browser from the computer desktop; then enter the following:

    http://*hostname*:5801

    where ***hostname*** is the IP address or host name of the server.

    The dialog box in Figure 10-5 appears.

Figure 10-5

From the top of the VNS session window, you can select from items such as setting session options and placing items in the clipboard.

From the session window, you can log in to a desktop environment on the server as root (or any other local user), or you can directly access YaST from the login dialog box.

2. Directly access YaST by selecting **Administration**.

3. Enter the root *password*; then select **OK**.

The YaST Control Center appears in the session window, and you are ready to begin administering the server from YaST.

4. When you finish performing administration tasks, exit YaST; then close the session by selecting **Disconnect**.

Exercise 10-2   Use Remote Administration

Do the following:

- Part I: Remotely Access a Text-Based Version of YaST
- Part II: Remotely Access the GUI Version of YaST
- Part III: Configure Remote Administration with YaST
- Part IV: Access Your Partner's Server Remotely

Part I: Remotely Access a Text-Based Version of YaST

Both you and a partner do the following:

1. From a terminal window, enter the following:

   ssh root@*your_partner_IP_address*

2. (Conditional) If you are prompted to accept your partner's ssh key, enter **yes**.

3. When prompted for the password, enter **novell**.

4. Launch the ncurses-based version of YaST by entering **yast2**.

   The text-based version of the YaST Control Center appears.

   Do not change any configurations on your partner's server.

5. Exit the YaST Control Center by pressing **Alt+Q**.

6. Close the ssh session by entering **exit**.

Part II: Remotely Access the GUI Version of YaST

Both you and a partner do the following:

1. From the terminal window, enter the following:

   ssh –X root@*your_partner_IP_address*

2. (Conditional) If you are prompted to accept your partner's ssh key, enter **yes**.

3. When prompted for the password, enter **novell**.

4. Launch the GUI-based version of YaST by entering **yast2**.

   The GUI-based version of the YaST Control Center appears.

   Do not change any configurations on your partner's server.

5. Close the YaST Control Center.

6. Close the ssh session by entering **exit**.

Part III: Configure Remote Administration with YaST

Both you and a partner do the following:

1. From the KDE desktop, select the **YaST** icon; then enter a root password of **novell** and select **OK**.

   The YaST Control Center appears.

2. Select **Network Services > Remote Administration**.

   The Remote Administration dialog box appears.

3. Select **Allow Remote Administration**; then select **Finish**.

   A dialog box appears for restarting the display manager.

4. Close the dialog box by selecting **OK**.

5. Close any open applications; then display a console by pressing **Ctrl+Alt+F2**.

6. Log in as **root** with a password of **novell**.

7. Restart the display manager by entering **rcxdm restart**.

   After a few moments, a graphical login is displayed.

8. Log in to the desktop as **geeko**.

9. From a terminal window, su to root (**su –**) with a password of **novell**.

10. Restart xinetd by entering **rcxinetd restart**.

    Your SUSE Linux Enterprise Server is ready to be accessed remotely for administration.

Part IV: Access Your Partner's Server Remotely

To access the server from a Web browser, you and a partner each do the following:

1. From the KDE desktop, open the Konqueror Web browser.

2. In the Location field, enter the following:

   http://*your_partner_IP_address*:5801

   A VNC Authentication dialog box appears.

CAUTION

If this step does not work, make sure that the ALL: ALL: line in the file /etc/hosts.deny is commented out or deleted (you did this in Exercise 9-3).

Although a password is requested, it is not required.

3. Continue by selecting **OK**.

4. Log in to the remote server's desktop as **geeko** with a password of **N0v3ll**.

   The desktop for your partner's geeko user appears.

5. When you finish testing the desktop, close the VNC session by selecting **Disconnect** (top of the screen).

6. Close all open windows.

OBJECTIVE 3   CONFIGURE A NETWORK INSTALLATION

10

As you migrate computers in your network to SUSE Linux, you can install SUSE Linux from a DVD or CDs on individual machines or configure a SUSE Linux Enterprise Server as an installation server.

To provide remote installation from a SUSE Linux Enterprise Server, you need to know the following:

- How to Prepare for the Installation
- SUSE Linux Installation Basics
- How to Configure an Installation Server

How to Prepare for the Installation

After installing SUSE Linux, some system configurations can be hard to change.

To make sure you are prepared to install SUSE Linux with the configuration settings you need, you should consider the following:

- **Hardware compatibility.** SUSE Linux Enterprise Server 9 supports most enterprise hardware for servers. Although it also supports hardware for desktops, some laptop computer hardware might not be compatible.

  To verify that your hardware is compatible with SUSE Linux Enterprise Server 9, you can use the following Web site:

  www.novell.com/partnerguide/section/481.html

- **File system types.** SUSE Linux Enterprise Server 9 supports various file system types.

Make sure you select the file system type that is right for your particular needs and requirements.

For details on file system types, see Section 3, *Select a Linux File System*.

■ **Partitioning scheme.** Make sure you plan for the appropriate partitions and partition sizes before starting your installation (if you are using traditional instead of virtual partitions).

Modifying partition sizes after installation can be impossible or difficult to achieve.

It's also easier to configure Software RAID or LVM during installation. This is especially true of configuring the root file system.

■ **Software package selection.** Although you can install software packages after installation, it can be easier to decide ahead of time which packages you want installed and do the configuration during SUSE Linux installation.

You should consider every installed software package as a potential security risk. To increase the security of your system, make sure you install only required services on your computer.

■ **Dual-boot system.** If you plan on installing a dual-boot system on your computer (with SUSE Linux Enterprise Server 9 as one of the systems), it is often better to install SUSE Linux Enterprise Server 9 first.

For example, if you install SUSE Linux Enterprise Server 9, and then install a Windows operating system, SUSE Linux recognizes the Windows operating system and automatically provides a dual boot screen after installing Windows.

SUSE Linux Installation Basics

SUSE Linux lets you install from a variety of sources, including a CD-ROM or DVD-ROM drive, a hard drive, or over the network (such as using an Installation server). You can also use AutoYaST to automate installations.

You can use a YaST GUI interface or a text-based interface (ncurses). Early YaST installations were text-based. The interface of the text-based YaST installation looked similar to Figure 10-6.

Figure 10-6

Currently, the GUI-based YaST interface is the standard installation tool, as illustrated in Figure 10-7.

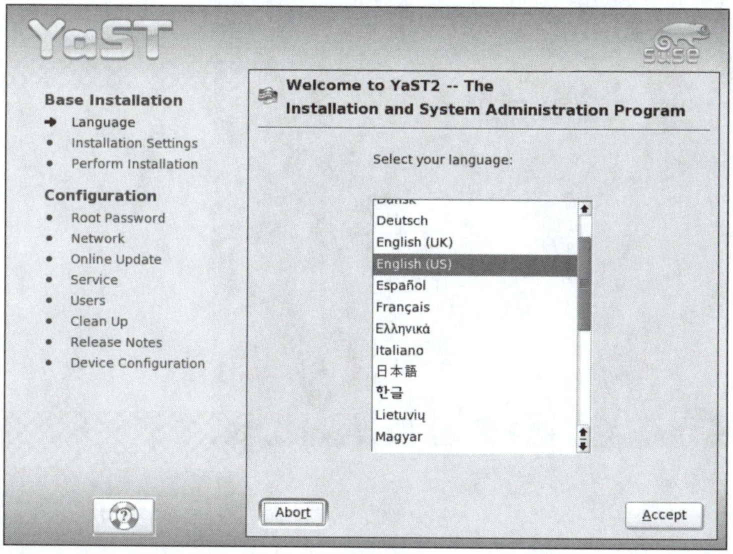

10

Figure 10-7

CAUTION

For certain computers and software, you might need to use the text-based YaST interface for installation.

For example, VMware Workstation currently supports only the text-based installation interface.

A SUSE Linux installation is run by two components—Linuxrc and YaST. To understand the SUSE Linux installation process, you need to know the following:

- The Role of Linuxrc
- Virtual Consoles
- YaST Installation Log File

The Role of Linuxrc

The Linuxrc program is a tool to define installation settings and to load hardware drivers (in the form of kernel modules).

After doing so, Linuxrc hands over control to YaST, which starts the actual installation of system software and applications.

Linuxrc is a text-based program that has the following features available from its main menu, shown in Figure 10-8.

```
>>> Linuxrc v1.6 (Kernel 2.6.5-7.51-default) (c) 1996-2004 SUSE LINU


                        Main Menu


                         Settings
                     System Information
              Kernel Modules (Hardware Drivers)
               Start Installation or System
                         Eject CD
                       Exit or Reboot
                         Power off


              OK                    Back
```

Figure 10-8

The following describes the options on the Linuxrc main menu:

- **Settings.** Provides settings that you can configure when using Linuxrc to perform tasks such as debugging or installation.

- **System Information.** This option displays a menu that lets you view kernel messages and other technical details.

  For example, you can check the I/O ports used by PCI cards and the memory size as detected by the Linux kernel.

- **Kernel Modules (Hardware Drivers).** This option displays a menu that lets you select the modules (drivers) you need from a list.

The name of the module is displayed with a brief description of the hardware supported by the driver. For some components, Linuxrc offers several drivers or newer alpha versions of them.

- **Start Installation or System.** After setting up the kernel (driver) support for your hardware, you can display the Start Installation or System menu which lets you select from several options, including the following:

  - Start Installation or Update
  - Boot Installed System
  - Start Rescue System

- **Eject CD.** Ejects the CD or DVD in the drive.

- **Exit or Reboot.** Lets you exit the Linuxrc main menu or reboot the system.

  For example, after selecting kernel (driver) devices, you might want to reboot the system to test the drivers.

- **Power Off.** Shuts down the Linux operating system.

Virtual Consoles

While the installation is running, you might need to access a command-line prompt (called a *shell prompt* in Linux) from a virtual console.

However, you need to be careful that you don't interrupt the installation process when using the shell prompt.

Accessing virtual consoles is also possible following a completed installation. By default, the Linux system provides six virtual consoles with text logins. If a desktop such as KDE or Gnome is running (the X Window system), it is normally assigned to console number 7.

You can switch between virtual consoles by pressing **Ctrl+Alt+F***x* (where *x* is the console number). To return to the X Window system (the desktop), press **Ctrl+Alt+F7**.

Some virtual consoles can provide additional information, such as F3 (the installation log) and F4 (system messages).

NOTE

YaST Installation Log File

A detailed installation log file (y2log) is written during installation and stored in /var/log/ YaST2/. This log can be invaluable when troubleshooting or documenting a SUSE Linux Enterprise Server 9 installation.

You can view the contents of the file from a shell prompt by entering the following:

```
more /var/log/YaST2/y2log
```

If you want to view the last few lines of the installation log file, you can enter the following:

```
tail /var/log/YaST2/y2log
```

How to Configure an Installation Server

A YaST installation server supports HTTP, FTP, and NFS. With the help of the Service Location Protocol (SLP), your installation server can be made known to all clients in the network.

This means that there is no need to select the installation source manually on the clients.

To configure the installation server, do the following:

1. From the KDE desktop, start the YaST Installation Server module by doing one of the following:

   - Select the **YaST** icon, enter the root *password*, and select **OK**; then select **Misc > Installation Server**.

     or

   - Open a terminal window and enter **sux –** and the root *password*; then enter **yast2 instserver**.

   The dialog box shown in Figure 10-9 appears.

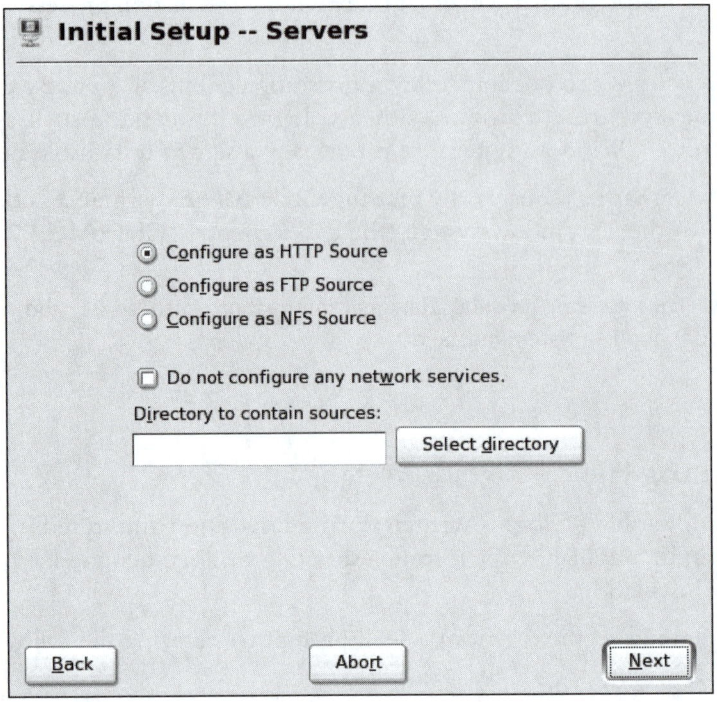

Figure 10-9

From this dialog box you select an installation server service type (HTTP, FTP, or NFS) and indicate the directory where you want to store the installation source files.

2. Select the *server type*.

   After you finish configuring the server, the selected service type is started automatically every time you start up the system.

3. (Conditional) If a service of the type that you want to use (such as FTP) is already running on your system, then deactivate the automatic configuration of the server service with YaST by selecting **Do not configure any network services**.

   If you select this option, you will need to perform any necessary configuration tasks on your own after you have completed the YaST configuration.

   This option is useful if you have already configured the installation server and want to add another installation source (program CDs or a DVD on the local hard drive) to the server.

4. In the **Directory to contain sources** field, browse to and select (**Select directory**) or enter the *directory* where you want to copy the installation files for all your installation resources.

   If this directory does not exist, YaST creates it for you.

5. When you finish, continue by selecting **Next**.

   A dialog box is displayed that lets you enter configuration information for the specific service type you selected.

   This dialog box is skipped if you deactivate automatic configuration (**Do not configure any network services**).

6. Configure the service type by following these guidelines:

   ■ **HTTP or FTP.** If you select HTTP or FTP, you need to configure an alias for the root directory of the FTP or HTTP server where the installation data will be stored.

   The installation source will be located under **ftp:// *Server-IP/Alias/Name*** (FTP) or under **http:// *Server-IP/Alias/Name*** (HTTP).

   Name is the name of the installation source, which you define in the following step.

   ■ **NFS.** If you select NFS, you need to configure wildcards and exports options. The NFS server will be accessible under **nfs:// *Server-IP/Name***.

7. When you finish, continue by selecting Next.

   The dialog box shown in Figure 10-10 appears.

10

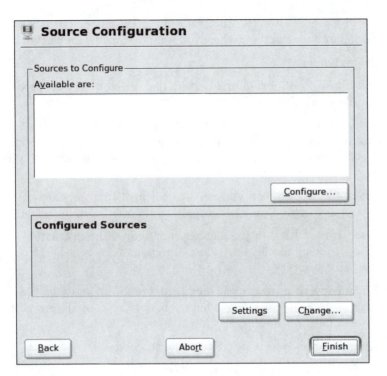

Figure 10-10

You configure the installation sources in this dialog box. Installation sources are generally individual CDs, a DVD, or CD ISOs that you copy to the installation server.

8. Configure an installation source by selecting **Configure**.

The dialog box in Figure 10-11 appears.

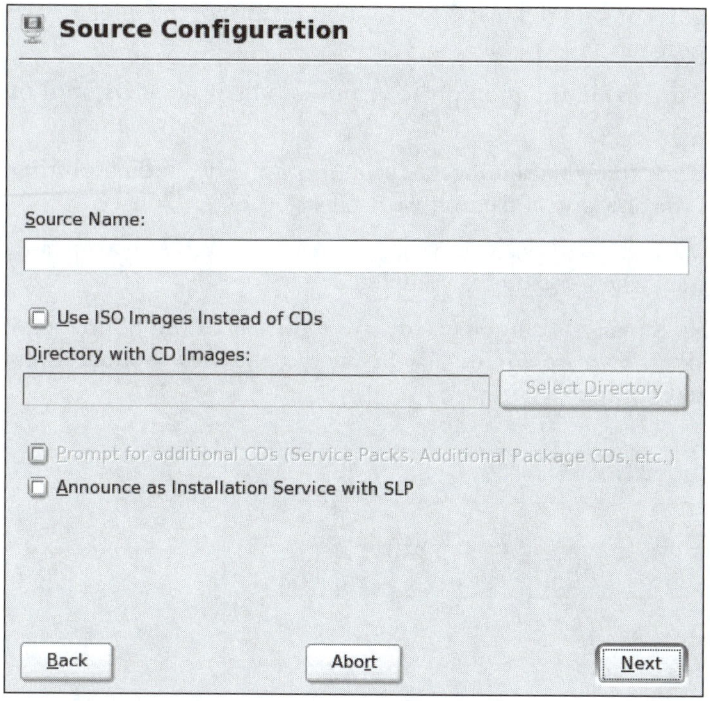

Figure 10-11

9. In the **Source Name** field, enter a *name* for the installation source (such as an easily remembered abbreviation of the product and version name).

   This name is used by YaST to create a directory under which all product CDs are copied and managed.

10. (Conditional) If you want to use ISO images of the media instead of copies of the SUSE Linux CDs, select **Use ISO Images Instead of CDs**; then enter the local *directory path* where the ISO images are stored.

11. (Conditional) If you require more add-on CDs or service pack CDs in order to complete the installation, select **Prompt for additional CDs**.

    YaST will automatically remind you to supply these media when copying the files.

12. (Optional) If you want to announce your installation server in the network through SLP, select **Announce as Installation Service with SLP**.

13. When you are ready to begin copying CDs (or ISO images) to the local hard drive, select **Next**.

    A dialog box prompts you to insert CD1.

14. Insert the first CD; then begin copying by selecting **Continue**.

YaST begins copying the first CD to a subdirectory of the directory created with the source name.

15. Continue following the prompts to remove and replace CDs until the copying is complete.

    This process can take a significant amount of time depending on the number of CDs and the amount of data on each CD.

    A Konqueror dialog box is displayed for each copied CD. You can close these dialog boxes when copying is complete.

    When the copying is complete, you are returned to the Source Configuration dialog box shown in Figure 10-12 where the new source is listed under Configured Sources.

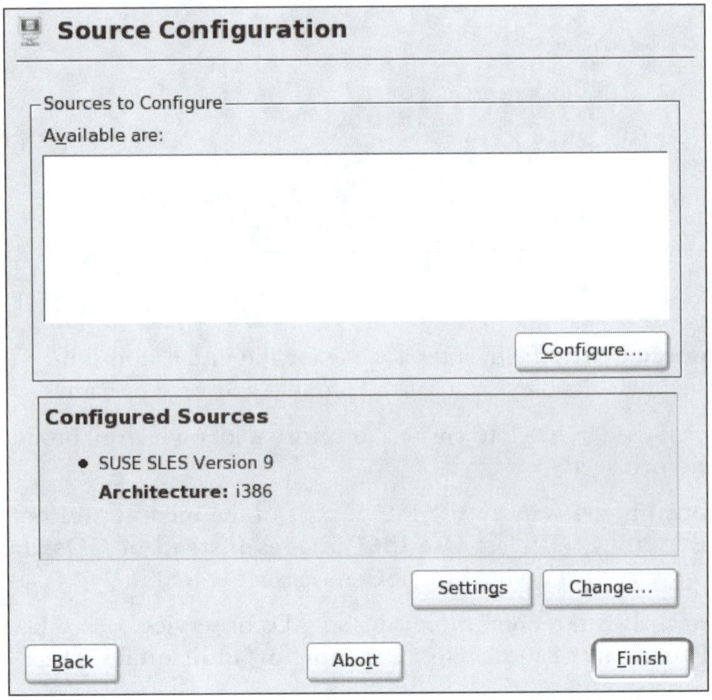

Figure 10-12

16. (Optional) If you want to edit the configured source before continuing, select **Configure**; then select the *resource* and select **Edit**.

    If you want to change the resource name, be aware that you will need to rename the directory to the new resource name.

17. (Optional) If you want to change the server settings (such as service type) before continuing, select **Settings**.

18. Finalize the configuration by selecting **Finish**.

19. (Conditional) Close the YaST Control Center.

Your configuration server is now fully configured and ready for service. It is automatically started every time the system is started.

NOTE

If you want to deactivate an installation source, start the **Installation Server** module, select **Change**, select the *installation source* from the list, and then select **Delete**.

Although the installation source is deleted from the list, the installation data still remains on the local hard drive. You need to remove this manually.

How to Start a Remote Installation

As soon as the installation server is available with the required installation data in the network, all computers in the local network can access the data.

To start the installation from a computer, you need a bootable media such as the DVD with SUSE Linux Enterprise Server 9, a set of bootable CDs, or a set of bootable floppy disks you can create with the YaST Create a Boot, Rescue, or Module Floppy module (on the System menu).

To start the installation, do the following:

1. Insert the *boot media* and restart your computer.

   The dialog box shown in Figure 10-13 appears.

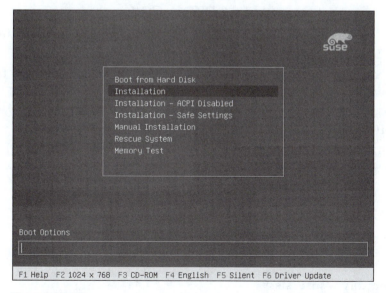

Figure 10-13

2. With the down-arrow key, scroll to and highlight **Installation** (*do not* press Enter to select the option).

3. Press **F3**; then select the service type (**FTP**, **HTTP**, **NFS**, or **SLP**) you configured for the installation server.

    Select SLP if you configured the installation server to broadcast the service over the network.

4. (Conditional) If you select FTP, HTTP, or NFS, enter the server (IP address or domain name) and full path to the directory where the installation files are stored; then select **OK**.

5. When you are ready to install, select **Installation**.

6. (Conditional) If you selected SLP, and there are several services being advertised by SLP, you need to select the installation resource before continuing.

    The installation files are accessed from the installation server, and a normal installation begins.

7. Follow the installation prompts until the installation is complete.

Exercise 10-3 Install SLES 9 from an Installation Server

To prepare for the LiveFire exercise in Section 11, you need to re-install your SLES 9 server.

In this exercise, you use server DA1 (10.0.0.254) and AutoYaST to automate the SLES 9 installation.

Do the following:

1. Boot the server from the *SLES 9 DVD or CD 1*.

2. When the GRUB installation screen appears, highlight the **Installation** option.

    You have 20 seconds to highlight the option before GRUB boots from the hard drive.

3. Set the display resolution by pressing **F2**; then select a display resolution of at least **1024x768**.

    If a resolution of 1024x768 is not available, select the highest resolution available (such as 640x480).

4. Select the installation source by pressing **F3**; then select **HTTP**.

    An HTTP Installation dialog box appears.

5. Enter the following:

    - Server: **10.0.0.254**

    - Directory: **/suse/sles9**

6. When you finish, continue by selecting **OK**.

7. In the Boot Options field, type **autoyast=http://10.0.0.254/suse/sles9/ yast/student.xml**; then press **Enter**.

YaST accesses the file student.xml from DA1 and installs SLES 9 from DA1 based on the configuration settings in the XML file.

This file is a structured XML file that contains all the configuration settings necessary for installing the SLES 9 server you need for the LiveFire exercise.

A Novell Software License Agreement dialog box appears. YaST takes care of accepting this agreement and interfacing with all other dialog boxes during installation.

After the system automatically reboots and finishes configuring, a GUI login screen appears.

8. Log in to your server as **root** with a password of **novell**.

Depending on your hardware, the SUSE Hardware Detection utility will probably find new hardware to configure (such as sound cards, mouse devices, and modems) and display "New Hardware Found!" dialog boxes.

9. Deselect **Keep me informed about new hardware**.

10. Do one of the following:

- Configure a hardware device by selecting **yes**; then enter the appropriate settings in the dialog boxes.

    or

- Skip configuring the hardware device (such as a sound card) by selecting **No**.

11. Verify that the DNS configuration and Internet connection work:

a. From a terminal window, test an A record type in the forward zone by entering the following:

dig da10.digitalairlines.com

Make sure an ANSWER SECTION is displayed in the output.

b. Test a record in the reverse zone by entering the following:

host 10.0.0.10

Make sure the output returns record information instead of "not found."

c. Test Internet connection by pinging a valid Internet site (such as **ping www.novell.com**) or by entering the a valid Internet site in a Web browser (such as Konqueror).

d. (Conditional) If you use the command ping, you can stop the ping process by pressing **Ctrl+C**.

12. Set your language and time zone with YaST.

The student.xml file sets your server to US English and Mountain Standard Time (US).

If you need to change these settings, do the following:

a. Select **KDE Menu > System > YaST**.

b. From the YaST Control Center, select **System > Language**.

A Language selection dialog box appears.

c. Select *your language*; then select **Accept**.

d. From the YaST Control Center, select **System > Date and Time**.

e. Select *your region* and *your time zone*; then from the Hardware clock drop-down list, select **UTC**.

f. When you finish, select **Accept**.

13. (Optional) Set your monitor and resolution

During installation, YaST selects a graphics card driver and resolution automatically. However, you might want to change these as YaST dialog boxes (and the terminal window) display best at a 1152 x 768 or a 1024 x 768 resolution.

Do one of the following:

- Right-click the desktop and select **Configure Desktop**; then select **Size & Orientation**. From the Screen size drop-down list, select **1152 x 768** or **1024 x 768**; then select **OK > Accept Configuration**.

    or

- If either of these is not available, try using the YaST Graphics Card and Monitor module (**Hardware > Graphics Card and Monitor**) to configure the resolution or select a more appropriate driver for your graphics card.

14. When you finish the hardware configuration and verification, log out as root by selecting **KDE Menu > Logout > Logout**.

You are returned to the GUI login screen.

15. Log in as **geeko** with a password of **N0v3ll**.

You are now ready to start the LiveFire exercise.

Chapter Summary

❑ The SSH daemon (sshd) provides a secure alternative to telnet, r-tools, and FTP by encrypting traffic. SLES uses OpenSSH to provide SSH services.

❑ The **scp** and **sftp** commands can be used to copy files between remote hosts using SSH, whereas the **ssh** command may be used to obtain an SSH terminal from a remote host.

❏ SSH uses a combination of asymmetric and symmetric encryption and supports several standard encryption algorithms. SSH version 2 uses HMAC to ensure the integrity of transmitted data.

❏ You can configure the SSH type, authentication, and encryption types in the SSH server configuration file /etc/ssh/sshd_config. SSH client options are stored in the /etc/ssh/ssh_config file. User-specific SSH client options are stored in ~/.ssh/config.

❏ You may generate asymmetric SSH encryption keys using the **ssh-keygen** command and view them using the **ssh-keyscan** command. Public encryption keys from remote hosts are stored ~/.ssh/known_hosts on the SSH client and /etc/ssh/ssh_known_hosts on the SSH server.

❏ You may use the YaST Remote Administration module to configure a VNC server that may be used to graphically administer your system remotely using a Web browser, Konqueror, or the **krdc** command. VNC does not use encryption.

❏ Prior to installing SLES, you should carefully plan the server role and hardware compatibility as well as the boot, partition, and filesystem configuration.

❏ Linuxrc provides a text-based installation program, whereas YaST is used to perform a graphical installation. You may switch to a virtual console during the installation to view and troubleshoot installation problems.

❏ YaST may be used to set up an installation server that hosts the SLES media using the HTTP, FTP, or NFS protocol. Clients can then boot from a SLES DVD, CD, or boot floppy to connect to the installation server.

10

KEY TERMS

/etc/ssh/ssh_config — The system-wide ssh client program configuration file.

/etc/ssh/sshd_config — The SSH daemon configuration file.

/var/log/YaST2/y2log — The SLES installation log file.

~/.ssh/config — The ssh client program configuration file.

Advanced Encryption Standard (AES) — A common symmetric encryption algorithm that uses up to 256-bit keys and is intended to replace 3DES.

asymmetric encryption — A type of encryption that uses a public and private key pair. Information encrypted with the public key can be decrypted using the private key and vice versa.

Blowfish — A common symmetric encryption algorithm that uses up to 448-bit keys.

chroot command — Runs a command or shell under a different root directory.

Data Encryption Standard (DES) — A common symmetric encryption algorithm that uses 56-bit keys.

Diffie-Hellman — A common asymmetric encryption algorithm.

Digital Signature Algorithm (DSA) — A common asymmetric encryption algorithm.

Hash Message Authentication Code (HMAC) — A feature of SSH version 2 that prevents attackers from compromising SSH data during transit.

Host Key Pair (HK) — An asymmetric encryption key pair that is generated for the computer itself and stored in a file.

International Data Encryption Algorithm (IDEA) — A common symmetric encryption algorithm that uses up to 128-bit keys.

krdc command — Used to connect to a remote computer using VNC.

Linuxrc — The program that performs a text-based SLES installation.

OpenSSH — The default package used to provide SSH services in SLES.

private key — An asymmetric encryption key that can be used to decrypt data encrypted using a public key. The private key can also be used to encrypt data.

public key — An asymmetric encryption key that can be used to decrypt data encrypted using a private key. The public key is typically used to encrypt data.

Rivest Shamir Adleman (RSA) — A common asymmetric encryption algorithm.

rlogin — Used to obtain a shell on a remote computer.

rsh — Used to obtain a shell or run a program on a remote computer.

r-tools — The rsh, rlogin, and rcp programs.

scp command — Used to copy files from one host to another using SSH.

Secure SHell (SSH) — A software service that provides encrypted communications to and from remote computers.

Server Process Key Pair (SK) — An asymmetric encryption key pair that is generated when the SSH daemon is started. This key pair is never stored in a file and is regenerated each time the daemon is restarted.

sftp command — Used to copy files from one host to another using SSH.

ssh command — Used to obtain a shell from a remote SSH server.

ssh-add command — Used to register new RSA and DSA keys for use by the **ssh-agent** command.

ssh-agent command — Used to perform SSH authentication.

ssh-keygen command — Used to generate RSA and DSA keys for use with SSH.

ssh-keyscan command — Displays asymmetric public keys used by SSH.

symmetric encryption — A type of encryption that uses the same key to encrypt and decrypt data.

Triple-DES (3DES) — A common symmetric encryption algorithm that uses 112- or 168-bit keys.

virtual console — Provides separate terminals for user logins in Linux.

Virtual Network Computing (VNC) — An open protocol that is used to obtain graphical interfaces from remote operating systems.

REVIEW QUESTIONS

1. What type of encryption uses a key pair to encrypt and decrypt data?
   _____

2. What version of SSH supports HMAC?
   a. Version 1
   b. Version 2
   c. Both Versions 1 and 2
   d. Neither Version 1 nor 2; it is an independent component

3. When you type **telnet localhost 22**, you notice that the SSH server responds with SSH 1.99-OpenSSH_3.8p1. What versions of SSH are supported by your SSH server? _____

4. What file could you view to determine the version of SSH on your computer?
   _____

5. What type of authentication in the /etc/ssh/sshd_config file uses the /etc/hosts.equiv file?
   a. Host-based
   b. Host-based RSA
   c. Public key (RSA/DSA)
   d. Password

6. What option to the **ssh** command would you use if you plan to run graphical applications remotely? _____

7. Which command could you use to view the public key on the computer **arfa**?
   a. ssh-keyscan arfa
   b. ssh-agent arfa
   c. ssh-keygen arfa
   d. ssh-add arfa

8. What port does VNC listen to?
   a. 53
   b. 1066
   c. 31173
   d. 5901

9. What would you enter in the Konqueror search dialog box to connect to the computer **arfa** using VNC? _____

10

10. Which of the following hardware configurations has the least support for SLES?

    a. Server class computer hardware

    b. Client computer hardware

    c. Desktop computer hardware

    d. Laptop/Portable computer hardware

11. What key combination would you use during installation to view system-related messages? _____

12. What key combination would you use during installation to view the installation log? _____

13. After you boot from your SLES installation DVD, what key would you press to select a network installation source?

    a. F1

    b. F2

    c. F3

    d. F4

14. What types of network installation are supported by SLES? (Choose all that apply.)

    a. VNC

    b. HTTP

    c. NFS

    d. FTP

15. What log file can you check following installation for installation-related problems? _____

Discovery Exercises

Exploring SSH

View the /etc/ssh/sshd_config file on your system. Most lines in this file are commented using a # character, but represent default values for the SSH daemon. What type of authentication is disabled by default? What port is used by default? What versions of SSH are supported by default? What syslog system area does SSH log to?

Next, view the /etc/ssh/ssh_config file on your system. View the cipher lines. What types of symmetric encryption beyond those mentioned in this chapter are available? Notice that many of them use cbc (cipher block chaining). Use the Internet to find out what functionality cbc adds to these algorithms.

Using VNC in a Multi-OS Environment

VNC may be used to manage multiple operating systems in your network environment. Provided that you have access to a Windows, UNIX, or Macintosh computer, download and install VNC server on a different OS and access it from your SLES computer. You can obtain VNC on the Internet from *www.realvnc.com*.

Creating an SLES Installation Server

Download the ISO image files for SLES to your hard disk. Next, use the Installation Server module in YaST to configure your system as a remote HTTP installation server for SLES, using the ISO images on your hard disk. Then, perform a network installation from these ISO images on another computer on your network.

10

LiveFire Exercise

The Digital Airlines Corporation has decided to implement SUSE Linux Enterprise Server 9 (SLES 9) in each corporate office. At this phase of the project, all of the requirements have been identified, and the company is ready to roll out a pilot program of SLES 9.

As system administrator for your Digital Airlines office, you have received the SLES 9 software and the following information for setting up the pilot program on two servers:

- Network Services Requirements
- System Installation Requirements
- Services Setup

Read through this information thoroughly before setting up the pilot program. You will need to work with a partner to set up and test the SLES 9 pilot program.

NETWORK SERVICES REQUIREMENTS

Figure 11-1 gives an overview of the required network services and where they should be placed.

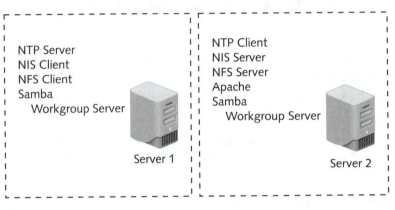

NTP Server
NIS Client
NFS Client
Samba
    Workgroup Server

Server 1

NTP Client
NIS Server
NFS Server
Apache
Samba
    Workgroup Server

Server 2

Figure 11-1

Use this diagram as a guide when setting up the services on each server.

SYSTEM INSTALLATION REQUIREMENTS

In Section 10, you performed a network installation of SLES 9 on both servers. However, before you begin configuring services, you need to complete the post-installation tasks listed in Table 11-1.

Table 11-1

Item	Task
Static IP address setup	Obtain two IP addresses (one for each server) from the instructor, along with the subnet mask, default gateway, and DNS server, and then configure each server statically with a domain name of **digitalairlines.com**
Hard disk layout	Check the hard disk layout on both servers to make sure they meet the following partitioning requirements: • **/dev/hda1** Partition type: Swap Size: 1.5 GB • **/dev/hda2** Mount: / Size: 10 GB File System: Reiser

Table 11-1 (continued)

Item	Task
Software package selection	Check both servers to make sure the appropriate packages are installed, based on the service requirements listed under Services Setup
User account setup	Check both servers to make sure you have the following user accounts created: • **root** (with a password of **novell**) • **geeko** Full User Name: **Geeko Novell** User Login: **geeko** Password: **N0v3ll** Keep all other settings at the default values.

SERVICES SETUP

The following are the services (and requirements) you need to set up on your SLES 9 servers to complete the pilot program setup:

- User Accounts
- Network Time
- Logical Volume Management (LVM)
- Network File System (NFS)
- Network Information Service (NIS)
- Samba Workgroup
- Apache Web Server
- OpenSSH

Before starting, obtain a group number from your instructor. You will use this number when configuring NIS and Samba.

After you complete and test these requirements, have your instructor conduct a final system check.

User Accounts

Do the following on *Server 2 only*:

- Create a group named **migration** that is assigned to all new user accounts
- Configure the system to create a directory named **migration** in the home directory of any new user account

11

- Create five accounts named **pilot1-pilot5** with a password of **novell** and each user's home directory set to **/export/home/pilotx** (such as **/export/home/pilot1** for user account pilot1)

- Make sure all pilot user accounts are assigned to the default groups plus the group migration

- Make sure all pilot users have a subdirectory migration in their home directories

Do the following on *both servers*:

- Display the following terminal message for all user logins:

```
==================================================
```

Reminder: This pilot program will run from Jun 1 to Aug 1.

```
==================================================
```

Network Time

Do the following:

- **NTP server configuration**

  Configure Server 1 as an NTP time server that uses its hardware clock as a reference.

- **NTP client configuration**

  Configure Server 2 as an NTP client that gets its time from Server 1.

Logical Volume Management (LVM)

Create the following LVM configuration on both servers:

- Create four physical volumes at 4 GB each (16 GB total)

- Set the volume group to **apps**, with all physical volumes assigned to the group

- Create two 6 GB logical volumes named **project** (file system: reiser) and **backup** (file system: ext3) and mount each as **/export/project** and **/export/backup**

- Set the mode on the directory /export/project so that the group owner is **migration** and user/group/other can read and write to the directory

  Set the permissions so that when a file is created in the directory /export/project, the group migration is automatically assigned as the group owner

- Set the mode on the directory /export/backup so that the group owner is **migration** and only user/group can read and write to the directory

  Set the permissions so that when a file is created in the directory /export/backup, the group migration is automatically assigned as the group owner

- Copy the project files from the instructor's server (DA1) into the /export/project and /export/backup directories, verifying that the group owner is migration

Network File System (NFS)

Do the following:

- **Configure the NFS server**

  Configure Server 2 as an NFS server. Export the following directories:

  - **/export/home** as read/write

  - **/export/project** as read-only

  - **/export/backup** as read/writable limited to mounting by the root user only

- **Configure the NFS client**

  Configure Server 1 as an NFS client to Server 2. Edit the file /etc/fstab so that the three file systems exported from Server 2 are mounted when Server 1 boots.

  Mount the remote /export/home directory locally as **/export/home**.

Network Information Service (NIS)

Do the following:

- **Configure the NIS server**

  Configure an NIS master server on Server 2. Set the domain name to **NIS-*group_number***.

- **Configure the NIS client**

  Configure Server 1 as an NIS client to the NIS domain hosted on Server 2. Pilot program users should be able to log in to Server 1.

Samba Workgroup

Add the five pilot program users as Samba users to **both servers**, then configure Samba on both servers to meet the following requirements:

- Share the directory **/export/project** directory so that it is read/write for all users

  Verify that all pilot program users can write to this directory.

- Set the workgroup name to **CIFS-*group_number***.

Apache Web Server

Configure Server 2 as an Apache Web server that allows symbolic links to be followed. Create a symbolic link named **project** from the root of the Web server (**http://server/project**) that points to the directory **/export/project**.

OpenSSH

Configure key-based authentication so that when the user pilot1 performs an ssh login as **pilot1** to Server 2 from Server 1, only the passphrase **secret** is required (not a password).

APPENDIX A

SUSE LINUX ENTERPRISE SERVER 9 INSTALLATION

The following are steps for manually installing SLES 9 to replicate the configuration of a student server at the beginning of the SUSE Linux Enterprise Server Administration course (3037).

NOTE

These steps are designed to use in a classroom environment for installing a student SLES 9 server.

For details on setting up your own SLES 9 server at home for self-study, see the *SUSE Linux Administration Self-Study Workbook* on your *3037 Course DVD*.

To install SLES 9 manually for classroom use, do the following:

1. Boot the server from the *SLES 9 DVD*.

2. In the SUSE Linux Enterprise Server welcome screen, scroll down through the menu options to stop the booting from hard disk process.

3. Select the highest screen resolution available by pressing **F2**; then select the highest resolution listed.

   For example, if 1024x768 screen resolution is available, select it from the drop-down list.

NOTE

If 640x 480 is the highest resolution available, the ncurses (text user interface) of the YaST installation will be displayed instead of a GUI interface.

4. Continue by selecting **Installation**.

NOTE

If your server reboots to the Welcome screen, there might be problems with the display (such as the graphics card driver). Try selecting **Installation - Safe Settings**.

   The Linux kernel loads and YaST starts.

   If the screen resolution cannot support a YaST GUI interface, a message appears indicating that the text front-end of YaST will be used during installation.

5. (Conditional) If the text front-end installation message appears, continue by selecting **OK**.

   After a few moments, a Novell Software License Agreement dialog appears.

6. Accept the license agreement by selecting **I Agree**.

   A YaST Welcome screen appears. YaST is the installation and system administration program provided by SUSE Linux.

7. Select *your language*; then select **Accept**.

If you already have SUSE Linux installed on your server, a dialog appears with installation options.

8. (Conditional) If this dialog appears, continue by selecting **New installation**; then select **OK**.

An Installation Settings screen appears with several headings such as System, Mode, Keyboard Layout, and Mouse.

Because this installation screen is designed in a hub and spoke configuration, each heading (headline) provides a link to a configuration screen you can use to reconfigure the default installation settings.

9. Make sure the **System**, **Mode**, **Keyboard Layout**, and **Mouse** settings are correct (the defaults are normally correct).

10. (Conditional) If a setting is not correct, select the heading and make the necessary changes.

Under the Partitioning heading are default settings for partitioning your hard drive.

To set up partitioning for the exercises in this course, you need to create a custom partitioning.

11. Remove any partitions from the hard drive by doing the following:

a. Select **Partitioning**.

b. Select **Create custom partition setup**; then select **Next**.

c. Select **Custom Partitioning -- for experts**; then select **Next**.

d. Remove any existing partitions by selecting the device **/dev/hda**; then select **Delete**.

A dialog appears asking if you really want to delete all the partitions on /dev/hda.

e. Confirm the deletion by selecting **Yes**.

All partitions are removed from the list.

12. Define a swap partition by doing the following:

a. Make sure **/dev/hda** is selected in the list; then select **Create**.

b. Select **Primary Partition**; then select **OK**.

A primary partition configuration dialog appears.

c. Select **Format**; then from the File system drop-down menu select **Swap**.

d. In the End field of the Size section, enter **+1GB**.

e. Make sure the Mount Point field is set to **swap**; then select **OK**.

13. Define a root partition by doing the following:

   a. Make sure **/dev/hda** is selected in the list (*not* /dev/hda1); then select **Create**.

   b. Select **Primary Partition**; then select **OK**.

     A primary partition configuration dialog appears.

   c. Select **Format**; then from the File system drop-down menu select **Swap**.

   d. In the End field of the Size section, enter **+10GB**.

   e. Make sure the Mount Point field is set to **/**; then select **OK**.

     You should have 3 entries in the Expert Partitioner list: **/dev/hda**, **/dev/hda1** (Linux swap), and **/dev/hda2** (Linux native - Reiser).

   f. Return to the Installation Settings screen by selecting **Next**.

14. Scroll down and select **Software**.

   A Software Selection screen appears.

15. Select **Full Installation**; then return to the Installation Settings screen by selecting **Accept**.

16. Scroll down and select **Time zone**.

   A Clock and Time Zone Configuration screen appears.

17. Select *your region* and *your time zone*.

18. From the **Hardware clock set to** field drop-down list select **UTC**; then select **Accept**.

   You are returned to the Hardware Settings screen.

19. Make sure that the following settings are selected:

   ■ Booting (boot loader type): **GRUB**

   ■ Language: *your language*

   ■ Default Runlevel: **5: Full multiuser with network and xdm**

20. (Conditional) If a setting is not correct, select the heading and make the necessary changes.

21. When you are satisfied with the installation settings, select **Accept**.

   A message appears indicating that YaST2 has all the information necessary to begin installing.

22. Start the installation by selecting **Yes, install**.

   YaST begins preparing your hard disk and installing SLES 9.

23. If you are installing SLES from CDs, at certain points, YaST will request a particular SLES 9 installation CD.

    Insert the requested SLES 9 CD; then continue by selecting **OK**.

24. The installation screen keeps you updated on the installation progress (time remaining and percentage completed).

    After copying files from the CDs or DVD, YaST performs tasks such as updating the configuration, copying files to the installed system, installing the boot manager, and preparing for a system boot.

    When these tasks are completed, YaST begins rebooting the system.

25. Remove the DVD or the SLES 9 CD from the drive, and wait for the system to boot.

26. (Conditional) If you receive another YaST message about displaying a text-based installation, continue by selecting **OK**.

    A password for root screen appears.

    The root user (like the Admin user in eDirectory or the Administrator user in Windows) has all administrative rights to the SUSE Linux Enterprise Server.

    Because of this, it is common practice to only log in to Linux as root when performing administrative tasks. Even then, many administrative tasks can be performed while logged in as a normal user by switching to root or entering the root password.

27. Enter a root password of **novell** (twice); then select **Next**.

    You are warned that the password is too simple.

28. Continue by selecting **Yes**.

    You are warned that you are only using lowercase letters.

29. Continue by selecting **Yes**.

    A Network Configuration screen appears with the network card configured for DHCP.

30. Keep the default settings and continue the installation by selecting **Next**.

    Wait while the configuration settings are saved. After a few moments, a Test Internet Connection dialog appears.

31. Select **No, Skip This Test**; then select **Next**.

    A Service Configuration dialog appears.

32. Select **Skip Configuration**; then select **Next**.

    A User Authentication dialog appears.

33. Because no central configuration store has been configured for NIS or LDAP, make sure **Local (/etc/passwd)** is selected; then select **Next**.

An Add New Local User dialog appears. This is the normal user you will log in as to perform the majority of your Linux administration tasks.

34. Enter the following information:

    ■ Full User Name: **Geeko Novell**

    ■ User login: **geeko**

    ■ Password: **N0v3ll** (enter twice)

    The password should be uppercase **N**, a zero, lowercase **v**, **3**, and two lowercase **l**'s.

35. Make sure that the **Auto Login** option is deselected; then continue by selecting **Next**.

    Notice that the password warning messages do not appear because you have entered a password that follows a model of a secure password (such as uppercase and lowercase letters and numbers).

    YaST begins writing the system configuration using SuSEconfig.

    A screen of release notes appears.

36. Review the release notes; then continue by selecting **Next**.

    YaST begins analyzing your system.

    A Hardware Configuration screen appears.

37. Check the **Graphics Card** information.

    You should have a minimum resolution and color setting of 1024x768@16bit to run the GUI interface for SLES 9.

38. (Conditional) If the Graphics Card settings *do not* meet these requirements, change the resolution and color settings by doing the following (otherwise, go to step Accept the hardware settings):

    a. Select **Graphics Cards**.

    Data for drivers is loaded.

NOTE

If your monitor is not detected, a warning dialog appears. Configure your monitor by selecting **Yes**, selecting **Properties**, and selecting the monitor model or entering the correct properties; then continue.

    b. On the left expand **Desktop**; then select **Color and Resolution**.

    c. At the bottom of the screen select **Change Configuration**.

    d. Make sure your desktop is selected; then select **Properties**.

    A dialog appears with tabs for Colors, Resolution, and Expert.

A

e. Select **Colors**; then make sure **65536 (16 bit)** is selected from the drop-down list.

f. Select **Resolution**; then select **1024x768**.

g. When you finish, select **Ok**; then select **Finish**.

h. Continue by selecting **Finalize >>**,

i. Test the new configuration by selecting **Test**.

   A test screen appears.

NOTE

If the display is corrupted or does not display at all, press **Ctrl+Alt+Backspace** and try adjusting the colors and resolution again.

j. Make any position or size adjustments and select **Save**.

   A message indicates that the settings have been saved and will be displayed the next time you restart the graphics system.

k. Select **Ok**.

39. Accept the hardware settings by selecting **Next**.

    YaST begins writing the configuration. An Installation Completed dialog appears.

40. Continue by selecting **Finish**.

    The system reboots and a GUI login screen appears.

    You are ready to begin using SLES 9 for Exercise 1-1.

B

NETWORK COMPONENTS AND ARCHITECTURE

One of the essential characteristics of human beings is their highly developed capacity for communication. Communication is dependent on and part of social interaction.

If you imagine the people involved in a conversation as points and their social interactions as lines, the result is a simple kind of network.

A computer network can be defined as a number of hosts connected to each other that exchange information across a connection (such as a cable or wireless medium).

A host does not need to be a computer. It can also be a network-capable printer or a terminal. In most networks, hosts are separated into clients and servers.

A server is a host providing a specific network service. A client is a host that requests the use of a network service. It is not always possible to strictly distinguish between both, because a server also often acts as a client (or vice versa).

However, hosts and network connections alone are not enough to guarantee successful communication. Hosts must also use the same network protocol (such as TCP/IP) to transmit data. In other words, hosts must speak a common language.

Before connecting your SUSE Linux Enterprise Server as a host to a network, you need to understand the following networking basics:

- Network Types
- Client/Server and Peer-to-Peer Computing
- Network Topology
- Elements of a Network
- TCP/IP Layer Model

Network Types

On the basis of the geographical area covered, a network can be classified into the following types:

- Local Area Network (LAN)
- Metropolitan Area Network (MAN)
- Wide Area Network (WAN)

Local Area Network (LAN)

A *LAN* is the simplest form of a network in which computers in a single location are connected using cables or a wireless medium.

Figure B-1 shows a LAN.

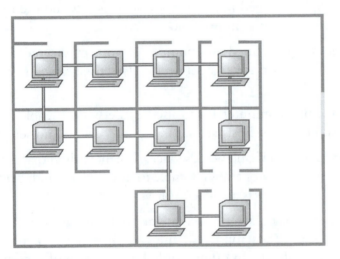

Figure B-1

A LAN connects computers located in a relatively small area. You can create a LAN within a single building or cover a group of buildings.

For example, suppose the employees of the Sales division of Digital Airlines need to frequently access information related to sales. This data is stored on different computers within the same building.

To enable easy access to the stored information, you can use a LAN to connect the computers.

Metropolitan Area Network (MAN)

A *MAN* is an extended version of a LAN. It covers a group of nearby buildings.

Figure B-2 shows a MAN connecting two organizations located in different buildings.

Organization A   Organization B

Figure B-2

For example, suppose the Marketing division of Digital Airlines is located in another building of the same city.

You can create a MAN to enable the Marketing employees to access data from the computers in the Sales division.

Wide Area Network (WAN)

A *WAN* connects multiple LANs and spans a large geographical area by using fiber optic cables and wireless. On a WAN, networks are connected normally through specialists such as Internet Service Providers (ISPs).

Figure B-3 shows two divisions of an organization connected through a satellite.

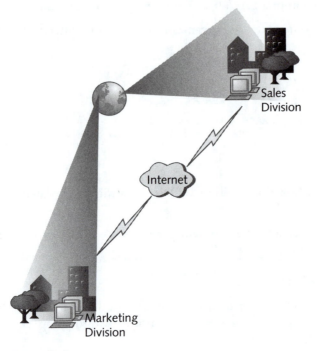

Figure B-3

For example, suppose Digital Airlines has decided to open marketing departments in different parts of the world. The employees in these departments require the information stored on the computers of the Sales division.

To enable the employees to access the required information, a WAN is created by connecting the LANs of the marketing departments to the network of the Sales division.

The technologies used to link WANs are provided by a WAN service provider.

There are two types of WANs:

- **Enterprise.** This connects the LANs of an organization that has divisions and departments in various cities of the world. For example, an organization can have an enterprise WAN for connecting its Sales offices in various cities.

- **Global.** This spans the earth and includes the networks of several organizations. An example of a global WAN is the Internet.

Client/Server and Peer-to-Peer Computing

The following are the common implementations of the computing models used to create networks:

- Client/Server Network
- Peer-to-Peer Network

Client/Server Network

A *client/server network* combines the processing and storage features of both the centralized and distributed computing models. In this model, several computers (known as clients) are connected to a server.

On a network, a computer requests services. The computer that provides the requested services to the client is called a *server*.

On a client/server network, you can to run programs such as spreadsheet or word-processing applications on a client and save data on a server.

The client/server network uses network operating systems (NOSs), such as SUSE Linux, Novell NetWare, or Windows NT/2000/XP/2003.

The classification of clients and servers introduces the concept of the *server-centric network*. On this type of network, a server is assigned the role of a service provider. The client performs the role of a service requester.

This type of network also allows for backup services and reduces network traffic.

Peer-to-Peer Network

A *peer-to-peer network* consists of peers—computers that can act both as service providers and requesters.

On a peer-to-peer network, any computer can request and provide network resources. Software used in peer-to-peer networks is designed in a way that peers can perform similar functions for each other.

A negative aspect of a peer-to-peer network is that there is no need for server-level security.

You can create a peer-to-peer network using operating systems such as SUSE Linux, Novell NetWare, Windows XP, and Windows 2000 Professional.

Network Topology

A *topology* is a pictorial representation of the layout of a network. Selecting an appropriate network topology enables you to create an efficient, reliable, and cost-effective network.

The following are the types of network topologies:

- Bus
- Ring

- Star
- Mesh
- Wireless

Bus

In a *bus* topology, all devices are connected to a central cable. This central cable is called the *bus* or the *backbone*. This topology is mainly used for small networks.

Figure B-4 shows the arrangement of computers in the bus topology.

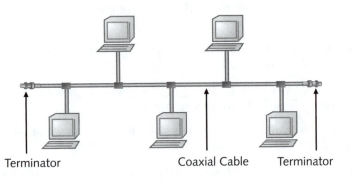

Terminator   Coaxial Cable   Terminator

Figure B-4

You implement this topology using coaxial cables.

When a computer in the bus topology wants to transmit a signal, the computer checks whether the bus is free for transmission.

If the bus is free and no other computer is transmitting a signal, the signal is sent to each computer on the network.

These signals carry information about the destination address with them. When all computers on the same bus receive the signal, the computers check the destination address against their own addresses.

When a workstation receives a signal with a different destination address than its own, the signal is dropped.

This topology is easy and relatively inexpensive to implement. In addition, networks using the bus topology can be easily extended.

A disadvantage of using this topology is that the strength of signals is reduced considerably as they travel the cable. This limits the number of devices that can be attached to a bus to 30.

If the cable or bus is damaged, the network stops functioning. Therefore, networks based on the bus topology are difficult to troubleshoot. In addition, heavy traffic deteriorates the performance of the network.

Ring

In a *ring* topology, all computers are connected to one another in the shape of a closed loop. This creates a ring in which each computer is connected directly to two other computers, one on either side.

Ring topology was designed by IBM, and is illustrated in Figure B-5.

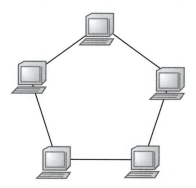

Figure B-5

It is not practical to have pure ring topology implementations because a network based on a ring topology cannot be easily reconfigured. To add or remove computers from a network using the ring topology, you have to break the ring.

A network based on the ring topology uses a method called *token passing* to transmit data. In this method, an empty token is passed around the ring. Tokens travel around a 600-meter ring about 477,000 times per second.

The device that wants to transmit data signals acquires the token. Data signals pass through each device on the ring and reach the destination computer. When the destination device receives the data, it sends back a signal acknowledging receipt of data to the source device.

The signal is called as an *acknowledgement signal*. After receiving an acknowledgement signal, the token is emptied and passed to another device on the network that wants to start data transmission.

A network based on the ring topology uses unshielded twisted pair and fiber optic cables. The cost of a network based on this topology varies depending upon the type of cable used. This topology is not used widely because it requires expensive and specialized equipment.

Data transmission on this type of network is fast. The network does not weaken the strength of the signal and enables data to travel large distances. Therefore, a large number of devices can be attached to the network.

However, the failure of a computer or a cable segment can cause the entire network to stop functioning. Therefore, a network based on a ring topology is not easy to troubleshoot.

Star

In a *star* topology, all computers are connected to a switch, and all data passes through the switch before reaching its destination. Although a switch is involved, the underlying topology is still a bus or a ring.

A star topology is the most popular technology used to network computers. Networks using the star topology are easy to install and manage.

Figure B-6 shows the arrangement of computers in a star topology.

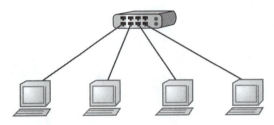

Figure B-6

A network using the star topology is implemented using twisted pair cables with the switch.

In a network based on the star topology, the signals are amplified using switches. This eliminates the problem of weak signals.

You can increase the number of devices used by adding more switches to the network. This enables you to expand the network easily.

When compared with the bus topology, the star topology is easier to troubleshoot. If one computer on the network fails and is disconnected, the network is not affected.

A disadvantage is that all data on the network must pass through the switch. If the central switch fails, all devices attached to the switch are disconnected from the network.

Mesh

In a *mesh* topology, all devices are connected through many redundant interconnections between network nodes. Every node has a connection to every other node on the network.

A mesh topology is a theoretical concept. Its practical implementation is limited to a few devices. The interconnection between each device makes the physical design of the network too complex and difficult to troubleshoot.

The Internet is an example of a mesh network. Various routers on the Internet interface with different networks.

The mesh topology is classified into the following two types:

- **Full mesh.** In a *full mesh* topology, every computer on the network is connected to every other computer or device. This creates dedicated connections between all the computers.

  Mesh networks are interconnected using WAN or MAN links.

  Figure B-7 shows the arrangement of computers in a full mesh topology.

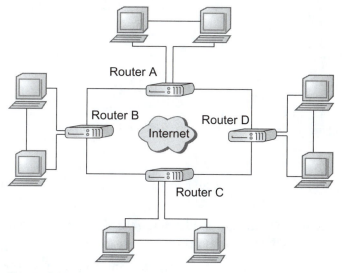

Figure B-7

If any two computers on the network are unable to communicate, the cable connecting the two computers would develop a fault.

The full mesh topology offers alternative paths for transmitting data when one of the devices on the network fails. The data can be sent through any other device attached to the active device.

However, full mesh topology is impractical and can be expensive to implement.

- **Partial mesh.** In a *partial mesh* topology, each computer is not connected to all other computers or devices. A few devices are connected using the full mesh topology, and the others are connected to one or two devices on the network.

Figure B-8 shows the arrangement of computers in a partial mesh topology.

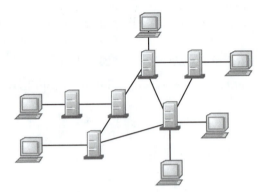

Figure B-8

The partial mesh topology is less expensive than the full mesh topology.

Wireless

In a *wireless* topology, all devices are connected to each other through an access point without a physical cable.

In the wireless topology, geographic areas are divided into *cells*. Each cell represents the area of the network where a specific connection operates.

Devices within a cell communicate with a switch. Switches, in turn, are interconnected to route data across the network.

Figure B-9 shows the cells in a wireless topology.

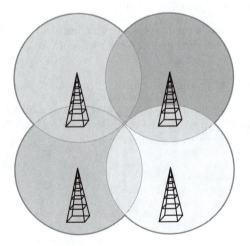

Figure B-9

B

This topology does not depend on the interconnection of cables. It depends on the location of the wireless switches.

A device can roam from one cell to another and still maintain a network connection.

On a network based on the wireless topology, complex and expensive devices are required to ensure communication.

The failure of any access point affects the network. However, you can easily troubleshoot the network because there is no physical interconnection between devices.

In addition, you can easily reconfigure the network because it supports mobile devices.

Elements of a Network

The following are the elements of a network:

- Network Nodes
- Transmission Media
- Network Protocols
- Network Connections (Sockets)
- Network Services

Network Nodes

Network nodes are processing locations on a network. A node can be a computer or a device, such as a printer. Every node on a network has a unique address, distinguishing it from other nodes.

Transmission Media

Transmission media are the paths used by network components to access data or resources. Transmission media provide a transmission path for data.

Transmission media include **bounded** and **unbounded** technologies. Bounded technologies use cables for transmission purposes; unbounded technologies use radio waves for transmission.

Figure B-10 shows how transmission media provide a path for data on a network.

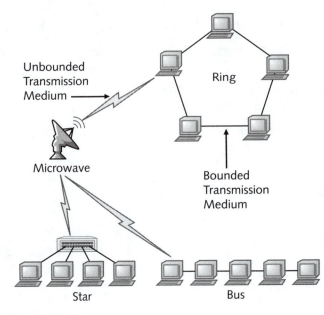

Figure B-10

The following are commonly used transmission media:

- Copper wire cabling (bounded)
- Radio waves or microwave (unbounded)
- Fiber optic cable (bounded)

Network Protocols

Network protocols enable network elements to communicate with each other.

To understand the basics of protocols, consider this example. Suppose two people are trying to communicate with each other without knowing each other's language. They would require an interpreter to facilitate communication.

Similarly, protocols ensure communication between different network nodes. Protocols are sets of rules that enable different network nodes to communicate.

Protocols can have different capabilities, depending on the purpose for which they are designed, and can be classified into the following types:

- **Routable protocols.** These enable communication between networks connected to each other through a device known as a router.

    Routable protocols are like phone services that allow you to make local and long-distance phone calls. Routable protocols can communicate across routers.

B

- **Nonroutable protocols.** These are limited to networks composed of a small number of computers.

  Nonroutable protocols are like phone services that allow you to make only local phone calls. Nonroutable protocols cannot communicate across routers.

For details on routable and nonroutable protocols, see *Internet Layer*.

NOTE

Protocols can be further classified as follows:

- **Connection-oriented.** These inform the sender that the delivery of data was successfully delivered by sending an acknowledgement when data is received at the destination.

  Connection-oriented protocols act like courier services that send packages. When you send a package by a courier service, you receive a delivery receipt after the package is delivered.

  Consider an example of using a connection-oriented protocol. During an online stock transaction, it is important to have all the data packets required for a complete transaction. If any data packet is lost, the stock transaction does not occur.

  In this example, you can use a connection-oriented protocol to make sure all data packets reach the destination.

- **Connectionless.** These send data across networks but do not provide feedback about the successful data delivery.

  Connectionless protocols function like a postal service. When you mail a letter at the post office, you do not get feedback about its arrival at the destination.

  For example, connectionless protocols are used when sending streaming video files. Even if a packet is lost during transmission, the loss creates only a small blip in the video image. The video image can still be viewed and understood.

  Connectionless protocols involve smaller overhead and are faster than connection-oriented protocols.

For details on connection and connectionless protocols, see *Internet Layer* and *Transport Layer*.

NOTE

Network Connections (Sockets)

In UNIX and some other operating systems, a software object that connects an application to a network protocol is called a *socket*. This enables two-way communication between programs on a network.

For example, a program can send and receive TCP/IP messages by opening a socket and reading data to and writing data from the socket.

This simplifies program development because the programmer only needs to worry about working with the socket and can rely on the operating system to actually transport messages across the network correctly.

Each socket gets bound to a given port, which lets the transport layer protocol (such as TCP or UDP) identify which application to send data to.

For TCP and UDP protocols, a socket on a host is defined as the combination of an *IP address* and a *port number* (such as **http://192.168.1.1:5801**).

NOTE   Another type of socket used by POSIX compliant systems (called POSIX Local IPC Sockets or simply IPC sockets) facilitates interprocess communication. These connections are from the local computer to itself, and not a connection over a physical network.

NOTE   For details on TCP and UDP protocols see Transmission Control Protocol (TCP) and User Datagram Protocol (UDP).

Network Services

Network services are programs that let users share network resources. On a network, nodes use network services to communicate using transmission media, such as cables.

Network services require resources and processing capabilities to accomplish a task, such as data processing.

Some examples of network services are CUPS (for printing), DNS (for name resolution), and NFS (for network file services).

TCP/IP Layer Model

Over the years, the functions of networks have grown in complexity due to different types of networks needing to be connected and the increasing number and requirements of applications.

Because of this increasing complexity, an attempt has been made to combine individual tasks within a network into groups and implement these as packages.

In the network environment, these packages are organized as layers stacked on top of each other. The overall model is referred to as the *layer model*.

One of the best-know layer models is the OSI (Open Systems Interconnection) reference model for open systems. In this model, a communication system is divided into seven layers.

However, as shown in Figure B-11, another well-known model, the TCP/IP layer model, has only four layers.

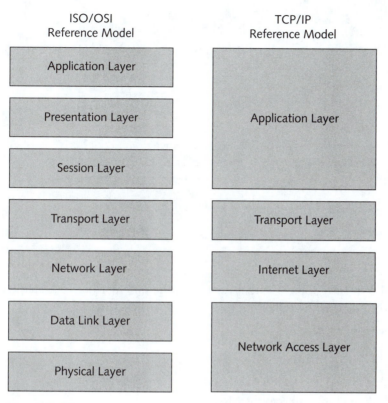

Figure B-11

With the TCP/IP model, the three upper layers of the OSI model are combined into the application layer and the two lower layers into the network access layer.

The following describe the layers in the TCP/IP model:

- Network Access Layer
- Internet Layer
- Transport Layer
- Application Layer

Network Access Layer

In the TCP/IP layer model, the physical layer and the data link layer of the OSI model are combined into the network access layer, as shown in Figure B-12.

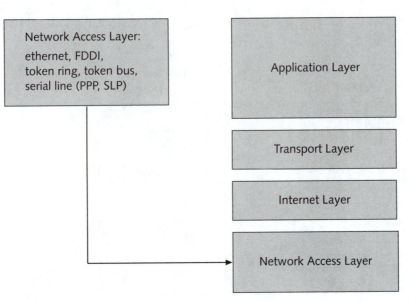

Figure B-12

One reason TCP/IP is so popular is that it runs on the different network architectures for WANs and LANs, such as the following:

- Ethernet
- Token bus
- Token ring
- ATM (Asynchronous Transfer Mode)
- FDDI (Fiber Distributed Data Interface)

It also provides the following solutions via telephone for IP:

- PPP (Point to Point Protocol)
- SLIP (Serial Line Interface Protocol)

Internet Layer

The Internet layer of the TCP/IP model ensures the connection between individual hosts in the network beyond the limits of individual networks in the Internet, as shown in Figure B-13.

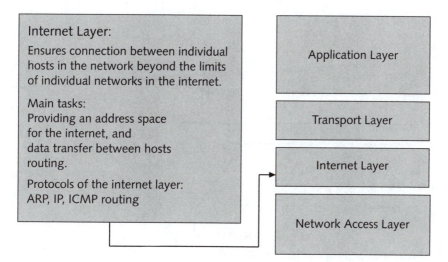

Figure B-13

The main tasks of the Internet layer are providing an address space for the Internet, routing, and data transfer between end systems (host computers).

The following are protocols of the Internet layer (with IP as the most popular):

- Address Resolution Protocol (ARP)
- Internet Protocol (IP)
- Internet Control Message Protocol (ICMP)

Address Resolution Protocol (ARP)   ARP (Address Resolution Protocol) (RFC 826) resolves IP addresses to hardware addresses (MAC addresses, Medium Access Control).

The MAC address is always composed of 6 bytes (in hexadecimal notation). The first 3 bytes indicate the manufacturer, and the last 3 bytes are the serial number of the network card.

If there are 2 network cards present, both with the same serial number, you can specify (under Linux) which MAC address the network card should use to reply.

As illustrated in Figure B-14, a special MAC address (all bits to 1: ff:ff:ff:ff:ff:ff) is used for the ARP broadcast.

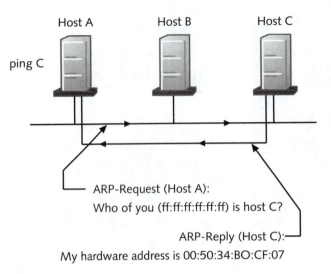

Host A   Host B   Host C

ping C

ARP-Request (Host A):
Who of you (ff:ff:ff:ff:ff:ff) is host C?

ARP-Reply (Host C):
My hardware address is 00:50:34:BO:CF:07

Figure B-14

The following describes the process:

1. Host A issues a query to all computers through an ARP broadcast request via **ping C**: "Who is host C?"

2. Host C replies (ARP reply): "My hardware address is 00:50:34:B0:CF:07."

3. The communication is established.

Host A memorizes the reply to its query in a cache. You can view this cache with the command *arp* (/sbin/arp\). The command also provides options for editing the cache, such as deleting an invalid assignment of a MAC address to an IP address (*arp –d hostname*).

For details on the command arp, enter **man arp**.

NOTE

You can use the program *arpwatch* (/usr/sbin/arpwatch) to monitor ARP requests and replies. By doing this, you can locate errors in the ARP traffic.

Internet Protocol (IP)   IP provides the underlying services for transferring data between end systems in TCP/IP networks and is specified in RFC 791.

Data is transported through the network in packet form (also called *datagrams*). The main characteristics of this protocol are that it is connectionless and unreliable.

The fact that IP is a connectionless protocol means that no end-to-end connection of communication partners is set up for data transfer.

In addition, IP is an unreliable protocol because it has no mechanisms for error detection or error correction. In other words, unreliable means that IP cannot guarantee delivery of data.

However, if data arrives at the destination host, the data is correct. This is guaranteed by the Network Access layer.

The following are the basic tasks performed by IP:

- Specifies datagrams that form the basic units for transferring data in the Internet
- Defines the addressing scheme
- Routes, exchanges, and transfers datagrams through the network
- Fragments and assembles datagrams

Every packet or datagram transmitted over the TCP/IP network has an IP header. Figure B-15 shows how the header of an IP datagram is constructed.

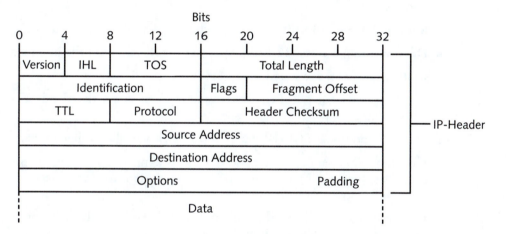

Figure B-15

The following describes the elements of the IP header:

- **Version (4 bits).** Specifies the format of the IP packet header.
- **IHL (Internet Header Length, 4 bits).** Specifies the length of the IP packet header.
- **TOS (Type of Services, 8 bits).** Specifies the parameters for the type of service requested, such as priority, reliability, and monetary cost.
- **Total length (16 bits).** Contains the length of the datagram.
- **Identification (16 bits).** Identifies the fragments of one datagram from those of another.
- **Flags (3 bits).** Include the following:
  - **R (Reserved, 1 bit)**

- **DF (Don't Fragment, 1 bit).** Controls the fragmentation of the datagram.

- **MF (More Fragments, 1 bit).** Indicates if the datagram contains additional fragments.

- **Fragment Offset (13 bits).** Used to direct the reassembly of a fragmented datagram.

- **TTL (Time To Live, 8 bits).** Used to track the lifetime of the datagram.

  When traversing a router, the TTL of a datagram is reduced by 1. If the TTL is 0, it will be discarded by a router.

- **Protocol (8 Bits).** Specifies the next encapsulated protocol (such as ICMP, TCP, UDP).

- **Header Checksum (16 bits).** Specifies the checksum of the IP header and IP options.

- **Source Address (32 bits).** Specifies the IP address of the sender.

- **Destination Address (32 Bits).** Specifies the IP address of the intended receiver.

- **Options.** Of variable length.

- **Padding (variable length).** Used as a filter to guarantee that the data starts at the 32 bit boundary.

The following are additional TCP/IP topics with which you should be familiar:

- **Routing.** The main characteristic of IP is its connectionless data transfer (packet exchange) between two computers. This means that for each packet a new path through the network is sought.

  The advantage of this approach lies in its robustness. If a cable fails for any reason, packets can take a different route (if there is one).

  The task of routing is to find a path through the Internet for each packet to send from machine A to machine B. To do this, routing protocols and algorithms are used.

- **IP addresses.** In IP-based networks, each computer (or each network interface of a computer) has a unique, 32-bit IP address.

  For the sake of readability, these 32 bits are not shown as a sequence of 32 zeros and ones, but are divided into 4 bytes.

  These four bytes, called *octets*, are separated by dots (32-bit/4-byte dot notation, or dotted quad notation) and are recorded either as decimal or binary numbers.

  For example, 32 bits "in sequence" from the machine's point of view looks like the following:

  ```
  11000000 10000001 00110010 00000001
  ```

  Readable IP representation in decimal format looks like the following:

  ```
  192.129.50.1
  ```

B

An IP address consists of the **network prefix** (the front part of the IP address) and a **host number** (the end part of the IP address).

The network prefix helps to determine the network class in which the host is located. By means of the IP address, data is delivered to the required host in the destination network.

- **IPv6.** The principle reason for changing the IP protocol is the limited address space, which causes a shortage of addresses in the foreseeable future.

Because of these demands and the problems with IPv4, the IETF (Internet Engineering Task Force) began working on a new version of IP in 1990: Internet Protocol Version 6—**IPv6** (IP Next Generation).

The basic aims of the project are:

- Support of billions of hosts, even if address space is used inefficiently
- Reduction in size of Internet routing tables
- Simplification of the protocol to allow packets to be processed by a router more quickly
- Higher security (authentication and data security) than today's IP
- More emphasis on types of service, especially for real-time applications
- Support for multicasting
- Openness of the protocol for future developments

NOTE

For details on IPv6, see *www.ipv6.org/*.

Internet Control Message Protocol (ICMP)   Internet Protocol (IP) was not designed for the purpose of ensuring faultless data transmission.

In the event of a communication problem during the transmission of an IP datagram, the sender of the datagram receives a corresponding error report through ICMP.

However, this error report can only be transmitted to the sender of the IP datagram if a gateway or the recipient of the IP datagram can analyze the error that occurred.

Because of this, ICMP (as defined in RFC 792) is a protocol that is usually used for transmitting error reports to the senders of IP datagrams.

For example, an IP datagram should be sent to a specific destination network through a specific router. However, the router in question is not able to reach the destination, so a **destination unreachable** message is sent.

Or, if the router notices that the received packet can reach the destination quicker via another path (another gateway), a *redirect* message is sent.

The analysis tool *ping* also uses the ICMP protocol for transmitting ping control messages (*echo request* and *echo reply*).

In turn, ICMP uses IP for transmitting the control messages, and packs the control messages into the data section of the IP header.

ICMP places the type ID of the control message in the first octet of the data section in the IP header. The type IP classifies the control message and defines which and how much data is contained in the subsequent bytes of the datagram.

ICMP uses the message types shown in Table B–1.

Table B-1

Type	Name	Description
0	Echo Reply	Answers the request (Type 8).
3	Destination Unreachable	A destination (host/network/protocol/port) cannot be reached.
4	Source Quench	The destination or a gateway currently is not able to process the IP datagrams (for example, due to overload).
5	Redirect Message	A gateway informs the sender of an IP datagram about a shorter route to the destination.
8	Echo Request	Sends a request for a response (Type 0: Echo Reply).
11	Time Exceeded	The TTL (Time-To-Live) of an IP datagram has reached the value 0. The datagram was discarded.
12	Parameter Problem	An IP datagram was discarded due to invalid parameters.
13	Timestamp Request	Sends a request for a response, including the time in milliseconds since 0:00 UT.
14	Timestamp Reply	Replies to the request (type 13) and sends its own time in milliseconds since 0:00 UT.

Figure B-16 shows how an ICMP packet header is constructed.

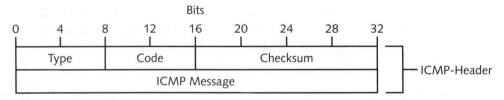

Figure B-16

The following describes each component of the header:

- **Type (8 bits).** Specifies the format of the ICMP message, such as Type 0 (echo reply) or Type 8 (echo request).
- **Code (8 bits).** Further qualifies the ICMP message.
- **Checksum (16 bits).** Of the ICMP message.
- **ICMP Message (variable length).** Contains the data specific to the message type indicated by the Type and Code fields.

Transport Layer

The third layer in the TCP/IP architecture is the transport layer, as illustrated in Figure B-17.

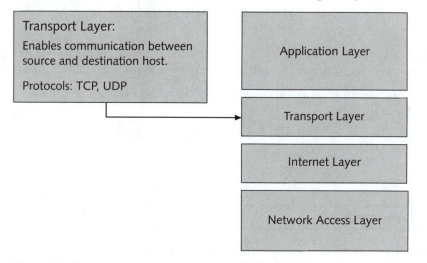

Figure B-17

The transport layer enables communication between source and destination hosts, and uses the following end-to-end protocols:

- Transmission Control Protocol (TCP)
- User Datagram Protocol (UDP)

In addition, you need to know about the following:

- Ports and Port Numbers

Transmission Control Protocol (TCP)   The Transmission Control Protocol (TCP) is a reliable, connection-oriented byte stream protocol.

The protocol was originally defined in RFC 793. Over the course of time, these definitions were improved by removing errors and inconsistencies (RFC 1122) and expanded with a number of requirements (RFC 1323).

The main task of TCP is to provide secure transport of data through the network.

TCP provides reliability of the data transfer with a mechanism referred to as Positive Acknowledgement with Retransmission (PAR).

The sending system repeats the transfer of data until it receives positive confirmation from the receiver that the data has been received.

The data units exchanged between the sending and receiving TCP units are called *packets*. A TCP packet consists of a protocol header, at least 20 bytes in size, and the data to transmit.

Each of these packets includes a *checksum* by means of which the receiver can check to see if the data is error-free.

In the case of an error-free transmission, the receiver sends a confirmation of receipt to the sender. Otherwise, the packet is discarded and no confirmation of receipt is sent.

If, after a specific length of time (timeout period) no receipt has arrived, the sender resends the packet in question.

Figure B-18 shows how a TCP packet header is constructed.

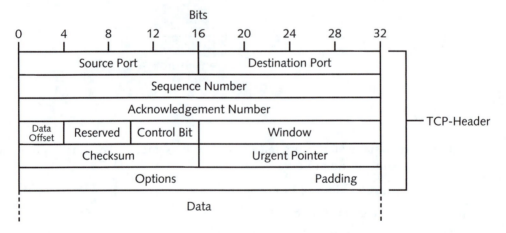

Figure B-18

The following describes the components of a TCP Packet header:

- **Source Port (16 bits).** Specifies the port of the sender.

- **Destination Port (16 bits).** Specifies the port of the receiver.

- **Sequence Number (32 bits).** Sequence number of the first data byte in this segment.

If the SYN bit is set, the sequence number is the initial sequence number, and the first data byte is the initial sequence number +1.

- **Acknowledgement Number (32 bits).** If the ACK bit is set, this field contains the value of the next sequence number the sender of the segment is expecting to receive.

Once a connection is established, this is always sent.

- **Data Offset (4 bits).** Indicates where the data begins. The length of the TCP header is always a multiple of 32 bits.

- **Reserved (4 bits).** Must be set to zero.

- **Control Bit (6 bits).** For example, it can be ACK, SYN, FIN.

- **Window (16 bits).** The number of data bytes, beginning with the one indicated in the acknowledgement field, that the sender of this segment is willing to accept.

- **Checksum (16 bits).** The complement sum of a *pseudoheader* of information from the IP header, TCP header, and the data, padded as needed with 0 bytes at the end to make a multiple of 2 bytes.

The pseudoheader contains the source address, destination address, IP protocol, and total length.

- **Urgent Pointer (16 bits).** If the URG bit is set, this field points to the sequence number of the last byte in a sequence of urgent data.

- **Options (0–44 bytes).** Occupies space at the end of the TCP header. All options are included in the checksum.

- **Padding.** The TCP header must be padded with zeros to make the header length a multiple of 32 bits.

Because TCP is a connection-oriented byte-stream protocol, a client-server dialog connection is required before data can be transmitted.

The process of setting up this connection is referred to as the TCP handshake or three-way handshake, as shown in Figure B-19.

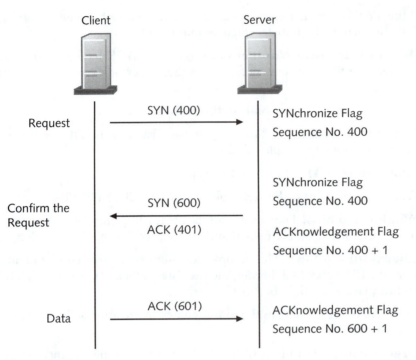

Figure B-19

The following describes the TCP handshake process:

1. The client sends a TCP packet to the server with the SYN flag set.

   This tells the server that the client wants to synchronize a connection. The SYN flag is used to synchronize the connection.

2. If the opposite side accepts the connection, the server receives the packet and takes out the sequence number (400).

3. The server sends a TCP packet to the client with a SYN flag set (with sequence number 600) and an ACK flag with sequence number 401 (Client SYN +1).

   With this, the server acknowledges the receipt of the client packet and tells the client that it wants to synchronize the connection.

4. The client receives the packet and knows that the server is ready for the data transmission.

   It starts the transmission of the first data packet in which the ACK flag is set with the sequence number 601 (Server-SYN +1), acknowledging the receipt of the last TCP packet from the server.

5. All additional packets are exchanged in this way between client and server, increasing the sequence number by 1 each time.

If the client or the server closes the connection, an additional TCP handshake takes place.

During the transmission of the last 3 packets, the FIN flag will be set instead of the SYN flag, signaling the end of the transmission.

User Datagram Protocol (UDP)   The User Datagram Protocol (UDP) is an unreliable, connectionless datagram protocol. The main task of UDP is to make available a simple and fast transport of data available through the network.

In this case, "unreliable" means that UDP has no mechanism to guarantee the delivery of a datagram. Applications that use UDP must implement their own routines on the application layer for guaranteeing the correct transmission of data.

"Connectionless" means that no computer-to-computer connection is established for transmitting UDP datagrams. Instead, UDP datagrams are sent by the sender without the destination machine making any further checks.

Figure B-20 shows how a UDP packet header is constructed (RFC 0768).

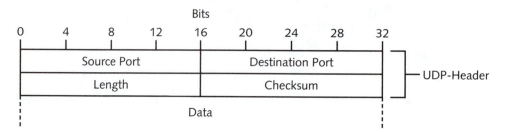

Figure B-20

The following describes the components of a UDP packet header:

- **Source Port (16 bits).** Port of the sender. This is an optional field.

- **Destination Port (16 bits).** Port of the receiver.

- **Length (16 bits) (In Bytes).** Length of the UDP header and the encapsulated data. The minimum value is 8.

- **Checksum (16 bits).** Consists of the complement sum of a pseudoheader of information from the IP header, UDP header, and the data.

  The checksum is padded as needed with 0 bytes at the end to make a multiple of 2 bytes.

Individual units sent by UDP are called *datagrams*. UDP is mainly used where a rapid and efficient protocol is needed to transfer data.

In certain cases, it is not worth the trouble involved when sending packets by TCP, as the transmission is considerably less economical due to the larger size of the TCP header.

Ports and Port Numbers   To enable specific services to be addressed, communication on the transport layer is carried out through *ports*. Because port numbers are 16 bits in length, there is a maximum of 65536 different ports.

To simplify communication and to avoid collisions, fixed port numbers (well-known ports) are assigned by the Internet Assigned Numbers Authority (IANA) for widely-used services.

All important network services run on privileged ports (ports from 0 to 1023). They are referred to as "privileged" because the associated services must be started with root permissions.

The upper ports (from 1024 to 65535) are nonprivileged ports.

The following lists some well-known ports registered with IANA:

- **FTP.** Ports 20, 21
- **SSH.** Port 22
- **Telnet.** Port 23
- **SMTP.** Port 25
- **DNS.** Port 53
- **HTTP.** Port 80
- **POP3.** Port 110
- **NNTP.** Port 119
- **NETBIOS-SSN.** Port 139
- **IMAP.** Port 143
- **SNMP.** Port 161

For TCP and UDP, the port numbers are assigned separately. For example, port 4912 for UDP can specify a different service from the same port number for TCP.

Almost all Internet services are constructed according to the client-server principle—each service has a server, which provides the service, and one or more clients, which access it.

On a Linux computer, there are normally a variety of daemons running simultaneously, which are all waiting for incoming connections on the various ports and form the server part of the client-server structure.

For a table listing the port numbers of frequently used services, see the file */etc/services*.

NOTE

Application Layer

The application layer combines all the higher-level protocols of the TCP/IP model (protocols based on the TCP/IP protocols), as shown in Figure B-21.

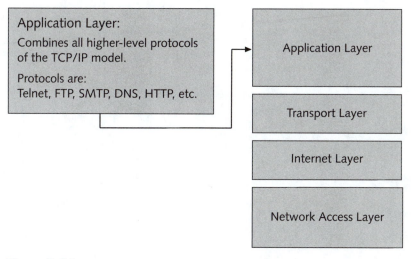

Figure B-21

Experience has shown that it was a wise decision to combine the three application-related layers from the OSI model into one, as layers 5 and 6 from that model are seldom used.

Protocols used in the application layer include the following:

- FTP (file transfer)
- SMTP (for sending email)
- DNS (Domain Name System)
- HTTP (Hypertext Transfer Protocol)
- SMB (Server Message Block)

C

NOVELL **CLP** AND **LPI** REQUIREMENTS

This appendix provides information about the LPI Level 1 objectives covered in this and the other Novell CLP certification courses.

LPI objectives named **1.*xxx.y*** are part of exams 101 and 102 (LPI Certification Level 1). LPI objectives named **2.*xxx.y*** are part of exams 201 and 202 (LPI Certification Level 2). CLP courses include the section (such as **3037/3** for Course 3037 Section 3).

Because Novell CLP courses use SUSE Linux exclusively, there are some differences in the software used in those courses and those covered by the LPI objectives (such as CUPS for printing in SLES 9 and lpr in the LPI objectives).

Table C-1

LPI Objective	CLP Courses
Topic 101: Hardware & Architecture	
1.101.1 Configure fundamental BIOS settings	not applicable
1.101.3 Configure modem and sound cards	not applicable
1.101.4 Setup SCSI devices	not applicable
1.101.5 Setup different PC expansion cards	not applicable
1.101.6 Configure communication devices	not applicable
1.101.7 Configure USB devices	not applicable
Topic 102: Linux Installation and Package Management	
1.102.1 Design hard disk layout	3037/3, 3038/1
1.102.2 Install a boot manager	3037/5, 3038/5
1.102.3 Make and install programs from source	3038/7
1.102.4 Manage shared libraries	3037/4
1.102.5 Use Debian package management	not applicable
1.102.6 Use RPM Package Manager (RPM)	3036/5, 3037/4
Topic 103: GNU and Unix Commands	
1.103.1 Work on the command line	3036/3, 3036/5
1.103.2 Process text streams using filters	3036/6
1.103.3 Perform basic file management	3036/6
1.103.4 Use streams, pipes, and redirects	3036/5, 3036/6
1.103.5 Create, monitor, and kill processes	3036/8, 3037/6, 3038/8
1.103.6 Modify process execution priorities	3036/8, 3037/6, 3038/8
1.103.7 Search text files using regular expressions	3036/6
1.103.8 Perform basic file editing operations using vi	3036/7
Topic 104: Devices, Linux Filesystems, Filesystem Hierarchy Standard	
1.104.1 Create partitions and filesystems	3037/3, 3038/1
1.104.2 Maintain the integrity of filesystems	3037/3
1.104.3 Control mounting and unmounting filesystems	3036/6, 3037/3
1.104.4 Managing disk quota	3037/3
1.104.5 Use file permissions to control access to files	3036/6, 3037/2
1.104.6 Manage file ownership	3036/6, 3037/2
1.104.7 Create and change hard and symbolic links	3036
1.104.8 Find system files and place files in the correct location	3036/6
Topic 105: Kernel	
1.105.1 Manage/query kernel and kernel modules at runtime	3037/5
1.105.2 Reconfigure, build, and install a custom kernel and kernel modules	not applicable
Topic 106: Boot, Installation, Shutdown and Runlevels	
1.106.1 Boot the system	3037/5, 3038/5
1.106.2 Change runlevels and shutdown or reboot system	3036/8, 3037/5, 3037/6
Topic 107: Printing	
1.107.2 Manage printers and print queues	3037/8
1.107.3 Print files	3037/8
1.107.4 Install and configure local and remote printers	3037/8

Table C-1   (continued)

LPI Objective	CLP Courses
Topic 108: Documentation	
1.108.1 Use and manage local system documentation	3036/3
1.108.2 Find Linux documentation on the Internet	3036/3
1.108.5 Notify users on system-related issues	3036/2
Topic 109: Shells, Scripting, Programming and Compiling	
1.109.1 Customize and use the shell environment	3036/5, 3038/6
1.109.2 Customize or write simple scripts	3038/6
Topic 110: X	
1.110.1 Install and configure XFree86	not applicable
1.110.2 Setup a display manager	not applicable
1.110.4 Install and customize a window manager environment	not applicable
Topic 111: Administrative Tasks	
1.111.1 Manage users and group accounts and related system files	3036/5, 3037/2
1.111.2 Tune the user environment and system environment variables	3036/5, 3037/2
1.111.3 Configure and use system log files to meet administrative and security needs	3037/6, 3038/8
1.111.4 Automate system administration tasks by scheduling jobs to run in the future	3036/8, 3037/6
1.111.5 Maintain an effective data backup strategy	3036/6, 3037/3, 3038/5
1.111.6 Maintain system time	3037/8
Topic 112: Networking Fundamentals	
1.112.1 Fundamentals of TCP/IP	3036/9, 3037/7
1.112.3 TCP/IP configuration and troubleshooting	3036/9, 3037/7, 3038/1
1.112.4 Configure Linux as a PPP client	not applicable
Topic 113: Networking Services	
1.113.1 Configure and manage inetd, xinetd, and related services	3037/9
1.113.2 Operate and perform basic configuration of sendmail	not applicable
1.113.3 Operate and perform basic configuration of Apache	3037/8, 3038/3
1.113.4 Properly manage the NFS, smb, and nmb daemons	3037/9, 3038/3
1.113.5 Setup and configure basic DNS services	3038/1
1.113.7 Setup secure shell (OpenSSH)	3037/10
Topic 114: Security	
1.114.1 Perform security administration tasks	3038/4
1.114.2 Setup host security	3038/4
1.114.3 Setup user level security	3037/2, 3038/4
Topic 201: Linux Kernel	
2.201.1 Kernel components	not applicable
2.201.2 Compiling a kernel	not applicable
2.201.3 Patching a kernel	not applicable

C

Table C-1 (continued)

LPI Objective	CLP Courses
2.201.4 Customizing a kernel	not applicable
Topic 202: System Startup	
2.202.1 Customizing system startup and boot process	3037/5, 3037/6
2.202.2 System recovery	3038/5
Topic 203: Filesystem	
2.203.1 Operate the Linux filesystem	3037/3
2.203.2 Maintaining a Linux filesystem	3037/3
2.203.3 Creating and configuring filesystem options	3037/3
Topic 204: Hardware	
2.204.1 Configuring RAID	3038/1
2.204.2 Adding new hardware	3038/9
2.204.3 Software and kernel configuration	3038/1
2.204.4 Configuring PCMCIA devices	not applicable
Topic 205: Networking	
2.205.1 Basic network configuration	3036/9, 3037/7, 3038/1
2.205.2 Advanced network configuration and troubleshooting	3036/9, 3037/7, 3038/1
Topic 206: Mail and News	
2.206.1 Configuring mailing lists	not applicable
2.206.2 Using sendmail	not applicable
2.206.3 Managing mail traffic	not applicable
2.206.4 Serving news	not applicable
Topic 207: DNS	
2.207.1 Basic BIND 8 configuration	not applicable
2.207.2 Create and maintain DNS zones	3038/1
2.207.3 Securing a DNS server	3038/1
Topic 208: Web Services	
2.208.1 Implementing a web server	3037/9, 3038/3
2.208.2 Maintaining a web server	3037/9, 3038/3
2.208.3 Implementing a proxy server	not applicable
Topic 209: File and Service Sharing	
2.209.1 Configuring a samba server	3037/8, 3038/3
2.209.2 Configuring an NFS server	3037/8
Topic 210: Network Client Management	
2.210.1 DHCP configuration	not applicable
2.210.2 NIS configuration	3037/8
2.210.3 LDAP configuration	3037/8, 3038/2
2.210.4 PAM authentication	3037/2
Topic 211: System Maintenance	
2.211.1 System logging	3037/6, 3038/8
2.211.2 Packaging software	not applicable
2.211.3 Backup operations	3038/5
Topic 212: System Security	
2.212.2 Configuring a router	not applicable

Table C-1   (continued)

LPI Objective	CLP Courses
2.212.3 Securing FTP servers	not applicable
2.212.4 Secure Shell (OpenSSH)	3037/10
2.212.5 TCP wrappers	3037/9
2.212.6 Security tasks	3038/4
Topic 213: System Customization and Automation	
2.213.1 Automating tasks using scripts	3037/6, 3038/6
Topic 214: Troubleshooting	
2.214.2 Creating recovery disks	3037/3, 3038/5
2.214.3 Identifying boot stages	3037/5, 3038/5
2.214.4 Troubleshooting LILO	not applicable
2.214.5 General troubleshooting	3038/5
2.214.6 Troubleshooting system resources	3037/5
2.214.7 Troubleshooting network issues	3037/7, 3038/1
2.214.8 Troubleshooting environment configurations	3038/5

C

D

NOVELL ZENWORKS LINUX MANAGEMENT (ZLM)

This appendix provides an overview of Novell ZENworks® Linux Management (ZLM) and contains the following:

- ◆ What ZLM Is
- ◆ ZLM Architecture
- ◆ Supported Linux Clients
- ◆ How to Install and Activate the ZLM Client

In addition to upgrading SLES 9 through a YaST Online Update (YOU) server, Novell also provides a ZLM channel for upgrading SLES 9 (and installing additional software packages such as Novell GroupWise).

SLES 9 includes the client daemon and other software modules necessary to interface with Novell's ZLM server channel for SLES 9.

In addition to upgrading SLES 9 through a ZLM channel, you might also consider purchasing the complete ZLM package for managing all software installations and upgrades on your enterprise network.

For additional details on ZLM, see the ***Novell ZENworks Linux Management Administration Guide*** on your ***3037 Course DVD***.

What ZLM Is

As a system or network administrator, you want to maximize security and convenience as you distribute software updates and new programs to your Linux network.

You don't have the budget or time to develop your own tools, and the standard package management systems are developed for individual computers rather than complete networks.

ZENworks Linux Management lets you manage dozens or thousands of individual client machines from a central server located within your firewall for maximum convenience and security.

Using the Web interface or command-line tools, you can create groups of individual machines and channels of software, and then distribute that software to the machines.

You can delegate authority to multiple administrators, follow progress with the built-in reporting system, and maintain your network with a minimum of cost and effort.

ZENworks Linux Management 6.6 offers several enhancements and new features, including:

- Support for SUSE Linux Enterprise Server 9
- Ability to manage and deploy SUSE patch files to your SUSE 9 servers
- YaST integration for patch management

ZLM Architecture

The simplest ZENworks Linux Management deployment consists of a single server and a single client machine.

The client runs the Red Carpet Daemon (rcd), and fetches updates automatically or at the user's direction, using the rug or red-carpet programs.

The ZLM server uses an XML–RPC interface to communicate with a variety of clients and other systems, as illustrated in Figure D-1.

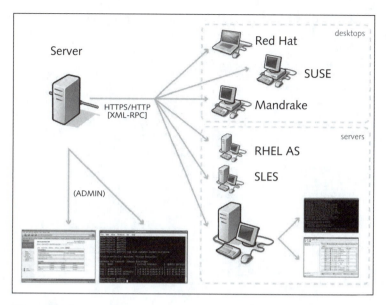

Figure D-1

The XML-RPC interface feeds into the core components of the server, which work with Apache, a database, and the package repository, as illustrated in Figure D-2.

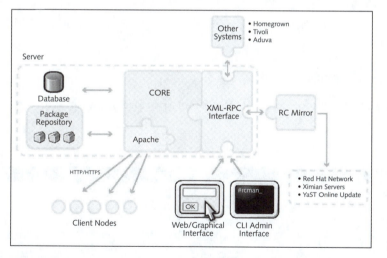

Figure D-2

The client daemon, rcd, also uses an XML–RPC interface to accept commands from rug and red–carpet, remotely or locally, as illustrated in Figure D-3.

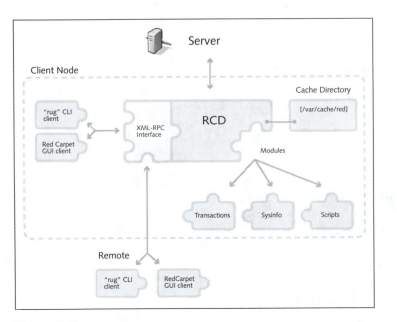

Figure D-3

Additional modules provide the client with the ability to interact with the ZLM server for extended functionality.

Supported Linux Clients

The Red Carpet client is supported on the Linux platforms and architectures listed in Table D-1.

Table D-1

Platform	Architectures
SUSE Linux Enterprise Server 9	• 32-bit Intel • 64-bit AMD Opteron • 64-bit Intel XEON EMT • 64-bit Intel Itanium • IBM zSeries, iSeries, pSeries
SUSE Linux Enterprise Server 8	• 32-bit Intel
Novell Linux Desktop	• 32-bit Intel • 64-bit AMD Opteron • 64-bit Intel XEON EMT
SUSE Linux 9.2	• 32-bit Intel • 64-bit AMD Opteron • 64-bit Intel XEON EMT

Table D-1   (continued)

Platform	Architectures
SUSE Linux 9.1	• 32-bit Intel • 64-bit AMD Opteron • 64-bit Intel XEON EMT
SUSE Linux Desktop 1	• 32-bit Intel
Red Hat Enterprise Linux 3 AS, ES, WS	• 32-bit Intel • 64-bit AMD Opteron • 64-bit Intel XEON EMT

The Red Carpet graphical user interface (GUI) is supported on all client platforms, with the exception of SUSE Linux Enterprise Server 8 and Red Hat Enterprise Linux 2.1 AS, ES, and WS.

How to Install and Activate the ZLM Client

The process of installing the ZLM client on your SLES 9 server includes the following tasks:

- Install and Start the Red Carpet Client
- Activate the Client and Subscribe to the SLES 9 Upgrade Channel

Install and Start the Red Carpet Client

To install the Red Carpet software packages on your SLES 9 server and start the Red Carpet daemon, do the following:

1. From a Linux desktop (such as KDE), start **YaST**.

2. (Conditional) If requested, enter the *root password*.

3. From the YaST Control Center, select **Software > Install and Remove Software**.

4. From the software installation dialog box, make sure **Search** is selected from the filter drop-down list.

5. In the Search field, enter **carpet**; then select **Search**.

   All the software packages for the Red Carpet client are displayed to the right in the package list.

6. Select all the packages; then select **Accept**.

   A dialog box appears listing the packages that have been changed to resolve dependencies.

7. Continue by selecting **Continue**.

   YaST requests a DVD or one or more SLES 9 installation CDs.

8. Insert each CD or DVD; then select **OK**.

   YaST installs the software and you are returned to the YaST Control Center.

9. Close the YaST Control Center.

10. Open a terminal window and su to root (**su -**).

11. Start the Red Carpet daemon by entering the following:

    /etc/init.d/rcd start

    The rcd daemon is started and added to the system start-up services to load automatically when the machine is started.

    By default, rcd requires verified SSL certificates.

12. Make sure you have Internet access, then configure rcd to contact Novell's ZLM server for SLES 9 updates by entering the following:

    rug service-add https://red-carpet.americas.novell.com/data

    This setting is stored in the file /var/lib/rcd/services.xml.

13. (Conditional) If you are using a proxy, you need to configure the proxy by entering the following commands:

    rug set proxy-url http://*hostname:port*

    rug set proxy-username *username*

    rug set proxy-password *password*

The Red Carpet client is now ready to be activated.

Activate the Client and Subscribe to the SLES 9 Upgrade Channel

Before your Red Carpet client can receive SLES 9 upgrades from Novell's ZLM server, you need to activate the client and subscribe to the SLES 9 upgrade channel.

Before activating the client, you should have already purchased SLES 9, activated a SUSE portal account (the account code comes with your SLES 9 package), and received an activation key from Novell.

You can activate the client and subscribe to the channel using one of the following methods:

- Activate and Subscribe from the Command Line
- Activate and Subscribe from a GUI Interface

Activate and Subscribe from the Command Line   You can activate the client and subscribe to the SLES 9 upgrade channel from the command line by doing the following:

1. From a terminal console, log in as **root**; from a terminal window, su to root (**su -**).

2. Activate the Red Carpet client by entering the following (all on one line):

   rug activate -s https://red-carpet.americas.novell.com/data *activation_key your_email-address*

   A "System successfully activated" and refresh messages appear.

3. List the channels available by entering **rug ch**.

   A list of Red Carpet channels appears with an alias and a name.

4. Subscribe to the SLES 9 upgrade channel by entering the following:

   rug sub sles-9-i586

   A message indicates that you have successfully subscribed to the channel.

At this point, you can use rug to perform several tasks.

For example, to download and install all packages from the sles-9-i586 channel, you would enter the following:

rug install ---entire-channel sles-9-i586

To download all the software packages but not install them, you would enter the following:

rug install -d sles-9-i586

> **NOTE**
>
> For details on these and other rug commands, enter **man rug** or **rug --help**.

Activate and Subscribe from a GUI Interface   You can activate the Red Carpet client and subscribe to the SLES 9 upgrade channel from a GUI interface by doing the following:

1. From a desktop (such as KDE), open a terminal window.

2. Switch to the root user by entering **sux –** and the *root password*.

3. Start the Red Carpet GUI client by entering **red-carpet**.

   The Red Carpet client dialog box appears.

4. Select **File > Activate**.

   A Group Activation dialog box appears.

5. From the drop-down list, select **ZLMAmericas**.

6. In the provided fields, enter your *email address* and *activation key (code)*; then select **Activate**.

7. When the activation is successful, select the **Channels** icon from the toolbar.

   A dialog box appears with a list of available channels.

8. Scroll down and select the **sles-9-i586** channel; then select **Close**.

   After a few moments, a list of available software packages is displayed on the Updates tab page.

9. Do one of the following:

- Download and install all packages by selecting **Update All** (above the list).

  or

- Update selected packages by selecting a package in the **Action** column.

The packages to be updated are listed in the Pending Actions list (to the left).

10. When you are ready to update, select **Run Now** from the toolbar.

The software packages are downloaded and installed on your SLES 9 server.

For additional details on using the Red Carpet GUI client, select **Help > Contents**.

Glossary

& — A special character used to start a program in the background.

/boot/grub.conf — The file that contains information about GRUB components.

/boot/grub/menu.lst — The configuration file for the GRUB boot Loader in SLES.

/etc/at.allow — A file that lists users who can use the at command.

/etc/at.deny — A file that lists users who cannot use the at command.

/etc/cron.d — A directory that contains additional system cron tables.

/etc/crontab — The system cron table.

/etc/cups/cupsd.conf — The main CUPS configuration file.

/etc/cups/lpoptions — The file that stores system-wide print options set by the root user.

/etc/cups/ppd — The directory that stores the active PPD files used for a particular printer.

/etc/cups/printers.conf — Contains CUPS printer definitions.

/etc/default/passwd — A file that contains default values used when changing passwords such as encryption algorithm.

/etc/default/useradd — A file that contains default values used when creating user accounts.

/etc/defaultdomain — A file that stores the default NIS domain name.

/etc/exports — The file that lists exported directories on an NFS server.

/etc/fstab — A file used to store information used to mount file systems.

/etc/group — The file that contains system groups and their members.

/etc/HOSTNAME — A file that contains the name of the host.

/etc/hosts — A file used for local name resolution.

/etc/hosts.allow — A text file used by tcpd listing hosts that are allowed to connect to network daemons.

/etc/hosts.deny — A text file used by tcpd listing hosts that are not allowed to connect to network daemons.

/etc/inetd.conf — The main configuration file for inetd.

/etc/init.d — The directory that contains the scripts used to start and stop most daemons.

/etc/init.d/boot — The script used to activate file systems and swap during system initialization.

/etc/init.d/network — The script that activates network interfaces at system initialization.

/etc/init.d/rc — The script used to start and stop daemons based on runlevel.

/etc/init.d/skeleton — A sample script that may be copied to create scripts used to start a daemon.

/etc/inittab — The configuration file for the init daemon.

/etc/issue — A text file that contains a message for users that log into a command-line terminal.

/etc/ld.so.cache — A file that contains a list of shared library locations.

/etc/ld.so.conf — A file that is used to create entries in the /etc/ld.so.cache file.

/etc/lilo.conf — The LILO configuration file.

/etc/localtime — A file that specifies the time zone used by a SLES system.

/etc/login.defs — A file that contains default values used when creating user accounts.

/etc/logrotate.conf — The configuration file for the logrotate command. It typically uses parameters listed in the /etc/logrotate.d directory for each log file.

/etc/logrotate.d — The directory that stores log file-specific information for use by the logrotate command.

/etc/modprobe.conf — Used at system initialization to load kernel modules.

/etc/motd — A text file that contains a message (or "message of the day") for users that log into a command-line terminal.

/etc/mtab — A file that contains a list of mounted file systems.

/etc/nsswitch.conf — A file that determines when NIS maps are used to configure system information.

/etc/ntp.conf — The NTP configuration file.

/etc/ntp/drift — A file that contains a value for time drift that was detected by the NTP daemon.

/etc/pam.d — The directory that stores PAM configuration information for PAM programs.

/etc/passwd — The file that contains user account information such as name, UID, primary group, home directory, and shell.

/etc/permissions.easy — A file that lists the least secure file permission restrictions for system files.

/etc/permissions.local — A file that lists user-defined file permission restrictions for system files.

/etc/permissions.paranoid — A file that lists the most secure file permission restrictions for system files.

/etc/permissions.secure — A file that lists secure file permission restrictions for system files.

/etc/powertweak/tweaks — The configuration file for the Powertweak daemon.

/etc/pure-ftpd/pure-ftpd.conf — The main PureFTPd configuration file.

/etc/rc.d/rc*n*.d — The directories used by the init daemon to start and kill daemons in each runlevel (*n*).

/etc/resolv.conf — A file that lists up to three DNS servers that may be contacted to resolve a remote hostname to an IP address.

/etc/rpmrc — Contains configuration information that is written to the /usr/lib/rpm/rpmrc file.

/etc/samba/smb.conf — The main Samba configuration file.

/etc/security — The directory that stores PAM configuration information for PAM modules.

/etc/shadow — The file that typically contains encrypted passwords and password expiry information for user accounts on the system.

/etc/shells — A file that lists valid system shells such as /bin/bash.

/etc/skel — A directory that contains files and directories that are copied to all new users' home directories after they are created.

/etc/ssh/ssh_config — The system-wide ssh client program configuration file.

/etc/ssh/sshd_config — The SSH daemon configuration file.

/etc/sudoers — A file that lists the users who are allowed to run certain commands as other users.

/etc/sysconfig — The directory that stores most system configuration settings.

/etc/sysconfig Editor — A YaST utility that may be used to change system configuration settings in the /etc/sysconfig directory.

/etc/sysconfig/backup — The configuration file that controls automatic system backups.

/etc/sysconfig/clock — A file that stores time and time-zone configuration information.

/etc/sysconfig/cron — A file that contains parameters for the cron daemon.

/etc/sysconfig/hardware — The directory that contains hardware device information for system devices, such as network interfaces used to load and initialize devices by the Linux kernel.

/etc/sysconfig/network — The directory that contains most network configuration information.

/etc/sysconfig/network/ifcfg.template — A template file that may be used to create the TCP/IP configuration for a network interface.

/etc/sysconfig/network/ifroute-*interface* — A file that stores static routes for a specific *interface*.

/etc/sysconfig/network/routes — A file that stores static routes for use on the system.

/etc/sysconfig/onlineupdate — The configuration file used by a YOU Client.

/etc/sysconfig/ypserv — Stores NIS server options.

/etc/xinetd.conf — The main configuration file for xinetd. It loads configuration files from the /etc/xinetd.d directory.

/etc/xinetd.d — The directory that stores most xinetd configuration.

/etc/youservers — A text file that lists the names of YOU servers on the network.

/etc/yp.conf — A file that stores the location of NIS servers.

/etc/ypserv.conf — The main NIS server configuration file.

/home — The default directory used to store user home directories.

/lib/modules/*version***/kernel** — The directory that stores most kernel modules in SLES.

/lost+found — A directory on every ext2 and ext3 file system used to store damaged file fragments. The fsck command stores files that could not be repaired in this directory.

/proc — A directory stored in RAM that contains information about system hardware and processes exported by the Linux kernel.

/proc/driver/rtc — A file that stores the current hardware clock time in SLES.

/proc/file systems — A text file that contains a list of supported file systems in SLES.

/proc/mounts — A file that contains mounted file system information from the Linux kernel.

/proc/sys — A virtual directory in memory that stores running system settings.

/proc/sys/net/ipv4/ip_forward — A file that is used to enable routing on a router.

/root — The root user's home directory.

/srv/www/cgi-bin — The default location for CGI scripts in SLES.

/srv/www/htdocs — The default DocumentRoot in SLES.

/usr/lib/rpm/rpmrc — The main RPM configuration file.

/usr/lib/zoneinfo/localtime — A link to /etc/localtime.

/usr/share/cups/model — The directory that stores sample PPD files used for a particular printer.

/usr/share/zoneinfo/ — The directory that stores time-zone definitions.

/var/adm/backup/rpmdb — The directory that stores backup copies of the RPM database.

/var/lib/named — The directory that stores zone files in SLES.

/var/lib/nfs/etab — A file that lists currently exported directories on an NFS server.

/var/lib/rpm — The directory that stores the RPM database.

/var/log/apache2/access_log — A file that stores information about every access attempt for the Apache Web server.

/var/log/apache2/error_log — A file that stores information from the Apache daemon.

/var/log/boot.msg — A text file that stores information regarding system initialization.

/var/log/cups/access_log — A CUPS log file that stores information about network print requests.

/var/log/cups/error_log — A CUPS log file that stores information about the CUPS daemon.

/var/log/faillog — A text file that lists failed login attempts.

/var/log/wtmp — A text file that lists successful login attempts.

/var/log/YaST2/y2log — The SLES installation log file.

/var/spool/cron/allow — A file that lists users who can use the crontab command.

/var/spool/cron/deny — A file that lists users who cannot use the crontab command.

/var/spool/cron/lastrun — The directory used to store information about system cron jobs run in the past.

/var/spool/cups — The default print queue directory in SLES.

/var/yp/Makefile — A file whose settings are used to create NIS maps.

/var/yp/nicknames — A file that contains aliases for NIS maps.

/var/yp/securenets — A file on a NIS server that lists valid networks for NIS clients.

/var/yp/ypservers — A file on a NIS master server that lists NIS slave servers.

~/.lpoptions — The file that stores user-defined print options.

~/.rpmrc — Contains configuration information that is written to the /usr/lib/rpm/rpmrc file.

~/.ssh/config — The ssh client program configuration file.

accept command — Allows print jobs to enter the print queue.

adjtimex command — Used to change the algorithm in the Linux kernel to count system time in order to adjust for time drift.

Advanced Encryption Standard (AES) — A common symmetric encryption algorithm that uses up to 256-bit keys and is intended to replace 3DES.

Apache — The default Web server software in SLES.

Application Programming Interfaces (APIs) — Sets of routines in an operating system that are available to software programs.

aquota.group — A file that stores group quota information for a file system.

aquota.user — A file that stores user quota information for a file system.

asymmetric encryption — A type of encryption that uses a public and private key pair. Information encrypted with the public key can be decrypted using the private key and vice versa.

at command — Used to schedule commands to run at a certain time in the future and manipulate at jobs.

atq command — Used to view scheduled at jobs.

atrm command — Used to remove a scheduled at job.

attributes — Special flags on a file or directory that modify its usage. The read-only attribute prevents contents from being changed.

background process — A process that runs unnoticed in your terminal and does not interfere with your command-line interface.

basic input/output system (BIOS) — The program located in mainboard ROM that is used to perform the POST and locate a boot loader or boot manager.

bg command — Used to start a process in the background.

block — The unit of data commonly used by a file system. Also called a data block.

Blowfish — An encryption method used to encrypt Linux passwords.

boot loader — The program used to load and start the operating system kernel at system startup.

boot manager — A program used to load and start one of several different operating systems at system start-up.

broadcast — A message destined for all computers on a TCP/IP network.

broadcasting — The process whereby an NTP time provider broadcasts time to NTP time consumers.

cancel command — Used to remove a print job from the print queue.

chattr — Used to change the attributes on a file or directory.

chgrp (change group) command — Used to change the group owner of a file or directory.

child process — A process that is started by another process.

chkconfig command — Used to set the startup status of a service in Linux.

chmod (change mode) command — Used to change the mode (permissions) of a file or directory.

chown (change owner) command — Used to change the owner and group owner of a file or directory.

chroot command — Runs a command or shell under a different root directory.

Class A address — An IP address that uses the first byte to identify the TCP/IP network.

Class B address — An IP address that uses the first two bytes to identify the TCP/IP network.

Class C address — An IP address that uses the first three bytes to identify the TCP/IP network.

Class D address — An IP address that is used for communicating to several hosts simultaneously using multicast packets.

Class E address — An IP address that should not be used on a TCP/IP network and is intended for research purposes only.

Common Gateway Interface (CGI) — A standard used to define programs that interface with a Web server.

Common Internet File System (CIFS) — A file- and printer-sharing protocol used by Windows systems.

Common Unix Printing System (CUPS) — The default printing system in SLES.

container — An LDAP object used to organize leaf objects.

cron — The system service that executes commands regularly in the future, based on information in crontabs.

crontab (cron table) — A file specifying the commands to be run by the cron daemon and the schedule to run them.

crontab command — Used to schedule commands to occur regularly using the cron service.

cuckoo egg — A file that, when executed, creates a security problem.

CUPS Web Administration Tools — A series of CUPS administration utilities that may be accessed using a Web browser on port 631.

daemon process — A system process that is not associated with a terminal. It stands for Disk and Execution Monitor.

data block — See **block**.

Data Encryption Standard (DES) — The default encryption method used in SLES for passwords.

date command — Used to view and set the system time.

dd command — Used to convert and copy files to other locations.

default gateway — The router that connects a network to other networks. Hosts send packets destined for remote networks to this default gateway router.

default route — See **default gateway**.

depmod command — Used to create and update the module dependency database.

device file — A file used to identify hardware devices such as hard disks and serial ports.

df command — Displays disk usage by file system.

Diffie-Hellman — A common asymmetric encryption algorithm.

Digital Signature Algorithm (DSA) — A common asymmetric encryption algorithm.

directories — Special files that are used to organize other files on the file system.

Directory Information Tree (DIT) — The hierarchical structure of an LDAP database.

disable command — Prevents print jobs in the print queue from being sent to the printer.

Distinguished Name (DN) — A full pathname to an LDAP leaf object.

DocumentRoot — A directory that stores HTTP content on a Web server.

domain name — A name that identifies the portion of DNS that your host belongs to.

Domain Name System (DNS) — The naming system used on the Internet. Each host is identified by a host name and domain name.

drift — The deviance that system time or a hardware clock experiences over time.

du command — Displays disk usage by directory.

dumpe2fs command — Used to obtain file system information from ext2 and ext3 file systems.

Dynamic Host Configuration Protocol (DHCP) — A protocol that is used to assign TCP/IP configuration information to a host on the network.

dynamic software libraries — Files that contain software functions that are shared by several different programs. They are also called shared libraries.

e2fsck command — Used to check ext2 and ext3 file systems for errors.

edquota command — Used to specify quota limits for users and groups.

effective group — See **primary group**.

enable command — Allows print jobs in the print queue to be sent to the printer.

Ethereal — A graphical program used to capture and examine IP packets on the network.

Ethernet — The standard method used to access network media today. Most network adapters on networks use Ethernet.

execute permission — Allows you to execute files as well as access directory contents.

exportfs command — Used to temporarily export directories on an NFS server.

ext2 — A traditional nonjournaling file system used on older Linux systems.

ext3 — A journaling version of the ext2 file system.

extended partition — A partition on a hard disk drive that stores logical partitions.

faillog command — Displays the contents of /var/log/faillog.

fdisk command — Used to view and change hard disk partitions.

fg command — Used to force a background process to run in the foreground.

FIFOs — See **named pipes**.

file system — A structure used to organize blocks on a device such that they can be used by the operating system to store data.

File Transfer Protocol (FTP) — A part of the TCP/IP suite that is used for Internet file transfer.

Filesystem Hierarchy Standard (FHS) — A Linux standard that defines the names, locations, and contents of key directories on the system.

finger command — Displays information about local user accounts.

firewall — A software feature that allows a host to drop IP packets that meet a certain criteria or are harmful.

foreground process — A process that runs in your terminal and must finish execution before you receive your shell prompt.

fsck command — Used to check and repair file systems.

fuser command — Used to identify users and processes using a particular file or directory.

gateway route — See **network route**.

General Electric Comprehensive Operating System (GECOS) — Represents a description of a user account stored in the comments field of /etc/passwd.

getty — A program used to display a login prompt on a character-based terminal.

GhostScript — A system used to format information for non-PostScript printers in SLES.

grace period — The amount of time a user can exceed a quota limit.

Grand Unified Boot Loader (GRUB) — The default boot manager in SLES.

Greenwich mean time (GMT) — See **Universal Time Coordinated (UTC)**.

group — When referring to a long file or directory listing, it represents the group ownership of a file or directory.

Group ID (GID) — A number that uniquely identifies system groups.

groupadd command — Used to add a group to the system.

groupdel command — Used to delete a group from the system.

groupmod command — Used to modify the name, membership, or GID of a group on the system.

groups command — Displays the groups that a user is a member of.

gzip command — A common compression utility in Linux.

halt command — Used to quickly bring a system to runlevel 0.

hard limit — A quota limit that cannot be exceeded.

hardware clock — The device that maintains time within the system BIOS on a computer mainboard.

Hash Message Authentication Code (HMAC) — A feature of SSH version 2 that prevents attackers from compromising SSH data during transit.

hdparm command — Used to view and change hard disk settings.

hdparm command — Used to view and manage hard disk settings.

host — A computer that can communicate on a network.

host ID — The part of an IP address that uniquely identifies the host on a network.

Host Key Pair (HK) — An asymmetric encryption key pair that is generated for the computer itself and stored in a file.

host route — A route that specifies the router that must be sent packets destined for a particular host.

HPFS — The native OS/2 file system.

hwclock command — Used to view and set the hardware clock.

hwinfo command — Generates a report for various hardware devices in your computer.

Hypertext Markup Language (HTML) — The format used by documents on the Internet.

Hypertext Transfer Protocol (HTTP) — The TCP/IP protocol used to send documents to Web browsers on the Internet.

id command — Displays the UID and GIDs associated with a user account.

ifconfig command — Used to view, configure, and manage IP addresses on a network interface.

ifdown command — Used to deactivate a network interface.

ifstatus command — Used to display the status of a network interface.

ifup command — Used to activate a network interface.

inetd — The Internet Super Daemon used to start other network daemons on Linux systems.

init — The first daemon started by the Linux kernel; it is responsible for starting and stopping other daemons.

init command — Used to change the system runlevel.

initrd — A ramdisk image that contains device drivers that are loaded during system initialization.

inode — That portion of a file that stores information on the file's attributes, access permissions, location, ownership, and file type.

inode table — That portion of a file system that stores the inodes for files and directories.

insane time source — An NTP time provider that has a time difference of more than 17 minutes with the NTP time consumer.

insmod command — Used to insert a module into the Linux kernel.

insserv command — Used to enable scripts used to start daemons.

International Data Encryption Algorithm (IDEA) — A common symmetric encryption algorithm that uses up to 128-bit keys.

Internet Control Message Protocol (ICMP) — A TCP/IP core protocol used to notify hosts of network error conditions. It is also used for network diagnostics by programs such as ping.

Internet Printing Protocol (IPP) — A printing protocol that allows print jobs to be sent across the Internet using a Web browser.

Internet Protocol (IP) address — A unique address used to identify a computer on a TCP/IP network.

Internet Protocol (IP) packet — A unit of information sent on a TCP/IP network.

interval-controlled daemon — A daemon that is started at a certain time on a regular basis.

iostat command — Displays Input/Output statistics for various system devices.

IP aliases — Additional IP addresses that are assigned to a network interface.

ip command — Used to view, configure, and manage network interfaces and the routing table.

JFS — A journaling file system that supports large file system sizes.

jitter — The deviance between system times on an NTP time provider and an NTP time consumer.

job identifier (job ID) — The ID given to a background process that may be used in commands that manipulate the process during exection.

jobs command — Used to view background processes in your terminal.

journaling — A file system feature that records all file system transactions in a small transaction log on the file system for tracking and troubleshooting purposes.

KDE Info Center — A graphical utility that displays system information.

KDE System Guard — A graphical application that may be used to view CPU and system statistics.

kdesu command — A KDE version of the su command that may be used to start a graphical program as another user.

kdf command — Starts the KDiskFree utility.

KDiskFree — A graphical utility that displays free space by filesystem.

kernel — The core component of the operating system. Different kernels provide different hardware features. The version of the Linux kernel in SLES is 2.6.

kill command — Used to send a signal to a process by PID or job ID.

killall command — Used to send a signal to a process by name.

kinfocenter command — Starts the KDE Info Center utility.

kmod — The process used to load and unload kernel modules.

kprinter — A graphical utility that is invoked when a graphical application creates a print job. It may also be used to change printing options such as resolution.

krdc command — Used to connect to a remote computer using VNC.

last command — Displays the most recent users who have logged into the system from entries in /var/log/wtmp.

lastlog command — Displays the most recent users who have logged into the system from entries in /var/log/lastlog.

ld.so — A Linux run-time linker.

ldconfig command — Updates the /etc/ld.so.cache file; it is typically run at system initialization.

ldd command — Displays the shared libraries required by a certain program.

ld-linux.so.2 — A Linux runtime linker.

leaf — An LDAP object that represents a network resource.

Lightweight Directory Access Protocol (LDAP) — A protocol used to provide central authentication and distribute information to network computers.

lilo command — Used to reinstall the LILO boot manager after configuration changes.

Line Printer Daemon (LPD) — A common printing protocol used on older Linux and UNIX computers.

links — Files that point to other files on the file system.

Linux Loader (LILO) — The traditional boot manager used on Linux systems.

Linux Standard Base (LSB) — A standard that defines the system and package structure for Linux systems.

linuxrc — A program used to load device drivers within the initrd during system initialization.

listener — A process that listens for network traffic on a port and forwards that traffic to a daemon.

local time — A time that is set on the local computer and not synchronized from other computers.

locate command — Used to search for files on the system via a pre-indexed database.

logical group — A virtual volume created by LVM that can be resized or manipulated following creation.

logical partition — A subpartition inside an extended partition on a hard disk drive.

logical volume management (LVM) — A set of components that allow you to create virtual or logical volumes in Linux.

loopback — An IP address that is used to test the local host.

lp command — Used to create a print job.

lpadmin command — Used to create and manage CUPS printers.

lpoptions command — Used to create or change printing options such as resolution.

lppasswd — Used to create CUPS passwords and configure access to the CUPS Web Administration Tools.

lpq command — Used to view print jobs in the print queue.

lpr command — Used to create a print job.

lprm command — Used to remove a print job from the print queue.

lpstat command — Used to view print jobs in the print queue.

LS_LIBRARY_PATH — An environment variable that may be used to add the location of a shared library.

lsattr — Used to list the attributes on a file or directory.

lsmod command — Used to list modules loaded into the Linux kernel.

lsof (list open files) command — Displays the files that processes are using.

lspci command — Displays information about devices using the PCI bus on your system.

make command — Used to generate NIS maps using the Makefile.

map files — Used by a boot manager or boot loader to locate physical data on the hard disk.

maps — NIS database files containing information that is central to the network, such as user accounts and host names.

Master Boot Record (MBR) — The first area of a hard disk that stores the partition table and bootable partition.

master server — A NIS server that contains the maps used to configure NIS clients.

Message Digest 5 (MD5) — An encryption method used to encrypt Linux passwords.

metadata — The section of a file system that is not used to store user data.

minix — A traditional nonjournaling file system used on older Linux systems.

mkfs command — Used to create most file systems in Linux.

mkpasswd command — Used to create an encrypted password for use with user or group accounts.

mkreiserfs command — Used to create ReiserFS file systems.

modinfo command — Used to list information about specific modules.

modprobe command — Used to insert a module and its dependent modules into the Linux kernel.

module disk — A floppy disk that contains additional device drivers for a SLES system.

mount command — Used to mount file systems on devices to mount point directories.

mount point — A directory to which a device is mounted.

mounting — The process of associating a device (e.g., CD-ROM) to a directory (e.g., /media/cdrom). Once a device has been mounted, it may be accessed by navigating to the appropriate directory.

MS-DOS — See **VFAT**.

mt (magnetic tape) command — Used to manage tape devices.

Multipurpose Internet Mail Extensions (MIME) — A standard used to identify content sent across the Internet.

name server — A server that contains records for hosts on a network. It may be queried to resolve a host name to an IP address.

named pipes — Temporary connections that send information from one command or process in memory to another; they can also be represented by files on the file system. Named pipes are also called FIFO (First In First Out) files.

ncurses — A text-based menuing interface in Linux.

NetBIOS — A Windows protocol that uses unique 15-character computer names to identify network hosts. Short for *Network Basic Input Output System*.

netcat command — Used to test communication among hosts using TCP or UDP.

netdate command — Used to obtain and set the system time from a remote computer.

netstat command — Displays network statistics for network interfaces on the system.

NetWare Core Protocol (NCP) — A file-sharing protocol used to share files on Novell Netware systems.

Network File System (NFS) — A file-sharing protocol used by UNIX and Linux systems.

network ID — The part of an IP address that identifies the network a host is on.

Network Information Service (NIS) — A service that allows the centralization of Linux and UNIX configuration.

network mask — See **subnet mask**.

network route — A route that specifies the router that must be sent packets destined for a particular network.

Network Time Protocol (NTP) — A standard protocol in the TCP/IP suite used to maintain consistent time on a network.

newgrp command — Used to change the current primary group for a user account.

NFS client — A computer that accesses exported files on an NFS server using the NFS protocol.

NFS server — A computer that hosts (exports) files using the NFS protocol.

nice command — Used to change the priority of a process as it is started.

nice value — Represents the priority of a process. A higher nice value reduces the priority of the process.

NIS client — A computer that authenticates or obtains its configuration information from a master or slave NIS server.

nmblookup command — Displays NetBIOS computer names for hosts.

node — See **host**.

nohup command — Used to prevent a process from stopping when the shell that started it has exited.

normal files — Commonly used files such as text files, graphic files, data files, and executable programs.

NTFS — The Windows NT file system.

ntpd — The NTP daemon on older Linux systems.

ntpdate command — Used to obtain and set the system time from a remote computer using NTP.

ntpq command — Displays NTP daemon statistics.

ntptrace command — Identifies the servers in each stratum that are used to provide time information to an NTP time consumer.

object — A component of an LDAP database. The two main object types are container objects and leaf objects.

object class — A type of object within an LDAP database.

online_update command — Used to obtain software updates from a YOU Server.

OpenSSH — The default package used to provide SSH services in SLES.

others — When referring to a long file or directory listing, it represents all users on the Linux system that are not the owner or a member of the group on the file or directory.

owner — The user whose name appears in a long listing of a file or directory and who typically has the most permissions to that file or directory.

parent process — A process that has started another process.

Parent Process ID (PPID) — The PID of the parent process of a process.

partition — A physical division of a hard disk drive.

passwd command — Used to modify user passwords and expiry information as well as lock and unlock user accounts.

Patch RPM — An RPM package that is designed to update an existing RPM package.

physical volume — A hard disk or hard disk partition.

ping command — Used to test network connectivity using ICMP.

Plug and Play (PnP) — A system used by the BIOS, hardware devices, and the operating system to automatically configure hardware resources for hardware devices in the computer.

Pluggable Authentication Modules (PAM) — A set of components that allow programs to access user account information.

pnpdump command — Displays information about PnP devices and their configuration.

polling — The process whereby an NTP time consumer polls its NTP time provider for time information.

portmapper — The service that provides for RPCs in Linux.

PostScript — A printing format that is widely used by many printers and printing systems.

PostScript Printer Description (PPD) — A file that stores PostScript printing instructions for a printer.

Power On Self Test (POST) — A simple hardware test performed by the BIOS at system initialization.

poweroff command — Used to quickly bring a system to runlevel 0 and power off the system.

Powertweak — A system that consists of a daemon and YaST utility that may be used to change running system settings.

Powertweak Configuration — A YaST utility that may be used to change running system settings.

primary group — The group specified for a user in the /etc/passwd file that becomes the group owner on newly created files and directories.

primary partition — A main partition on a hard disk drive. There are four primary partitions.

private key — An asymmetric encryption key that can be used to decrypt data encrypted using a public key. The private key can also be used to encrypt data.

private scheme — A method that, during user creation, creates a new group for each user that can be managed by the user.

process — A program currently loaded into memory and running on the CPU.

Process ID (PID) — A unique identifier assigned to every process.

program — A file that may be executed to create a process.

ps command — Used to list processes that are running on the system.

pstree command — Used to list processes that are running on the system as well as their parent and child relationships.

public key — An asymmetric encryption key that can be used to decrypt data encrypted using a private key. The public key is typically used to encrypt data.

public scheme — A method that places new users in a common group that is managed by the root user.

PureFTPd — An advanced FTP server for Linux systems.

pure-ftpd command — Used to configure PureFTPd.

pure-pw command — Used to configure PureFTPd user accounts.

pwck command — Used to check the validity of the /etc/passwd and /etc/shadow files.

pwconv command — Used to convert entries from the /etc/passwd file to the /etc/shadow file.

queue — A directory used to store print jobs before they are sent to the physical printer.

quotacheck command — Used to update the quota database files.

quotaoff command — Used to deactivate disk quotas.

quotaon command — Used to activate disk quotas.

quotas — File system usage limits that may be imposed on users and groups.

Read permission — Allows you to open and read files as well as list directory contents.

reboot command — Used to quickly bring a system to runlevel 6.

Red Hat Package Manager (RPM) — A format used to distribute software packages on most Linux systems.

regular users — User accounts that may be used to log in to the system interactively.

ReiserFS — A journaling file system that uses dynamic inode tables and has fast data access.

reiserfsck command — Used to check and repair ReiserFS file systems.

reiserfstune command — Used to configure file system settings on ReiserFS file systems.

reject command — Prevents print jobs from entering the print queue.

Relative Distinguished Name (RDN) — The simple name of an object in LDAP.

Remote Procedure Call (RPC) — A routine that is executed on a remote computer.

renice command — Used to change the priority of a running process.

repquota command — Used to produce a report on quotas for a particular file system.

Rescue Disk — A floppy disk used to repair a SLES system.

resize_reiserfs command — Used to resize ReiserFS file systems.

Rivest Shamir Adleman (RSA) — A common asymmetric encryption algorithm.

rlogin — Used to obtain a shell on a remote computer.

rmmod command — Used to remove a module from the Linux kernel.

route command — Used to view and modify the routing table.

router — A device that is used to relay IP packets from one TCP/IP network to another.

routing — The process of sending IP packets from one IP network to another.

routing table — A table that is stored on each host and which contains a list of local and remote networks and routers.

rpcinfo command — Displays RPC ports and their associated services.

rpm command — Used to install, remove, and find information on RPM software packages.

rsh — Used to obtain a shell or run a program on a remote computer.

rsync command — Used to copy files and directories to a different location on the local computer or to a remote computer across a network.

r-tools — The rsh, rlogin, and rcp programs.

runlevel — A category that describes the number and type of daemons on a Linux system.

runlevel command — Used to display the current and most recent runlevel.

runtime linker — A system component that is used to locate shared libraries when an executable program is run.

Samba — A set of services in Linux that provides the SMB and CIFS protocols for file and printer sharing with Windows computers.

scalability — The ease with which a system is able to support larger sets of hardware, data, and users.

schema — The list of object and object properties for an LDAP database.

scp command — Used to copy files from one host to another using SSH.

scsiinfo command — Used to view information about SCSI devices on your system.

Secure SHell (SSH) — A software service that provides encrypted communications to and from remote computers.

Server Level Security — A Samba share security level that requires a valid login to another server in order to access a shared directory or printer.

Server Message Block (SMB) — A file- and printer-sharing protocol used by Windows systems.

Server Process Key Pair (SK) — An asymmetric encryption key pair that is generated when the SSH daemon is started. This key pair is never stored in a file and is regenerated each time the daemon is restarted.

service — See **Daemon Process**.

Service Location Protocol (SLP) — A protocol that may be used to locate services on other computers.

Set Group ID (SGID) — A special permission set on executable files and directories. When you run an executable program that has the SGID permission set, you become the group owner of the executable file for the duration of the program. On a directory, the SGID sets the group that gets attached to newly created files.

Set User ID (SUID) — A special permission set on executable files. When you run an executable program that has the SUID permission set, you become the owner of the executable file for the duration of the program.

sftp command — Used to copy files from one host to another using SSH.

shadow passwords — Passwords that are stored in the /etc/shadow file instead of the /etc/passwd file.

Share Level Security — A Samba share security level that requires a password in order to access a shared directory.

shared libraries — See **dynamic software libraries**.

showmount command — Displays exported directories on an NFS server.

shutdown command — Used to change to runlevel 0 at a certain time.

siga command — Displays information about system hardware devices and installed software applications.

signal — A termination request that is sent to a process.

signal-controlled daemon — A daemon that is started when an event occurs on the system.

slave server — A NIS server that contains a copy of the maps from the master server and uses them to configure NIS clients.

slewing — A gradual adjustment of system time from an NTP time provider. It is used to adjust smaller time differences.

smbclient command — Used to view and access Windows file and printer shares.

smbpasswd command — Sets a Windows-formatted password for Linux user accounts.

smbstatus command — Displays current Samba server connections.

socket — An established network connection between two hosts. TCP uses STREAM sockets, whereas UDP uses DGRAM sockets.

soft limit — A quota limit that can be exceeded for a certain period of time.

ssh command — Used to obtain a shell from a remote SSH server.

ssh-add command — Used to register new RSA and DSA keys for use by the ssh-agent command.

ssh-agent command — Used to perform SSH authentication.

ssh-keygen command — Used to generate RSA and DSA keys for use with SSH.

ssh-keyscan command — Displays asymmetric public keys used by SSH.

standard boot disk — A floppy disk used to start a SLES system.

static route — Identifies a remote network and the router that must be used to forward packets to it.

static software libraries — Software functions that are contained within the software program itself after compile time and not shared with other programs.

station — See **host**.

stepping — A fast adjustment of system time from an NTP time provider. It is used to adjust larger time differences.

sticky bit — A special permission that is set on directories that prevents users from removing files that they do not own.

stratum — A measurement of distance from a reliable NTP time source. A stratum of 1 is the most reliable.

su (switch user) command — Used to change the current user account.

subnet mask — A number used to determine which portions of an IP address are the network ID and host ID.

sudo command — Used to run commands as another user via entries in /etc/sudoers.

sulogin — A runlevel 1 program used to display a login prompt on a character-based terminal for the root user only.

superblock — The section of a file system that stores the file system structure.

SuSEconfig — A software utility that configures the system using entries in the /etc/sysconfig directory.

SuSEPlugger — A graphical utility that displays hardware device information by category.

symmetric encryption — A type of encryption that uses the same key to encrypt and decrypt data.

sysctl command — Used to change running system settings.

system time — The time used by an operating system after system initialization.

system users — User accounts that may be used by system services and cannot be used by users to log in to the system interactively.

tar (tape archiver) command — A command-line utility that may be used to archive files and directories.

TCP wrapper (tcpd) — A small program that is used to start network daemons via inetd or xinetd. It provides additional security by using the /etc/hosts.allow and /etc/hosts.deny files to control access.

tcpdchk command — Used to report on the configuration of the tcpd program.

tcpdmatch command — Used to test the behavior of the tcpd program.

tcpdump command — Used to capture and examine IP packets on the network.

testparm command — Checks the syntax of /etc/samba/smb.conf.

TeX Directory Structure (TDS) — A Linux standard for the implementation of the TeX typesetting system.

time consumer — A computer that obtains NTP time information from other computers.

time provider — A computer that provides NTP time information to other computers.

timer interrupt — The interrupt used to maintain time by the Linux kernel.

top command — Used to view, renice, and kill the processes on the system that are using the most CPU time.

traceroute command — Used to identify the route an IP packet takes to a remote host.

Transmission Control Protocol (TCP) — A part of the TCP/IP protocol suite that provides reliable communication between hosts on a network.

Transmission Control Protocol / Internet Protocol (TCP/IP) — A suite of protocols that are used to communicate with other computers on a network.

trapdoor algorithm — An algorithm that encrypts data but cannot be used to decrypt it.

Triple-DES (3DES) — A common symmetric encryption algorithm that uses 112- or 168-bit keys.

tune2fs command — Used to configure file system settings on ext2 and ext3 file systems.

umask — A system variable that removes permissions on all new files and directories.

umask command — Used to view and change the system umask.

umount command — Used to unmount a device from a mount point directory.

uname command — Displays brief system information such as host name and kernel version.

Uniform Resource Locator (URL) — The address of a resource on the Internet. It consists of a protocol, domain, and resource name.

Universal Time Coordinated (UTC) — A standard time system used to coordinate time across the world by referring to the difference in time from Greenwich, England.

updatedb command — Used to update the database used by the locate command.

uptime command — Displays system uptime and process activity.

usbmodules command — Displays information about the USB device modules used on the system.

User Datagram Protocol (UDP) — A part of the TCP/IP protocol suite that provides fast but unreliable communication between hosts on a network.

user ID (UID) — A number that uniquely identifies each system user account.

User Level Security — A Samba share security level that requires a valid Linux login in order to access a shared directory.

user process — A process begun by a user that runs on a terminal.

useradd command — Used to add a user account to the system.

userdel command — Used to remove a user account from the system.

usermod command — Used to modify the properties of a user account on the system.

VFAT — A Linux version of the Microsoft FAT file system.

virtual console — Provides separate terminals for user logins in Linux.

virtual file system — See **Virtual Filesystem Switch (VFS)**.

Virtual Filesystem Switch (VFS) — A Linux component that applications write data to that is eventually written to the file system itself. It is also referred to as a virtual file system.

Virtual Network Computing (VNC) — An open protocol that is used to obtain graphical interfaces from remote operating systems.

visudo command — Used to edit the /etc/sudoers file with the vi text editor.

volume group — A system resource that logical volumes can use.

VxFS — A journaling file system that supports large data and virtual volumes.

w command — Displays the users currently logged in to the system and their processes.

who command — Displays the users currently logged in to the system. It also can be used to display the contents of the /var/log/wtmp file.

Windows Internet Naming Service (WINS) — A Windows service that is used to resolve NetBIOS names to IP addresses. Samba can be configured as a WINS server or client.

workgroup — A name that identifies a group of computers in a Windows network that are not part of a domain.

write permission — Allows you to open and edit files as well as add or remove directory contents.

XFS — A journaling file system that uses fast allocation groups to manage data.

xinetd — The Extended Internet Super Daemon used to start other network daemons on Linux systems. It is the default Internet Super Daemon used in SLES.

xntpd — The NTP daemon in SLES.

Xosview — A small graphical utility that displays CPU, memory, swap, and network statistics.

YaST — The main configuration tool in SLES. It may be run in graphical or text (ncurses) mode.

YaST Boot Loader Configuration — A graphical program that may be used to configure LILO and GRUB.

YaST Online Update (YOU) Client — A computer that accesses software updates on a YOU Server.

YaST Online Update (YOU) Server — A computer that hosts software updates for other SUSE Linux computers.

YaST Runlevel Editor — A graphical program that may be used to configure the daemons that start in each runlevel.

ypbind — The NIS client program. This program also runs on NIS servers.

ypcat command — Displays the contents of NIS maps.

ypchfn command — Used to change user account descriptions on a NIS server.

ypchsh command — Used to change the default user account shell on a NIS server.

ypdomainname command — Used to set the NIS domain name for a computer.

ypinit command — The NIS slave server program.

ypmatch command — Used to query NIS maps for specific information.

yppasswd command — Used to change a user password on a NIS server.

yppoll command — Displays NIS map ID numbers.

yppush command — Copies NIS maps from master servers to slave servers.

ypserv — The NIS server program.

ypwhich command — Displays the NIS server used by a host.

Index